COLLEGE MATHEMATICS I

Second Custom Edition

Robert Blitzer

Edited by Brian K. Saltzer

Taken from
Algebra and Trigonometry, Second Edition
by Robert Blitzer

Cover Art: *Big Wheel*, by Barry Cronin.

Taken from:

Algebra and Trigonometry, Second Edition
by Robert Blitzer
Copyright © 2004, 2001 by Pearson Education, Inc.
Published by Prentice-Hall
Upper Saddle River, New Jersey 07458

This special edition published in cooperation with Pearson Custom Publishing.

Printed in the United States of America

10 9 8

ISBN 0-536-80999-2

BA 999065

JP

Please visit our web site at *www.pearsoncustom.com*

PEARSON CUSTOM PUBLISHING
75 Arlington Street, Suite 300, Boston, MA 02116
A Pearson Education Company

Contents

Preface

I've written **Algebra and Trigonometry**, **Second Edition, Vols I and II** to help diverse students, with different backgrounds and future goals to succeed. These books have three fundamental goals:

1. To help students acquire a solid foundation in algebra and trigonometry, preparing them for other courses such as calculus, business calculus, and finite mathematics.
2. To show students how algebra and trigonometry can model and solve authentic real-world problems.
3. To enable students to develop problem-solving skills, while fostering critical thinking, within an interesting setting.

One major obstacle in the way of achieving these goals is the fact that very few students actually read their textbook. This has been a regular source of frustration for me and my colleagues in the classroom. Anecdotal evidence gathered over years highlights two basic reasons that students do not take advantage of their textbook:

- "I'll never use this information."
- "I can't follow the explanations."

As a result, I've written every page of these books with the intent of eliminating these two objections.

A Brief Note on Technology

Technology, and specifically the use of a graphing utility, is covered thoroughly, although its coverage by an instructor is optional. If you require the use of a graphing utility in the course, you will find support for this approach, particularly in the wide selection of clearly designated technology exercises in each exercise set. If you wish to minimize or eliminate the discussion or use of a graphing utility, these books are written to enable you to do so. Regardless of the role technology plays in your course, the technology boxes with TI-83 screens that appear throughout the books should allow your students to understand what graphing utilities can do, enabling them to visualize, verify, or explore what they have already graphed or manipulated by hand. The books' technology coverage is intended to reinforce, but never replace, algebraic solutions.

Acknowledgments

I wish to express my appreciation to all of the reviewers of my precalculus series for their helpful criticisms and suggestions, frequently transmitted with wit, humor, and intelligence. In particular, I would like to thank the following for reviewing **College Algebra**, **Algebra and Trigonometry,** and **Precalculus.**

Reviewers for the Previous Editions

Kayoko Yates Barnhill, *Clark College*
Lloyd Best, *Pacific Union College*
Diana Colt, *University of Minnesota-Duluth*
Yvelyne Germain-McCarthy, *University of New Orleans*
Cynthia Glickman, *Community College of Southern Nevada*
Sudhir Kumar Goel, *Valdosta State University*
Donald Gordon, *Manatee Community College*
David L. Gross, *University of Connecticut*
Joel K. Haack, *University of Northern Iowa*
Mike Hall, *Univeristy of Mississippi*
Christopher N. Hay-Jahans, *University of South Dakota*
Celeste Hernandez, *Richland College*
Winfield A. Ihlow, *SUNY College at Oswego*
Nancy Raye Johnson, *Manatee Community College*
James Miller, *West Virginia University*
Debra A. Pharo, *Northwestern Michigan College*
Gloria Phoenix, *North Carolina Agricultural and Technical State University*
Juha Pohjanpelto, *Oregon State University*
Richard E. Van Lommel, *California State University-Sacramento*
Dan Van Peursem, *University of South Dakota*
David White, *The Victoria College*

Reviewers for the Current Edition

Timothy Beaver, *Isothermal Community College*
Bill Burgin, *Gaston College*
Jimmy Chang, *St. Petersburg College*
Donna Densmore, *Bossier Parish Community College*
Disa Enegren, *Rose State College*
Nancy Fisher, *University of Alabama*
Jeremy Haefner, *University of Colorado*
Joyce Hague, *University of Wisconsin at River Falls*
Mary Leesburg, *Manatee Community College*
Christine Heinecke Lehmann, *Purdue University North Central*
Alexander Levichev, *Boston University*
Zongzhu Lin, *Kansas State University*
Benjamin Marlin, *Northwestern Oklahoma State University*
Marilyn Massey, *Collin County Community College*
David Platt, *Front Range Community College*
Janice Rech, *University of Nebraska at Omaha*
Judith Salmon, *Fitchburg State College*
Cynthia Schultz, *Illinois Valley Community College*
Chris Stump, *Bethel College*
Pamela Trim, *Southwest Tennessee Community College*
Chris Turner, *Arkansas State University*
Philip Van Veldhuizen, *University of Nevada at Reno*
Tracy Wienckowski, *Univesity of Buffalo*

To the Student

I've written these two volumes so that you can learn about the power of algebra and trigonometry and how it relates directly to your life outside the classroom. All concepts are carefully explained, important definitions and procedures are set off in boxes, and worked-out examples that present solutions in a step-by-step manner appear in every section. Each example is followed by a similar matched problem, called a Check Point, for you to try so that you can actively participate in the learning process as you read the books. (Answers to all Check Points appear in the back of each book.) Study Tips offer hints and suggestions and often point out common errors to avoid. A great deal of attention has been given to applying algebra and trigonometry to your life to make your learning experience both interesting and relevant.

As you begin your studies, I would like to offer some specific suggestions for using these books and for being successful in this course:

1. **Attend all lectures.** No book is intended to be a substitute for valuable insights and interactions that occur in the classroom. In addition to arriving for lectures on time and being prepared, you will find it useful to read the section before it is covered in the lecture. This will give you a clear idea of the new material that will be discussed.

2. **Read the book.** Read each section with pen (or pencil) in hand. Move through the illustrative examples with great care. These worked-out examples provide a model for doing exercises in the exercise sets. As you proceed through the reading, do not give up if you do not understand every single word. Things will become clearer as you read on and see how various procedures are applied to specific worked-out examples.

3. **Work problems every day and check your answers.** The way to learn mathematics is by doing mathematics, which means working the Check Points and assigned exercises in the exercise sets. The more exercises you work, the better you will understand the material.

4. **Prepare for chapter exams.** After completing a chapter, study the summary, work the exercises in the Chapter Review, and work the exercises in the Chapter Test. Answers to all these exercises are given in the back of each book.

5. **Use the supplements available with this book.** A solutions manual containing worked-out solutions to each book's odd-numbered exercises, all review exercises, and all Check Points; a dynamic web page; and videotapes and CD-ROMs created for every section of the books are among the supplements created to help you tap into the power of mathematics. Ask your instructor or bookstore which supplements are available and where you can find them.

I wrote this book in beautiful and pristine Point Reyes National Seashore, north of San Francisco. It was my hope to convey the beauty of mathematics using nature as a source of inspiration and creativity. Enjoy the pages that follow as you empower yourself with the algebra and trigonometry needed to succeed in college, your career, and your life.

Regards,
Bob
Robert Blitzer

About the Author

Bob Blitzer is a native of Manhattan and received a Bachelor of Arts degree with dual majors in mathematics and psychology (minor: English literature) from the City College of New York. His unusual combination of academic interests led him toward a Master of Arts in mathematics from the University of Miami and a doctorate in behavioral sciences from Nova University. Bob is most energized by teaching mathematics and has taught a variety of mathematics courses at Miami-Dade Community College for nearly 30 years. He has received numerous teaching awards, including Innovator of the Year from the League for Innovations in the Community College, and was among the first group of recipients at Miami-Dade Community College for an endowed chair based on excellence in the classroom. In addition to *Algebra and Trigonometry*, Bob has written *Introductory Algebra for College Students*, *Intermediate Algebra for College Students*, *Introductory and Intermediate Algebra for College Students*, *Algebra for College Students*, *Thinking Mathematically*, *College Algebra*, and *Precalculus*, all published by Prentice Hall.

Finally, Bob loves to spend time with his pal, Harley, pictured to the right. He's so cute (Harley, not Bob) that we couldn't resist including him.

TUTORIAL

Blitzer M@thP@k

An Integrated Learning Environment

Today's textbooks offer a wide variety of ancillary materials to students, from solutions manuals to tutorial software to text-specific Websites. Making the most of all of these resources can be difficult. Blitzer **M@thP@k** helps students get it together. **M@thP@k** seamlessly integrates the following key products into **an integrated learning environment:**

MathPro 5

MathPro 5 is online, customizable tutorial software integrated with the text at the Learning Objective level. MathPro 5's "watch" feature integrates lecture videos into the algorithmic tutorial environment. The easy-to-use course management system enables instructors to track and assess student performance on tutorial work, quizzes, and tests. A robust reports wizard provides a grade book, individual student reports, and class summaries. The customizable syllabus allows instructors to remove and reorganize chapters, sections, and objectives. MathPro 5's messaging system enhances communication between students and instructors. The combination of MathPro 5's richly integrated tutorial, testing, and robust course management tools provides an unparalleled tutorial experience for students, and new assessment and time-saving tools for instructors.

The Blitzer M@thP@k Website

This robust passcode-protected site features quizzes, homework starters, live animated examples, graphing calculator manuals, and much more. It offers the student many ways to test and reinforce their understanding of the course material.

Student Solutions Manual

The *Student Solutions Manual* offers thorough, accurate solutions that are consistent with the precise mathematics found in the text.

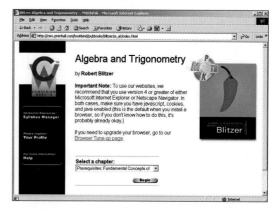

GREAT SUPPORT

Blitzer M@thP@k.
Helping Students Get it Together.

Problem Solving for Students.
Solving Problems for You.

Students need to practice solving problems—The more they practice, the better problem solvers they become. Professors want relief from the tedium of grading.

That's why we created **PH GradeAssist**. It's...

✓ online—available anytime, anywhere.
✓ text-specific—tied directly to your Prentice Hall Precalculus or Calculus text.
✓ algorithmic—contains unlimited questions and assignments for practice and assessment.
✓ customizable—completely unique to your course—edit questions and add yours.

How does PH GradeAssist work for the instructor?

- You create quizzes or homework assignments from question banks specific to your text. Choose the problems you prefer, edit them, or add your own.
- Your students go online and work the assignments that you have created.
- The problems let students work with real math, not just multiple choice.
- Many problems are algorithmically generated, so each student gets a slightly different problem with a different answer.
- PH GradeAssist scores these assignments for you, using a sophisticated math parser, which recognizes algebraic, numeric, and unit equivalents.
- Results can be easily accessed in a central gradebook.

**For a demonstration, contact your local Prentice Hall representative
or visit us online at www.prenhall.com/phga**

Applications Index

Prerequisites: Fundamental Concepts of Algebra

This chapter reviews fundamental concepts of algebra that are prerequisites for the study of college algebra. Algebra, like all of mathematics, provides the tools to help you recognize, classify, and explore the hidden patterns of your world, revealing its underlying structure. Throughout the new millennium, literacy in algebra will be a prerequisite for functioning in a meaningful way personally, professionally, and as a citizen.

Listening to the radio on the way to work, you hear candidates in the upcoming election discussing the problem of the country's 5.6 trillion dollar deficit. It seems like this is a real problem, but then you realize that you don't really know what that number means. How can you look at this deficit in the proper perspective? If the national debt were evenly divided among all citizens of the country, how much would each citizen have to pay? Does the deficit seem like such a significant problem now?

SECTION P.1 *Real Numbers and Algebraic Expressions*

Objectives

1. Recognize subsets of the real numbers.
2. Use inequality symbols.
3. Evaluate absolute value.
4. Use absolute value to express distance.
5. Evaluate algebraic expressions.
6. Identify properties of the real numbers.
7. Simplify algebraic expressions.

The U.N. Building is designed with three golden rectangles.

The United Nations Building in New York was designed to represent its mission of promoting world harmony. Viewed from the front, the building looks like three rectangles stacked upon each other. In each rectangle, the ratio of the width to height is $\sqrt{5} + 1$ to 2, approximately 1.618 to 1. The ancient Greeks believed that such a rectangle, called a **golden rectangle,** was the most visually pleasing of all rectangles.

The ratio 1.618 to 1 is approximate because $\sqrt{5}$ is an irrational number, a special kind of real number. Irrational? Real? Let's make sense of all this by describing the kinds of numbers you will encounter in this course.

1 Recognize subsets of the real numbers.

The Set of Real Numbers

Before we describe the set of real numbers, let's be sure you are familiar with some basic ideas about sets. A **set** is a collection of objects whose contents can be clearly determined. The objects in a set are called the **elements** of the set. For example, the set of numbers used for counting can be represented by

$$\{1, 2, 3, 4, 5, \ldots\}.$$

The braces, { }, indicate that we are representing a set. This form of representing a set uses commas to separate the elements of the set. The set of numbers used for counting is called the set of **natural numbers.** The three dots after the 5 indicate that there is no final element and that the listing goes on forever.

The sets that make up the real numbers are summarized in Table P.1. We refer to these sets as **subsets** of the real numbers, meaning that all elements in each subset are also elements in the set of real numbers.

Notice the use of the symbol $\approx$ in the examples of irrational numbers. The symbol means "is approximately equal to." Thus,

$$\sqrt{2} \approx 1.414214.$$

We can verify that this is only an approximation by multiplying 1.414214 by itself. The product is very close to, but not exactly, 2:

$$1.414214 \times 1.414214 = 2.0000012378.$$

Technology

A calculator with a square root key gives a decimal approximation for $\sqrt{2}$, not the exact value.

Real numbers ℝ

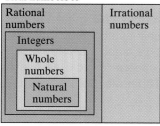

This diagram shows that every real number is rational or irrational.

Table P.1   Important Subsets of the Real Numbers

Name	Description	Examples
Natural numbers ℕ	$\{1, 2, 3, 4, 5, \ldots\}$ These numbers are used for counting.	$2, 3, 5, 17$
Whole numbers 𝕎	$\{0, 1, 2, 3, 4, 5, \ldots\}$ The set of whole numbers is formed by adding 0 to the set of natural numbers.	$0, 2, 3, 5, 17$
Integers ℤ	$\{\ldots, -5, -4, -3, -2, -1, 0, 1, 2, 3, 4, 5, \ldots\}$ The set of integers is formed by adding negatives of the natural numbers to the set of whole numbers.	$-17, -5, -3, -2, 0,$ $2, 3, 5, 17$
Rational numbers ℚ	The set of rational numbers is the set of all numbers which can be expressed in the form, where a and b are integers and b is not equal to 0, written $b \neq 0$. Rational numbers can be expressed as terminating or repeating decimals.	$-17 = \frac{-17}{1}, -5 = \frac{-5}{1}, -3, -2,$ $0, 2, 3, 5, 17,$ $\frac{2}{5} = 0.4,$ $\frac{-2}{3} = -0.6666\cdots = -0.\overline{6}$
Irrational numbers 𝕀	This is the set of all numbers whose decimal representations are neither terminating nor repeating. Irrational numbers cannot be expressed as a quotient of integers.	$\sqrt{2} \approx 1.414214$ $-\sqrt{3} \approx -1.73205$ $\pi \approx 3.142$ $-\frac{\pi}{2} \approx -1.571$

Study Tip

Not all square roots are irrational numbers. For example, $\sqrt{25} = 5$ because $5 \times 5 = 25$. Thus, $\sqrt{25}$ is a natural number, a whole number, an integer, and a rational number $\left(\sqrt{25} = \frac{5}{1}\right)$.

The set of **real numbers** is formed by combining the rational numbers and the irrational numbers. Thus, every real number is either rational or irrational.

The Real Number Line

The **real number line** is a graph used to represent the set of real numbers. An arbitrary point, called the **origin,** is labeled 0; units to the right of the origin are **positive** and units to the left of the origin are **negative.** The real number line is shown in Figure P.1.

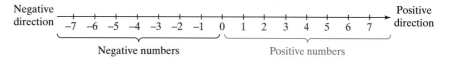

Figure P.1 The real number line

Real numbers are **graphed** on a number line by placing a dot at the correct location for each number. The integers are easiest to locate. In Figure P.2, we've graphed the integers −3, 0, and 4.

Figure P.2 Graphing −3, 0, and 4 on a number line

Every real number corresponds to a point on the number line and every point on the number line corresponds to a real number. We say there is a **one-to-one correspondence** between all the real numbers and all points on a real number line. If you draw a point on the real number line corresponding to a real number, you are **plotting** the real number. In Figure P.2, we are plotting the real numbers −3, 0, and 4.

2 Use inequality symbols.

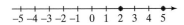

-5 -4 -3 -2 -1 0 1 2 3 4 5

Figure P.3

Study Tip

The symbols $<$ and $>$ always point to the lesser of the two real numbers when the inequality is true.

$2 < 5$ The symbol points to 2, the lesser number.

$5 > 2$ The symbol points to 2, the lesser number.

Ordering the Real Numbers

On the real number line, the real numbers increase from left to right. The lesser of two real numbers is the one farther to the left on a number line. The greater of two real numbers is the one farther to the right on a number line.

Look at the number line in Figure P.3. The integers 2 and 5 are plotted. Observe that 2 is to the left of 5 on the number line. This means that 2 is less than 5:

$2 < 5$:   2 is less than 5 because 2 is to the *left* of 5 on the number line.

In Figure P.3, we can also observe that 5 is to the right of 2 on the number line. This means that 5 is greater than 2:

$5 > 2$:   5 is greater than 2 because 5 is to the right of 2 on the number line.

The symbols $<$ and $>$ are called **inequality symbols.** They may be combined with an equal sign, as shown in the following table:

Symbols	Meaning	Example	Explanation
$a \leq b$	a is less than or equal to b.	$3 \leq 7$	Because $3 < 7$
		$7 \leq 7$	Because $7 = 7$
$b \geq a$	b is greater than or equal to a.	$7 \geq 3$	Because $7 > 3$
		$-5 \geq -5$	Because $-5 = -5$

3 Evaluate absolute value.

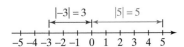

-5 -4 -3 -2 -1 0 1 2 3 4 5

Figure P.4 Absolute value as the distance from 0

Absolute Value

The **absolute value** of a real number a, denoted by $|a|$, is the distance from 0 to a on the number line. This distance is always taken to be nonnegative. For example, the real number line in Figure P.4 shows that

$$|-3| = 3 \quad \text{and} \quad |5| = 5.$$

The absolute value of -3 is 3 because -3 is 3 units from 0 on the number line. The absolute value of 5 is 5 because 5 is 5 units from 0 on the number line. The absolute value of a positive real number or 0 is the number itself. The absolute value of a negative real number, such as -3, is the number without the negative sign.

We can define the absolute value of the real number x without referring to a number line. The algebraic definition of the absolute value of x is given as follows:

> ### Definition of Absolute Value
>
> $$|x| = \begin{cases} x & \text{if } x \geq 0 \\ -x & \text{if } x < 0 \end{cases}$$

If x is nonnegative (that is $x \geq 0$), the absolute value of x is the number itself. For example,

$$|5| = 5 \qquad |\pi| = \pi \qquad \left|\frac{1}{3}\right| = \frac{1}{3} \qquad |0| = 0.$$

Zero is the only number whose absolute value is 0.

If x is a negative number (that is, $x < 0$), the absolute value of x is the opposite of x. This makes the absolute value positive. For example,

$$|-3| = -(-3) = 3 \qquad |-\pi| = -(-\pi) = \pi \qquad \left|-\frac{1}{3}\right| = -\left(-\frac{1}{3}\right) = \frac{1}{3}.$$

This middle step is usually omitted.

EXAMPLE 1 Evaluating Absolute Value

Rewrite each expression without absolute value bars:

a. $\left|\sqrt{3} - 1\right|$ **b.** $|2 - \pi|$ **c.** $\dfrac{|x|}{x}$ if $x < 0$.

Solution

a. Because $\sqrt{3} \approx 1.7$, the expression inside the absolute value bars, $\sqrt{3} - 1$, is positive. The absolute value of a positive number is the number itself. Thus,
$$\left|\sqrt{3} - 1\right| = \sqrt{3} - 1.$$

b. Because $\pi \approx 3.14$, the number inside the absolute value bars, $2 - \pi$, is negative. The absolute value of x when $x < 0$ is $-x$. Thus,
$$|2 - \pi| = -(2 - \pi) = \pi - 2.$$

c. If $x < 0$, then $|x| = -x$. Thus,
$$\frac{|x|}{x} = \frac{-x}{x} = -1.$$

Study Tip

After working each Check Point, check your answer in the answer section before continuing your reading.

Discovery

Verify the triangle inequality if $a = 4$ and $b = 5$. Verify the triangle inequality if $a = 4$ and $b = -5$.

When does equality occur in the triangle inequality and when does inequality occur? Verify your observation with additional number pairs.

4 Use absolute value to express distance.

Check Point 1 Rewrite each expression without absolute value bars:

a. $\left|1 - \sqrt{2}\right|$ **b.** $|\pi - 3|$ **c.** $\dfrac{|x|}{x}$ if $x > 0$.

Listed below are several basic properties of absolute value. Each of these properties can be derived from the definition of absolute value.

Properties of Absolute Value

For all real numbers a and b,

1. $|a| \geq 0$ **2.** $|-a| = |a|$ **3.** $a \leq |a|$

4. $|ab| = |a||b|$ **5.** $\left|\dfrac{a}{b}\right| = \dfrac{|a|}{|b|}, \quad b \neq 0$

6. $|a + b| \leq |a| + |b|$ (called the triangle inequality)

Distance between Points on a Real Number Line

Absolute value is used to find the distance between two points on a real number line. If a and b are any real numbers, the **distance between a and b** is the absolute value of their difference. For example, the distance between 4 and 10 is 6. Using absolute value, we find this distance in one of two ways:

$$|10 - 4| = |6| = 6 \quad \text{or} \quad |4 - 10| = |-6| = 6.$$

The distance between 4 and 10 on the real number line is 6.

Notice that we obtain the same distance regardless of the order in which we subtract.

> ### Distance between Two Points on the Real Number Line
> If a and b are any two points on a real number line, then the distance between a and b is given by
> $$|a - b| \quad \text{or} \quad |b - a|.$$

EXAMPLE 2   Distance between Two Points on a Number Line

Find the distance between −5 and 3 on the real number line.

Solution   Because the distance between a and b is given by $|a - b|$, the distance between −5 and 3 is

$$|-5 - 3| = |-8| = 8.$$

$a = -5$ $b = 3$

$$\overset{8}{\longleftrightarrow}$$

−5 −4 −3 −2 −1 0 1 2 3 4 5

Figure P.5 The distance between −5 and 3 is 8.

Figure P.5 verifies that there are 8 units between −5 and 3 on the real number line. We obtain the same distance if we reverse the order of the subtraction:

$$|3 - (-5)| = |8| = 8.$$

Check Point 2   Find the distance between −4 and 5 on the real number line.

Algebraic Expressions

Algebra uses letters, such as x and y, to represent real numbers. Such letters are called **variables.** For example, imagine that you are basking in the sun on the beach. We can let x represent the number of minutes that you can stay in the sun without burning with no sunscreen. With a number 6 sunscreen, exposure time without burning is six times as long, or 6 times x. This can be written $6 \cdot x$, but it is usually expressed as $6x$. Placing a number and a letter next to one another indicates multiplication.

Notice that $6x$ combines the number 6 and the variable x using the operation of multiplication. A combination of variables and numbers using the operations of addition, subtraction, multiplication, or division, as well as powers or roots (which are discussed later in this chapter), is called an **algebraic expression.** Here are some examples of algebraic expressions:

$$x + 6, \quad x - 6, \quad 6x, \quad \frac{x}{6}, \quad 3x + 5, \quad \sqrt{x} + 7.$$

5 Evaluate algebraic expressions.

Evaluating Algebraic Expressions

Evaluating an algebraic expression means to find the value of the expression for a given value of the variable. For example, we can evaluate $6x$ (from the sun-screen example) when $x = 15$. We substitute 15 for x. We obtain $6 \cdot 15$, or 90. This means if you can stay in the sun for 15 minutes without burning when you don't put on any lotion, then with a number 6 lotion, you can "cook" for 90 minutes without burning.

Many algebraic expressions involve more than one operation. Evaluating an algebraic expression without a calculator involves carefully applying the following order of operations agreement:

The Order of Operations Agreement

1. Perform operations within the innermost parentheses and work outward. If the algebraic expression involves a fraction, treat the numerator and the denominator as if they were each enclosed in parentheses.
2. Evaluate all exponential expressions.
3. Perform multiplications and divisions as they occur, working from left to right.
4. Perform additions and subtractions as they occur, working from left to right.

EXAMPLE 3   Evaluating an Algebraic Expression

The algebraic expression $2.35x + 179.5$ describes the population of the United States, in millions, x years after 1960. Evaluate the expression for $x = 40$. Describe what the answer means in practical terms.

Solution   We begin by substituting 40 for x. Because $x = 40$, we will be finding the U.S. population 40 years after 1960, in the year 2000.

$$2.35x + 179.5$$

Replace x with 40.

$$= 2.35(40) + 179.5$$
$$= 94 + 179.5 \qquad \text{Perform the multiplication: } 2.35(40) = 94.$$
$$= 273.5 \qquad \text{Perform the addition.}$$

According to the given algebraic expression, in 2000 the population of the United States was 273.5 million.

According to the U.S. Bureau of the Census, in 2000 the population of the United States was 281.4 million. Notice that the algebraic expression in Example 3 provides an approximate, but not an exact, description of the actual population.

Check Point 3   Evaluate the algebraic expression in Example 3 for $x = 30$. Describe what your answer means in practical terms.

6 Identify properties of the real numbers.

Properties of Real Numbers and Algebraic Expressions

When you use your calculator to add two real numbers, you can enter them in any order. The fact that two real numbers can be added in any order is called the **commutative property of addition.** You probably use this property, as well as other properties of real numbers listed in Table P.2 on the next page, without giving it much thought. The properties of the real numbers are especially useful when working with algebraic expressions. For each property listed in Table P.2, a, b, and c represent real numbers, variables, or algebraic expressions.

Table P.2   Properties of the Real Numbers

Name	Meaning	Examples
Commutative Property of Addition	Two real numbers can be added in any order. $a + b = b + a$	• $13 + 7 = 7 + 13$ • $13x + 7 = 7 + 13x$
Commutative Property of Multiplication	Two real numbers can be multiplied in any order. $ab = ba$	• $\sqrt{2} \cdot \sqrt{5} = \sqrt{5} \cdot \sqrt{2}$ • $x \cdot 6 = 6x$
Associative Property of Addition	If three real numbers are added, it makes no difference which two are added first. $(a + b) + c = a + (b + c)$	• $3 + (8 + x) = (3 + 8) + x$ $= 11 + x$
Associative Property of Multiplication	If three real numbers are multiplied, it makes no difference which two are multiplied first. $(a \cdot b) \cdot c = a \cdot (b \cdot c)$	• $-2(3x) = (-2 \cdot 3)x = -6x$
Distributive Property of Multiplication over Addition	Multiplication distributes over addition. $a \cdot (b + c) = a \cdot b + a \cdot c$	• $7(4 + \sqrt{3}) = 7 \cdot 4 + 7 \cdot \sqrt{3}$ $= 28 + 7\sqrt{3}$ • $5(3x + 7) = 5 \cdot 3x + 5 \cdot 7$ $= 15x + 35$
Identity Property of Addition	Zero can be deleted from a sum. $a + 0 = a$ $0 + a = a$	• $\sqrt{3} + 0 = \sqrt{3}$ • $0 + 6x = 6x$
Identity Property of Multiplication	One can be deleted from a product. $a \cdot 1 = a$ $1 \cdot a = a$	• $1 \cdot \pi = \pi$ • $13x \cdot 1 = 13x$
Inverse Property of Addition	The sum of a real number and its additive inverse gives 0, the additive identity. $a + (-a) = 0$ $(-a) + a = 0$	• $\sqrt{5} + (-\sqrt{5}) = 0$ • $-\pi + \pi = 0$ • $6x + (-6x) = 0$ • $(-4y) + 4y = 0$
Inverse Property of Multiplication	The product of a nonzero real number and its multiplicative inverse gives 1, the multiplicative identity. $a \cdot \dfrac{1}{a} = 1, \quad a \neq 0$ $\dfrac{1}{a} \cdot a = 1, \quad a \neq 0$	• $7 \cdot \dfrac{1}{7} = 1$ • $\left(\dfrac{1}{x-3}\right)(x-3) = 1, \ x \neq 3$

The Associative Property and the English Language

In the English language, phrases can take on different meanings depending on the way the words are associated with commas.

Here are two examples.

• *Woman, without her man, is nothing.*
  Woman, without her, man is nothing.
• *What's the latest dope?*
  What's the latest, dope?

Commutative Words and Sentences

The commutative property states that a change in order produces no change in the answer. The words and sentences listed here suggest a characteristic of the commutative property; they read the same from left to right and from right to left!

dad

repaper

never odd or even

Draw, o coward!

Dennis sinned.

Ma is a nun, as I am.

Revolting is error. Resign it, lover.

Naomi, did I moan?

Al lets Della call Ed Stella.

The properties in Table P.2 apply to the operations of addition and multiplication. Subtraction and division are defined in terms of addition and multiplication.

Definitions of Subtraction and Division

Let a and b represent real numbers.

Subtraction: $a - b = a + (-b)$
We call $-b$ the **additive inverse** or **opposite** of b.

Division: $a \div b = a \cdot \frac{1}{b}$, where $b \neq 0$
We call $\frac{1}{b}$ the **multiplicative inverse** or **reciprocal** of b. The quotient of a and b, $a \div b$, can be written in the form $\frac{a}{b}$, where a is the **numerator** and b the **denominator** of the fraction.

Because subtraction is defined in terms of adding an inverse, the distributive property can be applied to subtraction:

$$a(b - c) = ab - ac$$
$$(b - c)a = ba - ca.$$

For example,

$$4(2x - 5) = 4 \cdot 2x - 4 \cdot 5 = 8x - 20.$$

7 Simplify algebraic expressions.

Simplifying Algebraic Expressions

The **terms** of an algebraic expression are those parts that are separated by addition. For example, consider the algebraic expression

$$7x - 9y - 3,$$

which can be expressed as

$$7x + (-9y) + (-3).$$

This expression contains three terms, namely $7x$, $-9y$, and -3.

The numerical part of a term is called its **numerical coefficient.** In the term $7x$, the 7 is the numerical coefficient. In the term $-9y$, the -9 is the numerical coefficient.

A term that consists of just a number is called a **constant term.** The constant term of $7x - 9y - 3$ is -3.

A term indicates a product. The expressions that are multiplied to form the term are called its **factors. Like terms** have the same variable factors with the same exponents on the variables. For example, $7x$ and $3x$ are like terms because they have the same variable factor, x. The distributive property (in reverse) can be used to add these terms:

$$7x + 3x = (7 + 3)x = 10x.$$

Study Tip

To add like terms, add their numerical coefficients. Use this result as the numerical coefficient of the terms' common variable(s).

An algebraic expression is **simplified** when parentheses have been removed and like terms have been combined.

EXAMPLE 4 Simplifying an Algebraic Expression

Simplify: $6(2x - 4y) + 10(4x + 3y)$.

Solution

$$6(2x - 4y) + 10(4x + 3y)$$
$$= 6 \cdot 2x - 6 \cdot 4y + 10 \cdot 4x + 10 \cdot 3y \quad \text{Use the distributive property to remove the parentheses.}$$
$$= 12x - 24y + 40x + 30y \quad \text{Multiply.}$$
$$= (12x + 40x) + (30y - 24y) \quad \text{Group like terms.}$$
$$= 52x + 6y \quad \text{Combine like terms.}$$

Check Point 4 Simplify: $7(4x - 3y) + 2(5x + y)$.

Properties of Negatives

The distributive property can be extended to cover more than two terms within parentheses. For example,

> This sign represents subtraction.

> This sign tells us that −3 is negative.

$$-3(4x - 2y + 6) = -3 \cdot 4x - (-3) \cdot 2y - 3 \cdot 6$$
$$= -12x - (-6y) - 18$$
$$= -12x + 6y - 18.$$

The voice balloons illustrate that negative signs can appear side by side. They can represent the operation of subtraction or the fact that a real number is negative. Here is a list of properties of negatives and how they are applied to algebraic expressions:

Properties of Negatives

Let a and b represent real numbers, variables, or algebraic expressions.

Property	Examples
1. $(-1)a = -a$	$(-1)4xy = -4xy$
2. $-(-a) = a$	$-(-6y) = 6y$
3. $(-a)b = -ab$	$(-7)4xy = -7 \cdot 4xy = -28xy$
4. $a(-b) = -ab$	$5x(-3y) = -5x \cdot 3y = -15xy$
5. $-(a + b) = -a - b$	$-(7x + 6y) = -7x - 6y$
6. $-(a - b) = -a + b$ $= b - a$	$-(3x - 7y) = -3x + 7y$ $= 7y - 3x$

Do you notice that properties 5 and 6 in the box are related? In general, expressions within parentheses that are preceded by a negative can be simplified by dropping the parentheses and changing the sign of every term inside the parentheses.
For example,

$$-(3x - 2y + 5z - 6) = -3x + 2y - 5z + 6.$$

EXERCISE SET P.1

 Practice Exercises

*In Exercises 1–4, list all numbers from the given set that are **a.** natural numbers, **b.** whole numbers, **c.** integers, **d.** rational numbers, **e.** irrational numbers.*

1. $\{-9, -\frac{4}{5}, 0, 0.25, \sqrt{3}, 9.2, \sqrt{100}\}$
2. $\{-7, -0.\overline{6}, 0, \sqrt{49}, \sqrt{50}\}$
3. $\{-11, -\frac{5}{6}, 0, 0.75, \sqrt{5}, \pi, \sqrt{64}\}$
4. $\{-5, -0.\overline{3}, 0, \sqrt{2}, \sqrt{4}\}$

5. Give an example of a whole number that is not a natural number.
6. Give an example of a rational number that is not an integer.
7. Give an example of a number that is an integer, a whole number, and a natural number.
8. Give an example of a number that is a rational number, an integer, and a real number.

Determine whether each statement in Exercises 9–14 is true or false.

9. $-13 \leq -2$
10. $-6 > 2$
11. $4 \geq -7$
12. $-13 < -5$
13. $-\pi \geq -\pi$
14. $-3 > -13$

In Exercises 15–24, rewrite each expression without absolute value bars.

15. $|300|$
16. $|-203|$
17. $|12 - \pi|$
18. $|7 - \pi|$
19. $|\sqrt{2} - 5|$
20. $|\sqrt{5} - 13|$
21. $\dfrac{-3}{|-3|}$
22. $\dfrac{-7}{|-7|}$
23. $||-3| - |-7||$
24. $||-5| - |-13||$

In Exercises 25–30, evaluate each algebraic expression for $x = 2$ and $y = -5$.

25. $|x + y|$
26. $|x - y|$
27. $|x| + |y|$
28. $|x| - |y|$
29. $\dfrac{y}{|y|}$
30. $\dfrac{|x|}{x} + \dfrac{|y|}{y}$

In Exercises 31–38, express the distance between the given numbers using absolute value. Then find the distance by evaluating the absolute value expression.

31. 2 and 17
32. 4 and 15
33. -2 and 5
34. -6 and 8
35. -19 and -4
36. -26 and -3
37. -3.6 and -1.4
38. -5.4 and -1.2

In Exercises 39–48, evaluate each algebraic expression for the given value of the variable or variables.

39. $5x + 7$; $x = 4$
40. $9x + 6$; $x = 5$
41. $4(x + 3) - 11$; $x = -5$
42. $6(x + 5) - 13$; $x = -7$
43. $\dfrac{5}{9}(F - 32)$; $F = 77$
44. $\dfrac{5}{9}(F - 32)$; $F = 50$
45. $\dfrac{5(x + 2)}{2x - 14}$; $x = 10$
46. $\dfrac{7(x - 3)}{2x - 16}$; $x = 9$
47. $\dfrac{2x + 3y}{x + 1}$; $x = -2$ and $y = 4$
48. $\dfrac{2x + y}{xy - 2x}$; $x = -2$ and $y = 4$

In Exercises 49–58, state the name of the property illustrated.

49. $6 + (-4) = (-4) + 6$
50. $11 \cdot (7 + 4) = 11 \cdot 7 + 11 \cdot 4$
51. $6 + (2 + 7) = (6 + 2) + 7$
52. $6 \cdot (2 \cdot 3) = 6 \cdot (3 \cdot 2)$
53. $(2 + 3) + (4 + 5) = (4 + 5) + (2 + 3)$
54. $7 \cdot (11 \cdot 8) = (11 \cdot 8) \cdot 7$
55. $2(-8 + 6) = -16 + 12$
56. $-8(3 + 11) = -24 + (-88)$
57. $\dfrac{1}{(x + 3)}(x + 3) = 1$, $x \neq -3$
58. $(x + 4) + [-(x + 4)] = 0$

In Exercises 59–68, simplify each algebraic expression.

59. $5(3x + 4) - 4$
60. $2(5x + 4) - 3$
61. $5(3x - 2) + 12x$
62. $2(5x - 1) + 14x$
63. $7(3y - 5) + 2(4y + 3)$
64. $4(2y - 6) + 3(5y + 10)$

65. $5(3y - 2) - (7y + 2)$ **66.** $4(5y - 3) - (6y + 3)$

67. $7 - 4[3 - (4y - 5)]$ **68.** $6 - 5[8 - (2y - 4)]$

In Exercises 69–74, write each algebraic expression without parentheses.

69. $-(-14x)$ **70.** $-(-17y)$

71. $-(2x - 3y - 6)$ **72.** $-(5x - 13y - 1)$

73. $\frac{1}{3}(3x) + [(4y) + (-4y)]$ **74.** $\frac{1}{2}(2y) + [(-7x) + 7x]$

Application Exercises

75. Are first putting on your left shoe and then putting on your right shoe commutative?

76. Are first getting undressed and then taking a shower commutative?

77. Give an example of two things that you do that are not commutative.

78. Give an example of two things that you do that are commutative.

79. The algebraic expression $81 - 0.6x$ approximates the percentage of American adults who smoked cigarettes x years after 1900. Evaluate the expression for $x = 100$. Describe what the answer means in practical terms.

80. The algebraic expression $1527x + 31{,}290$ approximates average yearly earnings for elementary and secondary teachers in the United States x years after 1990. Evaluate the algebraic expression for $x = 10$. Describe what the answer means in practical terms.

81. The optimum heart rate is the rate that a person should achieve during exercise for the exercise to be most beneficial. The algebraic expression

$$0.6(220 - a)$$

describes a person's optimum heart rate, in beats per minute, where a represents the age of the person.

a. Use the distributive property to rewrite the algebraic expression without parentheses.

b. Use each form of the algebraic expression to determine the optimum heart rate for a 20-year-old runner.

Writing in Mathematics

Writing about mathematics will help you learn mathematics. For all writing exercises in this book, use complete sentences to respond to the question. Some writing exercises can be answered in a sentence; others require a paragraph or two. You can decide how much you need to write as long as your writing clearly and directly answers the question in the exercise. Standard references such as a dictionary and a thesaurus should be helpful.

82. How do the whole numbers differ from the natural numbers?

83. Can a real number be both rational and irrational? Explain your answer.

84. If you are given two real numbers, explain how to determine which one is the lesser.

85. How can $\dfrac{|x|}{x}$ be equal to 1 or -1?

86. What is an algebraic expression? Give an example with your explanation.

87. Why is $3(x + 7) - 4x$ not simplified? What must be done to simplify the expression?

88. You can transpose the letters in the word "conversation" to form the phrase "voices rant on." From "total abstainers" we can form "sit not at ale bars." What two algebraic properties do each of these transpositions (called anagrams) remind you of? Explain your answer.

Critical Thinking Exercises

89. Which one of the following statements is true?

a. Every rational number is an integer.

b. Some whole numbers are not integers.

c. Some rational numbers are not positive.

d. Irrational numbers cannot be negative.

90. Which of the following is true?

a. The term x has no numerical coefficient.

b. $5 + 3(x - 4) = 8(x - 4) = 8x - 32$

c. $-x - x = -x + (-x) = 0$

d. $x - 0.02(x + 200) = 0.98x - 4$

In Exercises 91–93, insert either $<$ or $>$ in the box between the numbers to make the statement true.

91. $\sqrt{2} \,\square\, 1.5$ **92.** $-\pi \,\square\, -3.5$

93. $-\dfrac{3.14}{2} \,\square\, -\dfrac{\pi}{2}$

94. A business that manufactures small alarm clocks has a weekly fixed cost of $5000. The average cost per clock for the business to manufacture x clocks is described by

$$\frac{0.5x + 5000}{x}.$$

a. Find the average cost when $x = 100$, 1000, and 10,000.

b. Like all other businesses, the alarm clock manufacturer must make a profit. To do this, each clock must be sold for at least 50¢ more than what it costs to manufacture. Due to competition from a larger company, the clocks can be sold for $1.50 each and no more. Our small manufacturer can only produce 2000 clocks weekly. Does this business have much of a future? Explain.

SECTION P.2 Exponents and Scientific Notation

Objectives

1. Understand and use integer exponents.
2. Use properties of exponents.
3. Simplify exponential expressions.
4. Use scientific notation.

1 Understand and use integer exponents.

Powers of Ten

$$10 = 10^1$$
$$100 = 10^2$$
$$1000 = 10^3$$
$$10,000 = 10^4$$
$$100,000 = 10^5$$
$$1,000,000 = 10^6 \quad \text{million}$$
$$10,000,000 = 10^7$$
$$100,000,000 = 10^8$$
$$1,000,000,000 = 10^9 \quad \text{billion}$$

Technology

You can use a calculator to evaluate exponential expressions. For example, to evaluate 5^3, press the following keys:

Many Scientific Calculators

5 $\boxed{y^x}$ 3 $\boxed{=}$

Many Graphing Calculators

5 $\boxed{\wedge}$ 3 $\boxed{\text{ENTER}}$.

Although calculators have special keys to evaluate powers of ten and squaring bases, you can always use one of the sequences shown here.

Although people do a great deal of talking, the total output since the beginning of gabble to the present day, including all baby talk, love songs, and congressional debates, only amounts to about 10 million billion words. This can be expressed as 16 factors of 10, or 10^{16} words.

Exponents such as 2, 3, 4, and so on are used to indicate repeated multiplication. For example,

$$10^2 = 10 \cdot 10 = 100,$$
$$10^3 = 10 \cdot 10 \cdot 10 = 1000, \quad 10^4 = 10 \cdot 10 \cdot 10 \cdot 10 = 10,000.$$

The 10 that is repeated when multiplying is called the **base.** The small numbers above and to the right of the base are called **exponents** or **powers.** The exponent tells the number of times the base is to be used when multiplying. In 10^3, the base is 10 and the exponent is 3.

Any number with an exponent of 1 is the number itself. Thus, $10^1 = 10$.

Multiplications that are expressed in exponential notation are read as follows:

10^1: "ten to the first power"

10^2: "ten to the second power" or "ten squared"

10^3: "ten to the third power" or "ten cubed"

10^4: "ten to the fourth power"

10^5: "ten to the fifth power"

Any real number can be used as the base. Thus,

$$7^2 = 7 \cdot 7 = 49 \quad \text{and} \quad (-3)^4 = (-3)(-3)(-3)(-3) = 81.$$

The bases are 7 and -3, respectively. Do not confuse $(-3)^4$ and -3^4.

$$-3^4 = -3 \cdot 3 \cdot 3 \cdot 3 = -81$$

The negative is not taken to the power because it is not inside parentheses.

EXAMPLE 1 Evaluating an Exponential Expression

Evaluate: $(-2)^3 \cdot 3^2$.

Solution

$$(-2)^3 \cdot 3^2 = (-2)(-2)(-2) \cdot 3 \cdot 3 = -8 \cdot 9 = -72$$

This is $(-2)^3$, read "-2 cubed." This is 3^2, read "3 squared."

Check Point 1 Evaluate: $(-4)^3 \cdot 2^2$.

The formal algebraic definition of a natural number exponent summarizes our discussion:

Definition of a Natural Number Exponent

If b is a real number and n is a natural number,

Exponent

$$b^n = \underbrace{b \cdot b \cdot b \cdot \cdots \cdot b.}_{b \text{ appears as a factor } n \text{ times.}}$$

Base

b^n is read "the nth power of b" or "b to the nth power." Thus, the nth power of b is defined as the product of n factors of b.
Furthermore, $b^1 = b$.

Negative Integers as Exponents

A nonzero base can be raised to a negative power using the following definition:

The Negative Exponent Rule

If b is any real number other than 0 and n is a natural number, then

$$b^{-n} = \frac{1}{b^n}.$$

EXAMPLE 2 Evaluating Expressions Containing Negative Exponents

Evaluate: **a.** 5^{-3} **b.** $\dfrac{1}{4^{-2}}$.

Solution

a. $5^{-3} = \dfrac{1}{5^3} = \dfrac{1}{5 \cdot 5 \cdot 5} = \dfrac{1}{125}$

b. $\dfrac{1}{4^{-2}} = \dfrac{1}{\dfrac{1}{4^2}} = 4^2 = 4 \cdot 4 = 16$

Study Tip

When a negative integer appears as an exponent, switch the position of the base (from numerator to denominator or from denominator to numerator) and make the exponent positive.

Check Point 2 Evaluate: **a.** 2^{-3} **b.** $\dfrac{1}{6^{-2}}$.

Zero as an Exponent

A nonzero base can be raised to the 0 power using the following definition:

The Zero Exponent Rule

If b is any real number other than 0,
$$b^0 = 1.$$

Here are three examples involving simplification using the zero exponent rule:
$$7^0 = 1 \qquad (-5)^0 = 1 \qquad -5^0 = -1.$$

Only 5 is raised to the zero power.

2 Use properties of exponents.

The Product Rule

Consider the multiplication of two exponential expressions, such as $2^4 \cdot 2^3$. We are multiplying 4 factors of 2 and 3 factors of 2. We have a total of 7 factors of 2. Thus,
$$2^4 \cdot 2^3 = 2^7.$$

We can quickly find the exponent on the product, 7, by adding 4 and 3, the original exponents. This suggests the following rule:

The Product Rule

$$b^m \cdot b^n = b^{m+n}$$

When multiplying exponential expressions with the same base, add the exponents. Use this sum as the exponent of the common base.

A Number with 369 Million Digits

The largest number that can be expressed with only three digits is

$$9^{(9^9)} \text{ or } 9^{387,420,489}.$$

This number begins with $428124773\dots$, has 369 million digits, and would take around 70 years to read.

EXAMPLE 3 Using the Product Rule

Use the product rule to simplify each expression:

a. $2^2 \cdot 2^3$ **b.** $4^2 \cdot 4^{-5}$ **c.** $x^{-3} \cdot x^7$.

Solution

a. $2^2 \cdot 2^3 = 2^{2+3} = 2^5 = 32$ **b.** $4^2 \cdot 4^{-5} = 4^{2+(-5)} = 4^{-3} = \dfrac{1}{4^3} = \dfrac{1}{64}$

c. $x^{-3} \cdot x^7 = x^{-3+7} = x^4$

Check Point 3 Use the product rule to simplify each expression:

a. $3^3 \cdot 3^2$ **b.** $2^4 \cdot 2^{-7}$ **c.** $x^{-5} \cdot x^{11}$.

The Power Rule

The next property of exponents applies when an expression containing a power is itself raised to a power.

The Power Rule (Powers to Powers)

$$(b^m)^n = b^{mn}$$

When an exponential expression is raised to a power, multiply the exponents. Place the product of the exponents on the base and remove the parentheses.

EXAMPLE 4 Using the Power Rule

Use the power rule to simplify each expression:

a. $(2^2)^3$ **b.** $(y^5)^6$ **c.** $(x^{-3})^4$.

Solution

a. $(2^2)^3 = 2^{2 \cdot 3} = 2^6 = 64$ **b.** $(y^5)^6 = y^{5 \cdot 6} = y^{30}$

c. $(x^{-3})^4 = x^{-3 \cdot 4} = x^{-12} = \dfrac{1}{x^{12}}$

Check Point 4 Use the power rule to simplify each expression:

a. $(3^3)^2$ **b.** $(y^7)^4$ **c.** $(x^{-4})^2$.

The Quotient Rule

The next property of exponents applies when we are dividing exponential expressions with the same base.

The Quotient Rule

$$\frac{b^m}{b^n} = b^{m-n}, \; b \neq 0$$

When dividing exponential expressions with the same nonzero base, subtract the exponent in the denominator from the exponent in the numerator. Use this difference as the exponent of the common base.

EXAMPLE 5   Using the Quotient Rule

Use the quotient rule to simplify each expression:

a. $\dfrac{2^8}{2^4}$ **b.** $\dfrac{x^3}{x^7}$ **c.** $\dfrac{y^9}{y^{-5}}.$

Solution

a. $\dfrac{2^8}{2^4} = 2^{8-4} = 2^4 = 16$ **b.** $\dfrac{x^3}{x^7} = x^{3-7} = x^{-4} = \dfrac{1}{x^4}$

c. $\dfrac{y^9}{y^{-5}} = y^{9-(-5)} = y^{9+5} = y^{14}$

Study Tip

$\dfrac{4^3}{4^5}$ and $\dfrac{4^5}{4^3}$ represent different numbers:

$\dfrac{4^3}{4^5} = 4^{3-5} = 4^{-2} = \dfrac{1}{4^2} = \dfrac{1}{16}$

$\dfrac{4^5}{4^3} = 4^{5-3} = 4^2 = 16.$

Check Point 5   Use th&e quotient rule to simplify each expression:

a. $\dfrac{3^6}{3^4}$ **b.** $\dfrac{x^5}{x^{12}}$ **c.** $\dfrac{y^2}{y^{-7}}.$

Products Raised to Powers

The next property of exponents applies when we are raising a product to a power.

Products to Powers

$$(ab)^n = a^n b^n$$

When a product is raised to a power, raise each factor to that power.

EXAMPLE 6   Raising a Product to a Power

Simplify: $(-2y)^4.$

Solution $(-2y)^4 = (-2)^4 y^4 = 16y^4$

Check Point 6   Simplify: $(-4x)^3.$

The rule for products of powers can be extended to cover three or more factors. For example,

$$(-2xy)^3 = (-2)^3 x^3 y^3 = -8x^3 y^3.$$

Quotients Raised to Powers

Our final exponential property applies when we are raising a quotient to a power.

Quotients to Powers

$$\left(\dfrac{a}{b}\right)^n = \dfrac{a^n}{b^n}, \; b \neq 0$$

When a quotient is raised to a power, raise the numerator to that power and divide by the denominator to that power.

EXAMPLE 7 Raising Quotients to Powers

Simplify by raising each quotient to the given power:

a. $\left(\dfrac{2}{5}\right)^4$ **b.** $\left(-\dfrac{3}{x}\right)^3$.

Solution

a. $\left(\dfrac{2}{5}\right)^4 = \dfrac{2^4}{5^4} = \dfrac{16}{625}$ **b.** $\left(-\dfrac{3}{x}\right)^3 = \dfrac{(-3)^3}{x^3} = \dfrac{-27}{x^3}$

Check Point 7 Simplify: **a.** $\left(\dfrac{3}{4}\right)^3$ **b.** $\left(-\dfrac{2}{y}\right)^5$.

3 Simplify exponential expressions.

Simplifying Exponential Expressions

Properties of exponents are used to simplify exponential expressions. Here is a summary of the properties we have discussed.

Properties of Exponents

1. $b^{-n} = \dfrac{1}{b^n}$ **2.** $b^0 = 1$ **3.** $b^m \cdot b^n = b^{m+n}$ **4.** $(b^m)^n = b^{mn}$

5. $\dfrac{b^m}{b^n} = b^{m-n}$ **6.** $(ab)^n = a^n b^n$ **7.** $\left(\dfrac{a}{b}\right)^n = \dfrac{a^n}{b^n}$

An exponential expression is **simplified** when

- No parentheses appear.
- No powers are raised to powers.
- Each base occurs only once.
- No negative exponents appear.

EXAMPLE 8 Simplifying Exponential Expressions

Simplify:

a. $(-3x^4y^5)^3$ **b.** $(-7xy^4)(-2x^5y^6)$ **c.** $\dfrac{-35x^2y^4}{5x^6y^{-8}}$ **d.** $\left(\dfrac{4x^2}{y}\right)^{-3}$.

Solution

a. $(-3x^4y^5)^3 = (-3)^3(x^4)^3(y^5)^3$ Raise each factor inside the parentheses to the third power.

$= (-3)^3 x^{4\cdot3} y^{5\cdot3}$ Multiply powers to powers.

$= -27x^{12}y^{15}$ $(-3)^3 = (-3)(-3)(-3) = -27$

b. $(-7xy^4)(-2x^5y^6) = (-7)(-2)xx^5y^4y^6$ Group factors with the same base.

$= 14x^{1+5}y^{4+6}$ When multiplying expressions with the same base, add the exponents.

$= 14x^6y^{10}$ Simplify.

c. $\dfrac{-35x^2y^4}{5x^6y^{-8}} = \left(\dfrac{-35}{5}\right)\left(\dfrac{x^2}{x^6}\right)\left(\dfrac{y^4}{y^{-8}}\right)$ Group factors with the same base.

$= -7x^{2-6}y^{4-(-8)}$ When dividing an expression with the same base, subtract the exponents.

$= -7x^{-4}y^{12}$ Simplify. Notice that
$4 - (-8) = 4 + 8 = 12.$

$= \dfrac{-7y^{12}}{x^4}$ Move x^{-4}, the factor with the negative exponent, from the numerator to the denominator.

d. $\left(\dfrac{4x^2}{y}\right)^{-3} = \dfrac{4^{-3}(x^2)^{-3}}{y^{-3}}$ Raise each factor inside the parentheses to the -3 power.

$= \dfrac{4^{-3}x^{-6}}{y^{-3}}$ Multiply powers to powers.

$= \dfrac{y^3}{4^3x^6}$ Move factors with negative exponents from the numerator to the denominator (or vice versa) by changing the sign of the exponent.

$= \dfrac{y^3}{64x^6}$ $4^3 = 4 \cdot 4 \cdot 4 = 64$

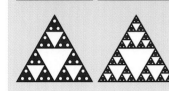

Visualizing Powers of 3

The triangles contain $3, 3^2, 3^3,$ and 3^4 circles.

Check Point 8   Simplify:
a. $(2x^3y^6)^4$ **b.** $(-6x^2y^5)(3xy^3)$ **c.** $\dfrac{100x^{12}y^2}{20x^{16}y^{-4}}$ **d.** $\left(\dfrac{5x}{y^4}\right)^{-2}$.

Study Tip

Try to avoid the following common errors that can occur when simplifying exponential expressions.

Correct	Incorrect	Description of Error
$b^3 \cdot b^4 = b^7$	$b^3 \cdot b^4 = b^{12}$	The exponents should be added, not multiplied.
$3^2 \cdot 3^4 = 3^6$	$3^2 \cdot 3^4 = 9^6$	The common base should be retained, not multiplied.
$\dfrac{5^{16}}{5^4} = 5^{12}$	$\dfrac{5^{16}}{5^4} = 5^4$	The exponents should be subtracted, not divided.
$(4a)^3 = 64a^3$	$(4a)^3 = 4a^3$	Both factors should be cubed.
$b^{-n} = \dfrac{1}{b^n}$	$b^{-n} = -\dfrac{1}{b^n}$	Only the exponent should change sign.
$(a + b)^{-1} = \dfrac{1}{a+b}$	$(a + b)^{-1} = \dfrac{1}{a} + \dfrac{1}{b}$	The exponent applies to the entire expression $a + b$.

4   Use scientific notation.

Scientific Notation

The national debt of the United States is about \$5.6 trillion. A stack of \$1 bills equaling the national debt would rise to twice the distance from the Earth to the moon. Because a trillion is 10^{12}, the national debt can be expressed as

$$5.6 \times 10^{12}.$$

The number 5.6×10^{12} is written in a form called *scientific notation*. A number in **scientific notation** is expressed as a number greater than or equal to 1 and less than 10 multiplied by some power of 10. It is customary to use the multiplication symbol, $\times$, rather than a dot, to indicate multiplication in scientific notation. Here are two examples of numbers in scientific notation:

- Each day, 2.6×10^7 pounds of dust from the atmosphere settle on Earth.
- The diameter of a hydrogen atom is 1.016×10^{-8} centimeter.

We can use the exponent on the 10 to change a number in scientific notation to decimal notation. If the exponent is *positive*, move the decimal point in the number to the *right* the same number of places as the exponent. If the exponent is *negative*, move the decimal point in the number to the *left* the same number of places as the exponent.

EXAMPLE 9 Converting from Scientific to Decimal Notation

Write each number in decimal notation:

a. 2.6×10^7 **b.** 1.016×10^{-8}.

Solution

a. We express 2.6×10^7 in decimal notation by moving the decimal point in 2.6 seven places to the right. We need to add six zeros.

$$2.6 \times 10^7 = 26,000,000$$

b. We express 1.016×10^{-8} in decimal notation by moving the decimal point in 1.016 eight places to the left. We need to add seven zeros to the right of the decimal point.

$$1.016 \times 10^{-8} = 0.00000001016$$

Check Point 9 Write each number in decimal notation:

a. 7.4×10^9 **b.** 3.017×10^{-6}.

To convert from decimal notation to scientific notation, we reverse the procedure of Example 9.

- Move the decimal point in the given number to obtain a number greater than or equal to 1 and less than 10.
- The number of places the decimal point moves gives the exponent on 10; the exponent is positive if the given number is greater than 10 and negative if the given number is between 0 and 1.

EXAMPLE 10 Converting from Decimal Notation to Scientific Notation

Write each number in scientific notation:

a. 4,600,000   **b.** 0.00023.

Solution

a. $4,600,000 = 4.6 \times 10^?$ $\xrightarrow{\text{Decimal point moves 6 places.}}$ 4.6×10^6

b. $0.00023 = 2.3 \times 10^{-?}$ $\xrightarrow{\text{Decimal point moves 4 places.}}$ 2.3×10^{-4}

Technology

You can use your calculator's EE (enter exponent) or EXP key to convert from decimal to scientific notation. Here is how it's done for 0.00023:

Many Scientific Calculators

Keystrokes	Display
.00023 EE =	2.3 − 04

Many Graphing Calculators

Use the mode setting for scientific notation.

Keystrokes	Display
.00023 ENTER	2.3E−4

Check Point 10

Write each number in scientific notation:

a. 7,410,000,000　　　　**b.** 0.000000092.

Technology

$(3.4 \times 10^9)(2 \times 10^{-5})$
On a Calculator:

Many Scientific Calculators

3.4 [EE] 9 [×] 2 [EE] 5 [+/−] [=]

Display

6.8　04

Many Graphing Calculators

3.4 [EE] 9 [×] 2 [EE] [(−)] 5 [ENTER]

Display (in scientific notation mode)

6.8E 4

Computations with Scientific Notation

The product and quotient rules for exponents can be used to multiply or divide numbers that are expressed in scientific notation. For example, here's how to find the product of 3.4×10^9 and 2×10^{-5}.

$$(3.4 \times 10^9)(2 \times 10^{-5}) = (3.4 \times 2) \times (10^9 \times 10^{-5})$$
$$= 6.8 \times 10^{9+(-5)}$$
$$= 6.8 \times 10^4 \quad \text{or} \quad 68,000$$

In our next example, we use the quotient of two numbers in scientific notation to help put a number into perspective. The number is our national debt. The United States began accumulating large deficits in the 1980s. To finance the deficit, the government had borrowed $5.6 trillion as of the end of 2000. The graph in Figure P.6 shows the national debt increasing over time.

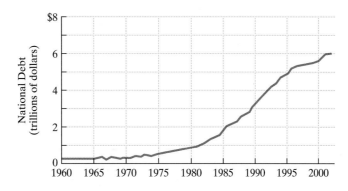

Figure P.6 The national debt

Source: Office of Management and Budget

EXAMPLE 11　The National Debt

As of the end of 2000, the national debt was $5.6 trillion, or 5.6×10^{12} dollars. At that time, the U.S. population was approximately 280,000,000 (280 million), or 2.8×10^8. If the national debt were evenly divided among every individual in the United States, how much would each citizen have to pay?

Technology

Here is the keystroke sequence for solving Example 11 using a calculator:

5.6 [EE] 12 [÷] 2.8 [EE] 8.

The quotient is displayed by pressing [=] on a scientific calculator and [ENTER] on a graphing calculator. The answer can be displayed in scientific or decimal notation. Consult your manual.

Solution　The amount each citizen must pay is the total debt, 5.6×10^{12} dollars, divided by the number of citizens, 2.8×10^8.

$$\frac{5.6 \times 10^{12}}{2.8 \times 10^8} = \left(\frac{5.6}{2.8}\right) \times \left(\frac{10^{12}}{10^8}\right)$$
$$= 2 \times 10^{12-8}$$
$$= 2 \times 10^4$$
$$= 20,000$$

Every U.S. citizen would have to pay about $20,000 to the federal government to pay off the national debt. A family of three would owe $60,000.

Check Point 11 In 2000, Americans spent 3.6×10^9 dollars on full-fat ice cream. At that time, the U.S. population was approximately 280 million, or 2.8×10^8. If ice cream spending is evenly divided, how much did each American spend?

EXERCISE SET P.2

Practice Exercises

Evaluate each exponential expression in Exercises 1–22.

1. $5^2 \cdot 2$ **2.** $6^2 \cdot 2$

3. $(-2)^6$ **4.** $(-2)^4$

5. -2^6 **6.** -2^4

7. $(-3)^0$ **8.** $(-9)^0$

9. -3^0 **10.** -9^0

11. 4^{-3} **12.** 2^{-6}

13. $2^2 \cdot 2^3$ **14.** $3^3 \cdot 3^2$

15. $(2^2)^3$ **16.** $(3^3)^2$

17. $\dfrac{2^8}{2^4}$ **18.** $\dfrac{3^8}{3^4}$

19. $3^{-3} \cdot 3$ **20.** $2^{-3} \cdot 2$

21. $\dfrac{2^3}{2^7}$ **22.** $\dfrac{3^4}{3^7}$

Simplify each exponential expression in Exercises 23–64.

23. $x^{-2}y$ **24.** xy^{-3}

25. x^0y^5 **26.** x^7y^0

27. $x^3 \cdot x^7$ **28.** $x^{11} \cdot x^5$

29. $x^{-5} \cdot x^{10}$ **30.** $x^{-6} \cdot x^{12}$

31. $(x^3)^7$ **32.** $(x^{11})^5$

33. $(x^{-5})^3$ **34.** $(x^{-6})^4$

35. $\dfrac{x^{14}}{x^7}$ **36.** $\dfrac{x^{30}}{x^{10}}$

37. $\dfrac{x^{14}}{x^{-7}}$ **38.** $\dfrac{x^{30}}{x^{-10}}$

39. $(8x^3)^2$ **40.** $(6x^4)^2$

41. $\left(-\dfrac{4}{x}\right)^3$ **42.** $\left(-\dfrac{6}{y}\right)^3$

43. $(-3x^2y^5)^2$ **44.** $(-3x^4y^6)^3$

45. $(3x^4)(2x^7)$ **46.** $(11x^5)(9x^{12})$

47. $(-9x^3y)(-2x^6y^4)$ **48.** $(-5x^4y)(-6x^7y^{11})$

49. $\dfrac{8x^{20}}{2x^4}$ **50.** $\dfrac{20x^{24}}{10x^6}$

51. $\dfrac{25a^{13}b^4}{-5a^2b^3}$ **52.** $\dfrac{35a^{14}b^6}{-7a^7b^3}$

53. $\dfrac{14b^7}{7b^{14}}$ **54.** $\dfrac{20b^{10}}{10b^{20}}$

55. $(4x^3)^{-2}$ **56.** $(10x^2)^{-3}$

57. $\dfrac{24x^3y^5}{32x^7y^{-9}}$ **58.** $\dfrac{10x^4y^9}{30x^{12}y^{-3}}$

59. $\left(\dfrac{5x^3}{y}\right)^{-2}$ **60.** $\left(\dfrac{3x^4}{y}\right)^{-3}$

61. $\left(\dfrac{-15a^4b^2}{5a^{10}b^{-3}}\right)^3$ **62.** $\left(\dfrac{-30a^{14}b^8}{10a^{17}b^{-2}}\right)^3$

63. $\left(\dfrac{3a^{-5}b^2}{12a^3b^{-4}}\right)^0$ **64.** $\left(\dfrac{4a^{-5}b^3}{12a^3b^{-5}}\right)^0$

In Exercises 65–72, write each number in decimal notation.

65. 4.7×10^3 **66.** 9.12×10^5

67. 4×10^6 **68.** 7×10^6

69. 7.86×10^{-4} **70.** 4.63×10^{-5}

71. 3.18×10^{-6} **72.** 5.84×10^{-7}

In Exercises 73–80, write each number in scientific notation.

73. 3600   **74.** 2700

75. 220,000,000   **76.** 370,000,000,000

77. 0.027   **78.** 0.014

79. 0.000763   **80.** 0.000972

In Exercises 81–88, perform the indicated operation and express the answer in decimal notation.

81. $(2 \times 10^3)(3 \times 10^2)$ **82.** $(5 \times 10^2)(4 \times 10^4)$

83. $(4.1 \times 10^2)(3 \times 10^{-4})$ **84.** $(1.2 \times 10^3)(2 \times 10^{-5})$

85. $\dfrac{12 \times 10^6}{4 \times 10^2}$ **86.** $\dfrac{20 \times 10^{26}}{10 \times 10^{15}}$

87. $\dfrac{6.3 \times 10^3}{3 \times 10^5}$ **88.** $\dfrac{9.6 \times 10^2}{3 \times 10^{-3}}$

In Exercises 89–92, write each number in scientific notation and use scientific notation to perform the operation(s). Express the answer in scientific notation.

89. $\dfrac{480,000,000,000}{0.00012}$ **90.** $\dfrac{282,000,000,000}{0.00141}$

91. $\dfrac{0.00072 \times 0.003}{0.00024}$ **92.** $\dfrac{66,000 \times 0.001}{0.003 \times 0.002}$

Application Exercises

Use 10^{12} for one trillion and 2.8×10^8 for the U.S. population in 2000 to solve Exercises 93–95.

93. In 2000, the government collected approximately $1.9 trillion in taxes. What was the per capita tax burden, or the amount that each U.S. citizen paid in taxes? Round to the nearest hundred dollars.

94. In 2000, U.S. personal income was $8 trillion. What was the per capita income, or the income per U.S. citizen? Round to the nearest hundred dollars.

95. In the United States, we spend an average of $4000 per person each year on health care—the highest in the world. What do we spend each year on health care nationwide? Express the answer in scientific notation.

96. Approximately 2×10^4 people run in the New York City Marathon each year. Each runner runs a distance of 26 miles. Write the total distance covered by all the runners (assuming that each person completes the marathon) in scientific notation.

97. The mass of one oxygen molecule is 5.3×10^{-23} gram. Find the mass of 20,000 molecules of oxygen. Express the answer in scientific notation.

98. The mass of one hydrogen atom is 1.67×10^{-24} gram. Find the mass of 80,000 hydrogen atoms. Express the answer in scientific notation.

Writing in Mathematics

99. Describe what it means to raise a number to a power. In your description, include a discussion of the difference between -5^2 and $(-5)^2$.

100. Explain the product rule for exponents. Use $2^3 \cdot 2^5$ in your explanation.

101. Explain the power rule for exponents. Use $(3^2)^4$ in your explanation.

102. Explain the quotient rule for exponents. Use $\dfrac{5^8}{5^2}$ in your explanation.

103. Why is $(-3x^2)(2x^{-5})$ not simplified? What must be done to simplify the expression?

104. How do you know if a number is written in scientific notation?

105. Explain how to convert from scientific to decimal notation and give an example.

106. Explain how to convert from decimal to scientific notation and give an example.

Critical Thinking Exercises

107. Which one of the following is true?

   a. $4^{-2} < 4^{-3}$ **b.** $5^{-2} > 2^{-5}$

   c. $(-2)^4 = 2^{-4}$ **d.** $5^2 \cdot 5^{-2} > 2^5 \cdot 2^{-5}$

108. The mad Dr. Frankenstein has gathered enough bits and pieces (so to speak) for $2^{-1} + 2^{-2}$ of his creature-to-be. Write a fraction that represents the amount of his creature that must still be obtained.

109. If $b^A = MN$, $b^C = M$, and $b^D = N$, what is the relationship among $A, C,$ and D?

Group Exercise

110. Putting Numbers into Perspective. A large number can be put into perspective by comparing it with another number. For example, we put the $5.6 trillion national debt into perspective by comparing it to the number of U.S. citizens. The total distance covered by all the runners in the New York City Marathon (Exercise 96) can be put into perspective by comparing this distance with, say, the distance from New York to San Francisco.

   For this project, each group member should consult an almanac, a newspaper, or the World Wide Web to find a number greater than one million. Explain to other members of the group the context in which the large number is used. Express the number in scientific notation. Then put the number into perspective by comparing it with another number.

SECTION P.3   Radicals and Rational Exponents

Objectives

1. Evaluate square roots.
2. Use the product rule to simplify square roots.
3. Use the quotient rule to simplify square roots.
4. Add and subtract square roots.
5. Rationalize denominators.
6. Evaluate and perform operations with higher roots.
7. Understand and use rational exponents.

What is the maximum speed at which a racing cyclist can turn a corner without tipping over? The answer, in miles per hour, is given by the algebraic expression $4\sqrt{x}$, where x is the radius of the corner, in feet. Algebraic expressions containing roots describe phenomena as diverse as a wild animal's territorial area, evaporation on a lake's surface, and Albert Einstein's bizarre concept of how an astronaut moving close to the speed of light would barely age relative to friends watching from Earth. No description of your world can be complete without roots and radicals. In this section, we review the basics of radical expressions and the use of rational exponents to indicate radicals.

1   Evaluate square roots.

Square Roots

The **principal square root** of a nonnegative real number b, written $\sqrt{b}$, is that number whose square equals b. For example,

$$\sqrt{100} = 10 \text{ because } 10^2 = 100 \quad \text{and} \quad \sqrt{0} = 0 \text{ because } 0^2 = 0.$$

Observe that the principal square root of a positive number is positive and the principal square root of 0 is 0.

The symbol $\sqrt{}$ that we use to denote the principal square root is called a **radical sign**. The number under the radical sign is called the **radicand**. Together we refer to the radical sign and its radicand as a **radical.**

The following definition summarizes our discussion:

> **Definition of the Principal Square Root**
>
> If a is a nonnegative real number, the nonnegative number b such that $b^2 = a$, denoted by $b = \sqrt{a}$, is the **principal square root** of a.

In the real number system, negative numbers do not have square roots. For example, $\sqrt{-9}$ is not a real number because there is no real number whose square is -9.

If a number is nonnegative $(a \geq 0)$, then $\left(\sqrt{a}\right)^2 = a$. For example,

$$\left(\sqrt{2}\right)^2 = 2, \quad \left(\sqrt{3}\right)^2 = 3, \quad \left(\sqrt{4}\right)^2 = 4, \quad \text{and} \left(\sqrt{5}\right)^2 = 5.$$

A number that is the square of a rational number is called a **perfect square.** For example,

64 is a perfect square because $64 = 8^2$.

$\frac{1}{9}$ is a perfect square because $\frac{1}{9} = \left(\frac{1}{3}\right)^2$.

The following rule can be used to find square roots of perfect squares:

> **Square Roots of Perfect Squares**
> $$\sqrt{a^2} = |a|$$

For example, $\sqrt{6^2} = 6$ and $\sqrt{(-6)^2} = |-6| = 6$.

2   Use the product rule to simplify square roots.

The Product Rule for Square Roots

A square root is **simplified** when its radicand has no factors other than 1 that are perfect squares. For example, $\sqrt{500}$ is not simplified because it can be expressed as $\sqrt{100 \cdot 5}$ and $\sqrt{100}$ is a perfect square. The **product rule for square roots** can be used to simplify $\sqrt{500}$.

> **The Product Rule for Square Roots**
> If a and b represent nonnegative real numbers, then
> $$\sqrt{ab} = \sqrt{a}\sqrt{b} \text{ and } \sqrt{a}\sqrt{b} = \sqrt{ab}.$$
> The square root of a product is the product of the square roots.

Example 1 shows how the product rule is used to remove from the square root any perfect squares that occur as factors.

EXAMPLE 1   **Using the Product Rule to Simplify Square Roots**

Simplify: **a.** $\sqrt{500}$ **b.** $\sqrt{6x} \cdot \sqrt{3x}$.

Solution

a. $\sqrt{500} = \sqrt{100 \cdot 5}$ 100 is the largest perfect square factor of 500.

$\qquad\quad = \sqrt{100}\sqrt{5}$ $\sqrt{ab} = \sqrt{a}\sqrt{b}$

$\qquad\quad = 10\sqrt{5}$ $\sqrt{100} = 10$

b. We can simplify $\sqrt{6x} \cdot \sqrt{3x}$ using the power rule only if $6x$ and $3x$ represent nonnegative real numbers. Thus, $x \geq 0$.

$\sqrt{6x} \cdot \sqrt{3x} = \sqrt{6x \cdot 3x}$ $\sqrt{a}\sqrt{b} = \sqrt{ab}$

$\qquad\qquad = \sqrt{18x^2}$ Multiply.

$\qquad\qquad = \sqrt{9x^2 \cdot 2}$ 9 is the largest perfect square factor of 18.

$\qquad\qquad = \sqrt{9x^2}\sqrt{2}$ $\sqrt{ab} = \sqrt{a}\sqrt{b}$

$\qquad\qquad = \sqrt{9}\sqrt{x^2}\sqrt{2}$ Split $\sqrt{9x^2}$ into two square roots.

$\qquad\qquad = 3x\sqrt{2}$ $\sqrt{9} = 3$ (because $3^2 = 9$) and $\sqrt{x^2} = x$ because $x \geq 0$.

Check Point 1 Simplify:
  a. $\sqrt{3^2}$ **b.** $\sqrt{5x} \cdot \sqrt{10x}$.

3 Use the quotient rule to simplify square roots.

The Quotient Rule for Square Roots

Another property for square roots involves division.

> **The Quotient Rule for Square Roots**
>
> If a and b represent nonnegative real numbers and $b \neq 0$, then
> $$\frac{\sqrt{a}}{\sqrt{b}} = \sqrt{\frac{a}{b}} \quad \text{and} \quad \sqrt{\frac{a}{b}} = \frac{\sqrt{a}}{\sqrt{b}}.$$
> The square root of a quotient is the quotient of the square roots.

EXAMPLE 2 Using the Quotient Rule to Simplify Square Roots

Simplify: **a.** $\sqrt{\dfrac{100}{9}}$ **b.** $\dfrac{\sqrt{48x^3}}{\sqrt{6x}}$.

Solution

a. $\sqrt{\dfrac{100}{9}} = \dfrac{\sqrt{100}}{\sqrt{9}} = \dfrac{10}{3}$

b. We can simplify the quotient of $\sqrt{48x^3}$ and $\sqrt{6x}$ using the quotient rule only if $48x^3$ and $6x$ represent nonnegative real numbers. Thus, $x \geq 0$.

$$\frac{\sqrt{48x^3}}{\sqrt{6x}} = \sqrt{\frac{48x^3}{6x}} = \sqrt{8x^2} = \sqrt{4x^2}\sqrt{2} = \sqrt{4}\sqrt{x^2}\sqrt{2} = 2x\sqrt{2}$$

$\sqrt{x^2} = x$ because $x \geq 0$.

Check Point 2 Simplify: **a.** $\sqrt{\dfrac{25}{16}}$ **b.** $\dfrac{\sqrt{150x^3}}{\sqrt{2x}}$.

4 Add and subtract square roots.

Adding and Subtracting Square Roots

Two or more square roots can be combined provided that they have the same radicand. Such radicals are called **like radicals.** For example,
$$7\sqrt{11} + 6\sqrt{11} = (7 + 6)\sqrt{11} = 13\sqrt{11}.$$

EXAMPLE 3 Adding and Subtracting Like Radicals

Add or subtract as indicated:
  a. $7\sqrt{2} + 5\sqrt{2}$ **b.** $\sqrt{5x} - 7\sqrt{5x}$.

Solution

a. $7\sqrt{2} + 5\sqrt{2} = (7 + 5)\sqrt{2}$ Apply the distributive property.

      $= 12\sqrt{2}$ Simplify.

b. $\sqrt{5x} - 7\sqrt{5x} = 1\sqrt{5x} - 7\sqrt{5x}$ Write $\sqrt{5x}$ as $1\sqrt{5x}$.

      $= (1 - 7)\sqrt{5x}$ Apply the distributive property.

      $= -6\sqrt{5x}$ Simplify.

Check Point 3   Add or subtract as indicated:

   a. $8\sqrt{13} + 9\sqrt{13}$ **b.** $\sqrt{17x} - 20\sqrt{17x}.$

In some cases, radicals can be combined once they have been simplified. For example, to add $\sqrt{2}$ and $\sqrt{8}$, we can write $\sqrt{8}$ as $\sqrt{4 \cdot 2}$ because 4 is a perfect square factor of 8.

$$\sqrt{2} + \sqrt{8} = \sqrt{2} + \sqrt{4 \cdot 2} = 1\sqrt{2} + 2\sqrt{2} = (1 + 2)\sqrt{2} = 3\sqrt{2}$$

EXAMPLE 4   Combining Radicals That First Require Simplification

Add or subtract as indicated:

   a. $7\sqrt{3} + \sqrt{12}$ **b.** $4\sqrt{50x} - 6\sqrt{32x}.$

Solution

a. $7\sqrt{3} + \sqrt{12}$

      $= 7\sqrt{3} + \sqrt{4 \cdot 3}$ Split 12 into two factors such that one is a perfect square.

      $= 7\sqrt{3} + 2\sqrt{3}$ $\sqrt{4 \cdot 3} = \sqrt{4}\sqrt{3} = 2\sqrt{3}$

      $= (7 + 2)\sqrt{3}$ Apply the distributive property. You will find that this step is usually done mentally.

      $= 9\sqrt{3}$ Simplify.

b. $4\sqrt{50x} - 6\sqrt{32x}$

      $= 4\sqrt{25 \cdot 2x} - 6\sqrt{16 \cdot 2x}$ 25 is the largest perfect square factor of 50 and 16 is the largest perfect square factor of 32.

      $= 4 \cdot 5\sqrt{2x} - 6 \cdot 4\sqrt{2x}$ $\sqrt{25 \cdot 2} = \sqrt{25}\sqrt{2} = 5\sqrt{2}$ and $\sqrt{16 \cdot 2} = \sqrt{16}\sqrt{2} = 4\sqrt{2}.$

      $= 20\sqrt{2x} - 24\sqrt{2x}$ Multiply.

      $= (20 - 24)\sqrt{2x}$ Apply the distributive property.

      $= -4\sqrt{2x}$ Simplify.

Check Point 4   Add or subtract as indicated:

   a. $5\sqrt{27} + \sqrt{12}$ **b.** $6\sqrt{18x} - 4\sqrt{8x}.$

5 Rationalize denominators.

Rationalizing Denominators

You can use a calculator to compare the approximate values for $\dfrac{1}{\sqrt{3}}$ and $\dfrac{\sqrt{3}}{3}$.

The two approximations are the same. This is not a coincidence:

$$\frac{1}{\sqrt{3}} = \frac{1}{\sqrt{3}} \cdot \boxed{\frac{\sqrt{3}}{\sqrt{3}}} = \frac{\sqrt{3}}{\sqrt{9}} = \frac{\sqrt{3}}{3}.$$

Any number divided by itself is 1.
Multiplication by 1 does not
change the value of $\dfrac{1}{\sqrt{3}}$.

This process involves rewriting a radical expression as an equivalent expression in which the denominator no longer contains a radical. The process is called **rationalizing the denominator.** If the denominator contains the square root of a natural number that is not a perfect square, **multiply the numerator and denominator by the smallest number that produces the square root of a perfect square in the denominator.**

EXAMPLE 5   Rationalizing Denominators

Rationalize the denominator: **a.** $\dfrac{15}{\sqrt{6}}$ **b.** $\dfrac{12}{\sqrt{8}}$.

Solution

a. If we multiply numerator and denominator by $\sqrt{6}$, the denominator becomes $\sqrt{6} \cdot \sqrt{6} = \sqrt{36} = 6$. Therefore, we multiply by 1, choosing $\dfrac{\sqrt{6}}{\sqrt{6}}$ for 1.

$$\frac{15}{\sqrt{6}} = \frac{15}{\sqrt{6}} \cdot \frac{\sqrt{6}}{\sqrt{6}} = \frac{15\sqrt{6}}{\sqrt{36}} = \frac{15\sqrt{6}}{6} = \frac{5\sqrt{6}}{2}$$

Multiply by 1.

Simplify: $\dfrac{15}{6} = \dfrac{15 \div 3}{6 \div 3} = \dfrac{5}{2}$.

b. The *smallest* number that will produce a perfect square in the denominator of $\dfrac{12}{\sqrt{8}}$ is $\sqrt{2}$, because $\sqrt{8} \cdot \sqrt{2} = \sqrt{16} = 4$. We multiply by 1, choosing $\dfrac{\sqrt{2}}{\sqrt{2}}$ for 1.

$$\frac{12}{\sqrt{8}} = \frac{12}{\sqrt{8}} \cdot \frac{\sqrt{2}}{\sqrt{2}} = \frac{12\sqrt{2}}{\sqrt{16}} = \frac{12\sqrt{2}}{4} = 3\sqrt{2}$$

Check Point 5   Rationalize the denominator: **a.** $\dfrac{5}{\sqrt{3}}$ **b.** $\dfrac{6}{\sqrt{12}}$.

How can we rationalize a denominator if the denominator contains two terms? In general,

$$\left(\sqrt{a} + \sqrt{b}\right)\left(\sqrt{a} - \sqrt{b}\right) = \left(\sqrt{a}\right)^2 - \left(\sqrt{b}\right)^2 = a - b.$$

Notice that the product does not contain a radical. Here are some specific examples.

The Denominator Contains:	Multiply by:	The New Denominator Contains:
$7 + \sqrt{5}$	$7 - \sqrt{5}$	$7^2 - \left(\sqrt{5}\right)^2 = 49 - 5 = 44$
$\sqrt{3} - 6$	$\sqrt{3} + 6$	$\left(\sqrt{3}\right)^2 - 6^2 = 3 - 36 = -33$
$\sqrt{7} + \sqrt{3}$	$\sqrt{7} - \sqrt{3}$	$\left(\sqrt{7}\right)^2 - \left(\sqrt{3}\right)^2 = 7 - 3 = 4$

EXAMPLE 6 **Rationalizing a Denominator Containing Two Terms**

Rationalize the denominator: $\dfrac{7}{5 + \sqrt{3}}$.

Solution   If we multiply the numerator and denominator by $5 - \sqrt{3}$, the denominator will not contain a radical. Therefore, we multiply by 1, choosing $\dfrac{5 - \sqrt{3}}{5 - \sqrt{3}}$ for 1.

$$\frac{7}{5 + \sqrt{3}} = \frac{7}{5 + \sqrt{3}} \cdot \frac{5 - \sqrt{3}}{5 - \sqrt{3}} = \frac{7\left(5 - \sqrt{3}\right)}{5^2 - \left(\sqrt{3}\right)^2} = \frac{7\left(5 - \sqrt{3}\right)}{25 - 3}$$

Multiply by 1.

$$= \frac{7\left(5 - \sqrt{3}\right)}{22} \quad \text{or} \quad \frac{35 - 7\sqrt{3}}{22}.$$

In either form of the answer, there is no radical in the denominator.

 Check Point 6   Rationalize the denominator: $\dfrac{8}{4 + \sqrt{5}}$.

6 Evaluate and perform operations with higher roots.

Other Kinds of Roots

We define the **principal nth root** of a real number a, symbolized by $\sqrt[n]{a}$, as follows:

Definition of the Principal nth Root of a Real Number

$$\sqrt[n]{a} = b \text{ means that } b^n = a.$$

If n, the **index**, is even, then a is nonnegative ($a \geq 0$) and b is also nonnegative ($b \geq 0$). If n is odd, a and b can be any real numbers.

For example,

$$\sqrt[3]{64} = 4 \text{ because } 4^3 = 64 \quad \text{and} \quad \sqrt[5]{-32} = -2 \text{ because } (-2)^5 = -32.$$

The same vocabulary that we learned for square roots applies to nth roots. The symbol $\sqrt[n]{a}$ is called a **radical** and a is called the **radicand**.

A number that is the nth power of a rational number is called a **perfect nth power**. For example, 8 is a perfect third power, or perfect cube, because $8 = 2^3$. In general, one of the following rules can be used to find nth roots of perfect nth powers:

Finding nth Roots of Perfect nth Powers

If n is odd, $\sqrt[n]{a^n} = a$.
If n is even, $\sqrt[n]{a^n} = |a|$.

For example,

$$\sqrt[3]{(-2)^3} = -2 \quad \text{and} \quad \sqrt[4]{(-2)^4} = |-2| = 2.$$

> Absolute value is not needed with odd roots, but is necessary with even roots.

The Product and Quotient Rules for Other Roots

The product and quotient rules apply to cube roots, fourth roots, and all higher roots.

The Product and Quotient Rules for nth Roots

For all real numbers, where the indicated roots represent real numbers,

$$\sqrt[n]{a} \cdot \sqrt[n]{b} = \sqrt[n]{ab} \quad \text{and} \quad \frac{\sqrt[n]{a}}{\sqrt[n]{b}} = \sqrt[n]{\frac{a}{b}}, \quad b \neq 0.$$

EXAMPLE 7 Simplifying, Multiplying, and Dividing Higher Roots

Simplify: **a.** $\sqrt[3]{24}$ **b.** $\sqrt[4]{8} \cdot \sqrt[4]{4}$ **c.** $\sqrt[4]{\dfrac{81}{16}}$.

Solution

a. $\sqrt[3]{24} = \sqrt[3]{8 \cdot 3}$ Find the largest perfect cube that is a factor of 24. $\sqrt[3]{8} = 2$, so 8 is a perfect cube and is the largest perfect cube factor of 24.

Study Tip

Some higher even and odd roots occur so frequently that you might want to memorize them.

Cube Roots	
$\sqrt[3]{1} = 1$	$\sqrt[3]{125} = 5$
$\sqrt[3]{8} = 2$	$\sqrt[3]{216} = 6$
$\sqrt[3]{27} = 3$	$\sqrt[3]{1000} = 10$
$\sqrt[3]{64} = 4$	

Fourth Roots	Fifth Roots
$\sqrt[4]{1} = 1$	$\sqrt[5]{1} = 1$
$\sqrt[4]{16} = 2$	$\sqrt[5]{32} = 2$
$\sqrt[4]{81} = 3$	$\sqrt[5]{243} = 3$
$\sqrt[4]{256} = 4$	
$\sqrt[4]{625} = 5$	

$$= \sqrt[3]{8} \cdot \sqrt[3]{3} \qquad \sqrt[n]{ab} = \sqrt[n]{a}\,\sqrt[n]{b}$$
$$= 2\sqrt[3]{3}$$

b. $\sqrt[4]{8} \cdot \sqrt[4]{4} = \sqrt[4]{8 \cdot 4}$ $\qquad \sqrt[n]{a} \cdot \sqrt[n]{b} = \sqrt[n]{ab}$

$$= \sqrt[4]{32} \qquad \text{Find the largest perfect fourth power that is a factor of 32.}$$

$$= \sqrt[4]{16 \cdot 2} \qquad \sqrt[4]{16} = 2, \text{ so 16 is a perfect fourth power and is the largest perfect fourth power that is a factor of 32.}$$

$$= \sqrt[4]{16} \cdot \sqrt[4]{2} \qquad \sqrt[n]{ab} = \sqrt[n]{a} \cdot \sqrt[n]{b}$$

$$= 2\sqrt[4]{2}$$

c. $\sqrt[4]{\dfrac{81}{16}} = \dfrac{\sqrt[4]{81}}{\sqrt[4]{16}} \qquad \sqrt[n]{\dfrac{a}{b}} = \dfrac{\sqrt[n]{a}}{\sqrt[n]{b}}$

$$= \dfrac{3}{2} \qquad \sqrt[4]{81} = 3 \text{ because } 3^4 = 81 \text{ and } \sqrt[4]{16} = 2 \text{ because } 2^4 = 16.$$

Check Point 7 Simplify: **a.** $\sqrt[3]{40}$ **b.** $\sqrt[5]{8} \cdot \sqrt[5]{8}$ **c.** $\sqrt[3]{\dfrac{125}{27}}$.

We have seen that adding and subtracting square roots often involves simplifying terms. The same idea applies to adding and subtracting *n*th roots.

EXAMPLE 8 Combining Cube Roots

Subtract: $5\sqrt[3]{16} - 11\sqrt[3]{2}$.

Solution

$$5\sqrt[3]{16} - 11\sqrt[3]{2}$$

$$= 5\sqrt[3]{8 \cdot 2} - 11\sqrt[3]{2} \qquad \text{Because } 16 = 8 \cdot 2 \text{ and } \sqrt[3]{8} = 2, \text{ 8 is the largest perfect cube that is a factor of 16.}$$

$$= 5 \cdot 2\sqrt[3]{2} - 11\sqrt[3]{2} \qquad \sqrt[3]{8 \cdot 2} = \sqrt[3]{8}\,\sqrt[3]{2} = 2\sqrt[3]{2}$$

$$= 10\sqrt[3]{2} - 11\sqrt[3]{2} \qquad \text{Multiply.}$$

$$= (10 - 11)\sqrt[3]{2} \qquad \text{Apply the distributive property.}$$

$$= -1\sqrt[3]{2} \text{ or } -\sqrt[3]{2} \qquad \text{Simplify.}$$

Check Point 8 Subtract: $3\sqrt[3]{81} - 4\sqrt[3]{3}$.

7 Understand and use rational exponents.

Rational Exponents

Animals in the wild have regions to which they confine their movement, called their territorial area. Territorial area, in square miles, is related to an animal's body weight. If an animal weighs W pounds, its territorial area is

$$W^{141/100}$$

square miles.

W to the *what* power?! How can we interpret the information given by this algebraic expression?

In the last part of this section, we turn our attention to rational exponents such as $\frac{141}{100}$ and their relationship to roots of real numbers.

Definition of Rational Exponents

If $\sqrt[n]{a}$ represents a real number and $n \geq 2$ is an integer, then

$$a^{1/n} = \sqrt[n]{a}.$$

Furthermore,

$$a^{-1/n} = \frac{1}{a^{1/n}} = \frac{1}{\sqrt[n]{a}}, \; a \neq 0.$$

EXAMPLE 9   Using the Definition of $a^{1/n}$

Simplify: **a.** $64^{1/2}$ **b.** $8^{1/3}$ **c.** $64^{-1/3}$.

Solution

  a. $64^{1/2} = \sqrt{64} = 8$ **b.** $8^{1/3} = \sqrt[3]{8} = 2$

  c. $64^{-1/3} = \dfrac{1}{64^{1/3}} = \dfrac{1}{\sqrt[3]{64}} = \dfrac{1}{4}$

Check Point 9   Simplify: **a.** $81^{1/2}$ **b.** $27^{1/3}$ **c.** $32^{-1/5}$.

Note that every rational exponent in Example 9 has a numerator of 1 or -1. We now define rational exponents with any integer in the numerator.

Definition of Rational Exponents

If $\sqrt[n]{a}$ represents a real number, $\dfrac{m}{n}$ is a rational number reduced to lowest terms, and $n \geq 2$ is an integer, then

$$a^{m/n} = \left(\sqrt[n]{a}\right)^m = \sqrt[n]{a^m}.$$

The exponent m/n consists of two parts: the denominator n is the root and the numerator m is the exponent. Furthermore,

$$a^{-m/n} = \frac{1}{a^{m/n}}.$$

EXAMPLE 10   Using the Definition of $a^{m/n}$

Simplify: **a.** $27^{2/3}$ **b.** $9^{3/2}$ **c.** $16^{-3/4}$.

Technology

Solution

a. $27^{2/3} = \left(\sqrt[3]{27} \right)^2 = 3^2 = 9$

The denominator of $\frac{2}{3}$ is the root and the numerator is the exponent.

b. $9^{3/2} = \left(\sqrt{9} \right)^3 = 3^3 = 27$

c. $16^{-3/4} = \dfrac{1}{16^{3/4}} = \dfrac{1}{\left(\sqrt[4]{16} \right)^3} = \dfrac{1}{2^3} = \dfrac{1}{8}$

> **Check Point 10** Simplify: **a.** $4^{3/2}$ **b.** $32^{-2/5}$.

Properties of exponents can be applied to expressions containing rational exponents.

EXAMPLE 11   Simplifying Expressions with Rational Exponents

Simplify using properties of exponents:

a. $\left(5x^{1/2} \right)\left(7x^{3/4} \right)$ **b.** $\dfrac{32x^{5/3}}{16x^{3/4}}$.

Solution

a. $\left(5x^{1/2} \right)\left(7x^{3/4} \right) = 5 \cdot 7x^{1/2} \cdot x^{3/4}$ Group factors with the same base.

$= 35x^{(1/2)+(3/4)}$ When multiplying expressions with the same base, add the exponents.

$= 35x^{5/4}$ $\frac{1}{2} + \frac{3}{4} = \frac{2}{4} + \frac{3}{4} = \frac{5}{4}$

b. $\dfrac{32x^{5/3}}{16x^{3/4}} = \left(\dfrac{32}{16} \right)\left(\dfrac{x^{5/3}}{x^{3/4}} \right)$ Group factors with the same base.

$= 2x^{(5/3)-(3/4)}$ When dividing expressions with the same base, subtract the exponents.

$= 2x^{11/12}$ $\frac{5}{3} - \frac{3}{4} = \frac{20}{12} - \frac{9}{12} = \frac{11}{12}$

> **Check Point 11** Simplify: **a.** $\left(2x^{4/3} \right)\left(5x^{8/3} \right)$ **b.** $\dfrac{20x^4}{5x^{3/2}}$.

Rational exponents are sometimes useful for simplifying radicals by reducing their index.

EXAMPLE 12 Reducing the Index of a Radical

Simplify: $\sqrt[9]{x^3}$.

Solution $\sqrt[9]{x^3} = x^{3/9} = x^{1/3} = \sqrt[3]{x}$

Check Point 12 Simplify: $\sqrt[6]{x^3}$.

EXERCISE SET P.3

Practice Exercises

Evaluate each expression in Exercises 1–6 or indicate that the root is not a real number.

1. $\sqrt{36}$ **2.** $\sqrt{25}$
3. $\sqrt{-36}$ **4.** $\sqrt{-25}$
5. $\sqrt{(-13)^2}$ **6.** $\sqrt{(-17)^2}$

Use the product rule to simplify the expressions in Exercises 7–16. In Exercises 11–16, assume that variables represent nonnegative real numbers.

7. $\sqrt{50}$ **8.** $\sqrt{27}$
9. $\sqrt{45x^2}$ **10.** $\sqrt{125x^2}$
11. $\sqrt{2x} \cdot \sqrt{6x}$ **12.** $\sqrt{10x} \cdot \sqrt{8x}$
13. $\sqrt{x^3}$ **14.** $\sqrt{y^3}$
15. $\sqrt{2x^2} \cdot \sqrt{6x}$ **16.** $\sqrt{6x} \cdot \sqrt{3x^2}$

Use the quotient rule to simplify the expressions in Exercises 17–26. Assume that $x > 0$.

17. $\sqrt{\dfrac{1}{81}}$ **18.** $\sqrt{\dfrac{1}{49}}$

19. $\sqrt{\dfrac{49}{16}}$ **20.** $\sqrt{\dfrac{121}{9}}$

21. $\dfrac{\sqrt{48x^3}}{\sqrt{3x}}$ **22.** $\dfrac{\sqrt{72x^3}}{\sqrt{8x}}$

23. $\dfrac{\sqrt{150x^4}}{\sqrt{3x}}$ **24.** $\dfrac{\sqrt{24x^4}}{\sqrt{3x}}$

25. $\dfrac{\sqrt{200x^3}}{\sqrt{10x^{-1}}}$ **26.** $\dfrac{\sqrt{500x^3}}{\sqrt{10x^{-1}}}$

In Exercises 27–38, add or subtract terms whenever possible.

27. $7\sqrt{3} + 6\sqrt{3}$ **28.** $8\sqrt{5} + 11\sqrt{5}$
29. $6\sqrt{17x} - 8\sqrt{17x}$ **30.** $4\sqrt{13x} - 6\sqrt{13x}$
31. $\sqrt{8} + 3\sqrt{2}$ **32.** $\sqrt{20} + 6\sqrt{5}$
33. $\sqrt{50x} - \sqrt{8x}$ **34.** $\sqrt{63x} - \sqrt{28x}$
35. $3\sqrt{18} + 5\sqrt{50}$ **36.** $4\sqrt{12} - 2\sqrt{75}$
37. $3\sqrt{8} - \sqrt{32} + 3\sqrt{72} - \sqrt{75}$

38. $3\sqrt{54} - 2\sqrt{24} - \sqrt{96} + 4\sqrt{63}$

In Exercises 39–48, rationalize the denominator.

39. $\dfrac{1}{\sqrt{7}}$ **40.** $\dfrac{2}{\sqrt{10}}$

41. $\dfrac{\sqrt{2}}{\sqrt{5}}$ **42.** $\dfrac{\sqrt{7}}{\sqrt{3}}$

43. $\dfrac{13}{3 + \sqrt{11}}$ **44.** $\dfrac{3}{3 + \sqrt{7}}$

45. $\dfrac{7}{\sqrt{5} - 2}$ **46.** $\dfrac{5}{\sqrt{3} - 1}$

47. $\dfrac{6}{\sqrt{5} + \sqrt{3}}$ **48.** $\dfrac{11}{\sqrt{7} - \sqrt{3}}$

Evaluate each expression in Exercises 49–60, or indicate that the root is not a real number.

49. $\sqrt[3]{125}$ **50.** $\sqrt[3]{8}$
51. $\sqrt[3]{-8}$ **52.** $\sqrt[3]{-125}$
53. $\sqrt[4]{-16}$ **54.** $\sqrt[4]{-81}$
55. $\sqrt[4]{(-3)^4}$ **56.** $\sqrt[4]{(-2)^4}$
57. $\sqrt[5]{(-3)^5}$ **58.** $\sqrt[5]{(-2)^5}$
59. $\sqrt[5]{-\frac{1}{32}}$ **60.** $\sqrt[6]{\frac{1}{64}}$

Simplify the radical expressions in Exercises 61–68.

61. $\sqrt[3]{32}$ **62.** $\sqrt[3]{150}$

63. $\sqrt[3]{x^4}$ **64.** $\sqrt[3]{x^5}$

65. $\sqrt[3]{9} \cdot \sqrt[3]{6}$ **66.** $\sqrt[3]{12} \cdot \sqrt[3]{4}$

67. $\dfrac{\sqrt[5]{64x^6}}{\sqrt[5]{2x}}$ **68.** $\dfrac{\sqrt[4]{162x^5}}{\sqrt[4]{2x}}$

In Exercises 69–76, add or subtract terms whenever possible.

69. $4\sqrt[5]{2} + 3\sqrt[5]{2}$ **70.** $6\sqrt[5]{3} + 2\sqrt[5]{3}$
71. $5\sqrt[3]{16} + \sqrt[3]{54}$ **72.** $3\sqrt[3]{24} + \sqrt[3]{81}$
73. $\sqrt[3]{54xy^3} - y\sqrt[3]{128x}$ **74.** $\sqrt[3]{24xy^3} - y\sqrt[3]{81x}$
75. $\sqrt{2} + \sqrt[3]{8}$ **76.** $\sqrt{3} + \sqrt[3]{15}$

In Exercises 77–84, evaluate each expression without using a calculator.

77. $36^{1/2}$ **78.** $121^{1/2}$

79. $8^{1/3}$ **80.** $27^{1/3}$

81. $125^{2/3}$ **82.** $8^{2/3}$

83. $32^{-4/5}$ **84.** $16^{-5/2}$

In Exercises 85–94, simplify using properties of exponents.

85. $(7x^{1/3})(2x^{1/4})$ **86.** $(3x^{2/3})(4x^{3/4})$

87. $\dfrac{20x^{1/2}}{5x^{1/4}}$ **88.** $\dfrac{72x^{3/4}}{9x^{1/3}}$

89. $(x^{2/3})^3$ **90.** $(x^{4/5})^5$

91. $(25x^4y^6)^{1/2}$ **92.** $(125x^9y^6)^{1/3}$

93. $\dfrac{(3y^{1/4})^3}{y^{1/12}}$ **94.** $\dfrac{(2y^{1/5})^4}{y^{3/10}}$

In Exercises 95–102, simplify by reducing the index of the radical.

95. $\sqrt[4]{5^2}$ **96.** $\sqrt[4]{7^2}$

97. $\sqrt[3]{x^6}$ **98.** $\sqrt[4]{x^{12}}$

99. $\sqrt[6]{x^4}$ **100.** $\sqrt[9]{x^6}$

101. $\sqrt[9]{x^6y^3}$ **102.** $\sqrt[12]{x^4y^8}$

Application Exercises

103. The algebraic expression $2\sqrt{5L}$ is used to estimate the speed of a car prior to an accident, in miles per hour, based on the length of its skid marks, L, in feet. Find the speed of a car that left skid marks 40 feet long, and write the answer in simplified radical form.

104. The time, in seconds, that it takes an object to fall a distance d, in feet, is given by the algebraic expression $\sqrt{\dfrac{d}{16}}$. Find how long it will take a ball dropped from the top of a building 320 feet tall to hit the ground. Write the answer in simplified radical form.

105. The early Greeks believed that the most pleasing of all rectangles were golden rectangles whose ratio of width to height is

$$\frac{w}{h} = \frac{2}{\sqrt{5} - 1}.$$

Rationalize the denominator for this ratio and then use a calculator to approximate the answer correct to the nearest hundredth.

106. The amount of evaporation, in inches per day, of a large body of water can be described by the algebraic expression

$$\frac{w}{20\sqrt{a}}$$

where

    a = surface area of the water, in square miles

    w = average wind speed of the air over the water, in miles per hour.

Determine the evaporation on a lake whose surface area is 9 square miles on a day when the wind speed over the water is 10 miles per hour.

107. In the Peanuts cartoon shown below, Woodstock appears to be working steps mentally. Fill in the missing steps that show how to go from $\dfrac{7\sqrt{2 \cdot 2 \cdot 3}}{6}$ to $\dfrac{7}{3}\sqrt{3}$.

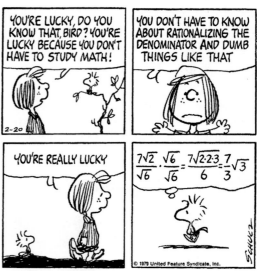

PEANUTS reprinted by permission of United Feature Syndicate, Inc.

108. The algebraic expression $152a^{-1/5}$ describes the percentage of U.S. taxpayers who are a years old who file early. Evaluate the algebraic expression for $a = 32$. Describe what the answer means in practical terms.

109. The algebraic expression $0.07d^{3/2}$ describes the duration of a storm, in hours, whose diameter is d miles. Evaluate the algebraic expression for $d = 9$. Describe what the answer means in practical terms.

 ## Writing in Mathematics

110. Explain how to simplify $\sqrt{10} \cdot \sqrt{5}$.

111. Explain how to add $\sqrt{3} + \sqrt{12}$.

112. Describe what it means to rationalize a denominator. Use both $\dfrac{1}{\sqrt{5}}$ and $\dfrac{1}{5 + \sqrt{5}}$ in your explanation.

113. What difference is there in simplifying $\sqrt[3]{(-5)^3}$ and $\sqrt[4]{(-5)^4}$?

114. What does $a^{m/n}$ mean?

115. Describe the kinds of numbers that have rational fifth roots.

116. Why must a and b represent nonnegative numbers when we write $\sqrt{a} \cdot \sqrt{b} = \sqrt{ab}$? Is it necessary to use this restriction in the case of $\sqrt[3]{a} \cdot \sqrt[3]{b} = \sqrt[3]{ab}$? Explain.

 Technology Exercises

117. The algebraic expression
$$\frac{73t^{1/3} - 28t^{2/3}}{t}$$
describes the percentage of people in the United States applying for jobs t years after 1985 who tested positive for illegal drugs. Use a calculator to find the percentage who tested positive from 1986 through 2001. Round answers to the nearest hundredth of a percent. What trend do you observe for the percentage of potential employees testing positive for illegal drugs over time?

118. The territorial area of an animal in the wild is defined to be the area of the region to which the animal confines its movements. The algebraic expression $W^{1.41}$ describes the territorial area, in square miles, of an animal that weighs W pounds. Use a calculator to find the territorial area of animals weighing 25, 50, 150, 200, 250, and 300 pounds. What do the values indicate about the relationship between body weight and territorial area?

 Critical Thinking Exercises

119. Which one of the following is true?

   a. Neither $(-8)^{1/2}$ nor $(-8)^{1/3}$ represent real numbers.

   b. $\sqrt{x^2 + y^2} = x + y$

   c. $8^{-1/3} = -2$

   d. $2^{1/2} \cdot 2^{1/2} = 2$

In Exercises 120–121, fill in each box to make the statement true.

120. $\left(5 + \sqrt{\square}\right)\left(5 - \sqrt{\square}\right) = 22$

121. $\sqrt{\square x^{\square}} = 5x^7$

122. Find exact value of $\sqrt{13 + \sqrt{2} + \dfrac{7}{3 + \sqrt{2}}}$ without the use of a calculator.

123. Place the correct symbol, $>$ or $<$, in the box between each of the given numbers. *Do not use a calculator.* Then check your result with a calculator.

   a. $3^{1/2} \;\square\; 3^{1/3}$ **b.** $\sqrt{7} + \sqrt{18} \;\square\; \sqrt{7 + 18}$

SECTION P.4 *Polynomials*

Objectives

1. Understand the vocabulary of polynomials.

2. Add and subtract polynomials.

3. Multiply polynomials.

4. Use FOIL in polynomial multiplication.

5. Use special products in polynomial multiplication.

6. Perform operations with polynomials in several variables.

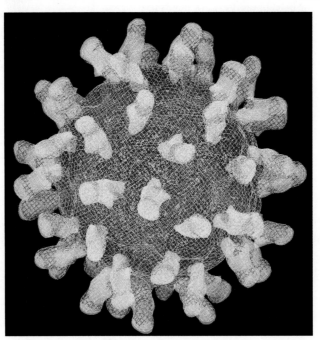

This computer-simulated model of the common cold virus was developed by researchers at Purdue University. Their discovery of how the virus infects human cells could lead to more effective treatment for the illness.

Runny nose? Sneezing? You are probably familiar with the unpleasant onset of a cold. We "catch cold" when the cold virus enters our bodies, where it multiplies. Fortunately, at a certain point the virus begins to die. The algebraic expression $-0.75x^4 + 3x^3 + 5$ describes the billions of viral particles in our bodies after x days of invasion. The expression enables mathematicians to determine the day on which there is a maximum number of viral particles and, consequently, the day we feel sickest.

The algebraic expression $-0.75x^4 + 3x^3 + 5$ is an example of a polynomial. A **polynomial** is a single term or the sum of two or more terms containing variables with whole number exponents. This particular polynomial contains three terms. Equations containing polynomials are used in such diverse areas as science, business, medicine, psychology, and sociology. In this section, we review basic ideas about polynomials and their operations.

1 Understand the vocabulary of polynomials.

The Vocabulary of Polynomials

Consider the polynomial

$$7x^3 - 9x^2 + 13x - 6.$$

We can express this polynomial as

$$7x^3 + (-9x^2) + 13x + (-6).$$

The polynomial contains four terms. It is customary to write the terms in the order of descending powers of the variable. This is the **standard form** of a polynomial.

We begin this section by limiting our discussion to polynomials containing only one variable. Each term of a polynomial in x is of the form ax^n. The **degree** of ax^n is n. For example, the degree of the term $7x^3$ is 3.

Study Tip

We can express 0 in many ways, including $0x$, $0x^2$, and $0x^3$. It is impossible to assign a single exponent on the variable. This is why 0 has no defined degree.

The Degree of ax^n

If $a \neq 0$, the degree of ax^n is n. The degree of a nonzero constant is 0. The constant 0 has no defined degree.

Here is an example of a polynomial and the degree of each of its four terms:

$$6x^4 - 3x^3 + 2x - 5.$$

| degree 4 | degree 3 | degree 1 | degree of non-zero constant: 0 |

Notice that the exponent on x for the term $2x$ is understood to be 1: $2x^1$. For this reason, the degree of $2x$ is 1. You can think of -5 as $-5x^0$; thus, its degree is 0.

A polynomial which when simplified has exactly one term is called a **monomial**. A **binomial** is a simplified polynomial that has two terms, each with a different exponent. A **trinomial** is a simplified polynomial with three terms, each with a different exponent. Simplified polynomials with four or more terms have no special names.

The **degree of a polynomial** is the highest degree of all the terms of the polynomial. For example, $4x^2 + 3x$ is a binomial of degree 2 because the degree of the first term is 2, and the degree of the other term is less than 2. Also, $7x^5 - 2x^2 + 4$ is a trinomial of degree 5 because the degree of the first term is 5, and the degrees of the other terms are less than 5.

Up to now, we have used x to represent the variable in a polynomial. However, any letter can be used. For example,

- $7x^5 - 3x^3 + 8$ is a polynomial (in x) of degree 5.
- $6y^3 + 4y^2 - y + 3$ is a polynomial (in y) of degree 3.
- $z^7 + \sqrt{2}$ is a polynomial (in z) of degree 7.

Not every algebraic expression is a polynomial. Algebraic expressions whose variables do not contain whole number exponents such as

$$3x^{-2} + 7 \quad \text{and} \quad 5x^{3/2} + 9x^{1/2} + 2$$

are not polynomials. Furthermore, a quotient of polynomials such as

$$\frac{x^2 + 2x + 5}{x^3 - 7x^2 + 9x - 3}$$

is not a polynomial because the form of a polynomial involves only addition and subtraction of terms, not division.

We can tie together the threads of our discussion with the formal definition of a polynomial in one variable. In this definition, the coefficients of the terms are represented by a_n (read "a sub n"), a_{n-1} (read "a sub n minus 1"), a_{n-2}, and so on. The small letters to the lower right of each a are called **subscripts** and are *not exponents*. Subscripts are used to distinguish one constant from another when a large and undetermined number of such constants are needed.

Definition of a Polynomial in x

A **polynomial in x** is an algebraic expression of the form

$$a_n x^n + a_{n-1} x^{n-1} + a_{n-2} x^{n-2} + \cdots + a_1 x + a_0,$$

where $a_n, a_{n-1}, a_{n-2}, \ldots, a_1$, and a_0 are real numbers, $a_n \neq 0$, and n is a nonnegative integer. The polynomial is of **degree n**, a_n is the **leading coefficient,** and a_0 is the **constant term.**

---

2   Add and subtract polynomials.

Adding and Subtracting Polynomials

Polynomials are added and subtracted by combining like terms. For example, we can combine the monomials $-9x^3$ and $13x^3$ using addition as follows:

$$-9x^3 + 13x^3 = (-9 + 13)x^3 = 4x^3.$$

EXAMPLE 1   Adding and Subtracting Polynomials

Perform the indicated operations and simplify:

    a. $(-9x^3 + 7x^2 - 5x + 3) + (13x^3 + 2x^2 - 8x - 6)$
    b. $(7x^3 - 8x^2 + 9x - 6) - (2x^3 - 6x^2 - 3x + 9)$.

Solution

    a. $(-9x^3 + 7x^2 - 5x + 3) + (13x^3 + 2x^2 - 8x - 6)$

$$= (-9x^3 + 13x^3) + (7x^2 + 2x^2) \qquad \text{\textit{Group like terms.}}$$
$$+ (-5x - 8x) + (3 - 6)$$
$$= 4x^3 + 9x^2 + (-13x) + (-3) \qquad \text{\textit{Combine like terms.}}$$
$$= 4x^3 + 9x^2 - 13x - 3 \qquad\qquad\quad \text{\textit{Simplify.}}$$

Study Tip

You can also arrange like terms in columns and combine vertically:

$$\begin{array}{r} 7x^3 - 8x^2 + 9x - 6 \\ -2x^3 + 6x^2 + 3x - 9 \\ \hline 5x^3 - 2x^2 + 12x - 15 \end{array}$$

The like terms can be combined by adding their coefficients and keeping the same variable factor.

b. $(7x^3 - 8x^2 + 9x - 6) - (2x^3 - 6x^2 - 3x + 9)$

$= (7x^3 - 8x^2 + 9x - 6) + (-2x^3 + 6x^2 + 3x - 9)$ Rewrite subtraction as addition of the additive inverse. Be sure to change the sign of each term inside parentheses preceded by the negative sign.

$= (7x^3 - 2x^3) + (-8x^2 + 6x^2)$ Group like terms.
$\quad + (9x + 3x) + (-6 - 9)$
$= 5x^3 + (-2x^2) + 12x + (-15)$ Combine like terms.
$= 5x^3 - 2x^2 + 12x - 15$ Simplify.

Check Point 1 Perform the indicated operations and simplify:

a. $(-17x^3 + 4x^2 - 11x - 5) + (16x^3 - 3x^2 + 3x - 15)$
b. $(13x^3 - 9x^2 - 7x + 1) - (-7x^3 + 2x^2 - 5x + 9)$.

3 Multiply polynomials.

Multiplying Polynomials

The product of two monomials is obtained by using properties of exponents. For example,

$$(-8x^6)(5x^3) = -8 \cdot 5x^{6+3} = -40x^9.$$

Multiply coefficients and add exponents.

Furthermore, we can use the distributive property to multiply a monomial and a polynomial that is not a monomial. For example,

$$3x^4(2x^3 - 7x + 3) = 3x^4 \cdot 2x^3 - 3x^4 \cdot 7x + 3x^4 \cdot 3 = 6x^7 - 21x^5 + 9x^4.$$

monomial   trinomial

How do we multiply two polynomials if neither is a monomial? For example, consider

$$(2x + 3)(x^2 + 4x + 5).$$

binomial   trinomial

One way to perform this multiplication is to distribute $2x$ throughout the trinomial

$$2x(x^2 + 4x + 5)$$

and 3 throughout the trinomial

$$3(x^2 + 4x + 5).$$

Then combine the like terms that result.

Multiplying Polynomials when Neither is a Monomial

Multiply each term of one polynomial by each term of the other polynomial. Then combine like terms.

EXAMPLE 2 **Multiplying a Binomial and a Trinomial**

Multiply: $(2x + 3)(x^2 + 4x + 5)$.

Solution

$(2x + 3)(x^2 + 4x + 5)$

$= 2x(x^2 + 4x + 5) + 3(x^2 + 4x + 5)$ | Multiply the trinomial by each term of the binomial.

$= 2x \cdot x^2 + 2x \cdot 4x + 2x \cdot 5 + 3 \cdot x^2 + 3 \cdot 4x + 3 \cdot 5$ | Use the distributive property.

$= 2x^3 + 8x^2 + 10x + 3x^2 + 12x + 15$ | Multiply the monomials: multiply coefficients and add exponents.

$= 2x^3 + 11x^2 + 22x + 15$ | Combine like terms: $8x^2 + 3x^2 = 11x^2$ and $10x + 12x = 22x$.

Another method for solving Example 2 is to use a vertical format similar to that used for multiplying whole numbers.

$$
\begin{array}{r}
x^2 + 4x + 5 \\
2x + 3 \\
\hline
3x^2 + 12x + 15 \\
2x^3 + 8x^2 + 10x \\
\hline
2x^3 + 11x^2 + 22x + 15
\end{array}
$$

Write like terms in the same column.

$3(x^2 + 4x + 5)$

$2x(x^2 + 4x + 5)$

Combine like terms.

Check Point 2   Multiply: $(5x - 2)(3x^2 - 5x + 4)$.

4 Use FOIL in polynomial multiplication.

The Product of Two Binomials: FOIL

Frequently we need to find the product of two binomials. We can use a method called FOIL, which is based on the distributive property, to do so. For example, we can find the product of the binomials $3x + 2$ and $4x + 5$ as follows:

$(3x + 2)(4x + 5) = 3x(4x + 5) + 2(4x + 5)$ First, distribute $3x$ over $4x + 5$. Then distribute 2.

$= 3x(4x) + 3x(5) + 2(4x) + 2(5)$

$= 12x^2 + 15x + 8x + 10.$

Two binomials can be quickly multiplied by using the FOIL method, in which F represents the product of the **first** terms in each binomial, O represents the product of the **outside** terms, I represents the product of the two **inside** terms, and L represents the product of the **last,** or second, terms in each binomial.

$$(3x + 2)(4x + 5) = 12x^2 + 15x + 8x + 10$$

$$= 12x^2 + 23x + 10$$ Combine like terms.

In general, here is how to use the FOIL method to find the product of $ax + b$ and $cx + d$:

Using the FOIL Method to Multiply Binomials

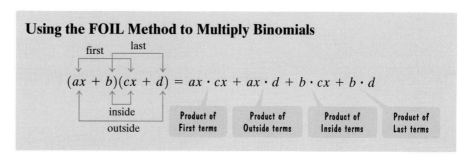

$$(ax + b)(cx + d) = ax \cdot cx + ax \cdot d + b \cdot cx + b \cdot d$$

| Product of First terms | Product of Outside terms | Product of Inside terms | Product of Last terms |

EXAMPLE 3 **Using the FOIL Method**

Multiply: $(3x + 4)(5x - 3)$.

Solution

$$
\begin{aligned}
(3x + 4)(5x - 3) &= \overset{F}{3x \cdot 5x} + \overset{O}{3x(-3)} + \overset{I}{4 \cdot 5x} + \overset{L}{4(-3)} \\
&= 15x^2 - 9x + 20x - 12 \\
&= 15x^2 + 11x - 12 \quad \textit{Combine like terms.}
\end{aligned}
$$

Check Point 3 Multiply: $(7x - 5)(4x - 3)$.

---

5 Use special products in polynomial multiplication.

Multiplying the Sum and Difference of Two Terms

We can use the FOIL method to multiply $A + B$ and $A - B$ as follows:

$$(A + B)(A - B) = \overset{F}{A^2} - \overset{O}{AB} + \overset{I}{AB} - \overset{L}{B^2} = A^2 - B^2.$$

Notice that the outside and inside products have a sum of 0 and the terms cancel. The FOIL multiplication provides us with a quick rule for multiplying the sum and difference of two terms, referred to as a special-product formula.

The Product of the Sum and Difference of Two Terms

$$(A + B)(A - B) = A^2 - B^2$$

The product of the sum and the difference of the same two terms   is   the square of the first term minus the square of the second term.

EXAMPLE 4 Finding the Product of the Sum and Difference of Two Terms

Find each product:

a. $(4y + 3)(4y - 3)$ **b.** $(5a^4 + 6)(5a^4 - 6)$.

Solution Use the special-product formula shown.

$$(A + B)(A - B) = A^2 - B^2$$

First term squared − Second term squared = Product

a. $(4y + 3)(4y - 3) = (4y)^2 - 3^2 = 16y^2 - 9$

b. $(5a^4 + 6)(5a^4 - 6) = (5a^4)^2 - 6^2 = 25a^8 - 36$

Check Point 4 Find each product:

a. $(7x + 8)(7x - 8)$ **b.** $(2y^3 - 5)(2y^3 + 5)$.

The Square of a Binomial

Let us find $(A + B)^2$, the square of a binomial sum. To do so, we begin with the FOIL method and look for a general rule.

F O I L

$$(A + B)^2 = (A + B)(A + B) = A \cdot A + A \cdot B + A \cdot B + B \cdot B$$
$$= A^2 + 2AB + B^2$$

This result implies the following rule, which is another example of a special-product formula:

The Square of a Binomial Sum

$$(A + B)^2 = A^2 + 2AB + B^2$$

The square of a binomial sum is first term squared plus 2 times the product of the terms plus last term squared.

Study Tip

Caution! The square of a sum is *not* the sum of the squares.

$(A + B)^2 \neq A^2 + B^2$

The middle term 2AB is missing

$(x + 3)^2 \neq x^2 + 9$

Incorrect

Show that $(x + 3)^2$ and $x^2 + 9$ are not equal by substituting 5 for x in each expression and simplifying.

EXAMPLE 5 Finding the Square of a Binomial Sum

Square each binomial:

a. $(x + 3)^2$ **b.** $(3x + 7)^2$.

Solution   Use the special-product formula shown.

$$(A + B)^2 = \quad A^2 \quad + \quad 2AB \quad + \quad B^2$$

Square a Sum	(First Term)^2	$+$	2 · Product of the Terms	$+$	(Last Term)^2	= Product
a. $(x + 3)^2 =$	x^2	$+$	$2 \cdot x \cdot 3$	$+$	3^2	$= x^2 + 6x + 9$
b. $(3x + 7)^2 =$	$(3x)^2$	$+$	$2(3x)(7)$	$+$	7^2	$= 9x^2 + 42x + 49$

Check Point 5   Square each binomial:

a. $(x + 10)^2$ **b.** $(5x + 4)^2$.

Using the FOIL method on $(A - B)^2$, the square of a binomial difference, we obtain the following rule:

The Square of a Binomial Difference

$$(A - B)^2 \quad = \quad A^2 \quad - \quad 2AB \quad + \quad B^2$$

The square of a binomial difference is first term squared minus 2 times the product of the terms plus last term squared.

EXAMPLE 6   **Finding the Square of a Binomial Difference**

Square each binomial:

a. $(x - 4)^2$ **b.** $(5y - 6)^2$.

Solution   Use the special-product formula shown.

$$(A - B)^2 = \quad A^2 \quad - \quad 2AB \quad + \quad B^2$$

Square a Difference	(First Term)^2	$-$	2 · Product of the Terms	$+$	(Last Term)^2	= Product
a. $(x - 4)^2 =$	x^2	$-$	$2 \cdot x \cdot 4$	$+$	4^2	$= x^2 - 8x + 16$
b. $(5y - 6)^2 =$	$(5y)^2$	$-$	$2(5y)(6)$	$+$	6^2	$= 25y^2 - 60y + 36$

Check Point 6   Square each binomial:

a. $(x - 9)^2$ **b.** $(7x - 3)^2$.

Special Products

There are several products that occur so frequently that it's convenient to memorize the form, or pattern, of these formulas.

Special Products

Let A and B represent real numbers, variables, or algebraic expressions.

Special Product	Example
Sum and Difference of Two Terms	
$(A + B)(A - B) = A^2 - B^2$	$(2x + 3)(2x - 3) = (2x)^2 - 3^2$
	$= 4x^2 - 9$
Squaring a Binomial	
$(A + B)^2 = A^2 + 2AB + B^2$	$(y + 5)^2 = y^2 + 2 \cdot y \cdot 5 + 5^2$
	$= y^2 + 10y + 25$
$(A - B)^2 = A^2 - 2AB + B^2$	$(3x - 4)^4$
	$= (3x)^2 - 2 \cdot 3x \cdot 4 + 4^2$
	$= 9x^2 - 24x + 16$
Cubing a Binomial	
$(A + B)^3 = A^3 + 3A^2B + 3AB^2 + B^3$	$(x + 4)^3$
	$= x^3 + 3x^2(4) + 3x(4)^2 + 4^3$
	$= x^3 + 12x^2 + 48x + 64$
$(A - B)^3 = A^3 - 3A^2B + 3AB^2 - B^3$	$(x - 2)^3$
	$= x^3 - 3x^2(2) + 3x(2)^2 - 2^3$
	$= x^3 - 6x^2 + 12x - 8$

Study Tip

Although it's convenient to memorize these forms, the FOIL method can be used on all five examples in the box. To cube $x + 4$, you can first square $x + 4$ using FOIL and then multiply this result by $x + 4$. In short, you do not necessarily have to utilize these special formulas. What is the advantage of knowing and using these forms?

6 Perform operations with polynomials in several variables.

Polynomials in Several Variables

The next time you visit the lumber yard and go rummaging through piles of wood, think *polynomials*, although polynomials a bit different from those we have encountered so far. The construction industry uses a polynomial in two variables to determine the number of board feet that can be manufactured from a tree with a diameter of x inches and a length of y feet. This polynomial is

$$\tfrac{1}{4}x^2y - 2xy + 4y.$$

In general, a **polynomial in two variables,** x and y, contains the sum of one or more monomials in the form ax^ny^m. The constant, a, is the **coefficient.** The exponents, n and m, represent whole numbers. The **degree** of the monomial ax^ny^m is $n + m$. We'll use the polynomial from the construction industry to illustrate these ideas.

The coefficients are $\frac{1}{4}$, **−2**, and **4.**

$$\tfrac{1}{4}x^2y \qquad -2xy \qquad +4y$$

| Degree of monomial: $2 + 1 = 3$ | Degree of monomial: $1 + 1 = 2$ | Degree of monomial: $0 + 1 = 1$ |

The **degree of a polynomial in two variables** is the highest degree of all its terms. For the preceding polynomial, the degree is 3.

Polynomials containing two or more variables can be added, subtracted, and multiplied just like polynomials that contain only one variable.

EXAMPLE 7   Subtracting Polynomials in Two Variables

Subtract as indicated:

$$(5x^3 - 9x^2y + 3xy^2 - 4) - (3x^3 - 6x^2y - 2xy^2 + 3).$$

Solution

$(5x^3 - 9x^2y + 3xy^2 - 4) - (3x^3 - 6x^2y - 2xy^2 + 3)$

$= (5x^3 - 9x^2y + 3xy^2 - 4) + (-3x^3 + 6x^2y + 2xy^2 - 3)$

Change the sign of each term in the second polynomial and add the two polynomials.

$= (5x^3 - 3x^3) + (-9x^2y + 6x^2y) + (3xy^2 + 2xy^2) + (-4 - 3)$

Group like terms.

$= 2x^3 - 3x^2y + 5xy^2 - 7$ Combine like terms by combining coefficients and keeping the same variable factors.

Check Point 7   Subtract: $(x^3 - 4x^2y + 5xy^2 - y^3) - (x^3 - 6x^2y + y^3).$

EXAMPLE 8   Multiplying Polynomials in Two Variables

Multiply: **a.** $(x + 4y)(3x - 5y)$ **b.** $(5x + 3y)^2.$

Solution   We will perform the multiplication in part (a) using the FOIL method. We will multiply in part (b) using the formula for the square of a binomial sum, $(A + B)^2$.

a. $(x + 4y)(3x - 5y)$ Multiply these binomials using the FOIL method.

F   O   I   L

$= (x)(3x) + (x)(-5y) + (4y)(3x) + (4y)(-5y)$
$= 3x^2 - 5xy + 12xy - 20y^2$
$= 3x^2 + 7xy - 20y^2$ Combine like terms.

$(A + B)^2 = A^2 + 2 \cdot A \cdot B + B^2$

b. $(5x + 3y)^2 = (5x)^2 + 2(5x)(3y) + (3y)^2$
$= 25x^2 + 30xy + 9y^2$

Check Point 8   Multiply:

a. $(7x - 6y)(3x - y)$ **b.** $(x^2 + 5y)^2.$

EXERCISE SET P.4

Practice Exercises

In Exercises 1–4, is the algebraic expression a polynomial? If it is, write the polynomial in standard form.

1. $2x + 3x^2 - 5$ **2.** $2x + 3x^{-1} - 5$

3. $\dfrac{2x + 3}{x}$ **4.** $x^2 - x^3 + x^4 - 5$

In Exercises 5–8, find the degree of the polynomial.

5. $3x^2 - 5x + 4$ **6.** $-4x^3 + 7x^2 - 11$

7. $x^2 - 4x^3 + 9x - 12x^4 + 63$

8. $x^2 - 8x^3 + 15x^4 + 91$

In Exercises 9–14, perform the indicated operations. Write the resulting polynomial in standard form and indicate its degree.

9. $(-6x^3 + 5x^2 - 8x + 9) + (17x^3 + 2x^2 - 4x - 13)$

10. $(-7x^3 + 6x^2 - 11x + 13) + (19x^3 - 11x^2 + 7x - 17)$

11. $(17x^3 - 5x^2 + 4x - 3) - (5x^3 - 9x^2 - 8x + 11)$

12. $(18x^4 - 2x^3 - 7x + 8) - (9x^4 - 6x^3 - 5x + 7)$

13. $(5x^2 - 7x - 8) + (2x^2 - 3x + 7) - (x^2 - 4x - 3)$

14. $(8x^2 + 7x - 5) - (3x^2 - 4x) - (-6x^3 - 5x^2 + 3)$

In Exercises 15–58, find each product.

15. $(x + 1)(x^2 - x + 1)$ **16.** $(x + 5)(x^2 - 5x + 25)$

17. $(2x - 3)(x^2 - 3x + 5)$ **18.** $(2x - 1)(x^2 - 4x + 3)$

19. $(x + 7)(x + 3)$ **20.** $(x + 8)(x + 5)$

21. $(x - 5)(x + 3)$ **22.** $(x - 1)(x + 2)$

23. $(3x + 5)(2x + 1)$ **24.** $(7x + 4)(3x + 1)$

25. $(2x - 3)(5x + 3)$ **26.** $(2x - 5)(7x + 2)$

27. $(5x^2 - 4)(3x^2 - 7)$ **28.** $(7x^2 - 2)(3x^2 - 5)$

29. $(8x^3 + 3)(x^2 - 5)$ **30.** $(7x^3 + 5)(x^2 - 2)$

31. $(x + 3)(x - 3)$ **32.** $(x + 5)(x - 5)$

33. $(3x + 2)(3x - 2)$ **34.** $(2x + 5)(2x - 5)$

35. $(5 - 7x)(5 + 7x)$ **36.** $(4 - 3x)(4 + 3x)$

37. $(4x^2 + 5x)(4x^2 - 5x)$ **38.** $(3x^2 + 4x)(3x^2 - 4x)$

39. $(1 - y^5)(1 + y^5)$ **40.** $(2 - y^5)(2 + y^5)$

41. $(x + 2)^2$ **42.** $(x + 5)^2$

43. $(2x + 3)^2$ **44.** $(3x + 2)^2$

45. $(x - 3)^2$ **46.** $(x - 4)^2$

47. $(4x^2 - 1)^2$ **48.** $(5x^2 - 3)^2$

49. $(7 - 2x)^2$ **50.** $(9 - 5x)^2$

51. $(x + 1)^3$ **52.** $(x + 2)^3$

53. $(2x + 3)^3$ **54.** $(3x + 4)^3$

55. $(x - 3)^3$ **56.** $(x - 1)^3$

57. $(3x - 4)^3$ **58.** $(2x - 3)^3$

In Exercises 59–66, perform the indicated operations. Indicate the degree of the resulting polynomial.

59. $(5x^2y - 3xy) + (2x^2y - xy)$

60. $(-2x^2y + xy) + (4x^2y + 7xy)$

61. $(4x^2y + 8xy + 11) + (-2x^2y + 5xy + 2)$

62. $(7x^4y^2 - 5x^2y^2 + 3xy) + (-18x^4y^2 - 6x^2y^2 - xy)$

63. $(x^3 + 7xy - 5y^2) - (6x^3 - xy + 4y^2)$

64. $(x^4 - 7xy - 5y^3) - (6x^4 - 3xy + 4y^3)$

65. $(3x^4y^2 + 5x^3y - 3y) - (2x^4y^2 - 3x^3y - 4y + 6x)$

66. $(5x^4y^2 + 6x^3y - 7y) - (3x^4y^2 - 5x^3y - 6y + 8x)$

In Exercises 67–82, find each product.

67. $(x + 5y)(7x + 3y)$ **68.** $(x + 9y)(6x + 7y)$

69. $(x - 3y)(2x + 7y)$ **70.** $(3x - y)(2x + 5y)$

71. $(3xy - 1)(5xy + 2)$ **72.** $(7x^2y + 1)(2x^2y - 3)$

73. $(7x + 5y)^2$ **74.** $(9x + 7y)^2$

75. $(x^2y^2 - 3)^2$ **76.** $(x^2y^2 - 5)^2$

77. $(x - y)(x^2 + xy + y^2)$ **78.** $(x + y)(x^2 - xy + y^2)$

79. $(3x + 5y)(3x - 5y)$ **80.** $(7x + 3y)(7x - 3y)$

81. $(7xy^2 - 10y)(7xy^2 + 10y)$

82. $(3xy^2 - 4y)(3xy^2 + 4y)$

Application Exercises

83. The polynomial $0.018x^2 - 0.757x + 9.047$ describes the amount, in thousands of dollars, that a person earning x thousand dollars a year feels underpaid. Evaluate the polynomial for $x = 40$. Describe what the answer means in practical terms.

84. The polynomial $104.5x^2 - 1501.5x + 6016$ describes the death rate per year, per 100,000 men, for men averaging x hours of sleep each night. Evaluate the polynomial for $x = 10$. Describe what the answer means in practical terms.

85. The polynomial $-1.45x^2 + 38.52x + 470.78$ describes the number of violent crimes in the United States, per 100,000 inhabitants, x years after 1975. Evaluate the polynomial for $x = 25$. Describe what the answer means in practical terms. How well does the polynomial describe the crime rate for the appropriate year shown in the bar graph?

Violent Crime in the United States

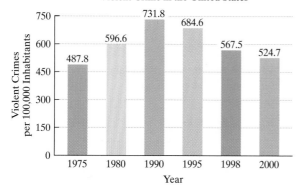

Source: F.B.I.

86. The polynomial $-0.02A^2 + 2A + 22$ is used by coaches to get athletes fired up so that they can perform well. The polynomial represents the performance level related to various levels of enthusiasm, from $A = 1$ (almost no enthusiasm) to $A = 100$ (maximum level of enthusiasm). Evaluate the polynomial for $A = 20$, $A = 50$, and $A = 80$. Describe what happens to performance as we get more and more fired up.

87. The number of people who catch a cold t weeks after January 1 is $5t - 3t^2 + t^3$. The number of people who recover t weeks after January 1 is $t - t^2 + \frac{1}{3}t^3$. Write a polynomial in standard form for the number of people who are still ill with a cold t weeks after January 1.

88. The weekly cost, in thousands of dollars, for producing x stereo headphones is $30x + 50$. The weekly revenue, in thousands of dollars, for selling x stereo headphones is $90x^2 - x$. Write a polynomial in standard form for the weekly profit, in thousands of dollars, for producing and selling x stereo headphones.

In Exercises 89–90, write a polynomial in standard form that represents the area of the shaded region of each figure.

89.

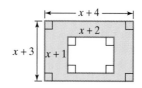

90.

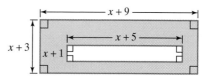

Writing in Mathematics

91. What is a polynomial in x?

92. Explain how to subtract polynomials.

93. Explain how to multiply two binomials using the FOIL method. Give an example with your explanation.

94. Explain how to find the product of the sum and difference of two terms. Give an example with your explanation.

95. Explain how to square a binomial difference. Give an example with your explanation.

96. Explain how to find the degree of a polynomial in two variables.

97. For Exercise 86, explain why performance levels do what they do as we get more and more fired up. If possible, describe an example of a time when you were too enthused and thus did poorly at something you were hoping to do well.

Technology Exercises

98. The common cold is caused by a rhinovirus. The polynomial

$$-0.75x^4 + 3x^3 + 5$$

describes the billions of viral particles in our bodies after x days of invasion. Use a calculator to find the number of viral particles after 0 days (the time of the cold's onset), 1 day, 2 days, 3 days, and 4 days. After how many days is the number of viral particles at a maximum and consequently the day we feel the sickest? By when should we feel completely better?

99. Using data from the National Institute on Drug Abuse, the polynomial

$$0.0032x^3 + 0.0235x^2 - 2.2477x + 61.1998$$

approximately describes the percentage of U.S. high school seniors in the class of x who had ever used marijuana, where x is the number of years after 1980. Use a calculator to find the percentage of high school seniors from the class of 1980 through the class of 2000 who had used marijuana. Round to the nearest tenth of a percent. Describe the trend in the data.

Critical Thinking Exercises

In Exercises 100–103, perform the indicated operations.

100. $(x - y)^2 - (x + y)^2$

101. $[(7x + 5) + 4y][(7x + 5) - 4y]$

102. $[(3x + y) + 1]^2$

103. $(x + y)(x - y)(x^2 + y^2)$

104. Express the area of the plane figure shown as a polynomial in standard form.

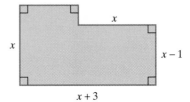

SECTION P.5 *Factoring Polynomials*

Objectives

1. Factor out the greatest common factor of a polynomial.
2. Factor by grouping.
3. Factor trinomials.
4. Factor the difference of squares.
5. Factor perfect square trinomials.
6. Factor the sum and difference of cubes.
7. Use a general strategy for factoring polynomials.
8. Factor algebraic expressions containing fractional and negative exponents.

A two-year-old boy is asked, "Do you have a brother?" He answers, "Yes." "What is your brother's name?" "Tom." Asked if Tom has a brother, the two-year-old replies, "No." The child can go in the direction from self to brother, but he cannot reverse this direction and move from brother back to self.

As our intellects develop, we learn to reverse the direction of our thinking. Reversibility of thought is found throughout algebra. For example, we can multiply polynomials and show that

$$(2x + 1)(3x - 2) = 6x^2 - x - 2.$$

We can also reverse this process and express the resulting polynomial as

$$6x^2 - x - 2 = (2x + 1)(3x - 2).$$

Factoring is the process of writing a polynomial as the product of two or more polynomials. The factors of $6x^2 - x - 2$ are $2x + 1$ and $3x - 2$.

In this section, we will be **factoring over the set of integers,** meaning that the coefficients in the factors are integers. Polynomials that cannot be factored using integer coefficients are called **irreducible over the integers,** or **prime.**

The goal in factoring a polynomial is to use one or more factoring techniques until each of the polynomial's factors is prime or irreducible. In this situation, the polynomial is said to be **factored completely.**

We will now discuss basic techniques for factoring polynomials.

1 Factor out the greatest common factor of a polynomial.

Common Factors

In any factoring problem, the first step is to look for the *greatest common factor.* The **greatest common factor,** abbreviated GCF, is an expression of the highest degree that divides each term of the polynomial. The distributive property in the reverse direction

$$ab + ac = a(b + c)$$

can be used to factor out the greatest common factor.

EXAMPLE 1 Factoring out the Greatest Common Factor

Factor: **a.** $18x^3 + 27x^2$ **b.** $x^2(x + 3) + 5(x + 3)$.

Solution

a. We begin by determining the greatest common factor. 9 is the greatest integer that divides 18 and 27. Furthermore, x^2 is the greatest expression that divides x^3 and x^2. Thus, the greatest common factor of the two terms in the polynomial is $9x^2$.

$$18x^3 + 27x^2$$
$$= 9x^2(2x) + 9x^2(3) \quad \text{Express each term as the product of the greatest common factor and its other factor.}$$
$$= 9x^2(2x + 3) \quad \text{Factor out the greatest common factor.}$$

b. In this situation, the greatest common factor is the common binomial factor $(x + 3)$. We factor out this common factor as follows:

$$x^2(x + 3) + 5(x + 3) = (x + 3)(x^2 + 5). \quad \text{Factor out the common binomial factor.}$$

Study Tip

The variable part of the greatest common factor always contains the *smallest* power of a variable or algebraic expression that appears in all terms of the polynomial.

Check Point 1 Factor:

a. $10x^3 - 4x^2$ **b.** $2x(x - 7) + 3(x - 7)$.

2 Factor by grouping.

Factoring by Grouping

Some polynomials have only a greatest common factor of 1. However, by a suitable rearrangement of the terms, it still may be possible to factor. This process, called **factoring by grouping,** is illustrated in Example 2.

EXAMPLE 2 Factoring by Grouping

Factor: $x^3 + 4x^2 + 3x + 12$.

Solution   Group terms that have a common factor:

$$\boxed{x^3 + 4x^2} \quad + \quad \boxed{3x + 12}.$$

Common
factor is x².

Common
factor is 3.

We now factor the given polynomial as follows.

$x^3 + 4x^2 + 3x + 12$

$= (x^3 + 4x^2) + (3x + 12)$ *Group terms with common factors.*

$= x^2(x + 4) + 3(x + 4)$ *Factor out the greatest common factor from the grouped terms. The remaining two terms have x + 4 as a common binomial factor.*

$= (x + 4)(x^2 + 3)$ *Factor (x + 4) out of both terms.*

Thus, $x^3 + 4x^2 + 3x + 12 = (x + 4)(x^2 + 3)$. Check the factorization by multiplying the right side of the equation using the FOIL method. If the factorization is correct, you will obtain the original polynomial.

Discovery

In Example 2, group the terms as follows:

$$\left(x^3 + 3x\right) + \left(4x^2 + 12\right).$$

Factor out the greatest common factor from each group and complete the factoring process. Describe what happens. What can you conclude?

Check Point 2   Factor: $x^3 + 5x^2 - 2x - 10$.

3 Factor trinomials.

Factoring Trinomials

To factor a trinomial of the form $ax^2 + bx + c$, a little trial and error may be necessary.

A Strategy for Factoring $ax^2 + bx + c$

(Assume, for the moment, that there is no greatest common factor.)

1. Find two **First** terms whose product is ax^2:

$$(\square x + \quad)(\square x + \quad) = ax^2 + bx + c.$$

2. Find two **Last** terms whose product is c:

$$(x + \square)(x + \square) = ax^2 + bx + c.$$

3. By trial and error, perform steps 1 and 2 until the sum of the **Outside** product and **Inside** product is bx:

$$(\square x + \square)(\square x + \square) = ax^2 + bx + c.$$

$\llcorner$ I $\lrcorner$

O

(sum of O + I)

If no such combinations exist, the polynomial is prime.

EXAMPLE 3 Factoring Trinomials Whose Leading Coefficients Are 1

Factor: **a.** $x^2 + 6x + 8$ **b.** $x^2 + 3x - 18$.

Solution

a. The factors of the first term are x and x :
$$x^2 + 6x + 8 = (x \quad)(x \quad).$$

Factors of 8	8, 1	4, 2	−8, −1	−4, −2
Sum of Factors	9	6	−9	−6

This is the desired sum.

To find the second term of each factor, we must find two numbers whose product is 8 and whose sum is 6. From the table in the margin, we see that 4 and 2 are the required integers. Thus,
$$x^2 + 6x + 8 = (x + 4)(x + 2) \text{ or } (x + 2)(x + 4).$$

b. We begin with
$$x^2 + 3x - 18 = (x \quad)(x \quad).$$

Factors of −18	18, −1	−18, 1	9, −2	−9, 2	6, −3	−6, 3
Sum of factors	17	−17	7	−7	3	−3

This is the desired sum.

To find the second term of each factor, we must find two numbers whose product is −18 and whose sum is 3. From the table in the margin, we see that 6 and −3 are the required integers. Thus,
$$x^2 + 3x - 18 = (x + 6)(x - 3)$$
$$\text{or } (x - 3)(x + 6).$$

Check Point 3 Factor:

a. $x^2 + 13x + 40$ **b.** $x^2 - 5x - 14$.

EXAMPLE 4 Factoring a Trinomial Whose Leading Coefficient Is Not 1

Factor: $8x^2 - 10x - 3$.

Solution

Step 1 Find two *First* terms whose product is $8x^2$.
$$8x^2 - 10x - 3 \overset{?}{=} (8x \quad)(x \quad)$$
$$8x^2 - 10x - 3 \overset{?}{=} (4x \quad)(2x \quad)$$

Step 2 Find two *Last* terms whose product is −3. The possible factorizations are $1(-3)$ and $-1(3)$.

Step 3 Try various combinations of these factors. The correct factorization of $8x^2 - 10x - 3$ is the one in which the sum of the *Outside* and *Inside* products is equal to $-10x$. Here is a list of the possible factorizations:

Possible Factorizations of $8x^2 - 10x - 3$	Sum of *Outside* and *Inside* Products (Should Equal $-10x$)
$(8x + 1)(x - 3)$	$-24x + x = -23x$
$(8x - 3)(x + 1)$	$8x - 3x = 5x$
$(8x - 1)(x + 3)$	$24x - x = 23x$
$(8x + 3)(x - 1)$	$-8x + 3x = -5x$
$(4x + 1)(2x - 3)$	$-12x + 2x = -10x$
$(4x - 3)(2x + 1)$	$4x - 6x = -2x$
$(4x - 1)(2x + 3)$	$12x - 2x = 10x$
$(4x + 3)(2x - 1)$	$-4x + 6x = 2x$

This is the required middle term.

Thus,
$$8x^2 - 10x - 3 = (4x + 1)(2x - 3) \quad \text{or} \quad (2x - 3)(4x + 1).$$

Show that this factorization is correct by multiplying the factors using the FOIL method. You should obtain the original trinomial.

Check Point 4 Factor: $6x^2 + 19x - 7$.

4 Factor the difference of squares.

Factoring the Difference of Two Squares

A method for factoring the difference of two squares is obtained by reversing the special product for the sum and difference of two terms.

The Difference of Two Squares
If A and B are real numbers, variables, or algebraic expressions, then
$$A^2 - B^2 = (A + B)(A - B).$$
In words: The difference of the squares of two terms factors as the product of a sum and a difference of those terms.

EXAMPLE 5   Factoring the Difference of Two Squares
Factor: **a.** $x^2 - 4$ **b.** $81x^2 - 49$.

Solution   We must express each term as the square of some monomial. Then we use the formula for factoring $A^2 - B^2$.

a. $x^2 - 4 = x^2 - 2^2 = (x + 2)(x - 2)$

$$A^2 - B^2 = (A + B)(A - B)$$

b. $81x^2 - 49 = (9x)^2 - 7^2 = (9x + 7)(9x - 7)$

Check Point 5 Factor:

   a. $x^2 - 81$ **b.** $36x^2 - 25$.

We have seen that a polynomial is factored completely when it is written as the product of prime polynomials. To be sure that you have factored completely, check to see whether the factors can be factored.

Study Tip

Factoring $x^4 - 81$ as
$$(x^2 + 9)(x^2 - 9)$$
is not a complete factorization. The second factor, $x^2 - 9$, is itself a difference of two squares and can be factored.

EXAMPLE 6   A Repeated Factorization
Factor completely: $x^4 - 81$.

Solution
$$x^4 - 81 = (x^2)^2 - 9^2$$ Express as the difference of two squares.
$$= (x^2 + 9)(x^2 - 9)$$ The factors are the sum and difference of the squared terms.

$$= (x^2 + 9)(x^2 - 3^2)$$ The factor $x^2 - 9$ is the difference of two squares and can be factored.

$$= (x^2 + 9)(x + 3)(x - 3)$$ The factors of $x^2 - 9$ are the sum and difference of the squared terms.

Check Point 6 Factor completely: $81x^4 - 16$.

5 Factor perfect square trinomials.

Factoring Perfect Square Trinomials

Our next factoring technique is obtained by reversing the special products for squaring binomials. The trinomials that are factored using this technique are called **perfect square trinomials.**

Factoring Perfect Square Trinomials

Let A and B be real numbers, variables, or algebraic expressions.

1. $A^2 + 2AB + B^2 = (A + B)^2$

Same sign

2. $A^2 - 2AB + B^2 = (A - B)^2$

Same sign

The two items in the box show that perfect square trinomials come in two forms: one in which the middle term is positive and one in which the middle term is negative. Here's how to recognize a perfect square trinomial:

1. The first and last terms are squares of monomials or integers.
2. The middle term is twice the product of the expressions being squared in the first and last terms.

EXAMPLE 7 Factoring Perfect Square Trinomials

Factor: **a.** $x^2 + 6x + 9$ **b.** $25x^2 - 60x + 36$.

Solution

a. $x^2 + 6x + 9 = x^2 + 2 \cdot x \cdot 3 + 3^2 = (x + 3)^2$ The middle term has a positive sign.

$A^2 + 2AB + B^2 = (A + B)^2$

b. We suspect that $25x^2 - 60x + 36$ is a perfect square trinomial because $25x^2 = (5x)^2$ and $36 = 6^2$. The middle term can be expressed as twice the product of $5x$ and 6.

$$25x^2 - 60x + 36 = (5x)^2 - 2 \cdot 5x \cdot 6 + 6^2 = (5x - 6)^2$$

$A^2 - 2AB + B^2 = (A - B)^2$

Check Point 7 Factor:

    a. $x^2 + 14x + 49$ **b.** $16x^2 - 56x + 49$.

6 Factor the sum and difference of cubes.

Factoring the Sum and Difference of Two Cubes

We can use the following formulas to factor the sum or the difference of two cubes:

Factoring the Sum and Difference of Two Cubes

1. Factoring the Sum of Two Cubes

$$A^3 + B^3 = (A + B)(A^2 - AB + B^2)$$

2. Factoring the Difference of Two Cubes

$$A^3 - B^3 = (A - B)(A^2 + AB + B^2)$$

EXAMPLE 8 Factoring Sums and Differences of Two Cubes

Factor: **a.** $x^3 + 8$ **b.** $64x^3 - 125$.

Solution

    a. $x^3 + 8 = x^3 + 2^3 = (x + 2)(x^2 - x \cdot 2 + 2^2) = (x + 2)(x^2 - 2x + 4)$

$$A^3 + B^3 = (A + B)(A^2 - AB + B^2)$$

    b. $64x^3 - 125 = (4x)^3 - 5^3 = (4x - 5)[(4x)^2 + (4x)(5) + 5^2]$

$$A^3 - B^3 = (A - B)(A^2 + AB + B^2)$$

$$= (4x - 5)(16x^2 + 20x + 25)$$

Check Point 8 Factor:

    a. $x^3 + 1$ **b.** $125x^3 - 8$.

7 Use a general strategy for factoring polynomials.

A Strategy for Factoring Polynomials

It is important to practice factoring a wide variety of polynomials so that you can quickly select the appropriate technique. The polynomial is factored completely when all its polynomial factors, except possibly for monomial factors, are prime. Because of the commutative property, the order of the factors does not matter.

A Strategy for Factoring a Polynomial

1. If there is a common factor, factor out the GCF.

2. Determine the number of terms in the polynomial and try factoring as follows:

 a. If there are two terms, can the binomial be factored by one of the following special forms?

   Difference of two squares: $A^2 - B^2 = (A + B)(A - B)$
   Sum of two cubes: $A^3 + B^3 = (A + B)(A^2 - AB + B^2)$
   Difference of two cubes: $A^3 - B^3 = (A - B)(A^2 + AB + B^2)$

 b. If there are three terms, is the trinomial a perfect square trinomial? If so, factor by one of the following special forms:

$$A^2 + 2AB + B^2 = (A + B)^2$$
$$A^2 - 2AB + B^2 = (A - B)^2.$$

   If the trinomial is not a perfect square trinomial, try factoring by trial and error.

 c. If there are four or more terms, try factoring by grouping.

3. Check to see if any factors with more than one term in the factored polynomial can be factored further. If so, factor completely.

EXAMPLE 9 **Factoring a Polynomial**

Factor: $2x^3 + 8x^2 + 8x$.

Solution

Step 1 **If there is a common factor, factor out the GCF.** Because $2x$ is common to all terms, we factor it out.

$$2x^3 + 8x^2 + 8x = 2x(x^2 + 4x + 4) \quad \text{\textit{Factor out the GCF.}}$$

Step 2 **Determine the number of terms and factor accordingly.** The factor $x^2 + 4x + 4$ has three terms and is a perfect square trinomial. We factor using $A^2 + 2AB + B^2 = (A + B)^2$.

$$2x^3 + 8x^2 + 8x = 2x(x^2 + 4x + 4)$$

$$= 2x(x^2 + 2 \cdot x \cdot 2 + 2^2)$$

$$\underbrace{A^2 + 2\,A\,B + B^2}$$

$$= 2x(x + 2)^2 \qquad \text{\textit{$A^2 + 2AB + B^2 = (A + B)^2$}}$$

Step 3 **Check to see if factors can be factored further.** In this problem, they cannot. Thus,

$$2x^3 + 8x^2 + 8x = 2x(x + 2)^2.$$

Check Point 9 Factor: $3x^3 - 30x^2 + 75x$.

EXAMPLE 10   Factoring a Polynomial

Factor: $x^2 - 25a^2 + 8x + 16$.

Solution

Step 1   If there is a common factor, factor out the GCF. Other than 1 or –1, there is no common factor.

Step 2   Determine the number of terms and factor accordingly. There are four terms. We try factoring by grouping. Grouping into two groups of two terms does not result in a common binomial factor. Let's try grouping as a difference of squares.

$$x^2 - 25a^2 + 8x + 16$$
$$= (x^2 + 8x + 16) - 25a^2 \qquad \text{Rearrange terms and group as a perfect square trinomial minus } 25a^2 \text{ to obtain a difference of squares.}$$

$$= (x + 4)^2 - (5a)^2 \qquad \text{Factor the perfect square trinomial.}$$
$$= (x + 4 + 5a)(x + 4 - 5a) \qquad \text{Factor the difference of squares. The factors are the sum and difference of the expressions being squared.}$$

Step 3   Check to see if factors can be factored further. In this case, they cannot, so we have factored completely.

Check Point 10   Factor: $x^2 - 36a^2 + 20x + 100$.

8 Factor algebraic expressions containing fractional and negative exponents.

Factoring Algebraic Expressions Containing Fractional and Negative Exponents

Although expressions containing fractional and negative exponents are not polynomials, they can be simplified using factoring techniques.

EXAMPLE 11   Factoring Involving Fractional and Negative Exponents

Factor and simplify: $x(x + 1)^{-3/4} + (x + 1)^{1/4}$.

Solution   The greatest common factor is $x + 1$ with the *smallest exponent* in the two terms. Thus, the greatest common factor is $(x + 1)^{-3/4}$.

$$x(x + 1)^{-3/4} + (x + 1)^{1/4}$$

$$= (x + 1)^{-3/4}x + (x + 1)^{-3/4}(x + 1) \qquad \text{Express each term as the product of the greatest common factor and its other factor.}$$

$$= (x + 1)^{-3/4}[x + (x + 1)] \qquad \text{Factor out the greatest common factor.}$$

$$= \frac{2x + 1}{(x + 1)^{3/4}} \qquad \qquad b^{-n} = \frac{1}{b^n}$$

Check
Point
11

Factor and simplify: $x(x - 1)^{-1/2} + (x - 1)^{1/2}$.

EXERCISE SET P.5

Practice Exercises

In Exercises 1–10, factor out the greatest common factor.

1. $18x + 27$ **2.** $16x - 24$

3. $3x^2 + 6x$ **4.** $4x^2 - 8x$

5. $9x^4 - 18x^3 + 27x^2$ **6.** $6x^4 - 18x^3 + 12x^2$

7. $x(x + 5) + 3(x + 5)$ **8.** $x(2x + 1) + 4(2x + 1)$

9. $x^2(x - 3) + 12(x - 3)$ **10.** $x^2(2x + 5) + 17(2x + 5)$

In Exercises 11–16, factor by grouping.

11. $x^3 - 2x^2 + 5x - 10$ **12.** $x^3 - 3x^2 + 4x - 12$

13. $x^3 - x^2 + 2x - 2$ **14.** $x^3 + 6x^2 - 2x - 12$

15. $3x^3 - 2x^2 - 6x + 4$ **16.** $x^3 - x^2 - 5x + 5$

In Exercises 17–30, factor each trinomial, or state that the trinomial is prime.

17. $x^2 + 5x + 6$ **18.** $x^2 + 8x + 15$

19. $x^2 - 2x - 15$ **20.** $x^2 - 4x - 5$

21. $x^2 - 8x + 15$ **22.** $x^2 - 14x + 45$

23. $3x^2 - x - 2$ **24.** $2x^2 + 5x - 3$

25. $3x^2 - 25x - 28$ **26.** $3x^2 - 2x - 5$

27. $6x^2 - 11x + 4$ **28.** $6x^2 - 17x + 12$

29. $4x^2 + 16x + 15$ **30.** $8x^2 + 33x + 4$

In Exercises 31–40, factor the difference of two squares.

31. $x^2 - 100$ **32.** $x^2 - 144$

33. $36x^2 - 49$ **34.** $64x^2 - 81$

35. $9x^2 - 25y^2$ **36.** $36x^2 - 49y^2$

37. $x^4 - 16$ **38.** $x^4 - 1$

39. $16x^4 - 81$ **40.** $81x^4 - 1$

In Exercises 41–48, factor any perfect square trinomials, or state that the polynomial is prime.

41. $x^2 + 2x + 1$ **42.** $x^2 + 4x + 4$

43. $x^2 - 14x + 49$ **44.** $x^2 - 10x + 25$

45. $4x^2 + 4x + 1$ **46.** $25x^2 + 10x + 1$

47. $9x^2 - 6x + 1$ **48.** $64x^2 - 16x + 1$

In Exercises 49–56, factor using the formula for the sum or difference of two cubes.

49. $x^3 + 27$ **50.** $x^3 + 64$

51. $x^3 - 64$ **52.** $x^3 - 27$

53. $8x^3 - 1$ **54.** $27x^3 - 1$

55. $64x^3 + 27$ **56.** $8x^3 + 125$

In Exercises 57–84, factor completely, or state that the polynomial is prime.

57. $3x^3 - 3x$ **58.** $5x^3 - 45x$

59. $4x^2 - 4x - 24$ **60.** $6x^2 - 18x - 60$

61. $2x^4 - 162$ **62.** $7x^4 - 7$

63. $x^3 + 2x^2 - 9x - 18$ **64.** $x^3 + 3x^2 - 25x - 75$

65. $2x^2 - 2x - 112$ **66.** $6x^2 - 6x - 12$

67. $x^3 - 4x$ **68.** $9x^3 - 9x$

69. $x^2 + 64$ **70.** $x^2 + 36$

71. $x^3 + 2x^2 - 4x - 8$ **72.** $x^3 + 2x^2 - x - 2$

73. $y^5 - 81y$ **74.** $y^5 - 16y$

75. $20y^4 - 45y^2$ **76.** $48y^4 - 3y^2$

77. $x^2 - 12x + 36 - 49y^2$ **78.** $x^2 - 10x + 25 - 36y^2$

79. $9b^2x - 16y - 16x + 9b^2y$

80. $16a^2x - 25y - 25x + 16a^2y$

81. $x^2y - 16y + 32 - 2x^2$ **82.** $12x^2y - 27y - 4x^2 + 9$

83. $2x^3 - 8a^2x + 24x^2 + 72x$

84. $2x^3 - 98a^2x + 28x^2 + 98x$

In Exercises 85–94, factor and simplify each algebraic expression.

85. $x^{3/2} - x^{1/2}$ **86.** $x^{3/4} - x^{1/4}$

87. $4x^{-2/3} + 8x^{1/3}$ **88.** $12x^{-3/4} + 6x^{1/4}$

89. $(x + 3)^{1/2} - (x + 3)^{3/2}$

90. $(x^2 + 4)^{3/2} + (x^2 + 4)^{7/2}$

91. $(x + 5)^{-1/2} - (x + 5)^{-3/2}$

92. $(x^2 + 3)^{-2/3} + (x^2 + 3)^{-5/3}$

93. $(4x - 1)^{1/2} - \frac{1}{3}(4x - 1)^{3/2}$

94. $-8(4x + 3)^{-2} + 10(5x + 1)(4x + 3)^{-1}$

Application Exercises

95. Your computer store is having an incredible sale. The price on one model is reduced by 40%. Then the sale price is reduced by another 40%. If x is the computer's original price, the sale price can be represented by

$$(x - 0.4x) - 0.4(x - 0.4x).$$

a. Factor out $(x - 0.4x)$ from each term. Then simplify the resulting expression.

b. Use the simplified expression from part (a) to answer these questions: With a 40% reduction followed by a 40% reduction, is the computer selling at 20% of its original price? If not, at what percentage of the original price is it selling?

96. The polynomial $8x^2 + 20x + 2488$ describes the number, in thousands, of high school graduates in the United States x years after 1993.

a. According to this polynomial, how many students will graduate from U.S. high schools in 2003?

b. Factor the polynomial.

c. Use the factored form of the polynomial in part (b) to find the number of high school graduates in 2003. Do you get the same answer as you did in part (a)? If so, does this prove that your factorization is correct? Explain.

97. A rock is dropped from the top of a 256-foot cliff. The height, in feet, of the rock above the water after t seconds is described by the polynomial $256 - 16t^2$. Factor this expression completely.

98. The amount of sheet metal needed to manufacture a cylindrical tin can, that is, its surface area, S, is $S = 2\pi r^2 + 2\pi rh$. Express the surface area, S, in factored form.

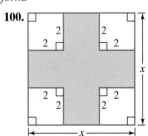

In Exercises 99–100, find the formula for the area of the shaded region and express it in factored form.

99.

100.
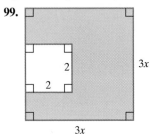

Writing in Mathematics

101. Using an example, explain how to factor out the greatest common factor of a polynomial.

102. Suppose that a polynomial contains four terms. Explain how to use factoring by grouping to factor the polynomial.

103. Explain how to factor $3x^2 + 10x + 8$.

104. Explain how to factor the difference of two squares. Provide an example with your explanation.

105. What is a perfect square trinomial and how is it factored?

106. Explain how to factor $x^3 + 1$.

107. What does it mean to factor completely?

Critical Thinking Exercises

108. Which one of the following is true?

a. Because $x^2 + 1$ is irreducible over the integers, it follows that $x^3 + 1$ is also irreducible.

b. One correct factored form for $x^2 - 4x + 3$ is $x(x - 4) + 3$.

c. $x^3 - 64 = (x - 4)^3$

d. None of the above is true.

In Exercises 109–112, factor completely.

109. $x^{2n} + 6x^n + 8$ **110.** $-x^2 - 4x + 5$

111. $x^4 - y^4 - 2x^3y + 2xy^3$

112. $(x - 5)^{-1/2}(x + 5)^{-1/2} - (x + 5)^{1/2}(x - 5)^{-3/2}$

In Exercises 113–114, find all integers b so that the trinomial can be factored.

113. $x^2 + bx + 15$ **114.** $x^2 + 4x + b$

Group Exercise

115. Without looking at any factoring problems in the book, create five factoring problems. Make sure that some of your problems require at least two factoring techniques. Next, exchange problems with another person in your group. Work to factor your partner's problems. Evaluate the problems as you work: Are they too easy? Too difficult? Can the polynomials really be factored? Share your response with the person who wrote the problems. Finally, grade each other's work in factoring the polynomials. Each factoring problem is worth 20 points. You may award partial credit. If you take off points, explain why points are deducted and how you decided to take off a particular number of points for the error(s) that you found.

SECTION P.6   *Rational Expressions*

Objectives

1. Specify numbers that must be excluded from the domain of rational expressions.
2. Simplify rational expressions.
3. Multiply rational expressions.
4. Divide rational expressions.
5. Add and subtract rational expressions.
6. Simplify complex rational expressions.

How do we describe the costs of reducing environmental pollution? We often use algebraic expressions involving quotients of polynomials. For example, the algebraic expression

$$\frac{250x}{100 - x}$$

describes the cost, in millions of dollars, to remove x percent of the pollutants that are discharged into a river. Removing a modest percentage of pollutants, say 40%, is far less costly than removing a substantially greater percentage, such as 95%. We see this by evaluating the algebraic expression for $x = 40$ and $x = 95$.

Discovery

What happens if you try substituting 100 for x in

$$\frac{250x}{100 - x}?$$

What does this tell you about the cost of cleaning up all of the river's pollutants?

Evaluating $\dfrac{250x}{100 - x}$ for

$x = 40$:

Cost is $\dfrac{250(40)}{100 - 40} \approx 167.$

$x = 95$:

Cost is $\dfrac{250(95)}{100 - 95} = 4750.$

The cost increases from approximately \$167 million to a possibly prohibitive \$4750 million, or \$4.75 billion. Costs spiral upward as the percentage of removed pollutants increases.

Many algebraic expressions that describe costs of environmental projects are examples of rational expressions. First we will define rational expressions. Then we will review how to perform operations with such expressions.

1 Specify numbers that must be excluded from the domain of rational expressions.

Rational Expressions

A **rational expression** is the quotient of two polynomials. Some examples are

$$\frac{x - 2}{4}, \quad \frac{4}{x - 2}, \quad \frac{x}{x^2 - 1}, \quad \text{and} \quad \frac{x^2 + 1}{x^2 + 2x - 3}.$$

The set of real numbers for which an algebraic expression is defined is the **domain** of the expression. Because rational expressions indicate division and division by zero is undefined, we must exclude numbers from a rational expression's domain that make the denominator zero.

EXAMPLE 1 Excluding Numbers from the Domain

Find all the numbers that must be excluded from the domain of each rational expression:

$$\textbf{a. } \frac{4}{x-2} \qquad \textbf{b. } \frac{x}{x^2-1}.$$

Solution To determine the numbers that must be excluded from each domain, examine the denominators.

$$\textbf{a. } \frac{4}{x-2} \qquad\qquad \textbf{b. } \frac{x}{x^2-1} = \frac{x}{(x+1)(x-1)}$$

This denominator
would equal
zero if x = 2.

This factor
would equal
zero if x = −1.

This factor
would equal
zero if x = 1.

For the rational expression in part (a), we must exclude 2 from the domain. For the rational expression in part (b), we must exclude both −1 and 1 from the domain. These excluded numbers are often written to the right of a rational expression.

$$\frac{4}{x-2}, x \ne 2 \qquad \frac{x}{x^2-1}, x \ne -1, x \ne 1$$

Check Point 1 Find all the numbers that must be excluded from the domain of each rational expression:

$$\textbf{a. } \frac{7}{x+5} \qquad \textbf{b. } \frac{x}{x^2-36}.$$

2 Simplify rational expressions.

Simplifying Rational Expressions

A rational expression is **simplified** if its numerator and denominator have no common factors other than 1 or −1. The following procedure can be used to simplify rational expressions:

> **Simplifying Rational Expressions**
> 1. Factor the numerator and denominator completely.
> 2. Divide both the numerator and denominator by the common factors.

EXAMPLE 2 Simplifying Rational Expressions

Simplify: $\textbf{a. } \dfrac{x^3+x^2}{x+1} \qquad \textbf{b. } \dfrac{x^2+6x+5}{x^2-25}.$

Solution

a. $\dfrac{x^3 + x^2}{x + 1} = \dfrac{x^2(x + 1)}{x + 1}$ Factor the numerator. Because the denominator is x + 1, x ≠ −1.

$= \dfrac{x^2 \overset{1}{\cancel{(x + 1)}}}{\underset{1}{\cancel{x + 1}}}$ Divide out the common factor, x + 1.

$= x^2, x \neq -1$ Denominators of 1 need not be written because $\frac{a}{1} = a$.

b. $\dfrac{x^2 + 6x + 5}{x^2 - 25} = \dfrac{(x + 5)(x + 1)}{(x + 5)(x - 5)}$ Factor the numerator and denominator. Because the denominator is (x + 5)(x − 5), x ≠ −5 and x ≠ 5.

$= \dfrac{\overset{1}{\cancel{(x + 5)}}(x + 1)}{\underset{1}{\cancel{(x + 5)}}(x - 5)}$ Divide out the common factor, x + 5.

$= \dfrac{x + 1}{x - 5}, \quad x \neq -5, \quad x \neq 5$

Check Point 2 Simplify:

a. $\dfrac{x^3 + 3x^2}{x + 3}$ **b.** $\dfrac{x^2 - 1}{x^2 + 2x + 1}.$

3 Multiply rational expressions.

Multiplying Rational Expressions

The product of two rational expressions is the product of their numerators divided by the product of their denominators. Here is a step-by-step procedure for multiplying rational expressions:

Multiplying Rational Expressions

1. Factor all numerators and denominators completely.

2. Divide numerators and denominators by common factors.

3. Multiply the remaining factors in the numerator and multiply the remaining factors in the denominator.

EXAMPLE 3 **Multiplying Rational Expressions**

Multiply and simplify:

$$\dfrac{x - 7}{x - 1} \cdot \dfrac{x^2 - 1}{3x - 21}.$$

Solution

$$\frac{x-7}{x-1} \cdot \frac{x^2-1}{3x-21}$$

This is the given multiplication problem.

$$= \frac{x-7}{x-1} \cdot \frac{(x+1)(x-1)}{3(x-7)}$$

Factor all numerators and denominators. Because the denominator has factors of x − 1 and x − 7, x ≠ 1 and x ≠ 7.

$$= \frac{\overset{1}{\cancel{x-7}}}{\underset{1}{\cancel{x-1}}} \cdot \frac{(x+1)\overset{1}{\cancel{(x-1)}}}{3\underset{1}{\cancel{(x-7)}}}$$

Divide numerators and denominators by common factors.

$$= \frac{x+1}{3}, x \neq 1, x \neq 7$$

Multiply the remaining factors in the numerator and denominator.

These excluded numbers from the domain must also be excluded from the simplified expression's domain.

Check Point 3 Multiply and simplify:

$$\frac{x+3}{x^2-4} \cdot \frac{x^2-x-6}{x^2+6x+9}.$$

4 Divide rational expressions.

Dividing Rational Expressions

We find the quotient of two rational expressions by inverting the divisor and multiplying.

EXAMPLE 4 Dividing Rational Expressions

Divide and simplify:

$$\frac{x^2-2x-8}{x^2-9} \div \frac{x-4}{x+3}.$$

Solution

$$\frac{x^2-2x-8}{x^2-9} \div \frac{x-4}{x+3}$$

This is the given division problem.

$$= \frac{x^2-2x-8}{x^2-9} \cdot \frac{x+3}{x-4}$$

Invert the divisor and multiply.

$$= \frac{(x-4)(x+2)}{(x+3)(x-3)} \cdot \frac{x+3}{x-4}$$

Factor throughout. For nonzero denominators, x ≠ −3, x ≠ 3, and x ≠ 4.

$$= \frac{\overset{1}{\cancel{(x-4)}}(x+2)}{\underset{1}{\cancel{(x+3)}}(x-3)} \cdot \frac{\overset{1}{\cancel{(x+3)}}}{\underset{1}{\cancel{(x-4)}}}$$

Divide numerators and denominators by common factors.

$$= \frac{x+2}{x-3}, x \neq -3, x \neq 3, x \neq 4$$

Multiply the remaining factors in the numerator and the denominator.

Check Point 4 Divide and simplify:

$$\frac{x^2-2x+1}{x^3+x} \div \frac{x^2+x-2}{3x^2+3}.$$

5 Add and subtract rational expressions.

Adding and Subtracting Rational Expressions with the Same Denominator

We add or subtract rational expressions with the same denominator by (1) adding or subtracting the numerators, (2) placing this result over the common denominator, and (3) simplifying, if possible.

> **EXAMPLE 5** Subtracting Rational Expressions with the Same Denominator

Subtract: $\dfrac{5x + 1}{x^2 - 9} - \dfrac{4x - 2}{x^2 - 9}$.

Solution

$\dfrac{5x + 1}{x^2 - 9} - \dfrac{4x - 2}{x^2 - 9} = \dfrac{5x + 1 - (4x - 2)}{x^2 - 9}$ Subtract numerators and include parentheses to indicate that both terms are subtracted. Place this difference over the common denominator.

$= \dfrac{5x + 1 - 4x + 2}{x^2 - 9}$ Remove parentheses and then change the sign of each term.

$= \dfrac{x + 3}{x^2 - 9}$ Combine like terms.

$= \dfrac{\overset{1}{\cancel{x + 3}}}{\underset{1}{\cancel{(x + 3)}}(x - 3)}$ Factor and simplify ($x \neq -3$ and $x \neq 3$).

$= \dfrac{1}{x - 3}, x \neq -3, x \neq 3$

Study Tip

Example 5 shows that when a numerator is being subtracted, we must subtract every term in that expression.

> **Check Point 5** Subtract: $\dfrac{x}{x + 1} - \dfrac{3x + 2}{x + 1}$.

Adding and Subtracting Rational Expressions with Different Denominators

Rational expressions that have no common factors in their denominators can be added or subtracted using one of the following properties:

$$\frac{a}{b} + \frac{c}{d} = \frac{ad + bc}{bd} \qquad \frac{a}{b} - \frac{c}{d} = \frac{ad - bc}{bd}, b \neq 0, d \neq 0.$$

The denominator, bd, is the product of the factors in the two denominators. Because we are looking at rational expressions that have no common factors in their denominators, the product bd gives the least common denominator.

> **EXAMPLE 6** Subtracting Rational Expressions Having No Common Factors in Their Denominators

Subtract: $\dfrac{x + 2}{2x - 3} - \dfrac{4}{x + 3}$.

Solution We need to find the least common denominator. This is the product of the distinct factors in each denominator, namely $(2x - 3)(x + 3)$. We can therefore use the subtraction property given previously as follows:

$$\frac{a}{b} - \frac{c}{d} = \frac{ad - bc}{bd}$$

$$\frac{x + 2}{2x - 3} - \frac{4}{x + 3} = \frac{(x + 2)(x + 3) - (2x - 3)4}{(2x - 3)(x + 3)}$$

Observe that $a = x + 2$, $b = 2x - 3$, $c = 4$, and $d = x + 3$.

$$= \frac{x^2 + 5x + 6 - (8x - 12)}{(2x - 3)(x + 3)}$$

Multiply.

$$= \frac{x^2 + 5x + 6 - 8x + 12}{(2x - 3)(x + 3)}$$

Remove parentheses and then change the sign of each term.

$$= \frac{x^2 - 3x + 18}{(2x - 3)(x + 3)}, x \neq \frac{3}{2}, x \neq -3$$

Combine like terms in the numerator.

Check Point 6   Add: $\dfrac{3}{x + 1} + \dfrac{5}{x - 1}$.

The **least common denominator,** or LCD, of several rational expressions is a polynomial consisting of the product of all prime factors in the denominators, with each factor raised to the greatest power of its occurrence in any denominator. When adding and subtracting rational expressions that have different denominators with one or more common factors in the denominators, it is efficient to find the least common denominator first.

Finding the Least Common Denominator

1. Factor each denominator completely.
2. List the factors of the first denominator.
3. Add to the list in step 2 any factors of the second denominator that do not appear in the list.
4. Form the product of each different factor from the list in step 3. This product is the least common denominator.

EXAMPLE 7   Finding the Least Common Denominator

Find the least common denominator of

$$\frac{7}{5x^2 + 15x} \quad \text{and} \quad \frac{9}{x^2 + 6x + 9}.$$

Solution

Step 1   Factor each denominator completely.

$$5x^2 + 15x = 5x(x + 3)$$
$$x^2 + 6x + 9 = (x + 3)^2$$

Step 2   List the factors of the first denominator.

$$5, x, (x + 3)$$

Step 3   Add any unlisted factors from the second denominator.   The second denominator is $(x + 3)^2$ or $(x + 3)(x + 3)$. One factor of $x + 3$ is already in our list, but the other factor is not. We add $x + 3$ to the list. We have

$$5, x, (x + 3), (x + 3).$$

Step 4   The least common denominator is the product of all factors in the final list.   Thus,

$$5x(x + 3)(x + 3), \quad \text{or} \quad 5x(x + 3)^2$$

is the least common denominator.

Check Point 7   Find the least common denominator of

$$\frac{3}{x^2 - 6x + 9} \quad \text{and} \quad \frac{7}{x^2 - 9}.$$

Finding the least common denominator for two (or more) rational expressions is the first step needed to add or subtract the expressions.

Adding and Subtracting Rational Expressions That Have Different Denominators with Shared Factors

1. Find the least common denominator.

2. Write all rational expressions in terms of the least common denominator. To do so, multiply both the numerator and the denominator of each rational expression by any factor(s) needed to convert the denominator into the least common denominator.

3. Add or subtract the numerators, placing the resulting expression over the least common denominator.

4. If necessary, simplify the resulting rational expression.

EXAMPLE 8   Adding Rational Expressions with Different Denominators

Add: $\dfrac{x + 3}{x^2 + x - 2} + \dfrac{2}{x^2 - 1}.$

Solution

Step 1   Find the least common denominator.   Start by factoring the denominators.

$$x^2 + x - 2 = (x + 2)(x - 1)$$
$$x^2 - 1 = (x + 1)(x - 1)$$

The factors of the first denominator are $x + 2$ and $x - 1$. The only factor from the second denominator that is not listed is $x + 1$. Thus, the least common denominator is

$$(x + 2)(x - 1)(x + 1).$$

Step 2 Write all rational expressions in terms of the least common denominator. We do so by multiplying both the numerator and the denominator by any factor(s) needed to convert the denominator into the least common denominator.

$$\frac{x + 3}{x^2 + x - 2} + \frac{2}{x^2 - 1}$$

$$= \frac{x + 3}{(x + 2)(x - 1)} + \frac{2}{(x + 1)(x - 1)}$$

The least common denominator is $(x + 2)(x - 1)(x + 1)$.

$$= \frac{(x + 3)(x + 1)}{(x + 2)(x - 1)(x + 1)} + \frac{2(x + 2)}{(x + 2)(x - 1)(x + 1)}$$

Multiply each numerator and denominator by the extra factor required to form $(x + 2)(x - 1)(x + 1)$, the least common denominator.

Step 3 Add numerators, putting this sum over the least common denominator.

$$= \frac{(x + 3)(x + 1) + 2(x + 2)}{(x + 2)(x - 1)(x + 1)}$$

$$= \frac{x^2 + 4x + 3 + 2x + 4}{(x + 2)(x - 1)(x + 1)}$$

Perform the multiplications in the numerator.

$$= \frac{x^2 + 6x + 7}{(x + 2)(x - 1)(x + 1)}, x \neq -2, x \neq 1, x \neq -1$$

Combine like terms in the numerator.

Step 4 If necessary, simplify. Because the numerator is prime, no further simplification is possible.

Check Point 8 Subtract: $\dfrac{x}{x^2 - 10x + 25} - \dfrac{x - 4}{2x - 10}$.

6 Simplify complex rational expressions.

Complex Rational Expressions

Complex rational expressions, also called **complex fractions,** have numerators or denominators containing one or more rational expressions. Here are two examples of such expressions:

$$\frac{1 + \dfrac{1}{x}}{1 - \dfrac{1}{x}}$$

Separate rational expressions occur in the numerator and denominator.

$$\frac{\dfrac{1}{x + h} - \dfrac{1}{x}}{h}$$

Separate rational expressions occur in the numerator.

One method for simplifying a complex rational expression is to combine its numerator into a single expression and combine its denominator into a single expression. Then perform the division by inverting the denominator and multiplying.

EXAMPLE 9   **Simplifying a Complex Rational Expression**

Simplify: $\dfrac{1 + \dfrac{1}{x}}{1 - \dfrac{1}{x}}$.

Solution

$$\dfrac{1 + \dfrac{1}{x}}{1 - \dfrac{1}{x}} = \dfrac{\dfrac{x}{x} + \dfrac{1}{x}}{\dfrac{x}{x} - \dfrac{1}{x}}, \; x \neq 0$$

The terms in the numerator and in the denominator are each combined by performing the addition and subtraction. The least common denominator is x.

$$= \dfrac{\dfrac{x+1}{x}}{\dfrac{x-1}{x}}$$

Perform the addition in the numerator and the subtraction in the denominator.

$$= \dfrac{x+1}{x} \div \dfrac{x-1}{x}$$

Rewrite the main fraction bar as ÷.

$$= \dfrac{x+1}{x} \cdot \dfrac{x}{x-1}$$

Invert the divisor and multiply (x ≠ 0 and x ≠ 1).

$$= \dfrac{x+1}{\overset{}{\underset{1}{x}}} \cdot \dfrac{\overset{1}{x}}{x-1}$$

Divide a numerator and denominator by the common factor, x.

$$= \dfrac{x+1}{x-1}, \; x \neq 0, \; x \neq 1$$

Multiply the remaining factors in the numerator and in the denominator.

Check Point 9   Simplify: $\dfrac{\dfrac{1}{x} - \dfrac{3}{2}}{\dfrac{1}{x} + \dfrac{3}{4}}$.

  A second method for simplifying a complex rational expression is to find the least common denominator of all the rational expressions in its numerator and denominator. Then multiply each term in its numerator and denominator by this least common denominator. Here we use this method to simplify the complex rational expression in Example 9.

$$\dfrac{1 + \dfrac{1}{x}}{1 - \dfrac{1}{x}} = \dfrac{\left(1 + \dfrac{1}{x}\right)}{\left(1 - \dfrac{1}{x}\right)} \cdot \dfrac{x}{x}$$

The least common denominator of all the rational expressions is x. Multiply the numerator and denominator by x. Because $\dfrac{x}{x} = 1$, we are not changing the complex fraction (x ≠ 0).

$$= \dfrac{1 \cdot x + \dfrac{1}{x} \cdot x}{1 \cdot x - \dfrac{1}{x} \cdot x}$$

Use the distributive property. Be sure to distribute x to every term.

$$= \dfrac{x+1}{x-1}, \; x \neq 0, \; x \neq 1$$

Multiply. The complex rational expression is now simplified.

EXERCISE SET P.6

 Practice Exercises

In Exercises 1–6, find all numbers that must be excluded from the domain of each rational expression.

1. $\dfrac{7}{x - 3}$

2. $\dfrac{13}{x + 9}$

3. $\dfrac{x + 5}{x^2 - 25}$

4. $\dfrac{x + 7}{x^2 - 49}$

5. $\dfrac{x - 1}{x^2 + 11x + 10}$

6. $\dfrac{x - 3}{x^2 + 4x - 45}$

In Exercises 7–14, simplify each rational expression. Find all numbers that must be excluded from the domain of the simplified rational expression.

7. $\dfrac{3x - 9}{x^2 - 6x + 9}$

8. $\dfrac{4x - 8}{x^2 - 4x + 4}$

9. $\dfrac{x^2 - 12x + 36}{4x - 24}$

10. $\dfrac{x^2 - 8x + 16}{3x - 12}$

11. $\dfrac{y^2 + 7y - 18}{y^2 - 3y + 2}$

12. $\dfrac{y^2 - 4y - 5}{y^2 + 5y + 4}$

13. $\dfrac{x^2 + 12x + 36}{x^2 - 36}$

14. $\dfrac{x^2 - 14x + 49}{x^2 - 49}$

In Exercises 15–32, multiply or divide as indicated.

15. $\dfrac{x - 2}{3x + 9} \cdot \dfrac{2x + 6}{2x - 4}$

16. $\dfrac{6x + 9}{3x - 15} \cdot \dfrac{x - 5}{4x + 6}$

17. $\dfrac{x^2 - 9}{x^2} \cdot \dfrac{x^2 - 3x}{x^2 + x - 12}$

18. $\dfrac{x^2 - 4}{x^2 - 4x + 4} \cdot \dfrac{2x - 4}{x + 2}$

19. $\dfrac{x^2 - 5x + 6}{x^2 - 2x - 3} \cdot \dfrac{x^2 - 1}{x^2 - 4}$

20. $\dfrac{x^2 + 5x + 6}{x^2 + x - 6} \cdot \dfrac{x^2 - 9}{x^2 - x - 6}$

21. $\dfrac{x^3 - 8}{x^2 - 4} \cdot \dfrac{x + 2}{3x}$

22. $\dfrac{x^2 + 6x + 9}{x^3 + 27} \cdot \dfrac{1}{x + 3}$

23. $\dfrac{x + 1}{3} \div \dfrac{3x + 3}{7}$

24. $\dfrac{x + 5}{7} \div \dfrac{4x + 20}{9}$

25. $\dfrac{x^2 - 4}{x} \div \dfrac{x + 2}{x - 2}$

26. $\dfrac{x^2 - 4}{x - 2} \div \dfrac{x + 2}{4x - 8}$

27. $\dfrac{4x^2 + 10}{x - 3} \div \dfrac{6x^2 + 15}{x^2 - 9}$

28. $\dfrac{x^2 + x}{x^2 - 4} \div \dfrac{x^2 - 1}{x^2 + 5x + 6}$

29. $\dfrac{x^2 - 25}{2x - 2} \div \dfrac{x^2 + 10x + 25}{x^2 + 4x - 5}$

30. $\dfrac{x^2 - 4}{x^2 + 3x - 10} \div \dfrac{x^2 + 5x + 6}{x^2 + 8x + 15}$

31. $\dfrac{x^2 + x - 12}{x^2 + x - 30} \cdot \dfrac{x^2 + 5x + 6}{x^2 - 2x - 3} \div \dfrac{x + 3}{x^2 + 7x + 6}$

32. $\dfrac{x^3 - 25x}{4x^2} \cdot \dfrac{2x^2 - 2}{x^2 - 6x + 5} \div \dfrac{x^2 + 5x}{7x + 7}$

In Exercises 33–54, add or subtract as indicated.

33. $\dfrac{4x + 1}{6x + 5} + \dfrac{8x + 9}{6x + 5}$

34. $\dfrac{3x + 2}{3x + 4} + \dfrac{3x + 6}{3x + 4}$

35. $\dfrac{x^2 - 2x}{x^2 + 3x} + \dfrac{x^2 + x}{x^2 + 3x}$

36. $\dfrac{x^2 - 4x}{x^2 - x - 6} + \dfrac{4x - 4}{x^2 - x - 6}$

37. $\dfrac{4x - 10}{x - 2} - \dfrac{x - 4}{x - 2}$

38. $\dfrac{2x + 3}{3x - 6} - \dfrac{3 - x}{3x - 6}$

39. $\dfrac{x^2 + 3x}{x^2 + x - 12} - \dfrac{x^2 - 12}{x^2 + x - 12}$

40. $\dfrac{x^2 - 4x}{x^2 - x - 6} - \dfrac{x - 6}{x^2 - x - 6}$

41. $\dfrac{3}{x + 4} + \dfrac{6}{x + 5}$

42. $\dfrac{8}{x - 2} + \dfrac{2}{x - 3}$

43. $\dfrac{3}{x + 1} - \dfrac{3}{x}$

44. $\dfrac{4}{x} - \dfrac{3}{x + 3}$

45. $\dfrac{2x}{x + 2} + \dfrac{x + 2}{x - 2}$

46. $\dfrac{3x}{x - 3} - \dfrac{x + 4}{x + 2}$

47. $\dfrac{x + 5}{x - 5} + \dfrac{x - 5}{x + 5}$

48. $\dfrac{x + 3}{x - 3} + \dfrac{x - 3}{x + 3}$

49. $\dfrac{4}{x^2 + 6x + 9} + \dfrac{4}{x + 3}$

50. $\dfrac{3}{5x + 2} + \dfrac{5x}{25x^2 - 4}$

51. $\dfrac{3x}{x^2 + 3x - 10} - \dfrac{2x}{x^2 + x - 6}$

52. $\dfrac{x}{x^2 - 2x - 24} - \dfrac{x}{x^2 - 7x + 6}$

53. $\dfrac{4x^2 + x - 6}{x^2 + 3x + 2} - \dfrac{3x}{x + 1} + \dfrac{5}{x + 2}$

54. $\dfrac{6x^2 + 17x - 40}{x^2 + x - 20} + \dfrac{3}{x - 4} - \dfrac{5x}{x + 5}$

In Exercise 55–64, simplify each complex rational expression.

55. $\dfrac{\dfrac{x}{3} - 1}{x - 3}$

56. $\dfrac{\dfrac{x}{4} - 1}{x - 4}$

57. $\dfrac{1 + \dfrac{1}{x}}{3 - \dfrac{1}{x}}$

58. $\dfrac{8 + \dfrac{1}{x}}{4 - \dfrac{1}{x}}$

59. $\dfrac{\dfrac{1}{x} + \dfrac{1}{y}}{x + y}$

60. $\dfrac{1 - \dfrac{1}{x}}{xy}$

61. $\dfrac{x - \dfrac{x}{x + 3}}{x + 2}$

62. $\dfrac{x - 3}{x - \dfrac{3}{x - 2}}$

63. $\dfrac{\dfrac{3}{x - 2} - \dfrac{4}{x + 2}}{\dfrac{7}{x^2 - 4}}$

64. $\dfrac{\dfrac{x}{x - 2} + 1}{\dfrac{3}{x^2 - 4} + 1}$

Application Exercises

65. The rational expression

$$\frac{130x}{100 - x}$$

describes the cost, in millions of dollars, to inoculate x percent of the population against a particular strain of flu.

a. Evaluate the expression for $x = 40$, $x = 80$, and $x = 90$. Describe the meaning of each evaluation in terms of percentage inoculated and cost.

b. For what value of x is the expression undefined?

c. What happens to the cost as x approaches 100%? How can you interpret this observation?

66. Doctors use the rational expression

$$\frac{DA}{A + 12}$$

to determine the dosage of a drug prescribed for children. In this expression, A = child's age, and D = adult dosage. What is the difference in the child's dosage for a 7-year-old child and a 3-year-old child? Express the answer as a single rational expression in terms of D. Then describe what your answer means in terms of the variables in the rational expression.

67. Anthropologists and forensic scientists classify skulls using

$$\frac{L + 60W}{L} - \frac{L - 40W}{L}$$

where L is the skull's length and W is its width.

a. Express the classification as a single rational expression.

b. If the value of the rational expression in part (a) is less than 75, a skull is classified as long. A medium skull has a value between 75 and 80, and a round skull has a value over 80. Use your rational expression from part (a) to classify a skull that is 5 inches wide and 6 inches long.

68. The polynomial

$$6t^4 - 207t^3 + 2128t^2 - 6622t + 15{,}220$$

describes the annual number of drug convictions in the United States t years after 1984. The polynomial

$$28t^4 - 711t^3 + 5963t^2 - 1695t + 27{,}424$$

describes the annual number of drug arrests in the United States t years after 1984. Write a rational expression that describes the conviction rate for drug arrests in the United States t years after 1984.

69. The average speed on a round-trip commute having a one-way distance d is given by the complex rational expression

$$\frac{2d}{\dfrac{d}{r_1} + \dfrac{d}{r_2}}$$

in which r_1 and r_2 are the speeds on the outgoing and return trips, respectively. Simplify the expression. Then find the average speed for a person who drives from home to work at 30 miles per hour and returns on the same route averaging 20 miles per hour. Explain why the answer is not 25 miles per hour.

Writing in Mathematics

70. What is a rational expression?

71. Explain how to determine which numbers must be excluded from the domain of a rational expression.

72. Explain how to simplify a rational expression.

73. Explain how to multiply rational expressions.

74. Explain how to divide rational expressions.

75. Explain how to add or subtract rational expressions with the same denominators.

76. Explain how to add rational expressions having no common factors in their denominators. Use $\dfrac{3}{x+5} + \dfrac{7}{x+2}$ in your explanation.

77. Explain how to find the least common denominator for denominators of $x^2 - 100$ and $x^2 - 20x + 100$.

78. Describe two ways to simplify $\dfrac{\dfrac{3}{x}+\dfrac{2}{x^2}}{\dfrac{1}{x^2}+\dfrac{2}{x}}$.

Explain the error in Exercises 79–81. Then rewrite the right side of the equation to correct the error that now exists.

79. $\dfrac{1}{a}+\dfrac{1}{b}=\dfrac{1}{a+b}$

80. $\dfrac{1}{x}+7=\dfrac{1}{x+7}$

81. $\dfrac{a}{x}+\dfrac{a}{b}=\dfrac{a}{x+b}$

82. A politician claims that each year the conviction rate for drug arrests in the United States is increasing. Explain how to use the polynomials in Exercise 68 to verify this claim.

Technology Exercises

83. How much are your monthly payments on a loan? If P is the principal, or amount borrowed, i is the monthly interest rate, and n is the number of monthly payments, then the amount, A, of each monthly payment is
$$A = \dfrac{Pi}{1 - \dfrac{1}{(1+i)^n}}.$$

a. Simplify the complex rational expression for the amount of each payment.

b. You purchase a $20,000 automobile at 1% monthly interest to be paid over 48 months. How much do you pay each month? Use the simplified rational expression from part (a) and a calculator. Round to the nearest dollar.

Critical Thinking Exercises

84. Which one of the following is true?

a. $\dfrac{x^2-25}{x-5}=x-5$

b. $\dfrac{x}{y}\div\dfrac{y}{x}=1$, if $x\neq0$ and $y\neq0$.

c. The least common denominator needed to find $\dfrac{1}{x}+\dfrac{1}{x+3}$ is $x+3$.

d. The rational expression
$$\dfrac{x^2-16}{x-4}$$
is not defined for $x=4$. However, as x gets closer and closer to 4, the value of the expression approaches 8.

In Exercises 85–86, find the missing expression.

85. $\dfrac{3x}{x-5}+\dfrac{\boxed{}}{5-x}=\dfrac{7x+1}{x-5}$

86. $\dfrac{4}{x-2}-\boxed{}=\dfrac{2x+8}{(x-2)(x+1)}$

87. In one short sentence, five words or less, explain what
$$\dfrac{\dfrac{1}{x}+\dfrac{1}{x^2}+\dfrac{1}{x^3}}{\dfrac{1}{x^4}+\dfrac{1}{x^5}+\dfrac{1}{x^6}}$$
does to each number x.

CHAPTER SUMMARY, REVIEW, AND TEST

Summary: Basic Formulas

Definition of Absolute Value

$$|x| = \begin{cases} x & \text{if } x \geq 0 \\ -x & \text{if } x < 0 \end{cases}$$

Distance between Points a and b on a Number Line

$$|a - b| \quad \text{or} \quad |b - a|$$

Properties of Algebra

Commutative	$a + b = b + a, \quad ab = ba$
Associative	$(a + b) + c = a + (b + c)$
	$(ab)c = a(bc)$
Distributive	$a(b + c) = ab + ac$
Identity	$a + 0 = a \quad a \cdot 1 = a$
Inverse	$a + (-a) = 0 \quad a \cdot \dfrac{1}{a} = 1, a \neq 0$

Properties of Exponents

$$b^{-n} = \frac{1}{b^n}, \quad b^0 = 1, \quad b^m \cdot b^n = b^{m+n},$$

$$(b^m)^n = b^{mn}, \quad \frac{b^m}{b^n} = b^{m-n}, \quad (ab)^n = a^n b^n, \quad \left(\frac{a}{b}\right)^n = \frac{a^n}{b^n}$$

Product and Quotient Rules for nth Roots

$$\sqrt[n]{a} \cdot \sqrt[n]{b} = \sqrt[n]{ab} \qquad \frac{\sqrt[n]{a}}{\sqrt[n]{b}} = \sqrt[n]{\frac{a}{b}}$$

Rational Exponents

$$a^{1/n} = \sqrt[n]{a}, \quad a^{-1/n} = \frac{1}{a^{1/n}} = \frac{1}{\sqrt[n]{a}},$$

$$a^{m/n} = \left(\sqrt[n]{a}\right)^m = \sqrt[n]{a^m}, \quad a^{-m/n} = \frac{1}{a^{m/n}}$$

Special Products

$$(A + B)(A - B) = A^2 - B^2$$
$$(A + B)^2 = A^2 + 2AB + B^2$$
$$(A - B)^2 = A^2 - 2AB + B^2$$
$$(A + B)^3 = A^3 + 3A^2B + 3AB^2 + B^3$$
$$(A - B)^3 = A^3 - 3A^2B + 3AB^2 - B^3$$

Factoring Formulas

$$A^2 - B^2 = (A + B)(A - B)$$
$$A^2 + 2AB + B^2 = (A + B)^2$$
$$A^2 - 2AB + B^2 = (A - B)^2$$
$$A^3 + B^3 = (A + B)(A^2 - AB + B^2)$$
$$A^3 - B^3 = (A - B)(A^2 + AB + B^2)$$

Review Exercises

You can use these review exercises, like the review exercises at the end of each chapter, to test your understanding of the chapter's topics. However, you can also use these exercises as a prerequisite test to check your mastery of the fundamental algebra skills needed in this book.

P.1

1. Consider the set:

$$\left\{-17, -\tfrac{9}{13}, 0, 0.75, \sqrt{2}, \pi, \sqrt{81}\right\}.$$

List all numbers from the set that are **a.** natural numbers, **b.** whole numbers, **c.** integers, **d.** rational numbers, **e.** irrational numbers.

In Exercises 2–4, rewrite each expression without absolute value bars.

2. $|-103|$

3. $|\sqrt{2} - 1|$

4. $|3 - \sqrt{17}|$

5. Express the distance between the numbers -17 and 4 using absolute value. Then evaluate the absolute value.

In Exercises 6–7, evaluate each algebraic expression for the given value of the variable.

6. $\frac{5}{9}(F - 32)$; $F = 68$ **7.** $\frac{8(x + 5)}{3x + 8}$, $x = 2$

In Exercises 8–13, state the name of the property illustrated.

8. $3 + 17 = 17 + 3$ **9.** $(6 \cdot 3) \cdot 9 = 6 \cdot (3 \cdot 9)$

10. $\sqrt{3}(\sqrt{5} + \sqrt{3}) = \sqrt{15} + 3$

11. $(6 \cdot 9) \cdot 2 = 2 \cdot (6 \cdot 9)$

12. $\sqrt{3}(\sqrt{5} + \sqrt{3}) = (\sqrt{5} + \sqrt{3})\sqrt{3}$

13. $(3 \cdot 7) + (4 \cdot 7) = (4 \cdot 7) + (3 \cdot 7)$

In Exercises 14–15, simplify each algebraic expression.

14. $3(7x - 5y) - 2(4y - x + 1)$

15. $\frac{1}{5}(5x) + [(3y) + (-3y)] - (-x)$

P.2

Evaluate each exponential expression in Exercises 16–19.

16. $(-3)^3(-2)^2$ **17.** $2^{-4} + 4^{-1}$

18. $5^{-3} \cdot 5$ **19.** $\frac{3^3}{3^6}$

Simplify each exponential expression in Exercises 20–23.

20. $(-2x^4y^3)^3$ **21.** $(-5x^3y^2)(-2x^{-11}y^{-2})$

22. $(2x^3)^{-4}$ **23.** $\frac{7x^5y^6}{28x^{15}y^{-2}}$

In Exercises 24–25, write each number in decimal notation.

24. 3.74×10^4 **25.** 7.45×10^{-5}

In Exercises 26–27, write each number in scientific notation.

26. 3,590,000   **27.** 0.00725

In Exercises 28–29, perform the indicated operation and write the answer in decimal notation.

28. $(3 \times 10^3)(1.3 \times 10^2)$ **29.** $\frac{6.9 \times 10^3}{3 \times 10^5}$

30. If you earned $1 million per year ($10^6$), how long would it take to accumulate $1 billion ($10^9$)?

31. If the population of the United States is 2.8×10^8 and each person spends about $150 per year going to the movies (or renting movies), express the total annual spending on movies in scientific notation.

P.3

Use the product rule to simplify the expressions in Exercises 32–35. In Exercises 34–35, assume that variables represent nonnegative real numbers.

32. $\sqrt{300}$ **33.** $\sqrt{12x^2}$

34. $\sqrt{10x} \cdot \sqrt{2x}$ **35.** $\sqrt{r^3}$

Use the quotient rule to simplify the expressions in Exercises 36–37.

36. $\sqrt{\frac{121}{4}}$

37. $\frac{\sqrt{96x^3}}{\sqrt{2x}}$ (Assume that $x > 0$.)

In Exercises 38–40, add or subtract terms whenever possible.

38. $7\sqrt{5} + 13\sqrt{5}$ **39.** $2\sqrt{50} + 3\sqrt{8}$

40. $4\sqrt{72} - 2\sqrt{48}$

In Exercises 41–44, rationalize the denominator.

41. $\frac{30}{\sqrt{5}}$ **42.** $\frac{\sqrt{2}}{\sqrt{3}}$

43. $\frac{5}{6 + \sqrt{3}}$ **44.** $\frac{14}{\sqrt{7} - \sqrt{5}}$

Evaluate each expression in Exercises 45–48 or indicate that the root is not a real number.

45. $\sqrt[3]{125}$ **46.** $\sqrt[5]{-32}$

47. $\sqrt[4]{-125}$ **48.** $\sqrt[4]{(-5)^4}$

Simplify the radical expressions in Exercises 49–53.

49. $\sqrt[3]{81}$ **50.** $\sqrt[3]{y^5}$

51. $\sqrt[4]{8} \cdot \sqrt[4]{10}$ **52.** $4\sqrt[3]{16} + 5\sqrt[3]{2}$

53. $\frac{\sqrt[4]{32x^5}}{\sqrt[4]{16x}}$ (Assume that $x > 0$.)

In Exercises 54–59, evaluate each expression.

54. $16^{1/2}$ **55.** $25^{-1/2}$

56. $125^{1/3}$ **57.** $27^{-1/3}$

58. $64^{2/3}$ **59.** $27^{-4/3}$

In Exercises 60–62, simplify using properties of exponents.

60. $(5x^{2/3})(4x^{1/4})$ **61.** $\frac{15x^{3/4}}{5x^{1/2}}$

62. $(125x^6)^{2/3}$

63. Simplify by reducing the index of the radical: $\sqrt[6]{y^3}$.

P.4

In Exercises 64–65, perform the indicated operations. Write the resulting polynomial in standard form and indicate its degree.

64. $(-6x^3 + 7x^2 - 9x + 3) + (14x^3 + 3x^2 - 11x - 7)$

65. $(13x^4 - 8x^3 + 2x^2) - (5x^4 - 3x^3 + 2x^2 - 6)$

In Exercises 66–72, find each product.

66. $(3x - 2)(4x^2 + 3x - 5)$ **67.** $(3x - 5)(2x + 1)$

68. $(4x + 5)(4x - 5)$ **69.** $(2x + 5)^2$

70. $(3x - 4)^2$ **71.** $(2x + 1)^3$

72. $(5x - 2)^3$

In Exercises 73–74, perform the indicated operations. Indicate the degree of the resulting polynomial.

73. $(7x^2 - 8xy + y^2) + (-8x^2 - 9xy - 4y^2)$

74. $(13x^3y^2 - 5x^2y - 9x^2) - (-11x^3y^2 - 6x^2y + 3x^2 - 4)$

In Exercises 75–79, find each product.

75. $(x + 7y)(3x - 5y)$ **76.** $(3x - 5y)^2$

77. $(3x^2 + 2y)^2$ **78.** $(7x + 4y)(7x - 4y)$

79. $(a - b)(a^2 + ab + b^2)$

P.5

In Exercises 80–96, factor completely, or state that the polynomial is prime.

80. $15x^3 + 3x^2$ **81.** $x^2 - 11x + 28$

82. $15x^2 - x - 2$ **83.** $64 - x^2$

84. $x^2 + 16$ **85.** $3x^4 - 9x^3 - 30x^2$

86. $20x^7 - 36x^3$ **87.** $x^3 - 3x^2 - 9x + 27$

88. $16x^2 - 40x + 25$ **89.** $x^4 - 16$

90. $y^3 - 8$ **91.** $x^3 + 64$

92. $3x^4 - 12x^2$ **93.** $27x^3 - 125$

94. $x^5 - x$ **95.** $x^3 + 5x^2 - 2x - 10$

96. $x^2 + 18x + 81 - y^2$

In Exercises 97–99, factor and simplify each algebraic expression.

97. $16x^{-3/4} + 32x^{1/4}$

98. $(x^2 - 4)(x^2 + 3)^{1/2} - (x^2 - 4)^2(x^2 + 3)^{3/2}$

99. $12x^{-1/2} + 6x^{-3/2}$

P.6

In Exercises 100–102, simplify each rational expression. Also, list all numbers that must be excluded from the domain.

100. $\dfrac{x^3 + 2x^2}{x + 2}$ **101.** $\dfrac{x^2 + 3x - 18}{x^2 - 36}$

102. $\dfrac{x^2 + 2x}{x^2 + 4x + 4}$

In Exercises 103–105, multiply or divide as indicated.

103. $\dfrac{x^2 + 6x + 9}{x^2 - 4} \cdot \dfrac{x + 3}{x - 2}$ **104.** $\dfrac{6x + 2}{x^2 - 1} \div \dfrac{3x^2 + x}{x - 1}$

105. $\dfrac{x^2 - 5x - 24}{x^2 - x - 12} \div \dfrac{x^2 - 10x + 16}{x^2 + x - 6}$

In Exercises 106–109, add or subtract as indicated.

106. $\dfrac{2x - 7}{x^2 - 9} - \dfrac{x - 10}{x^2 - 9}$ **107.** $\dfrac{3x}{x + 2} + \dfrac{x}{x - 2}$

108. $\dfrac{x}{x^2 - 9} + \dfrac{x - 1}{x^2 - 5x + 6}$

109. $\dfrac{4x - 1}{2x^2 + 5x - 3} - \dfrac{x + 3}{6x^2 + x - 2}$

In Exercises 110–112, simplify each complex rational expression.

110. $\dfrac{\dfrac{1}{x} - \dfrac{1}{2}}{\dfrac{1}{3} - \dfrac{x}{6}}$ **111.** $\dfrac{3 + \dfrac{12}{x}}{1 - \dfrac{16}{x^2}}$ **112.** $\dfrac{3 - \dfrac{1}{x + 3}}{3 + \dfrac{1}{x + 3}}$

Chapter P Test

1. List all the rational numbers in this set:
$$\{-7, -\tfrac{4}{5}, 0, 0.25, \sqrt{3}, \sqrt{4}, \tfrac{22}{7}, \pi\}.$$

In Exercises 2–3, state the name of the property illustrated.

2. $3(2 + 5) = 3(5 + 2)$ **3.** $6(7 + 4) = 6 \cdot 7 + 6 \cdot 4$

4. Express in scientific notation: 0.00076.

Simplify each expression in Exercises 5–11.

5. $9(10x - 2y) - 5(x - 4y + 3)$

6. $\dfrac{30x^3y^4}{6x^9y^{-4}}$

7. $\sqrt{6r}\,\sqrt{3r}$ (Assume that $r \geq 0$.)

8. $4\sqrt{50} - 3\sqrt{18}$ **9.** $\dfrac{3}{5 + \sqrt{2}}$

10. $\sqrt[3]{16x^4}$ **11.** $\dfrac{x^2 + 2x - 3}{x^2 - 3x + 2}$

12. Evaluate: $27^{-5/3}$.

In Exercises 13–14, find each product.

13. $(2x - 5)(x^2 - 4x + 3)$ **14.** $(5x + 3y)^2$

In Exercises 15–20, factor completely, or state that the polynomial is prime.

15. $x^2 - 9x + 18$

16. $x^3 + 2x^2 + 3x + 6$

17. $25x^2 - 9$

18. $36x^2 - 84x + 49$

19. $y^3 - 125$

20. $x^2 + 10x + 25 - 9y^2$

21. Factor and simplify:

$$x(x + 3)^{-3/5} + (x + 3)^{2/5}.$$

In Exercises 22–25, perform the operations and simplify, if possible.

22. $\dfrac{2x + 8}{x - 3} \div \dfrac{x^2 + 5x + 4}{x^2 - 9}$

23. $\dfrac{x}{x + 3} + \dfrac{5}{x - 3}$

24. $\dfrac{2x + 3}{x^2 - 7x + 12} - \dfrac{2}{x - 3}$

25. $\dfrac{\dfrac{1}{x} - \dfrac{1}{3}}{\dfrac{1}{x}}$

Equations, Inequalities, and Mathematical Models

Formulas like those that describe the height a child will attain as an adult are frequently obtained from actual data. Formulas can be used to explain what is happening in the present and to make predictions about what might occur in the future. Knowing how to create and use formulas will help you recognize patterns, logic, and order in a world that can appear chaotic to the untrained eye. In many ways, algebra will provide you with a new way of looking at your world.

Sitting in the biology department office, you overhear two of the professors discussing the possible adult heights of their respective children. Looking at the blackboard that they've been writing on, you see that there are formulas that can estimate the height a child will attain as an adult. If the child is x years old and h inches tall, that child's adult height, H, in inches, is approximated by one of the following formulas:

Girls: $$H = \frac{h}{0.00028x^3 - 0.0071x^2 + 0.0926x + 0.3524}$$

Boys: $$H = \frac{h}{0.00011x^3 - 0.0032x^2 + 0.0604x + 0.3796}.$$

SECTION 1.1 *Graphs and Graphing Utilities*

Objectives

1. Plot points in the rectangular coordinate system.
2. Graph equations in the rectangular coordinate system.
3. Interpret information about a graphing utility's viewing rectangle.
4. Use a graph to determine intercepts.
5. Interpret information given by graphs.

The beginning of the seventeenth century was a time of innovative ideas and enormous intellectual progress in Europe. English theatergoers enjoyed a succession of exciting new plays by Shakespeare. William Harvey proposed the radical notion that the heart was a pump for blood rather than the center of emotion. Galileo, with his new-fangled invention called the telescope, supported the theory of Polish astronomer Copernicus that the sun, not the Earth, was the center of the solar system. Monteverdi was writing the world's first grand operas. French mathematicians Pascal and Fermat invented a new field of mathematics called probability theory.

Into this arena of intellectual electricity stepped French aristocrat René Descartes (1596–1650). Descartes, propelled by the creativity surrounding him, developed a new branch of mathematics that brought together algebra and geometry in a unified way—a way that visualized numbers as points on a graph, equations as geometric figures, and geometric figures as equations. This new branch of mathematics, called *analytic geometry*, established Descartes as one of the founders of modern thought and among the most original mathematicians and philosophers of any age. We begin this section by looking at Descartes's deceptively simple idea, called the **rectangular coordinate system** or (in his honor) the **Cartesian coordinate system.**

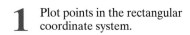

1 Plot points in the rectangular coordinate system.

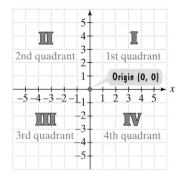

Figure 1.1 The rectangular coordinate system

Points and Ordered Pairs

Descartes used two number lines that intersect at right angles at their zero points, as shown in Figure 1.1. The horizontal number line is the **x-axis.** The vertical number line is the **y-axis.** The point of intersection of these axes is their zero points, called the **origin.** Positive numbers are shown to the right and above the origin. Negative numbers are shown to the left and below the origin. The axes divide the plane into four quarters, called **quadrants.** The points located on the axes are not in any quadrant.

Each point in the rectangular coordinate system corresponds to an **ordered pair** of real numbers, (x, y). Examples of such pairs are $(4, 2)$ and $(-5, -3)$. The first number in each pair, called the **x-coordinate,** denotes the distance and direction from the origin along the x-axis. The second number, called the **y-coordinate,** denotes vertical distance and direction along a line parallel to the y-axis or along the y-axis itself.

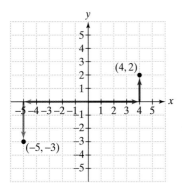

Figure 1.2 Plotting $(4, 2)$ and $(-5, -3)$

Figure 1.2 shows how we **plot,** or locate, the points corresponding to the ordered pairs $(4, 2)$ and $(-5, -3)$. We plot $(4, 2)$ by going 4 units from 0 to the right along the x-axis. Then we go 2 units up parallel to the y-axis. We plot $(-5, -3)$ by going 5 units from 0 to the left along the x-axis and 3 units down parallel to the y-axis. The phrase "the point corresponding to the ordered pair $(-5, -3)$" is often abbreviated as "the point $(-5, -3)$."

EXAMPLE 1 Plotting Points in the Rectangular Coordinate System

Plot the points: $A(-3, 5)$, $B(2, -4)$, $C(5, 0)$, $D(-5, -3)$, $E(0, 4)$, and $F(0, 0)$.

Solution See Figure 1.3. We move from the origin and plot the points in the following way:

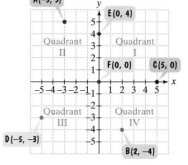

$A(-3, 5)$:   3 units left, 5 units up

$B(2, -4)$:   2 units right, 4 units down

$C(5, 0)$:   5 units right, 0 units up or down

$D(-5, -3)$:   5 units left, 3 units down

$E(0, 4)$:   0 units right or left, 4 units up

$F(0, 0)$:   0 units right or left, 0 units up or down

Figure 1.3 Plotting points

The phrase *ordered pair* is used because **order is important.** For example, the points $(2, 5)$ and $(5, 2)$ are not the same. To plot $(2, 5)$, move 2 units right and 5 units up. To plot $(5, 2)$, move 5 units right and 2 units up. The points $(2, 5)$ and $(5, 2)$ are in different locations. **The order in which coordinates appear makes a difference in a points location.**

Check Point 1   Plot the points:

$$A(-2, 4), B(4, -2), C(-3, 0), \text{ and } D(0, -3).$$

Graphs of Equations

A relationship between two quantities can be expressed as an **equation in two variables,** such as

$$y = x^2 - 4.$$

2 Graph equations in the rectangular coordinate system.

A **solution** of this equation is an ordered pair of real numbers with the following property: When the x-coordinate is substituted for x and the y-coordinate is substituted for y in the equation, we obtain a true statement. For example, if we let $x = 3$, then $y = 3^2 - 4 = 9 - 4 = 5$. The ordered pair $(3, 5)$ is a solution of the equation $y = x^2 - 4$. We also say that $(3, 5)$ **satisfies** the equation.

We can generate as many ordered-pair solutions as desired of $y = x^2 - 4$ by substituting numbers for x and then finding the values for y. The **graph of the equation** is the set of all points whose coordinates satisfy the equation.

One method for graphing an equation such as $y = x^2 - 4$ is the **point-plotting method.** First, we find several ordered pairs that are solutions of the equation. Next, we plot these ordered pairs as points in the rectangular coordinate system. Finally, we connect the points with a smooth curve or line. This often gives us a picture of all ordered pairs that satisfy the equation.

EXAMPLE 2 **Graphing an Equation Using the Point-Plotting Method**

Graph $y = x^2 - 4$. Select integers for x, starting with -3 and ending with 3.

Solution For each value of x we find the corresponding value for y.

x	$y = x^2 - 4$	(x, y)
-3	$y = (-3)^2 - 4 = 9 - 4 = 5$	$(-3, 5)$
-2	$y = (-2)^2 - 4 = 4 - 4 = 0$	$(-2, 0)$
-1	$y = (-1)^2 - 4 = 1 - 4 = -3$	$(-1, -3)$
0	$y = 0^2 - 4 = 0 - 4 = -4$	$(0, -4)$
1	$y = 1^2 - 4 = 1 - 4 = -3$	$(1, -3)$
2	$y = 2^2 - 4 = 4 - 4 = 0$	$(2, 0)$
3	$y = 3^2 - 4 = 9 - 4 = 5$	$(3, 5)$

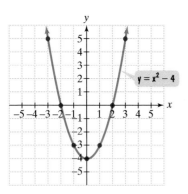

Figure 1.4 The graph of $y = x^2 - 4$

Now we plot the ordered pairs that are solutions of the equation and join the points with a smooth curve, as shown in Figure 1.4. The graph of $y = x^2 - 4$ is a curve where the part of the graph to the right of the y-axis is a reflection of the part to the left of it, and vice versa. The arrows on the left and the right of the curve indicate that it extends indefinitely in both directions.

Check Point 2 Graph $y = 2x - 4$. Select integers for x, starting with -1 and ending with 3.

Do you see a difference between the equations in Example 2 and Check Point 2? The equation in Example 2, $y = x^2 - 4$, involves a polynomial of degree 2. All such equations have graphs that are shaped like cups, such as the graph in Figure 1.4. These U-shaped "cups" can open upward, like the one in Figure 1.4, or downward. By contrast, the equation in Check Point 2, $y = 2x - 4$, involves a polynomial of degree 1. All such equations have graphs that are straight lines.

Study Tip

In Chapters 2 and 3, we will be studying graphs of equations in two variables in which

$$y = \text{a polynomial in } x.$$

Do not be concerned that we have not yet learned techniques, other than plotting points, for graphing such equations. As you solve some of the equations in this chapter, we will display graphs simply to enhance your visual understanding of your work. For now, think of graphs of first-degree polynomials as lines and graphs of second-degree polynomials as symmetric U-shaped cups.

3 Interpret information about a graphing utility's viewing rectangle.

Graphing Equations Using a Graphing Utility

Graphing calculators or graphing software packages for computers are referred to as **graphing utilities** or graphers. A graphing utility is a powerful tool that quickly generates the graph of an equation in two variables. Figure 1.5 shows two such graphs for the equations in Example 2 and Check Point 2.

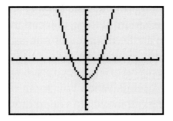

Figure 1.5(a)
The graph of $y = x^2 - 4$

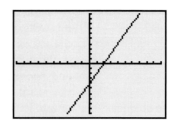

Figure 1.5(b)
The graph of $y = 2x - 4$

Study Tip

Even if you are not using a graphing utility in the course, read this part of the section. Knowing about viewing rectangles will enable you to understand the graphs that we display in the technology boxes throughout the book.

What differences do you notice between these graphs and graphs that we draw by hand? They do seem a bit "jittery." Arrows do not appear on the left and right ends of the graphs. Furthermore, numbers are not given along the axes. For both graphs in Figure 1.5, the x-axis extends from -10 to 10 and the y-axis also extends from -10 to 10. The distance represented by each consecutive tick mark is one unit. We say that the **viewing rectangle** is $[-10, 10, 1]$ by $[-10, 10, 1]$.

$$[-10, \qquad 10, \qquad 1] \quad \text{by} \quad [-10, \qquad 10, \qquad 1]$$

| The minimum x-value along the x-axis is −10. | The maximum x-value along the x-axis is 10. | Distance between consecutive tick marks on the x-axis is one unit. | The minimum y-value along the y-axis is −10. | The maximum y-value along the y-axis is 10. | Distance between consecutive tick marks on the y-axis is one unit. |

To graph an equation in x and y using a graphing utility, enter the equation and specify the size of the viewing rectangle. The size of the viewing rectangle sets minimum and maximum values for both the x- and y-axes. Enter these values, as well as the values between consecutive tick marks on the respective axes. The $[-10, 10, 1]$ by $[-10, 10, 1]$ viewing rectangle used in Figure 1.5 is called the **standard viewing rectangle.**

EXAMPLE 3   Understanding the Viewing Rectangle

What is the meaning of a $[-2, 3, 0.5]$ by $[-10, 20, 5]$ viewing rectangle?

Solution   We begin with $[-2, 3, 0.5]$, which describes the x-axis. The minimum x-value is -2 and the maximum x-value is 3. The distance between consecutive tick marks is 0.5.

Next, consider $[-10, 20, 5]$, which describes the y-axis. The minimum y-value is -10 and the maximum y-value is 20. The distance between consecutive tick marks is 5.

Figure 1.6 illustrates a $[-2, 3, 0.5]$ by $[-10, 20, 5]$ viewing rectangle. To make things clearer, we've placed numbers by each tick mark. These numbers do not appear on the axes when you use a graphing utility to graph an equation.

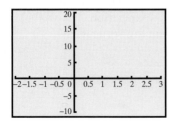

Figure 1.6 A $[-2, 3, 0.5]$ by $[-10, 20, 5]$ viewing rectangle

Check Point 3   What is the meaning of a $[-100, 100, 50]$ by $[-80, 80, 10]$ viewing rectangle? Create a figure like the one in Figure 1.6 that illustrates this viewing rectangle.

On most graphing utilities, the display screen is about two-thirds as high as it is wide. By using a square setting, you can make the distance of one unit along the *x*-axis the same as the distance of one unit along the *y*-axis. (This does not occur in the standard viewing rectangle.) Graphing utilities can also *zoom in* and *zoom out*. When you zoom in, you see a smaller portion of the graph, but you see it in greater detail. When you zoom out, you see a larger portion of the graph. Thus, zooming out may help you to develop a better understanding of the overall character of the graph. With practice, you will become more comfortable with graphing equations in two variables using your graphing utility. You will also develop a better sense of the size of the viewing rectangle that will reveal needed information about a particular graph.

4 Use a graph to determine intercepts.

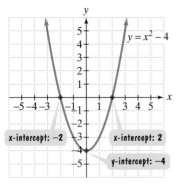

Figure 1.7 Intercepts of $y = x^2 - 4$

Intercepts

An ***x*-intercept** of a graph is the *x*-coordinate of a point where the graph intersects the *x*-axis. For example, look at the graph of $y = x^2 - 4$ in Figure 1.7. The graph crosses the *x*-axis at $(-2, 0)$ and $(2, 0)$. Thus, the *x*-intercepts are -2 and 2. **The *y*-coordinate corresponding to a graph's *x*-intercept is always zero.**

A ***y*-intercept** of a graph is the *y*-coordinate of a point where the graph intersects the *y*-axis. The graph of $y = x^2 - 4$ in Figure 1.7 shows that the graph crosses the *y*-axis at $(0, -4)$. Thus, the *y*-intercept is -4. **The *x*-coordinate corresponding to a graph's *y*-intercept is always zero.**

Figure 1.8 illustrates that a graph may have no intercepts or several intercepts.

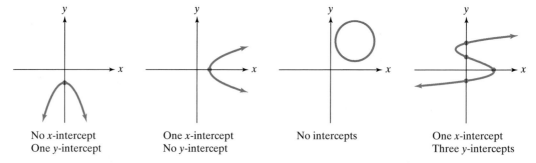

| No *x*-intercept
One *y*-intercept | One *x*-intercept
No *y*-intercept | No intercepts | One *x*-intercept
Three *y*-intercepts |

Figure 1.8

5 Interpret information given by graphs.

Interpreting Information Given by Graphs

Magazines and newspapers often display information using **line graphs** like the one in Figure 1.9. The graph shows the average age at which women in the United States married for the first time over a 110-year period. The years are listed on the horizontal axis and the ages are listed on the vertical axis.

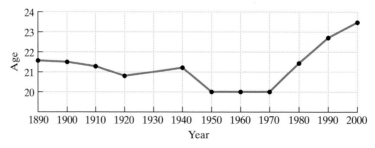

Figure 1.9 Average age at which U.S. women married for the first time
Source: U.S. Census Bureau

Like the graph in Figure 1.9, line graphs are often used to illustrate trends over time. Some measure of time, such as months or years, frequently appears on the horizontal axis. Amounts are generally listed on the vertical axis.

A line graph displays information in the first quadrant of a rectangular coordinate system. By identifying points on line graphs and their coordinates, you can interpret specific information given by the graph.

For example, Figure 1.10 shows how to find the average age at which women married for the first time in 1930. (Only the part of the graph that reveals what occurred through about 1940 is shown in the margin because we are interested in 1930.)

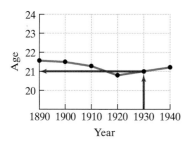

Figure 1.10 In 1930, women were 21 on average when they married for the first time.

Step 1 Locate 1930 on the horizontal axis.

Step 2 Locate the point above 1930.

Step 3 Read across to the corresponding age on the vertical axis.

The age is 21. The coordinates (1930, 21) tell us that in 1930, women in the United States married for the first time at an average age of 21.

EXAMPLE 4 Applying Estimation Techniques to a Line Graph

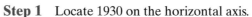
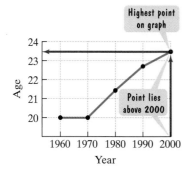

Figure 1.9 Shown again to show only 1960–2000

Use Figure 1.9 to estimate the maximum average age at which U.S. women married for the first time. When did this occur?

Solution The maximum average age at which U.S. women married for the first time can be found by locating the highest point on the graph. This point lies above 2000 on the horizontal axis. Read across to the corresponding age on the vertical axis. The age falls approximately midway between 23 and 24, at $23\frac{1}{2}$. The coordinates of the point are approximately $(2000, 23\frac{1}{2})$. Thus, according to the graph, the maximum average age at which U.S. women married for the first time is about $23\frac{1}{2}$. This occurred in 2000. Take another look at the complete line graph in Figure 1.9 at the bottom of page 80 that includes the years 1890 through 2000. Can you see that $23\frac{1}{2}$ is the oldest average age of first marriage over the 110-year period?

Check Point 4 Use the complete line graph in Figure 1.9 to estimate the maximum average age, for the period from 1900 through 1950, at which U.S. women married for the first time. When did this occur?

EXERCISE SET 1.1

Practice Exercises

In Exercises 1–12, plot the given point in a rectangular coordinate system.

1. $(1, 4)$
2. $(2, 5)$
3. $(-2, 3)$
4. $(-1, 4)$
5. $(-3, -5)$
6. $(-4, -2)$
7. $(4, -1)$
8. $(3, -2)$
9. $(-4, 0)$
10. $(0, -3)$
11. $(\frac{7}{2}, -\frac{3}{2})$
12. $(-\frac{5}{2}, \frac{3}{2})$

Graph each equation in Exercises 13–28. Let x = −3, −2, −1, 0, 1, 2, and 3.

13. $y = x^2 - 2$
14. $y = x^2 + 2$
15. $y = x - 2$
16. $y = x + 2$
17. $y = 2x + 1$
18. $y = 2x - 4$
19. $y = -\frac{1}{2}x$
20. $y = -\frac{1}{2}x + 2$
21. $y = |x|$
22. $y = 2|x|$
23. $y = |x| + 1$
24. $y = |x| - 1$
25. $y = 4 - x^2$
26. $y = 9 - x^2$
27. $y = x^3$
28. $y = x^3 - 1$

In Exercises 29–32, match the viewing rectangle with the correct figure. Then label the tick marks in the figure to illustrate this viewing rectangle.

29. $[-5, 5, 1]$ by $[-5, 5, 1]$

30. $[-10, 10, 2]$ by $[-4, 4, 2]$

31. $[-20, 80, 10]$ by $[-30, 70, 10]$

32. $[-40, 40, 20]$ by $[-1000, 1000, 100]$

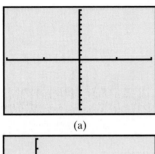

(a)

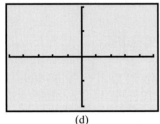

(b)

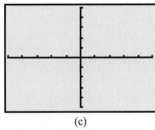

(c)

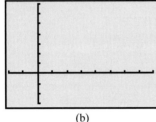

(d)

*In Exercises 33–38, use the graph and **a.** determine the x-intercepts, if any; **b.** determine the y-intercepts, if any. For each graph, tick marks along the axes represent one unit each.*

33.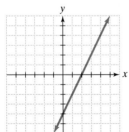

34.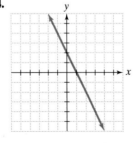

35.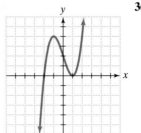

36.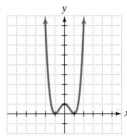

37.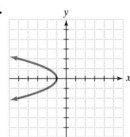

38.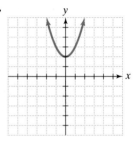

 Application Exercises

A football is thrown by a quarterback to a receiver. The points in the figure show the height of the football, in feet, above the ground in terms of its distance, in yards, from the quarterback. Use this information to solve Exercises 39–44.

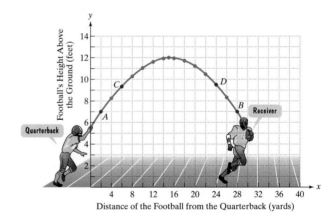

39. Find the coordinates of point A. Then interpret the coordinates in terms of the information given.

40. Find the coordinates of point B. Then interpret the coordinates in terms of the information given.

41. Estimate the coordinates of point C.

42. Estimate the coordinates of point D.

43. What is the football's maximum height? What is its distance from the quarterback when it reaches its maximum height?

44. What is the football's height when it is caught by the receiver? What is the receiver's distance from the quarterback when he catches the football?

The graph shows the percent distribution of divorces in the United States by number of years of marriage. Use the graph to solve Exercises 45–48.

Percent Distribution of Divorces by Number of Years of Marriage

Source: Divorce Center

45. During which years of marriage is the chance of divorce increasing?

46. During which years of marriage is the chance of divorce decreasing?

47. During which year of marriage is the chance of divorce the highest? Estimate, to the nearest percent, the percentage of divorces that occur during this year.

48. During which year of marriage is the chance of divorce the lowest? Estimate, to the nearest percent, the percentage of divorces that occur during this year.

Writing in Mathematics

49. What is the rectangular coordinate system?

50. Explain how to plot a point in the rectangular coordinate system. Give an example with your explanation.

51. Explain why $(5, -2)$ and $(-2, 5)$ do not represent the same point.

52. Explain how to graph an equation in the rectangular coordinate system.

53. What does a $[-20, 2, 1]$ by $[-4, 5, 0.5]$ viewing rectangle mean?

54. Describe the trend shown in the graph for Exercises 45–48. What explanations can you offer for this trend?

Technology Exercises

55. Use a graphing utility to verify each of your hand-drawn graphs in Exercises 13–28. Experiment with the size of the viewing rectangle to make the graph displayed by the graphing utility resemble your hand-drawn graph as much as possible.

56. The stated intent of the 1994 "don't ask, don't tell" policy was to reduce the number of discharges of gay men and lesbians from the military. The equation

$$y = 45.48x^2 - 334.35x + 1237.9$$

describes the number of gay service members, y, discharged from the military for homosexuality x years after 1990. Graph the equation in a $[0, 10, 1]$ by $[0, 2200, 200]$ viewing rectangle. Then describe something about the relationship between x and y that is revealed by looking at the graph that is not obvious from the equation. What does the graph reveal about the success or lack of success of "don't ask, don't tell"?

A graph of an equation is a complete graph *if it shows all of the important features of the graph. Use a graphing utility to graph the equations in Exercises 57–59 in each of the given viewing rectangles. Then choose which viewing rectangle gives a complete graph.*

57. $y = x^2 + 10$
   a. $[-5, 5, 1]$ by $[-5, 5, 1]$
   b. $[-10, 10, 1]$ by $[-10, 10, 1]$
   c. $[-10, 10, 1]$ by $[-50, 50, 1]$

58. $y = 0.1x^4 - x^3 + 2x^2$
   a. $[-5, 5, 1]$ by $[-8, 2, 1]$
   b. $[-10, 10, 1]$ by $[-10, 10, 1]$
   c. $[-8, 16, 1]$ by $[-16, 8, 1]$

59. $y = x^3 - 30x + 20$
   a. $[-10, 10, 1]$ by $[-10, 10, 1]$
   b. $[-10, 10, 1]$ by $[-50, 50, 10]$
   c. $[-10, 10, 1]$ by $[-50, 100, 10]$

Critical Thinking Exercises

60. Which one of the following is true?
   a. If the coordinates of a point satisfy the inequality $xy > 0$, then (x, y) must be in quadrant I.
   b. The ordered pair $(2, 5)$ satisfies $3y - 2x = -4$.
   c. If a point is on the x-axis, it is neither up nor down, so $x = 0$.
   d. None of the above is true.

In Exercises 61–64, match the story with the correct figure. The figures are labeled (a), (b), (c), and (d).

61. As the blizzard got worse, the snow fell harder and harder.

62. The snow fell more and more softly.

63. It snowed hard, but then it stopped. After a short time, the snow started falling softly.

64. It snowed softly, and then it stopped. After a short time, the snow started falling hard.

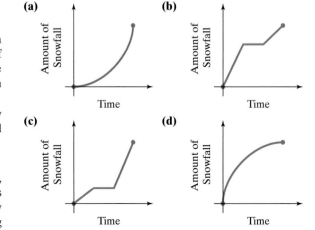

SECTION 1.2   *Linear Equations*

Objectives

1. Solve linear equations in one variable.
2. Solve equations with constants in denominators.
3. Solve equations with variables in denominators.
4. Recognize identities, conditional equations, and inconsistent equations.

Unfortunately, many of us have been fined for driving over the speed limit. The amount of the fine depends on how fast we are speeding. Suppose that a highway has a speed limit of 60 miles per hour. The amount that speeders are fined, F, is described by the statement of equality

$$F = 10x - 600$$

where x is the speed, in miles per hour. We can use this statement to determine the fine, F, for a speeder traveling at, say, 70 miles per hour. We substitute 70 for x in the given statement and then find the corresponding value for F.

$$F = 10(70) - 600 = 700 - 600 = 100$$

Thus, a person caught driving 70 miles per hour gets a $100 fine.

A friend, whom we shall call Leadfoot, borrows your car and returns a few hours later with a $400 speeding fine. Leadfoot is furious, protesting that the car was barely driven over the speed limit. Should you believe Leadfoot?

In order to decide if Leadfoot is telling the truth, use $F = 10x - 600$. Leadfoot was fined $400, so substitute 400 for F:

$$400 = 10x - 600.$$

In Example 1, we will find the value for x. This variable represents Leadfoot's speed, which resulted in the $400 fine.

An **equation** consists of two algebraic expressions joined by an equal sign. Thus, $400 = 10x - 600$ is an example of an equation. The equal sign divides the equation into two parts, the left side and the right side:

$$\boxed{400} \;=\; \boxed{10x - 600}.$$

Left side   Right side

The two sides of an equation can be reversed. So, we can also express this equation as

$$10x - 600 = 400.$$

Notice that the highest exponent on the variable is 1. Such an equation is called a *linear equation in one variable*. In this section, we will study how to solve linear equations.

1 Solve linear equations in one variable.

Solving Linear Equations in One Variable

We begin with a general definition of a linear equation in one variable.

Definition of a Linear Equation

A **linear equation in one variable** x is an equation that can be written in the form

$$ax + b = 0$$

where a and b are real numbers, and $a \neq 0$.

An example of a linear equation in one variable is $4x + 12 = 0$. **Solving an equation** in x involves determining all values of x that result in a true statement when substituted into the equation. Such values are **solutions,** or **roots,** of the equation. For example, substitute -3 into $4x + 12 = 0$. We obtain $4(-3) + 12 = 0$, or $-12 + 12 = 0$. This simplifies to the true statement $0 = 0$. Thus, -3 is a solution of the equation $4x + 12 = 0$. We also say that -3 **satisfies** the equation $4x + 12 = 0$, because when we substitute -3 for x, a true statement results. The set of all such solutions is called the equation's **solution set.** For example, the solution set of the equation $4x + 12 = 0$ is $\{-3\}$.

Equations that have the same solution set are called **equivalent equations.** For example, the equations $4x + 12 = 0$, $4x = -12$, and $x = -3$ are equivalent equations because the solution set for each is $\{-3\}$. To solve a linear equation in x, we transform the equation into an equivalent equation one or more times. Our final equivalent equation should be in the form $x = d$, where d is a real number. By inspection, we can see that the solution set of this equation is $\{d\}$.

To generate equivalent equations, we will use the following principles:

Study Tip

We can solve equations such as $3(x - 6) = 5x$ for a variable. However, we cannot solve for a variable in an algebraic expression such as $3(x - 6)$. We *simplify* algebraic expressions.

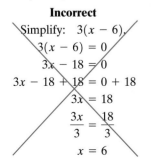

Correct

Simplify: $3(x - 6)$.
$3(x - 6) = 3x - 18$

Incorrect

Simplify: $3(x - 6)$.
$3(x - 6) = 0$
$3x - 18 = 0$
$3x - 18 + 18 = 0 + 18$
$3x = 18$
$\dfrac{3x}{3} = \dfrac{18}{3}$
$x = 6$

Generating Equivalent Equations

An equation can be transformed into an equivalent equation by one or more of the following operations:

Example

1. Simplify an expression by removing grouping symbols and combining like terms.

$$3(x - 6) = 6x - x$$
$$3x - 18 = 5x$$

2. Add (or subtract) the same real number or variable expression on *both* sides of the equation.

Subtract 3x from both sides of the equation.

$$3x - 18 = 5x$$
$$3x - 18 - 3x = 5x - 3x$$
$$-18 = 2x$$

3. Multiply (or divide) on *both* sides of the equation by the same *nonzero* quantity.

Divide both sides of the equation by 2.

$$-18 = 2x$$
$$\dfrac{-18}{2} = \dfrac{2x}{2}$$
$$-9 = x$$

4. Interchange the two sides of the equation.

$$-9 = x$$
$$x = -9$$

If you look closely at the equations in the box, you will notice that we have solved the equation $3(x - 6) = 6x - x$. The final equation, $x = -9$, with x isolated by itself on the left side, shows that $\{-9\}$ is the solution set. The idea in solving a linear equation is to get the variable by itself on one side of the equal sign and a number by itself on the other side.

EXAMPLE 1 Solving a Linear Equation (Is Leadfoot Telling the Truth?)

Solve the equation: $10x - 600 = 400$.

Solution   Remember that x represents Leadfoot's speed that resulted in the $400 fine. Our goal is to get x by itself on the left side. We do this by adding 600 to both sides to get $10x$ by itself. Then we isolate x from $10x$ by dividing both sides of the equation by 10.

$$10x - 600 = 400 \qquad \text{This is the given equation.}$$
$$10x - 600 + 600 = 400 + 600 \qquad \text{Add 600 to both sides.}$$
$$10x = 1000 \qquad \text{Combine like terms.}$$
$$\frac{10x}{10} = \frac{1000}{10} \qquad \text{Divide both sides by 10.}$$
$$x = 100 \qquad \text{Simplify.}$$

Can this possibly be correct? Was Leadfoot doing 100 miles per hour in the car he borrowed from you? To find out, check the proposed solution, 100, in the original equation. In other words, evaluate for $x = 100$.

Check 100:

$$10x - 600 = 400 \qquad \text{This is the original equation.}$$
$$10(100) - 600 \stackrel{?}{=} 400 \qquad \text{Substitute 100 for x. The question mark}$$
indicates that we do not yet know if the two sides are equal.
$$1000 - 600 \stackrel{?}{=} 400 \qquad \text{Multiply:} \quad 10(100) = 1000.$$

This statement is true. $400 = 400$ Subtract: $1000 - 600 = 400$.

The true statement $400 = 400$ indicates that 100 is the solution. This verifies that the solution set is $\{100\}$. Leadfoot was doing an outrageous 100 miles per hour, and lied by claiming that your car was barely driven over the speed limit.

Check Point 1   Solve and check: $5x - 8 = 72$.

We now present a step-by-step procedure for solving a linear equation in one variable. Not all of these steps are necessary to solve every equation.

Solving a Linear Equation

1. Simplify the algebraic expression on each side.
2. Collect the variable terms on one side and the constant terms on the other side.
3. Isolate the variable and solve.
4. Check the proposed solution in the original equation.

Study Tip

If your proposed solution is incorrect, you will get a false statement when you check your answer. For example, 65 is not a solution of $10x - 600 = 400$. Look what happens when we substitute 65 for x:

$$10x - 600 = 400$$
$$10(65) - 600 \stackrel{?}{=} 400$$
$$650 - 600 \stackrel{?}{=} 400$$
$$50 = 400 \qquad \text{False.}$$

The compact, symbolic notation of algebra enables us to use a clear step-by-step method for solving equations, designed to avoid the confusion shown in the painting.

EXAMPLE 2 Solving a Linear Equation

Solve the equation: $2(x - 3) - 17 = 13 - 3(x + 2)$.

Solution

Step 1 Simplify the algebraic expression on each side.

$$2(x - 3) - 17 = 13 - 3(x + 2) \qquad \text{This is given equation.}$$
$$2x - 6 - 17 = 13 - 3x - 6 \qquad \text{Use the distributive property.}$$
$$2x - 23 = -3x + 7 \qquad \text{Combine like terms.}$$

Step 2 Collect variable terms on one side and constant terms on the other side. We will collect variable terms on the left by adding $3x$ to both sides. We will collect the numbers on the right by adding 23 to both sides.

$$2x - 23 + 3x = -3x + 7 + 3x \qquad \text{Add } 3x \text{ to both sides.}$$
$$5x - 23 = 7 \qquad \text{Simplify.}$$
$$5x - 23 + 23 = 7 + 23 \qquad \text{Add 23 to both sides.}$$
$$5x = 30 \qquad \text{Simplify.}$$

Step 3 Isolate the variable and solve. We isolate x by dividing both sides by 5.

$$\frac{5x}{5} = \frac{30}{5} \qquad \text{Divide both sides by 5.}$$

$$x = 6 \qquad \text{Simplify.}$$

Step 4 Check the proposed solution in the original equation. Substitute 6 for x in the original equation.

$$2(x - 3) - 17 = 13 - 3(x + 2) \qquad \text{This is the original equation.}$$
$$2(6 - 3) - 17 \overset{?}{=} 13 - 3(6 + 2) \qquad \text{Substitute 6 for x.}$$
$$2(3) - 17 \overset{?}{=} 13 - 3(8) \qquad \text{Simplify inside parentheses.}$$
$$6 - 17 \overset{?}{=} 13 - 24 \qquad \text{Multiply.}$$
$$-11 = -11 \qquad \text{Subtract.}$$

The true statement $-11 = -11$ verifies that the solution set is $\{6\}$.

Discovery

Solve the equation in Example 2 by collecting terms with the variable on the right and numerical terms on the left. What do you observe?

Technology

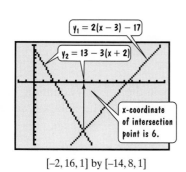

$y_1 = 2(x - 3) - 17$

$y_2 = 13 - 3(x + 2)$

x-coordinate of intersection point is 6.

$[-2, 16, 1]$ by $[-14, 8, 1]$

You can use a graphing utility to check the solution to a linear equation in one variable. **Graph the left side and graph the right side. The solution is the x-coordinate of the point where the graphs intersect.** For example, to verify that 6 is the solution of

$$2(x - 3) - 17 = 13 - 3(x + 2),$$

graph these two equations in the same viewing rectangle:

$$y_1 = 2(x - 3) - 17$$
$$\text{and} \quad y_2 = 13 - 3(x + 2).$$

Choose a large enough viewing rectangle so that you can see where the graphs intersect. The viewing rectangle on the left shows that the x-coordinate of the intersection point is 6, verifying that $\{6\}$ is the solution set for the equation in Example 2.

Solve and check: $4(2x + 1) - 29 = 3(2x - 5)$.

2 Solve equations with constants in denominators.

Linear Equations with Fractions

Equations are easier to solve when they do not contain fractions. How do we solve equations involving fractions? We begin by multiplying both sides of the equation by the least common denominator of all fractions in the equation. The least common denominator is the smallest number that all the denominators will divide into. Multiplying every term on both sides of the equation by the least common denominator will eliminate the fractions in the equation. Example 3 shows how we "clear an equation of fractions."

EXAMPLE 3 Solving a Linear Equation Involving Fractions

Solve the equation: $\dfrac{3x}{2} = \dfrac{x}{5} - \dfrac{39}{5}$.

Solution The denominators are 2, 5, and 5. The smallest number that is divisible by 2, 5, and 5 is 10. We begin by multiplying both sides of the equation by 10, the least common denominator.

$$\frac{3x}{2} = \frac{x}{5} - \frac{39}{5} \qquad \text{This is the given equation.}$$

$$10 \cdot \frac{3x}{2} = 10\left(\frac{x}{5} - \frac{39}{5}\right) \qquad \text{Multiply both sides by 10.}$$

$$10 \cdot \frac{3x}{2} = 10 \cdot \frac{x}{5} - 10 \cdot \frac{39}{5} \qquad \text{Use the distributive property and multiply each term by 10.}$$

$$\overset{5}{\cancel{10}} \cdot \frac{3x}{\underset{1}{\cancel{2}}} = \overset{2}{\cancel{10}} \cdot \frac{x}{\underset{1}{\cancel{5}}} - \overset{2}{\cancel{10}} \cdot \frac{39}{\underset{1}{\cancel{5}}} \qquad \text{Divide out common factors in each multiplication.}$$

$$15x = 2x - 78 \qquad \text{Complete the multiplications. The fractions are now cleared.}$$

At this point, we have an equation similar to those we previously solved. Collect the variable terms on one side and the constant terms on the other side.

$$15x - 2x = 2x - 2x - 78 \qquad \text{Subtract 2x to get the variable terms on the left.}$$

$$13x = -78 \qquad \text{Simplify.}$$

Isolate x by dividing both sides by 13.

$$\frac{13x}{13} = \frac{-78}{13} \qquad \text{Divide both sides by 13.}$$

$$x = -6 \qquad \text{Simplify.}$$

Check the proposed solution. Substitute -6 for x in the original equation. You should obtain $-9 = -9$. This true statement verifies that the solution set is $\{-6\}$.

Solve and check: $\dfrac{x}{4} = \dfrac{2x}{3} + \dfrac{5}{6}$.

3 Solve equations with variables in denominators.

Equations Involving Rational Expressions

In Example 3 we solved a linear equation with constants in denominators. Now, let's consider an equation such as

$$\frac{1}{x} = \frac{1}{5} + \frac{3}{2x}.$$

Can you see how this equation differs from the fractional equation that we solved earlier? The variable, x, appears in two of the denominators. The procedure for solving this equation still involves multiplying each side by the least common denominator. However, we must avoid any values of the variable that make a denominator zero. For example, examine the denominators in the equation

$$\frac{1}{x} = \frac{1}{5} + \frac{3}{2x}.$$

> This denominator would equal zero if x = 0.

> This denominator would equal zero if x = 0.

We see that x cannot equal zero. With this in mind, let's solve the equation.

EXAMPLE 4 Solving an Equation Involving Rational Expressions

Solve: $\dfrac{1}{x} = \dfrac{1}{5} + \dfrac{3}{2x}.$

Solution The denominators are x, 5, and $2x$. The least common denominator is $10x$. We begin by multiplying both sides of the equation by $10x$. We will also write the restriction that x cannot equal zero to the right of the equation.

$$\frac{1}{x} = \frac{1}{5} + \frac{3}{2x}, \quad x \neq 0 \qquad \text{This is the given equation.}$$

$$10x \cdot \frac{1}{x} = 10x\left(\frac{1}{5} + \frac{3}{2x}\right) \qquad \text{Multiply both sides by 10x.}$$

$$10x \cdot \frac{1}{x} = 10x \cdot \frac{1}{5} + 10x \cdot \frac{3}{2x} \qquad \text{Use the distributive property and multiply each term by 10x.}$$

$$10x \cdot \frac{1}{x} = \overset{2}{10}x \cdot \frac{1}{\underset{1}{5}} + \overset{5}{10}x \cdot \frac{3}{\underset{1}{2x}} \qquad \text{Divide out common factors in each multiplication.}$$

$$10 = 2x + 15 \qquad \text{Complete the multiplications.}$$

Observe that the resulting equation,

$$10 = 2x + 15,$$

is now cleared of fractions. With the variable term, $2x$, already on the right, we will collect constant terms on the left by subtracting 15 from both sides.

$$10 - 15 = 2x + 15 - 15 \qquad \text{Subtract 15 from both sides.}$$

$$-5 = 2x \qquad \text{Simplify.}$$

Finally, we isolate the variable, x, in $-5 = 2x$ by dividing both sides by 2.

$$\frac{-5}{2} = \frac{2x}{2} \qquad \text{Divide both sides by 2.}$$

$$-\frac{5}{2} = x \qquad \text{Simplify.}$$

We check our solution by substituting $-\frac{5}{2}$ into the original equation or by using a calculator. With a calculator, evaluate each side of the equation for $x = -\frac{5}{2}$, or for $x = -2.5$. Note that the original restriction that $x \neq 0$ is met. The solution set is $\left\{-\frac{5}{2}\right\}$.

Check Point 4 Solve: $\dfrac{5}{2x} = \dfrac{17}{18} - \dfrac{1}{3x}$.

EXAMPLE 5 Solving an Equation Involving Rational Expressions

Solve: $\dfrac{x}{x-3} = \dfrac{3}{x-3} + 9$.

Solution We must avoid any values of the variable x that make a denominator zero.

$$\frac{x}{x-3} = \frac{3}{x-3} + 9$$

These denominators are zero if
$x - 3 = 0$, or equivalently, if $x = 3$.

We see that x cannot equal 3. With denominators of $x - 3$, $x - 3$, and 1, the least common denominator is $x - 3$. We multiply both sides of the equation by $x - 3$. We also write the restriction that x cannot equal 3 to the right of the equation.

$$\frac{x}{x-3} = \frac{3}{x-3} + 9, \quad x \neq 3 \qquad \text{This is the given equation.}$$

$$(x-3) \cdot \frac{x}{x-3} = (x-3)\left[\frac{3}{x-3} + 9\right] \qquad \text{Multiply both sides by } x - 3.$$

$$(x-3) \cdot \frac{x}{x-3} = (x-3) \cdot \frac{3}{x-3} + (x-3) \cdot 9 \qquad \text{Use the distributive property.}$$

$$\cancel{(x-3)} \cdot \frac{x}{\cancel{x-3}} = \cancel{(x-3)} \cdot \frac{3}{\cancel{x-3}} + (x-3) \cdot 9 \qquad \text{Divide out common factors in each multiplication.}$$

$$x = 3 + (x-3) \cdot 9 \qquad \text{Simplify.}$$

The resulting equation, which can be expressed as

$$x = 3 + 9(x-3),$$

is cleared of fractions. We now solve for x.

$$x = 3 + 9x - 27 \qquad \text{Use the distributive property.}$$

$$x = 9x - 24 \qquad \text{Combine numerical terms.}$$

$$x - 9x = 9x - 24 - 9x \qquad \text{Subtract } 9x \text{ from both sides.}$$

$$-8x = -24 \qquad \text{Simplify.}$$

$$\frac{-8x}{-8} = \frac{-24}{-8} \qquad \text{Solve for x, dividing both sides by } -8.$$

$$x = 3 \qquad \text{Simplify.}$$

The proposed solution, 3, is *not* a solution because of the restriction that $x \neq 3$. There is *no solution to this equation.* The solution set for this equation contains no elements and is called the empty set, written $\varnothing$.

Check Point 5 Solve: $\dfrac{x}{x - 2} = \dfrac{2}{x - 2} - \dfrac{2}{3}.$

4 Recognize identities, conditional equations, and inconsistent equations.

Types of Equations

We tend to place things in categories, allowing us to order and structure the world. For example, you can categorize yourself by your age group, your ethnicity, your academic major, or your gender. Equations can be placed into categories that depend on their solution sets.

An equation that is true for all real numbers for which both sides are defined is called an **identity.** An example of an identity is

$$x + 3 = x + 2 + 1.$$

Every number plus 3 is equal to that number plus 2 plus 1. Therefore, the solution set to this equation is the set of all real numbers. Another example of an identity is

$$\frac{2x}{x} = 2.$$

Because division by 0 is undefined, this equation is true for all real number values of x except 0. The solution set is the set of nonzero real numbers.

An equation that is not an identity, but that is true for at least one real number, is called a **conditional equation.** The equation $10x - 600 = 400$ is an example of a conditional equation. The equation is not an identity and is true only if x is 100.

An **inconsistent equation** is an equation that is not true for even one real number. An example of an inconsistent equation is

$$x = x + 7.$$

There is no number that is equal to itself plus 7. Some inconsistent equations are less obvious than this. Consider the equation in Example 5,

$$\frac{x}{x - 3} = \frac{3}{x - 3} + 9.$$

This equation is not true for any real number and has no solution. Thus, it is inconsistent.

EXAMPLE 6   Categorizing an Equation

Determine whether the equation

$$2(x + 1) = 2x + 3$$

is an identity, a conditional equation, or an inconsistent equation.

Technology

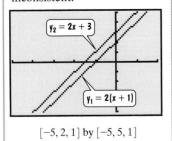

The graphs of $y_1 = 2(x + 1)$ and $y_2 = 2x + 3$ are parallel lines with no intersection point. This shows that the equation

$$2(x + 1) = 2x + 3$$

has no solution and is inconsistent.

$y_2 = 2x + 3$

$y_1 = 2(x + 1)$

$[-5, 2, 1]$ by $[-5, 5, 1]$

Solution   Let's see what happens if we try solving $2(x + 1) = 2x + 3$. Applying the distributive property on the left side, we obtain

$$2x + 2 = 2x + 3.$$

Does something look strange? Can doubling a number and increasing the product by 2 give the same result as doubling the same number and increasing the product by 3? No. Let's continue solving the equation by subtracting $2x$ from both sides.

$$2x + 2 - 2x = 2x + 3 - 2x$$

$$2 = 3$$

The false statement $2 = 3$ verifies that the given equation is inconsistent.

Check Point 6   Determine whether the equation

$$2(x + 1) = 2x + 2$$

is an identity, a conditional equation, or an inconsistent equation.

EXERCISE SET 1.2

Practice Exercises

In Exercises 1–16, solve and check each linear equation.

1. $7x - 5 = 72$

2. $6x - 3 = 63$

3. $11x - (6x - 5) = 40$

4. $5x - (2x - 10) = 35$

5. $2x - 7 = 6 + x$

6. $3x + 5 = 2x + 13$

7. $7x + 4 = x + 16$

8. $13x + 14 = 12x - 5$

9. $3(x - 2) + 7 = 2(x + 5)$

10. $2(x - 1) + 3 = x - 3(x + 1)$

11. $3(x - 4) - 4(x - 3) = x + 3 - (x - 2)$

12. $2 - (7x + 5) = 13 - 3x$

13. $16 = 3(x - 1) - (x - 7)$

14. $5x - (2x + 2) = x + (3x - 5)$

15. $25 - [2 + 5y - 3(y + 2)] = -3(2y - 5) - [5(y - 1) - 3y + 3]$

16. $45 - [4 - 2y - 4(y + 7)] = -4(1 + 3y) - [4 - 3(y + 2) - 2(2y - 5)]$

Exercises 17–30 contain equations with constants in denominators. Solve each equation.

17. $\dfrac{x}{3} = \dfrac{x}{2} - 2$

18. $\dfrac{x}{5} = \dfrac{x}{6} + 1$

19. $20 - \dfrac{x}{3} = \dfrac{x}{2}$

20. $\dfrac{x}{5} - \dfrac{1}{2} = \dfrac{x}{6}$

21. $\dfrac{3x}{5} = \dfrac{2x}{3} + 1$

22. $\dfrac{x}{2} = \dfrac{3x}{4} + 5$

23. $\dfrac{3x}{5} - x = \dfrac{x}{10} - \dfrac{5}{2}$

24. $2x - \dfrac{2x}{7} = \dfrac{x}{2} + \dfrac{17}{2}$

25. $\dfrac{x + 3}{6} = \dfrac{3}{8} + \dfrac{x - 5}{4}$

26. $\dfrac{x + 1}{4} = \dfrac{1}{6} + \dfrac{2 - x}{3}$

27. $\dfrac{x}{4} = 2 + \dfrac{x - 3}{3}$

28. $5 + \dfrac{x - 2}{3} = \dfrac{x + 3}{8}$

29. $\dfrac{x + 1}{3} = 5 - \dfrac{x + 2}{7}$

30. $\dfrac{3x}{5} - \dfrac{x - 3}{2} = \dfrac{x + 2}{3}$

Exercises 31–50 contain equations with variables in denominators. For each equation, **a.** *Write the value or values of the variable that make a denominator zero. These are the restrictions on the variable.* **b.** *Keeping the restrictions in mind, solve the equation.*

31. $\dfrac{4}{x} = \dfrac{5}{2x} + 3$

32. $\dfrac{5}{x} = \dfrac{10}{3x} + 4$

33. $\dfrac{2}{x} + 3 = \dfrac{5}{2x} + \dfrac{13}{4}$

34. $\dfrac{7}{2x} - \dfrac{5}{3x} = \dfrac{22}{3}$

35. $\dfrac{2}{3x} + \dfrac{1}{4} = \dfrac{11}{6x} - \dfrac{1}{3}$

36. $\dfrac{5}{2x} - \dfrac{8}{9} = \dfrac{1}{18} - \dfrac{1}{3x}$

37. $\dfrac{x - 2}{2x} + 1 = \dfrac{x + 1}{x}$

38. $\dfrac{4}{x} = \dfrac{9}{5} - \dfrac{7x - 4}{5x}$

39. $\dfrac{1}{x - 1} + 5 = \dfrac{11}{x - 1}$

40. $\dfrac{3}{x + 4} - 7 = \dfrac{-4}{x + 4}$

41. $\dfrac{8x}{x + 1} = 4 - \dfrac{8}{x + 1}$

42. $\dfrac{2}{x - 2} = \dfrac{x}{x - 2} - 2$

43. $\dfrac{3}{2x - 2} + \dfrac{1}{2} = \dfrac{2}{x - 1}$

44. $\dfrac{3}{x + 3} = \dfrac{5}{2x + 6} + \dfrac{1}{x - 2}$

45. $\dfrac{3}{x+2} + \dfrac{2}{x-2} = \dfrac{8}{(x+2)(x-2)}$

46. $\dfrac{5}{x+2} + \dfrac{3}{x-2} = \dfrac{12}{(x+2)(x-2)}$

47. $\dfrac{2}{x+1} - \dfrac{1}{x-1} = \dfrac{2x}{x^2-1}$

48. $\dfrac{4}{x+5} + \dfrac{2}{x-5} = \dfrac{32}{x^2-25}$

49. $\dfrac{1}{x-4} - \dfrac{5}{x+2} = \dfrac{6}{x^2-2x-8}$

50. $\dfrac{6}{x+3} - \dfrac{5}{x-2} = \dfrac{-20}{x^2+x-6}$

In Exercises 51–58, determine whether each equation is an identity, a conditional equation, or an inconsistent equation.

51. $4(x-7) = 4x - 28$ **52.** $4(x-7) = 4x + 28$

53. $2x + 3 = 2x - 3$ **54.** $\dfrac{7x}{x} = 7$

55. $4x + 5x = 8x$ **56.** $8x + 2x = 9x$

57. $\dfrac{2x}{x-3} = \dfrac{6}{x-3} + 4$ **58.** $\dfrac{3}{x-3} = \dfrac{x}{x-3} + 3$

The equations in Exercises 59–70 combine the types of equations we have discussed in this section. Solve each equation or state that it is true for all real numbers or no real numbers.

59. $\dfrac{x+5}{2} - 4 = \dfrac{2x-1}{3}$ **60.** $\dfrac{x+2}{7} = 5 - \dfrac{x+1}{3}$

61. $\dfrac{2}{x-2} = 3 + \dfrac{x}{x-2}$ **62.** $\dfrac{6}{x+3} + 2 = \dfrac{-2x}{x+3}$

63. $8x - (3x + 2) + 10 = 3x$

64. $2(x+2) + 2x = 4(x+1)$

65. $\dfrac{2}{x} + \dfrac{1}{2} = \dfrac{3}{4}$ **66.** $\dfrac{3}{x} - \dfrac{1}{6} = \dfrac{1}{3}$

67. $\dfrac{4}{x-2} + \dfrac{3}{x+5} = \dfrac{7}{(x+5)(x-2)}$

68. $\dfrac{1}{x-1} = \dfrac{1}{(2x+3)(x-1)} + \dfrac{4}{2x+3}$

69. $\dfrac{4x}{x+3} - \dfrac{12}{x-3} = \dfrac{4x^2+36}{x^2-9}$

70. $\dfrac{4}{x^2+3x-10} - \dfrac{1}{x^2+x-6} = \dfrac{3}{x^2-x-12}$

Application Exercises

71. The equation $d = 5000c - 525{,}000$ describes the relationship between the annual number of deaths, d, in the United States from heart disease and the average cholesterol level, c, of blood. (Cholesterol level, c, is expressed in milligrams per deciliter of blood.)

a. In 2000, 725,000 Americans died from heart disease. Substitute 725,000 for d in the given equation and then solve for c to determine the average cholesterol level in 2000.

b. Suppose that the average cholesterol level for people in the United States could be reduced to 180. Substitute 180 for c in the given equation and then compute the value for d to determine the number of annual deaths from heart disease with this reduced cholesterol level. Compared to the number of deaths in 2000, how many lives would be saved by this cholesterol reduction?

72. There is a relationship between the vocabulary of a child and the child's age. The equation $60A - V = 900$ describes this relationship, where A is the age of the child, in months, and V is the number of words that the child uses. Suppose that a child uses 1500 words. Determine the child's age, in months.

73. The equation

$$p = 15 + \dfrac{15d}{33}$$

describes the pressure of sea water, p, in pounds per square foot, at a depth of d feet below the surface. The record depth for breath-held diving, by Francisco Ferreras (Cuba) off Grand-Bahama Island, on November 14, 1993, involved pressure of 201 pounds per square foot. To what depth did Ferreras descend on this ill-advised venture? (He was underwater for 2 minutes and 9 seconds!)

74. The equation $P = -0.5d + 100$ describes the percentage, P, of lost hikers found in search and rescue missions when members of the search team walk parallel to one another separated by a distance of d yards. If a search and rescue team finds 70% of lost hikers, find the parallel distance of separation between members of the search party.

 ## Writing in Mathematics

75. What is a linear equation in one variable? Give an example of this type of equation.

76. What does it mean to solve an equation?

77. What is the solution set of an equation?

78. What are equivalent equations? Give an example.

79. What is the difference between solving an equation such as $2(x-4) + 5x = 34$ and simplifying an algebraic expression such as $2(x-4) + 5x$? If there is a difference, which topic should be taught first? Why?

80. Suppose that you solve $\dfrac{x}{5} - \dfrac{x}{2} = 1$ by multiplying both sides by 20, rather than the least common denominator of 5 and 2 (namely, 10). Describe what happens. If you get the correct solution, why do you think we clear the equation of fractions by multiplying by the *least* common denominator?

81. Suppose you are an algebra teacher grading the following solution on an examination:

$$-3(x - 6) = 2 - x$$
$$-3x - 18 = 2 - x$$
$$-2x - 18 = 2$$
$$-2x = -16$$
$$x = 8.$$

You should note that 8 checks, and the solution set is {8}. The student who worked the problem therefore wants full credit. Can you find any errors in the solution? If full credit is 10 points, how many points should you give the student? Justify your position.

82. Explain how to determine the restrictions on the variable for the equation

$$\frac{3}{x + 5} + \frac{4}{x - 2} = \frac{7}{(x + 5)(x - 2)}.$$

83. What is an identity? Give an example.

84. What is a conditional equation? Give an example.

85. What is an inconsistent equation? Give an example.

 Technology Exercises

For Exercises 86–89, use your graphing utility to graph each side of the equations in the same viewing rectangle. Based on the resulting graph, label each equation as conditional, inconsistent, or an identity. If the equation is conditional, use the x-coordinate of the intersection point to find the solution set. Verify this value by direct substitution into the equation.

86. $2(x - 6) + 3x = x + 6$

87. $9x + 3 - 3x = 2(3x + 1)$

88. $2\left(x + \frac{1}{2}\right) = 5x + 1 - 3x$

89. $\dfrac{2x - 1}{3} - \dfrac{x - 5}{6} = \dfrac{x - 3}{4}$

 Critical Thinking Exercises

90. Which one of the following is true?
  a. The equation $-7x = x$ has no solution.
  b. The equations $\dfrac{x}{x - 4} = \dfrac{4}{x - 4}$ and $x = 4$ are equivalent.
  c. The equations $3y - 1 = 11$ and $3y - 7 = 5$ are equivalent.
  d. If a and b are any real numbers, then $ax + b = 0$ always has one number in its solution set.

91. Solve for x: $ax + b = c$.

92. Write three equations that are equivalent to $x = 5$.

93. If x represents a number, write an English sentence about the number that results in an inconsistent equation.

94. Find b such that $\dfrac{7x + 4}{b} + 13 = x$ will have a solution set given by $\{-6\}$.

95. Find b such that $\dfrac{4x - b}{x - 5} = 3$ will have a solution set given by $\varnothing$.

Group Exercise

96. In your group, describe the best procedure for solving the following equation:

$$0.47x + \frac{19}{4} = -0.2 + \frac{2}{5}x.$$

Use this procedure to actually solve the equation. Then compare procedures with other groups working on this problem. Which group devised the most streamlined method?

SECTION 1.3 *Formulas and Applications*

Objectives

1. Solve problems using formulas.
2. Use linear equations to solve problems.
3. Solve for a variable in a formula.

Could you live to be 125? The number of Americans ages 100 or older could approach 850,000 by 2050. Some scientists predict that by 2100, our descendants could live to be 200 years of age. In this section, we will see how equations can be used to make these kinds of predictions as we turn to applications of linear equations.

1 Solve problems using formulas.

Formulas and Modeling Data

The graph in Figure 1.11 shows life expectancy in the United States by year of birth. For example, we can use the graph to find life expectancy for women born in 1980. Find the two bars for 1980 and then look at the bar on the right, representing females. The number printed on this bar is 77.4. Thus, the life expectancy for women born in 1980 is 77.4 years.

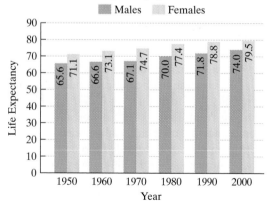

Life Expectancy by Year of Birth

Males   Females

Source: U.S. Bureau of the Census

Figure 1.11 Life expectancy by year of birth

The data for U.S. women in Figure 1.11 can be approximated by the equation

$$E = 0.177t + 71.35$$

where the variable E represents life expectancy for women born t years after 1950. This equation is an example of a *formula*. A **formula** is an equation that uses letters to express a relationship between two or more variables. The given formula expresses the relationship between the number of years born after 1950, t, and life expectancy for U.S. women, E.

EXAMPLE 1   Using a Formula

Use the formula

$$E = 0.177t + 71.35$$

to determine the year of birth for which U.S. women can expect to live 82 years.

Solution   We are given that the life expectancy for women is 82 years, so substitute 82 for E in the formula and solve for t.

$E = 0.177t + 71.35$	This is the given formula.
$82 = 0.177t + 71.35$	Replace E with 82 and solve for t.
$82 - 71.35 = 0.177t + 71.35 - 71.35$	Isolate the term containing t by subtracting 71.35 from both sides.
$10.65 = 0.177t$	Simplify.
$\dfrac{10.65}{0.177} = \dfrac{0.177t}{0.177}$	Divide both sides by 0.177.
$60 \approx t$	Simplify. Round to the nearest whole number.

The formula indicates that U.S. women born approximately 60 years after 1950, or in 2010, can expect to live 82 years.

The process of finding equations and formulas to describe real-world phenomena is called **mathematical modeling.** Such equations and formulas, together with the meaning assigned to the variables, are called **mathematical models.** One method of creating a mathematical model is to use available data and construct an equation that describes the behavior of the data. For example, consider the formula

$$E = 0.177t + 71.35$$

in which E is the life expectancy of the U.S. women born t years after 1950. This formula, or mathematical model, can be obtained from the data for women's life expectancy given in the bar graph in Figure 1.11 on the previous page. In Chapter 2, you will learn a modeling technique that will enable you to obtain the formula.

In creating mathematical models from data, we strive for both accuracy and simplicity. The formula $E = 0.177t + 71.35$ is relatively simple to use, but as we can see from Table 1.1, it is not an entirely accurate description of the data. Sometimes a mathematical model gives an estimate that is not a good approximation or is extended too far into the future, resulting in a prediction that does not make sense. In these cases, we say that **model breakdown** has occurred.

Table 1.1   Life Expectancy for U.S. Women

Birth Year	Actual Value	Value Predicted by $E = 0.177t + 71.35$
1950	71.1	71.35
1960	73.1	73.12
1970	74.7	74.89
1980	77.4	76.66
1990	78.8	78.43
2000	79.5	80.2

Check Point 1
The formula $W = 0.3x + 46.6$ models the average number of hours per week, W, that Americans worked x years after 1980. When will we average 55 hours of work per week?

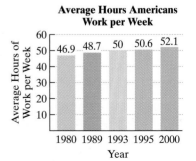

Average Hours Americans Work per Week

46.9   48.7   50   50.6   52.1

1980 1989 1993 1995 2000
Year

Source: U.S.A. Today

2 Use linear equations to solve problems.

Problem Solving with Linear Equations

Americans love their pets. The number of cats in the United States exceeds the number of dogs by 7.5 million. The number of cats and dogs combined is 114.7 million. So, how many dogs and cats are there in the United States?

Before answering the question, let's see if we can write a critical sentence that describes, or *models*, the problems conditions. The **verbal model** is

The number of dogs in the U.S.	plus	The number of cats in the U.S.	equals	114.7 million.
?	+	?	=	114.7 (million).

The question marks under the voice balloons indicate that we need algebraic expressions for these unknowns. Once we obtain these expressions, we will have an equation that models the verbal conditions. Because we are finding equations to describe real-world phenomena, we are engaged in mathematical modeling. The resulting equation, or mathematical model, is formed from a verbal model. Earlier, we mentioned that a mathematical model can be formed using actual data.

Here is a step-by-step strategy for solving problems using mathematical models that are created from verbal models:

Strategy for Problem Solving

Step 1 Read the problem carefully. Attempt to state the problem in your own words and state what the problem is looking for. Let x (or any variable) represent one of the quantities in the problem.

Step 2 If necessary, write expressions for any other unknown quantities in the problem in terms of x.

Step 3 Form a verbal model of the problems conditions and then write an equation in x that translates the verbal model.

Step 4 Solve the equation and answer the question in the problem.

Step 5 Check the proposed solution in the *original wording* of the problem, not in the equation obtained from the words.

U.S. Pet Population

Source: American Veterinary Medical Association

Americans spend more than $21 billion a year on their pets. 31.4% of households have cats and 34.3% have dogs.

EXAMPLE 2 Pet Population

The number of cats in the United States exceeds the number of dogs by 7.5 million. The number of cats and dogs combined is 114.7 million. Determine the number of dogs and cats in the United States.

Solution

Step 1 Let x represent one of the quantities. We know something about the number of cats; the cat population exceeds the dog population by 7.5 million. This means that there are 7.5 million more cats than dogs. We will let

x = the number, in millions, of dogs in the United States.

Step 2 Represent other quantities in terms of x. The other unknown quantity is the number of cats. Because there are 7.5 million more cats than dogs, let

$x + 7.5$ = the number, in millions, of cats in the United States.

Step 3 Write an equation in x that describes the conditions. The number of cats and dogs combined is 114.7 million.

The number (in millions) of dogs in the U.S.	plus	the number (in millions) of cats in the U.S.	equals	114.7 million.
x	$+$	$x + 7.5$	$=$	114.7

Step 4   Solve the equation and answer the question.

$$x + x + 7.5 = 114.7 \qquad \text{This is the equation that models the verbal conditions.}$$

$$2x + 7.5 = 114.7 \qquad \text{Combine like terms on the left side.}$$

$$2x + 7.5 - 7.5 = 114.7 - 7.5 \qquad \text{Subtract 7.5 from both sides.}$$

$$2x = 107.2 \qquad \text{Simplify.}$$

$$\frac{2x}{2} = \frac{107.2}{2} \qquad \text{Divide both sides by 2.}$$

$$x = 53.6 \qquad \text{Simplify.}$$

Because x represents the number, in millions, of dogs, there are 53.6 million dogs in the United States. Because $x + 7.5$ represents the number, in millions, of cats, there are $53.6 + 7.5$, or 61.1 million cats in the United States.

Step 5   Check the proposed solution in the original wording of the problem. The problem states that the number of cats and dogs combined is 114.7 million. By adding 53.6 million, the dog population, and 61.1 million, the cat population, we do, indeed, obtain a sum of 114.7 million.

 Check Point 2 Two of the top-selling music albums of all time are *Jagged Little Pill* (Alanis Morissette) and *Saturday Night Fever* (Bee Gees). The Morissette album sold 5 million more copies than that of the Bee Gees. Combined, the two albums sold 27 million copies. Determine the number of sales for each of the albums.

EXAMPLE 3   Selecting a Long-Distance Carrier

You are choosing between two long-distance telephone plans. Plan A has a monthly fee of $20 with a charge of $0.05 per minute for all long-distance calls. Plan B has a monthly fee of $5 with a charge of $0.10 per minute for all long-distance calls. For how many minutes of long-distance calls will the costs for the two plans be the same?

Solution

Step 1   Let x represent one of the quantities. Let

$x =$ the number of minutes of long-distance calls for the two plans to cost the same.

Step 2   Represent other quantities in terms of x. There are no other unknown quantities, so we can skip this step.

Step 3   Write an equation in x that describes the conditions. The monthly cost for plan A is the monthly fee, $20, plus the per minute charge, $0.05, times the number of minutes of long-distance calls, x. The monthly cost for plan B is the monthly fee, $5, plus the per-minute charge, $0.10, times the number of minutes of long-distance calls, x.

| The monthly cost for plan A | must equal | the monthly cost for plan B. |

$$20 + 0.05x = 5 + 0.10x$$

Step 4 Solve the equation and answer the question.

$$20 + 0.05x = 5 + 0.10x$$ This is the equation that models the verbal conditions.

$$20 + 0.05x - 0.05x = 5 + 0.10x - 0.05x$$ Subtract 0.05x from both sides.

$$20 = 5 + 0.05x$$ Simplify.

$$20 - 5 = 5 + 0.05x - 5$$ Subtract 5 from both sides.

$$15 = 0.05x$$ Simplify.

$$\frac{15}{0.05} = \frac{0.05x}{0.05}$$ Divide both sides by 0.05.

$$300 = x$$ Simplify.

Because x represents the number of minutes of long-distance calls for the two plans to cost the same, the costs will be the same with 300 minutes of long-distance calls.

Step 5 Check the proposed solution in the original wording of the problem. The problem states that the costs for the two plans should be the same. Let's see if they are with 300 minutes of long-distance calls:

$$\text{Cost for plan A} = \$20 + \$0.05(300) = \$20 + \$15 = \$35$$

| Monthly fee | Per-minute charge |

$$\text{Cost for plan B} = \$5 + \$0.10(300) = \$5 + \$30 = \$35$$

With 300 minutes, or 5 hours, of long-distance chatting, both plans cost $35 for the month. Thus, the proposed solution, 300 minutes, satisfies the problems conditions.

Check Point 3 You are choosing between two long-distance telephone plans. Plan A has a monthly fee of $15 with a charge of $0.08 per minute for all long-distance calls. Plan B has a monthly fee of $3 with a charge of $0.12 per minute for all long-distance calls. For how many minutes of long-distance calls will the costs for the two plans be the same?

Our next example involves simple interest. The annual simple interest that an investment earns is given by the formula

$$I = Pr$$

where I is the simple interest, P is the principal, and r is the simple interest rate, expressed in decimal form. Suppose, for example, that you deposit $2000 ($P = 2000$) in a savings account that has a simple interest rate of 6% ($r = 0.06$). The annual simple interest is computed as follows:

$$I = Pr = (2000)(0.06) = 120.$$

The annual interest is $120.

EXAMPLE 4 Solving a Simple Interest Problem

You inherit $16,000 with the stipulation that for the first year the money must be placed in two investments paying 6% and 8% annual interest, respectively. How much should be invested at each rate if the total interest earned for the year is to be $1180?

Solution

Step 1 Let x represent one of the quantities.

Let x = the amount invested at 6%.

Step 2 Represent other quantities in terms of x. The other quantity that we seek is the amount to be invested at 8%. Because the total amount to be invested is $16,000, and we already used up x,

$16,000 - x$ = the amount invested at 8%.

Step 3 Write an equation in x that describes the conditions. The interest for the two investments combined must be $1180. Interest is Pr or rP for each investment.

Interest from 6% investment	plus	interest from 8% investment		is	$1180.
$0.06x$	$+$	$0.08(16{,}000 - x)$		$=$	1180
rate times principal		rate times principal			

Step 4 Solve the equation and answer the question.

$$0.06x + 0.08(16{,}000 - x) = 1180 \qquad \text{This is the equation that models the verbal conditions.}$$

$$0.06x + 1280 - 0.08x = 1180 \qquad \text{Use the distributive property.}$$

$$-0.02x + 1280 = 1180 \qquad \text{Combine like terms.}$$

$$-0.02x + 1280 - 1280 = 1180 - 1280 \qquad \text{Subtract 1280 from both sides.}$$

$$-0.02x = -100 \qquad \text{Simplify.}$$

$$\frac{-0.02x}{-0.02} = \frac{-100}{-0.02} \qquad \text{Divide both sides by } -0.02.$$

$$x = 5000 \qquad \text{Simplify.}$$

Because x represents the amount invested at 6%, $5000 should be invested at 6%. Because $16,000 - x$ represents the amount invested at 8%, $16,000 - $5000, or $11,000, should be invested at 8%.

Step 5 Check the proposed solution in the original wording of the problem.
The problem states that the total interest should be $1180. The interest earned on $5000 at 6% is ($5000)(0.06), or $300. The interest earned on $11,000 at 8% is ($11,000)(0.08), or $880. The total interest is $300 + $880, or $1180, exactly as it should be.

 Check Point 4 Suppose that you invest $25,000, part at 9% simple interest and the remainder at 12%. If the total yearly interest from these investments was $2550, find the amount invested at each rate.

Solving geometry problems usually requires a knowledge of basic geometric ideas and formulas. Formulas for area, perimeter, and volume are given in Table 1.2.

Table 1.2   Common Formulas for Area, Perimeter, and Volume

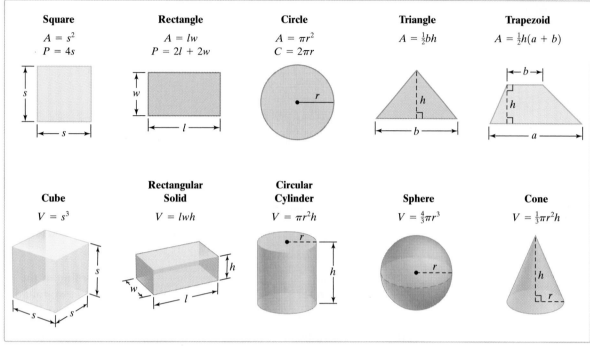

We will be using the formula for the perimeter of a rectangle, $P = 2l + 2w$, in our next example. A helpful verbal model for this formula is 2 times length plus 2 times width is a rectangles perimeter.

Figure 1.12 An American football field

EXAMPLE 5   Finding the Dimensions of an American Football Field

The length of an American football field is 200 feet more than the width. If the perimeter of the field is 1040 feet, what are its dimensions?

Solution

Step 1   Let x represent one of the quantities.   We know something about the length; the length is 200 feet more than the width. We will let

$$x = \text{the width.}$$

Step 2   Represent other quantities in terms of x.   Because the length is 200 feet more than the width, let

$$x + 200 = \text{the length.}$$

Figure 1.12 illustrates an American football field and its dimensions.

Step 3   Write an equation in x that describes the conditions.   Because the perimeter of the field is 1040 feet,

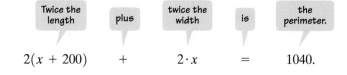

$$2(x + 200) \quad + \quad 2 \cdot x \quad = \quad 1040.$$

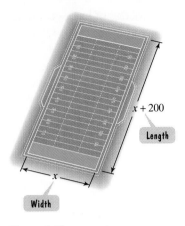

Figure 1.12, repeated

Step 4   Solve the equation and answer the question.

$$2(x + 200) + 2x = 1040$$

This is the equation that models the verbal conditions.

$$2x + 400 + 2x = 1040$$

Apply the distributive property.

$$4x + 400 = 1040$$

Combine like terms: $2x + 2x = 4x$.

$$4x + 400 - 400 = 1040 - 400$$

Subtract 400 from both sides.

$$4x = 640$$

Simplify.

$$\frac{4x}{4} = \frac{640}{4}$$

Divide both sides by 4.

$$x = 160$$

Simplify.

Thus,

$$\text{width} = x = 160.$$

$$\text{length} = x + 200 = 160 + 200 = 360.$$

The dimensions of an American football field are 360 feet by 160 feet. (The 360-foot length is usually described as 120 yards.)

Step 5   Check the proposed solution in the original wording of the problem.
The perimeter of the football field using the dimensions that we found is

$$2(360 \text{ feet}) + 2(160 \text{ feet}) = 720 \text{ feet} + 320 \text{ feet} = 1040 \text{ feet}.$$

Because the problems wording tells us that the perimeter is 1040 feet, our dimensions are correct.

Check Point 5   The length of a rectangular basketball court is 44 feet more than the width. If the perimeter of the basketball court is 288 feet, what are its dimensions?

3   Solve for a variable in a formula.

Solving for a Variable in a Formula

When working with formulas, such as the geometric formulas shown in Table 1.2 on the previous page, it is often necessary to solve for a specified variable. This is done by isolating the specified variable on one side of the equation. Begin by isolating all terms with the specified variable on one side of the equation and all terms without the specified variable on the other side. The next example shows how to do this.

EXAMPLE 6   Solving for a Variable in a Formula

Solve the formula $2l + 2w = P$ for w.

Solution   First, isolate $2w$ on the left by subtracting $2l$ from both sides. Then solve for w by dividing both sides by 2.

We need to isolate w.

$$2l + 2w = P$$

This is the given formula.

$$2l - 2l + 2w = P - 2l \qquad \text{Isolate 2w by subtracting 2l from both sides.}$$
$$2w = P - 2l \qquad \text{Simplify.}$$
$$\frac{2w}{2} = \frac{P - 2l}{2} \qquad \text{Isolate w by dividing both sides by 2.}$$

> You can divide both P and 2l by 2, expressing the answer as $w = \frac{P}{2} - l$.

$$w = \frac{P - 2l}{2} \qquad \text{Simplify.}$$

Check Point 6   Solve $y = mx + b$ for m.

EXAMPLE 7   Solving for a Variable That Occurs Twice in a Formula

Solve the formula $A = P + Prt$ for P.

Study Tip

You cannot solve $A = P + Prt$ for P by subtracting Prt from both sides and writing

$$A - Prt = P.$$

When a formula is solved for a specified variable, that variable must be isolated on one side. The variable P occurs on both sides of

$$A - Prt = P.$$

Solution   Notice that all terms with P already occur on the right side of the equation. Factor P from the two terms on the right to isolate P.

$$A = P + Prt \qquad \text{This is the given formula.}$$
$$A = P(1 + rt) \qquad \text{Factor P on the right side of the equation.}$$
$$\frac{A}{1 + rt} = \frac{P(1 + rt)}{1 + rt} \qquad \text{Divide both sides by 1 + rt.}$$
$$\frac{A}{1 + rt} = P \qquad \text{Simplify: } \frac{P\cancel{(1 + rt)}}{\cancel{(1 + rt)}} = \frac{P}{1} = P.$$

Check Point 7   Solve the formula $P = C + MC$ for C.

EXERCISE SET 1.3

Practice Exercises

In Exercises 1–14, let x represent the number. Write each English phrase as an algebraic expression.

1. The sum of a number and 9
2. A number increased by 13
3. A number subtracted from 20
4. 13 less than a number
5. 8 decreased by 5 times a number
6. 14 less than the product of 6 and a number
7. The quotient of 15 and a number
8. The quotient of a number and 15
9. The sum of twice a number and 20
10. Twice the sum of a number and 20
11. 30 subtracted from 7 times a number
12. The quotient of 12 and a number, decreased by 3 times the number

13. Four times the sum of a number and 12
14. Five times the difference of a number and 6

In Exercises 15–20, let x represent the number. Use the given conditions to write an equation. Solve the equation and find the number.

15. A number increased by 40 is equal to 450. Find the number.
16. The sum of a number and 29 is 54. Find the number.
17. Seven subtracted from five times a number is 123. Find the number.
18. Eight subtracted from six times a number is 184. Find the number.
19. Nine times a number is 30 more than three times that number. Find the number.
20. Five more than four times a number is that number increased by 35. Find the number.

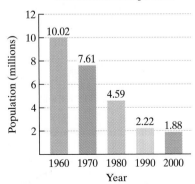

Application Exercises

Medical researchers have found that the desirable heart rate, R, in beats per minute, for beneficial exercise is modeled by the formulas

$$R = 143 - 0.65A \quad \text{for women}$$

$$R = 165 - 0.75A \quad \text{for men}$$

where A is the person's age. Use these formulas to solve Exercises 21–22.

21. If the desirable heart rate for a woman is 117 beats per minute, how old is she? How is the solution shown on the accompanying line graph?

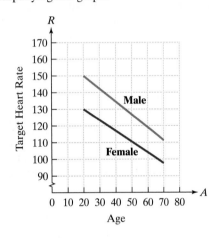

22. If the desirable heart rate for a man is 147 beats per minute, how old is he? How is the solution shown on the line graph?

Growth in human populations and economic activity threatens the continued existence of salmon in the Pacific Northwest. The bar graph shows the Pacific salmon population for various years. The data can be modeled by the formula

$$P = -0.22t + 9.6$$

in which P is the salmon population, in millions, t years after 1960. Use the formula to solve Exercises 23–24. Round to the nearest year.

Pacific Salmon Population

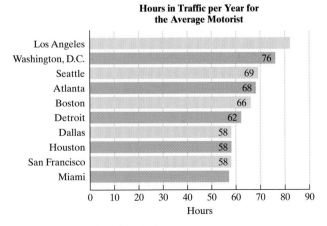

Source: U.S. Department of the Interior

23. When will the salmon population be reduced to 0.5 million?

24. When will there be no Pacific salmon?

25. The formula

$$\frac{W}{2} - 3H = 53$$

models the recommended weight W, in pounds, for a male, where H represents the man's height, in inches, over 5 feet. What is the recommended weight for a man who is 6 feet, 3 inches tall?

26. The International Panel on Climate Change is a U.N.-sponsored body made up of more than 1500 leading experts from 60 nations. According to their recent findings, increased levels of atmospheric carbon dioxide are affecting our climate. Global warming is under way and the effects could be catastrophic. The formula $C = 1.44t + 280$ models carbon dioxide concentration, C, in parts per million, t years after 1939. The preindustrial carbon dioxide concentration of 280 parts per million remained fairly constant until World War II, increasing after that due primarily to the burning of fossil fuels related to energy consumption. When will the concentration be double the preindustrial level? Round to the nearest year.

In Exercises 27–56, use the five-step strategy given in the box on page 97 to solve each problem.

27. Two of the most expensive movies ever made were *Titanic* and *Waterworld*. The cost to make *Titanic* exceeded the cost to make *Waterworld* by $40 million. The combined cost to make the two movies was $360 million. Find the cost of making each of these movies.

28. In 2001, the most populous countries in the world were China and India. In that year, China's population exceeded India's by 260 million. Combined, the two countries had a population of 2310 million. Determine the 2001 population for China and India.

29. Each year, Americans in 68 urban areas waste almost 7 billion gallons of fuel sitting in traffic. The bar graph shows the number of hours in traffic per year for the average motorist in ten cities. The average motorist in Los Angeles spends 32 hours less than twice that of the average motorist in Miami stuck in traffic each year. Together, the average motorist in Miami and the average motorist in Los Angeles spend 139 hours per year in traffic. How many hours are wasted in traffic by the average motorist in Los Angeles and Miami?

Hours in Traffic per Year for the Average Motorist

City	Hours
Los Angeles	
Washington, D.C.	76
Seattle	69
Atlanta	68
Boston	66
Detroit	62
Dallas	58
Houston	58
San Francisco	58
Miami	

Source: Texas Transportation Institute

30. The graph shows the five costliest natural disasters in U.S. history. The cost of the Northridge, California, earthquake exceeded Hurricane Hugo by $5.5 billion and the cost of Hurricane Andrew exceeded twice that of Hugo by $6 billion. The combined cost of the three natural disasters was $39.5 billion. Determine the cost of each.

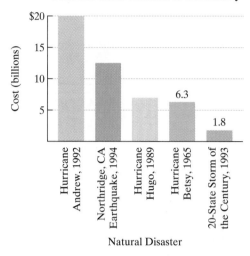

Costliest Natural Disasters in U.S. History

Source: Federal Emergency Management Agency

31. A car rental agency charges $200 per week plus $0.15 per mile to rent a car. How many miles can you travel in one week for $320?

32. A car rental agency charges $180 per week plus $0.25 per mile to rent a car. How many miles can you travel in one week for $395?

According to the National Center for Health Statistics, in 1990, 28% of babies in the United States were born to parents who were not married. Throughout the 1990s, this increased by approximately 0.6% per year. Use this information to solve Exercises 33–34.

33. If this trend continues, in which year will 37% of babies be born out of wedlock?

34. If this trend continues, in which year will 40% of babies be born out of wedlock?

35. The bus fare in a city is $1.25. People who use the bus have the option of purchasing a monthly coupon book for $21.00. With the coupon book, the fare is reduced to $0.50.
  a. Let x represent the number of times in a month the bus is used. Write algebraic expressions for the total monthly costs of using the bus x times both with and without the coupon book.
  b. Determine the number of times in a month the bus must be used so that the total monthly cost without the coupon book is the same as the total monthly cost with the coupon book.

36. A coupon book for a bridge costs $21 per month. The toll for the bridge is normally $2.50, but it is reduced to $1 for people who have purchased the coupon book.

  a. Let x represent the number of times in a month the bridge is used. Write algebraic expressions for the total monthly costs of using the bridge x times both with and without the coupon book.
  b. Determine the number of times in a month the bridge must be crossed so that the total monthly cost without the coupon book is the same as the total monthly cost with the coupon book.

37. You are choosing between two plans at a discount warehouse. Plan A offers an annual membership fee of $100 and you pay 80% of the manufacturer's recommended list price. Plan B offers an annual membership fee of $40 and you pay 90% of the manufacturer's recommended list price. How many dollars of merchandise would you have to purchase in a year to pay the same amount under both plans? What will be the cost for each plan?

38. You are choosing between two plans at a discount warehouse. Plan A offers an annual membership fee of $300 and you pay 70% of the manufacturer's recommended list price. Plan B offers an annual membership fee of $40 and you pay 90% of the manufacturer's recommended list price. How many dollars of merchandise would you have to purchase in a year to pay the same amount under both plans? What will be the cost for each plan?

39. Your grandmother needs your help. She has $50,000 to invest. Part of this money is to be invested in noninsured bonds paying 15% annual interest. The rest of this money is to be invested in a government-insured certificate of deposit paying 7% annual interest. She told you that she requires $6000 per year in extra income from both of these investments. How much money should be placed in each investment?

40. You inherit $18,750 with the stipulation that for the first year the money must be placed in two investments paying 10% and 12% annual interest, respectively. How much should be invested at each rate if the total interest earned for the year is to be $2117?

41. Things did not go quite as planned. You invested $8000, part of it in stock that paid 12% annual interest. However, the rest of the money suffered a 5% loss. If the total annual income from both investments was $620, how much was invested at each rate?

42. Things did not go quite as planned. You invested $12,000, part of it in stock that paid 14% annual interest. However, the rest of the money suffered a 6% loss. If the total annual income from both investments was $680, how much was invested at each rate?

43. The length of the rectangular tennis court at Wimbledon is 6 feet longer than twice the width. If the court's perimeter is 228 feet, what are the court's dimensions?

44. A rectangular soccer field is twice as long as it is wide. If the perimeter of the soccer field is 300 yards, what are its dimensions?

45. The height of the bookcase in the figure is 3 feet longer than the length of a shelf. If 18 feet of lumber is available for the entire unit, find the length and height of the unit.

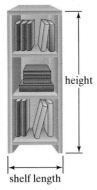

height

shelf length

46. A bookcase is to be constructed as shown in the figure. The length is to be 3 times the height. If 60 feet of lumber is available for the entire unit, find the length and height of the bookcase.

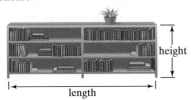

height

length

47. An automobile repair shop charged a customer $448, listing $63 for parts and the remainder for labor. If the cost of labor is $35 per hour, how many hours of labor did it take to repair the car?

48. A repair bill on a yacht came to $1603, including $532 for parts and the remainder for labor. If the cost of labor is $63 per hour, how many hours of labor did it take to repair the yacht?

The graph shows median, or average, income by level of education. Exercises 49–50 use the information in the bar graph.

Income by Level of Education

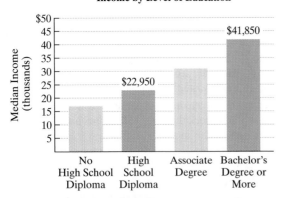

Source: U.S. Department of Commerce

49. The annual salary for people with a bachelor's degree or more is an increase of 35% of the annual salary for people with an associate degree. What is the average annual salary with an associate degree?

50. The annual salary for high school graduates is an increase of 35% of the annual salary for people without a high school diploma. What is the average annual salary without a high school diploma?

51. Answer the question in the following *Peanuts* cartoon strip. (*Note:* You may not use the answer given in the cartoon!)

PEANUTS reprinted by permission of United Features Syndicate, Inc.

52. After a graphing calculator's price is reduced by $\frac{1}{3}$ of its original price, you purchase it for $64. What was the graphing calculator's price before the reduction?

53. After a 12% price reduction, a car sold for $17,600. What was the car's price before the reduction?

54. Including 8% sales tax, an inn charges $162 per night. Find the inn's nightly cost before the tax is added.

55. An HMO pamphlet contains the following recommended weight for women: "Give yourself 100 pounds for the first 5 feet plus 5 pounds for every inch over 5 feet tall." Using this description, what height corresponds to a recommended weight of 135 pounds?

56. A job pays an annual salary of $33,150, which includes a holiday bonus of $750. If paychecks are issued twice a month, what is the gross amount for each paycheck?

In Exercises 57–76, solve each formula for the specified variable. Do you recognize the formula? If so, what does it describe?

57. $A = lw$ for w

58. $D = RT$ for R

59. $A = \frac{1}{2}bh$ for b

60. $V = \frac{1}{3}Bh$ for B

61. $I = Prt$ for P

62. $C = 2\pi r$ for r

63. $E = mc^2$ for m

64. $V = \pi r^2 h$ for h

65. $T = D + pm$ for p

66. $P = C + MC$ for M

67. $A = \frac{1}{2}h(a + b)$ for a

68. $A = \frac{1}{2}h(a + b)$ for b

69. $S = P + Prt$ for r

70. $S = P + Prt$ for t

71. $B = \dfrac{F}{S - V}$ for S

72. $S = \dfrac{C}{1 - r}$ for r

73. $IR + Ir = E$ for I

74. $A = 2lw + 2lh + 2wh$ for h

75. $\dfrac{1}{p} + \dfrac{1}{q} = \dfrac{1}{f}$ for f

76. $\dfrac{1}{R} = \dfrac{1}{R_1} + \dfrac{1}{R_2}$ for R_1

Writing in Mathematics

77. What is a formula?

78. We discussed formulas in this section after we considered procedures for solving linear equations. Doesn't working with a formula simply mean substituting given numbers into the formula and using the order of operations? Is it necessary to know how to solve equations to work with formulas? Explain.

79. In your own words, describe a step-by-step approach for solving algebraic word problems.

80. Did you have some difficulties solving some of the problems that were assigned in this exercise set? Discuss what you did if this happened to you. Did your course of action enhance your ability to solve algebraic word problems?

Technology Exercises

81. The formula $y = 28 + 0.6x$ models the percentage, y, of U.S. babies born out of wedlock x years after 1990. Graph the formula in a $[0, 20, 5]$ by $[0, 50, 10]$ viewing rectangle. Then use the TRACE or ZOOM feature to verify your answer in Exercise 33 or 34.

82. A tennis club offers two payment options. Members can pay a monthly fee of $30 plus $5 per hour for court rental time. The second option has no monthly fee, but court time costs $7.50 per hour.

   a. Write a mathematical model representing total monthly costs for each option for x hours of court rental time.

   b. Use a graphing utility to graph the two models in a $[0, 15, 1]$ by $[0, 120, 20]$ viewing rectangle.

   c. Use your utility's trace or intersection feature to determine where the two graphs intersect. Describe what the coordinates of this intersection point represent in practical terms.

   d. Verify part (c) using an algebraic approach by setting the two models equal to one another and determining how many hours one has to rent the court so that the two plans result in identical monthly costs.

Critical Thinking Exercises

83. At the north campus of a performing arts school, 10% of the students are music majors. At the south campus, 90% of the students are music majors. The campuses are merged into one east campus. If 42% of the 1000 students at the east campus are music majors, how many students did the north and south campuses have before the merger?

84. The price of a dress is reduced by 40%. When the dress still does not sell, it is reduced by 40% of the reduced price. If the price of the dress after both reductions is $72, what was the original price?

85. In a film, the actor Charles Coburn plays an elderly "uncle" character criticized for marrying a woman when he is 3 times her age. He wittily replies, "Ah, but in 20 years time I shall only be twice her age." How old is the "uncle" and the woman?

86. Suppose that we agree to pay you 8¢ for every problem in this chapter that you solve correctly and fine you 5¢ for every problem done incorrectly. If at the end of 26 problems we do not owe each other any money, how many problems did you solve correctly?

87. It was wartime when the Ricardos found out Mrs. Ricardo was pregnant. Ricky Ricardo was drafted and made out a will, deciding that $14,000 in a savings account was to be divided between his wife and his child-to-be. Rather strangely, and certainly with gender bias, Ricky stipulated that if the child were a boy, he would get twice the amount of the mother's portion. If it were a girl, the mother would get twice the amount the girl was to receive. We'll never know what Ricky was thinking of, for (as fate would have it) he did not return from war. Mrs. Ricardo gave birth to twins—a boy and a girl. How was the money divided?

88. Solve for C: $V = C - \dfrac{C - S}{L} N$.

Group Exercise

89. One of the best ways to learn how to *solve* a word problem in algebra is to *design* word problems of your own. Creating a word problem makes you very aware of precisely how much information is needed to solve the problem. You must also focus on the best way to present information to a reader and on how much information to give. As you write your problem, you gain skills that will help you solve problems created by others.

   The group should design five different word problems that can be solved using linear equations. All of the problems should be on different topics. For example, the group should not have more than one problem on simple interest. The group should turn in both the problems and their algebraic solutions.

SECTION 1.4 *Complex Numbers*

Objectives

1. Add and subtract complex numbers.
2. Multiply complex numbers.
3. Divide complex numbers.
4. Perform operations with square roots of negative numbers.

Who is this kid warning us about our eyeballs turning black if we attempt to find the square root of −9? Don't believe what you hear on the street. Although square roots of negative numbers are not real numbers, they do play a significant role in algebra. In this section, we move beyond the real numbers and discuss square roots with negative radicands.

The Imaginary Unit *i*

In the next section, we'll be studying equations whose solutions involve the square roots of negative numbers. Because the square of a real number is never negative, there is no real number x such that $x^2 = -1$. To provide a setting in which such equations have solutions, mathematicians invented an expanded system of numbers, the complex numbers. The *imaginary number i*, defined to be a solution of the equation $x^2 = -1$, is the basis of this new set.

The Imaginary Unit *i*

The **imaginary unit** *i* is defined as

$$i = \sqrt{-1}, \quad \text{where} \quad i^2 = -1.$$

Using the imaginary unit *i*, we can express the square root of any negative number as a real multiple of *i*. For example,

$$\sqrt{-25} = i\sqrt{25} = 5i.$$

We can check this result by squaring $5i$ and obtaining -25.

$$(5i)^2 = 5^2 i^2 = 25(-1) = -25$$

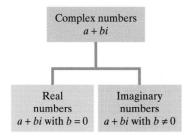

Complex numbers
$a + bi$

Real numbers
$a + bi$ with $b = 0$

Imaginary numbers
$a + bi$ with $b \neq 0$

Figure 1.13 The complex number system

A new system of numbers, called *complex numbers*, is based on adding multiples of i, such as $5i$, to the real numbers.

Complex Numbers

The set of all numbers in the form

$$a + bi$$

with real numbers a and b, and i, the imaginary unit, is called the set of **complex numbers.** The real number a is called the **real part,** and the real number b is called the **imaginary part,** of the complex number $a + bi$. If $b \neq 0$, then the complex number is called an **imaginary number** (Figure 1.13). An imaginary number in the form bi is called a **pure imaginary number.**

Here are some examples of complex numbers. Each number can be written in the form $a + bi$.

$$-4 + 6i \qquad\qquad 2i = 0 + 2i \qquad\qquad 3 = 3 + 0i$$

a, the real part, is −4. b, the imaginary part, is 6. a, the real part, is 0. b, the imaginary part, is 2. a, the real part, is 3. b, the imaginary part, is 0.

Can you see that b, the imaginary part, is not zero in the first two complex numbers? Because $b \neq 0$, these complex numbers are imaginary numbers. Furthermore, the imaginary number $2i$ is a pure imaginary number. By contrast, the imaginary part of the complex number on the right is zero. This complex number is not an imaginary number. The number 3, or $3 + 0i$, is a real number.

A complex number is said to be **simplified** if it is expressed in the **standard form** $a + bi$. If b is a radical, we usually write i before b. For example, we write $7 + i\sqrt{5}$ rather than $7 + \sqrt{5}i$, which could easily be confused with $7 + \sqrt{5i}$.

Expressed in standard form, two complex numbers are equal if and only if their real parts are equal and their imaginary parts are equal.

Equality of Complex Numbers

$a + bi = c + di$ if and only if $a = c$ and $b = d$.

1 Add and subtract complex numbers.

Operations with Complex Numbers

The form of a complex number $a + bi$ is like the binomial $a + bx$. Consequently, we can add, subtract, and multiply complex numbers using the same methods we used for binomials, remembering that $i^2 = -1$.

Adding and Subtracting Complex Numbers

1. $(a + bi) + (c + di) = (a + c) + (b + d)i$

In words, this says that you add complex numbers by adding their real parts, adding their imaginary parts, and expressing the sum as a complex number.

2. $(a + bi) - (c + di) = (a - c) + (b - d)i$

In words, this says that you subtract complex numbers by subtracting their real parts, subtracting their imaginary parts, and expressing the difference as a complex number.

EXAMPLE 1 Adding and Subtracting Complex Numbers

Perform the indicated operations, writing the result in standard form:

a. $(5 - 11i) + (7 + 4i)$ **b.** $(-5 + 7i) - (-11 - 6i)$.

Study Tip

The following examples, using the same integers as in Example 1, show how operations with complex numbers are just like operations with polynomials.

a. $(5 - 11x) + (7 + 4x)$
  $= 12 - 7x$

b. $(-5 + 7x) - (-11 - 6x)$
  $= -5 + 7x + 11 + 6x$
  $= 6 + 13x$

Solution

a. $(5 - 11i) + (7 + 4i)$

$= 5 - 11i + 7 + 4i$ *Remove the parentheses.*

$= 5 + 7 - 11i + 4i$ *Group real and imaginary terms.*

$= (5 + 7) + (-11 + 4)i$ *Add real parts and add imaginary parts.*

$= 12 - 7i$ *Simplify.*

b. $(-5 + 7i) - (-11 - 6i)$

$= -5 + 7i + 11 + 6i$ *Remove the parentheses.*

$= -5 + 11 + 7i + 6i$ *Group real and imaginary terms.*

$= (-5 + 11) + (7 + 6)i$ *Add real parts and add imaginary parts.*

$= 6 + 13i$ *Simplify.*

Check Point 1   Add or subtract as indicated:

a. $(5 - 2i) + (3 + 3i)$ **b.** $(2 + 6i) - (12 - 4i)$.

2 Multiply complex numbers.

Multiplication of complex numbers is performed the same way as multiplication of polynomials, using the distributive property and the FOIL method. After completing the multiplication, we replace i^2 with -1. This idea is illustrated in the next example.

EXAMPLE 2 Multiplying Complex Numbers

Find the products:

a. $4i(3 - 5i)$ **b.** $(7 - 3i)(-2 - 5i)$.

Solution

a. $4i(3 - 5i) = 4i(3) - 4i(5i)$ *Distribute 4i throughout the parentheses.*

$= 12i - 20i^2$ *Multiply.*

$= 12i - 20(-1)$ *Replace i^2 with -1.*

$= 20 + 12i$ *Simplify to 12i + 20 and write in standard form.*

b. $(7 - 3i)(-2 - 5i)$

     F   O   I   L

$= -14 - 35i + 6i + 15i^2$ *Use the FOIL method.*

$= -14 - 35i + 6i + 15(-1)$ *$i^2 = -1$*

$= -14 - 15 - 35i + 6i$ *Group real and imaginary terms.*

$= -29 - 29i$ *Combine real and imaginary terms.*

Check Point 2   Find the products:

a. $7i(2 - 9i)$ **b.** $(5 + 4i)(6 - 7i)$.

3 Divide complex numbers.

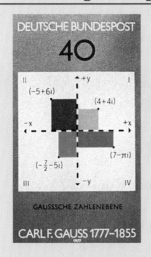
Complex Conjugates and Division

It is possible to multiply complex numbers and obtain a real number. This occurs when we multiply $a + bi$ and $a - bi$.

$$(a + bi)(a - bi) = a^2 - abi + abi - b^2 i^2 \quad \text{Use the FOIL method.}$$
$$= a^2 - b^2(-1) \quad i^2 = -1$$
$$= a^2 + b^2 \quad \text{Notice that this product eliminates } i.$$

For the complex number $a + bi$, we define its *complex conjugate* to be $a - bi$. The multiplication of complex conjugates results in a real number.

Conjugate of a Complex Number

The **complex conjugate** of the number $a + bi$ is $a - bi$, and the complex conjugate of $a - bi$ is $a + bi$. The multiplication of complex conjugates gives a real number.

$$(a + bi)(a - bi) = a^2 + b^2$$
$$(a - bi)(a + bi) = a^2 + b^2$$

Complex conjugates are used when dividing complex numbers. By multiplying the numerator and the denominator of the division by the complex conjugate of the denominator, you will obtain a real number in the denominator.

EXAMPLE 3   Using Complex Conjugates to Divide Complex Numbers

Divide and express the result in standard form: $\dfrac{7 + 4i}{2 - 5i}$.

Solution The complex conjugate of the denominator, $2 - 5i$, is $2 + 5i$. Multiplication of both the numerator and the denominator by $2 + 5i$ will eliminate i from the denominator.

$$\frac{7 + 4i}{2 - 5i} = \frac{(7 + 4i)}{(2 - 5i)} \cdot \frac{(2 + 5i)}{(2 + 5i)} \quad \text{Multiply the numerator and the denominator by the complex conjugate of the denominator.}$$

$$= \frac{14 + 35i + 8i + 20i^2}{2^2 + 5^2} \quad \text{Use the FOIL method in the numerator and } (a - bi)(a + bi) = a^2 + b^2 \text{ in the denominator.}$$

$$= \frac{14 + 43i + 20(-1)}{29} \quad \text{Combine imaginary terms and replace } i^2 \text{ with } -1.$$

$$= \frac{-6 + 43i}{29} \quad \text{Combine real terms in the numerator.}$$

$$= -\frac{6}{29} + \frac{43}{29}i \quad \text{Express the answer in standard form.}$$

Observe that the quotient is expressed in the standard form $a + bi$, with $a = -\frac{6}{29}$ and $b = \frac{43}{29}$.

Check Point 3 Divide and express the result in standard form: $\dfrac{5 + 4i}{4 - 2i}$.

4 Perform operations with square roots of negative numbers.

Roots of Negative Numbers

The square of $4i$ and the square of $-4i$ both result in -16.

$$(4i)^2 = 16i^2 = 16(-1) = -16 \qquad (-4i)^2 = 16i^2 = 16(-1) = -16$$

Consequently, in the complex number system -16 has two square roots, namely, $4i$ and $-4i$. We call $4i$ the **principal square root** of -16.

> **Principal Square Root of a Negative Number**
>
> For any positive number real number b, the **principal square root** of the negative number $-b$ is defined by
> $$\sqrt{-b} = i\sqrt{b}.$$

EXAMPLE 4 Operations Involving Square Roots of Negative Numbers

Perform the indicated operations and write the result in standard form:

a. $\sqrt{-18} - \sqrt{-8}$ **b.** $(-1 + \sqrt{-5})^2$ **c.** $\dfrac{-25 + \sqrt{-50}}{15}$.

Solution Begin by expressing all square roots of negative numbers in terms of i.

a. $\sqrt{-18} - \sqrt{-8} = i\sqrt{18} - i\sqrt{8} = i\sqrt{9 \cdot 2} - i\sqrt{4 \cdot 2}$
$$= 3i\sqrt{2} - 2i\sqrt{2} = i\sqrt{2}$$

$(A + B)^2 = A^2 + 2AB + B^2$

b. $(-1 + \sqrt{-5})^2 = (-1 + i\sqrt{5})^2 = (-1)^2 + 2(-1)(i\sqrt{5}) + (i\sqrt{5})^2$
$$= 1 - 2i\sqrt{5} + 5i^2$$
$$= 1 - 2i\sqrt{5} + 5(-1)$$
$$= -4 - 2i\sqrt{5}$$

c. $\dfrac{-25 + \sqrt{-50}}{15}$
$$= \dfrac{-25 + i\sqrt{50}}{15} \qquad \sqrt{-b} = i\sqrt{b}$$
$$= \dfrac{-25 + 5i\sqrt{2}}{15} \qquad \sqrt{50} = \sqrt{25 \cdot 2} = 5\sqrt{2}$$
$$= \dfrac{-25}{15} + \dfrac{5i\sqrt{2}}{15} \qquad \text{Write the complex number in standard form.}$$
$$= -\dfrac{5}{3} + i\dfrac{\sqrt{2}}{3} \qquad \text{Simplify.}$$

Study Tip

Do not apply the properties
$$\sqrt{b}\sqrt{c} = \sqrt{bc}$$
and
$$\dfrac{\sqrt{b}}{\sqrt{c}} = \sqrt{\dfrac{b}{c}}$$
to the pure imaginary numbers because these properties can only be used when b and c are positive.

Correct:
$$\sqrt{-25}\sqrt{-4} = i\sqrt{25}\,i\sqrt{4}$$
$$= (5i)(2i)$$
$$= 10i^2$$
$$= 10(-1)$$
$$= -10$$

Incorrect:
$$\sqrt{-25}\sqrt{-4} = \sqrt{(-25)(-4)}$$
$$= \sqrt{100}$$
$$= 10$$

One way to avoid confusion is to represent square roots of negative numbers in terms of i before performing any operations.

Check Point 4 Perform the indicated operations and write the result in standard form:

a. $\sqrt{-27} + \sqrt{-48}$ **b.** $(-2 + \sqrt{-3})^2$ **c.** $\dfrac{-14 + \sqrt{-12}}{2}$.

EXERCISE SET 1.4

Practice Exercises

In Exercises 1–8, add or subtract as indicated and write the result in standard form.

1. $(7 + 2i) + (1 - 4i)$ **2.** $(-2 + 6i) + (4 - i)$

3. $(3 + 2i) - (5 - 7i)$ **4.** $(-7 + 5i) - (-9 - 11i)$

5. $6 - (-5 + 4i) - (-13 - 11i)$

6. $7 - (-9 + 2i) - (-17 - 6i)$

7. $8i - (14 - 9i)$ **8.** $15i - (12 - 11i)$

In Exercises 9–20, find each product and write the result in standard form.

9. $-3i(7i - 5)$ **10.** $-8i(2i - 7)$

11. $(-5 + 4i)(3 + 7i)$ **12.** $(-4 - 8i)(3 + 9i)$

13. $(7 - 5i)(-2 - 3i)$ **14.** $(8 - 4i)(-3 + 9i)$

15. $(3 + 5i)(3 - 5i)$ **16.** $(2 + 7i)(2 - 7i)$

17. $(-5 + 3i)(-5 - 3i)$ **18.** $(-7 - 4i)(-7 + 4i)$

19. $(2 + 3i)^2$ **20.** $(5 - 2i)^2$

In Exercises 21–28, divide and express the result in standard form.

21. $\dfrac{2}{3 - i}$ **22.** $\dfrac{3}{4 + i}$

23. $\dfrac{2i}{1 + i}$ **24.** $\dfrac{5i}{2 - i}$

25. $\dfrac{8i}{4 - 3i}$ **26.** $\dfrac{-6i}{3 + 2i}$

27. $\dfrac{2 + 3i}{2 + i}$ **28.** $\dfrac{3 - 4i}{4 + 3i}$

In Exercises 29–44, perform the indicated operations and write the result in standard form.

29. $\sqrt{-64} - \sqrt{-25}$ **30.** $\sqrt{-81} - \sqrt{-144}$

31. $5\sqrt{-16} + 3\sqrt{-81}$ **32.** $5\sqrt{-8} + 3\sqrt{-18}$

33. $(-2 + \sqrt{-4})^2$ **34.** $(-5 - \sqrt{-9})^2$

35. $(-3 - \sqrt{-7})^2$ **36.** $(-2 + \sqrt{-11})^2$

37. $\dfrac{-8 + \sqrt{-32}}{24}$ **38.** $\dfrac{-12 + \sqrt{-28}}{32}$

39. $\dfrac{-6 - \sqrt{-12}}{48}$ **40.** $\dfrac{-15 - \sqrt{-18}}{33}$

41. $\sqrt{-8}(\sqrt{-3} - \sqrt{5})$ **42.** $\sqrt{-12}(\sqrt{-4} - \sqrt{2})$

43. $(3\sqrt{-5})(-4\sqrt{-12})$ **44.** $(3\sqrt{-7})(2\sqrt{-8})$

Writing in Mathematics

45. What is i?

46. Explain how to add complex numbers. Provide an example with your explanation.

47. Explain how to multiply complex numbers and give an example.

48. What is the complex conjugate of $2 + 3i$? What happens when you multiply this complex number by its complex conjugate?

49. Explain how to divide complex numbers. Provide an example with your explanation.

50. A stand-up comedian uses algebra in some jokes, including one about a telephone recording that announces "You have just reached an imaginary number. Please multiply by i and dial again." Explain the joke.

Explain the error in Exercises 51–52.

51. $\sqrt{-9} + \sqrt{-16} = \sqrt{-25} = i\sqrt{25} = 5i$

52. $\left(\sqrt{-9}\right)^2 = \sqrt{-9} \cdot \sqrt{-9} = \sqrt{81} = 9$

Critical Thinking Exercises

53. Which one of the following is true?

a. Some irrational numbers are not complex numbers.

b. $(3 + 7i)(3 - 7i)$ is an imaginary number.

c. $\dfrac{7 + 3i}{5 + 3i} = \dfrac{7}{5}$

d. In the complex number system, $x^2 + y^2$ (the sum of two squares) can be factored as $(x + yi)(x - yi)$.

In Exercises 54–56, perform the indicated operations and write the result in standard form.

54. $(8 + 9i)(2 - i) - (1 - i)(1 + i)$

55. $\dfrac{4}{(2 + i)(3 - i)}$ **56.** $\dfrac{1 + i}{1 + 2i} + \dfrac{1 - i}{1 - 2i}$

57. Evaluate $x^2 - 2x + 2$ for $x = 1 + i$.

SECTION 1.5 *Quadratic Equations*

Objectives

1. Solve quadratic equations by factoring.
2. Solve quadratic equations by the square root method.
3. Solve quadratic equations by completing the square.
4. Solve quadratic equations using the quadratic formula.
5. Use the discriminant to determine the number and type of solutions.
6. Determine the most efficient method to use when solving a quadratic equation.
7. Solve problems modeled by quadratic equations.

Serpico, 1973, starring Al Pacino, is a movie about police corruption.

In 2000, a police scandal shocked Los Angeles. A police officer who had been convicted of stealing cocaine held as evidence described how members of his unit behaved in ways that resembled the gangs they were targeting, assaulting and framing innocent people.

Is police corruption on the rise? The graph in Figure 1.14 shows the number of convictions of police officers throughout the United States for seven years.

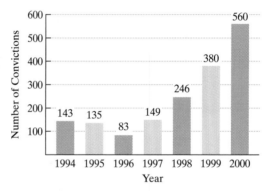

Figure 1.14
Source: F.B.I.

The data can be modeled by the formula

$$N = 23.4x^2 - 259.1x + 815.8$$

where N is the number of police officers convicted of felonies x years after 1990. If present trends continue, in which year will 1000 police officers be convicted of felonies? To answer the question, it is necessary to substitute 1000 for N in the formula and solve for x, the number of years after 1990:

$$1000 = 23.4x^2 - 259.1x + 815.8.$$

Do you see how this equation differs from a linear equation? The exponent on x is 2. Solving such an equation involves finding the set of numbers that make the equation a true statement. In this section, we study a number of methods for solving equations in the form $ax^2 + bx + c = 0$. We also look at applications of these equations.

The General Form of a Quadratic Equation

We begin by defining a quadratic equation.

> **Definition of a Quadratic Equation**
>
> A **quadratic equation** in x is an equation that can be written in the **general form**
> $$ax^2 + bx + c = 0$$
> where a, b, and c are real numbers, with $a \neq 0$. A quadratic equation in x is also called a **second-degree polynomial equation** in x.

    An example of a quadratic equation in general form is $x^2 - 7x + 10 = 0$. The coefficient of x^2 is $1\,(a = 1)$, the coefficient of x is $-7\,(b = -7)$, and the constant term is $10\,(c = 10)$.

1 Solve quadratic equations by factoring.

Solving Quadratic Equations by Factoring

We can factor the left side of the quadratic equation $x^2 - 7x + 10 = 0$. We obtain $(x - 5)(x - 2) = 0$. If a quadratic equation has zero on one side and a factored expression on the other side, it can be solved using the **zero-product principle.**

> **The Zero-Product Principle**
>
> If the product of two algebraic expressions is zero, then at least one of the factors is equal to zero.
> $$\text{If } AB = 0, \quad \text{then} \quad A = 0 \text{ or } B = 0.$$

For example, consider the equation $(x - 5)(x - 2) = 0$. According to the zero-product principle, this product can be zero only if at least one of the factors is zero. We set each individual factor equal to zero and solve each resulting equation for x.

$$(x - 5)(x - 2) = 0$$
$$x - 5 = 0 \quad \text{ or } \quad x - 2 = 0$$
$$x = 5 \qquad\qquad x = 2$$

We can check each of these proposed solutions in the original quadratic equation, $x^2 - 7x + 10 = 0$.

Check 5:
$$5^2 - 7 \cdot 5 + 10 \overset{?}{=} 0$$
$$25 - 35 + 10 \overset{?}{=} 0$$
$$0 = 0 \checkmark$$

Check 2:
$$2^2 - 7 \cdot 2 + 10 \overset{?}{=} 0$$
$$4 - 14 + 10 \overset{?}{=} 0$$
$$0 = 0 \checkmark$$

The resulting true statements, indicated by the checks, show that the solutions are 5 and 2. The solution set is $\{5, 2\}$. Note that with a quadratic equation, we can have two solutions, compared to the conditional linear equation that had one.

> **Solving a Quadratic Equation by Factoring**
>
> **1.** If necessary, rewrite the equation in the form $ax^2 + bx + c = 0$, moving all terms to one side, thereby obtaining zero on the other side.
> **2.** Factor.   (continues on the next page)

Solving a Quadratic Equation by Factoring (continued)

3. Apply the zero-product principle, setting each factor equal to zero.

4. Solve the equations in step 3.

5. Check the solutions in the original equation.

EXAMPLE 1 **Solving Quadratic Equations by Factoring**

Solve by factoring:

    a. $4x^2 - 2x = 0$ **b.** $2x^2 + 7x = 4$.

Solution

   a. We begin with $4x^2 - 2x = 0$.

Step 1 Move all terms to one side and obtain zero on the other side. All terms are already on the left and zero is on the other side, so we can skip this step.

Step 2 Factor. We factor out $2x$ from the two terms on the left side.

$$4x^2 - 2x = 0 \quad \text{This is the given equation.}$$

$$2x(2x - 1) = 0 \quad \text{Factor.}$$

Steps 3 and 4 Set each factor equal to zero and solve the resulting equations.

$$2x = 0 \quad \text{or} \quad 2x - 1 = 0$$

$$x = 0 \qquad\qquad 2x = 1$$

$$x = \tfrac{1}{2}$$

Step 5 Check the solutions in the original equation.

Check 0:
$$4x^2 - 2x = 0$$
$$4 \cdot 0^2 - 2 \cdot 0 \overset{?}{=} 0$$
$$0 - 0 \overset{?}{=} 0$$
$$0 = 0 \checkmark$$

Check $\tfrac{1}{2}$:
$$4x^2 - 2x = 0$$
$$4\left(\tfrac{1}{2}\right)^2 - 2\left(\tfrac{1}{2}\right) \overset{?}{=} 0$$
$$4\left(\tfrac{1}{4}\right) - 2\left(\tfrac{1}{2}\right) \overset{?}{=} 0$$
$$1 - 1 \overset{?}{=} 0$$
$$0 = 0 \checkmark$$

The solution set is $\left\{0, \tfrac{1}{2}\right\}$.

   b. Next, we solve $2x^2 + 7x = 4$.

Step 1 Move all terms to one side and obtain zero on the other side. Subtract 4 from both sides and write the equation in general form.

$$2x^2 + 7x = 4 \qquad \text{This is the given equation.}$$
$$2x^2 + 7x - 4 = 4 - 4 \qquad \text{Subtract 4 from both sides.}$$
$$2x^2 + 7x - 4 = 0 \qquad \text{Simplify.}$$

Step 2 Factor.

$$2x^2 + 7x - 4 = 0$$
$$(2x - 1)(x + 4) = 0$$

Steps 3 and 4 **Set each factor equal to zero and solve each resulting equation.**

$$2x - 1 = 0 \qquad \text{or} \qquad x + 4 = 0$$
$$2x = 1 \qquad\qquad\qquad x = -4$$
$$x = \tfrac{1}{2}$$

Step 5 **Check the solutions in the original equation.**

Check $\tfrac{1}{2}$:

$$2x^2 + 7x = 4$$
$$2\left(\tfrac{1}{2}\right)^2 + 7\left(\tfrac{1}{2}\right) \stackrel{?}{=} 4$$
$$\tfrac{1}{2} + \tfrac{7}{2} \stackrel{?}{=} 4$$
$$4 = 4 \ \checkmark$$

Check -4:

$$2x^2 + 7x = 4$$
$$2(-4)^2 + 7(-4) \stackrel{?}{=} 4$$
$$32 + (-28) \stackrel{?}{=} 4$$
$$4 = 4 \ \checkmark$$

The solution set is $\left\{-4, \tfrac{1}{2}\right\}$.

Check Point 1 Solve by factoring:

a. $3x^2 - 9x = 0$ **b.** $2x^2 + x = 1$.

Technology

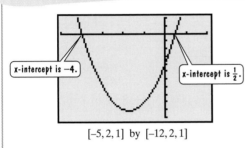

x-intercept is −4.

x-intercept is $\tfrac{1}{2}$.

$[-5, 2, 1]$ by $[-12, 2, 1]$

You can use a graphing utility to check the real solutions of a quadratic equation. **The solutions of $ax^2 + bx + c = 0$ correspond to the x-intercepts of the graph of $y = ax^2 + bx + c$.** For example, to check the solutions of $2x^2 + 7x = 4$, or $2x^2 + 7x - 4 = 0$, graph $y = 2x^2 + 7x - 4$. The cuplike U-shaped graph is shown on the left. Note that it is important to have all nonzero terms on one side of the quadratic equation before entering it into the graphing utility. The x-intercepts are -4 and $\tfrac{1}{2}$, and the graph of $y = 2x^2 + 7x - 4$ passes through $(-4, 0)$ and $\left(\tfrac{1}{2}, 0\right)$. This verifies that $\left\{-4, \tfrac{1}{2}\right\}$ is the solution set of $2x^2 + 7x - 4 = 0$.

2 Solve quadratic equations by the square root method.

Solving Quadratic Equations by the Square Root Method

Quadratic equations of the form $u^2 = d$, where $d > 0$ and u is an algebraic expression, can be solved by the **square root method.** First, isolate the squared expression u^2 on one side of the equation and the number d on the other side. Then take the square root of both sides. Remember, there are two numbers whose square is d. One number is positive and one is negative.

We can use factoring to verify that $u^2 = d$ has two solutions.

$$u^2 = d \qquad \text{This is the given equation.}$$
$$u^2 - d = 0 \qquad \text{Move all terms to one side and obtain}$$
$$\text{zero on the other side.}$$
$$(u + \sqrt{d})(u - \sqrt{d}) = 0 \qquad \text{Factor.}$$
$$u + \sqrt{d} = 0 \qquad \text{or} \qquad u - \sqrt{d} = 0 \qquad \text{Set each factor equal to zero.}$$
$$u = -\sqrt{d} \qquad\qquad u = \sqrt{d} \qquad \text{Solve the resulting equations.}$$

Because the solutions differ only in sign, we can write them in abbreviated notation as $u = \pm\sqrt{d}$. We read this as "u equals positive or negative the square root of d" or "u equals plus or minus the square root of d."

Now that we have verified these solutions, we can solve $u^2 = d$ directly by taking square roots. This process is called **the square root method.**

The Square Root Method

If u is an algebraic expression and d is a positive real number, then $u^2 = d$ has exactly two solutions:

$$\text{If } u^2 = d, \text{ then } u = \sqrt{d} \text{ or } u = -\sqrt{d}.$$

Equivalently,

$$\text{If } u^2 = d, \text{ then } u = \pm\sqrt{d}.$$

EXAMPLE 2 **Solving Quadratic Equations by the Square Root Method**

Solve by the square root method:

a. $4x^2 = 20$ **b.** $(x - 2)^2 = 6.$

Solution

a. In order to apply the square root method, we need a squared expression by itself on one side of the equation.

$$4x^2 = 20$$

> We want x^2 by itself.

We can get x^2 by itself if we divide both sides by 4.

$$\frac{4x^2}{4} = \frac{20}{4}$$

$$x^2 = 5$$

Now, we can apply the square root method.

$$x = \pm\sqrt{5}$$

By checking both values in the original equation, we can confirm that the solution set is $\{-\sqrt{5}, \sqrt{5}\}$.

b. $(x - 2)^2 = 6$

> The squared expression is by itself.

With the squared expression by itself, we can apply the square root method.

$$x - 2 = \pm\sqrt{6}$$

We solve for x by adding 2 to both sides.

$$x = 2 \pm \sqrt{6}$$

By checking both values in the original equation, we can confirm that the solution set is $\{2 + \sqrt{6}, 2 - \sqrt{6}\}$ or $\{2 \pm \sqrt{6}\}$.

Check Point 2   Solve by the square root method:

a. $3x^2 = 21$ **b.** $(x + 5)^2 = 11$.

3 Solve quadratic equations by completing the square.

Completing the Square

How do we solve an equation in the form $ax^2 + bx + c = 0$ if the trinomial $ax^2 + bx + c$ cannot be factored? We cannot use the zero-product principle in such a case. However, we can convert the equation into an equivalent equation that can be solved using the square root method. This is accomplished by **completing the square.**

Completing the Square

If $x^2 + bx$ is a binomial, then by adding $\left(\dfrac{b}{2}\right)^2$, which is the square of half the coefficient of x, a perfect square trinomial will result. That is,

$$x^2 + bx + \left(\frac{b}{2}\right)^2 = \left(x + \frac{b}{2}\right)^2.$$

EXAMPLE 3   Completing the Square

What term should be added to the binomial $x^2 + 8x$ so that it becomes a perfect square trinomial? Then write and factor the trinomial.

Solution   The term that should be added is the square of half the coefficient of x. The coefficient of x is 8. Thus, we will add $\left(\frac{8}{2}\right)^2 = 4^2$. A perfect square trinomial is the result.

$$x^2 + 8x + 4^2 = x^2 + 8x + 16 = (x + 4)^2$$

$$(\text{half})^2$$

Check Point 3   What term should be added to the binomial $x^2 - 14x$ so that it becomes a perfect square trinomial? Then write and factor the trinomial.

We can solve any quadratic equation by completing the square. If the coefficient of the x^2-term is one, we add the square of half the coefficient of x to both sides of the equation. **When you add a constant term to one side of the equation to complete the square, be certain to add the same constant to the other side of the equation.** These ideas are illustrated in Example 4.

EXAMPLE 4   Solving a Quadratic Equation by Completing the Square

Solve by completing the square: $x^2 - 6x + 2 = 0$.

Solution   We begin the procedure of solving $x^2 - 6x + 2 = 0$ by isolating the binomial, $x^2 - 6x$, so that we can complete the square. Thus, we subtract 2 from both sides of the equation.

$$x^2 - 6x + 2 = 0 \qquad \text{This is the given equation.}$$

$$x^2 - 6x + 2 - 2 = 0 - 2 \quad \text{Subtract 2 from both sides.}$$

$$x^2 - 6x = -2 \qquad \text{Simplify.}$$

> We need to add a constant to this binomial that will make it a perfect square trinomial.

What constant should we add? Add the square of half the coefficient of x.

$$x^2 - 6x = -2$$

> -6 is the coefficient of x.
> $$\left(\frac{-6}{2}\right)^2 = (-3)^2 = 9$$

Thus, we need to add 9 to $x^2 - 6x$. In order to obtain an equivalent equation, we must add 9 to both sides.

$$x^2 - 6x = -2 \qquad \text{This is the quadratic equation with the binomial isolated.}$$

$$x^2 - 6x + 9 = -2 + 9 \qquad \text{Add 9 to both sides to complete the square.}$$

$$(x - 3)^2 = 7 \qquad \text{Factor the perfect square trinomial.}$$

> In this step we have converted our equation into one that can be solved by the square root method.

$$x - 3 = \pm\sqrt{7} \qquad \text{Apply the square root method.}$$

$$x = 3 \pm \sqrt{7} \qquad \text{Add 3 to both sides.}$$

The solution set is $\{3 + \sqrt{7}, 3 - \sqrt{7}\}$ or $\{3 \pm \sqrt{7}\}$.

Check Point 4   Solve by completing the square: $x^2 - 2x - 2 = 0$.

If the coefficient of the x^2-term in a quadratic equation is not one, you must divide each side of the equation by this coefficient before completing the square. For example, to solve $3x^2 - 2x - 4 = 0$ by completing the square, first divide every term by 3:

$$\frac{3x^2}{3} - \frac{2x}{3} - \frac{4}{3} = \frac{0}{3}$$

$$x^2 - \frac{2}{3}x - \frac{4}{3} = 0.$$

Now that the coefficient of x^2 is one, we can solve by completing the square using the method of Example 4.

4 Solve quadratic equations using the quadratic formula.

Solving Quadratic Equations Using the Quadratic Formula

We can use the method of completing the square to derive a formula that can be used to solve all quadratic equations. The derivation given here also shows a particular quadratic equation, $3x^2 - 2x - 4 = 0$, to specifically illustrate each of the steps.

Deriving the Quadratic Formula

General Form of a Quadratic Equation	Comment	A Specific Example
$ax^2 + bx + c = 0, \quad a > 0$	This is the given equation.	$3x^2 - 2x - 4 = 0$
$x^2 + \dfrac{b}{a}x + \dfrac{c}{a} = 0$	Divide both sides by the coefficient of x^2.	$x^2 - \dfrac{2}{3}x - \dfrac{4}{3} = 0$
$x^2 + \dfrac{b}{a}x = -\dfrac{c}{a}$	Isolate the binomial by adding $-\dfrac{c}{a}$ on both sides.	$x^2 - \dfrac{2}{3}x = \dfrac{4}{3}$
$x^2 + \dfrac{b}{a}x + \left(\dfrac{b}{2a}\right)^2 = -\dfrac{c}{a} + \left(\dfrac{b}{2a}\right)^2$ (half)^2	Complete the square. Add the square of half the coefficient of x to both sides.	$x^2 - \dfrac{2}{3}x + \left(-\dfrac{1}{3}\right)^2 = \dfrac{4}{3} + \left(-\dfrac{1}{3}\right)^2$ (half)^2
$x^2 + \dfrac{b}{a}x + \dfrac{b^2}{4a^2} = -\dfrac{c}{a} + \dfrac{b^2}{4a^2}$		$x^2 - \dfrac{2}{3}x + \dfrac{1}{9} = \dfrac{4}{3} + \dfrac{1}{9}$
$\left(x + \dfrac{b}{2a}\right)^2 = -\dfrac{c}{a}\cdot\dfrac{4a}{4a} + \dfrac{b^2}{4a^2}$	Factor on the left side and obtain a common denominator on the right side.	$\left(x - \dfrac{1}{3}\right)^2 = \dfrac{4}{3}\cdot\dfrac{3}{3} + \dfrac{1}{9}$
$\left(x + \dfrac{b}{2a}\right)^2 = \dfrac{-4ac + b^2}{4a^2}$	Add fractions on the right side.	$\left(x - \dfrac{1}{3}\right)^2 = \dfrac{12 + 1}{9}$
$\left(x + \dfrac{b}{2a}\right)^2 = \dfrac{b^2 - 4ac}{4a^2}$		$\left(x - \dfrac{1}{3}\right)^2 = \dfrac{13}{9}$
$x + \dfrac{b}{2a} = \pm\sqrt{\dfrac{b^2 - 4ac}{4a^2}}$	Apply the square root method.	$x - \dfrac{1}{3} = \pm\sqrt{\dfrac{13}{9}}$
$x + \dfrac{b}{2a} = \pm\dfrac{\sqrt{b^2 - 4ac}}{2a}$	Take the square root of the quotient, simplifying the denominator.	$x - \dfrac{1}{3} = \pm\dfrac{\sqrt{13}}{3}$
$x = \dfrac{-b}{2a} \pm \dfrac{\sqrt{b^2 - 4ac}}{2a}$	Solve for x by subtracting $\dfrac{b}{2a}$ from both sides.	$x = \dfrac{1}{3} \pm \dfrac{\sqrt{13}}{3}$
$x = \dfrac{-b \pm \sqrt{b^2 - 4ac}}{2a}$	Combine fractions on the right.	$x = \dfrac{1 \pm \sqrt{13}}{3}$

The formula shown at the bottom of the left column is called the *quadratic formula*. A similar proof shows that the same formula can be used to solve quadratic equations if a, the coefficient of the x^2-term, is negative.

To Die at Twenty

Can the equations

$$7x^5 + 12x^3 - 9x + 4 = 0$$

and

$$8x^6 - 7x^5 + 4x^3 - 19 = 0$$

be solved using a formula similar to the quadratic formula? The first equation has five solutions and the second has six solutions, but they cannot be found using a formula. How do we know? In 1832, a 20-year-old Frenchman, Evariste Galois, wrote down a proof showing that there is no general formula to solve equations when the exponent on the variable is 5 or greater. Galois was jailed as a political activist several times while still a teenager. The day after his brilliant proof he fought a duel over a woman. The duel was a political setup. As he lay dying, Galois told his brother, Alfred, of the manuscript that contained his proof: "Mathematical manuscripts are in my room. On the table. Take care of my work. Make it known. Important. Don't cry, Alfred. I need all my courage—to die at twenty." (Our source is Leopold Infeld's biography of Galois, *Whom the Gods Love*. Some historians, however, dispute the story of Galois's ironic death the very day after his algebraic proof. Mathematical truths seem more reliable than historical ones!)

The Quadratic Formula

The solutions of a quadratic equation in standard form $ax^2 + bx + c = 0$, with $a \neq 0$, are given by the **quadratic formula**

$$x = \frac{-b \pm \sqrt{b^2 - 4ac}}{2a}.$$

x equals negative b, plus or minus the square root of $b^2 - 4ac$, all divided by 2a.

To use the quadratic formula, write the quadratic equation in general form if necessary. Then determine the numerical values for a (the coefficient of the squared term), b (the coefficient of the x-term), and c (the constant term). Substitute the values of a, b, and c in the quadratic formula and evaluate the expression. The $\pm$ sign indicates that there are two solutions of the equation.

EXAMPLE 5 Solving a Quadratic Equation Using the Quadratic Formula

Solve using the quadratic formula: $2x^2 - 6x + 1 = 0$.

Solution The given equation is in general form. Begin by identifying the values for a, b, and c.

$$2x^2 - 6x + 1 = 0$$

$a = 2$ $b = -6$ $c = 1$

$$x = \frac{-b \pm \sqrt{b^2 - 4ac}}{2a}$$

Use the quadratic formula.

$$= \frac{-(-6) \pm \sqrt{(-6)^2 - 4(2)(1)}}{2 \cdot 2}$$

Substitute the values for a, b, and c: $a = 2$, $b = -6$, and $c = 1$.

$$= \frac{6 \pm \sqrt{36 - 8}}{4}$$

$-(-6) = 6$ and $(-6)^2 = (-6)(-6) = 36$.

$$= \frac{6 \pm \sqrt{28}}{2}$$

Complete the subtraction under the radical.

$$= \frac{6 \pm 2\sqrt{7}}{4}$$

$\sqrt{28} = \sqrt{4 \cdot 7} = \sqrt{4}\sqrt{7} = 2\sqrt{7}$

$$= \frac{2(3 \pm \sqrt{7})}{4}$$

Factor out 2 from the numerator.

$$= \frac{3 \pm \sqrt{7}}{2}$$

Divide the numerator and denominator by 2.

The solution set is $\left\{ \dfrac{3 + \sqrt{7}}{2}, \dfrac{3 - \sqrt{7}}{2} \right\}$ or $\left\{ \dfrac{3 \pm \sqrt{7}}{2} \right\}$.

Check Point 5 Solve using the quadratic formula:

$$2x^2 + 2x - 1 = 0.$$

We have seen that a graphing utility can be used to check the solutions of the quadratic equation $ax^2 + bx + c = 0$. The x-intercepts of the graph of

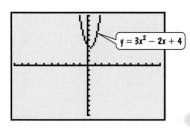

Figure 1.15 This graph has no *x*-intercepts.

$y = ax^2 + bx + c$ are the solutions. However, take a look at the graph of $y = 3x^2 - 2x + 4$, shown in Figure 1.15. Notice that the graph has no *x*-intercepts. Can you guess what this means about the solutions of the quadratic equation $3x^2 - 2x + 4 = 0$? If you're not sure, we'll answer this question in the next example.

EXAMPLE 6   **Solving a Quadratic Equation Using the Quadratic Formula**

Solve using the quadratic formula: $3x^2 - 2x + 4 = 0$.

Solution   The given equation is in general form. Begin by identifying the values for a, b, and c.

$$3x^2 - 2x + 4 = 0$$

$$a = 3 \qquad b = -2 \qquad c = 4$$

$$x = \frac{-b \pm \sqrt{b^2 - 4ac}}{2a}$$ Use the quadratic formula.

$$= \frac{-(-2) \pm \sqrt{(-2)^2 - 4(3)(4)}}{2(3)}$$ Substitute the values for a, b, and c: $a = 3$, $b = -2$, and $c = 4$.

$$= \frac{2 \pm \sqrt{4 - 48}}{6}$$ $-(-2) = 2$ and $(-2)^2 = (-2)(-2) = 4$.

$$= \frac{2 \pm \sqrt{-44}}{6}$$ Subtract under the radical. Because the number under the radical sign is negative, the solutions will not be real numbers.

$$= \frac{2 \pm 2i\sqrt{11}}{6}$$ $\sqrt{-44} = \sqrt{4(11)(-1)}$ $= 2i\sqrt{11}$

$$= \frac{2(1 \pm i\sqrt{11})}{6}$$ Factor 2 from the numerator.

$$= \frac{1 \pm i\sqrt{11}}{3}$$ Divide numerator and denominator by 2.

$$= \frac{1}{3} \pm i\frac{\sqrt{11}}{3}$$ Write the complex numbers in standard form.

Study Tip

Checking irrational and complex imaginary solutions can be time-consuming. The solutions given by the quadratic formula are always correct, unless you have made a careless error. Checking for computational errors or errors in simplification is sufficient.

The solutions are complex conjugates, and the solution set is $\left\{\frac{1}{3} + i\frac{\sqrt{11}}{3}, \frac{1}{3} - i\frac{\sqrt{11}}{3}\right\}$ or $\left\{\frac{1}{3} \pm i\frac{\sqrt{11}}{3}\right\}$.

If $ax^2 + bx + c = 0$ has complex imaginary solutions, the graph of $y = ax^2 + bx + c$ will not have *x*-intercepts. This is illustrated by the imaginary solutions of $3x^2 - 2x + 4 = 0$ in Example 6 and the graph in Figure 1.15.

Check Point 6   Solve using the quadratic formula:

$$x^2 - 2x + 2 = 0.$$

⑤ Use the discriminant to determine the number and type of solutions.

The Discriminant

The quantity $b^2 - 4ac$, which appears under the radical sign in the quadratic formula, is called the **discriminant.** In Example 5 the discriminant was 28, a positive number that is not a perfect square. The equation had two solutions that were irrational numbers. In Example 6, the discriminant was -44, a negative number. The equation had solutions that were complex imaginary numbers. These observations are generalized in Table 1.3.

Table 1.3   The Discriminant and the Kinds of Solutions to $ax^2 + bx + c = 0$

Discriminant $b^2 - 4ac$	Kinds of Solutions to $ax^2 + bx + c = 0$	Graph of $y = ax^2 + bx + c$
$b^2 - 4ac > 0$	**Two unequal real solutions;** if $a, b,$ and c are rational numbers and the discriminant is a perfect square, the solutions are rational. If the discriminant is not a perfect square, the solutions are irrational.	Two x-intercepts
$b^2 - 4ac = 0$	**One solution(a repeated solution) that is a real number;** If $a, b,$ and c are rational numbers, the repeated solution is also a rational number.	One x-intercepts
$b^2 - 4ac < 0$	**No real solution; two complex imaginary solutions;** The solutions are complex conjugates.	No x-intercepts

EXAMPLE 7   Using the Discriminant

Compute the discriminant of $4x^2 - 8x + 1 = 0$. What does the discriminant indicate about the number and type of solutions?

Solution   Begin by identifying the values for $a, b,$ and c.

$$4x^2 - 8x + 1 = 0$$

$a = 4$ $b = -8$ $c = 1$

Substitute and compute the discriminant:

$$b^2 - 4ac = (-8)^2 - 4 \cdot 4 \cdot 1 = 64 - 16 = 48.$$

The discriminant is 48. Because the discriminant is positive, the equation $4x^2 - 8x + 1 = 0$ has two unequal real solutions.

Compute the discriminant of $3x^2 - 2x + 5 = 0$. What does the discriminant indicate about the number and type of solutions?

6 Determine the most efficient method to use when solving a quadratic equation.

Determining Which Method to Use

All quadratic equations can be solved by the quadratic formula. However, if an equation is in the form $u^2 = d$, such as $x^2 = 5$ or $(2x + 3)^2 = 8$, it is faster to use the square root method, taking the square root of both sides. If the equation is not in the form $u^2 = d$, write the quadratic equation in general form $(ax^2 + bx + c = 0)$. Try to solve the equation by the factoring method. If $ax^2 + bx + c$ cannot be factored, then solve the quadratic equation by the quadratic formula.

Because we used the method of completing the square to derive the quadratic formula, we no longer need it for solving quadratic equations. However, we will use completing the square later in the book to help graph certain kinds of equations.

Table 1.4 summarizes our observations about which technique to use when solving a quadratic equation.

Table 1.4   Determining the Most Efficient Technique to Use When Solving a Quadratic Equation

Description and Form of the Quadratic Equation	Most Efficient Solution Method	Example
$ax^2 + bx + c = 0$ and $ax^2 + bx + c$ can be factored easily.	Factor and use the zero-product principle.	$3x^2 + 5x - 2 = 0$ $(3x - 1)(x + 2) = 0$ $3x - 1 = 0$ or $x + 2 = 0$ $x = \dfrac{1}{3}$ $x = -2$
$ax^2 + c = 0$ The quadratic equation has no x-term. $(b = 0)$	Solve for x^2 and apply the square root method.	$4x^2 - 7 = 0$ $4x^2 = 7$ $x^2 = \dfrac{7}{4}$ $x = \pm\dfrac{\sqrt{7}}{2}$
$(ax + c)^2 = d$; $ax + c$ is a first-degree polynomial.	Use the square root method.	$(x + 4)^2 = 5$ $x + 4 = \pm\sqrt{5}$ $x = -4 \pm \sqrt{5}$
$ax^2 + bx + c = 0$ and $ax^2 + bx + c$ cannot be factored or the factoring is too difficult.	Use the quadratic formula: $$x = \dfrac{-b \pm \sqrt{b^2 - 4ac}}{2a}.$$	$x^2 - 2x - 6 = 0$ $a = 1$ $b = -2$ $c = -6$ $x = \dfrac{-(-2) \pm \sqrt{(-2)^2 - 4(1)(-6)}}{2(1)}$ $= \dfrac{2 \pm \sqrt{4 - 4(1)(-6)}}{2(1)}$ $= \dfrac{2 \pm \sqrt{28}}{2} = \dfrac{2 \pm \sqrt{4}\sqrt{7}}{2}$ $= \dfrac{2 \pm 2\sqrt{7}}{2} = \dfrac{2(1 \pm \sqrt{7})}{2}$ $= 1 \pm \sqrt{7}$

7 Solve problems modeled by quadratic equations.

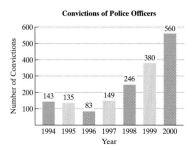

Convictions of Police Officers

Figure 1.14, repeated

Source: F.B.I.

Applications

We opened this section with a graph (Figure 1.14, repeated in the margin) showing the number of convictions of police officers throughout the United States from 1994 through 2000. The data can be modeled by the formula

$$N = 23.4x^2 - 259.1x + 815.8$$

where N is the number of police officers convicted of felonies x years after 1990. Notice that this formula contains an expression in the form $ax^2 + bx + c$ on the right side. If a formula contains such an expression, we can write and solve a quadratic equation to answer questions about the variable x. Our next example shows how this is done.

EXAMPLE 8 Convictions of Police Officers

Use the formula $N = 23.4x^2 - 259.1x + 815.8$ to answer this question: In which year will 1000 police officers be convicted of felonies?

Solution   Because we are interested in 1000 convictions, we substitute 1000 for N in the given formula. Then we solve for x, the number of years after 1990.

$N = 23.4x^2 - 259.1x + 815.8$ This is the given formula.

$1000 = 23.4x^2 - 259.1x + 815.8$ Substitute 1000 for N.

$0 = 23.4x^2 - 259.1x - 184.2$ Subtract 1000 from both sides and write the quadratic equation in general form.

$a = 23.4$ $b = -259.1$ $c = -184.2$

Because the trinomial on the right side of the equation is prime, we solve using the quadratic formula.

$$x = \frac{-b \pm \sqrt{b^2 - 4ac}}{2a}$$ Use the quadratic formula.

$$= \frac{-(-259.1) \pm \sqrt{(-259.1)^2 - 4(23.4)(-184.2)}}{2(23.4)}$$ Substitute the values for a, b, and c: a = 23.4, b = −259.1, c = −184.2.

$$= \frac{259.1 \pm \sqrt{84{,}373.93}}{46.8}$$ Use a calculator to simplify the radicand.

Thus,

$$x = \frac{259.1 + \sqrt{84{,}373.93}}{46.8} \quad \text{or} \quad x = \frac{259.1 - \sqrt{84{,}373.93}}{46.8}$$

$$x \approx 12 \qquad\qquad\qquad x \approx -1$$ Use a calculator and round to the nearest integer.

The model describes the number of convictions x years *after* 1990. Thus, we are interested only in the positive solution, 12. This means that approximately 12 years after 1990, in 2002, 1000 police officers will be convicted of felonies.

Technology

On most calculators, here is how to approximate

$$\frac{259.1 + \sqrt{84{,}373.93}}{46.8}:$$

Many Scientific Calculators

(259.1 + 84373.93 √

) ÷ 46.8 =

Many Graphing Calculators

(259.1 + √ 84373.93

) ÷ 46.8 ENTER.

Similar keystrokes can be used to approximate the other irrational solution in Example 8.

Check Point 8   Use the formula in Example 8 to answer this question: In which year after 1993 were 250 police officers convicted of felonies? How well does the formula model the actual number of convictions for that year shown in Figure 1.14?

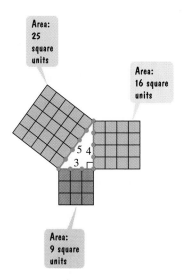

Area:
25 square units

Area:
16 square units

5 4
3

Area:
9 square units

Figure 1.16 The area of the large square equals the sum of the areas of the smaller squares.

In our next example, we will be using the *Pythagorean Theorem* to obtain a verbal model. The ancient Greek philosopher and mathematician Pythagoras (approximately 582–500 B.C.) founded a school whose motto was "All is number." Pythagoras is best remembered for his work with the **right triangle,** a triangle with one angle measuring 90°. The side opposite the 90° angle is called the **hypotenuse.** The other sides are called **legs.** Pythagoras found that if he constructed squares on each of the legs, as well as a larger square on the hypotenuse, the sum of the areas of the smaller squares is equal to the area of the larger square. This is illustrated in Figure 1.16.

This relationship is usually stated in terms of the lengths of the three sides of a right triangle and is called the **Pythagorean Theorem.**

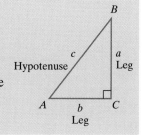

The Pythagorean Theorem

The sum of the squares of the lengths of the legs of a right triangle equals the square of the length of the hypotenuse.

If the legs have lengths a and b, and the hypotenuse has length c, then

$$a^2 + b^2 = c^2.$$

EXAMPLE 9 Using the Pythagorean Theorem

In a 25-inch television set, the length of the screen's diagonal is 25 inches. If the screen's height is 15 inches, what is its width?

Solution   Figure 1.17 shows a right triangle that is formed by the height, width, and diagonal. We can find w, the screen's width, using the Pythagorean Theorem.

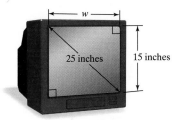

w

25 inches   15 inches

Figure 1.17 A right triangle is formed by the television's height, width, and diagonal.

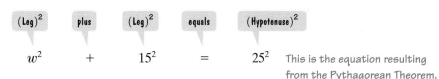

$(\text{Leg})^2$	plus	$(\text{Leg})^2$	equals	$(\text{Hypotenuse})^2$	
w^2	$+$	15^2	$=$	25^2	This is the equation resulting from the Pythagorean Theorem.

The equation $w^2 + 15^2 = 25^2$ can be solved most efficiently by the square root method.

$$w^2 + 15^2 = 25^2 \qquad \text{This is the equation that models the verbal conditions.}$$

$$w^2 + 225 = 625 \qquad \text{Square 15 and 25.}$$

$$w^2 + 225 - 225 = 625 - 225 \qquad \text{Isolate } w^2 \text{ by subtracting 225 from both sides.}$$

$$w^2 = 400 \qquad \text{Simplify.}$$

$$w = \pm\sqrt{400} \qquad \text{Apply the square root method.}$$

$$w = \pm 20 \qquad \text{Simplify.}$$

Because w represents the width of the television's screen, this dimension must be positive. We reject -20. Thus, the width of the television is 20 inches.

Check Point 9   What is the width in a 15-inch television set whose height is 9 inches?

EXERCISE SET 1.5

Practice Exercises

Solve each equation in Exercises 1–14 by factoring.

1. $x^2 - 3x - 10 = 0$ **2.** $x^2 - 13x + 36 = 0$

3. $x^2 = 8x - 15$ **4.** $x^2 = -11x - 10$

5. $6x^2 + 11x - 10 = 0$ **6.** $9x^2 + 9x + 2 = 0$

7. $3x^2 - 2x = 8$ **8.** $4x^2 - 13x = -3$

9. $3x^2 + 12x = 0$ **10.** $5x^2 - 20x = 0$

11. $2x(x - 3) = 5x^2 - 7x$ **12.** $16x(x - 2) = 8x - 25$

13. $7 - 7x = (3x + 2)(x - 1)$

14. $10x - 1 = (2x + 1)^2$

Solve each equation in Exercises 15–26 by the square root method.

15. $3x^2 = 27$ **16.** $5x^2 = 45$

17. $5x^2 + 1 = 51$ **18.** $3x^2 - 1 = 47$

19. $(x + 2)^2 = 25$ **20.** $(x - 3)^2 = 36$

21. $(3x + 2)^2 = 9$ **22.** $(4x - 1)^2 = 16$

23. $(5x - 1)^2 = 7$ **24.** $(8x - 3)^2 = 5$

25. $(3x - 4)^2 = 8$ **26.** $(2x + 8)^2 = 27$

In Exercises 27–38, determine the constant that should be added to the binomial so that it becomes a perfect square trinomial. Then write and factor the trinomial.

27. $x^2 + 12x$ **28.** $x^2 + 16x$

29. $x^2 - 10x$ **30.** $x^2 - 14x$

31. $x^2 + 3x$ **32.** $x^2 + 5x$

33. $x^2 - 7x$ **34.** $x^2 - 9x$

35. $x^2 - \frac{2}{3}x$ **36.** $x^2 + \frac{4}{5}x$

37. $x^2 - \frac{1}{3}x$ **38.** $x^2 - \frac{1}{4}x$

Solve each equation in Exercises 39–54 by completing the square.

39. $x^2 + 6x = 7$ **40.** $x^2 + 6x = -8$

41. $x^2 - 2x = 2$ **42.** $x^2 + 4x = 12$

43. $x^2 - 6x - 11 = 0$ **44.** $x^2 - 2x - 5 = 0$

45. $x^2 + 4x + 1 = 0$ **46.** $x^2 + 6x - 5 = 0$

47. $x^2 + 3x - 1 = 0$ **48.** $x^2 - 3x - 5 = 0$

49. $2x^2 - 7x + 3 = 0$ **50.** $2x^2 + 5x - 3 = 0$

51. $4x^2 - 4x - 1 = 0$ **52.** $2x^2 - 4x - 1 = 0$

53. $3x^2 - 2x - 2 = 0$ **54.** $3x^2 - 5x - 10 = 0$

Solve each equation in Exercises 55–64 using the quadratic formula.

55. $x^2 + 8x + 15 = 0$ **56.** $x^2 + 8x + 12 = 0$

57. $x^2 + 5x + 3 = 0$ **58.** $x^2 + 5x + 2 = 0$

59. $3x^2 - 3x - 4 = 0$ **60.** $5x^2 + x - 2 = 0$

61. $4x^2 = 2x + 7$ **62.** $3x^2 = 6x - 1$

63. $x^2 - 6x + 10 = 0$ **64.** $x^2 - 2x + 17 = 0$

Compute the discriminant of each equation in Exercises 65–72. What does the discriminant indicate about the number and type of solutions?

65. $x^2 - 4x - 5 = 0$ **66.** $4x^2 - 2x + 3 = 0$

67. $2x^2 - 11x + 3 = 0$ **68.** $2x^2 + 11x - 6 = 0$

69. $x^2 - 2x + 1 = 0$ **70.** $3x^2 = 2x - 1$

71. $x^2 - 3x - 7 = 0$ **72.** $3x^2 + 4x - 2 = 0$

Solve each equation in Exercises 73–98 by the method of your choice.

73. $2x^2 - x = 1$ **74.** $3x^2 - 4x = 4$

75. $5x^2 + 2 = 11x$ **76.** $5x^2 = 6 - 13x$

77. $3x^2 = 60$ **78.** $2x^2 = 250$

79. $x^2 - 2x = 1$ **80.** $2x^2 + 3x = 1$

81. $(2x + 3)(x + 4) = 1$ **82.** $(2x - 5)(x + 1) = 2$

83. $(3x - 4)^2 = 16$ **84.** $(2x + 7)^2 = 25$

85. $3x^2 - 12x + 12 = 0$ **86.** $9 - 6x + x^2 = 0$

87. $4x^2 - 16 = 0$ **88.** $3x^2 - 27 = 0$

89. $x^2 - 6x + 13 = 0$ **90.** $x^2 - 4x + 29 = 0$

91. $x^2 = 4x - 7$ **92.** $5x^2 = 2x - 3$

93. $2x^2 - 7x = 0$ **94.** $2x^2 + 5x = 3$

95. $\frac{1}{x} + \frac{1}{x + 2} = \frac{1}{3}$ **96.** $\frac{1}{x} + \frac{1}{x + 3} = \frac{1}{4}$

97. $\frac{2x}{x - 3} + \frac{6}{x + 3} = -\frac{28}{x^2 - 9}$

98. $\frac{3}{x - 3} + \frac{5}{x - 4} = \frac{x^2 - 20}{x^2 - 7x + 12}$

Application Exercises

A driver's age has something to do with his or her chance of getting into a fatal car crash. The bar graph shows the number of fatal vehicle crashes per 100 million miles driven for drivers of various age groups. For example, 25-year-old drivers are involved in 4.1 fatal crashes per 100 million miles driven. Thus, when a group of 25-year-old Americans have driven a total of 100 million miles, approximately 4 have been in accidents in which someone died.

Source: Insurance Institute for Highway Safety

The number of fatal vehicle crashes per 100 million miles, N, for drivers of age x can be modeled by the formula

$$N = 0.013x^2 - 1.19x + 28.24.$$

Use the formula to solve Exercises 99–100.

99. What age groups are expected to be involved in 10 fatal crashes per 100 million miles driven? How well does the formula model the trend in the actual data shown in the bar graph?

100. What age groups are expected to be involved in 3 fatal crashes per 100 million miles driven? How well does the formula model the trend in the actual data shown in the bar graph?

The Food Stamp Program is America's first line of defense against hunger for millions of families. Over half of all participants are children; one out of six is a low-income older adult. Exercises 101–104 involve the number of participants in the program from 1990 through 2000. The formula

$$y = -\frac{1}{2}x^2 + 4x + 19$$

models the number of people, y, in millions, receiving food stamps x years after 1990. Use the formula to solve Exercises 101–102.

101. In which year did 27 million people receive food stamps?

102. In which years did 19 million people receive food stamps?

The graph of the formula in Exercises 101–102 is shown. Use the graph to solve Exercises 103–104.

Number of People Receiving Food Stamps

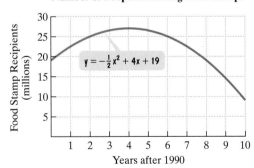

Source: New York Times

103. Identify your solution in Exercise 101 as a point on the graph. Describe what is significant about this point.

104. Identify your solution in Exercise 102 as one or more points on the graph. Then describe the trend shown by the graph.

The formula

$$N = 2x^2 + 22x + 320$$

models the number of inmates, N, in thousands, in U.S. state and federal prisons x years after 1980. The graph of the formula is shown in a [0, 20, 1] by [0, 1600, 100] viewing rectangle at the top of the next column. Use the formula to solve Exercises 105–106.

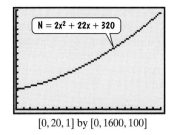

$[0, 20, 1]$ by $[0, 1600, 100]$

105. In which year were there 740 thousand inmates in U.S. state and federal prisons? Identify the solution as a point on the graph shown.

106. In which year were 1100 thousand inmates in U.S. state and federal prisons? Identify the solution as a point on the graph shown?

107. A baseball diamond is actually a square with 90-foot sides. What is the distance from home plate to second base?

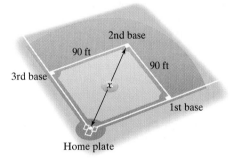

108. A 20-foot ladder is 15 feet from the house. How far up the house does the ladder reach?

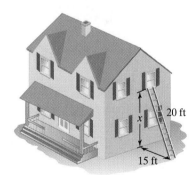

109. An 8-foot tree is supported by two wires that extend from the top of the tree to a point on the ground located 15 feet from the base of the tree. Find the total length of the two support wires.

110. A vertical pole is supported by three wires. Each wire is 13 yards long and is anchored 5 yards from the base of the pole. How far up the pole will the wires be attached?

111. The length of a rectangular garden is 5 feet greater than the width. The area of the garden is 300 square feet. Find the length and the width.

112. A rectangular parking lot has a length that is 3 yards greater than the width. The area of the rectangular lot is 180 square yards. Find the length and the width.

113. A machine produces open boxes using square sheets of metal. The figure illustrates that the machine cuts equal-sized squares measuring 2 inches on a side from the corners and then shapes the metal into an open box by turning up the sides. If each box must have a volume of 200 cubic inches, find the length of the side of the open square-bottom box.

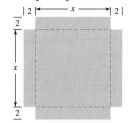

114. A machine produces open boxes using square sheets of metal. The machine cuts equal-sized squares measuring 3 inches on a side from the corners and then shapes the metal into an open box by turning up the sides. If each box must have a volume of 75 cubic inches, find the length of the side of the open square-bottom box.

115. A rain gutter is made from sheets of aluminum that are 20 inches wide. As shown in the figure, the edges are turned up to form right angles. Determine the depth of the gutter that will allow a cross-sectional area of 13 square inches. Show that there are two different solutions to the problem. Round to the nearest tenth of an inch.

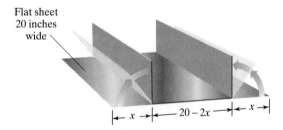

116. A piece of wire is 8 inches long. The wire is cut into two pieces and then each piece is bent into a square. Find the length of each piece if the sum of the areas of these squares is to be 2 square inches.

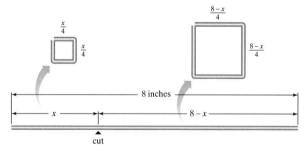

117. A painting measuring 10 inches by 16 inches is surrounded by a frame of uniform width. If the combined area of the painting and the frame is 280 square inches, determine the width of the frame.

Writing in Mathematics

118. What is a quadratic equation?

119. Explain how to solve $x^2 + 6x + 8 = 0$ using factoring and the zero-product principle.

120. Explain how to solve $x^2 + 6x + 8 = 0$ by completing the square.

121. Explain how to solve $x^2 + 6x + 8 = 0$ using the quadratic formula.

122. How is the quadratic formula derived?

123. What is the discriminant and what information does it provide about a quadratic equation?

124. If you are given a quadratic equation, how do you determine which method to use to solve it?

125. If $(x + 2)(x - 4) = 0$ indicates that $x + 2 = 0$ or $x - 4 = 0$, explain why $(x + 2)(x - 4) = 6$ does not mean $x + 2 = 6$ or $x - 4 = 6$. Could we solve the equation using $x + 2 = 3$ and $x - 4 = 2$ because $3 \cdot 2 = 6$?

126. Describe the trend shown by the data for the convictions of police officers in the graph in Figure 1.14 on page 114. Do you believe that this trend is likely to continue or might something occur that would make it impossible to extend the model into the future? Explain your answer.

Technology Exercises

127. If you have access to a calculator that solves quadratic equations, consult the owner's manual to determine how to use this feature. Then use your calculator to solve any five of the equations in Exercises 55–64.

128. Use a graphing utility and x-intercepts to verify any of the real solutions that you obtained for three of the quadratic equations in Exercises 55–64.

Critical Thinking Exercises

129. Which one of the following is true?
  a. The equation $(2x - 3)^2 = 25$ is equivalent to $2x - 3 = 5$.
  b. Every quadratic equation has two distinct numbers in its solution set.
  c. A quadratic equation whose coefficients are real numbers can never have a solution set containing one real number and one complex nonreal number.
  d. The equation $ax^2 + c = 0$ cannot be solved by the quadratic formula.

130. Solve the equation: $x^2 + 2\sqrt{3}x - 9 = 0$.

131. Write a quadratic equation in general form whose solution set is $\{-3, 5\}$.

132. A person throws a rock upward from the edge of an 80-foot cliff. The height, h, in feet, of the rock above the water at the bottom of the cliff after t seconds is described by the formula

$$h = -16t^2 + 64t + 80.$$

How long will it take for the rock to reach the water?

133. A rectangular swimming pool is 12 meters long and 8 meters wide. A tile border of uniform width is to be built around the pool using 120 square meters of tile. The tile is from a discontinued stock (so no additional materials are available), and all 120 square meters are to be used. How wide should the border be? Round to the nearest tenth of a meter. If zoning laws require at least a 2-meter-wide border around the pool, can this be done with the available tile?

Group Exercise

134. Each group member should find an "intriguing" algebraic formula that contains an expression in the form $ax^2 + bx + c$ on one side. Consult college algebra books or liberal arts mathematics books to do so. Group members should select four of the formulas. For each formula selected, write and solve a problem similar to Exercises 99–102 in this exercise set.

SECTION 1.6 *Other Types of Equations*

Objectives

1. Solve polynomial equations by factoring.
2. Solve radical equations.
3. Solve equations with rational exponents.
4. Solve equations that are quadratic in form.
5. Solve equations involving absolute value.

Marine iguanas of the Galápagos Islands

The Galápagos Islands are a volcanic chain of islands lying 600 miles west of Ecuador. They are famed for their extraordinary wildlife, which includes a rare flightless cormorant, marine iguanas, and giant tortoises weighing more than 600 pounds. It was here that naturalist Charles Darwin began to formulate his theory of evolution. Darwin made an enormous collection of the islands' plant species. The formula

$$S = 28.5\sqrt[3]{x}$$

describes the number of plant species, S, on the various islands of the Galápagos chain in terms of the area, x, in square miles, of a particular island.

How can we find the area of a Galápagos island with 57 species of plants? Substitute 57 for S in the formula and solve for x:

$$57 = 28.5\sqrt[3]{x}.$$

The resulting equation contains a variable in the radicand and is called a *radical equation*. In this section, in addition to radical equations, we will show you how to solve certain kinds of polynomial equations, equations involving rational exponents, and equations involving absolute value.

1 Solve polynomial equations by factoring.

Polynomial Equations

The linear and quadratic equations that we studied in the first part of this chapter can be thought of as polynomial equations of degrees 1 and 2, respectively. By contrast, consider the following polynomial equations of degree greater than 2:

$$3x^4 = 27x^2 \qquad\qquad x^3 + x^2 = 4x + 4$$

This equation is of degree 4 because 4 is the largest exponent.

This equation is of degree 3 because 3 is the largest exponent.

We can solve these equations by moving all terms to one side, thereby obtaining zero on the other side. We then use factoring and the zero-product principle.

EXAMPLE 1 Solving a Polynomial Equation by Factoring

Solve by factoring: $3x^4 = 27x^2$.

Solution

Step 1 Move all terms to one side and obtain zero on the other side. Subtract $27x^2$ from both sides.

$$3x^4 = 27x^2 \qquad \text{This is the given equation.}$$
$$3x^4 - 27x^2 = 27x^2 - 27x^2 \qquad \text{Subtract } 27x^2 \text{ from both sides.}$$
$$3x^4 - 27x^2 = 0 \qquad \text{Simplify.}$$

Step 2 Factor. We can factor $3x^2$ from each term.

$$3x^4 - 27x^2 = 0$$
$$3x^2(x^2 - 9) = 0$$

Study Tip

In solving $3x^4 = 27x^2$, be careful not to divide both sides by x^2. If you do, you'll lose 0 as a solution. In general, do not divide both sides of an equation by a variable because that variable might take on the value 0 and you cannot divide by 0.

Steps 3 and 4 Set each factor equal to zero and solve the resulting equations.

$$3x^2 = 0 \qquad \text{or} \qquad x^2 - 9 = 0$$
$$x^2 = 0 \qquad\qquad\qquad x^2 = 9$$
$$x = \pm\sqrt{0} \qquad\qquad\qquad x = \pm\sqrt{9}$$
$$x = 0 \qquad\qquad\qquad\qquad x = \pm 3$$

Step 5 Check the solutions in the original equation. Check the three solutions, $0, -3$, and 3, by substituting them into the original equation. Can you verify that the solution set is $\{-3, 0, 3\}$?

Check Point 1 Solve by factoring: $4x^4 = 12x^2$.

EXAMPLE 2 **Solving a Polynomial Equation by Factoring**

Solve by factoring: $x^3 + x^2 = 4x + 4$.

Solution

Step 1 **Move all terms to one side and obtain zero on the other side.** Subtract $4x$ and subtract 4 from both sides.

$$x^3 + x^2 = 4x + 4 \qquad \text{This is the given equation.}$$

$$x^3 + x^2 - 4x - 4 = 4x + 4 - 4x - 4 \qquad \text{Subtract 4x and 4 from both sides.}$$

$$x^3 + x^2 - 4x - 4 = 0 \qquad \text{Simplify.}$$

Step 2 **Factor.** Because there are four terms, we use factoring by grouping. Group terms that have a common factor.

$$\boxed{x^3 + x^2} + \boxed{-4x - 4} = 0$$

Common factor is x^2.　　Common factor is -4.

$$x^2(x + 1) - 4(x + 1) = 0 \qquad \text{Factor } x^2 \text{ from the first two terms and } -4 \text{ from the last two terms.}$$

$$(x + 1)(x^2 - 4) = 0 \qquad \text{Factor out the common binomial, } x + 1, \text{ from each term.}$$

Steps 3 and 4 **Set each factor equal to zero and solve the resulting equations.**

$$x + 1 = 0 \qquad \text{or} \qquad x^2 - 4 = 0$$
$$x = -1 \qquad\qquad x^2 = 4$$
$$x = \pm\sqrt{4} = \pm 2$$

Step 5 **Check the solutions in the original equation.** Check the three solutions, $-1, -2,$ and $2,$ by substituting them into the original equation. Can you verify that the solution set is $\{-2, -1, 2\}$?

Technology

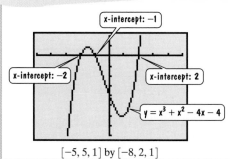

$[-5, 5, 1]$ by $[-8, 2, 1]$

You can use a graphing utility to check the solutions of $x^3 + x^2 - 4x - 4 = 0$. Graph $y = x^3 + x^2 - 4x - 4$, as shown on the left. The x-intercepts are $-2, -1,$ and $2,$ corresponding to the equation's solutions.

Check Point 2 Solve by factoring: $2x^3 + 3x^2 = 8x + 12$.

2 Solve radical equations.

Equations Involving Radicals

A **radical equation** is an equation in which the variable occurs in a square root, cube root, or any higher root. An example of a radical equation is

$$28.5\sqrt[3]{x} = 57.$$

The variable occurs in a cube root.

The equation $28.5\sqrt[3]{x} = 57$ can be used to find the area, x, in square miles, of a Galápagos island with 57 species of plants. First, we isolate the radical by dividing both sides of the equation by 28.5.

$$\frac{28.5\sqrt[3]{x}}{28.5} = \frac{57}{28.5}$$
$$\sqrt[3]{x} = 2$$

Next, we eliminate the radical by raising each side of the equation to a power equal to the index of the radical. Because the index is 3, we cube both sides of the equation.

$$\left(\sqrt[3]{x}\right)^3 = 2^3$$
$$x = 8$$

Thus, a Galápagos island with 57 species of plants has an area of 8 square miles.

The Galápagos equation shows that solving equations involving radicals involves raising both sides of the equation to a power equal to the radicals index. All solutions of the original equation are also solutions of the resulting equation. However, the resulting equation may have some extra solutions that do not satisfy the original equation. Because the resulting equation may not be equivalent to the original equation, we must check each proposed solution by substituting it into the original equation. Let's see exactly how this works.

Study Tip

Be sure to square *both sides* of an equation. Do *not* square each term.

Correct:
$$\left(\sqrt{26-11}\right)^2 = (4-x)^2$$

Incorrect:
$$\left(\sqrt{26-11}\right)^2 = 4^2 - x^2$$

Technology

The graph of
$$y = x + \sqrt{26-11x} - 4$$
is shown in a $[-10, 3, 1]$ by $[-4, 3, 1]$ viewing rectangle. The x-intercepts are -5 and 2, verifying $\{-5, 2\}$ as the solution set of
$$x + \sqrt{26-11x} = 4.$$

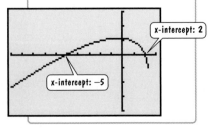

EXAMPLE 3 Solving an Equation Involving a Radical

Solve: $x + \sqrt{26 - 11x} = 4$.

Solution To solve this equation, we isolate the radical expression $\sqrt{26 - 11x}$ on one side of the equation. By squaring both sides of the equation, we can then eliminate the square root.

$$x + \sqrt{26 - 11x} = 4 \qquad \text{This is the given equation.}$$
$$x + \sqrt{26 - 11x} - x = 4 - x \qquad \text{Isolate the radical by subtracting } x \text{ from both sides.}$$
$$\sqrt{26 - 11x} = 4 - x \qquad \text{Simplify.}$$
$$\left(\sqrt{26 - 11x}\right)^2 = (4 - x)^2 \qquad \text{Square both sides.}$$
$$26 - 11x = 16 - 8x + x^2 \qquad \text{Use } (A - B)^2 = A^2 - 2AB + B^2 \text{ to square } 4 - x.$$

Next, we need to write this quadratic equation in general form. We can obtain zero on the left side by subtracting 26 and adding $11x$ on both sides.

$$26 - 26 - 11x + 11x = 16 - 26 - 8x + 11x + x^2$$
$$0 = x^2 + 3x - 10 \qquad \text{Simplify.}$$
$$0 = (x + 5)(x - 2) \qquad \text{Factor.}$$
$$x + 5 = 0 \quad \text{or} \quad x - 2 = 0 \qquad \text{Set each factor equal to zero.}$$
$$x = -5 \qquad\qquad x = 2 \qquad \text{Solve for x.}$$

We have not completed the solution process. Although -5 and 2 satisfy the squared equation, there is no guarantee that they satisfy the original equation. Thus, we must check the proposed solutions. We can do this using a graphing utility (see the technology box in the margin) or by substituting both proposed solutions into the given equation.

$$\textbf{CHECK } -5:$$
$$x + \sqrt{26 - 11x} = 4$$
$$-5 + \sqrt{26 - 11(-5)} \overset{?}{=} 4$$
$$-5 + \sqrt{81} \overset{?}{=} 4$$
$$-5 + 9 \overset{?}{=} 4$$
$$4 = 4 \checkmark$$

$$\textbf{CHECK } 2:$$
$$x + \sqrt{26 - 11x} = 4$$
$$2 + \sqrt{26 - 11 \cdot 2} \overset{?}{=} 4$$
$$2 + \sqrt{4} \overset{?}{=} 4$$
$$2 + 2 \overset{?}{=} 4$$
$$4 = 4 \checkmark$$

The solution set is $\{-5, 2\}$.

Check Point 3   Solve and check: $\sqrt{6x + 7} - x = 2$.

When solving a radical equation, extra solutions may be introduced when you raise both sides of the equation to an even power. Such solutions, which are not solutions of the given equation, are called **extraneous solutions.**
    The solution of radical equations with two or more square root expressions involves isolating a radical, squaring both sides, and then repeating this process. Let's consider an equation containing two square root expressions.

Study Tip

When solving equations by raising both sides to an even power, don't forget to check for extraneous solutions. Here is a simple example:

$x = 4$

$x^2 = 16$ Square both sides.

$x = \pm\sqrt{16}$ Use the square root method.

$x = \pm 4.$

However, -4 does not check in $x = 4$. Thus, -4 is an extraneous solution.

EXAMPLE 4   Solving an Equation Involving Two Radicals

Solve: $\sqrt{3x + 1} - \sqrt{x + 4} = 1$.

Solution

$$\sqrt{3x + 1} - \sqrt{x + 4} = 1 \qquad \text{This is the given equation.}$$

$$\sqrt{3x + 1} = \sqrt{x + 4} + 1 \qquad \begin{array}{l}\text{Isolate one of the radicals by} \\ \text{adding } \sqrt{x + 4} \text{ to both sides.}\end{array}$$

$$\left(\sqrt{3x + 1}\right)^2 = \left(\sqrt{x + 4} + 1\right)^2 \quad \text{Square both sides.}$$

Squaring the expression on the right side of the equation can be a bit tricky. We need to use the formula

$$(A + B)^2 = A^2 + 2AB + B^2.$$

Focusing on just the right side, here is how the squaring is done:

$$\underset{(A + B)^2}{} = \underset{A^2}{} + \underset{2}{} \cdot \underset{A}{} \cdot \underset{B}{} + \underset{B^2}{}$$

$$\left(\sqrt{x + 4} + 1\right)^2 = \left(\sqrt{x + 4}\right)^2 + 2 \cdot \sqrt{x + 4} \cdot 1 + 1^2.$$

This simplifies to $x + 4 + 2\sqrt{x + 4} + 1$. Thus, our equation $\left(\sqrt{3x + 1}\right)^2 = \left(\sqrt{x + 4} + 1\right)^2$ can be written as follows:

$$3x + 1 = x + 4 + 2\sqrt{x + 4} + 1.$$

$$3x + 1 = x + 5 + 2\sqrt{x + 4} \qquad \text{Combine numerical terms on the right.}$$

$$2x - 4 = 2\sqrt{x + 4} \qquad \begin{array}{l}\text{Isolate } 2\sqrt{x + 4}, \text{ the radical term, by} \\ \text{subtracting } x + 5 \text{ from both sides.}\end{array}$$

$$(2x - 4)^2 = \left(2\sqrt{x + 4}\right)^2 \qquad \text{Square both sides.}$$

Discovery

Divide each side of
$$2x - 4 = 2\sqrt{x + 4}$$
by 2 before squaring both sides. Solve the resulting equation. How does your solution compare to the one shown?

$$4x^2 - 16x + 16 = 4(x + 4)$$ Use $(A - B)^2 = A^2 - 2AB + B^2$ to square the left side. Use $(AB)^2 = A^2B^2$ to square the right side.

$$4x^2 - 16x + 16 = 4x + 16$$ Use the distributive property.

$$4x^2 - 20x = 0$$ Write the quadratic equation in general form by subtracting $4x + 16$ from both sides.

$$4x(x - 5) = 0$$ Factor.

$$4x = 0 \quad \text{or} \quad x - 5 = 0$$ Set each factor equal to zero.

$$x = 0 \qquad\qquad x = 5$$ Solve for x.

Technology

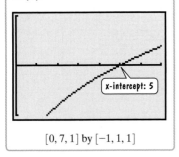

The graph of
$$y = \sqrt{3x + 1} - \sqrt{x + 4} - 1$$
has only one x-intercept at 5. This verifies that the solution set of $\sqrt{3x + 1} - \sqrt{x + 4} = 1$ is {5}.

[0, 7, 1] by [−1, 1, 1]

Complete the solution process by checking both proposed solutions. We can do this using a graphing utility (see the technology box in the margin) or by substituting both proposed solutions in the given equation.

Check 0:

$$\sqrt{3x + 1} - \sqrt{x + 4} = 1$$
$$\sqrt{3 \cdot 0 + 1} - \sqrt{0 + 4} \stackrel{?}{=} 1$$
$$\sqrt{1} - \sqrt{4} \stackrel{?}{=} 1$$
$$1 - 2 \stackrel{?}{=} 1$$
$$-1 = 1 \quad \text{False}$$

Check 5:

$$\sqrt{3x + 1} - \sqrt{x + 4} = 1$$
$$\sqrt{3 \cdot 5 + 1} - \sqrt{5 + 4} \stackrel{?}{=} 1$$
$$\sqrt{16} - \sqrt{9} \stackrel{?}{=} 1$$
$$4 - 3 \stackrel{?}{=} 1$$
$$1 = 1 \quad \checkmark$$

The false statement $-1 = 1$ indicates that 0 is not a solution. It is an extraneous solution brought about by squaring each side of the equation. The only solution is 5, and the solution set is {5}.

Check Point 4
Solve and check: $\sqrt{x + 5} - \sqrt{x - 3} = 2$.

Radicals and Windchill

The way that we perceive the temperature on a cold day depends on both air temperature and wind speed. The windchill temperature is what the air temperature would have to be with no wind to achieve the same chilling effect on the skin. The formula that describes windchill temperature, W, in terms of the velocity of the wind, v, in miles per hour, and the actual air temperature, t, in degrees Fahrenheit, is

$$W = 91.4 - \frac{(10.5 + 6.7\sqrt{v} - 0.45v)(457 - 5t)}{110}.$$

Use your calculator to describe how cold the air temperature feels (that is, the windchill temperature) when the temperature is 15° Fahrenheit and the wind is 5 miles per hour. Contrast this with a temperature of 40° Fahrenheit and a wind blowing at 50 miles per hour.

3 Solve equations with rational exponents.

Because $\sqrt[n]{b}$ can be expressed as $b^{1/n}$, radical equations can be written using rational exponents. For example, the Galápagos equation

$$28.5\sqrt[3]{x} = 57$$

can be written

$$28.5x^{1/3} = 57.$$

We solve this equation exactly as we did when it was expressed in radical form. First, isolate $x^{1/3}$.

$$\frac{28.5x^{1/3}}{28.5} = \frac{57}{28.5}$$

$$x^{1/3} = 2$$

Complete the solution process by raising both sides to the third power.

$$(x^{1/3})^3 = 2^3$$

$$x = 8$$

Solving Radical Equations of the Form $x^{m/n} = k$

Assume that m and n are positive integers, $\frac{m}{n}$ is in lowest terms, and k is a real number.

1. Isolate the expression with the rational exponent.
2. Raise both sides of the equation to the $\frac{n}{m}$ power.

If m is even:	**If m is odd:**
$x^{m/n} = k$	$x^{m/n} = k$
$(x^{m/n})^{n/m} = \pm k^{n/m}$	$(x^{m/n})^{n/m} = k^{n/m}$
$x = \pm k^{n/m}$	$x = k^{n/m}$

It is incorrect to insert the $\pm$ symbol when the numerator of the exponent is odd. An odd index has only one root.

3. Check all proposed solutions in the original equation to find out if they are actual solutions or extraneous solutions.

EXAMPLE 5 Solving Equations Involving Rational Exponents

Solve:

a. $3x^{3/4} - 6 = 0$ **b.** $x^{2/3} - \frac{3}{4} = -\frac{1}{2}$.

Solution

a. Our goal is to isolate $x^{3/4}$. Then we can raise both sides of the equation to the $\frac{4}{3}$ power because $\frac{4}{3}$ is the reciprocal of $\frac{3}{4}$.

$3x^{3/4} - 6 = 0$ This is the given equation; we will isolate $x^{3/4}$.

$3x^{3/4} = 6$ Add 6 to both sides.

$\frac{3x^{3/4}}{3} = \frac{6}{3}$ Divide both sides by 3.

$x^{3/4} = 2$ Simplify.

$(x^{3/4})^{4/3} = 2^{4/3}$ Raise both sides to the $\frac{4}{3}$ power. Because $\frac{m}{n} = \frac{3}{4}$ and m is odd, we do not use the $\pm$ symbol.

$x = 2^{4/3}$ Simplify the left side: $(x^{3/4})^{4/3} = x^{\frac{3\cdot4}{4\cdot3}} = x^{\frac{12}{12}} = x^1 = x.$

The proposed solution is $2^{4/3}$. Complete the solution process by checking this value in the given equation.

$$3x^{3/4} - 6 = 0 \qquad \text{This is the original equation.}$$
$$3(2^{4/3})^{3/4} - 6 \stackrel{?}{=} 0 \qquad \text{Substitute the proposed solution.}$$
$$3 \cdot 2 - 6 \stackrel{?}{=} 0 \qquad (2^{4/3})^{3/4} = 2^{\frac{4 \cdot 3}{3 \cdot 4}} = 2^{\frac{12}{12}} = 2^1 = 2.$$
$$0 = 0 \checkmark \qquad \text{The true statement shows that } 2^{4/3} \text{ is a solution.}$$

The solution is $2^{4/3} = \sqrt[3]{2^4} \approx 2.52$. The solution set is $\{2^{4/3}\}$.

b. To solve $x^{2/3} - \frac{3}{4} = -\frac{1}{2}$, our goal is to isolate $x^{2/3}$. Then we can raise both sides of the equation to the $\frac{3}{2}$ power because $\frac{3}{2}$ is the reciprocal of $\frac{2}{3}$.

$$x^{2/3} - \frac{3}{4} = -\frac{1}{2} \qquad \text{This is the given equation.}$$
$$x^{2/3} = \frac{1}{4} \qquad \text{Add } \frac{3}{4} \text{ to both sides.}$$
$$(x^{2/3})^{3/2} = \pm\left(\frac{1}{4}\right)^{3/2} \qquad \text{Raise both sides to the } \frac{3}{2} \text{ power. Because } \frac{m}{n} = \frac{2}{3}$$
$$\qquad \text{and } m \text{ is even, the } \pm \text{ symbol is necessary.}$$
$$x = \pm\frac{1}{8} \qquad \left(\frac{1}{4}\right)^{3/2} = \left(\sqrt{\frac{1}{4}}\right)^3 = \left(\frac{1}{2}\right)^3 = \frac{1}{8}$$

Take a moment to verify that the solution set is $\left\{-\frac{1}{8}, \frac{1}{8}\right\}$.

 Check Point 5 Solve and check:

a. $5x^{3/2} - 25 = 0$ **b.** $x^{2/3} - 8 = -4$.

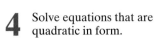 **4** Solve equations that are quadratic in form.

Equations That Are Quadratic in Form

Some equations that are not quadratic can be written as quadratic equations using an appropriate substitution. Here are some examples:

Given Equation	Substitution	New Equation
$x^4 - 8x^2 - 9 = 0$ or $(x^2)^2 - 8x^2 - 9 = 0$	$t = x^2$	$t^2 - 8t - 9 = 0$
$5x^{2/3} + 11x^{1/3} + 2 = 0$ or $5(x^{1/3})^2 + 11x^{1/3} + 2 = 0$	$t = x^{1/3}$	$5t^2 + 11t + 2 = 0$

An equation that is **quadratic in form** is one that can be expressed as a quadratic equation using an appropriate substitution. Both of the preceding given equations are quadratic in form.

Equations that are quadratic in form contain an expression to a power, the same expression to that power squared, and a constant term. By letting t equal the expression to the power, a quadratic equation in t will result. Now it's easy. Solve this quadratic equation for t. Finally, use your substitution to find the values for the variable in the given equation. Example 6 shows how this is done.

EXAMPLE 6 **Solving an Equation Quadratic in Form**

Solve: $x^4 - 8x^2 - 9 = 0$.

Solution Notice that the equation contains an expression to a power, x^2, the same expression to that power squared, x^4 or $(x^2)^2$, and a constant term, -9. We let t equal the expression to the power. Thus,

$$\text{let } t = x^2.$$

Now we write the given equation as a quadratic equation in t and solve for t.

$$x^4 - 8x^2 - 9 = 0 \qquad \text{This is the given equation.}$$
$$(x^2)^2 - 8x^2 - 9 = 0 \qquad \text{The given equation contains } x^2 \text{ and } x^2 \text{ squared.}$$
$$t^2 - 8t - 9 = 0 \qquad \text{Replace } x^2 \text{ with } t.$$
$$(t - 9)(t + 1) = 0 \qquad \text{Factor.}$$
$$t - 9 = 0 \quad \text{or} \quad t + 1 = 0 \qquad \text{Apply the zero-product principle.}$$
$$t = 9 \qquad\qquad t = -1 \qquad \text{Solve for } t.$$

We're not done! Why not? We were asked to solve for x and we have values for t. We use the original substitution, $t = x^2$, to solve for x. Replace t with x^2 in each equation shown, namely $t = 9$ and $t = -1$.

$$x^2 = 9 \qquad\qquad x^2 = -1$$
$$x = \pm\sqrt{9} \qquad\qquad x = \pm\sqrt{-1}$$
$$x = \pm 3 \qquad\qquad x = \pm i$$

The solution set is $\{-3, 3, -i, i\}$.

> **Check Point 6** Solve: $x^4 - 5x^2 + 6 = 0$.

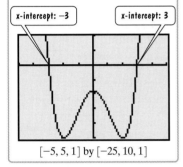
EXAMPLE 7 **Solving an Equation Quadratic in Form**

Solve: $5x^{2/3} + 11x^{1/3} + 2 = 0$.

Solution Notice that the equation contains an expression to a power, $x^{1/3}$, the same expression to that power squared, $x^{2/3}$ or $(x^{1/3})^2$, and a constant term, 2. We let t equal the expression to the power. Thus,

$$\text{let } t = x^{1/3}.$$

Now we write the given equation as a quadratic equation in t and solve for t.

$$5x^{2/3} + 11x^{1/3} + 2 = 0 \qquad \text{This is the given equation.}$$
$$5(x^{1/3})^2 + 11x^{1/3} + 2 = 0 \qquad \text{The given equation contains } x^{1/3} \text{ and } x^{1/3} \text{ squared.}$$
$$5t^2 + 11t + 2 = 0 \qquad \text{Replace } x^{1/3} \text{ with } t.$$
$$(5t + 1)(t + 2) = 0 \qquad \text{Factor.}$$
$$5t + 1 = 0 \quad \text{or} \quad t + 2 = 0 \qquad \text{Set each factor equal to 0.}$$
$$5t = -1 \qquad\qquad t = -2 \qquad \text{Solve for } t.$$
$$t = -\frac{1}{5}$$

Use the original substitution, $t = x^{1/3}$, to solve for x. Replace t with $x^{1/3}$ in each of the preceding equations, namely $t = -\frac{1}{5}$ and $t = -2$.

$$x^{1/3} = -\frac{1}{5} \qquad\qquad x^{1/3} = -2 \qquad \text{Replace } t \text{ with } x^{1/3}.$$

$$\left(x^{1/3}\right)^3 = \left(-\frac{1}{5}\right)^3 \qquad \left(x^{1/3}\right)^3 = (-2)^3 \qquad \text{Solve for } x \text{ by cubing both sides of each equation.}$$

$$x = -\frac{1}{125} \qquad\qquad x = -8$$

Check these values to verify that the solution set is $\{-\frac{1}{125}, -8\}$.

Check Point 7 Solve: $3x^{2/3} - 11x^{1/3} - 4 = 0$.

5 Solve equations involving absolute value.

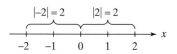

Figure 1.18 If $|x| = 2$, then $x = 2$ or $x = -2$.

Equations Involving Absolute Value

We have seen that the absolute value of x, $|x|$, describes the distance of x from zero on a number line. Now consider **absolute value equations,** such as

$$|x| = 2.$$

This means that we must determine real numbers whose distance from the origin on the number line is 2. Figure 1.18 shows that there are two numbers such that $|x| = 2$, namely, 2 or -2. We write $x = 2$ or $x = -2$. This observation can be generalized as follows:

> **Rewriting an Absolute Value Equation without Absolute Value Bars**
>
> If c is a positive real number and X represents any algebraic expression, then $|X| = c$ is equivalent to $X = c$ or $X = -c$.

Technology

You can use a graphing utility to verify the solution of an absolute value equation. Consider, for example,

$$|2x - 3| = 11$$

Graph $y_1 = |2x - 3|$ and $y_2 = 11$. The graphs are shown in a $[-10, 10, 1]$ by $[-1, 15, 1]$ viewing rectangle. The x-coordinates of the intersection points are -4 and 7, verifying that $\{-4, 7\}$ is the solution set.

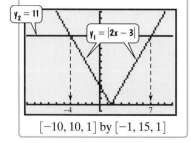

$[-10, 10, 1]$ by $[-1, 15, 1]$

EXAMPLE 8 Solving an Equation Involving Absolute Value

Solve: $|2x - 3| = 11$.

Solution

$|2x - 3| = 11$		This is the given equation.
$2x - 3 = 11$ or $2x - 3 = -11$		Rewrite the equation without absolute value bars.
$2x = 14$	$2x = -8$	Add 3 to both sides of each equation.
$x = 7$	$x = -4$	Divide both sides of each equation by 2.

Check 7:   **Check -4:**

$|2x - 3| = 11$	$|2x - 3| = 11$	This is the original equation.
$|2(7) - 3| \overset{?}{=} 11$	$|2(-4) - 3| \overset{?}{=} 11$	Substitute the proposed solutions.
$|14 - 3| \overset{?}{=} 11$	$|-8 - 3| \overset{?}{=} 11$	Perform operations inside the absolute value bars.
$|11| \overset{?}{=} 11$	$|-11| \overset{?}{=} 11$	
$11 = 11 \checkmark$	$11 = 11 \checkmark$	These true statements indicate that 7 and -4 are solutions.

The solution set is $\{-4, 7\}$.

Check
Point
8
Solve: $|2x - 1| = 5$.

The absolute value of a number is never negative. Thus, if X is an algebraic expression and c is a negative number, then $|X| = c$ has no solution. For example, the equation $|3x - 6| = -2$ has no solution because $|3x - 6|$ cannot be negative. The solution set is $\varnothing$, the empty set.

The absolute value of 0 is 0. Thus, if X is an algebraic expression and $|X| = 0$, the solution is found by solving $X = 0$. For example, the solution of $|x - 2| = 0$ is obtained by solving $x - 2 = 0$. The solution is 2 and the solution set is $\{2\}$.

To solve some absolute value equations, it is necessary to first isolate the expression containing the absolute value symbols. For example, consider the equation

$$3|2x - 3| - 8 = 25.$$

We need to isolate $|2x - 3|$.

How can we isolate $|2x - 3|$? Add 8 to both sides of the equation and then divide both sides by 3.

$$3|2x - 3| - 8 = 25 \quad \text{This is the given equation.}$$
$$3|2x - 3| = 33 \quad \text{Add 8 to both sides.}$$
$$|2x - 3| = 11 \quad \text{Divide both sides by 3.}$$

This results in the equation we solved in Example 8.

EXERCISE SET 1.6

Practice Exercises

Solve each polynomial equation in Exercises 1–10 by factoring and then using the zero-product principle.

1. $3x^4 - 48x^2 = 0$
2. $5x^4 - 20x^2 = 0$
3. $3x^3 + 2x^2 = 12x + 8$
4. $4x^3 - 12x^2 = 9x - 27$
5. $2x - 3 = 8x^3 - 12x^2$
6. $x + 1 = 9x^3 + 9x^2$
7. $4y^3 - 2 = y - 8y^2$
8. $9y^3 + 8 = 4y + 18y^2$
9. $2x^4 = 16x$
10. $3x^4 = 81x$

Solve each radical equation in Exercises 11–28. Check all proposed solutions.

11. $\sqrt{3x + 18} = x$
12. $\sqrt{20 - 8x} = x$
13. $\sqrt{x + 3} = x - 3$
14. $\sqrt{x + 10} = x - 2$
15. $\sqrt{2x + 13} = x + 7$
16. $\sqrt{6x + 1} = x - 1$
17. $x - \sqrt{2x + 5} = 5$
18. $x - \sqrt{x + 11} = 1$
19. $\sqrt{3x + 10} = x + 4$
20. $\sqrt{x - 3} = x - 9$
21. $\sqrt{x + 8} - \sqrt{x - 4} = 2$

22. $\sqrt{x + 5} - \sqrt{x - 3} = 2$
23. $\sqrt{x - 5} - \sqrt{x - 8} = 3$
24. $\sqrt{2x - 3} - \sqrt{x - 2} = 1$
25. $\sqrt{2x + 3} + \sqrt{x - 2} = 2$
26. $\sqrt{x + 2} + \sqrt{3x + 7} = 1$
27. $\sqrt{3\sqrt{x + 1}} = \sqrt{3x - 5}$
28. $\sqrt{1 + 4\sqrt{x}} = 1 + \sqrt{x}$

Solve and check each equation with rational exponents in Exercises 29–38.

29. $x^{3/2} = 8$
30. $x^{3/2} = 27$
31. $(x - 4)^{3/2} = 27$
32. $(x + 5)^{3/2} = 8$
33. $6x^{5/2} - 12 = 0$
34. $8x^{5/3} - 24 = 0$
35. $(x - 4)^{2/3} = 16$
36. $(x + 5)^{2/3} = 4$
37. $(x^2 - x - 4)^{3/4} - 2 = 6$
38. $(x^2 - 3x + 3)^{3/2} - 1 = 0$

Solve each equation in Exercises 39–58 by making an appropriate substitution.

39. $x^4 - 5x^2 + 4 = 0$

40. $x^4 - 13x^2 + 36 = 0$

41. $9x^4 = 25x^2 - 16$

42. $4x^4 = 13x^2 - 9$

43. $x - 13\sqrt{x} + 40 = 0$

44. $2x - 7\sqrt{x} - 30 = 0$

45. $x^{-2} - x^{-1} - 20 = 0$

46. $x^{-2} - x^{-1} - 6 = 0$

47. $x^{2/3} - x^{1/3} - 6 = 0$

48. $2x^{2/3} + 7x^{1/3} - 15 = 0$

49. $x^{3/2} - 2x^{3/4} + 1 = 0$

50. $x^{2/5} + x^{1/5} - 6 = 0$

51. $2x - 3x^{1/2} + 1 = 0$

52. $x + 3x^{1/2} - 4 = 0$

53. $(x - 5)^2 - 4(x - 5) - 21 = 0$

54. $(x + 3)^2 + 7(x + 3) - 18 = 0$

55. $(x^2 - x)^2 - 14(x^2 - x) + 24 = 0$

56. $(x^2 - 2x)^2 - 11(x^2 - 2x) + 24 = 0$

57. $\left(y - \dfrac{8}{y}\right)^2 + 5\left(y - \dfrac{8}{y}\right) - 14 = 0$

58. $\left(y - \dfrac{10}{y}\right)^2 + 6\left(y - \dfrac{10}{y}\right) - 27 = 0$

In Exercises 59–74, solve each absolute value equation or indicate the equation has no solution.

59. $|x| = 8$

60. $|x| = 6$

61. $|x - 2| = 7$

62. $|x + 1| = 5$

63. $|2x - 1| = 5$

64. $|2x - 3| = 11$

65. $2|3x - 2| = 14$

66. $3|2x - 1| = 21$

67. $7|5x| + 2 = 16$

68. $7|3x| + 2 = 16$

69. $|x + 1| + 5 = 3$

70. $|x + 1| + 6 = 2$

71. $|2x - 1| + 3 = 3$

72. $|3x - 2| + 4 = 4$

Hint for Exercises 73–74: Absolute value expressions are equal when the expressions inside the absolute value bars are equal to or opposites of each other.

73. $|3x - 1| = |x + 5|$ **74.** $|2x - 7| = |x + 3|$

Solve each equation in Exercises 75–84 by the method of your choice.

75. $x + 2\sqrt{x} - 3 = 0$ **76.** $x^3 + 3x^2 - 4x - 12 = 0$

77. $(x + 4)^{3/2} = 8$ **78.** $(x^2 - 1)^2 - 2(x^2 - 1) = 3$

79. $\sqrt{4x + 15} - 2x = 0$ **80.** $x^{2/5} - 1 = 0$

81. $|x^2 + 2x - 36| = 12$

82. $\sqrt{3x + 1} - \sqrt{x - 1} = 2$

83. $x^3 - 2x^2 = x - 2$ **84.** $|x^2 + 6x + 1| = 8$

Application Exercises

First the good news: The graph shows that U.S. seniors' scores in standard testing in science have improved since 1982. Now the bad news: The highest possible score is 500, and in 1970, the average test score was 304.

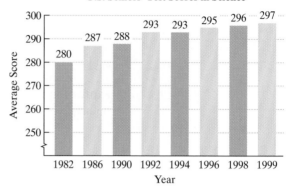

U.S. Seniors' Test Scores in Science

Source: National Assessment of Educational Progress

The formula

$$S = 4\sqrt{x} + 280$$

models the average science test score, S, x years after 1982. Use the formula to solve Exercises 85–86.

85. When will the average science score return to the 1970 average of 304?

86. When will the average science test score be 300?

Out of a group of 50,000 births, the number of people, y, surviving to age x is modeled by the formula

$$y = 5000\sqrt{100 - x}.$$

The graph of the formula is shown. Use the formula to solve Exercises 87–88.

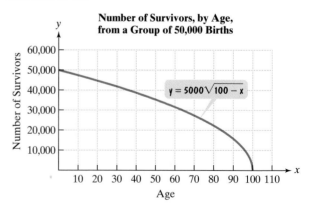

Number of Survivors, by Age, from a Group of 50,000 Births

$y = 5000\sqrt{100 - x}$

87. To what age will 40,000 people in the group survive? Identify the solution as a point on the graph of the formula.

88. To what age will 35,000 people in the group survive? Identify the solution as a point on the graph of the formula.

For each planet in our solar system, its year is the time it takes the planet to revolve once around the sun. The formula

$$E = 0.2x^{3/2}$$

models the number of Earth days in a planet's year, E, where x is the average distance of the planet from the sun, in millions of kilometers. Use the formula to solve Exercises 89–90.

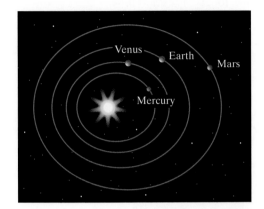

89. We, of course, have 365 Earth days in our year. What is the average distance of Earth from the sun? Use a calculator and round to the nearest million kilometers.

90. There are approximately 88 Earth days in the year of the planet Mercury. What is the average distance of Mercury from the sun? Use a calculator and round to the nearest million kilometers.

Use the Pythagorean Theorem to solve Exercises 91–92.

91. Two vertical poles of lengths 6 feet and 8 feet stand 10 feet apart (see the figure). A cable reaches from the top of one pole to some point on the ground between the poles and then to the top of the other pole. Where should this point be located to use 18 feet of cable?

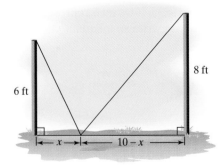

92. Towns *A* and *B* are located 6 miles and 3 miles, respectively, from a major expressway. The point on the expressway closest to town *A* is 12 miles from the point on the expressway closest to town *B*. Two new roads are to be built from *A* to the expressway and then to *B*. (See the figure at the top of the next column.)

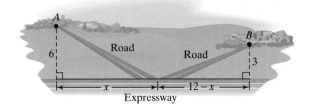

a. Find *x* if the length of the new roads is 15 miles.

b. Write a verbal description for the road crew telling them where to position the new roads based on your answer to part (a).

Writing in Mathematics

93. Without actually solving the equation, give a general description of how to solve $x^3 - 5x^2 - x + 5 = 0$.

94. In solving $\sqrt{3x + 4} - \sqrt{2x + 4} = 2$, why is it a good idea to isolate a radical term? What if we don't do this and simply square each side? Describe what happens.

95. What is an extraneous solution to a radical equation?

96. Explain how to recognize an equation that is quadratic in form. Provide two original examples with your explanation.

97. Describe two methods for solving this equation: $x - 5\sqrt{x} + 4 = 0$.

98. Explain how to solve an equation involving absolute value.

99. Explain why the procedure that you explained in Exercise 98 does not apply to the equation $|x - 2| = -3$. What is the solution set for this equation?

100. Describe the trend shown by the graph in Exercises 87–88. When is the rate of decrease most rapid? What does this mean about survival rate by age?

Technology Exercises

In Exercises 101–103, use a graphing utility and the graph's x-intercepts to solve each equation. Check by direct substitution. A viewing rectangle is given.

101. $x^3 + 3x^2 - x - 3 = 0$
$[-6, 6, 1]$ by $[-6, 6, 1]$

102. $-x^4 + 4x^3 - 4x^2 = 0$
$[-6, 6, 1]$ by $[-9, 2, 1]$

103. $\sqrt{2x + 13} - x - 5 = 0$
$[-5, 5, 1]$ by $[-5, 5, 1]$

104. Use a graphing utility to obtain the graph of the formula in Exercises 87–88. Then use the TRACE feature to trace along the curve until you reach the point that visually shows the solution to Exercise 87 or 88.

Critical Thinking Exercises

105. Which one of the following is true?
   a. Squaring both sides of $\sqrt{y+4} + \sqrt{y-1} = 5$ leads to $y + 4 + y - 1 = 25$, an equation with no radicals.
   b. The equation $(x^2 - 2x)^9 - 5(x^2 - 2x)^3 + 6 = 0$ is quadratic in form and should be solved by letting $t = (x^2 - 2x)^3$.
   c. If a radical equation has two proposed solutions and one of these values is not a solution, the other value is also not a solution.
   d. None of these statements is true.

106. Solve: $\sqrt{6x - 2} = \sqrt{2x + 3} - \sqrt{4x - 1}$.

107. Solve *without* squaring both sides:

$$5 - \frac{2}{x} = \sqrt{5 - \frac{2}{x}}.$$

108. Solve for x: $\sqrt[3]{x\sqrt{x}} = 9$.

109. Solve for x: $x^{5/6} + x^{2/3} - 2x^{1/2} = 0$.

SECTION 1.7   Linear Inequalities

Objectives

1. Graph an inequality's solution set.
2. Use set-builder and interval notations.
3. Use properties of inequalities to solve inequalities.
4. Solve compound inequalities.
5. Solve inequalities involving absolute value.

Rent-a-Heap, a car rental company, charges \$125 per week plus \$0.20 per mile to rent one of their cars. Suppose you are limited by how much money you can spend for the week: You can spend at most \$335. If we let x represent the number of miles you drive the heap in a week, we can write an inequality that models the given conditions.

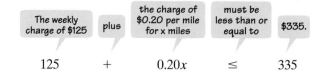

The weekly charge of \$125	plus	the charge of \$0.20 per mile for x miles	must be less than or equal to	\$335.
125	+	0.20x	≤	335

Using the commutative property of addition, we can express this inequality as $0.20x + 125 \leq 335$. The form of this inequality is $ax + b \leq c$, with $a = 0.20$, $b = 125$, and $c = 335$. Any inequality in this form is called a **linear inequality in one variable.** The greatest exponent on the variable in such an inequality is 1. The symbol between $ax + b$ and c can be $\leq$ (is less than or equal to), $<$ (is less than), $\geq$ (is greater than or equal to), or $>$ (is greater than).

In this section, we will study how to solve linear inequalities such as $0.20x + 125 \leq 335$. **Solving an inequality** is the process of finding the set of numbers that make the inequality a true statement. These numbers are called the **solutions** of the inequality, and we say that they **satisfy** the inequality. The set of all solutions is called the **solution set** of the inequality. We begin by discussing how to graph and how to represent these solution sets.

1 Graph an inequality's solution set.

Graphs of Inequalities; Interval Notation

There are infinitely many solutions to the inequality $x > -4$, namely all real numbers that are greater than -4. Although we cannot list all the solutions, we can make a drawing on a number line that represents these solutions. Such a drawing is called the **graph of the inequality.**

Graphs of solutions to linear inequalities are shown on a number line by shading all points representing numbers that are solutions. Parentheses indicate endpoints that are not solutions. Square brackets indicate endpoints that are solutions.

EXAMPLE 1   Graphing Inequalities

Graph the solutions of:

 a. $x < 3$ **b.** $x \geq -1$ **c.** $-1 < x \leq 3$.

Study Tip

An inequality symbol points to the smaller number. Thus, another way to express $x < 3$ (x is less than 3) is $3 > x$ (3 is greater than x).

Solution

 a. The solutions of $x < 3$ are all real numbers that are less than 3. They are graphed on a number line by shading all points to the left of 3. The parenthesis at 3 indicates that 3 is not a solution, but numbers such as 2.9999 and 2.6 are. The arrow shows that the graph extends indefinitely to the left.

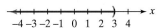

 b. The solutions of $x \geq -1$ are all real numbers that are greater than or equal to -1. We shade all points to the right of -1 and the point for -1 itself. The bracket at -1 shows that -1 is a solution of the given inequality. The arrow shows that the graph extends indefinitely to the right.

 c. The inequality $-1 < x \leq 3$ is read "-1 is less than x *and* x is less than or equal to 3," or "x is greater than -1 *and* less than or equal to 3." The solutions of $-1 < x \leq 3$ are all real numbers between -1 and 3, not including -1 but including 3. The parenthesis at -1 indicates that -1 is not a solution. By contrast, the bracket at 3 shows that 3 is a solution. Shading indicates the other solutions.

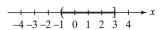

Check Point 1

Graph the solutions of:

a. $x \le 2$ **b.** $x > -4$ **c.** $2 \le x < 6$.

2 Use set-builder and interval notations.

Now that we know how to graph the solution set of an inequality such as $x > -4$, let's see how to represent the solution set. One method is with **set-builder notation.** Using this method, the solution set of $x > -4$ can be expressed as

$$\{x \mid x > -4\}.$$

The set of all x — such that

We read this as "the set of all real numbers x such that x is greater than -4."

Another method used to represent solution sets of inequalities is **interval notation.** Using this notation, the solution set of $x > -4$ is expressed as $(-4, \infty)$. The parenthesis at -4 indicates that -4 is not included in the interval. The infinity symbol, ∞, does not represent a real number. It indicates that the interval extends indefinitely to the right.

Table 1.5 lists nine possible types of intervals used to describe subsets of real numbers.

Table 1.5   Intervals on the Real Number Line

Let a and b be real numbers such that $a < b$.

Interval Notation	Set-Builder Notation	Graph
(a, b)	$\{x \mid a < x < b\}$	
$[a, b]$	$\{x \mid a \le x \le b\}$	
$[a, b)$	$\{x \mid a \le x < b\}$	
$(a, b]$	$\{x \mid a < x \le b\}$	
(a, ∞)	$\{x \mid x > a\}$	
$[a, \infty)$	$\{x \mid x \ge a\}$	
$(-\infty, b)$	$\{x \mid x < b\}$	
$(-\infty, b]$	$\{x \mid x \le b\}$	
$(-\infty, \infty)$	$\mathbb{R}$ (set of all real numbers)	

EXAMPLE 2   Intervals and Inequalities

Express the intervals in terms of inequalities and graph:

a. $(-1, 4]$ **b.** $[2.5, 4]$ **c.** $(-4, \infty)$.

Solution

a. $(-1, 4] = \{x \mid -1 < x \le 4\}$

b. $[2.5, 4] = \{x \mid 2.5 \le x \le 4\}$

c. $(-4, \infty) = \{x \mid x > -4\}$

Check Point 2 Express the intervals in terms of inequalities and graph:
a. $[-2, 5)$ **b.** $[1, 3.5]$ **c.** $(-\infty, -1)$.

3 Use properties of inequalities to solve inequalities.

Solving Linear Inequalities

Back to our question: How many miles can you drive your Rent-a-Heap car if you can spend at most $335 per week? We answer the question by solving

$$0.20x + 125 \leq 335$$

for x. The solution procedure is nearly identical to that for solving

$$0.20x + 125 = 335.$$

Our goal is to get x by itself on the left side. We do this by subtracting 125 from both sides to isolate $0.20x$:

$$0.20x + 125 \leq 335$$
$$0.20x + 125 - 125 \leq 335 - 125$$
$$0.20x \leq 210.$$

Finally, we isolate x from $0.20x$ by dividing both sides of the inequality by 0.20:

$$\frac{0.20x}{0.20} \leq \frac{210}{0.20}$$
$$x \leq 1050.$$

With at most $335 per week to spend, you can travel at most 1050 miles.

We started with the inequality $0.20x + 125 \leq 335$ and obtained the inequality $x \leq 1050$ in the final step. Both of these inequalities have the same solution set, namely $\{x \mid x \leq 1050\}$. Inequalities such as these, with the same solution set, are said to be **equivalent.**

We isolated x from $0.20x$ by dividing both sides of $0.20x \leq 210$ by 0.20, a positive number. Let's see what happens if we divide both sides of an inequality by a negative number. Consider the inequality $10 < 14$. Divide 10 and 14 by -2:

$$\frac{10}{-2} = -5 \quad \text{and} \quad \frac{14}{-2} = -7.$$

Because -5 lies to the right of -7 on the number line, -5 is greater than -7:

$$-5 > -7.$$

Notice that the direction of the inequality symbol is reversed:

$$10 < 14$$
$$-5 > -7.$$

In general, **when we multiply or divide both sides of an inequality by a negative number, the direction of the inequality symbol is reversed.** When we reverse the direction of the inequality symbol, we say that we change the *sense* of the inequality.

We can isolate a variable in a linear inequality the same way we can isolate a variable in a linear equation. The following properties are used to create equivalent inequalities:

Study Tip

English phrases such as "at least" and "at most" can be modeled by inequalities.

English Sentence	Inequality
x is at least 5.	$x \geq 5$
x is at most 5.	$x \leq 5$
x is between 5 and 7.	$5 < x < 7$
x is no more than 5.	$x \leq 5$
x is no less than 5.	$x \geq 5$

Properties of Inequalities

Property	The Property in Words	Example
Addition and Subtraction Properties If $a < b$, then $a + c < b + c$. If $a < b$, then $a - c < b - c$.	If the same quantity is added to or subtracted from both sides of an inequality, the resulting inequality is equivalent to the original one.	$2x + 3 < 7$ Subtract 3: $2x + 3 - 3 < 7 - 3$. Simplify: $2x < 4$.
Positive Multiplication and Division Properties If $a < b$ and c is positive, then $ac < bc$. If $a < b$ and c is positive, then $\dfrac{a}{c} < \dfrac{b}{c}$.	If we multiply or divide both sides of an inequality by the same positive quantity, the resulting inequality is equivalent to the original one.	$2x < 4$ Divide by 2: $\dfrac{2x}{2} < \dfrac{4}{2}$. Simplify: $x < 2$.
Negative Multiplication and Division Properties If $a < b$ and c is negative, then $ac > bc$. If $a < b$ and c is negative, then $\dfrac{a}{c} > \dfrac{b}{c}$.	If we multiply or divide both sides of an inequality by the same negative quantity and reverse the direction of the inequality symbol, the result is an equivalent inequality.	$-4x < 20$ Divide by -4 and reverse the sense of the inequality: $\dfrac{-4x}{-4} > \dfrac{20}{-4}$. Simplify: $x > -5$.

EXAMPLE 3 Solving a Linear Inequality

Solve and graph the solution set on a number line:

$$3 - 2x < 11.$$

Solution

$3 - 2x < 11$	This is the given inequality.
$3 - 2x - 3 < 11 - 3$	Subtract 3 from both sides.
$-2x < 8$	Simplify.
$\dfrac{-2x}{-2} > \dfrac{8}{-2}$	Divide both sides by -2 and reverse the sense of the inequality.
$x > -4$	Simplify.

Discovery

As a partial check, select one number from the solution set for the inequality in Example 3. Substitute that number into the original inequality. Perform the resulting computations. You should obtain a true statement.

   Is it possible to perform a partial check using a number that is not in the solution set? What should happen in this case? Try doing this.

The solution set consists of all real numbers that are greater than -4, expressed as $\{x \mid x > -4\}$ in set-builder notation. The interval notation for this solution set is $(-4, \infty)$. The graph of the solution set is shown as follows:

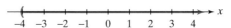

Check Point 3 Solve and graph the solution set on a number line:

$$2 - 3x \le 5.$$

EXAMPLE 4 Solving a Linear Inequality

Solve and graph the solution set: $7x + 15 \geq 13x + 51$.

Study Tip

You can solve

$$7x + 15 \geq 13x + 51$$

by isolating x on the right side. Subtract $7x$ from both sides.

$$7x + 15 - 7x$$

$$\geq 13x + 51 - 7x$$

$$15 \geq 6x + 51$$

Now subtract 51 from both sides.

$$15 - 51 \geq 6x + 51 - 51$$

$$-36 \geq 6x$$

Finally, divide both sides by 6.

$$\frac{-36}{6} \geq \frac{6x}{6}$$

$$-6 \geq x$$

This last inequality means the same thing as

$$x \leq -6.$$

Solution We will collect variable terms on the left and constant terms on the right.

$7x + 15$	$\geq$	$13x + 51$	This is the given inequality.
$7x + 15 - 13x$	$\geq$	$13x + 51 - 13x$	Subtract 13x from both sides.
$-6x + 15$	$\geq$	51	Simplify.
$-6x + 15 - 15$	$\geq$	$51 - 15$	Subtract 15 from both sides.
$-6x$	$\geq$	36	Simplify.
$\dfrac{-6x}{-6}$	$\leq$	$\dfrac{36}{-6}$	Divide both sides by -6 and reverse the sense of the inequality.
x	$\leq$	-6	Simplify.

The solution set consists of all real numbers that are less than or equal to -6, expressed as $\{x \mid x \leq -6\}$. The interval notation for this solution set is $(-\infty, -6]$. The graph of the solution set is shown as follows:

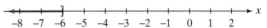

Check Point 4 Solve and graph the solution set: $6 - 3x \leq 5x - 2$.

Technology

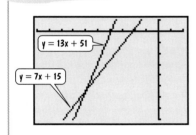

$y = 13x + 51$

$y = 7x + 15$

You can use a graphing utility to verify that $(-\infty, -6]$ is the solution set of

$$7x + 15 \qquad \geq \qquad 13x + 51.$$

> For what values of x does the graph of $y = 7x + 15$ lie above or on   the graph of $y = 13x + 51$?

The graphs are shown on the left in a $[-10, 2, 1]$ by $[-40, 5, 5]$ viewing rectangle. Look closely at the graphs. Can you see that the graph of $y = 7x + 15$ lies above or on the graph of $y = 13x + 51$ when $x \leq -6$, or on the interval $(-\infty, -6]$?

4 Solve compound inequalities.

Solving Compound Inequalities

We now consider two inequalities such as

$$-3 < 2x + 1 \text{ and } 2x + 1 \leq 3$$

expressed as a **compound inequality**

$$-3 < 2x + 1 \leq 3.$$

The word "and" does not appear when the inequality is written in the shorter form, although it is implied. The shorter form enables us to solve both inequalities at once. By performing the same operation on all three parts of the inequality, our goal is to **isolate x in the middle.**

Technology

To check Example 5, graph each part of

$$-3 < 2x + 1 \le 3.$$

The figure shows that the graph of $y_2 = 2x + 1$ lies above the graph of $y_1 = -3$ and on or below the graph of $y_3 = 3$ when x is in the interval $(-2, 1]$.

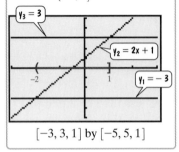

$[-3, 3, 1]$ by $[-5, 5, 1]$

EXAMPLE 5 Solving a Compound Inequality

Solve and graph the solution set:

$$-3 < 2x + 1 \le 3.$$

Solution We would like to isolate x in the middle. We can do this by first subtracting 1 from all three parts of the compound inequality. Then we isolate x from $2x$ by dividing all three parts of the inequality by 2.

$-3 < 2x + 1 \le 3$	This is the given inequality.
$-3 - 1 < 2x + 1 - 1 \le 3 - 1$	Subtract 1 from all three parts.
$-4 < 2x \le 2$	Simplify.
$\dfrac{-4}{2} < \dfrac{2x}{2} \le \dfrac{2}{2}$	Divide each part by 2.
$-2 < x \le 1$	Simplify.

The solution set consists of all real numbers greater than -2 and less than or equal to 1, represented by $\{x \mid -2 < x \le 1\}$ in set-builder notation and $(-2, 1]$ in interval notation. The graph is shown as follows:

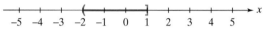

Check Point 5 Solve and graph the solution set: $1 \le 2x + 3 < 11.$

5 Solve inequalities involving absolute value.

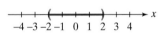

Figure 1.19 $|x| < 2$, so $-2 < x < 2$.

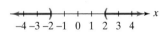

Figure 1.20 $|x| > 2$, so $x < -2$ or $x > 2$.

Solving Inequalities with Absolute Value

We know that $|x|$ describes the distance of x from zero on a real number line. We can use this geometric interpretation to solve an inequality such as

$$|x| < 2.$$

This means that the distance of x from 0 is *less than* 2, as shown in Figure 1.19. The interval shows values of x that lie less than 2 units from 0. Thus, x can lie between -2 and 2. That is, x is greater than -2 and less than 2. We write $(-2, 2)$ or $\{x \mid -2 < x < 2\}$.

Some absolute value inequalities use the "greater than" symbol. For example, $|x| > 2$ means that the distance of x from 0 is *greater than* 2, as shown in Figure 1.20. Thus, x can be less than -2 *or* greater than 2. We write $x < -2$ or $x > 2$.

These observations suggest the following principles for solving inequalities with absolute value:

Study Tip

In the $|X| < c$ case, we have one compound inequality to solve. In the $|X| > c$ case, we have two separate inequalities to solve.

Solving an Absolute Value Inequality

If X is an algebraic expression and c is a positive number,

1. The solutions of $|X| < c$ are the numbers that satisfy $-c < X < c$.
2. The solutions of $|X| > c$ are the numbers that satisfy $X < -c$ or $X > c$.

These rules are valid if $<$ is replaced by $\le$ and $>$ is replaced by $\ge$.

EXAMPLE 6 **Solving an Absolute Value Inequality with** <

Solve and graph the solution set: $|x - 4| < 3$.

Solution

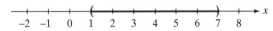

$$|X| < c \text{ means } -c < X < c.$$

$|x - 4| < 3$ means $-3 < x - 4 < 3$.

We solve the compound inequality by adding 4 to all three parts.

$$-3 < x - 4 < 3$$
$$-3 + 4 < x - 4 + 4 < 3 + 4$$
$$1 < x < 7$$

The solution set is all real numbers greater than 1 and less than 7, denoted by $\{x | 1 < x < 7\}$ or $(1, 7)$. The graph of the solution set is shown as follows:

```
  ─┼──┼──┼──(──┼──┼──┼──┼──)──┼──→ x
  -2 -1  0  1  2  3  4  5  6  7  8
```

Check Point 6   Solve and graph the solution set: $|x - 2| < 5$.

EXAMPLE 7 **Solving an Absolute Value Inequality with** ≥

Solve and graph the solution set: $|2x + 3| \geq 5$.

Solution $|X| \geq c$ means $X \leq -c$ or $X \geq c.$

$|2x + 3| \geq 5$ means $2x + 3 \leq -5$ or $2x + 3 \geq 5$.

We solve each of these inequalities separately.

$2x + 3 \leq -5$	or	$2x + 3 \geq 5$	These are the inequalities without absolute value bars.
$2x + 3 - 3 \leq -5 - 3$	or	$2x + 3 - 3 \geq 5 - 3$	Subtract 3 from both sides.
$2x \leq -8$	or	$2x \geq 2$	Simplify.
$\dfrac{2x}{2} \leq \dfrac{-8}{2}$	or	$\dfrac{2x}{2} \geq \dfrac{2}{2}$	Divide both sides by 2.
$x \leq -4$	or	$x \geq 1$	Simplify.

The solution set is $\{x | x \leq -4 \text{ or } x \geq 1\}$, that is, all x in $(-\infty, -4]$ or $[1, \infty)$. The graph of the solution set is shown as follows:

```
  ─┼──┼──┼──┼─]──┼──┼──┼──┼─[──┼──┼──→ x
  -7 -6 -5 -4 -3 -2 -1  0  1  2  3
```

Study Tip

The graph of the solution set for $|X| > c$ will be divided into two intervals. The graph of the solution set for $|X| < c$ will be a single interval.

Check Point 7   Solve and graph the solution set: $|2x - 5| \geq 3$.

Applications

Our next example shows how to use an inequality to select the better deal between two pricing options. We will use our five-step strategy for solving problems using mathematical models.

EXAMPLE 8   Creating and Comparing Mathematical Models

Acme Car rental agency charges $4 a day plus $0.15 a mile, whereas Interstate rental agency charges $20 a day and $0.05 a mile. Under what conditions is the daily cost of an Acme rental a better deal than an Interstate rental?

Solution

Step 1   Let x represent one of the quantities.   We are looking for the number of miles driven in a day to make Acme the better deal. Thus,

$$\text{let } x = \text{ the number of miles driven in a day.}$$

Step 2   Represent other quantities in terms of x.   We are not asked to find another quantity, so we can skip this step.

Step 3   Write an inequality in x that describes the conditions.

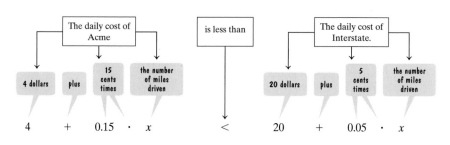

Technology

The graphs of the daily cost models for the car rental agencies

$$y_1 = 4 + 0.15x$$

and $y_2 = 20 + 0.05x$

are shown in a $[0, 300, 10]$ by $[0, 40, 4]$ viewing rectangle. The graphs intersect at $(160, 28)$. To the left of $x = 160$, the graph of Acme's daily cost lies below that of Interstate's daily cost. This shows that for fewer than 160 miles per day, Acme offers the better deal.

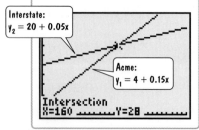

Step 4   Solve the inequality and answer the question.

$$4 + 0.15x < 20 + 0.05x \qquad \text{This is the inequality that models the verbal conditions.}$$

$$4 + 0.15x - 0.05x < 20 + 0.05x - 0.05x \qquad \text{Subtract 0.05x from both sides.}$$

$$4 + 0.1x < 20 \qquad \text{Simplify.}$$

$$4 + 0.1x - 4 < 20 - 4 \qquad \text{Subtract 4 from both sides.}$$

$$0.1x < 16 \qquad \text{Simplify.}$$

$$\frac{0.1x}{0.1} < \frac{16}{0.1} \qquad \text{Divide both sides by 0.1.}$$

$$x < 160 \qquad \text{Simplify.}$$

Thus, driving fewer than 160 miles per day makes Acme the better deal.

Step 5 Check the proposed solution in the original wording of the problem.
One way to do this is to take a mileage less than 160 miles per day to see if Acme is the better deal. Suppose that 150 miles are driven in a day.

$$\text{Cost for Acme} = 4 + 0.15(150) = 26.50$$

$$\text{Cost for Interstate} = 20 + 0.05(150) = 27.50$$

Acme has a lower daily cost, making it the better deal.

Check Point 8 A car can be rented from Basic Rental for $260 per week with no extra charge for mileage. Continental charges $80 per week plus 25 cents for each mile driven to rent the same car. Under what conditions is the rental cost for Basic Rental a better deal than Continental's?

EXERCISE SET 1.7

Practice Exercises

In Exercises 1–12, graph the solutions of each inequality on a number line.

1. $x > 6$

2. $x > -2$

3. $x < -4$

4. $x < 0$

5. $x \geq -3$

6. $x \geq -5$

7. $x \leq 4$

8. $x \leq 7$

9. $-2 < x \leq 5$

10. $-3 \leq x < 7$

11. $-1 < x < 4$

12. $-7 \leq x \leq 0$

In Exercises 13–26, express each interval in terms of an inequality and graph the interval on a number line.

13. $(1, 6]$

14. $(-2, 4]$

15. $[-5, 2)$

16. $[-4, 3)$

17. $[-3, 1]$

18. $[-2, 5]$

19. $(2, \infty)$

20. $(3, \infty)$

21. $[-3, \infty)$

22. $[-5, \infty)$

23. $(-\infty, 3)$

24. $(-\infty, 2)$

25. $(-\infty, 5.5)$

26. $(-\infty, 3.5]$

Solve each linear inequality in Exercises 27–48 and graph the solution set on a number line. Express the solution set using interval notation.

27. $5x + 11 < 26$

28. $2x + 5 < 17$

29. $3x - 7 \geq 13$

30. $8x - 2 \geq 14$

31. $-9x \geq 36$

32. $-5x \leq 30$

33. $8x - 11 \leq 3x - 13$

34. $18x + 45 \leq 12x - 8$

35. $4(x + 1) + 2 \geq 3x + 6$

36. $8x + 3 > 3(2x + 1) + x + 5$

37. $2x - 11 < -3(x + 2)$

38. $-4(x + 2) > 3x + 20$

39. $1 - (x + 3) \geq 4 - 2x$

40. $5(3 - x) \leq 3x - 1$

41. $\dfrac{x}{4} - \dfrac{3}{5} \leq \dfrac{x}{2} + 1$

42. $\dfrac{3x}{10} + 1 \geq \dfrac{1}{5} - \dfrac{x}{10}$

43. $1 - \dfrac{x}{2} > 4$

44. $7 - \dfrac{4}{5}x < \dfrac{3}{5}$

45. $\dfrac{x - 4}{6} \geq \dfrac{x - 2}{9} + \dfrac{5}{18}$

46. $\dfrac{4x - 3}{6} + 2 \geq \dfrac{2x - 1}{12}$

47. $4(3x - 2) - 3x < 3(1 + 3x) - 7$

48. $3(x - 8) - 2(10 - x) > 5(x - 1)$

Solve each inequality in Exercises 49–56 and graph the solution set on a number line. Express the solution set using interval notation.

49. $6 < x + 3 < 8$

50. $7 < x + 5 < 11$

51. $-3 \leq x - 2 < 1$

52. $-6 < x - 4 \leq 1$

53. $-11 < 2x - 1 \leq -5$

54. $3 \leq 4x - 3 < 19$

55. $-3 \leq \dfrac{2}{3}x - 5 < -1$

56. $-6 \leq \dfrac{1}{2}x - 4 < -3$

Solve each inequality in Exercises 57–84 by first rewriting each one as an equivalent inequality without absolute value bars. Graph the solution set on a number line. Express the solution set using interval notation.

57. $|x| < 3$

58. $|x| < 5$

59. $|x - 1| \leq 2$

60. $|x + 3| \leq 4$

61. $|2x - 6| < 8$

62. $|3x + 5| < 17$

63. $|2(x - 1) + 4| \leq 8$

64. $|3(x - 1) + 2| \leq 20$

65. $\left|\dfrac{2y + 6}{3}\right| < 2$

66. $\left|\dfrac{3(x - 1)}{4}\right| < 6$

67. $|x| > 3$

68. $|x| > 5$

69. $|x - 1| \geq 2$

70. $|x + 3| \geq 4$

71. $|3x - 8| > 7$

72. $|5x - 2| > 13$

73. $\left|\dfrac{2x + 2}{4}\right| \geq 2$

74. $\left|\dfrac{3x - 3}{9}\right| \geq 1$

75. $\left|3 - \dfrac{2}{3}x\right| > 5$

76. $\left|3 - \dfrac{3}{4}x\right| > 9$

77. $3|x - 1| + 2 \geq 8$

78. $-2|4 - x| \geq -4$

79. $3 < |2x - 1|$

80. $5 \geq |4 - x|$

81. $12 < \left|-2x + \dfrac{6}{7}\right| + \dfrac{3}{7}$

82. $1 < \left|x - \dfrac{11}{3}\right| + \dfrac{7}{3}$

83. $4 + \left|3 - \dfrac{x}{3}\right| \geq 9$

84. $\left|2 - \dfrac{x}{2}\right| - 1 \leq 1$

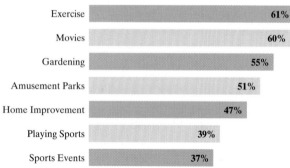

Application Exercises

The bar graph shows how we spend our leisure time. Let x represent the percentage of the population regularly participating in an activity. In Exercises 85–92, write the name or names of the activity described by the given inequality or interval.

Percentage of U.S. Population Participating in Each Activity on a Regular Basis

Activity	Percentage
Exercise	61%
Movies	60%
Gardening	55%
Amusement Parks	51%
Home Improvement	47%
Playing Sports	39%
Sports Events	37%

Source: U.S. Census Bureau

85. $x < 40\%$

86. $x < 50\%$

87. $[51\%, 61\%]$

88. $[47\%, 60\%]$

89. $(51\%, 61\%)$

90. $(47\%, 60\%)$

91. $(39\%, 55\%)$

92. $(37\%, 47\%)$

The line graph at the top of the next column shows the declining consumption of cigarettes in the United States. The data shown by the graph can be modeled by

$$N = 550 - 9x$$

where N is the number of cigarettes consumed, in billions, x years after 1988. Use this formula to solve Exercises 93–94.

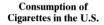
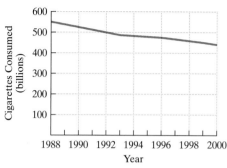

Consumption of Cigarettes in the U.S.

Source: Economic Research Service, USDA

93. How many years after 1988 will cigarette consumption be less than 370 billion cigarettes each year? Which years does this describe?

94. Describe how many years after 1988 cigarette consumption will be less than 325 billion cigarettes each year. Which years are included in your description?

95. The formula for converting Fahrenheit temperature, F, to Celsius temperature, C, is

$$C = \frac{5}{9}(F - 32).$$

If Celsius temperature ranges from 15° to 35°, inclusive, what is the range for the Fahrenheit temperature? Use interval notation to express this range.

96. The formula

$$T = 0.01x + 56.7$$

models the global mean temperature, T, in degrees Fahrenheit, of Earth x years after 1905. For which range of years was the global mean temperature at least 56.7°F and at most 57.2°F?

The three television programs viewed by the greatest percentage of U.S. households in the twentieth century are shown in the table. The data are from a random survey of 4000 TV households by Nielsen Media Research. In Exercises 97–98, let x represent the actual viewing percentage in the U.S. population.

TV Programs with the Greatest U.S. Audience Viewing Percentage of the Twentieth Century

Program	Viewing Percentage in Survey
1. "M*A*S*H" Feb. 28, 1983	60.2%
2. "Dallas" Nov. 21, 1980	53.3%
3. "Roots" Part 8 Jan. 30, 1977	51.1%

Source: Nielsen Media Research

97. The inequality $|x - 60.2| \leq 1.6$ describes the actual viewing percentage for "M*A*S*H" in the U.S. population. Solve the inequality and interpret the solution. Explain why the surveys *margin of error* is $\pm 1.6\%$.

98. The inequality $|x - 51.1| \leq 1.6$ describes the actual viewing percentage for "Roots" Part 8 in the U.S. population. Solve the inequality and interpret the solution. Explain why the surveys *margin of error* is $\pm 1.6\%$.

99. If a coin is tossed 100 times, we would expect approximately 50 of the outcomes to be heads. It can be demonstrated that a coin is unfair if h, the number of outcomes that result in heads, satisfies $\left| \dfrac{h - 50}{5} \right| \geq 1.645$. Describe the number of outcomes that determine an unfair coin that is tossed 100 times.

100. The inequality $|T - 57| \leq 7$ describes the range of monthly average temperature, T, in degrees Fahrenheit, for San Francisco, California. The inequality $|T - 50| \leq 22$ describes the range of monthly average temperature, T, in degrees Fahrenheit, for Albany, New York. Solve each inequality and interpret the solution. Then describe at least three differences between the monthly average temperatures for the two cities.

In Exercises 101–110, use the five-step strategy for solving word problems. Give a linear inequality that models the verbal conditions and then solve the problem.

101. A truck can be rented from Basic Rental for $50 a day plus $0.20 per mile. Continental charges $20 per day plus $0.50 per mile to rent the same truck. How many miles must be driven in a day to make the rental cost for Basic Rental a better deal then Continental's?

102. You are choosing between two long-distance telephone plans. Plan A has a monthly fee of $15 with a charge of $0.08 per minute for all long-distance calls. Plan B has a monthly fee of $3 with a charge of $0.12 per minute for all long-distance calls. How many minutes of long-distance calls in a month make plan A the better deal?

103. A city commission has proposed two tax bills. The first bill requires that a homeowner pay $1800 plus 3% of the assessed home value in taxes. The second bill requires taxes of $200 plus 8% of the assessed home value. What price range of home assessment would make the first bill a better deal?

104. A local bank charges $8 per month plus 5¢ per check. The credit union charges $2 per month plus 8¢ per check. How many check should be written each month to make the credit union a better deal?

105. A company manufactures and sells blank audiocassette tapes. The weekly fixed cost is $10,000 and it cost $0.40 to produce each tape. The selling price is $2.00 per tape. How many tapes must be produced and sold each week for the company to have a profit gain?

106. A company manufactures and sells personalized stationery. The weekly fixed cost is $3000 and it cost $3.00 to produce each package of stationery. The selling price is $5.50 per package. How many packages of stationery must be produced and sold each week for the company to have a profit gain?

107. An elevator at a construction site has a maximum capacity of 2800 pounds. If the elevator operator weighs 265 pounds and each cement bag weighs 65 pounds, how many bags of cement can be safely lifted on the elevator in one trip?

108. An elevator at a construction site has a maximum capacity of 3000 pounds. If the elevator operator weighs 245 pounds and each cement bag weighs 95 pounds, how many bags of cement can be safely lifted on the elevator in one trip?

109. On two examinations, you have grades of 86 and 88. There is an optional final examination, which counts as one grade. You decide to take the final in order to get a course grade of A, meaning a final average of at least 90.
   a. What must you get on the final to earn an A in the course?
   b. By taking the final, if you do poorly, you might risk the B that you have in the course based on the first two exam grades. If your final average is less than 80, you will lose your B in the course. Describe the grades on the final that will cause this happen.

110. Parts for an automobile repair cost $175. The mechanic charges $34 per hour. If you receive an estimate for at least $226 and at most $294 for fixing the car, what is the time interval that the mechanic will be working on the job?

Writing in Mathematics

111. When graphing the solutions of an inequality, what does a parenthesis signify? What does a bracket signify?

112. When solving an inequality, when is it necessary to change the sense of the inequality? Give an example.

113. Describe ways in which solving a linear inequality is similar to solving a linear equation.

114. Describe ways in which solving a linear inequality is different than solving a linear equation.

115. What is a compound inequality and how is it solved?

116. Describe how to solve an absolute value inequality involving the symbol $<$. Give an example.

117. Describe how to solve an absolute value inequality involving the symbol $>$. Give an example.

118. Explain why $|x| < -4$ has no solution.

119. Describe the solution set of $|x| > -4$.

120. The formula
$$V = 3.5x + 120$$
models Super Bowl viewers, V, in millions, x years after 1990. Use the formula to write a word problem that can be solved using a linear inequality. Then solve the problem.

Technology Exercises

In Exercises 121–122, solve each inequality using a graphing utility. Graph each side separately. Then determine the values of x for which the graph on the left side lies above the graph on the right side.

121. $-3(x - 6) > 2x - 2$ **122.** $-2(x + 4) > 6x + 16$

Use the same technique employed in Exercises 121–122 to solve each inequality in Exercises 123–124. In each case, what conclusion can you draw? What happens if you try solving the inequalities algebraically?

123. $12x - 10 > 2(x - 4) + 10x$

124. $2x + 3 > 3(2x - 4) - 4x$

125. A bank offers two checking account plans. Plan A has a base service charge of $4.00 per month plus 10¢ per check. Plan B charges a base service charge of $2.00 per month plus 15¢ per check.

   a. Write models for the total monthly costs for each plan if x checks are written.

   b. Use a graphing utility to graph the models in the same $[0, 50, 10]$ by $[0, 10, 1]$ viewing rectangle.

   c. Use the graphs (and the TRACE or intersection feature) to determine for what number of checks per month plan A will be better than plan B.

   d. Verify the result of part (c) algebraically by solving an inequality.

Critical Thinking Exercises

126. Which one of the following is true?

   a. The first step in solving $|2x - 3| > -7$ is to rewrite the inequality as $2x - 3 > -7$ or $2x - 3 < 7$.

   b. The smallest real number in the solution set of $2x > 6$ is 4.

   c. All irrational numbers satisfy $|x - 4| > 0$.

   d. None of these statements is true.

127. What's wrong with this argument? Suppose x and y represent two real numbers, where $x > y$.

$2 > 1$	This is a true statement.
$2(y - x) > 1(y - x)$	Multiply both sides by $y - x$.
$2y - 2x > y - x$	Use the distributive property.
$y - 2x > -x$	Subtract y from both sides.
$y > x$	Add 2x to both sides.

The final inequality, $y > x$, is impossible because we were initially given $x > y$.

128. The graphs of $y = 6$, $y = 3(-x - 5) - 9$, and $y = 0$ are shown in the figure. The graphs were obtained using a graphing utility and a $[-12, 1, 1]$ by $[-2, 8, 1]$ viewing rectangle. Use the graphs to write the solution set for the compound inequality. Express the solution set using interval notation.

$$0 < 3(-x - 5) - 9 < 6.$$

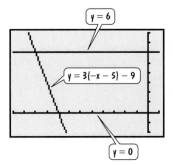

129. The percentage, p, of defective products manufactured by a company is given by $|p - 0.3\%| \le 0.2\%$. If 100,000 products are manufactured and the company offers a $5 refund for each defective product, describe the company's cost for refunds.

Group Exercise

130. Each group member should research one situation that provides two different pricing options. These can involve areas such as public transportation options (with or without coupon books) or long-distance telephone plans or anything of interest. Be sure to bring in all the details for each option. At a second group meeting, select the two pricing situations that are most interesting and relevant. Using each situation, write a word problem about selecting the better of the two options. The word problem should be one that can be solved using a linear inequality. The group should turn in the two problems and their solutions.

CHAPTER *SUMMARY*, REVIEW, AND TEST

Summary

DEFINITIONS AND CONCEPTS	EXAMPLES

1.1 Graphs and Graphing Utilities

a. The rectangular coordinate system consists of a horizontal number line, the x-axis, and a vertical number line, the y-axis, intersecting at their zero points, the origin. Each point in the system corresponds to an ordered pair of real numbers (x,y). The first number in the pair is the x-coordinate; the second number is the y-coordinate. See Figure 1.1 on page 76.

Ex. 1, p. 77

b. An ordered pair is a solution of an equation in two variables if replacing the variables by the corresponding coordinates results in a true statement. The ordered pair is said to satisfy the equation. The graph of the equation is the set of all points whose coordinates satisfy the equation. One method for graphing an equation is to plot ordered-pair solutions and connect them with a smooth curve or line.

Ex. 2, p. 78

c. An x-intercept of a graph is the x-coordinate of a point where the graph intersects the x-axis. The y-coordinate corresponding to a graphs x-intercept is always zero.

d. A y-intercept of a graph is the y-coordinate of a point where the graph intersects the y-axis. The x-coordinate corresponding to a graphs y-intercept is always zero.

1.2 Linear Equations

a. A linear equation in one variable x can be written in the form $ax + b = 0, a \neq 0$.

b. The procedure for solving a linear equation is given in the box on page 86.

Ex. 1, p. 86;
Ex. 2, p. 87

c. If an equation contains fractions, begin by multiplying both sides by the least common denominator, thereby clearing fractions.

Ex. 3, p. 88

d. If an equation contains rational expressions with variable denominators, avoid in the solution set any values of the variable that make a denominator zero.

Ex. 4, p. 89;
Ex. 5, p. 90

e. An identity is an equation that is true for all real numbers for which both sides are defined. A conditional equation is not an identity and is true for at least one real number. An inconsistent equation is an equation that is not true for even one real number.

Ex. 6, p. 91

1.3 Formulas and Applications

a. A formula is an equation that uses letters to express a relationship between two or more variables.

Ex. 1, p. 96

b. Mathematical modeling is the process of finding equations and formulas to describe real-world phenomena. Such equations and formulas, together with the meaning assigned to the variables, are called mathematical models. Mathematical models can be formed from verbal models or from actual data.

c. A five-step procedure for solving problems using mathematical models is given in the box on page 97.

Ex. 2, p. 97;
Ex. 3, p. 98;
Ex. 4, p. 100;
Ex. 5, p. 101

1.4 Complex Numbers

a. The imaginary unit i is defined as

$$i = \sqrt{-1}, \text{ where } i^2 = -1.$$

The set of numbers in the form $a + bi$ is called the set of complex numbers; a is the real part and b is the imaginary part. If $b = 0$, the complex number is a real number. If $b \neq 0$, the complex number is an imaginary number. Complex numbers in the form bi are called pure imaginary numbers.

b. Rules for adding and subtracting complex numbers are given in the box on page 109.

Ex. 1, p. 110

c. To multiply complex numbers, multiply as if they are polynomials. After completing the multiplication, replace i^2 with -1.

Ex. 2, p. 110

DEFINITIONS AND CONCEPTS	**EXAMPLES**

d. The complex conjugate of $a + bi$ is $a - bi$ and vice versa. The multiplication of complex conjugates gives a real number:

$$(a + bi)(a - bi) = a^2 + b^2.$$

e. To divide complex numbers, multiply the numerator and the denominator by the complex conjugate of the denominator. — Ex. 3, p. 111

f. When performing operations with square roots of negative numbers, begin by expressing all square roots in terms of i. The principal square root of $-b$ is defined by — Ex. 4, p. 112

$$\sqrt{-b} = i\sqrt{b}.$$

1.5 Quadratic Equations

a. A quadratic equation in x can be written in the general form $ax^2 + bx + c = 0, a \neq 0$.

b. The procedure for solving a quadratic equation by factoring and the zero-product principle is given in the box on pages 115–116. — Ex. 1, p. 116

c. The procedure for solving a quadratic equation by the square root method is given in the box on page 118. — Ex. 2, p. 118

d. All quadratic equations can be solved by completing the square. Isolate the binomial with the two variable terms on one side of the equation. If the coefficient of the x^2-term is not one, divide each side of the equation by this coefficient. Then add the square of half the coefficient of x to both sides. — Ex. 4, p. 119

e. All quadratic equations can be solved by the quadratic formula — Ex. 5, p. 122; Ex. 6, p. 123

$$x = \frac{-b \pm \sqrt{b^2 - 4ac}}{2a}.$$

The formula is derived by completing the square of the equation $ax^2 + bx + c = 0$.

f. The discriminant, $b^2 - 4ac$, indicates the number and type of solutions to the quadratic equation $ax^2 + bx + c = 0$, shown in Table 1.3 on page 124. — Ex. 7, p. 124

g. Table 1.4 on page 125 shows the most efficient technique to use when solving a quadratic equation. — Ex. 8, p. 126; Ex. 9, p. 127

1.6 Other Types of Equations

a. Some polynomial equations of degree 3 or greater can be solved by moving all terms to one side, obtaining zero on the other side, factoring, and using the zero-product principle. Factoring by grouping is often used. — Ex. 1, p. 132; Ex. 2, p. 133

b. A radical equation is an equation in which the variable occurs in a square root, cube root, and so on. A radical equation can be solved by isolating the radical and raising both sides of the equation to a power equal to the radicals index. When raising both sides to an even power, check all proposed solutions in the original equation. Eliminate extraneous solutions from the solution set. — Ex. 3, p. 134; Ex. 4, p. 135

c. A radical equation with rational exponents can be solved by isolating the expression with the rational exponent and raising both sides of the equation to a power that is the reciprocal of the rational exponent. See the details in the box on page 137. — Ex. 5, p. 137

d. An equation is quadratic in form if it can be written in the form $at^2 + bt + c = 0$, where t is an algebraic expression and $a \neq 0$. Solve for t and use the substitution that resulted in this equation to find the values for the variable in the given equation. — Ex. 6, p. 139; Ex. 7, p. 139

e. Absolute value equations in the form $|X| = c, c > 0$, can be solved by rewriting the equation without absolute value bars: $X = c$ or $X = -c$. — Ex. 8, p. 140

DEFINITIONS AND CONCEPTS	EXAMPLES

1.7 Linear Inequalities

a. A linear inequality in one variable x can be expressed as
$ax + b \leq c,\ ax + b < c,\ ax + b \geq c,$ or $ax + b > c,\ a \neq 0.$ — Ex. 1, p. 145

b. Graphs of solutions to inequalities are shown on a number line by shading all points representing numbers that are solutions. Parentheses exclude endpoints and square brackets include endpoints. — Ex. 2, p. 146

c. Solution sets of inequalities can be expressed in set-builder or interval notation. Table 1.5 on page 146 compares the notations. — Ex. 3, p. 148; Ex. 4, p. 149

d. A linear inequality is solved using a procedure similar to solving a linear equation. However, when multiplying or dividing by a negative number, reverse the sense of the inequality. — Ex. 5, p. 150

e. A compound inequality with three parts can be solved by isolating x in the middle.

f. Inequalities involving absolute value can be solved by rewriting the inequalities without absolute value bars. The ways to do this are shown in the box on page 150. — Ex. 6, p. 151; Ex. 7, p. 151

Review Exercises

1.1

Graph each equation in Exercises 1–4.

Let $x = -3, -2, -1, 0, 1, 2,$ and 3.

1. $y = 2x - 2$

2. $y = x^2 - 3$

3. $y = x$

4. $y = |x| - 2$

5. What does a $[-20, 40, 10]$ by $[-5, 5, 1]$ viewing rectangle mean? Draw axes with tick marks and label the tick marks to illustrate this viewing rectangle.

In Exercises 6–8, use the graph and determine the x-intercepts, if any, and the y-intercepts, if any. For each graph, tick marks along the axes represent one unit each.

6.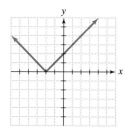

7.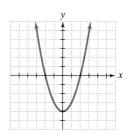

8.

The caseload of Alzheimer's disease in the United States is expected to explode as baby boomers head into their later years. The graph shows the percentage of Americans with the disease, by age. Use the graph to solve Exercises 9–11.

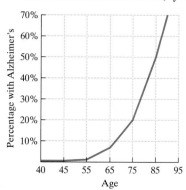

Alzheimer's Prevalence in the U.S., by Age

Source: Centers for Disease Control

9. What percentage of Americans who are 75 have Alzheimer's disease?

10. What age represents 50% prevalence of Alzheimer's disease?

11. Describe the trend shown by the graph.

1.2

In Exercises 12–17, solve and check each linear equation.

12. $2x - 5 = 7$

13. $5x + 20 = 3x$

14. $7(x - 4) = x + 2$

15. $1 - 2(6 - x) = 3x + 2$

16. $2(x - 4) + 3(x + 5) = 2x - 2$

17. $2x - 4(5x + 1) = 3x + 17$

Exercises 18–22 contain equations with constants in denominators. Solve each equation and check by the method of your choice.

18. $\dfrac{2x}{3} = \dfrac{x}{6} + 1$

19. $\dfrac{x}{2} - \dfrac{1}{10} = \dfrac{x}{5} + \dfrac{1}{2}$

20. $\dfrac{2x}{3} = 6 - \dfrac{x}{4}$

21. $\dfrac{x}{4} = 2 + \dfrac{x - 3}{3}$

22. $\dfrac{3x + 1}{3} - \dfrac{13}{2} = \dfrac{1 - x}{4}$

Exercises 23–26 contain equations with variables in denominators. **a.** *List the value or values representing restriction(s) on the variable.* **b.** *Solve the equation.*

23. $\dfrac{9}{4} - \dfrac{1}{2x} = \dfrac{4}{x}$

24. $\dfrac{7}{x - 5} + 2 = \dfrac{x + 2}{x - 5}$

25. $\dfrac{1}{x - 1} - \dfrac{1}{x + 1} = \dfrac{2}{x^2 - 1}$

26. $\dfrac{4}{x + 2} + \dfrac{2}{x - 4} = \dfrac{30}{x^2 - 2x - 8}$

In Exercises 27–29, determine whether each equation is an identity, a conditional equation, or an inconsistent equation.

27. $\dfrac{1}{x + 5} = 0$

28. $7x + 13 = 4x - 10 + 3x + 23$

29. $7x + 13 = 3x - 10 + 2x + 23$

1.3

30. The percentage, P, of U.S. adults who read the daily newspaper can be modeled by the formula

$$P = -0.7x + 80$$

where x is the number of years after 1965. In which year will 52% of U.S. adults read the daily newspaper?

31. Suppose you were to list in order, from least to most, the family income for every U.S. family. The median income is the income in the middle of this list of ranked data. This income can be modeled by the formula

$$I = 1321.7(x - 1980) + 21,153.$$

In this formula, I represents median family income in the United States and x is the actual year, beginning in 1980. When was the median income $47,587?

In Exercises 32–39, use the five-step strategy given in the box on page 97 to solve each problem.

32. The cost of raising a child through the age of 17 varies by income group. The cost in middle-income families exceeds that of low-income families by $63 thousand, and the cost of high-income families is $3 thousand less than twice that of low-income families. Three children, one in a low-income family, one in a middle-income family, and one in a high-income family, will cost a total of $756 thousand to raise through the age of 17. Find the cost of raising a child in each of the three income groups. (*Source: The World Almanac;* low annual income is less than $36,800, middle is $36,800–$61,900, and high exceeds $61,900.)

33. In 2000, the average weekly salary for workers in the United States was $567. If this amount is increasing by $15 yearly, in how many years after 2000 will the average salary reach $702. In which year will that be?

34. You are choosing between two long-distance telephone plans. One plan has a monthly fee of $15 with a charge of $0.05 per minute. The other plan has a monthly fee of $5 with a charge of $0.07 per minute. For how many minutes of long-distance calls will the costs for the two plans be the same?

35. You inherit $10,000 with the stipulation that for the first year the money must be placed in two investments paying 8% and 12% annual interest, respectively. How much should be invested at each rate if the total interest earned for the year is to be $950?

36. The length of a rectangular football field is 14 meters more than twice the width. If the perimeter is 346 meters, find the field's dimensions.

37. The bus fare in a city is $1.50. People who use the bus have the option of purchasing a monthly coupon book for $25.00. With the coupon book, the fare is reduced to $0.25. Determine the number of times in a month the bus must be used so that the total monthly cost without the coupon book is the same as the total monthly cost with the coupon book.

38. A salesperson earns $300 per week plus 5% commission of sales. How much must be sold to earn $800 in a week?

39. A study entitled *Performing Arts—The Economic Dilemma* documents the relationship between the number of concerts given by a major orchestra and the attendance per concert. For each additional concert given per year, attendance per concert drops by approximately eight people. If 50 concerts are given, attendance per concert is 2987 people. How many concerts should be given to ensure an audience of 2627 people at each concert?

In Exercises 40–42, solve each formula for the specified variable.

40. $V = \dfrac{1}{3}Bh$ for h

41. $F = f(1 - M)$ for M

42. $T = gr + gvt$ for g

1.4

In Exercises 43–52, perform the indicated operations and write the result in standard form.

43. $(8 - 3i) - (17 - 7i)$

44. $4i(3i - 2)$

45. $(7 - 5i)(2 + 3i)$

46. $(3 - 4i)^2$

47. $(7 + 8i)(7 - 8i)$

48. $\dfrac{6}{5 + i}$

49. $\dfrac{3 + 4i}{4 - 2i}$

50. $\sqrt{-32} - \sqrt{-18}$

51. $(-2 + \sqrt{-100})^2$

52. $\dfrac{4 + \sqrt{-8}}{2}$

1.5

Solve each equation in Exercises 53–54 by factoring.

53. $2x^2 + 15x = 8$

54. $5x^2 + 20x = 0$

Solve each equation in Exercises 55–56 by the square root method.

55. $2x^2 - 3 = 125$

56. $(3x - 4)^2 = 18$

In Exercises 57–58, determine the constant that should be added to the binomial so that it becomes a perfect square trinomial. Then write and factor the trinomial.

57. $x^2 + 20x$

58. $x^2 - 3x$

Solve each equation in Exercises 59–60 by completing the square.

59. $x^2 - 12x + 27 = 0$

60. $3x^2 - 12x + 11 = 0$

Solve each equation in Exercises 61–63 using the quadratic formula.

61. $x^2 = 2x + 4$

62. $x^2 - 2x + 19 = 0$

63. $2x^2 = 3 - 4x$

Compute the discriminant of each equation in Exercises 64–65. What does the discriminant indicate about the number and type of solutions?

64. $x^2 - 4x + 13 = 0$

65. $9x^2 = 2 - 3x$

Solve each equation in Exercises 66–71 by the method of your choice.

66. $2x^2 - 11x + 5 = 0$

67. $(3x + 5)(x - 3) = 5$

68. $3x^2 - 7x + 1 = 0$

69. $x^2 - 9 = 0$

70. $(x - 3)^2 - 25 = 0$

71. $3x^2 - x + 2 = 0$

72. The weight of a human fetus is modeled by the formula $W = 3t^2$, where W is the weight, in grams, and t is the time, in weeks, $0 \le t \le 39$. After how many weeks does the fetus weigh 1200 grams?

73. The alligator, an endangered species, is the subject of a protection program. The formula
$$P = -10x^2 + 475x + 3500$$
models the alligator population, P, after x years of the protection program, where $0 \le x \le 12$. After how many years is the population up to 7250?

74. The graph of the alligator population described in Exercise 73 is shown over time. Identify your solution in Exercise 73 as a point on the graph.

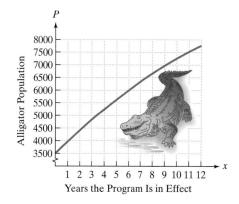

75. An architect is allowed 15 square yards of floor space to add a small bedroom to a house. Because of the room's design in relationship to the existing structure, the width of the rectangular floor must be 7 yards less than two times the length. Find the length and width of the rectangular floor that the architect is permitted.

76. A building casts a shadow that is double the length of its height. If the distance from the end of the shadow to the top of the building is 300 meters, how high is the building? Round to the nearest meter.

1.6

Solve each polynomial equation in Exercises 77–78.

77. $2x^4 = 50x^2$

78. $2x^3 - x^2 - 18x + 9 = 0$

Solve each radical equation in Exercises 79–80.

79. $\sqrt{2x - 3} + x = 3$

80. $\sqrt{x - 4} + \sqrt{x + 1} = 5$

Solve the equations with rational exponents in Exercises 81–82.

81. $3x^{3/4} - 24 = 0$

82. $(x - 7)^{2/3} = 25$

Solve each equation in Exercises 83–84 by making an appropriate substitution.

83. $x^4 - 5x^2 + 4 = 0$

84. $x^{1/2} + 3x^{1/4} - 10 = 0$

Solve the equations containing absolute value in Exercises 85–86.

85. $|2x + 1| = 7$

86. $2|x - 3| - 6 = 10$

Solve each equation in Exercises 87–90 by the method of your choice.

87. $3x^{4/3} - 5x^{2/3} + 2 = 0$

88. $2\sqrt{x - 1} = x$

89. $|2x - 5| - 3 = 0$ **90.** $x^3 + 2x^2 = 9x + 18$

91. The distance to the horizon that you can see, D, in miles, from the top of a mountain H feet high is modeled by the formula $D = \sqrt{2H}$. You've hiked to the top of a mountain with views extending 50 miles to the horizon. How high is the mountain?

1.7

In Exercises 92–94, graph the solutions of each inequality on a number line.

92. $x > 5$ **93.** $x \le 1$ **94.** $-3 \le x < 0$

In Exercises 95–97, express each interval in terms of an inequality, and graph the interval on a number line.

95. $(-2, 3]$ **96.** $[-1.5, 2]$ **97.** $(-1, \infty)$

Solve each linear inequality in Exercises 98–103 and graph the solution set on a number line. Express each solution set in interval notation.

98. $-6x + 3 \le 15$ **99.** $6x - 9 \ge -4x - 3$

100. $\dfrac{x}{3} - \dfrac{3}{4} - 1 > \dfrac{x}{2}$ **101.** $6x + 5 > -2(x - 3) - 25$

102. $3(2x - 1) - 2(x - 4) \ge 7 + 2(3 + 4x)$

103. $7 < 2x + 3 \le 9$

Solve each inequality in Exercises 104–106 by first rewriting each one as an equivalent inequality without absolute value bars. Graph the solution set on a number line. Express each solution set in interval notation.

104. $|2x + 3| \le 15$ **105.** $\left|\dfrac{2x + 6}{3}\right| > 2$

106. $|2x + 5| - 7 \ge -6$

107. Approximately 90% of the population sleeps h hours daily, where h is modeled by the inequality $|h - 6.5| \le 1$. Write a sentence describing the range for the number of hours that most people sleep. Do *not* use the phrase "absolute value" in your description.

108. The formula for converting Fahrenheit temperature, F, to Celsius temperature, C, is $C = \frac{5}{9}(F - 32)$. If Celsius temperature ranges from $10°$ to $25°$, inclusive, what is the range for the Fahrenheit temperature?

109. A person can choose between two charges on a checking account. The first method involves a fixed cost of $11 per month plus 6¢ for each check written. The second method involves a fixed cost of $4 per month plus 20¢ for each check written. How many checks should be written to make the first method a better deal?

110. A student has grades on three examinations of 75, 80, and 72. What must the student earn on a fourth examination in order to have an average of at least 80?

Chapter 1 Test

1. Graph $y = x^2 - 4$ by letting x equal integers from -3 through 3.

2. The graph of $y = -\frac{3}{2}x + 3$ is shown in a $[-6, 6, 1]$ by $[-6, 6, 1]$ viewing rectangle. Determine the x-intercepts, if any, and the y-intercepts, if any.

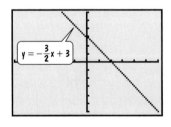

3. The graph shows the unemployment rate in the United States from 1990 through 2000. For the period shown, during which year did the unemployment rate reach a maximum? Estimate the percentage of the work force unemployed, to the nearest tenth of a percent, at that time.

U.S. Unemployment Rate

Source: Bureau of Labor Statistics

Find the solution set for each equation in Exercises 4–16.

4. $7(x - 2) = 4(x + 1) - 21$

5. $\dfrac{2x - 3}{4} = \dfrac{x - 4}{2} - \dfrac{x + 1}{4}$

6. $\dfrac{2}{x - 3} - \dfrac{4}{x + 3} = \dfrac{8}{x^2 - 9}$

7. $2x^2 - 3x - 2 = 0$ **8.** $(3x - 1)^2 = 75$

9. $x(x - 2) = 4$ **10.** $4x^2 = 8x - 5$

11. $x^3 - 4x^2 - x + 4 = 0$ **12.** $\sqrt{x - 3} + 5 = x$

13. $\sqrt{x + 4} + \sqrt{x - 1} = 5$ **14.** $5x^{3/2} - 10 = 0$

15. $x^{2/3} - 9x^{1/3} + 8 = 0$ **16.** $\left|\dfrac{2}{3}x - 6\right| = 2$

Solve each inequality in Exercises 17–22. Express the answer in interval notation and graph the solution set on a number line.

17. $3(x + 4) \geq 5x - 12$ **18.** $\dfrac{x}{6} + \dfrac{1}{8} \leq \dfrac{x}{2} - \dfrac{3}{4}$

19. $-3 \leq \dfrac{2x + 5}{3} < 6$ **20.** $|3x + 2| \geq 3$

21. $x^2 < x + 12$ **22.** $\dfrac{2x + 1}{x - 3} > 3$

In Exercises 23–25, perform the indicated operations and write the result in standard form.

23. $(6 - 7i)(2 + 5i)$ **24.** $\dfrac{5}{2 - i}$

25. $2\sqrt{-49} + 3\sqrt{-64}$

In Exercises 26–27, solve each formula for the specified variable.

26. $V = \dfrac{1}{3}lwh$ for h

27. $y - y_1 = m(x - x_1)$ for x

The male minority? The graphs show enrollment in U.S. colleges, with projections from 2000 to 2009. The trend indicated by the graphs is among the hottest topics of debate among college-admission officers. Some private liberal arts colleges have quietly begun special efforts to recruit men— including admissions preferences for them.

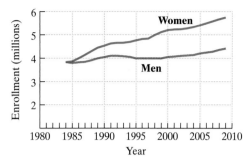

Enrollment in U.S. Colleges

Source: U.S. Department of Education

Exercises 28–29 are based on the data shown by the graphs.

28. The data for the men can be modeled by the formula

$$N = 0.01x + 3.9$$

where N represents enrollment, in millions, x years after 1984. According to the formula, when will the projected enrollment for men be 4.1 million? How well does the formula describe enrollment for that year shown by line graph?

29. The data for the women can be modeled from the following verbal description:

> In 1984, 4.1 million women were enrolled. Female enrollment has increased by 0.07 million per year since then.

According to the verbal model, when will the projected enrollment for women be 5.71 million? How well does the verbal model describe enrollment for that year shown by the line graph?

30. On average, the number of unhealthy air days per year in Los Angeles exceeds three times that of New York City by 48 days. If Los Angeles and New York City combined have 268 unhealthy air days per year, determine the number of unhealthy days for the two cities. (*Source:* U.S. Environmental Protection Agency)

31. The costs for two different kinds of heating systems for a three-bedroom home are given in the following table. After how many years will total costs for solar heating and electric heating be the same? What will be the cost at that time?

System	Cost to Install	Operating Cost/Year
Solar	$29,700	$150
Electric	$5000	$1100

32. You placed $10,000 in two investments paying 8% and 10% annual interest, respectively. At the end of the year, the total interest from these investments was $940. How much was invested at each rate?

33. The length of a rectangular carpet is 4 feet greater than twice its width. If the area is 48 square feet, find the carpet's length and width.

34. A vertical pole is to be supported by a wire that is 26 feet long and anchored 24 feet from the base of the pole. How far up the pole should the wire be attached?

35. You take a summer job selling medical supplies. You are paid $600 per month plus 4% of the sales price of all the supplies you sell. If you want to earn more than $2500 per month, what value of medical supplies must you sell?

Functions
and Graphs

Chapter 2

The cost of mailing a package depends on its weight. The probability that you and another person in a room share the same birthday depends on the number of people in the room. In both these situations, the relationship between variables can be described by a *function*. Understanding this concept will give you a new perspective on many ordinary situations.

'Tis the season and you've waited until the last minute to mail your holiday gifts. Your only option is overnight express mail. You realize that the cost of mailing a gift depends on its weight, but the mailing costs seem somewhat odd. Your packages that weigh 1.1 pounds, 1.5 pounds, and 2 pounds cost $15.75 each to send overnight. Packages that weigh 2.01 pounds and 3 pounds cost you $18.50 each. Finally, your heaviest gift is barely over 3 pounds and its mailing cost is $21.25. What sort of system is this in which costs increase by $2.75, stepping from $15.75 to $18.50 and from $18.50 to $21.25?

SECTION 2.1 *Lines and Slopes*

Objectives

1. Compute a line's slope.
2. Write the point-slope equation of a line.
3. Write and graph the slope-intercept equation of a line.
4. Recognize equations of horizontal and vertical lines.
5. Recognize and use the general form of a line's equation.
6. Find slopes and equations of parallel and perpendicular lines.
7. Model data with linear equation

Is there a relationship between literacy and child mortality? As the percentage of adult females who are literate increases, does the mortality of children under five decrease? Figure 2.1, based on data from the United Nations, indicates that this is, indeed, the case. Each point in the figure represents one country.

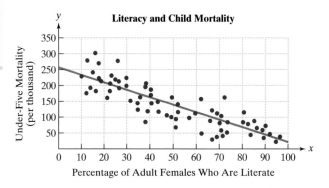

Figure 2.1
Source: United Nations

Data presented in a visual form as a set of points is called a **scatter plot.** Also shown in Figure 2.1 is a line that passes through or near the points. A line that best fits the data points in a scatter plot is called a **regression line.** By writing the equation of this line, we can obtain a model of the data and make predictions about child mortality based on the percentage of adult females in a country who are literate.

Data often fall on or near a line. In this section we will use equations to model such data and make predictions. We begin with a discussion of a line's steepness.

1 Calculate a line's slope.

The Slope of a Line

Mathematicians have developed a useful measure of the steepness of a line, called the *slope* of the line. Slope compares the vertical change (the **rise**) to the horizontal change (the **run**) when moving from one fixed point to another along the line. To calculate the slope of a line, we use a ratio that compares the change in y (the rise) to the corresponding change in x (the run).

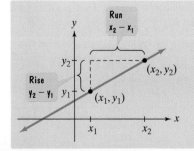

Definition of Slope

The **slope** of the line through the distinct points (x_1, y_1) and (x_2, y_2) is

$$\frac{\text{Change in } y}{\text{Change in } x} = \frac{\text{Rise}}{\text{Run}}$$

$$= \frac{y_2 - y_1}{x_2 - x_1}$$

where $x_2 - x_1 \neq 0$.

It is common notation to let the letter m represent the slope of a line. The letter m is used because it is the first letter of the French verb *monter*, meaning to rise, or to ascend.

Slope and the Streets of San Francisco

San Francisco's Filbert Street has a slope of 0.613, meaning that for every horizontal distance of 100 feet, the street ascends 61.3 feet vertically. With its 31.5° angle of inclination, the street is too steep to pave and is only accessible by wooden stairs.

EXAMPLE 1 Using the Definition of Slope

Find the slope of the line passing through each pair of points:

a. $(-3, -1)$ and $(-2, 4)$ **b.** $(-3, 4)$ and $(2, -2)$.

Solution

a. Let $(x_1, y_1) = (-3, -1)$ and $(x_2, y_2) = (-2, 4)$. We obtain a slope of

$$m = \frac{\text{Change in } y}{\text{Change in } x} = \frac{y_2 - y_1}{x_2 - x_1} = \frac{4 - (-1)}{-2 - (-3)} = \frac{5}{1} = 5.$$

The situation is illustrated in Figure 2.2(a). The slope of the line is 5, indicating that there is a vertical change, a rise, of 5 units for each horizontal change, a run, of 1 unit. The slope is positive, and the line rises from left to right.

Study Tip

When computing slope, it makes no difference which point you call (x_1, y_1) and which point you call (x_2, y_2). If we let $(x_1, y_1) = (-2, 4)$ and $(x_2, y_2) = (-3, -1)$, the slope is still 5:

$$m = \frac{y_2 - y_1}{x_2 - x_1} = \frac{-1 - 4}{-3 - (-2)} = \frac{-5}{-1} = 5.$$

However, you should not subtract in one order in the numerator $(y_2 - y_1)$ and then in a different order in the denominator $(x_1 - x_2)$. The slope is *not*

$$\frac{-1 - 4}{-2 - (-3)} = -5. \quad \text{Incorrect}$$

b. We can let $(x_1, y_1) = (-3, 4)$ and $(x_2, y_2) = (2, -2)$. The slope of the line shown in Figure 2.2(b) is computed as follows:

$$m = \frac{-2 - 4}{2 - (-3)} = \frac{-6}{5} = -\frac{6}{5}.$$

The slope of the line is $-\frac{6}{5}$. For every vertical change of -6 units (6 units down), there is a corresponding horizontal change of 5 units. The slope is negative and the line falls from left to right.

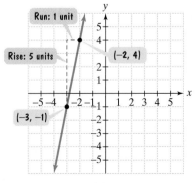

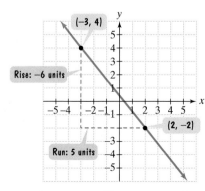

Figure 2.2 Visualizing slope   **(a)**   **(b)**

Check Point 1
Find the slope of the line passing through each pair of points:

    a. $(-3, 4)$ and $(-4, -2)$ **b.** $(4, -2)$ and $(-1, 5)$.

Example 1 illustrates that a line with a positive slope is rising from left to right and a line with a negative slope is falling from left to right. By contrast, a horizontal line neither rises nor falls and has a slope of zero. A vertical line has no horizontal change, so $x_2 - x_1 = 0$ in the formula for slope. Because we cannot divide by zero, the slope of a vertical line is undefined. This discussion is summarized in Table 2.1.

Table 2.1   Possibilities for a Line's Slope

Positive Slope	Negative Slope	Zero Slope	Undefined Slope
$m > 0$	$m < 0$	$m = 0$	m is undefined.
Line rises from left to right.	Line falls from left to right.	Line is horizontal.	Line is vertical.

2 Write the point-slope equation of a line.

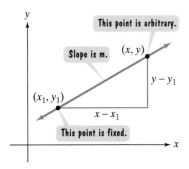

Figure 2.3 A line passing through (x_1, y_1) with slope m

The Point-Slope Form of the Equation of a Line

We can use the slope of a line to obtain various forms of the line's equation. For example, consider a nonvertical line with slope m that contains the point (x_1, y_1). Now, let (x, y) represent any other point on the line, shown in Figure 2.3. Keep in mind that the point (x, y) is arbitrary and is not in one fixed position. By contrast, the point (x_1, y_1) is fixed. Regardless of where the point (x, y) is located, the shape of the triangle in Figure 2.3 remains the same. Thus, the ratio for slope stays a constant m. This means that for all points along the line,

$$m = \frac{y - y_1}{x - x_1}, \quad x \neq x_1.$$

We can clear the fraction by multiplying both sides by $x - x_1$.

$$m(x - x_1) = \frac{y - y_1}{x - x_1} \cdot x - x_1$$

$$m(x - x_1) = y - y_1 \qquad \text{Simplify.}$$

Now, if we reverse the two sides, we obtain the *point-slope form* of the equation of a line.

> **Point-Slope Form of the Equation of a Line**
>
> The **point-slope equation** of a nonvertical line with slope m that passes through the point (x_1, y_1) is
>
> $$y - y_1 = m(x - x_1).$$

For example, an equation of the line passing through $(1, 5)$ with slope $2 (m = 2)$ is

$$y - 5 = 2(x - 1).$$

After we obtain the point-slope form of a line, it is customary to express the equation with y isolated on one side of the equal sign. Example 2 illustrates how this is done.

EXAMPLE 2 Writing the Point-Slope Equation of a Line

Write the point-slope form of the equation of the line passing through $(-1, 3)$ with slope 4. Then solve the equation for y.

Solution We use the point-slope equation of a line with $m = 4$, $x_1 = -1$, and $y_1 = 3$.

$$y - y_1 = m(x - x_1) \qquad \text{This is the point-slope form of the equation.}$$

$$y - 3 = 4[x - (-1)] \qquad \text{Substitute the given values.}$$

$$y - 3 = 4(x + 1) \qquad \text{We now have the point-slope form of the equation for the given line.}$$

We can solve this equation for y by applying the distributive property on the right side.

$$y - 3 = 4x + 4$$

Finally, we add 3 to both sides.

$$y = 4x + 7$$

Check Point 2 Write the point-slope form of the equation of the line passing through $(2, -5)$ with slope 6. Then solve the equation for y.

EXAMPLE 3 Writing the Point-Slope Equation of a Line

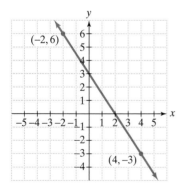

Figure 2.4 Write the point-slope equation of this line.

Write the point-slope form of the equation of the line passing through the points $(4, -3)$ and $(-2, 6)$. (See Figure 2.4.) Then solve the equation for y.

Solution To use the point-slope form, we need to find the slope. The slope is the change in the y-coordinates divided by the corresponding change in the x-coordinates.

$$m = \frac{6 - (-3)}{-2 - 4} = \frac{9}{-6} = -\frac{3}{2} \qquad \text{This is the definition of slope using } (4, -3) \text{ and } (-2, 6).$$

We can take either point on the line to be (x_1, y_1). Let's use $(x_1, y_1) = (4, -3)$. Now, we are ready to write the point-slope equation.

$$y - y_1 = m(x - x_1) \qquad \text{This is the point-slope form of the equation.}$$

$$y - (-3) = -\tfrac{3}{2}(x - 4) \qquad \text{Substitute: } (x_1, y_1) = (4, -3) \text{ and } m = -\tfrac{3}{2}.$$

$$y + 3 = -\tfrac{3}{2}(x - 4) \qquad \text{Simplify.}$$

We now have the point-slope form of the equation of the line shown in Figure 2.4. Now, we solve this equation for y.

Discovery

You can use either point for (x_1, y_1) when you write a line's point-slope equation. Rework Example 3 using $(-2, 6)$ for (x_1, y_1). Once you solve for y, you should still obtain

$$y = -\tfrac{3}{2}x + 3.$$

$$y + 3 = -\tfrac{3}{2}(x - 4) \qquad \text{This is the point-slope form of the equation.}$$

$$y + 3 = -\tfrac{3}{2}x + 6 \qquad \text{Use the distributive property.}$$

$$y = -\tfrac{3}{2}x + 3 \qquad \text{Subtract 3 from both sides.}$$

 Check Point 3 Write the point-slope form of the equation of the line passing through the points $(-2, -1)$ and $(-1, -6)$. Then solve the equation for y.

3 Write and graph the slope-intercept equation of a line.

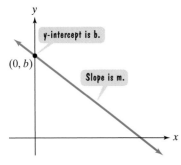

Figure 2.5 A line with slope m and y-intercept b

The Slope-Intercept Form of the Equation of a Line

Let's write the point-slope form of the equation of a nonvertical line with slope m and y-intercept b. The line is shown in Figure 2.5. Because the y-intercept is b, the line passes through $(0, b)$. We use the point-slope form with $x_1 = 0$ and $y_1 = b$.

$$y - y_1 = m(x - x_1)$$

Let $y_1 = b$.   Let $x_1 = 0$.

We obtain

$$y - b = m(x - 0).$$

Simplifying on the right side gives us

$$y - b = mx.$$

Finally, we solve for y by adding b to both sides.

$$y = mx + b$$

Thus, if a line's equation is written with y isolated on one side, the x-coefficient is the line's slope and the constant term is the y-intercept. This form of a line's equation is called the *slope-intercept form* of a line.

> **Slope-Intercept Form of the Equation of a Line**
>
> The **slope-intercept equation** of a nonvertical line with slope m and y-intercept b is
>
> $$y = mx + b.$$

EXAMPLE 4   Graphing by Using the Slope and y-Intercept

Graph the line whose equation is $y = \tfrac{2}{3}x + 2$.

Solution   The equation of the line is in the form $y = mx + b$. We can find the slope, m, by identifying the coefficient of x. We can find the y-intercept, b, by identifying the constant term.

$$y = \frac{2}{3}x + 2$$

The slope is $\tfrac{2}{3}$.   The y-intercept is 2.

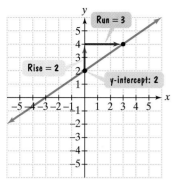

Figure 2.6 The graph of $y = \frac{2}{3}x + 2$

We need two points in order to graph the line. We can use the y-intercept, 2, to obtain the first point $(0, 2)$. Plot this point on the y-axis, shown in Figure 2.6.

We know the slope and one point on the line. We can use the slope, $\frac{2}{3}$, to determine a second point on the line. By definition,

$$m = \frac{2}{3} = \frac{\text{Rise}}{\text{Run}}.$$

We plot the second point on the line by starting at $(0, 2)$, the first point. Based on the slope, we move 2 units *up* (the rise) and 3 units to the *right* (the run). This puts us at a second point on the line, $(3, 4)$, shown in Figure 2.6.

We use a straightedge to draw a line through the two points. The graph of $y = \frac{2}{3}x + 2$ is shown in Figure 2.6.

Graphing $y = mx + b$ by Using the Slope and y-Intercept

1. Plot the y-intercept on the y-axis. This is the point $(0, b)$.
2. Obtain a second point using the slope, m. Write m as a fraction, and use rise over run, starting at the point containing the y-intercept, to plot this point.
3. Use a straightedge to draw a line through the two points. Draw arrowheads at the ends of the line to show that the line continues indefinitely in both directions.

Check Point 4 Graph the line whose equation is $y = \frac{3}{5}x + 1$.

4 Recognize equations of horizontal and vertical lines.

Equations of Horizontal and Vertical Lines

Some things change very little. For example, Figure 2.7 shows that the percentage of people in the United States satisfied with their lives remains relatively constant for all age groups. Shown in the figure is a horizontal line that passes near most tops of the six bars.

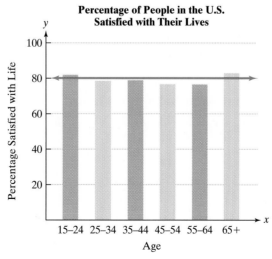

Figure 2.7
Source: Culture Shift in Advanced Industrial Society, Princeton University Press

We can use $y = mx + b$, the slope-intercept form of a line's equation, to write the equation of the horizontal line in Figure 2.7. We need the line's slope, m, and its y-intercept, b. Because the line is horizontal, $m = 0$. The line intersects the y-axis at $(0, 80)$, so its y-intercept is 80: $b = 80$.

Thus, an equation in the form $y = mx + b$ that models the percentage, y, of people at age x satisfied with their lives is

$$y = 0x + 80, \quad \text{or} \quad y = 80.$$

The percentage of people satisfied with their lives remains relatively constant in the United States for all age groups, at approximately 80%.

In general, if a line is horizontal, its slope is zero: $m = 0$. Thus, the equation $y = mx + b$ becomes $y = b$, where b is the y-intercept. All horizontal lines have equations of the form $y = b$.

EXAMPLE 5 Graphing a Horizontal Line

Graph $y = -4$ in the rectangular coordinate system.

Solution All points on the graph of $y = -4$ have a value of y that is always -4. No matter what the x-coordinate is, the y-coordinate for every point on the line is -4. Let us select three of the possible values for x: $-2, 0$, and 3. So, three of the points on the graph $y = -4$ are $(-2, -4)$, $(0, -4)$, and $(3, -4)$. Plot each of these points. Drawing a line that passes through the three points gives the horizontal line shown in Figure 2.8.

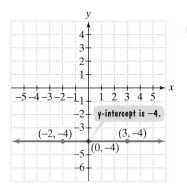

Figure 2.8 The graph of $y = -4$

Check Point 5 Graph $y = 3$ in the rectangular coordinate system.

Next, let's see what we can discover about the graph of an equation of the form $x = a$ by looking at an example.

EXAMPLE 6 Graphing a Vertical Line

Graph $x = 5$ in the rectangular coordinate system.

Solution All points on the graph of $x = 5$ have a value of x that is always 5. No matter what the y-coordinate is, the corresponding x-coordinate for every point on the line is 5. Let us select three of the possible values of y: $-2, 0$, and 3. So, three of the points on the graph of $x = 5$ are $(5, -2)$, $(5, 0)$, and $(5, 3)$. Plot each of these points. Drawing a line that passes through the three points gives the vertical line shown in Figure 2.9.

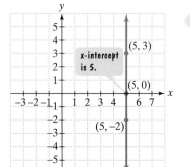

Figure 2.9 The graph $x = 5$

Horizontal and Vertical Lines

The graph of $y = b$ is a horizontal line. The y-intercept is b.

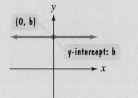

The graph of $x = a$ is a vertical line. The x-intercept is a.

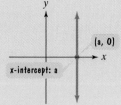

Check Point 6 Graph $x = -1$ in the rectangular coordinate system.

5 Recognize and use the general form of a line's equation.

The General Form of the Equation of a Line

The vertical line whose equation is $x = 5$ cannot be written in slope-intercept form, $y = mx + b$, because its slope is undefined. However, every line has an equation that can be expressed in the form $Ax + By + C = 0$. For example, $x = 5$ can be expressed as $1x + 0y - 5 = 0$, or $x - 5 = 0$. The equation $Ax + By + C = 0$ is called the *general form* of the equation of a line.

> ### General Form of the Equation of a Line
> Every line has an equation that can be written in the **general form**
> $$Ax + By + C = 0$$
> where A, B, and C are real numbers, and A and B are not both zero.

If the equation of a line is given in general form, it is possible to find the slope, m, and the y-intercept, b, for the line. We solve the equation for y, transforming it into the slope-intercept form $y = mx + b$. In this form, the coefficient of x is the slope of the line, and the constant term is its y-intercept.

EXAMPLE 7   Finding the Slope and the y-Intercept

Find the slope and the y-intercept of the line whose equation is $2x - 3y + 6 = 0$.

Solution The equation is given in general form. We begin by rewriting it in the form $y = mx + b$. We need to solve for y.

$$2x - 3y + 6 = 0 \quad \text{This is the given equation.}$$
$$2x + 6 = 3y \quad \text{To isolate the y-term, add 3y to both sides.}$$
$$3y = 2x + 6 \quad \text{Reverse the two sides. (This step is optional.)}$$
$$y = \frac{2}{3}x + 2 \quad \text{Divide both sides by 3.}$$

The coefficient of x, $\frac{2}{3}$, is the slope and the constant term, 2, is the y-intercept. This is the form of the equation that we graphed in Figure 2.6 on page 171.

Check Point 7 Find the slope and the y-intercept of the line whose equation is $3x + 6y - 12 = 0$. Then use the y-intercept and the slope to graph the equation.

We've covered a lot of territory. Let's take a moment to summarize the various forms for equations of lines.

> ### Equations of Lines
> 1. Point-slope form: $\quad y - y_1 = m(x - x_1)$
> 2. Slope-intercept form: $\quad y = mx + b$
> 3. Horizontal line: $\quad y = b$
> 4. Vertical line: $\quad x = a$
> 5. General form: $\quad Ax + By + C = 0$

6 Find slopes and equations of parallel and perpendicular lines.

Parallel and Perpendicular Lines

Two nonintersecting lines that lie in the same plane are **parallel.** If two lines do not intersect, the ratio of the vertical change to the horizontal change is the same for each line. Because two parallel lines have the same "steepness," they must have the same slope.

> **Slope and Parallel Lines**
>
> **1.** If two nonvertical lines are parallel, then they have the same slope.
> **2.** If two distinct nonvertical lines have the same slope, then they are parallel.
> **3.** Two distinct vertical lines, both with undefined slopes, are parallel.

EXAMPLE 8 **Writing Equations of a Line Parallel to a Given Line**

Write an equation of the line passing through $(-3, 2)$ and parallel to the line whose equation is $y = 2x + 1$. Express the equation in point-slope form and slope-intercept form.

Solution The situation is illustrated in Figure 2.10. We are looking for the equation of the line shown on the left. How do we obtain this equation? Notice that the line passes through the point $(-3, 2)$. Using the point-slope form of the line's equation, we have $x_1 = -3$ and $y_1 = 2$.

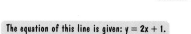

$$y - y_1 = m(x - x_1)$$

$y_1 = 2$ $x_1 = -3$

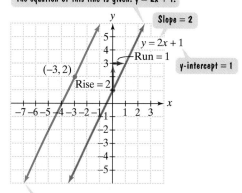

We must write the equation of this line.

Figure 2.10 Writing equations of a line parallel to a given line

Now, the only thing missing from the equation is m, the slope of the line on the left. Do we know anything about the slope of either line in Figure 2.10? The answer is yes; we know the slope of the line on the right, whose equation is given.

$$y = 2x + 1$$

The slope of the line on the right in Figure 2.10 is 2.

Parallel lines have the same slope. Because the slope of the line with the given equation is 2, $m = 2$ for the line whose equation we must write.

$$y - y_1 = m(x - x_1)$$

$y_1 = 2$ $m = 2$ $x_1 = -3$

The point-slope form of the line's equation is

$$y - 2 = 2[x - (-3)] \text{ or}$$

$$y - 2 = 2(x + 3).$$

Solving for y, we obtain the slope-intercept form of the equation.

$y - 2 = 2x + 6$ Apply the distributive property.

$y = 2x + 8$ Add 2 to both sides. This is the slope-intercept form, $y = mx + b$, of the equation.

Check Point 8   Write an equation of the line passing through $(-2, 5)$ and parallel to the line whose equation is $y = 3x + 1$. Express the equation in point-slope form and slope-intercept form.

Two lines that intersect at a right angle ($90°$) are said to be **perpendicular,** shown in Figure 2.11. There is a relationship between the slopes of perpendicular lines.

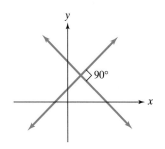

Figure 2.11 Perpendicular lines

Slope and Perpendicular Lines

1. If two nonvertical lines are perpendicular, then the product of their slopes is -1.
2. If the product of the slopes of two lines is -1, then the lines are perpendicular.
3. A horizontal line having zero slope is perpendicular to a vertical line having undefined slope.

An equivalent way of stating this relationship is to say that one line is perpendicular to another line if its slope is the *negative reciprocal* of the slope of the other. For example, if a line has slope 5, any line having slope $-\frac{1}{5}$ is perpendicular to it. Similarly, if a line has slope $-\frac{3}{4}$, any line having slope $\frac{4}{3}$ is perpendicular to it.

EXAMPLE 9   **Finding the Slope of a Line Perpendicular to a Given Line**

Find the slope of any line that is perpendicular to the line whose equation is $x + 4y - 8 = 0$.

Solution   We begin by writing the equation of the given line, $x + 4y - 8 = 0$, in slope-intercept form. Solve for y.

$x + 4y - 8 = 0$ *This is the given equation.*

$4y = -x + 8$ *To isolate the y-term, subtract x and add 8 on both sides.*

$y = -\frac{1}{4}x + 2$ *Divide both sides by 4.*

Slope is $-\frac{1}{4}$.

The given line has slope $-\frac{1}{4}$. Any line perpendicular to this line has a slope that is the negative reciprocal of $-\frac{1}{4}$. Thus, the slope of any perpendicular line is 4.

Check Point 9   Find the slope of any line that is perpendicular to the line whose equation is $x + 3y - 12 = 0$.

7 Model data with linear equations.

Applications

Slope is defined as the ratio of a change in y to a corresponding change in x. Our next example shows how slope can be interpreted as a **rate of change** in an applied situation.

EXAMPLE 10   Slope as a Rate of Change

A best guess at the look of our nation in the next decade indicates that the number of men and women living alone will increase each year. Figure 2.12 shows line graphs for the number of U.S. men and women living alone, projected through 2010. Find the slope of the line segment for the women. Describe what the slope represents.

Solution   We let x represent a year and y the number of women living alone in that year. The two points shown on the line segment for women have the following coordinates:

$$(1995, 14) \quad \text{and} \quad (2010, 17).$$

In 1995, 14 million U.S. women lived alone.

In 2010, 17 million U.S. women are projected to live alone.

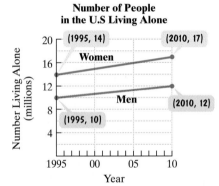

Number of People in the U.S Living Alone

Figure 2.12 *Source:* Forrester Research

Now we compute the slope:

$$m = \frac{\text{Change in } y}{\text{Change in } x} = \frac{17 - 14}{2010 - 1995}$$

The unit in the numerator is million people.

The unit in the denominator is year.

$$= \frac{3}{15} = \frac{1}{5} = \frac{0.2 \text{ million people}}{\text{year}}.$$

The slope indicates that the number of U.S. women living alone is projected to increase by 0.2 million each year. The rate of change is 0.2 million women per year.

Check Point 10   Use the graph in Example 10 to find the slope of the line segment for the men. Express the slope correct to two decimal places and describe what it represents.

If an equation in slope-intercept form models relationships between variables, then the slope and y-intercept have physical interpretations. For the equation $y = mx + b$, the y-intercept, b, tells us what is happening to y when x is 0. If x represents time, the y-intercept describes the value of y at the beginning, or when time equals 0. The slope represents the rate of change in y per unit change in x.

Using these ideas, we can develop a model for the data for women living alone, shown in Figure 2.12 on the previous page. We let x = the number of years after 1995. At the beginning of our data, or 0 years after 1995, 14 million women lived alone. Thus, $b = 14$. In Example 10, we found that $m = 0.2$ (rate of change is 0.2 million women per year). An equation of the form $y = mx + b$ that models the data is

$$y = 0.2x + 14,$$

where y is the number, in millions, of U.S. women living alone x years after 1995.

Linear equations are useful for modeling data in scatter plots that fall on or near a line. For example, Table 2.2 gives the population of the United States, in millions, in the indicated year. The data are displayed in a scatter plot as a set of six points in Figure 2.13.

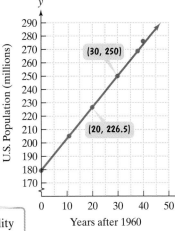

U.S. Population (millions)

Years after 1960

Figure 2.13

Table 2.2

Year	x (Years after 1960)	y (U.S. Population) (in millions)
1960	0	179.3
1970	10	203.3
1980	20	226.5
1990	30	250.0
1998	38	268.9
2000	40	281.4

Also shown in Figure 2.13 is a line that passes through or near the six points. By writing the equation of this line, we can obtain a model of the data and make predictions about the population of the United States in the future.

Technology

You can use a graphing utility to obtain a model for a scatter plot in which the data points fall on or near a straight line. The line that best fits the data is called the **regression line**. After entering the data in Table 2.2, a graphing utility displays a scatter plot of the data and the regression line.

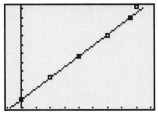

$[-5, 45, 5]$ by $[170, 285, 10]$

Also displayed is the regression line's equation.

```
LinReg
y=ax+b
a=2.45748031496
b=178.377952756
```

EXAMPLE 11   Modeling U.S. Population

Write the slope-intercept equation of the line shown in Figure 2.13. Use the equation to predict U.S. population in 2010.

Solution   The line in Figure 2.13 passes through $(20, 226.5)$ and $(30, 250)$. We start by finding the slope.

$$m = \frac{\text{Change in } y}{\text{Change in } x} = \frac{250 - 226.5}{30 - 20} = \frac{23.5}{10} = 2.35$$

The slope indicates that the rate of change in the U.S. population is 2.35 million people per year. Now we write the line's slope-intercept equation.

$y - y_1 = m(x - x_1)$	Begin with the point-slope form.
$y - 250 = 2.35(x - 30)$	Either ordered pair can be (x_1, y_1). Let $(x_1, y_1) = (30, 250)$. From above, $m = 2.35$.
$y - 250 = 2.35x - 70.5$	Apply the distributive property on the right.
$y = 2.35x + 179.5$	Add 250 to both sides and solve for y.

A linear equation that models U.S. population, y, in millions, x years after 1960 is
$$y = 2.35x + 179.5.$$

Now, let's use this equation to predict U.S. population in 2010. Because 2010 is 50 years after 1960, substitute 50 for x and compute y.
$$y = 2.35(50) + 179.5 = 297$$

Our equation predicts that the population of the United States in the year 2010 will be 297 million. (The projected figure from the U.S. Census Bureau is 297.716 million.)

Check Point 11 Use the data points $(10, 203.3)$ and $(20, 226.5)$ from Table 2.2 to write an equation that models U.S. population x years after 1960. Use the equation to predict U.S. population in 2020.

Cigarettes and Lung Cancer

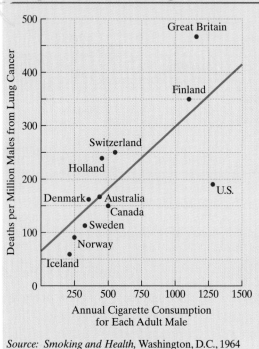

This scatter plot shows a relationship between cigarette consumption among males and deaths due to lung cancer per million males. The data are from 11 countries and date back to a 1964 report by the U.S. Surgeon General. The scatter plot can be modeled by a line whose slope indicates an increasing death rate from lung cancer with increased cigarette consumption. At that time, the tobacco industry argued that in spite of this regression line, tobacco use is not the cause of cancer. Recent data do, indeed, show a causal effect between tobacco use and numerous diseases.

Source: Smoking and Health, Washington, D.C., 1964

EXERCISE SET 2.1

Practice Exercises

In Exercises 1–10, find the slope of the line passing through each pair of points or state that the slope is undefined. Then indicate whether the line through the points rises, falls, is horizontal, or is vertical.

1. $(4, 7)$ and $(8, 10)$
2. $(2, 1)$ and $(3, 4)$
3. $(-2, 1)$ and $(2, 2)$
4. $(-1, 3)$ and $(2, 4)$
5. $(4, -2)$ and $(3, -2)$
6. $(4, -1)$ and $(3, -1)$
7. $(-2, 4)$ and $(-1, -1)$
8. $(6, -4)$ and $(4, -2)$

9. $(5, 3)$ and $(5, -2)$
10. $(3, -4)$ and $(3, 5)$

In Exercises 11–38, use the given conditions to write an equation for each line in point-slope form and slope-intercept form.

11. Slope = 2, passing through $(3, 5)$
12. Slope = 4, passing through $(1, 3)$
13. Slope = 6, passing through $(-2, 5)$
14. Slope = 8, passing through $(4, -1)$
15. Slope = -3, passing through $(-2, -3)$

16. Slope $= -5$, passing through $(-4, -2)$

17. Slope $= -4$, passing through $(-4, 0)$

18. Slope $= -2$, passing through $(0, -3)$

19. Slope $= -1$, passing through $\left(-\frac{1}{2}, -2\right)$

20. Slope $= -1$, passing through $\left(-4, -\frac{1}{4}\right)$

21. Slope $= \frac{1}{2}$, passing through the origin

22. Slope $= \frac{1}{3}$, passing through the origin

23. Slope $= -\frac{2}{3}$, passing through $(6, -2)$

24. Slope $= -\frac{3}{5}$, passing through $(10, -4)$

25. Passing through $(1, 2)$ and $(5, 10)$

26. Passing through $(3, 5)$ and $(8, 15)$

27. Passing through $(-3, 0)$ and $(0, 3)$

28. Passing through $(-2, 0)$ and $(0, 2)$

29. Passing through $(-3, -1)$ and $(2, 4)$

30. Passing through $(-2, -4)$ and $(1, -1)$

31. Passing through $(-3, -2)$ and $(3, 6)$

32. Passing through $(-3, 6)$ and $(3, -2)$

33. Passing through $(-3, -1)$ and $(4, -1)$

34. Passing through $(-2, -5)$ and $(6, -5)$

35. Passing through $(2, 4)$ with x-intercept $= -2$

36. Passing through $(1, -3)$ with x-intercept $= -1$

37. x-intercept $= -\frac{1}{2}$ and y-intercept $= 4$

38. x-intercept $= 4$ and y-intercept $= -2$

In Exercises 39–46, give the slope and y-intercept of each line whose equation is given. Then graph the line.

39. $y = 2x + 1$

40. $y = 3x + 2$

41. $y = -2x + 1$

42. $y = -3x + 2$

43. $y = \frac{3}{4}x - 2$

44. $y = \frac{3}{4}x - 3$

45. $y = -\frac{3}{5}x + 7$

46. $y = -\frac{2}{5}x + 6$

In Exercises 47–52, graph each equation in the rectangular coordinate system.

47. $y = -2$

48. $y = 4$

49. $x = -3$

50. $x = 5$

51. $y = 0$

52. $x = 0$

In Exercises 53–60,

   a. *Rewrite the given equation in slope-intercept form.*
   b. *Give the slope and y-intercept.*
   c. *Graph the equation.*

53. $3x + y - 5 = 0$

54. $4x + y - 6 = 0$

55. $2x + 3y - 18 = 0$

56. $4x + 6y + 12 = 0$

57. $8x - 4y - 12 = 0$

58. $6x - 5y - 20 = 0$

59. $3x - 9 = 0$

60. $4y + 28 = 0$

In Exercises 61–68, use the given conditions to write an equation for each line in point-slope form and slope-intercept form.

61. Passing through $(-8, -10)$ and parallel to the line whose equation is $y = -4x + 3$

62. Passing through $(-2, -7)$ and parallel to the line whose equation is $y = -5x + 4$

63. Passing through $(2, -3)$ and perpendicular to the line whose equation is $y = \frac{1}{5}x + 6$

64. Passing through $(-4, 2)$ and perpendicular to the line whose equation is $y = \frac{1}{3}x + 7$

65. Passing through $(-2, 2)$ and parallel to the line whose equation is $2x - 3y - 7 = 0$

66. Passing through $(-1, 3)$ and parallel to the line whose equation is $3x - 2y - 5 = 0$

67. Passing through $(4, -7)$ and perpendicular to the line whose equation is $x - 2y - 3 = 0$

68. Passing through $(5, -9)$ and perpendicular to the line whose equation is $x + 7y - 12 = 0$

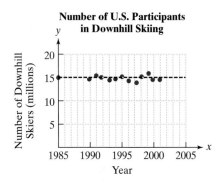

Application Exercises

69. The scatter plot shows that from 1985 to 2001, the number of Americans participating in downhill skiing remained relatively constant. Write an equation that models the number of participants in downhill skiing, y, in millions, for this period.

Number of U.S. Participants in Downhill Skiing

Source: National Ski Areas Association

If talk about a federal budget surplus sounded too good to be true, that's because it probably was. The Congressional Budget Office's estimates for 2010 range from a $1.2 trillion budget surplus to a $286 billion deficit. Use the information provided by the Congressional Budget Office graphs to solve Exercises 70–71.

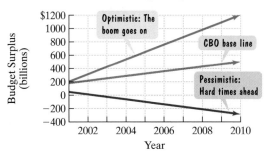

Federal Budget Projections

Source: Congressional Budget Office

70. Turn back a page and look at the line that indicates hard times ahead. Find the slope of this line using (2001, 50) and (2010, −286). Use a calculator and round to the nearest whole number. Describe what the slope represents.

71. Turn back a page and look at the line that indicates the boom goes on. Find the slope of this line using (2001, 200) and (2010, 1200). Use a calculator and round to the nearest whole number. Describe what the slope represents.

72. Horrified at the cost the last time you needed a prescription drug? The graph shows that the cost of the average retail prescription has been rising steadily since 1991.

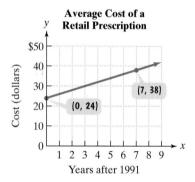

Average Cost of a Retail Prescription

Years after 1991

Source: Newsweek

a. According to the graph, what is the *y*-intercept? Describe what this represents in this situation.

b. Use the coordinates of the two points shown to compute the slope. What does this mean about the cost of the average retail prescription?

c. Write a linear equation in slope-intercept form that models the cost of the average retail prescription, *y*, *x* years after 1991.

d. Use your model from part (c) to predict the cost of the average retail prescription in 2010.

73. For 61 years, Social Security has been a huge success. It is the primary source of income for 66% of Americans over 65 and the only thing that keeps 42% of the elderly from poverty. However, the number of workers per Social Security beneficiary has been declining steadily since 1950.

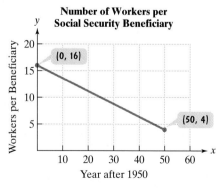

Number of Workers per Social Security Beneficiary

Year after 1950

Source: Social Security Administration

a. According to the graph, what is the *y*-intercept? Describe what this represents in this situation.

b. Use the coordinates of the two points shown to compute the slope. What does this mean about the number of workers per beneficiary?

c. Write a linear equation in slope-intercept form that models the number of workers per beneficiary, *y*, *x* years after 1950.

d. Use your model from part (c) to predict number of workers per beneficiary in 2010. For every 8 workers, how many beneficiaries will there be?

74. We seem to be fed up with being lectured at about our waistlines. The points in the graph show the average weight of American adults from 1990 through 2000. Also shown is a line that passes through or near the points.

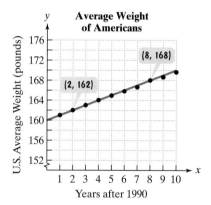

Average Weight of Americans

Years after 1990

Source: Diabetes Care

a. Use the two points whose coordinates are shown by the voice balloons to find the point-slope equation of the line that models average weight of Americans, *y*, in pounds, *x* years after 1990.

b. Write the equation in part (a) in slope-intercept form.

c. Use the slope-intercept equation to predict the average weight of Americans in 2008.

75. Films may not be getting any better, but in this era of moviegoing, the number of screens available for new films and the classics has exploded. The points in the graph show the number of screens in the United States from 1995 through 2000. Also shown is a line that passes through or near the points.

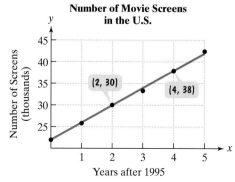

Number of Movie Screens in the U.S.

Years after 1995

Source: Motion Picture Association of America

a. Use the two points whose coordinates are shown by the voice balloons to find the point-slope equation of the line that models the number of screens, y, in thousands, x years after 1995.

b. Write the equation in part (a) in slope-intercept form.

c. Use the slope-intercept equation to predict the number of screens, in thousands, in 2008.

76. The scatter plot shows the relationship between the percentage of married women of child-bearing age using contraceptives and the births per woman in selected countries. Also shown is the regression line. Use two points on this line to write both its point-slope and slope-intercept equations. Then find the number of births per woman if 90% of married women of child-bearing age use contraceptives.

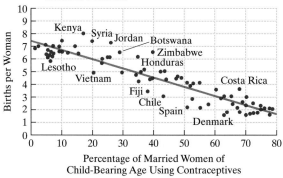

Contraceptive Prevalence and Births per Woman, Selected Countries

Source: Population Reference Bureau

77. Shown, again, is the scatter plot that indicates a relationship between the percentage of adult females in a country who are literate and the mortality of children under five. Also shown is a line that passes through or near the points. Find a linear equation that models the data by finding the slope-intercept equation of the line. Use the model to make a prediction about child mortality based on the percentage of adult females in a country who are literate.

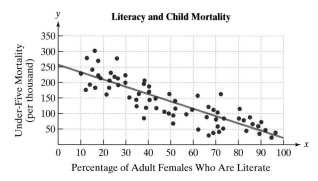

Literacy and Child Mortality

Source: United Nations

In Exercises 78–80, find a linear equation in slope-intercept form that models the given description. Describe what each variable in your model represents. Then use the model to make a prediction.

78. In 1995, the average temperature of Earth was 57.7°F and has increased at a rate of 0.01°F per year since then.

79. In 1995, 60% of U.S. adults read a newspaper and this percentage has decreased at a rate of 0.7% per year since then.

80. A computer that was purchased for $4000 is depreciating at a rate of $950 per year.

81. A business discovers a linear relationship between the number of shirts it can sell and the price per shirt. In particular, 20,000 shirts can be sold at $19 each, and 2000 of the same shirts can be sold at $55 each. Write the slope-intercept equation of the *demand line* that models the number of shirts that can be sold, y, at a price of x dollars. Then determine the number of shirts that can be sold at $50 each.

Writing in Mathematics

82. What is the slope of a line and how is it found?

83. Describe how to write the equation of a line if two points along the line are known.

84. Explain how to derive the slope-intercept form of a line's equation, $y = mx + b$, from the point-slope form

$$y - y_1 = m(x - x_1).$$

85. Explain how to graph the equation $x = 2$. Can this equation be expressed in slope-intercept form? Explain.

86. Explain how to use the general form of a line's equation to find the line's slope and y-intercept.

87. If two lines are parallel, describe the relationship between their slopes.

88. If two lines are perpendicular, describe the relationship between their slopes.

88. If you know a point on a line and you know the equation of a line perpendicular to this line, explain how to write the line's equation.

90. A formula in the form $y = mx + b$ models the cost, y, of a four-year college x years after 2003. Would you expect m to be positive, negative, or zero? Explain your answer.

91. We saw that the percentage of people satisfied with their lives remains relatively constant for all age groups. Exercise 69 showed that the number of skiers in the United States has remained relatively constant over time. Give another example of a real-world phenomenon that has remained relatively constant over time. Try writing an equation that models this phenomenon.

Technology Exercises

Use a graphing utility to graph each equation in Exercises 92–95. Then use the TRACE *feature to trace along the line and find the coordinates of two points. Use these points to compute the line's slope. Check your result by using the coefficient of x in the line's equation.*

92. $y = 2x + 4$

93. $y = -3x + 6$

94. $y = -\frac{1}{2}x - 5$

95. $y = \frac{3}{4}x - 2$

96. Is there a relationship between alcohol from moderate wine consumption and heart disease death rate? The table gives data from 19 developed countries.

France

Country	A	B	C	D	E	F	G
Liters of alcohol from drinking wine, per person, per year (x)	2.5	3.9	2.9	2.4	2.9	0.8	9.1
Deaths from heart disease, per 100,000 people per year (y)	211	167	131	191	220	297	71

U.S.

Country	H	I	J	K	L	M	N	O	P	Q	R	S
(x)	0.8	0.7	7.9	1.8	1.9	0.8	6.5	1.6	5.8	1.3	1.2	2.7
(y)	211	300	107	167	266	227	86	207	115	285	199	172

Source: New York Times, December 28, 1994

a. Use the statistical menu of your graphing utility to enter the 19 ordered pairs of data items shown in the table.

b. Use the DRAW menu and the scatter plot capability to draw a scatter plot of the data.

c. Select the linear regression option. Use your utility to obtain values for a and b for the equation of the regression line, $y = ax + b$. You may also be given a **correlation coefficient,** r. Values of r close to 1 indicate that the points can be described by a linear relationship and the regression line has a positive slope. Values of r close to -1 indicate that the points can be described by a linear relationship and the regression line has a negative slope. Values of r close to 0 indicate no linear relationship between the variables. In this case, a linear model does not accurately describe the data.

d. Use the appropriate sequence (consult your manual) to graph the regression equation on top of the points in the scatter plot.

Critical Thinking Exercises

97. Which one of the following is true?
a. A linear equation with nonnegative slope has a graph that rises from left to right.
b. The equations $y = 4x$ and $y = -4x$ have graphs that are perpendicular lines.
c. The line whose equation is $5x + 6y - 30 = 0$ passes through the point $(6, 0)$ and has slope $-\frac{5}{6}$.
d. The graph of $y = 7$ in the rectangular coordinate system is the single point $(7, 0)$.

98. Prove that the equation of a line passing through $(a, 0)$ and $(0, b)$ $(a \neq 0, b \neq 0)$ can be written in the form $\frac{x}{a} + \frac{y}{b} = 1$. Why is this called the *intercept form* of a line?

99. Use the figure shown to make the following lists.
a. List the slopes m_1, m_2, m_3, and m_4 in order of decreasing size.
b. List the y-intercepts b_1, b_2, b_3, and b_4 in order of decreasing size.

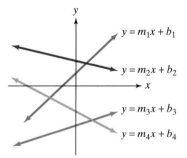

100. Excited about the success of celebrity stamps, post office officials were rumored to have put forth a plan to institute two new types of thermometers. On these new scales, $°E$ represents degrees Elvis and $°M$ represents degrees Madonna. If it is known that $40°E = 25°M$, $280°E = 125°M$, and degrees Elvis is linearly related to degrees Madonna, write an equation expressing E in terms of M.

Group Exercise

101. Group members should consult an almanac, newspaper, magazine, or the Internet to find data that lie approximately on or near a straight line. Working by hand or using a graphing utility, construct a scatter plot for the data. If working by hand, draw a line that approximately fits the data and then write its equation. If using a graphing utility, obtain the equation of the regression line. Then use the equation of the line to make a prediction about what might happen in the future. Are there circumstances that might affect the accuracy of this prediction? List some of these circumstances.

SECTION 2.2 *Distance and Midpoint Formulas; Circles*

Objectives

1. Find the distance between two points.
2. Find the midpoint of a line segment.
3. Write the standard form of a circle's equation.
4. Give the center and radius of a circle whose equation is in standard form.
5. Convert the general form of a circle's equation to standard form.

It's a good idea to know your way around a circle. Clocks, angles, maps, and compasses are based on circles. Circles occur everywhere in nature: in ripples on water, patterns on a butterfly's wings, and cross sections of trees. Some consider the circle to be the most pleasing of all shapes.

The rectangular coordinate system gives us a unique way of knowing a circle. It enables us to translate a circle's geometric definition into an algebraic equation. To do this, we must first develop a formula for the distance between any two points in rectangular coordinates.

① Find the distance between two points.

The Distance Formula

Using the Pythagorean Theorem, we can find the distance between the two points $P_1(x_1, y_1)$ and $P_2(x_2, y_2)$ in the rectangular coordinate system. The two points are illustrated in Figure 2.14.

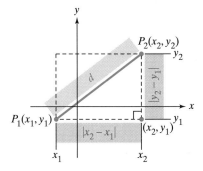

Figure 2.14

The distance that we need to find is represented by d and shown in blue. Notice that the distance between two points on the dashed horizontal line is the absolute value of the difference between the x-coordinates of the two points. This distance, $|x_2 - x_1|$, is shown in pink. Similarly, the distance between two points on the dashed vertical line is the absolute value of the difference between the y-coordinates of the two points. This distance, $|y_2 - y_1|$, is also shown in pink.

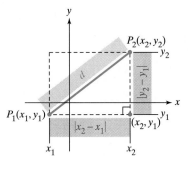

Figure 2.14, repeated

Because the dashed lines are horizontal and vertical, a right triangle is formed. Thus, we can use the Pythagorean Theorem to find distance d. By the Pythagorean Theorem,

$$d^2 = |x_2 - x_1|^2 + |y_2 - y_1|^2$$

$$d = \sqrt{|x_2 - x_1|^2 + |y_2 - y_1|^2}$$

$$d = \sqrt{(x_2 - x_1)^2 + (y_2 - y_1)^2}.$$

This result is called the **distance formula.**

The Distance Formula

The distance, d, between the points (x_1, y_1) and (x_2, y_2) in the rectangular coordinate system is

$$d = \sqrt{(x_2 - x_1)^2 + (y_2 - y_1)^2}.$$

When using the distance formula, it does not matter which point you call (x_1, y_1) and which you call (x_2, y_2).

EXAMPLE 1   Using the Distance Formula

Find the distance between $(-1, -3)$ and $(2, 3)$.

Solution   Letting $(x_1, y_1) = (-1, -3)$ and $(x_2, y_2) = (2, 3)$, we obtain

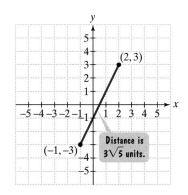

Figure 2.15 Finding the distance between two points

$$d = \sqrt{(x_2 - x_1)^2 + (y_2 - y_1)^2}$$ Use the distance formula.

$$= \sqrt{[2 - (-1)]^2 + [3 - (-3)]^2}$$ Substitute the given values.

$$= \sqrt{(2 + 1)^2 + (3 + 3)^2}$$ Apply the definition of subtraction within the grouping symbols.

$$= \sqrt{3^2 + 6^2}$$ Perform the resulting additions.

$$= \sqrt{9 + 36}$$ Square 3 and 6.

$$= \sqrt{45}$$ Add.

$$= 3\sqrt{5} \approx 6.71.$$ $\sqrt{45} = \sqrt{9 \cdot 5} = \sqrt{9}\sqrt{5} = 3\sqrt{5}$

The distance between the given points is $3\sqrt{5}$ units, or approximately 6.71 units. The situation is illustrated in Figure 2.15.

Check Point 1   Find the distance between $(2, -2)$ and $(5, 2)$.

2 Find the midpoint of a line segment.

The Midpoint Formula

The distance formula can be used to derive a formula for finding the midpoint of a line segment between two given points. The formula is given as follows:

The Midpoint Formula

Consider a line segment whose endpoints are (x_1, y_1) and (x_2, y_2). The coordinates of the segment's midpoint are

$$\left(\frac{x_1 + x_2}{2}, \frac{y_1 + y_2}{2} \right).$$

To find the midpoint, take the average of the two x-coordinates and the average of the two y-coordinates.

EXAMPLE 2   Using the Midpoint Formula

Find the midpoint of the line segment with endpoints $(1, -6)$ and $(-8, -4)$.

Solution   To find the coordinates of the midpoint, we average the coordinates of the endpoints.

$$\text{Midpoint} = \left(\frac{1 + (-8)}{2}, \frac{-6 + (-4)}{2} \right) = \left(\frac{-7}{2}, \frac{-10}{2} \right) = \left(-\frac{7}{2}, -5 \right)$$

Average the x-coordinates.   Average the y-coordinates.

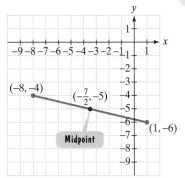

Figure 2.16 Finding a line segment's midpoint

Figure 2.16 illustrates that the point $(-\frac{7}{2}, -5)$ is midway between the points $(1, -6)$ and $(-8, -4)$.

Check Point 2   Find the midpoint of the line segment with endpoints $(1, 2)$ and $(7, -3)$.

Circles

Our goal is to translate a circle's geometric definition into an equation. We begin with this geometric definition.

Definition of a Circle

A **circle** is the set of all points in a plane that are equidistant from a fixed point, called the **center.** The fixed distance from the circle's center to any point on the circle is called the **radius.**

Figure 2.17 is our starting point for obtaining a circle's equation. We've placed the circle into a rectangular coordinate system. The circle's center is (h, k) and its radius is r. We let (x, y) represent the coordinates of any point on the circle.

What does the geometric definition of a circle tell us about point (x, y) in Figure 2.17? The point is on the circle if and only if its distance from the center is r. We can use the distance formula to express this idea algebraically:

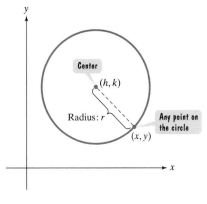

Figure 2.17 A circle centered at (h, k) with radius r

The distance between (x, y) and (h, k) is always   r.

$$\sqrt{(x - h)^2 + (y - k)^2} \qquad = \qquad r$$

Squaring both sides of $\sqrt{(x-h)^2 + (y-k)^2} = r$ yields the *standard form of the equation of a circle*.

> ### The Standard Form of the Equation of a Circle
> The **standard form of the equation of a circle** with center (h, k) and radius r is
> $$(x-h)^2 + (y-k)^2 = r^2.$$

3 Write the standard form of a circle's equation.

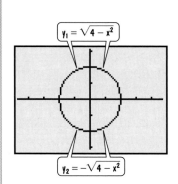

Figure 2.18 The graph of $x^2 + y^2 = 4$

EXAMPLE 3 Finding the Standard Form of a Circle's Equation

Write the standard form of the equation of the circle with center $(0, 0)$ and radius 2. Graph the circle.

Solution The center is $(0, 0)$. Because the center is represented as (h, k) in the standard form of the equation, $h = 0$ and $k = 0$. The radius is 2, so we will let $r = 2$ in the equation.

$$(x-h)^2 + (y-k)^2 = r^2 \quad \text{This is the standard form of a circle's equation.}$$

$$(x-0)^2 + (y-0)^2 = 2^2 \quad \text{Substitute 0 for } h, \text{ 0 for } k, \text{ and 2 for } r.$$

$$x^2 + y^2 = 4 \quad \text{Simplify.}$$

The standard form of the equation of the circle is $x^2 + y^2 = 4$. Figure 2.18 shows the graph.

Check Point 3 Write the standard form of the equation of the circle with center $(0, 0)$ and radius 4.

Technology

To graph a circle with a graphing utility, first solve the equation for y.

$$x^2 + y^2 = 4$$

$$y^2 = 4 - x^2$$

$$y = \pm\sqrt{4 - x^2}$$

Graph the two equations

$$y_1 = \sqrt{4 - x^2} \quad \text{and} \quad y_2 = -\sqrt{4 - x^2}$$

in the same viewing rectangle. The graph of $y_1 = \sqrt{4 - x^2}$ is the top semicircle because y is always positive. The graph of $y_2 = -\sqrt{4 - x^2}$ is the bottom semicircle because y is always negative. Use a $\boxed{\text{ZOOM SQUARE}}$ setting so that the circle looks like a circle. (Many graphing utilities have problems connecting the two semicircles because the segments directly across horizontally from the center become nearly vertical.)

Example 3 and Check Point 3 involved circles centered at the origin. The standard form of the equation of all such circles is $x^2 + y^2 = r^2$, where r is the circle's radius. Now, let's consider a circle whose center is not at the origin.

EXAMPLE 4   Finding the Standard Form of a Circle's Equation

Write the standard form of the equation of the circle with center $(-2, 3)$ and radius 4.

Solution   The center is $(-2, 3)$. Because the center is represented as (h, k) in the standard form of the equation, $h = -2$ and $k = 3$. The radius is 4, so we will let $r = 4$ in the equation.

$$(x - h)^2 + (y - k)^2 = r^2 \qquad \text{This is the standard form of a circle's equation.}$$
$$[x - (-2)]^2 + (y - 3)^2 = 4^2 \qquad \text{Substitute } -2 \text{ for } h, 3 \text{ for } k, \text{ and } 4 \text{ for } r.$$
$$(x + 2)^2 + (y - 3)^2 = 16 \qquad \text{Simplify.}$$

The standard form of the equation of the circle is $(x + 2)^2 + (y - 3)^2 = 16$.

> **Check Point 4**   Write the standard form of the equation of the circle with center $(5, -6)$ and radius 10.

4 Give the center and radius of a circle whose equation is in standard form.

EXAMPLE 5   Using the Standard Form of a Circle's Equation to Graph the Circle

Find the center and radius of the circle whose equation is
$$(x - 2)^2 + (y + 4)^2 = 9$$
and graph the equation.

Solution   In order to graph the circle, we need to know its center, (h, k), and its radius, r. We can find the values for h, k, and r by comparing the given equation to the standard form of the equation of a circle.

$$(x - 2)^2 + (y + 4)^2 = 9$$
$$(x - 2)^2 + [y - (-4)]^2 = 3^2$$

This is $(x - h)^2$, with $h = 2$.   This is $(y - k)^2$, with $k = -4$.   This is r^2, with $r = 3$.

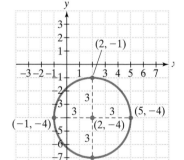

Figure 2.19 The graph of $(x - 2)^2 + (y + 4)^2 = 9$

We see that $h = 2$, $k = -4$, and $r = 3$. Thus, the circle has center $(h, k) = (2, -4)$ and a radius of 3 units. To graph this circle, first plot the center $(2, -4)$. Because the radius is 3, you can locate at least four points on the circle by going out three units to the right, to the left, up, and down from the center.

The points three units to the right and to the left of $(2, -4)$ are $(5, -4)$ and $(-1, -4)$, respectively. The points three units up and down from $(2, -4)$ are $(2, -1)$ and $(2, -7)$, respectively.

Using these points, we obtain the graph in Figure 2.19.

> **Check Point 5**   Find the center and radius of the circle whose equation is
> $$(x + 3)^2 + (y - 1)^2 = 4$$
> and graph the equation.

If we square $x - 2$ and $y + 4$ in the standard form of the equation from Example 5, we obtain another form for the circle's equation.

$$(x - 2)^2 + (y + 4)^2 = 9$$ *This is the standard form of the equation from Example 5.*

$$x^2 - 4x + 4 + y^2 + 8y + 16 = 9$$ *Square x − 2 and y + 4.*

$$x^2 + y^2 - 4x + 8y + 20 = 9$$ *Combine numerical terms and rearrange terms.*

$$x^2 + y^2 - 4x + 8y + 11 = 0$$ *Subtract 9 from both sides.*

This result suggests that an equation in the form $x^2 + y^2 + Dx + Ey + F = 0$ can represent a circle. This is called the *general form of the equation of a circle.*

The General Form of the Equation of a Circle

The **general form of the equation of a circle** is

$$x^2 + y^2 + Dx + Ey + F = 0.$$

---

5 Convert the general form of a circle's equation to standard form.

We can convert the general form of the equation of a circle to the standard form $(x - h)^2 + (y - k)^2 = r^2$. We do so by completing the square on x and y. Let's see how this is done.

EXAMPLE 6   **Converting the General Form of a Circle's Equation to Standard Form and Graphing the Circle**

Study Tip

To review completing the square, see Section 1.5, pages 119–120.

Write in standard form and graph: $x^2 + y^2 + 4x - 6y - 23 = 0$.

Solution   Because we plan to complete the square on both x and y, let's rearrange terms so that x-terms are arranged in descending order, y-terms are arranged in descending order, and the constant term appears on the right.

$$x^2 + y^2 + 4x - 6y - 23 = 0$$ *This is the given equation.*

$$(x^2 + 4x \quad) + (y^2 - 6y \quad) = 23$$ *Rewrite in anticipation of completing the square.*

$$(x^2 + 4x + 4) + (y^2 - 6y + 9) = 23 + 4 + 9$$ *Complete the square on x: $\frac{1}{2} \cdot 4 = 2$ and $2^2 = 4$, so add 4 to both sides. Complete the square on y: $\frac{1}{2}(-6) = -3$ and $(-3)^2 = 9$, so add 9 to both sides.*

Remember that numbers added on the left side must also be added on the right side.

$$(x + 2)^2 + (y - 3)^2 = 36$$ *Factor on the left and add on the right.*

This last equation is in standard form. We can identify the circle's center and radius by comparing this equation to the standard form of the equation of a circle, $(x - h)^2 + (y - k)^2 = r^2$.

$$(x + 2)^2 + (y - 3)^2 = 36$$
$$[x - (-2)]^2 + (y - 3)^2 = 6^2$$

This is $(x - h)^2$, with h = −2.   *This is $(y - k)^2$, with k = 3.*   *This is r^2, with r = 6.*

We use the center, $(h, k) = (-2, 3)$, and the radius, $r = 6$, to graph the circle. The graph is shown in Figure 2.20.

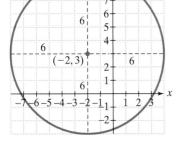

Figure 2.20 The graph of $(x + 2)^2 + (y - 3)^2 = 36$

Technology

To graph $x^2 + y^2 + 4x - 6y - 23 = 0$, rewrite the equation as a quadratic equation in y.

$$y^2 - 6y + (x^2 + 4x - 23) = 0$$

Now solve for y using the quadratic formula, with $a = 1$, $b = -6$, and $c = x^2 + 4x - 23$.

$$y = \frac{-b \pm \sqrt{b^2 - 4ac}}{2a} = \frac{-(-6) \pm \sqrt{(-6)^2 - 4 \cdot 1(x^2 + 4x - 23)}}{2 \cdot 1} = \frac{6 \pm \sqrt{36 - 4(x^2 + 4x - 23)}}{2}$$

Because we will enter these equations, there is no need to simplify. Enter

$$y_1 = \frac{6 + \sqrt{36 - 4(x^2 + 4x - 23)}}{2}$$

and

$$y_2 = \frac{6 - \sqrt{36 - 4(x^2 + 4x - 23)}}{2}.$$

Use a [ZOOM SQUARE] setting. The graph is shown on the right.

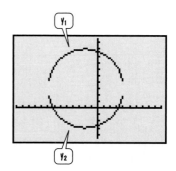

Check Point 6 Write in standard form and graph:
$$x^2 + y^2 + 4x - 4y - 1 = 0.$$

EXERCISE SET 2.2

 Practice Exercises

In Exercises 1–18, find the distance between each pair of points. If necessary, round answers to two decimals places.

1. $(2, 3)$ and $(14, 8)$
2. $(5, 1)$ and $(8, 5)$
3. $(4, 1)$ and $(6, 3)$
4. $(2, 3)$ and $(3, 5)$
5. $(0, 0)$ and $(-3, 4)$
6. $(0, 0)$ and $(3, -4)$
7. $(-2, -6)$ and $(3, -4)$
8. $(-4, -1)$ and $(2, -3)$
9. $(0, -3)$ and $(4, 1)$
10. $(0, -2)$ and $(4, 3)$
11. $(3.5, 8.2)$ and $(-0.5, 6.2)$
12. $(2.6, 1.3)$ and $(1.6, -5.7)$
13. $(0, -\sqrt{3})$ and $(\sqrt{5}, 0)$
14. $(0, -\sqrt{2})$ and $(\sqrt{7}, 0)$
15. $(3\sqrt{3}, \sqrt{5})$ and $(-\sqrt{3}, 4\sqrt{5})$
16. $(2\sqrt{3}, \sqrt{6})$ and $(-\sqrt{3}, 5\sqrt{6})$
17. $\left(\frac{7}{3}, \frac{1}{5}\right)$ and $\left(\frac{1}{3}, \frac{6}{5}\right)$
18. $\left(-\frac{1}{4}, -\frac{1}{7}\right)$ and $\left(\frac{3}{4}, \frac{6}{7}\right)$

In Exercises 19–30, find the midpoint of each line segment with the given endpoints.

19. $(6, 8)$ and $(2, 4)$
20. $(10, 4)$ and $(2, 6)$
21. $(-2, -8)$ and $(-6, -2)$
22. $(-4, -7)$ and $(-1, -3)$
23. $(-3, -4)$ and $(6, -8)$
24. $(-2, -1)$ and $(-8, 6)$
25. $\left(-\frac{7}{2}, \frac{3}{2}\right)$ and $\left(-\frac{5}{2}, -\frac{11}{2}\right)$
26. $\left(-\frac{2}{5}, \frac{7}{15}\right)$ and $\left(-\frac{2}{5}, -\frac{4}{15}\right)$
27. $(8, 3\sqrt{5})$ and $(-6, 7\sqrt{5})$
28. $(7\sqrt{3}, -6)$ and $(3\sqrt{3}, -2)$
29. $(\sqrt{18}, -4)$ and $(\sqrt{2}, 4)$
30. $(\sqrt{50}, -6)$ and $(\sqrt{2}, 6)$

In Exercises 31–40, write the standard form of the equation of the circle with the given center and radius.

31. Center $(0, 0), r = 7$
32. Center $(0, 0), r = 8$
33. Center $(3, 2), r = 5$
34. Center $(2, -1), r = 4$
35. Center $(-1, 4), r = 2$
36. Center $(-3, 5), r = 3$
37. Center $(-3, -1), r = \sqrt{3}$

38. Center $(-5, -3)$, $r = \sqrt{5}$

39. Center $(-4, 0)$, $r = 10$

40. Center $(-2, 0)$, $r = 6$

In Exercises 41–48, give the center and radius of the circle described by the equation and graph each equation.

41. $x^2 + y^2 = 16$

42. $x^2 + y^2 = 49$

43. $(x - 3)^2 + (y - 1)^2 = 36$

44. $(x - 2)^2 + (y - 3)^2 = 16$

45. $(x + 3)^2 + (y - 2)^2 = 4$

46. $(x + 1)^2 + (y - 4)^2 = 25$

47. $(x + 2)^2 + (y + 2)^2 = 4$

48. $(x + 4)^2 + (y + 5)^2 = 36$

In Exercises 49–56, complete the square and write the equation in standard form. Then give the center and radius of each circle and graph the equation.

49. $x^2 + y^2 + 6x + 2y + 6 = 0$

50. $x^2 + y^2 + 8x + 4y + 16 = 0$

51. $x^2 + y^2 - 10x - 6y - 30 = 0$

52. $x^2 + y^2 - 4x - 12y - 9 = 0$

53. $x^2 + y^2 + 8x - 2y - 8 = 0$

54. $x^2 + y^2 + 12x - 6y - 4 = 0$

55. $x^2 - 2x + y^2 - 15 = 0$

56. $x^2 + y^2 - 6y - 7 = 0$

Application Exercises

57. A rectangular coordinate system with coordinates in miles is placed on the map in the figure shown. Bangkok has coordinates $(-115, 170)$ and Phnom Penh has coordinates $(65, 70)$. How long will it take a plane averaging 400 miles per hour to fly directly from one city to the other? Round to the nearest tenth of an hour. Approximately how many minutes is the flight?

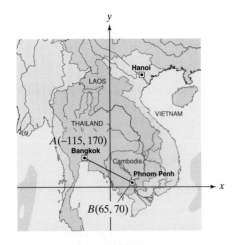

58. We refer to the driveway in the figure shown as being *circular*, meaning that it is bounded by two circles. The figure indicates that the radius of the larger circle is 52 feet and the radius of the smaller circle is 38 feet.

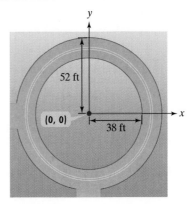

a. Use the coordinate system shown to write the equation of the smaller circle.

b. Use the coordinate system shown to write the equation of the larger circle.

59. The ferris wheel in the figure has a radius of 68 feet. The clearance between the wheel and the ground is 14 feet. The rectangular coordinate system shown has its origin on the ground directly below the center of the wheel. Use the coordinate system to write the equation of the circular wheel.

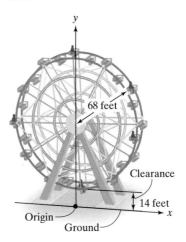

60. The circle formed by the middle lane of a circular running track can be described algebraically by $x^2 + y^2 = 4$, where all measurements are in miles. If you run around the track's middle lane twice, approximately how many miles have you covered?

Writing in Mathematics

61. In your own words, describe how to find the distance between two points in the rectangular coordinate system.

62. In your own words, describe how to find the midpoint of a line segment if its endpoints are known.

63. What is a circle? Without using variables, describe how the definition of a circle can be used to obtain a form of its equation.

64. Give an example of a circle's equation in standard form. Describe how to find the center and radius for this circle.

65. How is the standard form of a circle's equation obtained from its general form?

66. Does $(x - 3)^2 + (y - 5)^2 = 0$ represent the equation of a circle? If not, describe the graph of this equation.

67. Does $(x - 3)^2 + (y - 5)^2 = -25$ represent the equation of a circle? What sort of set is the graph of this equation?

 Technology Exercises

In Exercises 68–70, use a graphing utility to graph each circle whose equation is given.

68. $x^2 + y^2 = 25$

69. $(y + 1)^2 = 36 - (x - 3)^2$

70. $x^2 + 10x + y^2 - 4y - 20 = 0$

 Critical Thinking Exercises

71. Which one of the following is true?
   a. The equation of the circle whose center is at the origin with radius 16 is $x^2 + y^2 = 16$.
   b. The graph of $(x - 3)^2 + (y + 5)^2 = 36$ is a circle with radius 6 centered at $(-3, 5)$.
   c. The graph of $(x - 4) + (y + 6) = 25$ is a circle with radius 5 centered at $(4, -6)$.
   d. None of the above is true.

72. Show that the points $A(1, 1 + d)$, $B(3, 3 + d)$, and $C(6, 6 + d)$ are collinear (lie along a straight line) by showing that the distance from A to B plus the distance from B to C equals the distance from A to C.

73. Prove the midpoint formula by using the following procedure.
   a. Show that the distance between (x_1, y_1) and
   $$\left(\frac{x_1 + x_2}{2}, \frac{y_1 + y_2}{2} \right)$$ is equal to the distance between
   (x_2, y_2) and $\left(\frac{x_1 + x_2}{2}, \frac{y_1 + y_2}{2} \right)$.
   b. Use the procedure from Exercise 72 and the distances from part (a) to show that the points (x_1, y_1),
   $\left(\frac{x_1 + x_2}{2}, \frac{y_1 + y_2}{2} \right)$, and (x_2, y_2) are collinear.

In Exercises 74–75, write the standard form and the general form of the equation of each circle.

74. Center at $(3, -5)$ and passing through the point $(-2, 1)$

75. Passing through $(-7, 2)$ and $(1, 2)$; these points are endpoints of the diameter, the line that passes through the circle's center.

76. Find the area of the donut-shaped region bounded by the graphs of $(x - 2)^2 + (y + 3)^2 = 25$ and $(x - 2)^2 + (y + 3)^2 = 36$.

77. A **tangent line** to a circle is a line that intersects the circle at exactly one point. The tangent line is perpendicular to the radius of the circle at this point of contact. Write the point-slope equation of a line tangent to the circle whose equation is $x^2 + y^2 = 25$ at the point $(3, -4)$.

SECTION 2.3 *Basics of Functions*

Objectives

1. Find the domain and range of a relation.
2. Determine whether a relation is a function.
3. Determine whether an equation represents a function.
4. Evaluate a function.
5. Find and simplify a function's difference quotient.
6. Understand and use piecewise functions.
7. Find the domain of a function.

Jerry Orbach	$34,000
Charles Shaugnessy	$31,800
Andy Richter	$29,400
Norman Schwarzkopf	$28,000
Jon Stewart	$28,000

The answer: See the above list. The question: Who are *Celebrity Jeopardy's* five all-time highest earners? The list indicates a correspondence between the five all-time highest earners and their winnings. We can write this correspondence using a set of ordered pairs:

{(Orbach, $34,000), (Shaugnessy, $31,800), (Richter, $29,400), (Schwarzkopf, $28,000), (Stewart, $28,000)}.

1 Find the domain and range of a relation.

The mathematical term for a set of ordered pairs is a *relation*.

> **Definition of a Relation**
>
> A **relation** is any set of ordered pairs. The set of all first components of the ordered pairs is called the **domain** of the relation, and the set of all second components is called the **range** of the relation.

EXAMPLE 1   Finding the Domain and Range of a Relation

Find the domain and range of the relation:

{(Orbach, $34,000), (Shaugnessy, $31,800), (Richter, $29,400),
(Schwarzkopf, $28,000), (Stewart, $28,000)}.

Solution   The domain is the set of all first components. Thus, the domain is

{Orbach, Shaugnessy, Richter, Schwarzkopf, Stewart}.

The range is the set of all second components. Thus, the range is

{$34,000, $31,800, $29,400, $28,000}.

Check Point 1   Find the domain and the range of the relation:

$\{(5, 12.8), (10, 16.2), (15, 18.9), (20, 20.7), (25, 21.8)\}.$

As you worked Check Point 1, did you wonder if there was a rule that assigned the "inputs" in the domain to the "outputs" in the range? For example, for the ordered pair (15, 18.9), how does the output 18.9 depend on the input 15? Think paid vacation days! The first number in each ordered pair is the number of years a full-time employee has been employed by a medium to large U.S. company. The second number is the average number of paid vacation days each year. Consider, for example, the ordered pair (15, 18.9).

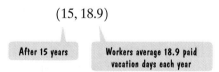

The relation in the vacation-days example can be pictured as follows:

Average Number of Paid Vacation Days for Full-Time Workers at Medium to Large U.S. Companies

Figure 2.21 The graph of a relation showing a correspondence between years with a company and paid vacation days

Source: Bureau of Labor Statistics

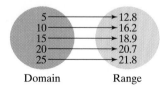

A scatter plot, like the one shown in Figure 2.21, is another way to represent the relation.

2 Determine whether a relation is a function.

Jerry Orbach $34,000
Charles Shaugnessy $31,800
Andy Richter $29,400
Norman Schwarzkopf $28,000
Jon Stewart $28,000

Functions

Shown, again, in the margin are *Celebrity Jeopardy's* five all-time highest winners and their winnings. We've used this information to define two relations. Figure 2.22(a) shows a correspondence between winners and their winnings. Figure 2.22(b) shows a correspondence between winnings and winners.

Figure 2.22(a)
Winners correspond to winnings

Figure 2.22(b)
Winnings correspond to winners

A relation in which each member of the domain corresponds to exactly one member of the range is a **function**. Can you see that the relation in Figure 2.22(a) is a function? Each winner in the domain corresponds to exactly one winning amount in the range. If we know the winner, we can be sure of the amount won. Notice that more than one element in the domain can correspond to the same element in the range. (Schwarzkopf and Stewart both won $28,000.)

Is the relation in Figure 2.22(b) a function? Does each member of the domain correspond to precisely one member of the range? This relation is not a function because there is a member of the domain that corresponds to two members of the range:

($28,000, Schwarzkopf)   ($28,000, Stewart).

The member of the domain, $28,000, corresponds to both Schwarzkopf and Stewart in the range. If we know the amount won, $28,000, we cannot be sure of the winner. Because **a function is a relation in which no two ordered pairs have the same first component and different second components,** the ordered pairs ($28,000, Schwarzkopf) and ($28,000, Stewart) are not ordered pairs of a function.

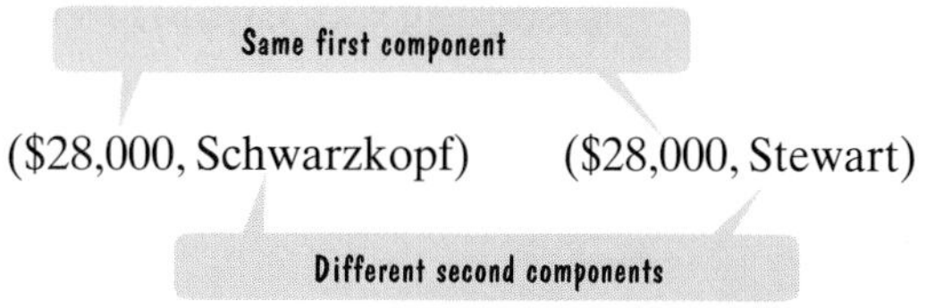

Same first component

($28,000, Schwarzkopf)   ($28,000, Stewart)

Different second components

Definition of a Function

A **function** is a correspondence from a first set, called the **domain,** to a second set, called the **range,** such that each element in the domain corresponds to *exactly one* element in the range.

Example 2 illustrates that not every correspondence between sets is a function.

EXAMPLE 2   Determining Whether a Relation is a Function

Determine whether each relation is a function:

a. $\{(1, 6), (2, 6), (3, 8), (4, 9)\}$ **b.** $\{(6, 1), (6, 2), (8, 3), (9, 4)\}$.

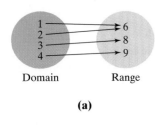

Domain   Range

(a)

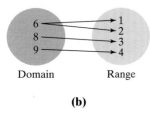

Domain   Range

(b)

Figure 2.23

Study Tip

The word "range" can mean many things, from a chain of mountains to a cooking stove. For functions, it means the set of all function values. For graphing utilities, it means the setting used for the viewing rectangle. Try not to confuse these meanings.

Solution   We will make a figure for each relation that shows the domain and the range.

a. We begin with the relation $\{(1, 6), (2, 6), (3, 8), (4, 9)\}$. Figure 2.23(a) shows that every element in the domain corresponds to exactly one element in the range. The element 1 in the domain corresponds to the element 6 in the range. Furthermore, 2 corresponds to 6, 3 corresponds to 8, and 4 corresponds to 9. No two ordered pairs in the given relation have the same first component and different second components. Thus, the relation is a function.

b. We now consider the relation $\{(6, 1), (6, 2), (8, 3), (9, 4)\}$. Figure 2.23(b) shows that 6 corresponds to both 1 and 2. If any element in the domain corresponds to more than one element in the range, the relation is not a function. This relation is not a function; two ordered pairs have the same first component and different second components.

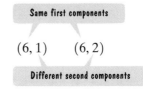

Look at Figure 2.23 again. The fact that 1 and 2 in the domain have the same image, 6, in the range does not violate the definition of a function. **A function can have two different first components with the same second component.** By contrast, a relation is not a function when two different ordered pairs have the same first component and different second components. Thus, the relation in Example 2(b) is not a function.

> **Check Point 2**   Determine whether each relation is a function:
> **a.** $\{(1, 2), (3, 4), (5, 6), (5, 8)\}$
> **b.** $\{(1, 2), (3, 4), (6, 5), (8, 5)\}$.

3 Determine whether an equation represents a function.

Functions as Equations

Functions are usually given in terms of equations rather than as sets of ordered pairs. For example, here is an equation that models paid vacation days each year as a function of years working for a company:

$$y = -0.016x^2 + 0.93x + 8.5.$$

The variable x represents years working for a company. The variable y represents the average number of vacation days each year. The variable y is a function of the variable x. For each value of x, there is one and only one value of y. The variable x is called the **independent variable** because it can be assigned any value from the domain. Thus, x can be assigned any positive integer representing the number of years working for a company. The variable y is called the **dependent variable** because its value depends on x. Paid vacation days depend on years working for a company. The value of the dependent variable, y, is calculated after selecting a value for the independent variable, x.

We have seen that not every set of ordered pairs defines a function. Similarly, not all equations with the variables x and y define a function. If an equation is solved for y and more than one value of y can be obtained for a given x, then the equation does not define y as a function of x.

> **EXAMPLE 3** **Determining Whether an Equation Represents a Function**

Determine whether each equation defines y as a function of x:

    a. $x^2 + y = 4$ **b.** $x^2 + y^2 = 4$.

Solution Solve each equation for y in terms of x. If two or more values of y can be obtained for a given x, the equation is not a function.

    a. $x^2 + y = 4$ This is the given equation.

        $x^2 + y - x^2 = 4 - x^2$ Solve for y by subtracting x² from both sides.

                $y = 4 - x^2$ Simplify.

From this last equation we can see that for each value of x, there is one and only one value of y. For example, if $x = 1$, then $y = 4 - 1^2 = 3$. The equation defines y as a function of x.

    b. $x^2 + y^2 = 4$ This given equation describes a circle.

        $x^2 + y^2 - x^2 = 4 - x^2$ Isolate y² by subtracting x² from both sides.

              $y^2 = 4 - x^2$ Simplify.

            $y = \pm\sqrt{4 - x^2}$ Apply the square root method.

The $\pm$ in this last equation shows that for certain values of x (all values between -2 and 2), there are two values of y. For example, if $x = 1$, then $y = \pm\sqrt{4 - 1^2} = \pm\sqrt{3}$. For this reason, the equation does not define y as a function of x.

> **Check Point 3** Solve each equation for y and then determine whether the equation defines y as a function of x:
>
>   **a.** $2x + y = 6$ **b.** $x^2 + y^2 = 1$.

4 Evaluate a function.

Function Notation

When an equation represents a function, the function is often named by a letter such as $f, g, h, F, G,$ or H. Any letter can be used to name a function. Suppose that f names a function. Think of the domain as the set of the function's inputs and the range as the set of the function's outputs. As shown in Figure 2.24, the input is represented by x and the output by $f(x)$. The special notation $f(x)$, read "f of x" or "f at x," represents the **value of the function at the number x.**

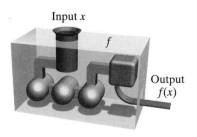

Figure 2.24 A function as a machine with inputs and outputs

Let's make this clearer by considering a specific example. We know that the equation

$$y = -0.016x^2 + 0.93x + 8.5$$

defines y as a function of x. We'll name the function f. Now, we can apply our new function notation.

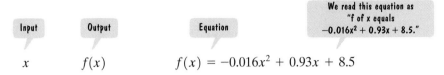

| Input | Output | Equation | We read this equation as "f of x equals $-0.016x^2 + 0.93x + 8.5$." |

$$x \qquad f(x) \qquad f(x) = -0.016x^2 + 0.93x + 8.5$$

Technology

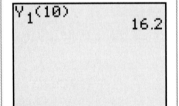

Suppose we are interested in finding $f(10)$, the function's output when the input is 10. To find the value of the function at 10, we substitute 10 for x. We are **evaluating the function** at 10.

$$f(x) = -0.016x^2 + 0.93x + 8.5 \qquad \text{This is the given function.}$$

$$f(10) = -0.016(10)^2 + 0.93(10) + 8.5 \qquad \text{Replace each occurrence of x with 10.}$$

$$= -0.016(100) + 0.93(10) + 8.5 \qquad \text{Evaluate the exponential expression: } 10^2 = 100.$$

$$= -1.6 + 9.3 + 8.5 \qquad \text{Perform the multiplications.}$$

$$= 16.2 \qquad \text{Add from left to right.}$$

The statement $f(10) = 16.2$, read "f of 10 equals 16.2," tells us that the value of the function at 10 is 16.2. When the function's input is 10, its output is 16.2 (After 10 years, workers average 16.2 vacation days each year.) To find other function values, such as $f(15)$, $f(20)$, or $f(23)$, substitute the specified input values for x into the function's equation.

If a function is named f and x represents the independent variable, the notation $f(x)$ corresponds to the y-value for a given x. Thus,

$$f(x) = -0.016x^2 + 0.93x + 8.5 \quad \text{and} \quad y = -0.016x^2 + 0.93x + 8.5$$

define the same function. This function may be written as

$$y = f(x) = -0.016x^2 + 0.93x + 8.5.$$

EXAMPLE 4   Evaluating a Function

If $f(x) = x^2 + 3x + 5$, evaluate:

   a. $f(2)$ **b.** $f(x + 3)$ **c.** $f(-x)$.

Solution   We substitute 2, $x + 3$, and $-x$ for x in the definition of f. When replacing x with a variable or an algebraic expression, you might find it helpful to think of the function's equation as

$$f(\boxed{x}) = \boxed{x}^2 + 3\boxed{x} + 5.$$

a. We find $f(2)$ by substituting 2 for x in the equation.

$$f(\boxed{2}) = \boxed{2}^2 + 3 \cdot \boxed{2} + 5 = 4 + 6 + 5 = 15$$

Thus, $f(2) = 15$.

b. We find $f(x + 3)$ by substituting $x + 3$ for x in the equation.

$$f(\boxed{x + 3}) = \boxed{(x + 3)}^2 + 3\boxed{(x + 3)} + 5$$

Equivalently,

$$f(x + 3) = (x + 3)^2 + 3(x + 3) + 5$$
$$= x^2 + 6x + 9 + 3x + 9 + 5 \quad \text{Square } x + 3 \text{ using } (A + B)^2 = A^2 + 2AB + B^2.$$
$$\text{Distribute 3 throughout the parentheses.}$$
$$= x^2 + 9x + 23. \quad \text{Combine like terms.}$$

c. We find $f(-x)$ by substituting $-x$ for x in the equation.

$$f(\boxed{-x}) = \boxed{(-x)}^2 + 3 \boxed{(-x)} + 5$$

Equivalently,

$$f(-x) = (-x)^2 + 3(-x) + 5$$
$$= x^2 - 3x + 5.$$

Discovery

Using $f(x) = x^2 + 3x + 5$ and the answers in parts (b) and (c):

1. Is $f(x + 3)$ equal to $f(x) + f(3)$?

2. Is $f(-x)$ equal to $-f(x)$?

Check Point 4   If $f(x) = x^2 - 2x + 7$, evaluate:

    a. $f(-5)$ **b.** $f(x + 4)$ **c.** $f(-x)$.

5   Find and simplify a function's difference quotient.

Functions and Difference Quotients

We have seen how slope can be interpreted as a rate of change. In the next section, we will be studying the average rate of change of a function. A ratio, called the *difference quotient*, plays an important role in understanding the rate at which functions change.

> **Definition of a Difference Quotient**
>
> The expression
>
> $$\frac{f(x + h) - f(x)}{h}$$
>
> for $h \neq 0$ is called the **difference quotient**.

EXAMPLE 5   **Evaluating and Simplifying a Difference Quotient**

If $f(x) = x^2 + 3x + 5$, find and simplify:

    a. $f(x + h)$ **b.** $\dfrac{f(x + h) - f(x)}{h}, h \neq 0.$

Solution

    a. We find $f(x + h)$ by replacing x with $x + h$ each time that x appears in the equation.

$$f(x) \quad = \quad x^2 \quad + \quad 3x \quad + \quad 5$$

Replace x with $x + h$.   Replace x with $x + h$.   Replace x with $x + h$.   Copy the 5. There is no x in this term.

$$f(x + h) \quad = \quad (x + h)^2 \quad + \quad 3(x + h) \quad + \quad 5$$
$$= x^2 + 2xh + h^2 + 3x + 3h \quad + \quad 5$$

b. Using our result from part (a), we obtain the following:

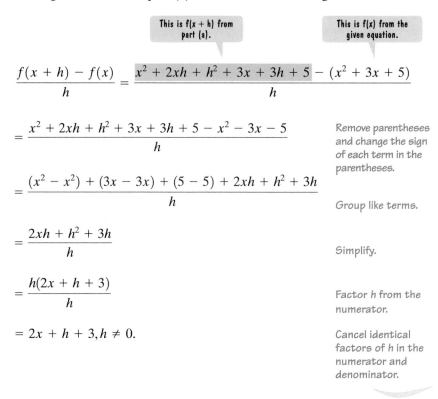

$$\frac{f(x+h)-f(x)}{h} = \frac{x^2+2xh+h^2+3x+3h+5-(x^2+3x+5)}{h}$$

$$= \frac{x^2+2xh+h^2+3x+3h+5-x^2-3x-5}{h}$$

Remove parentheses and change the sign of each term in the parentheses.

$$= \frac{(x^2-x^2)+(3x-3x)+(5-5)+2xh+h^2+3h}{h}$$

Group like terms.

$$= \frac{2xh+h^2+3h}{h}$$

Simplify.

$$= \frac{h(2x+h+3)}{h}$$

Factor h from the numerator.

$$= 2x+h+3, h \neq 0.$$

Cancel identical factors of h in the numerator and denominator.

Check Point 5 If $f(x)=x^2-7x+3$, find and simplify:

a. $f(x+h)$ **b.** $\dfrac{f(x+h)-f(x)}{h}, h \neq 0.$

6   Understand and use piecewise functions.

Piecewise Functions

The early part of the twentieth century was the golden age of immigration in America. More than 13 million people migrated to the United States between 1900 and 1914. By 1910, foreign-born residents accounted for 15% of the total U.S. population. The graph in Figure 2.25 shows the percentage of Americans who were foreign born throughout the twentieth century.

We can model the data from 1910 through 2000 with two equations, one from 1910 through 1970, years in which the percentage was decreasing, and one from 1970 through 2000, years in which the percentage was increasing. These two trends can be approximated by the function

Percentage of Americans Who Were Foreign Born in the Twentieth Century

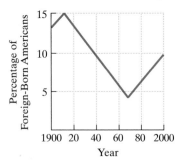

Figure 2.25 *Source*: U.S. Census Bureau

$$P(t) = \begin{cases} -\dfrac{11}{60}t + 15 & \text{if } 0 \le t < 60 \\[2ex] \dfrac{1}{5}t - 8 & \text{if } 60 \le t \le 90 \end{cases}$$

in which t represents the number of years after 1910 and $P(t)$ is the percentage of foreign-born Americans. A function that is defined by two (or more) equations over a specified domain is called a **piecewise function**.

EXAMPLE 6 Evaluating a Piecewise Function

Use the function $P(t)$, described previously, to find and interpret:

   a. $P(30)$ **b.** $P(80)$.

Solution

a. To find $P(30)$, we let $t = 30$. Because 30 is less than 60, we use the first line of the piecewise function.

$$P(t) = -\tfrac{11}{60}t + 15 \qquad \text{This is the function's equation for } 0 \le t < 60.$$

$$P(30) = -\tfrac{11}{60} \cdot 30 + 15 \qquad \text{Replace } t \text{ with 60.}$$

$$= 9.5$$

This means that 30 years after 1910, in 1940, 9.5% of Americans were foreign born.

b. To find $P(80)$, we let $t = 80$. Because 80 is between 60 and 90, we use the second line of the piecewise function.

$$P(t) = \frac{1}{5}t - 8 \qquad \text{This is the function's equation for } 60 \le t \le 90.$$

$$P(80) = \tfrac{1}{5} \cdot 80 - 8 \qquad \text{Replace } t \text{ with 80.}$$

$$= 8$$

This means that 80 years after 1910, in 1990, 8% of Americans were foreign born.

Check Point 6 If $f(x) = \begin{cases} x^2 + 3 & \text{if } x < 0 \\ 5x + 3 & \text{if } x \ge 0 \end{cases}$, find:

   a. $f(-5)$ **b.** $f(6)$.

7 Find the domain of a function.

The Domain of a Function

Let's reconsider the function that models the percentage of foreign-born Americans t years after 1910, up through and including 2000. The domain of this function is

$$\{0, \ 1, \ 2, \ 3, \ \ldots, \ 90\}.$$

0 years after 1910 is 1910.   3 years after 1910 is 1913.   90 years after 1910 brings the domain up to the year 2000.

    Functions that model data often have their domains explicitly given along with the function's equation. However, for most functions, only an equation is given, and the domain is not specified. In cases like this, the domain of f is the largest set of real numbers for which the value of $f(x)$ is a real number. For example, consider the function

$$f(x) = \frac{1}{x - 3}.$$

Because division by 0 is undefined (and not a real number), the denominator $x - 3$ cannot be 0. Thus, x cannot equal 3. The domain of the function consists of all real numbers other than 3, represented by $\{x \mid x \ne 3\}$. We say that f is not defined at 3, or $f(3)$ does not exist.

Just as the domain of a function must exclude real numbers that cause division by zero, it must also exclude real numbers that result in an even root of a negative number. For example, consider the function

$$g(x) = \sqrt{x}.$$

The equation tells us to take the square root of x. Because only nonnegative numbers have real square roots, the expression under the radical sign, x, must be greater than or equal to 0. The domain of g is $\{x \mid x \geq 0\}$, or the interval $[0, \infty)$.

Finding a Function's Domain

If a function f does not model data or verbal conditions, its domain is the largest set of real numbers for which the value of $f(x)$ is a real number. Exclude from a function's domain real numbers that cause division by zero and real numbers that result in an even root of a negative number.

EXAMPLE 7   Finding the Domain of a Function

Find the domain of each function:

a. $f(x) = x^2 - 7x$ **b.** $g(x) = \dfrac{6x}{x^2 - 9}$ **c.** $h(x) = \sqrt{3x + 12}$.

Solution

a. The function $f(x) = x^2 - 7x$ contains neither division nor an even root. The domain of f is the set of all real numbers.

b. The function $g(x) = \dfrac{6x}{x^2 - 9}$ contains division. Because division by 0 is undefined, we must exclude from the domain values of x that cause $x^2 - 9$ to be 0. Thus, x cannot equal -3 or 3. The domain of g is $\{x \mid x \neq -3, x \neq 3\}$.

c. The function $h(x) = \sqrt{3x + 12}$ contains an even root. Because only nonnegative numbers have real square roots, the quantity under the radical sign, $3x + 12$, must be greater than or equal to 0.

$$3x + 12 \geq 0$$

$$3x \geq -12$$

$$x \geq -4$$

The domain of h is $\{x \mid x \geq -4\}$, or the interval $[-4, \infty)$.

Technology

You can graph a function and often get hints about its domain. For example, $h(x) = \sqrt{3x + 12}$, or $y = \sqrt{3x + 12}$, appears only for $x \geq -4$, verifying $[-4, \infty)$ as the domain.

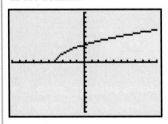

Check Point 7   Find the domain of each function:

a. $f(x) = x^2 + 3x - 17$ **b.** $g(x) = \dfrac{5x}{x^2 - 49}$

c. $h(x) = \sqrt{9x - 27}$.

EXERCISE SET 2.3

 Practice Exercises

In Exercises 1–8, determine whether each relation is a function. Give the domain and range for each relation.

1. $\{(1,2),(3,4),(5,5)\}$ **2.** $\{(4,5),(6,7),(8,8)\}$

3. $\{(3,4),(3,5),(4,4),(4,5)\}$

4. $\{(5,6),(5,7)\,(6,6),(6,7)\}$

5. $\{(-3,-3),(-2,-2),(-1,-1),(0,0)\}$

6. $\{(-7,-7),(-5,-5),(-3,-3),(0,0)\}$

7. $\{(1,4),(1,5),(1,6)\}$ **8.** $\{(4,1),(5,1),(6,1)\}$

In Exercises 9–20, determine whether each equation defines y as a function of x.

9. $x + y = 16$ **10.** $x + y = 25$

11. $x^2 + y = 16$ **12.** $x^2 + y = 25$

13. $x^2 + y^2 = 16$ **14.** $x^2 + y^2 = 25$

15. $x = y^2$ **16.** $4x = y^2$

17. $y = \sqrt{x + 4}$ **18.** $y = -\sqrt{x + 4}$

19. $x + y^3 = 8$ **20.** $x + y^3 = 27$

In Exercises 21–32, evaluate each function at the given values of the independent variable and simplify.

21. $f(x) = 4x + 5$
  a. $f(6)$ **b.** $f(x + 1)$ **c.** $f(-x)$

22. $f(x) = 3x + 7$
  a. $f(4)$ **b.** $f(x + 1)$ **c.** $f(-x)$

23. $g(x) = x^2 + 2x + 3$
  a. $g(-1)$ **b.** $g(x + 5)$ **c.** $g(-x)$

24. $g(x) = x^2 - 10x - 3$
  a. $g(-1)$ **b.** $g(x + 2)$ **c.** $g(-x)$

25. $h(x) = x^4 - x^2 + 1$
  a. $h(2)$ **b.** $h(-1)$
  c. $h(-x)$ **d.** $h(3a)$

26. $h(x) = x^3 - x + 1$
  a. $h(3)$ **b.** $h(-2)$
  c. $h(-x)$ **d.** $h(3a)$

27. $f(r) = \sqrt{r + 6} + 3$
  a. $f(-6)$ **b.** $f(10)$ **c.** $f(x - 6)$

28. $f(r) = \sqrt{25 - r} - 6$
  a. $f(16)$ **b.** $f(-24)$ **c.** $f(25 - 2x)$

29. $f(x) = \dfrac{4x^2 - 1}{x^2}$
  a. $f(2)$ **b.** $f(-2)$ **c.** $f(-x)$

30. $f(x) = \dfrac{4x^3 + 1}{x^3}$
  a. $f(2)$ **b.** $f(-2)$ **c.** $f(-x)$

31. $f(x) = \dfrac{x}{|x|}$
  a. $f(6)$ **b.** $f(-6)$ **c.** $f(r^2)$

32. $f(x) = \dfrac{|x + 3|}{x + 3}$
  a. $f(5)$ **b.** $f(-5)$ **c.** $f(-9 - x)$

In Exercises 33–44, find and simplify the difference quotient

$$\frac{f(x + h) - f(x)}{h}, \ h \neq 0$$

for the given function.

33. $f(x) = 4x$ **34.** $f(x) = 7x$

35. $f(x) = 3x + 7$ **36.** $f(x) = 6x + 1$

37. $f(x) = x^2$ **38.** $f(x) = 2x^2$

39. $f(x) = x^2 - 4x + 3$ **40.** $f(x) = x^2 - 5x + 8$

41. $f(x) = 6$ **42.** $f(x) = 7$

43. $f(x) = \dfrac{1}{x}$ **44.** $f(x) = \dfrac{1}{2x}$

In Exercises 45–50, evaluate each piecewise function at the given values of the independent variable.

45. $f(x) = \begin{cases} 3x + 5 & \text{if } x < 0 \\ 4x + 7 & \text{if } x \geq 0 \end{cases}$
  a. $f(-2)$ **b.** $f(0)$ **c.** $f(3)$

46. $f(x) = \begin{cases} 6x - 1 & \text{if } x < 0 \\ 7x + 3 & \text{if } x \geq 0 \end{cases}$
  a. $f(-3)$ **b.** $f(0)$ **c.** $f(4)$

47. $g(x) = \begin{cases} x + 3 & \text{if } x \geq -3 \\ -(x + 3) & \text{if } x < -3 \end{cases}$
  a. $g(0)$ **b.** $g(-6)$ **c.** $g(-3)$

48. $g(x) = \begin{cases} x + 5 & \text{if } x \geq -5 \\ -(x + 5) & \text{if } x < -5 \end{cases}$
  a. $g(0)$ **b.** $g(-6)$ **c.** $g(-5)$

49. $h(x) = \begin{cases} \dfrac{x^2 - 9}{x - 3} & \text{if } x \neq 3 \\ 6 & \text{if } x = 3 \end{cases}$
  a. $h(5)$ **b.** $h(0)$ **c.** $h(3)$

50. $h(x) = \begin{cases} \dfrac{x^2 - 25}{x - 5} & \text{if } x \neq 5 \\ 10 & \text{if } x = 5 \end{cases}$
  a. $h(7)$ **b.** $h(0)$ **c.** $h(5)$

In Exercises 51–74, find the domain of each function.

51. $f(x) = 4x^2 - 3x + 1$

52. $f(x) = 8x^2 - 5x + 2$

53. $g(x) = \dfrac{3}{x - 4}$

54. $g(x) = \dfrac{2}{x + 5}$

55. $h(x) = \dfrac{7x}{x^2 - 16}$

56. $h(x) = \dfrac{12x}{x^2 - 36}$

57. $f(x) = \dfrac{2}{(x + 3)(x - 7)}$

58. $f(x) = \dfrac{15}{(x + 8)(x - 3)}$

59. $H(r) = \dfrac{4}{r^2 + 11r + 24}$

60. $H(r) = \dfrac{5}{6r^2 + r - 2}$

61. $f(t) = \dfrac{3}{t^2 + 4}$

62. $f(t) = \dfrac{5}{t^2 + 9}$

63. $f(x) = \sqrt{x - 3}$

64. $f(x) = \sqrt{x + 2}$

65. $f(x) = \dfrac{1}{\sqrt{x - 3}}$

66. $f(x) = \dfrac{1}{\sqrt{x + 2}}$

67. $g(x) = \sqrt{5x + 35}$

68. $g(x) = \sqrt{7x - 70}$

69. $f(x) = \sqrt{24 - 2x}$

70. $f(x) = \sqrt{84 - 6x}$

71. $f(x) = \sqrt{x^2 - 5x - 14}$

72. $f(x) = \sqrt{x^2 - 5x - 24}$

73. $f(x) = \dfrac{\sqrt{x - 2}}{x - 5}$

74. $f(x) = \dfrac{\sqrt{x - 3}}{x - 6}$

Application Exercises

75. The bar graph shows the percentage of people in the United States using the Internet by education level. Write five ordered pairs for

(education level, percentage using Internet)

as a relation. Find the domain and the range of the relation. Is this relation a function? Explain your answer.

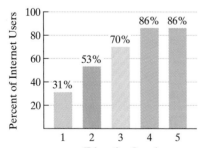

Internet Use in the U.S. by Education Level

Source: U.C.L.A. Center for Communication Policy

The table shows the ten longest-running television shows of the twentieth century. Use the information in the table to solve Exercises 76–78.

Ten Longest-Running National Network TV Series of the Twentieth Century

Program	Number of Seasons the Show Ran
"Walt Disney"	33
"60 Minutes"	33
"The Ed Sullivan Show"	24
"Gunsmoke"	20
"The Red Skelton Show"	20
"Meet the Press"	18
"What's My Line?"	18
"I've Got a Secret"	17
"Lassie"	17
"The Lawrence Welk Show"	17

Source: Nielsen Media Research

76. Consider the relation for which the domain represents the ten longest-running series and the range represents the number of seasons the series ran. Is this relation a function? Explain your answer.

77. Consider the relation for which the domain represents the number of seasons the ten longest-running series ran and the range represents the ten longest-running series. Is this relation a function? Explain your answer.

78. Use your answers from Exercises 76 and 77 to answer the following question: If the components in a function's ordered pairs are reversed, must the resulting relation also be a function?

79. The function

$$P(x) = 0.72x^2 + 9.4x + 783$$

models the gray wolf population in the United States, $P(x)$, x years after 1960. Find and interpret $P(30)$. How well does the function model the actual value shown in the bar graph?

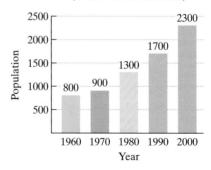

Gray Wolf Population (to the Nearest Hundred)

Source: U.S. Department of the Interior

80. As the use of the Internet increases, so has the number of computer infections from viruses. The function

$$N(x) = 0.2x^2 - 1.2x + 2$$

models the number of infections per month for every 1000 computers, $N(x)$, x years after 1990. Find and interpret $N(10)$. How well does the function model the actual value shown in the bar graph?

Computer Infection Rates

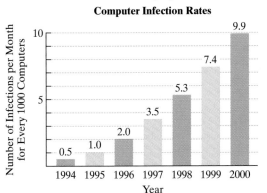

Source: Jupiter Communications

The function

$$P(t) = 6.85\sqrt{t} + 19$$

models the percentage of U.S. households online, P(t), t years after 1997. In Exercises 81–84, use this function to find and interpret the given expression. If necessary, use a calculator and round to the nearest whole percent. How well does the function model the actual data shown in the bar graph?

Percentage of U.S. Households Online

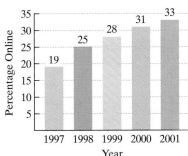

Source: Forrester Research

81. $P(0)$ **82.** $P(4)$

83. $P(3) - P(1)$ **84.** $P(2) - P(1)$

The number of lawyers in the United States can be modeled by the function

$$f(x) = \begin{cases} 6.5x + 200 & \text{if } 0 \le x < 23 \\ 26.2x - 252 & \text{if } x \ge 23 \end{cases}$$

where x represents the number of years after 1951 and f(x) represents the number of lawyers, in thousands. In Exercises 85–88, use this function to find and interpret each of the following.

85. $f(0)$ **86.** $f(10)$

87. $f(50)$ **88.** $f(60)$

During a particular year, the taxes owed, T(x), in dollars, filing separately with an adjusted gross income of x dollars is given by the piecewise function

$$T(x) = \begin{cases} 0.15x & \text{if } 0 \le x < 17{,}900 \\ 0.28(x - 17{,}900) + 2685 & \text{if } 17{,}900 \le x < 43{,}250 \\ 0.31(x - 43{,}250) + 9783 & \text{if } x \ge 43{,}250 \end{cases}$$

In Exercises 89–90, use this function to find and interpret each of the following.

89. $T(40{,}000)$ **90.** $T(70{,}000)$

In Exercises 91–94, you will be developing functions that model given conditions.

91. A company that manufactures bicycles has a fixed cost of $100,000. It costs $100 to produce each bicycle. The total cost for the company is the sum of its fixed cost and variable costs. Write the total cost, C, as a function of the number of bicycles produced. Then find and interpret $C(90)$.

92. A car was purchased for $22,500. The value of the car decreases by $3200 per year for the first six years. Write a function that describes the value of the car, V, after x years, where $0 \le x \le 7$. Then find and interpret $V(3)$.

93. You commute to work a distance of 40 miles and return on the same route at the end of the day. Your average rate on the return trip is 30 miles per hour faster than your average rate on the outgoing trip. Write the total time, T, in hours, devoted to your outgoing and return trips as a function of your rate on the outgoing trip. Then find and interpret $T(30)$. Hint:

$$\text{Time traveled} = \frac{\text{Distance traveled}}{\text{Rate of travel}}.$$

94. A chemist working on a flu vaccine needs to mix a 10% sodium-iodine solution with a 60% sodium-iodine solution to obtain a 50-milliliter mixture. Write the amount of sodium iodine in the mixture, S, in milliliters, as a function of the number of milliliters of the 10% solution used. Then find and interpret $S(30)$.

Writing in Mathematics

95. If a relation is represented by a set of ordered pairs, explain how to determine whether the relation is a function.

96. How do you determine if an equation in x and y defines y as a function of x?

97. A student in introductory algebra hears that functions are studied in subsequent algebra courses. The student asks you what a function is. Provide the student with a clear, relatively concise response.

98. Describe one advantage of using $f(x)$ rather than y in a function's equation.

99. Explain how to find the difference quotient,

$$\frac{f(x + h) - f(x)}{h}, \text{ if a function's equation is given.}$$

100. What is a piecewise function?

101. How is the domain of a function determined?

102. For people filing a single return, federal income tax is a function of adjusted gross income because for each value of adjusted gross income there is a specific tax to be paid. On the other hand, the price of a house is not a function of the lot size on which the house sits because houses on same-sized lots can sell for many different prices.

    a. Describe an everyday situation between variables that is a function.

    b. Describe an everyday situation between variables that is not a function.

Technology Exercises

Use a graphing utility to find the domain of each function in Exercises 103–105. Then verify your observation algebraically.

103. $f(x) = \sqrt{x-1}$ **104.** $g(x) = \sqrt{2x+6}$

105. $h(x) = \sqrt{15-3x}$

Critical Thinking Exercises

106. Write a function defined by an equation in x whose domain is $\{x \mid x \neq -4, x \neq 11\}$.

107. Write a function defined by an equation in x whose domain is $[-6, \infty)$.

108. Give an example of an equation that does not define y as a function of x but that does define x as a function of y.

109. If $f(x) = ax^2 + bx + c$ and $r_1 = \dfrac{-b + \sqrt{b^2 - 4ac}}{2a}$, find $f(r_1)$ without doing any algebra and explain how you arrived at your result.

Group Exercise

110. Almanacs, newspapers, magazines, and the Internet contain bar graphs and line graphs that describe how things are changing over time. For example, the graphs in Exercises 79–82 show how various phenomena are changing over time. Find a bar or line graph showing yearly changes that you find intriguing. Describe to the group what interests you about this data. The group should select their two favorite graphs. For each graph selected:

    a. Rewrite the data so that they are presented as a relation in the form of a set of ordered pairs.

    b. Determine whether the relation in part (a) is a function. Explain why the relation is a function, or why it is not.

SECTION 2.4 *Graphs of Functions*

Objectives

1. Graph functions by plotting points.

2. Obtain information about a function from its graph.

3. Use the vertical line test to identify functions.

4. Identify intervals on which a function increases, decreases, or is constant.

5. Use graphs to locate relative maxima or minima.

6. Find a function's average rate of change.

7. Identify even or odd functions and recognize their symmetries.

8. Graph step functions.

Have you ever seen a gas-guzzling car from the 1950s, with its huge fins and overstated design? The worst year for automobile fuel efficiency was 1958, when cars averaged a dismal 12.4 miles per gallon. The function

$$f(x) = 0.0075x^2 - 0.2672x + 14.8$$

models the average number of miles per gallon for U.S. automobiles, $f(x)$, x years after 1940. If we could see the graph of the function's equation, we would get a much better idea of the relationship between time and fuel efficiency. In this section, we will learn how to use the graph of a function to obtain useful information about the function.

Graphs of Functions

A graph enables us to visualize a function's behavior. The graph shows the relationship between the function's two variables more clearly than the function's equation does. The **graph of a function** is the graph of its ordered pairs. For example, the graph of $f(x) = \sqrt{x}$ is the set of points (x, y) in the rectangular coordinate system satisfying the equation $y = \sqrt{x}$. Thus, one way to graph a function is by plotting several of its ordered pairs and drawing a line or smooth curve through them. With the function's graph, we can picture its domain on the x-axis and its range on the y-axis. Our first example illustrates how this is done.

1 Graph functions by plotting points.

EXAMPLE 1   Graphing a Function by Plotting Points

Graph $f(x) = x^2 + 1$. To do so, use integer values of x from the set $\{-3, -2, -1, 0, 1, 2, 3\}$ to obtain seven ordered pairs. Plot each ordered pair and draw a smooth curve through the points. Use the graph to specify the function's domain and range.

Solution   The graph of $f(x) = x^2 + 1$ is, by definition, the graph of $y = x^2 + 1$. We begin by setting up a partial table of coordinates.

x	$f(x) = x^2 + 1$	(x, y) or $(x, f(x))$
-3	$f(-3) = (-3)^2 + 1 = 10$	$(-3, 10)$
-2	$f(-2) = (-2)^2 + 1 = 5$	$(-2, 5)$
-1	$f(-1) = (-1)^2 + 1 = 2$	$(-1, 2)$
0	$f(0) = 0^2 + 1 = 1$	$(0, 1)$
1	$f(1) = 1^2 + 1 = 2$	$(1, 2)$
2	$f(2) = 2^2 + 1 = 5$	$(2, 5)$
3	$f(3) = 3^2 + 1 = 10$	$(3, 10)$

Now, we plot the seven points and draw a smooth curve through them, as shown in Figure 2.26. The graph of f has a cuplike shape. The points on the graph of f have x-coordinates that extend indefinitely to the left and to the right. Thus, the domain consists of all real numbers, represented by $(-\infty, \infty)$. By contrast, the points on the graph have y-coordinates that start at 1 and extend indefinitely upward. Thus, the range consists of all real numbers greater than or equal to 1, represented by $[1, \infty)$.

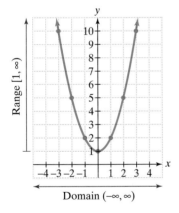

Figure 2.26 The graph of $f(x) = x^2 + 1$

Check Point 1   Graph $f(x) = x^2 - 2$, using integers from -3 to 3 for x in the partial table of coordinates. Use the graph to specify the function's domain and range.

Technology

Does your graphing utility have a [TABLE] feature? If so, you can use it to create tables of coordinates for a function. You will need to enter the equation of the function and specify the starting value for x, [TblStart], and the increment between successive x-values, [ΔTbl]. For the table of coordinates in Example 1, we start the table at $x = -3$ and increment by 1. Using the up- or down-arrow keys, you can scroll through the table and determine as many ordered pairs of the graph as desired.

2 Obtain information about a function from its graph.

Obtaining Information from Graphs

You can obtain information about a function from its graph. At the right or left of a graph, you will find closed dots, open dots, or arrows.

- A closed dot indicates that the graph does not extend beyond this point and the point belongs to the graph.

- An open dot indicates that the graph does not extend beyond this point and the point does not belong to the graph.

- An arrow indicates that the graph extends indefinitely in the direction in which the arrow points.

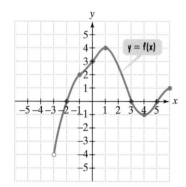

Figure 2.27

EXAMPLE 2   Obtaining Information from a Function's Graph

Use the graph of the function f, shown in Figure 2.27, to answer the following questions:

a. What are the function values $f(-1)$ and $f(1)$?

b. What is the domain of f?

c. What is the range of f?

Solution

a. Because $(-1, 2)$ is a point on the graph of f, the y-coordinate, 2, is the value of the function at the x-coordinate, -1. Thus, $f(-1) = 2$. Similarly, because $(1, 4)$ is also a point on the graph of f, this indicates that $f(1) = 4$.

b. The open dot on the left shows that $x = -3$ is not in the domain of f. By contrast, the closed dot on the right shows that $x = 6$ is in the domain of f. We determine the domain of f by noticing that the points on the graph of f have x-coordinates between -3, excluding -3, and 6, including 6. For each number x between -3 and 6, there is a point $(x, f(x))$ on the graph. Thus, the domain of f is $\{x \mid -3 < x \leq 6\}$, or the interval $(-3, 6]$.

c. The points on the graph all have y-coordinates between -4, not including -4, and 4, including 4. The graph does not extend below $y = -4$ or above $y = 4$. Thus, the range of f is $\{y \mid -4 < y \leq 4\}$, or the interval $(-4, 4]$.

Check Point 2   Use the graph of function f, shown below, to find $f(4)$, the domain, and the range.

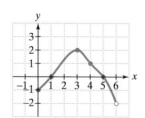

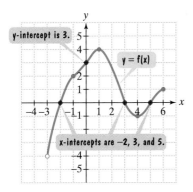

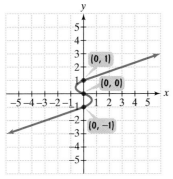

Figure 2.28 Identifying intercepts

3 Use the vertical line test to identify functions.

Figure 2.29 y is not a function of x because 0 is paired with three values of y, namely, 1, 0, and -1.

Figure 2.28 illustrates how we can identify a graph's intercepts. To find the x-intercepts, look for the points at which the graph crosses the x-axis. There are three such points: $(-2, 0)$, $(3, 0)$, and $(5, 0)$. Thus, the x-intercepts are -2, 3, and 5. We express this in function notation by writing $f(-2) = 0$, $f(3) = 0$, and $f(5) = 0$. We say that -2, 3, and 5 are the *zeros of the function*. The **zeros of a function**, f, are the x-values for which $f(x) = 0$.

To find the y-intercept, look for the point at which the graph crosses the y-axis. This occurs at $(0, 3)$. Thus, the y-intercept is 3. We express this in function notation by writing $f(0) = 3$.

By the definition of a function, for each value of x we can have at most one value for y. What does this mean in terms of intercepts? **A function can have more than one x-intercept but at most one y-intercept.**

The Vertical Line Test

Not every graph in the rectangular coordinate system is the graph of a function. The definition of a function specifies that no value of x can be paired with two or more different values of y. Consequently, if a graph contains two or more different points with the same first coordinate, the graph cannot represent a function. This is illustrated in Figure 2.29. Observe that points sharing a common first coordinate are vertically above or below each other.

This observation is the basis of a useful test for determining whether a graph defines y as a function of x. The test is called the **vertical line test.**

> ### The Vertical Line Test for Functions
> If any vertical line intersects a graph in more than one point, the graph does not define y as a function of x.

EXAMPLE 3 Using the Vertical Line Test

Use the vertical line test to identify graphs in which y is a function of x.

a.

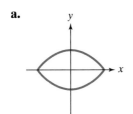

b.

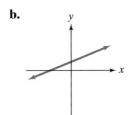

c.

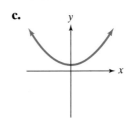

d.

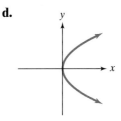

Solution y is a function of x for the graphs in **b** and **c**.

a.

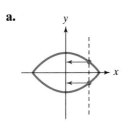

b.

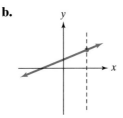

c.

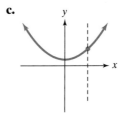

d.

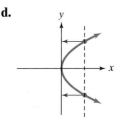

y is **not a function of** x.
Two values of y
correspond to an x-value.

y **is a function of** x.

y **is a function of** x.

y is **not a function of** x.
Two values of y
correspond to an x-value.

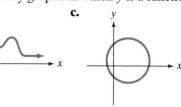

Use the vertical line test to identify graphs in which y is a function of x.

Average Number of Paid Vacation Days for Full-Time Workers at Medium to Large U.S. Companies

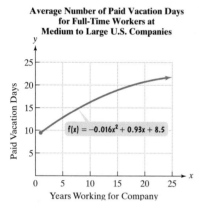

Figure 2.30 *Source*: Bureau of Labor Statistics

EXAMPLE 4 Analyzing the Graph of a Function

The function

$$f(x) = -0.016x^2 + 0.93x + 8.5$$

models the average number of paid vacation days each year, $f(x)$, for full-time workers at medium to large U.S. companies after x years. The graph of f is shown in Figure 2.30.

a. Explain why f represents the graph of a function.
b. Use the graph to find a reasonable estimate of $f(5)$.
c. For what value of x is $f(x) = 20$?
d. Describe the general trend shown by the graph.

Solution

a. No vertical line intersects the graph of f more than once. By the vertical line test, f represents the graph of a function.

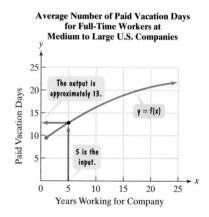

b. To find $f(5)$, or f of 5, we locate 5 on the x-axis. The figure shows the point on the graph of f for which 5 is the first coordinate. From this point, we look to the y-axis to find the corresponding y-coordinate. A reasonable estimate of the y-coordinate is 13. Thus, $f(5) \approx 13$. After 5 years, a worker can expect approximately 13 paid vacation days.

c. To find the value of x for which $f(x) = 20$, we locate 20 on the y-axis. The figure shows that there is one point on the graph of f for which 20 is the second coordinate. From this point, we look to the x-axis to find the corresponding x-coordinate. A reasonable estimate of the x-coordinate is 18. Thus, $f(x) = 20$ for $x \approx 18$. A worker with 20 paid vacation days has been with the company approximately 18 years.

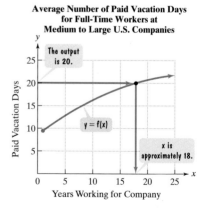

d. The graph of f is rising from left to right. This shows that paid vacation days increase as time with the company increases. However, the rate of increase is slowing down as the graph moves to the right. This means that the increase in paid vacation days takes place more slowly the longer an employee is with the company.

Check Point 4

a. Use the graph of f in Figure 2.30 to find a reasonable estimate of $f(10)$.

b. For what value of x is $f(x) = 15$? Round to the nearest whole number.

Increasing and Decreasing Functions

4 Identify intervals on which a function increases, decreases, or is constant.

Too late for that flu shot now! It's only 8 A.M. and you're feeling lousy. Your temperature is 101°F. Fascinated by the way that algebra models the world (your author is projecting a bit here), you decide to construct graphs showing your body temperature as a function of the time of day. You decide to let x represent the number of hours after 8 A.M. and $f(x)$ your temperature at time x.

At 8 A.M. your temperature is 101°F and you are not feeling well. However, your temperature starts to decrease. It reaches normal (98.6°F) by 11 A.M. Feeling energized, you construct the graph shown on the right, indicating decreasing temperature for $\{x \mid 0 < x < 3\}$, or on the interval $(0, 3)$.

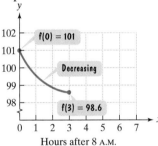

Hours after 8 A.M.

Temperature decreases on $(0, 3)$, reaching 98.6° by 11 A.M.

Did creating that first graph drain you of your energy? Your temperature starts to rise after 11 A.M. By 1 P.M., 5 hours after 8 A.M., your temperature reaches 100°F. However, you keep plotting points on your graph. At right, we can see that your temperature increases for $\{x \mid 3 < x < 5\}$, or on the interval $(3, 5)$.

The graph of f is decreasing to the left of $x = 3$ and increasing to the right of $x = 3$. Thus, your temperature 3 hours after 8 A.M. was at a relative minimum. Your relative minimum temperature was 98.6°.

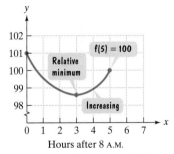

Hours after 8 A.M.

Temperature increases on $(3, 5)$.

By 3 P.M., your temperature is no worse than it was at 1 P.M.: It is still 100°F. (Of course, it's no better, either.) Your temperature remained the same, or constant, for $\{x \mid 5 < x < 7\}$, or on the interval $(5, 7)$.

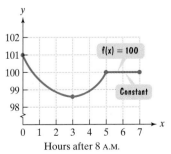

Hours after 8 A.M.

Temperature remains constant at 100° on $(5, 7)$.

The time-temperature flu scenario illustrates that a function f is increasing when its graph rises, decreasing when its graph falls, and remains constant when it neither rises nor falls. Let's now provide a more algebraic description for these intuitive concepts.

Increasing, Decreasing, and Constant Functions

1. A function is **increasing** on an open interval, I, if for any x_1 and x_2 in the interval, where $x_1 < x_2$, then $f(x_1) < f(x_2)$.
2. A function is **decreasing** on an open interval, I, if for any x_1 and x_2 in the interval, where $x_1 < x_2$, then $f(x_1) > f(x_2)$.
3. A function is **constant** on an open interval, I, if for any x_1 and x_2 in the interval, where $x_1 < x_2$, then $f(x_1) = f(x_2)$.

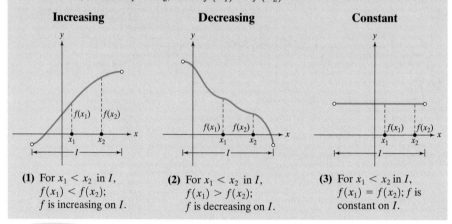

Increasing	Decreasing	Constant

(1) For $x_1 < x_2$ in I, $f(x_1) < f(x_2)$; f is increasing on I.

(2) For $x_1 < x_2$ in I, $f(x_1) > f(x_2)$; f is decreasing on I.

(3) For $x_1 < x_2$ in I, $f(x_1) = f(x_2)$; f is constant on I.

EXAMPLE 5 **Intervals on Which a Function Increases, Decreases, or Is Constant**

Give the intervals on which each function whose graph is shown is increasing, decreasing, or constant.

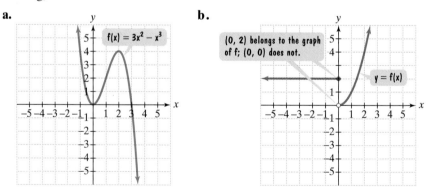

a. $f(x) = 3x^2 - x^3$

b. $(0, 2)$ belongs to the graph of f; $(0, 0)$ does not. $y = f(x)$

Solution

a. The function is decreasing on the interval $(-\infty, 0)$, increasing on the interval $(0, 2)$, and decreasing on the interval $(2, \infty)$.

b. Although the function's equations are not given, the graph indicates that the function is defined in two pieces. The part of the graph to the left of the y-axis shows that the function is constant on the interval $(-\infty, 0)$. The part to the right of the y-axis shows that the function is increasing on the interval $(0, \infty)$.

Check Point 5 Give the intervals on which the function whose graph is shown is increasing, decreasing, or constant.

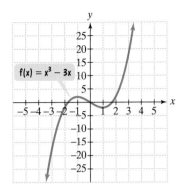

5 Use graphs to locate relative maxima or minima.

Relative Maxima and Relative Minima

The points at which a function changes its increasing or decreasing behavior can be used to find the *relative maximum* or *relative minimum* values of the function. For example, consider the function with which we opened this section:

$$f(x) = 0.0075x^2 - 0.2672x + 14.8.$$

Recall that the function models the average number of miles per gallon of U.S. automobiles, $f(x)$, x years after 1940. The graph of this function is shown as a continuous curve in Figure 2.31. (It can also be shown as a series of points, each point representing a year and miles per gallon for that year.)

The graph of f is decreasing to the left of $x = 18$ and increasing to the right of $x = 18$. Thus, 18 years after 1940, in 1958, fuel efficiency was at a minimum. We say that the relative minimum fuel efficiency is $f(18)$, or approximately 12.4 miles per gallon. Mathematicians use the word "relative" to suggest that relative to an open interval about 18, the value $f(18)$ is smallest.

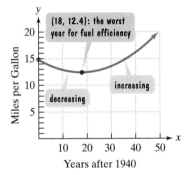

Figure 2.31 Fuel efficiency of U.S. automobiles over time

Study Tip

The word *local* is sometimes used instead of *relative* when describing maxima or minima. If f has a relative, or local, maximum at a, *f(a)* is greater than the values of f near a. If f has a relative, or local, minimum at b, *f(b)* is less than the values of f near b.

Definitions of Relative Maximum and Relative Minimum

1. A function value $f(a)$ is a **relative maximum** of f if there exists an open interval about a such that $f(a) > f(x)$ for all x in the open interval.

2. A function value $f(b)$ is a **relative minimum** of f if there exists an open interval about b such that $f(b) < f(x)$ for all x in the open interval.

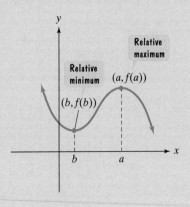

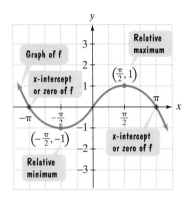

Figure 2.32 Using a graph to locate where f has a relative maximum or minimum

If the graph of a function is given, we can often visually locate the number(s) at which the function has a relative maximum or a relative minimum. For example, the graph of f in Figure 2.32 shows that:

• f has a relative maximum at $\dfrac{\pi}{2}$.

  The relative maximum is $f\left(\dfrac{\pi}{2}\right) = 1$.

• f has a relative minimum at $-\dfrac{\pi}{2}$.

  The relative minimum is $f\left(-\dfrac{\pi}{2}\right) = -1$.

Notice that f does not have a relative maximum or minimum at $-\pi$ and π, the x-intercepts, or zeros, of the function.

6 Find a function's average rate of change.

The Average Rate of Change of a Function

We have seen that the slope of a line can be interpreted as its rate of change. If the graph of a function is not a straight line, we speak of an **average rate of change** between any two points on its graph. To find the average rate of change, calculate the slope of the line containing the two points. This line is called a **secant line.**

The Average Rate of Change of a Function

Let $(x_1, f(x_1))$ and $(x_2, f(x_2))$ be distinct points on the graph of a function f. (See Figure 2.33.) The **average rate of change of f** from x_1 to x_2 is

$$\frac{f(x_2) - f(x_1)}{x_2 - x_1}.$$

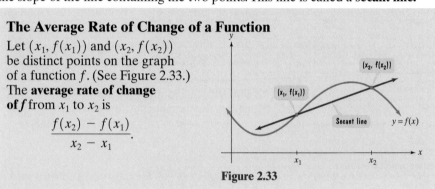

Figure 2.33

EXAMPLE 6 Finding the Average Rate of Change

Find the average rate of change of $f(x) = x^2$ from:

a. $x_1 = 0$ to $x_2 = 1$ **b.** $x_1 = 1$ to $x_2 = 2$ **c.** $x_1 = -2$ to $x_2 = 0.$

Solution

a. The average rate of change of $f(x) = x^2$ from $x_1 = 0$ to $x_2 = 1$ is

$$\frac{f(x_2) - f(x_1)}{x_2 - x_1} = \frac{f(1) - f(0)}{1 - 0} = \frac{1^2 - 0^2}{1} = 1.$$

Figure 2.34(a) shows the secant line of $f(x) = x^2$ from $x_1 = 0$ to $x_2 = 1$. The average rate of change is positive, and the function is increasing on the interval $(0, 1)$.

b. The average rate of change of $f(x) = x^2$ from $x_1 = 1$ to $x_2 = 2$ is

$$\frac{f(x_2) - f(x_1)}{x_2 - x_1} = \frac{f(2) - f(1)}{2 - 1} = \frac{2^2 - 1^2}{1} = 3.$$

Figure 2.34(b) shows the secant line of $f(x) = x^2$ from $x_1 = 1$ to $x_2 = 2$. The average rate of change is positive, and the function is increasing on the interval $(1, 2)$. Can you see that the graph rises more steeply on the interval $(1, 2)$ than on $(0, 1)$? This is because the average rate of change from $x_1 = 1$ to $x_2 = 2$ is greater than the average rate of change from $x_1 = 0$ to $x_2 = 1$.

c. The average rate of change of $f(x) = x^2$ from $x_1 = -2$ to $x_2 = 0$ is

$$\frac{f(x_2) - f(x_1)}{x_2 - x_1} = \frac{f(0) - f(-2)}{0 - (-2)} = \frac{0^2 - (-2)^2}{2} = \frac{-4}{2} = -2.$$

Figure 2.34(c) shows the secant line of $f(x) = x^2$ from $x_1 = -2$ to $x_2 = 0$. The average rate of change is negative, and the function is decreasing on the interval $(-2, 0)$.

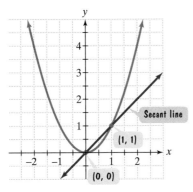

Figure 2.34(a) The secant line of $f(x) = x^2$ from $x_1 = 0$ to $x_2 = 1$

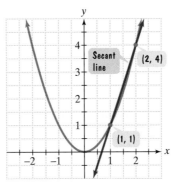

Figure 2.34(b) The secant line of $f(x) = x^2$ from $x_1 = 1$ to $x_2 = 2$

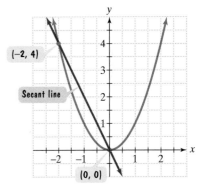

Figure 2.34(c) The secant line of $f(x) = x^2$ from $x_1 = -2$ to $x_2 = 0$

Check Point 6   Find the average rate of change of $f(x) = x^3$ from

a. $x_1 = 0$ to $x_2 = 1$

b. $x_1 = 1$ to $x_2 = 2$

c. $x_1 = -2$ to $x_2 = 0$.

Suppose we are interested in the average rate of change of f from $x_1 = x$ to $x_2 = x + h$. In this case, the average rate of change is

$$\frac{f(x_2) - f(x_1)}{x_2 - x_1} = \frac{f(x + h) - f(x)}{x + h - x} = \frac{f(x + h) - f(x)}{h}.$$

Do you recognize the last expression? It is the difference quotient that you used in the previous section to practice evaluating functions. Thus, the difference quotient gives the average rate of change of a function from x to $x + h$. In the difference quotient, h is thought of as a number very close to 0. In this way, the average rate of change can be found for a very short interval.

7 Identify even or odd functions and recognize their symmetries.

Even and Odd Functions and Symmetry

Is beauty in the eye of the beholder? Or are there certain objects (or people) that are so well balanced and proportioned that they are universally pleasing to the eye? What constitutes an attractive human face? In Figure 2.35, we've drawn lines between paired features and marked the midpoints. Notice how the features line up almost perfectly. Each half of the face is a mirror image of the other half through the white vertical line.

Did you know that graphs of some equations exhibit exactly the kind of symmetry shown by the attractive face in Figure 2.35? The word *symmetry* comes from the Greek *symmetria*, meaning "the same measure." We can identify graphs with symmetry by looking at a function's equation and determining if the function is *even* or *odd*.

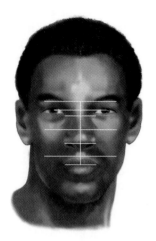

Figure 2.35 To most people, an attractive face is one in which each half is an almost perfect mirror image of the other half

Definition of Even and Odd Functions

The function f is an **even function** if

$$f(-x) = f(x) \quad \text{for all } x \text{ in the domain of } f.$$

The right side of the equation of an even function does not change if x is replaced with $-x$.

The function f is an **odd function** if

$$f(-x) = -f(x) \quad \text{for all } x \text{ in the domain of } f.$$

Every term in the right side of the equation of an odd function changes sign if x is replaced with $-x$.

EXAMPLE 7   Identifying Even or Odd Functions

Identify each of the following functions as even, odd, or neither:

a. $f(x) = x^3$ **b.** $g(x) = x^4 - 2x^2$ **c.** $h(x) = x^2 + 2x + 1$.

Solution   In each case, replace x with $-x$ and simplify. If the right side of the equation stays the same, the function is even. If every term on the right changes sign, the function is odd.

a. We use the given function's equation, $f(x) = x^3$, to find $f(-x)$.

Use $f(x) = x^3$.

Replace x with −x.   Replace x with −x.

$$f(-x) = (-x)^3 = (-x)(-x)(-x) = -x^3$$

There is only one term in the equation $f(x) = x^3$, and the term changed signs when we replaced x with $-x$. Because $f(-x) = -f(x)$, f is an odd function.

b. We use the given function's equation, $g(x) = x^4 - 2x^2$, to find $g(-x)$.

Use $g(x) = x^4 - 2x^2$.

Replace x with −x.

$$g(-x) = (-x)^4 - 2(-x)^2 = (-x)(-x)(-x)(-x) - 2(-x)(-x)$$
$$= x^4 - 2x^2$$

The right side of the equation of the given function, $g(x) = x^4 - 2x^2$, did not change when we replaced x with $-x$. Because $g(-x) = g(x)$, g is an even function.

c. We use the given function's equation, $h(x) = x^2 + 2x + 1$, to find $h(-x)$.

Use $h(x) = x^2 + 2x + 1$.

Replace x with −x.

$$h(-x) = (-x)^2 + 2(-x) + 1 = x^2 - 2x + 1$$

The right side of the equation of the given function, $h(x) = x^2 + 2x + 1$, changed when we replaced x with $-x$. Thus, $h(-x) \neq h(x)$, so h is not an even function. The sign of *each* of the three terms in the equation for $h(x)$ did not change when we replaced x with $-x$. Only the second term changed signs. Thus, $h(-x) \neq -h(x)$, so h is not an odd function. We conclude that h is neither an even nor an odd function.

Check Point 7 Determine whether each of the following functions is even, odd, or neither:

a. $f(x) = x^2 + 6$ **b.** $g(x) = 7x^3 - x$ **c.** $h(x) = x^5 + 1$.

Now, let's see what even and odd functions tell us about a function's graph. Begin with the even function $f(x) = x^2 - 4$, shown in Figure 2.36. The function is even because

$$f(-x) = (-x)^2 - 4 = x^2 - 4 = f(x).$$

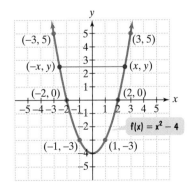

Figure 2.36 y-axis symmetry with $f(-x) = f(x)$

Examine the pairs of points shown, such as $(3, 5)$ and $(-3, 5)$. Notice that we obtain the same y-coordinate whenever we evaluate the function at a value of x and the value of its opposite, $-x$. Like the attractive face, each half of the graph is a mirror image of the other half through the y-axis. If we were to fold the paper along the y-axis, the two halves of the graph would coincide. This causes the graph to be *symmetric with respect to the y-axis*. A graph is **symmetric with respect to the y-axis** if, for every point (x, y) on the graph, the point $(-x, y)$ is also on the graph. All even functions have graphs with this kind of symmetry.

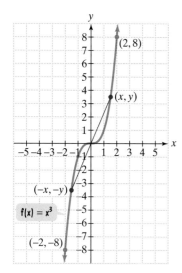

Figure 2.37 Origin symmetry with $f(-x) = -f(x)$

Even Functions and y-Axis Symmetry

The graph of an even function in which $f(-x) = f(x)$ is symmetric with respect to the y-axis.

Now, consider the graph of the function $f(x) = x^3$. In Example 5, we saw that $f(-x) = -f(x)$, so this is an odd function. Although the graph in Figure 2.37 is not symmetric with respect to the y-axis, it is symmetric in another way. Look at the pairs of points, such as $(2, 8)$ and $(-2, -8)$. For each point (x, y) on the graph, the point $(-x, -y)$ is also on the graph. The points $(2, 8)$ and $(-2, -8)$ are reflections of one another in the origin. This means that:

- the points are the same distance from the origin, and
- the points lie on a line through the origin.

A graph is **symmetric with respect to the origin** if, for every point (x, y) on the graph, the point $(-x, -y)$ is also on the graph. Observe that the first- and third-quadrant portions of $f(x) = x^3$ are reflections of one another with respect to the origin. Notice that $f(x)$ and $f(-x)$ have opposite signs, so that $f(-x) = -f(x)$. All odd functions have graphs with origin symmetry.

Odd Functions and Origin Symmetry

The graph of an odd function in which $f(-x) = -f(x)$ is symmetric with respect to the origin.

8 Graph step functions.

Step Functions

Have you ever mailed a letter that seemed heavier than usual? Perhaps you worried that the letter would not have enough postage. Costs for mailing a letter weighing up to 5 ounces are given in Table 2.3. If your letter weighs an ounce or less, the cost is $0.37. If your letter weighs 1.05 ounces, 1.50 ounces, 1.90 ounces, or 2.00 ounces, the cost "steps" to $0.60. The cost does not take on any value between $0.37 and $0.60. If your letter weighs 2.05 ounces, 2.50 ounces, 2.90 ounces, or 3 ounces, the cost "steps" to $0.83. Cost increases are $0.23 per step.

Now, let's see what the graph of the function that models this situation looks like. Let

$$x = \text{the weight of the letter, in ounces, and}$$

$$y = f(x) = \text{the cost of mailing a letter weighing } x \text{ ounces.}$$

Table 2.3 Cost of First-Class Mail (Effective June 30, 2002)

Weight Not Over	Cost
1 ounce	$0.37
2 ounces	0.60
3 ounces	0.83
4 ounces	1.06
5 ounces	1.29

Source: U.S. Postal Service

The graph is shown in Figure 2.38. Notice how it consists of a series of steps that jump vertically 0.23 unit at each integer. The graph is constant between each pair of consecutive integers.

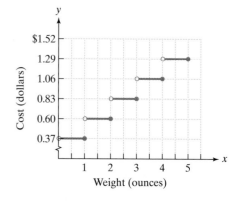

Figure 2.38

Mathematicians have defined functions that describe situations where function values graphically form discontinuous steps. One such function is called the **greatest integer function,** symbolized by int(x) or $[x]$. And what is int(x)?

int(x) = the greatest integer that is less than or equal to x.

For example,

$$\text{int}(1) = 1, \quad \text{int}(1.3) = 1, \quad \text{int}(1.5) = 1, \quad \text{int}(1.9) = 1.$$

1 is the greatest integer that is less than or equal to 1, 1.3, 1.5, and 1.9.

Here are some additional examples:

$$\text{int}(2) = 2, \quad \text{int}(2.3) = 2, \quad \text{int}(2.5) = 2, \quad \text{int}(2.9) = 2.$$

2 is the greatest integer that is less than or equal to 2, 2.3, 2.5, and 2.9.

Notice how we jumped from 1 to 2 in the function values for int(x). In particular,

$$\text{If } 1 \le x < 2, \quad \text{then} \quad \text{int}(x) = 1.$$
$$\text{If } 2 \le x < 3, \quad \text{then} \quad \text{int}(x) = 2.$$

The graph of $f(x) = \text{int}(x)$ is shown in Figure 2.39. The graph of the greatest integer function jumps vertically one unit at each integer. However, the graph is constant between each pair of consecutive integers. The rightmost horizontal step shown in the graph illustrates that

$$\text{If } 5 \le x < 6, \quad \text{then} \quad \text{int}(x) = 5.$$

In general,

$$\text{If } n \le x < n + 1, \text{ where } n \text{ is an integer,} \quad \text{then} \quad \text{int}(x) = n.$$

By contrast to the graph for the cost of first-class mail, the graph of the greatest integer function includes the point on the left of each horizontal step, but does not include the point on the right. The domain of $f(x) = \text{int}(x)$ is the set of all real numbers, $(-\infty, \infty)$. The range is the set of all integers.

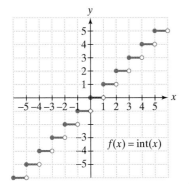

Figure 2.39 The graph of the greatest integer function

Technology

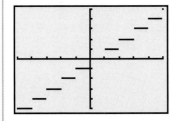

The graph of $f(x) = \text{int}(x)$, shown on the left, was obtained with a graphing utility. By graphing in "dot" mode, we can see the discontinuities at the integers. By looking at the graph, it is impossible to tell that, for each step, the point on the left is included and the point on the right is not. We must trace along the graph to obtain such information.

EXERCISE SET 2.4

Practice Exercises

Graph the function in Exercises 1–14. Use the integer values of x given to the right of the function to obtain ordered pairs. Use the graph to specify the function's domain and range.

1. $f(x) = x^2 + 2$ $x = -3, -2, -1, 0, 1, 2, 3$
2. $f(x) = x^2 - 1$ $x = -3, -2, -1, 0, 1, 2, 3$
3. $g(x) = \sqrt{x} - 1$ $x = 0, 1, 4, 9$
4. $g(x) = \sqrt{x} + 2$ $x = 0, 1, 4, 9$
5. $h(x) = \sqrt{x - 1}$ $x = 1, 2, 5, 10$
6. $h(x) = \sqrt{x + 2}$ $x = -2, -1, 2, 7$
7. $f(x) = |x| - 1$ $x = -3, -2, -1, 0, 1, 2, 3$
8. $f(x) = |x| + 1$ $x = -3, -2, -1, 0, 1, 2, 3$
9. $g(x) = |x - 1|$ $x = -3, -2, -1, 0, 1, 2, 3$
10. $g(x) = |x + 1|$ $x = -3, -2, -1, 0, 1, 2, 3$
11. $f(x) = 5$ $x = -3, -2, -1, 0, 1, 2, 3$
12. $f(x) = 3$ $x = -3, -2, -1, 0, 1, 2, 3$
13. $f(x) = x^3 - 2$ $x = -2, -1, 0, 1, 2$
14. $f(x) = x^3 + 2$ $x = -2, -1, 0, 1, 2$

*In Exercises 15–30, use the graph to determine **a.** the function's domain; **b.** the function's range; **c.** the x-intercepts, if any; **d.** the y-intercept, if any; and **e.** the function values indicated below some of the graphs.*

15.

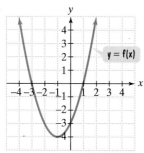

16.

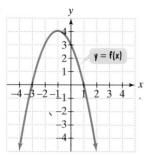

17.

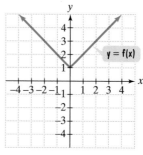

$f(-1) = ?$ $f(3) = ?$

18.

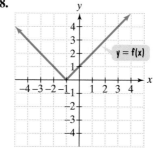

$f(-4) = ?$ $f(3) = ?$

19.

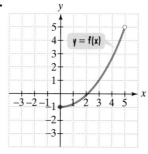

$f(3) = ?$

20.

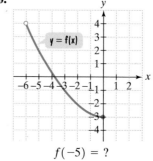

$f(-5) = ?$

21.

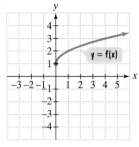

$f(4) = ?$

22.

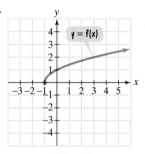

$f(3) = ?$

23.

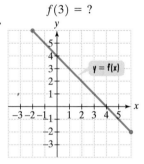

$f(-1) = ?$

24.

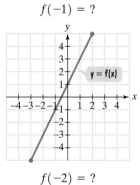

$f(-2) = ?$

25.

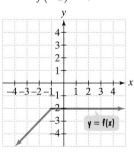

$f(-4) = ?$ $f(4) = ?$

26.

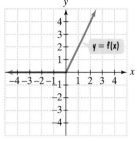

$f(-2) = ?$ $f(2) = ?$

27.

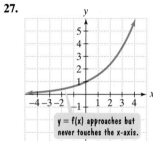

28.

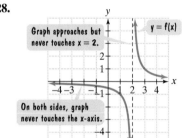

29.

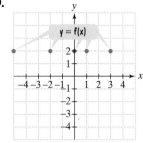

30.

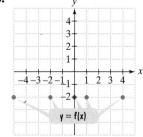

In Exercises 31–38, use the vertical line test to identify graphs in which y is a function of x.

31.

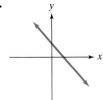

32.

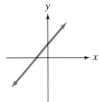

33.

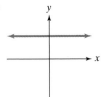

34.

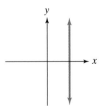

35.

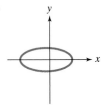

36.

37.

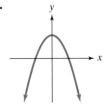

38.

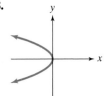

47.

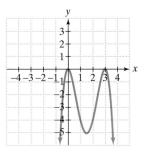

48.

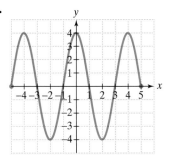

49.

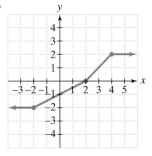

In Exercises 39–50, use the graph to determine:

   a. *intervals on which the function is increasing, if any.*

   b. *intervals on which the function is decreasing, if any.*

   c. *intervals on which the function is constant, if any.*

39. Use the graph in Exercise 15.

40. Use the graph in Exercise 16.

41. Use the graph in Exercise 21.

42. Use the graph in Exercise 22.

43. Use the graph in Exercise 23.

44. Use the graph in Exercise 24.

45. Use the graph in Exercise 25.

46. Use the graph in Exercise 26.

50.

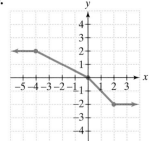

In Exercises 51–54, the graph of a function f is given. Use the graph to find:

a. The numbers, if any, at which f has a relative maximum. What are these relative maxima?

b. The numbers, if any, at which f has a relative minimum. What are these relative minima?

51.

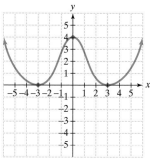

52.

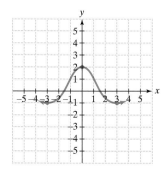

53.

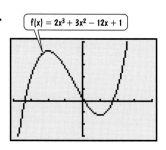

$f(x) = 2x^3 + 3x^2 - 12x + 1$

[-4, 4, 1] by [-15, 25, 5]

54.

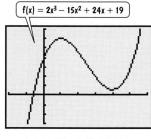

$f(x) = 2x^3 - 15x^2 + 24x + 19$

[-2, 6, 1] by [-15, 35, 5]

In Exercises 55–60, find the average rate of change of the function from x_1 to x_2.

55. $f(x) = 3x$ from $x_1 = 0$ to $x_2 = 5$
56. $f(x) = 6x$ from $x_1 = 0$ to $x_2 = 4$
57. $f(x) = x^2 + 2x$ from $x_1 = 3$ to $x_2 = 5$
58. $f(x) = x^2 - 2x$ from $x_2 = 3$ to $x_2 = 6$
59. $f(x) = \sqrt{x}$ from $x_1 = 4$ to $x_2 = 9$
60. $f(x) = \sqrt{x}$ from $x_1 = 9$ to $x_2 = 16$

In Exercises 61–72, determine whether each function is even, odd, or neither.

61. $f(x) = x^3 + x$ **62.** $f(x) = x^3 - x$
63. $g(x) = x^2 + x$ **64.** $g(x) = x^2 - x$
65. $h(x) = x^2 - x^4$ **66.** $h(x) = 2x^2 + x^4$
67. $f(x) = x^2 - x^4 + 1$ **68.** $f(x) = 2x^2 + x^4 + 1$
69. $f(x) = \frac{1}{5}x^6 - 3x^2$ **70.** $f(x) = 2x^3 - 6x^5$
71. $f(x) = x\sqrt{1 - x^2}$ **72.** $f(x) = x^2\sqrt{1 - x^2}$

In Exercises 73–66, use possible symmetry to determine whether each graph is the graph of an even function, an odd function, or a function that is neither even nor odd.

73.

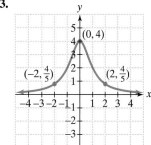

74.

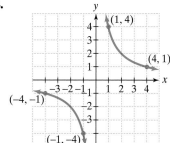

75.

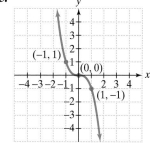

76.

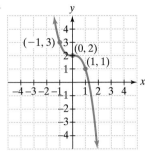

In Exercises 77–82, if $f(x) = int(x)$, find each function value.

77. $f(1.06)$ **78.** $f(2.99)$

79. $f(\frac{1}{3})$ **80.** $f(-1.5)$

81. $f(-2.3)$ **82.** $f(-99.001)$

Application Exercises

The figure shows the percentage of the U.S. population made up of Jewish Americans, $f(x)$, as a function of time, x, where x is the number of years after 1900. Use the graph to solve Exercises 83–90.

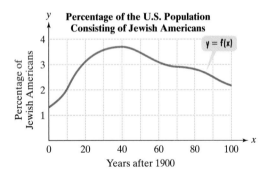

Source: American Jewish Yearbook

83. Use the graph to find a reasonable estimate of $f(60)$. What does this mean in terms of the variables in this situation?

84. Use the graph to find a reasonable estimate of $f(100)$. What does this mean in terms of the variables in this situation?

85. For what value or values of x is $f(x) = 3$? Round to the nearest year. What does this mean in terms of the variables in this situation?

86. For what value or values of x is $f(x) = 2.5$? Round to the nearest year. What does this mean in terms of the variables in this situation?

87. In which year did the percentage of Jewish Americans in the U.S. population reach a maximum? What is a reasonable estimate of the percentage for that year?

88. In which year was the percentage of Jewish Americans in the U.S. population at a minimum? What is a reasonable estimate of the percentage for that year?

89. Explain why f represents the graph of a function.

90. Describe the general trend shown by the graph.

The function

$$f(x) = 0.4x^2 - 36x + 1000$$

models the number of accidents, $f(x)$, per 50 million miles driven as a function of the driver's age, x, in years, where x includes drivers from ages 16 through 74. The graph of f is shown. Use the graph of f, and possibly the equation, to solve Exercises 91–93.

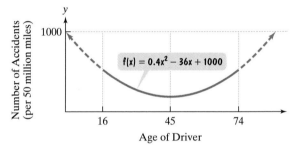

91. State the intervals on which the function is increasing and decreasing and describe what this means in terms of the variables modeled by the function.

92. For what value of x does the graph reach its lowest point? What is the minimum value of y? Describe the practical significance of this minimum value.

93. Use the graph to identify two different ages for which drivers have the same number of accidents. Use the equation for f to find the number of accidents for drivers at each of these ages.

94. Based on a study by Vance Tucker (*Scientific American*, May 1969), the power expenditure of migratory birds in flight is a function of their flying speed, x, in miles per hour, modeled by $f(x) = 0.67x^2 - 27.74x + 387$. Power expenditure, $f(x)$, is measured in calories, and migratory birds generally fly between 12 and 30 miles per hour. The graph of f is shown in the figure on the next page, with a domain of $[12, 30]$.

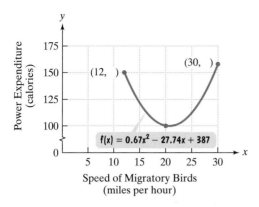

Speed of Migratory Birds
(miles per hour)

$f(x) = 0.67x^2 - 27.74x + 387$

(12,)   (30,)

a. State the intervals on which the function is increasing and decreasing and describe what this means in terms of the variables modeled by the function.

b. For what approximate value of x does the graph reach its lowest point? What is the minimum value of y? Describe the practical significance of this minimum value.

95. The cost of a telephone call between two cities is $0.10 for the first minute and $0.05 for each additional minute or portion of a minute. Draw a graph of the cost, C, in dollars, of the phone call as a function of time, t, in minutes, on the interval $(0, 5]$.

96. A cargo service charges a flat fee of $4 plus $1 for each pound or fraction of a pound to mail a package. Let $C(x)$ represent the cost to mail a package that weighs x pounds. Graph the cost function on the interval $(0, 5]$.

97. Researchers at Yale University have suggested that levels of passion and commitment in human relations are functions of time. Based on the shapes of the graphs shown, which do you think depicts passion and which represents commitment? Explain how you arrived at your answer.

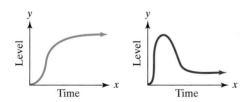

Writing in Mathematics

98. Discuss one disadvantage to using point plotting as a method for graphing functions.

99. Explain how to use a function's graph to find the function's domain and range.

100. Explain how the vertical line test is used to determine whether a graph is a function.

101. What does it mean if function f is increasing on an interval?

102. Suppose that a function f is increasing on (a, b) and decreasing on (b, c). Describe what occurs at $x = b$. What does the function value $f(b)$ represent?

103. What is a secant line?

104. What is the average rate of change of a function?

105. If you are given a function's equation, how do you determine if the function is even, odd, or neither?

106. If you are given a function's graph, how do you determine if the function is even, odd, or neither?

107. What is a step function? Give an example of an everyday situation that can be modeled using such a function. Do not use the cost-of-mail example.

108. Explain how to find int(-3.000004).

Technology Exercises

109. The function
$$f(x) = -0.00002x^3 + 0.008x^2 - 0.3x + 6.95$$
models the number of annual physician visits, $f(x)$, by a person of age x. Graph the function in a $[0, 100, 5]$ by $[0, 40, 2]$ viewing rectangle. What does the shape of the graph indicate about the relationship between one's age and the number of annual physician visits? Use the TRACE or minimum function capability to find the coordinates of the minimum point on the graph of the function. What does this mean?

In Exercises 110–115, use a graphing utility to graph each function. Use a $[-5, 5, 1]$ by $[-5, 5, 1]$ viewing rectangle. Then find the intervals on which the function is increasing, decreasing, or constant.

110. $f(x) = x^3 - 6x^2 + 9x + 1$ **111.** $g(x) = |4 - x^2|$

112. $h(x) = |x - 2| + |x + 2|$ **113.** $f(x) = x^{1/3}(x - 4)$

114. $g(x) = x^{2/3}$ **115.** $h(x) = 2 - x^{2/5}$

116. a. Graph the functions $f(x) = x^n$ for $n = 2, 4$, and 6 in a $[-2, 2, 1]$ by $[-1, 3, 1]$ viewing rectangle.

b. Graph the functions $f(x) = x^n$ for $n = 1, 3$, and 5 in a $[-2, 2, 1]$ by $[-2, 2, 1]$ viewing rectangle.

c. If n is even, where is the graph of $f(x) = x^n$ increasing and where is it decreasing?

d. If n is odd, what can you conclude about the graph of $f(x) = x^n$ in terms of increasing or decreasing behavior.

e. Graph all six functions in a $[-1, 3, 1]$ by $[-1, 3, 1]$ viewing rectangle. What do you observe about the graphs in terms of how flat or how steep they are?

Critical Thinking Exercises

117. Which one of the following is true based on the graph of f in the figure?

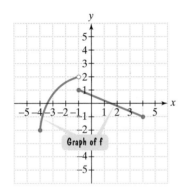

Graph of f

a. The domain of f is $[-4, 1)$ or $(1, 4]$.
b. The range of f is $[-2, 2]$.
c. $f(-1) - f(4) = 2$
d. $f(0) = 2.1$

118. Sketch the graph of f using the following properties. (More than one correct graph is possible.) f is a piecewise function that is decreasing on $(-\infty, 2)$, $f(2) = 0$, f is increasing on $(2, \infty)$, and the range of f is $[0, \infty)$.

119. Define a piecewise function on the intervals $(-\infty, 2]$, $(2, 5)$, and $[5, \infty)$ that does not "jump" at 2 or 5 such that one piece is a constant function, another piece is an increasing function, and the third piece is a decreasing function.

120. Suppose that $h(x) = \dfrac{f(x)}{g(x)}$. The function f can be even, odd, or neither. The same is true for the function g.

a. Under what conditions is h definitely an even function?

b. Under what conditions is h definitely an odd function?

121. Take another look at the cost of first-class mail and its graph (Table 2.3 and Figure 2.38 on page 226. Change the description of the heading in the left column of Table 2.3 so that the graph includes the point on the left of each horizontal step, but does not include the point on the right.

Group Exercise

122. In Exercise 97, passion and commitment are graphed over time. For this activity, you will be creating a graph of a particular experience that involved your feelings of love, anger, sadness, or any other emotion you choose. The horizontal axis should be labeled time and the vertical axis the emotion you are graphing. You will not be using your algebra skills to create your graph; however, you should try to make the graph as precise as possible. You may use negative numbers on the vertical axis, if appropriate. After each group member has created a graph, pool together all of the graphs and study them to see if there are any similarities in the graphs for a particular emotion or for all emotions.

SECTION 2.5 *Transformations of Functions*

Objectives

1. Recognize graphs of common functions.
2. Use vertical shifts to graph functions.
3. Use horizontal shifts to graph functions.
4. Use reflections to graph functions.
5. Use vertical stretching and shrinking to graph functions.
6. Graph functions involving a sequence of transformations.

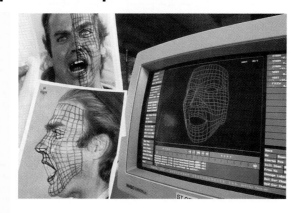

Have you seen *Terminator 2*, *The Mask*, or *The Matrix*? These were among the first films to use spectacular effects in which a character or object having one shape was transformed in a fluid fashion into a quite different shape. The name for such a transformation is **morphing.** The effect allows a real actor to be seamlessly transformed into a computer-generated animation. The animation can be made to perform impossible feats before it is morphed back to the conventionally filmed image.

Like transformed movie images, the graph of one function can be turned into the graph of a different function. To do this, we need to rely on a function's equation. Knowing that a graph is a transformation of a familiar graph makes graphing easier.

1 Recognize graphs of common functions.

Graphs of Common Functions

Table 2.4 below and on page 226 gives names to six frequently encountered functions in algebra. The table shows each function's graph and lists characteristics of the function. Study the shape of each graph and take a few minutes to verify the function's characteristics from its graph. Knowing these graphs is essential for analyzing their transformations into more complicated graphs.

Table 2.4   Algebra's Common Graphs

Constant Function	Identity Function	Standard Quadratic Function
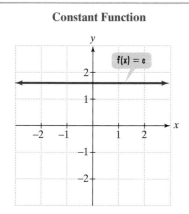	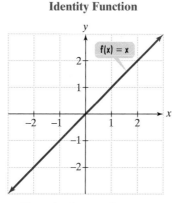	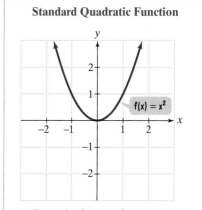
• Domain: $(-\infty, \infty)$	• Domain: $(-\infty, \infty)$	• Domain: $(-\infty, \infty)$
• Range: the single number c	• Range: $(-\infty, \infty)$	• Range: $[0, \infty)$
• Constant on $(-\infty, \infty)$	• Increasing on $(-\infty, \infty)$	• Decreasing on $(-\infty, 0)$ and increasing on $(0, \infty)$
• Even function	• Odd function	• Even function

Table 2.4 Algebra's Common Graphs (*continued*)

Standard Cubic Function	Square Root Function	Absolute Value Function
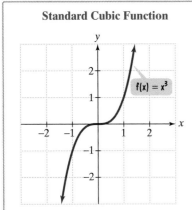	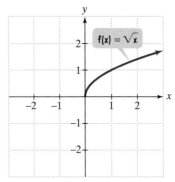	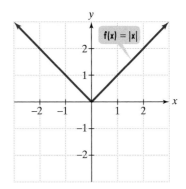
• Domain: $(-\infty, \infty)$	• Domain: $[0, \infty)$	• Domain: $(-\infty, \infty)$
• Range: $(-\infty, \infty)$	• Range: $[0, \infty)$	• Range: $[0, \infty)$
• Increasing on $(-\infty, \infty)$	• Increasing on $(0, \infty)$	• Decreasing on $(-\infty, 0)$ and increasing on $(0, \infty)$
• Odd function	• Neither even nor odd	• Even function

Discovery

The study of how changing a function's equation can affect its graph can be explored with a graphing utility. Use your graphing utility to verify the hand-drawn graphs as you read this section.

2 Use vertical shifts to graph functions.

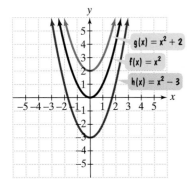

Figure 2.40 Vertical shifts

The graph of $f(x) = x^2$ can be gradually morphed into the graph of $g(x) = x^2 + 2$ by using animation to graph $f(x) = x^2 + c$ for $0 \le c \le 2$. By selecting many values for c, we can create an animated sequence in which change appears to occur continuously.

Vertical Shifts

Let's begin by looking at three graphs whose shapes are the same. Figure 2.40 shows the graphs. The black graph in the middle is the standard quadratic function, $f(x) = x^2$. Now, look at the blue graph on the top. The equation of this graph, $g(x) = x^2 + 2$, adds 2 to the right side of $f(x) = x^2$. What effect does this have on the graph of f? It shifts the graph vertically up by 2 units.

$$g(x) = x^2 + 2 = f(x) + 2$$

The graph of g ⟶ shifts the graph of f up 2 units.

Finally, look at the red graph on the bottom of Figure 2.40. The equation of this graph, $h(x) = x^2 - 3$, subtracts 3 from the right side of $f(x) = x^2$. What effect does this have on the graph of f? It shifts the graph vertically down by 3 units.

$$h(x) = x^2 - 3 = f(x) - 3$$

The graph of h ⟶ shifts the graph of f down 3 units.

In general, if c is positive, $y = f(x) + c$ shifts the graph of f upward c units and $y = f(x) - c$ shifts the graph of f downward c units. These are called **vertical shifts** of the graph of f.

Vertical Shifts

Let f be a function and c a positive real number.
- The graph of $y = f(x) + c$ is the graph of $y = f(x)$ shifted c units vertically upward.
- The graph of $y = f(x) - c$ is the graph of $y = f(x)$ shifted c units vertically downward.

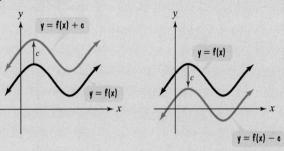

EXAMPLE 1   Vertical Shift Down

Use the graph of $f(x) = |x|$ to obtain the graph of $g(x) = |x| - 4$.

Solution   The graph of $g(x) = |x| - 4$ has the same shape as the graph of $f(x) = |x|$. However, it is shifted down vertically 4 units. We have constructed a table showing some of the coordinates for f and g. The graphs of f and g are shown in Figure 2.41.

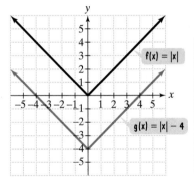

x	$y = f(x) = |x|$	$(x, f(x))$	$y = g(x)$ $= |x| - 4 = f(x) - 4$	$(x, g(x))$
-2	$|-2| = 2$	$(-2, 2)$	$|-2| - 4 = -2$	$(-2, -2)$
-1	$|-1| = 1$	$(-1, 1)$	$|-1| - 4 = -3$	$(-1, -3)$
0	$|0| = 0$	$(0, 0)$	$|0| - 4 = -4$	$(0, -3)$
1	$|1| = 1$	$(1, 1)$	$|1| - 4 = -3$	$(1, -3)$
2	$|2| = 2$	$(2, 2)$	$|2| - 4 = -2$	$(2, -2)$

Figure 2.41

Check Point 1   Use the graph of $f(x) = |x|$ to obtain the graph of $g(x) = |x| + 3$.

3 Use horizontal shifts to graph functions.

Horizontal Shifts

We return to the graph of $f(x) = x^2$, the standard quadratic function. In Figure 2.42 on the next page, the graph of function f is in the middle of the three graphs. Turn the page and verify this observation.

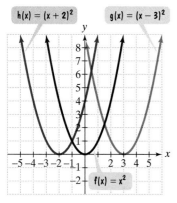

Figure 2.42 Horizontal shifts

By contrast to the vertical shift situation, this time there are graphs to the left and to the right of the graph of f. Look at the blue graph on the right. The equation of this graph, $g(x) = (x - 3)^2$, subtracts 3 from each value of x in the domain of $f(x) = x^2$. What effect does this have on the graph of f? It shifts the graph horizontally to the right by 3 units.

$$g(x) = (x - 3)^2 = f(x - 3)$$

The graph of g   shifts the graph of f 3 units to the right.

Now, look at the red graph on the left in Figure 2.42. The equation of this graph, $h(x) = (x + 2)^2$, adds 2 to each value of x in the domain of $f(x) = x^2$. What effect does this have on the graph of f? It shifts the graph horizontally to the left by 2 units.

$$h(x) = (x + 2)^2 = f(x + 2)$$

The graph of h   shifts the graph of f 2 units to the left.

In general, if c is positive, $y = f(x + c)$ shifts the graph of f to the left c units and $y = f(x - c)$ shifts the graph of f to the right c units. These are called **horizontal shifts** of the graph of f.

Study Tip

We know that positive numbers are to the right of zero on a number line and negative numbers are to the left of zero. This positive-negative orientation does not apply to horizontal shifts. A *positive* number causes a shift to the *left* and a *negative* number causes a shift to the *right*.

Horizontal Shifts

Let f be a function and c a positive real number.
- The graph of $y = f(x + c)$ is the graph of $y = f(x)$ shifted to the left c units.
- The graph of $y = f(x - c)$ is the graph of $y = f(x)$ shifted to the right c units.

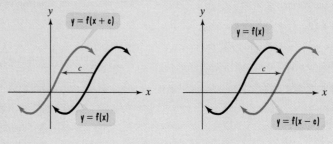

EXAMPLE 2   Horizontal Shift to the Left

Use the graph of $f(x) = \sqrt{x}$ to obtain the graph of $g(x) = \sqrt{x + 5}$.

Solution Compare the equations for $f(x) = \sqrt{x}$ and $g(x) = \sqrt{x + 5}$. The equation for g adds 5 to each value of x in the domain of f.

$$y = g(x) = \sqrt{x + 5} = f(x + 5)$$

The graph of g   shifts the graph of f 5 units to the left.

The graph of $g(x) = \sqrt{x + 5}$ has the same shape as the graph of $f(x) = \sqrt{x}$. However, it is shifted horizontally to the left 5 units. We have created tables on the next page showing some of the coordinates for f and g. As shown in Figure 2.43, every point in the graph of g is exactly 5 units to the left of a corresponding point on the graph of f.

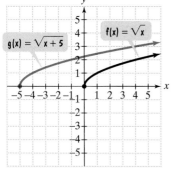

Figure 2.43 Shifting $f(x) = \sqrt{x}$ five units left

x	$y = f(x) = \sqrt{x}$	$(x, f(x))$
0	$\sqrt{0} = 0$	$(0, 0)$
1	$\sqrt{1} = 1$	$(1, 1)$
4	$\sqrt{4} = 2$	$(4, 2)$

x	$y = g(x) = \sqrt{x + 5}$	$(x, g(x))$
-5	$\sqrt{-5 + 5} = \sqrt{0} = 0$	$(-5, 0)$
-4	$\sqrt{-4 + 5} = \sqrt{1} = 1$	$(-4, 1)$
-1	$\sqrt{-1 + 5} = \sqrt{4} = 2$	$(-1, 2)$

Check Point 2   Use the graph of $f(x) = \sqrt{x}$ to obtain the graph of $g(x) = \sqrt{x - 4}$.

Some functions can be graphed by combining horizontal and vertical shifts. These functions will be variations of a function whose equation you know how to graph, such as the standard quadratic function, the standard cubic function, the square root function, or the absolute value function.

In our next example, we will use the graph of the standard quadratic function, $f(x) = x^2$, to obtain the graph of $h(x) = (x + 1)^2 - 3$. We will graph three functions:

$$f(x) = x^2 \qquad g(x) = (x + 1)^2 \qquad h(x) = (x + 1)^2 - 3.$$

Start by graphing the standard quadratic function.

Shift the graph of f horizontally one unit to the left.

Shift the graph of g vertically down 3 units.

Discovery

Work Example 3 by first shifting the graph of $f(x) = x^2$ three units down, graphing $g(x) = x^2 - 3$. Now, shift this graph one unit left to graph $h(x) = (x + 1)^2 - 3$. Did you obtain the graph in Figure 2.44(c)? What can you conclude?

EXAMPLE 3   Combining Horizontal and Vertical Shifts

Use the graph of $f(x) = x^2$ to obtain the graph of $h(x) = (x + 1)^2 - 3$.

Solution

Step 1   Graph $f(x) = x^2$.   The graph of the standard quadratic function is shown in Figure 2.44(a). We've identified three points on the graph.

Step 2   Graph $g(x) = (x + 1)^2$.   Because we add 1 to each value of x in the domain of the standard quadratic function, $f(x) = x^2$, we shift the graph of f horizontally one unit to the left. This is shown in Figure 2.44(b). Notice that every point in the graph in Figure 2.44(b) has an x-coordinate that is one less than the x-coordinate for the corresponding point in the graph in Figure 2.44(a).

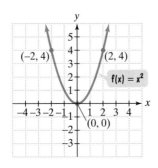

(a) The graph of $f(x) = x^2$

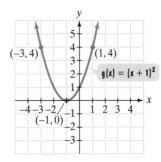

(b) The graph of $g(x) = (x + 1)^2$

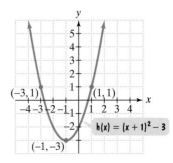

(c) The graph of $h(x) = (x + 1)^2 - 3$

Figure 2.44

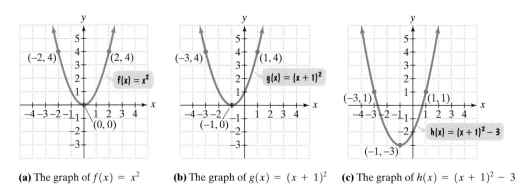

(a) The graph of $f(x) = x^2$ **(b)** The graph of $g(x) = (x + 1)^2$ **(c)** The graph of $h(x) = (x + 1)^2 - 3$

Figure 2.44, repeated

Step 3   Graph $h(x) = (x + 1)^2 - 3$.   Because we subtract 3, we shift the graph in Figure 2.44(b) vertically down 3 units. The graph is shown in Figure 2.44(c). Notice that every point in the graph in Figure 2.44(c) has a y-coordinate that is three less than the y-coordinate of the corresponding point in the graph in Figure 2.44(b).

Check Point 3   Use the graph of $f(x) = \sqrt{x}$ to obtain the graph of $h(x) = \sqrt{x - 1} - 2$.

4 Use reflections to graph functions.

Reflections of Graphs

This photograph shows a reflection of an old bridge in a Maryland river. This perfect reflection occurs because the surface of the water is absolutely still. A mild breeze rippling the water's surface would distort the reflection.

Is it possible for graphs to have mirror-like qualities? Yes. Figure 2.45 shows the graphs of $f(x) = x^2$ and $g(x) = -x^2$. The graph of g is a **reflection about the x-axis** of the graph of f. In general, the graph of $y = -f(x)$ reflects the graph of f about the x-axis. Thus, the graph of g is a reflection of the graph of f about the x-axis because

$$g(x) = -x^2 = -f(x).$$

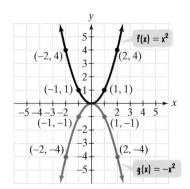

Figure 2.45 Reflections about the x-axis

Reflection about the x-Axis
The graph of $y = -f(x)$ is the graph of $y = f(x)$ reflected about the x-axis.

EXAMPLE 4 Reflection about the x-Axis

Use the graph of $f(x) = \sqrt{x}$ to obtain the graph of $g(x) = -\sqrt{x}$.

Solution Compare the equations for $f(x) = \sqrt{x}$ and $g(x) = -\sqrt{x}$. The graph of g is a reflection about the x-axis of the graph of f because

$$g(x) = -\sqrt{x} = -f(x).$$

We have created a table showing some of the coordinates for f and g. The graphs of f and g are shown in Figure 2.46.

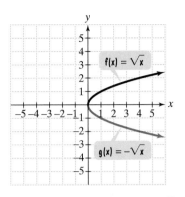

Figure 2.46 Reflecting $f(x) = \sqrt{x}$ about the x-axis

x	$f(x) = \sqrt{x}$	$(x, f(x))$	$g(x) = -\sqrt{x}$	$(x, g(x))$
0	$\sqrt{0} = 0$	$(0, 0)$	$-\sqrt{0} = 0$	$(0, 0)$
1	$\sqrt{1} = 1$	$(1, 1)$	$-\sqrt{1} = -1$	$(1, -1)$
4	$\sqrt{4} = 2$	$(4, 2)$	$-\sqrt{4} = -2$	$(4, -2)$

> **Check Point 4** Use the graph of $f(x) = |x|$ to obtain the graph of $g(x) = -|x|$.

It is also possible to reflect graphs about the y-axis.

Reflection about the y-Axis

The graph of $y = f(-x)$ is the graph of $y = f(x)$ reflected about the y-axis.

EXAMPLE 5 Reflection about the y-Axis

Use the graph of $f(x) = \sqrt{x}$ to obtain the graph of $h(x) = \sqrt{-x}$.

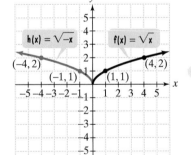

Figure 2.47 Reflecting $f(x) = \sqrt{x}$ about the y-axis

Solution Compare the equations for $f(x) = \sqrt{x}$ and $h(x) = \sqrt{-x}$. The graph of h is a reflection about the y-axis of the graph of f because

$$h(x) = \sqrt{-x} = f(-x).$$

We have created tables showing some of the coordinates for f and h. The graphs of f and h are shown in Figure 2.47.

x	$f(x) = \sqrt{x}$	$(x, f(x))$
0	$\sqrt{0} = 0$	$(0, 0)$
1	$\sqrt{1} = 1$	$(1, 1)$
4	$\sqrt{4} = 2$	$(4, 2)$

x	$h(x) = \sqrt{-x}$	$(x, h(x))$
0	$\sqrt{-0} = \sqrt{0} = 0$	$(0, 0)$
-1	$\sqrt{-(-1)} = \sqrt{1} = 1$	$(-1, 1)$
-4	$\sqrt{-(-4)} = \sqrt{4} = 2$	$(-4, 2)$

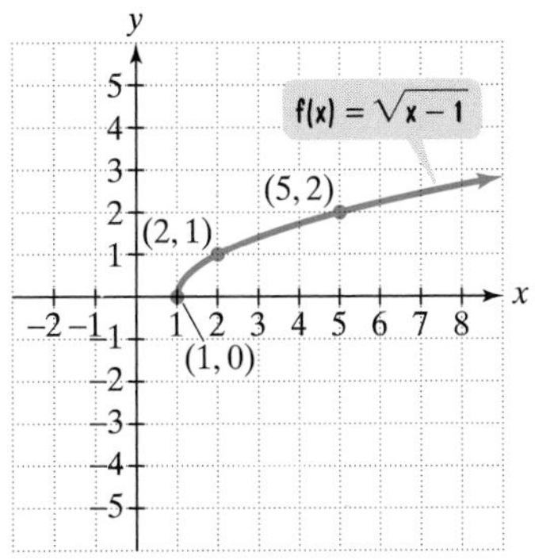

Figure 2.48

> **Check Point 5** Use the graph of $f(x) = \sqrt{x} - 1$ in Figure 2.48 to obtain the graph of $h(x) = \sqrt{-x} - 1$.

5 Use vertical stretching and shrinking to graph functions.

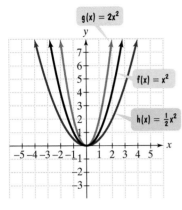

$$g(x) = 2x^2$$

$$f(x) = x^2$$

$$h(x) = \tfrac{1}{2}x^2$$

Figure 2.49 Stretching and shrinking $f(x) = x^2$

Vertical Stretching and Shrinking

Morphing does much more than move an image horizontally, vertically, or about an axis. An object having one shape is transformed into a different shape. Horizontal shifts, vertical shifts, and reflections do not change the basic shape of a graph. How can we shrink and stretch graphs, thereby altering their basic shapes?

Look at the three graphs in Figure 2.49. The black graph in the middle is the graph of the standard quadratic function, $f(x) = x^2$. Now, look at the blue graph on the top. The equation of this graph is $g(x) = 2x^2$. Thus, for each x, the y-coordinate of g is 2 times as large as the corresponding y-coordinate on the graph of f. The result is a narrower graph. We say that the graph of g is obtained by vertically *stretching* the graph of f. Now, look at the red graph on the bottom. The equation of this graph is $h(x) = \tfrac{1}{2}x^2$, or $h(x) = \tfrac{1}{2}f(x)$. Thus, for each x, the y-coordinate of h is one-half as large as the corresponding y-coordinate on the graph of f. The result is a wider graph. We say that the graph of h is obtained by vertically *shrinking* the graph of f.

These observations can be summarized as follows:

Stretching and Shrinking Graphs

Let f be a function and c a positive real number.
- If $c > 1$, the graph of $y = cf(x)$ is the graph of $y = f(x)$ vertically stretched by multiplying each of its y-coordinates by c.
- If $0 < c < 1$, the graph of $y = cf(x)$ is the graph of $y = f(x)$ vertically shrunk by multiplying each of its y-coordinates by c.

EXAMPLE 6 Vertically Stretching a Graph

Use the graph of $f(x) = |x|$ to obtain the graph of $g(x) = 2|x|$.

Solution The graph of $g(x) = 2|x|$ is obtained by vertically stretching the graph of $f(x) = |x|$. We have constructed a table showing some of the coordinates for f and g. Observe that the y-coordinate on the graph of g is twice as large as the corresponding y-coordinate on the graph of f. The graphs of f and g are shown in Figure 2.50.

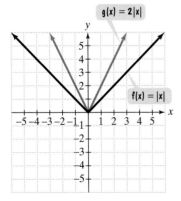

$$g(x) = 2|x|$$

$$f(x) = |x|$$

Figure 2.50 Stretching $f(x) = |x|$

x	$f(x) = \lvert x \rvert$	$(x, f(x))$	$g(x) = 2\lvert x \rvert = 2f(x)$	$(x, g(x))$
-2	$\lvert -2 \rvert = 2$	$(-2, 2)$	$2\lvert -2 \rvert = 4$	$(-2, 4)$
-1	$\lvert -1 \rvert = 1$	$(-1, 1)$	$2\lvert -1 \rvert = 2$	$(-1, 2)$
0	$\lvert 0 \rvert = 0$	$(0, 0)$	$2\lvert 0 \rvert = 0$	$(0, 0)$
1	$\lvert 1 \rvert = 1$	$(1, 1)$	$2\lvert 1 \rvert = 2$	$(1, 2)$
2	$\lvert 2 \rvert = 2$	$(2, 2)$	$2\lvert 2 \rvert = 4$	$(2, 4)$

Check Point 6 Use the graph of $f(x) = |x|$ to obtain the graph of $g(x) = 3|x|$.

EXAMPLE 7 Vertically Shrinking a Graph

Use the graph of $f(x) = |x|$ to obtain the graph of $h(x) = \frac{1}{2}|x|$.

Solution   The graph of $h(x) = \frac{1}{2}|x|$ is obtained by vertically shrinking the graph of $f(x) = |x|$. We have constructed a table showing some of the coordinates for f and h. Observe that the y-coordinate on the graph of h is one-half the corresponding y-coordinate on the graph of f. The graphs of f and h are shown in Figure 2.51.

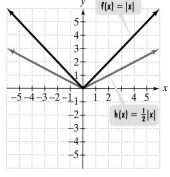

Figure 2.51 Shrinking $f(x) = |x|$

x	$f(x) = |x|$	$(x, f(x))$	$h(x) = \frac{1}{2}|x| = \frac{1}{2}f(x)$	$(x, h(x))$
-2	$|-2| = 2$	$(-2, 2)$	$\frac{1}{2}|-2| = 1$	$(-2, 1)$
-1	$|-1| = 1$	$(-1, 1)$	$\frac{1}{2}|-1| = \frac{1}{2}$	$(-1, \frac{1}{2})$
0	$|0| = 0$	$(0, 0)$	$\frac{1}{2}|0| = 0$	$(0, 0)$
1	$|1| = 1$	$(1, 1)$	$\frac{1}{2}|1| = \frac{1}{2}$	$(1, \frac{1}{2})$
2	$|2| = 2$	$(2, 2)$	$\frac{1}{2}|2| = 1$	$(2, 1)$

Check Point 7   Use the graph of $f(x) = |x|$ to obtain the graph of $h(x) = \frac{1}{4}|x|$.

6 Graph functions involving a sequence of transformations.

Sequences of Transformations

Table 2.5 summarizes the procedures for transforming the graph of $y = f(x)$.

Table 2.5   Summary of Transformations
In each case, c represents a positive real number.

To Graph:	Draw the Graph of f and:	Changes in the Equation of $y = f(x)$
Vertical shifts		
$y = f(x) + c$	Raise the graph of f by c units.	c is added to $f(x)$.
$y = f(x) - c$	Lower the graph of f by c units.	c is subtracted from $f(x)$.
Horizontal shifts		
$y = f(x + c)$	Shift the graph of f to the left c units.	x is replaced with $x + c$.
$y = f(x - c)$	Shift the graph of f to the right c units.	x is replaced with $x - c$.
Reflection about the x-axis $y = -f(x)$	Reflect the graph of f about the x-axis.	$f(x)$ is multiplied by -1.
Reflection about the y-axis $y = f(-x)$	Reflect the graph of f about the y-axis.	x is replaced with $-x$.
Vertical stretching or shrinking		
$y = cf(x), c > 1$	Multiply each y-coordinate of $y = f(x)$ by c, vertically stretching the graph of f.	$f(x)$ is multiplied by $c, c > 1$.
$y = cf(x), 0 < c < 1$	Multiply each y-coordinate of $y = f(x)$ by c, vertically shrinking the graph of f.	$f(x)$ is multiplied by $c, 0 < c < 1$.

A function involving more than one transformation can be graphed by performing transformations in the following order:

1. Horizontal shifting
2. Vertical stretching or shrinking
3. Reflecting
4. Vertical shifting

EXAMPLE 8 Graphing Using a Sequence of Transformations

Use the graph of $f(x) = \sqrt{x}$ to graph $g(x) = \sqrt{1 - x} + 3$.

Solution The following sequence of steps is illustrated in Figure 2.52. We begin with the graph of $f(x) = \sqrt{x}$.

Step 1   Horizontal Shifting   Graph $y = \sqrt{x + 1}$.   Because x is replaced with $x + 1$, the graph of $f(x) = \sqrt{x}$ is shifted 1 unit to the left.

Step 2   Vertical Stretching or Shrinking   Because the equation $y = \sqrt{x + 1}$ is not multiplied by a constant in $g(x) = \sqrt{1 - x} + 3$, no stretching or shrinking is involved.

Step 3   Reflecting   We are interested in graphing $y = \sqrt{1 - x} + 3$, or $y = \sqrt{-x + 1} + 3$. We have now graphed $y = \sqrt{x + 1}$. We can graph $y = \sqrt{-x + 1}$ by noting that x is replaced with $-x$. Thus, we graph $y = \sqrt{-x + 1}$ by reflecting the graph of $y = \sqrt{x + 1}$ about the y-axis.

Step 4   Vertical Shifting   We can use the graph of $y = \sqrt{1 - x}$ to get the graph of $g(x) = \sqrt{1 - x} + 3$. Because 3 is added, shift the graph of $y = \sqrt{1 - x}$ up 3 units.

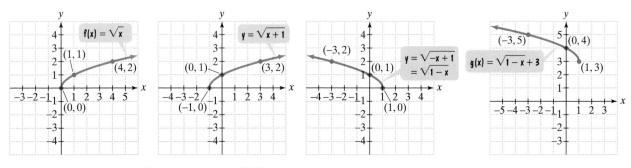

Figure 2.52 Using $f(x) = \sqrt{x}$ to graph $g(x) = \sqrt{1 - x} + 3$

Check Point 8   Use the graph of $f(x) = x^2$ to graph $g(x) = -(x - 2)^2 + 3$.

EXERCISE SET 2.5

Practice Exercises

In Exercises 1–10, begin by graphing the standard quadratic function, $f(x) = x^2$. Then use transformations of this graph to graph the given function.

1. $g(x) = x^2 - 2$
2. $g(x) = x^2 - 1$
3. $g(x) = (x - 2)^2$
4. $g(x) = (x - 1)^2$
5. $h(x) = -(x - 2)^2$
6. $h(x) = -(x - 1)^2$
7. $h(x) = (x - 2)^2 + 1$
8. $h(x) = (x - 1)^2 + 2$
9. $g(x) = 2(x - 2)^2$
10. $g(x) = \frac{1}{2}(x - 1)^2$

In Exercises 11–22, begin by graphing the square root function, $f(x) = \sqrt{x}$. Then use transformations of this graph to graph the given function.

11. $g(x) = \sqrt{x} + 2$

12. $g(x) = \sqrt{x} + 1$

13. $g(x) = \sqrt{x + 2}$

14. $g(x) = \sqrt{x + 1}$

15. $h(x) = -\sqrt{x + 2}$

16. $h(x) = -\sqrt{x + 1}$

17. $h(x) = \sqrt{-x + 2}$

18. $h(x) = \sqrt{-x + 1}$

19. $g(x) = \frac{1}{2}\sqrt{x + 2}$

20. $g(x) = 2\sqrt{x + 1}$

21. $h(x) = \sqrt{x + 2} - 2$

22. $h(x) = \sqrt{x + 1} - 1$

In Exercises 23–34, begin by graphing the absolute value function, $f(x) = |x|$. Then use transformations of this graph to graph the given function.

23. $g(x) = |x| + 4$

24. $g(x) = |x| + 3$

25. $g(x) = |x + 4|$

26. $g(x) = |x + 3|$

27. $h(x) = |x + 4| - 2$

28. $h(x) = |x + 3| - 2$

29. $h(x) = -|x + 4|$

30. $h(x) = -|x + 3|$

31. $g(x) = -|x + 4| + 1$

32. $g(x) = -|x + 4| + 2$

33. $h(x) = 2|x + 4|$

34. $h(x) = 2|x + 3|$

In Exercises 35–44, begin by graphing the standard cubic function, $f(x) = x^3$. Then use transformations of this graph to graph the given function.

35. $g(x) = x^3 - 3$

36. $g(x) = x^3 - 2$

37. $g(x) = (x - 3)^3$

38. $g(x) = (x - 2)^3$

39. $h(x) = -x^3$

40. $h(x) = -(x - 2)^3$

41. $h(x) = \frac{1}{2}x^3$

42. $h(x) = \frac{1}{4}x^3$

43. $r(x) = (x - 3)^3 + 2$

44. $r(x) = (x - 2)^3 + 1$

In Exercises 45–52, use the graph of the function f to sketch the graph of the given function g.

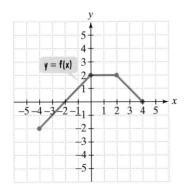

45. $g(x) = f(x) + 1$

46. $g(x) = f(x) + 2$

47. $g(x) = f(x + 1)$

48. $g(x) = f(x + 2)$

49. $g(x) = -f(x)$

50. $g(x) = \frac{1}{2}f(x)$

51. $g(x) = \frac{1}{2}f(x + 1)$

52. $g(x) = -f(x + 2)$

In Exercises 53–56, write a possible equation for the function whose graph is shown. Each graph shows a transformation of a common function.

53.

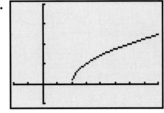

[–2, 8, 1] by [–1, 4, 1]

54.

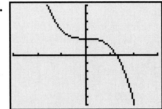

[–3, 3, 1] by [–6, 6, 1]

55.

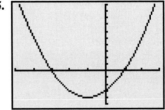

[–5, 3, 1] by [–5, 10, 1]

56.

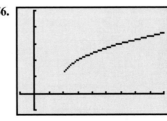

[–1, 9, 1] by [–1, 5, 1]

Application Exercises

57. The function $f(x) = 2.9\sqrt{x} + 20.1$ models the median height, $f(x)$, in inches, of boys who are x months of age. The graph of f is shown.

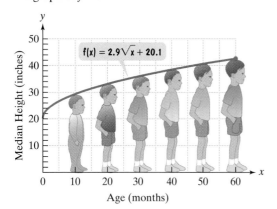

$f(x) = 2.9\sqrt{x} + 20.1$

a. Describe how the graph can be obtained using transformations of the square root function $f(x) = \sqrt{x}$.

b. According to the model, what is the median height of boys who are 48 months, or four years, old? Use a calculator and round to the nearest tenth of an inch. The actual median height for boys at 48 months is 40.8 inches. How well does the model describe the actual height?

c. Use the model to find the average rate of change, in inches per month, between birth and 10 months. Round to the nearest tenth.

d. Use the model to find the average rate of change, in inches per month, between 50 and 60 months. Round to the nearest tenth. How does this compare with your answer in part (c)? How is this difference shown by the graph?

58. The graph shows the amount of money, in billions of dollars, of new student loans from 1993 through 2000.

Amount of New Student Loans

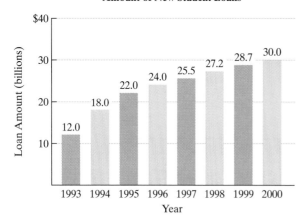

Source: U.S. Department of Education

The data shown can be modeled by the function $f(x) = 6.75\sqrt{x} + 12$, where $f(x)$ is the amount, in billion of dollars, of new student loans x years after 1993.

a. Describe how the graph of f can be obtained using transformations of the square root function $f(x) = \sqrt{x}$. Then sketch the graph of f over the interval $0 \le x \le 9$. If applicable, use a graphing utility to verify your hand-drawn graph.

b. According to the model, how much was loaned in 2000? Round to the nearest tenth of a billion. How well does the model describe the actual data?

c. Use the model to find the average rate of change, in billions of dollars per year, between 1993 and 1995 Round to the nearest tenth.

d. Use the model to find the average rate of change, in billions of dollars per year, between 1998 and 2000. Round to the nearest tenth. How does this compare with you answer in part (c)? How is this difference shown by your graph?

e. Rewrite the function so that it represents the amount, $f(x)$, in billions of dollars, of new student loans x years after 1995.

Writing in Mathematics

59. What must be done to a function's equation so that its graph is shifted vertically upward?

60. What must be done to a function's equation so that its graph is shifted horizontally to the right?

61. What must be done to a function's equation so that its graph is reflected about the x-axis?

62. What must be done to a function's equation so that its graph is reflected about the y-axis?

63. What must be done to a function's equation so that its graph is stretched?

Technology Exercises

64. a. Use a graphing utility to graph $f(x) = x^2 + 1$.

b. Graph $f(x) = x^2 + 1$, $g(x) = f(2x)$, $h(x) = f(3x)$, and $k(x) = f(4x)$ in the same viewing rectangle.

c. Describe the relationship among the graphs of f, g, h, and k, with emphasis on different values of x for points on all four graphs that give the same y-coordinate.

d. Generalize by describing the relationship between the graph of f and the graph of g, where $g(x) = f(cx)$ for $c > 1$.

e. Try out your generalization by sketching the graphs of $f(cx)$ for $c = 1$, $c = 2$, $c = 3$, and $c = 4$ for a function of your choice.

65. a. Use a graphing utility to graph $f(x) = x^2 + 1$.

b. Graph $f(x) = x^2 + 1$, and $g(x) = f(\frac{1}{2}x)$, and $h(x) = f(\frac{1}{4}x)$ in the same viewing rectangle.

c. Describe the relationship among the graphs of f, g, and h, with emphasis on different values of x for points on all three graphs that give the same y-coordinate.

d. Generalize by describing the relationship between the graph of f and the graph of g, where $g(x) = f(cx)$ for $0 < c < 1$.

e. Try out your generalization by sketching the graphs of $f(cx)$ for $c = 1$, and $c = \frac{1}{2}$, and $c = \frac{1}{4}$ for a function of your choice.

Critical Thinking Exercises

66. Which one of the following is true?

   a. If $f(x) = |x|$ and $g(x) = |x + 3| + 3$, then the graph of g is a translation of three units to the right and three units upward of the graph of f.

   b. If $f(x) = -\sqrt{x}$ and $g(x) = \sqrt{-x}$, then f and g have identical graphs.

   c. If $f(x) = x^2$ and $g(x) = 5(x^2 - 2)$, then the graph of g can be obtained from the graph of f by stretching f five units followed by a downward shift of two units.

   d. If $f(x) = x^3$ and $g(x) = -(x - 3)^3 - 4$, then the graph of g can be obtained from the graph of f by moving f three units to the right, reflecting in the x-axis, and then moving the resulting graph down four units.

In Exercises 67–70, functions f and g are graphed in the same rectangular coordinate system. If g is obtained from f through a sequence of transformations, find an equation for g.

67.

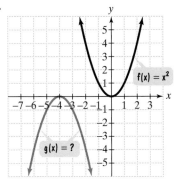

68.

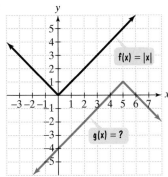

69.

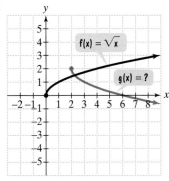

70.

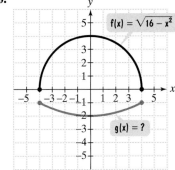

For Exercises 71–74, assume that (a, b) is a point on the graph of f. What is the corresponding point on the graph of each of the following functions?

71. $y = f(-x)$ **72.** $y = 2f(x)$

73. $y = f(x - 3)$ **74.** $y = f(x) - 3$

Group Exercise

75. This activity is a group research project on morphing and should result in a presentation made by group members to the entire class. Be sure to include morphing images that will intrigue class members. You should have no problem finding an array of fascinating images online. Also include a discussion of films using spectacular morphing effects. Rent videos of these films and show appropriate excerpts.

SECTION 2.6   *Combinations of Functions; Composite Functions*

Objectives

1. Combine functions arithmetically, specifying domains.
2. Form composite functions.
3. Determine domains for composite functions.
4. Write functions as compositions.

They say a fool and his money are soon parted and the rest of us just wait to be taxed. It's hard to believe that the United States was a low-tax country in the early part of the twentieth century. Figure 2.53 shows how the tax burden has grown since then. We can use the information shown to illustrate how two functions can be combined to form a new function. In this section, you will learn how to combine functions to obtain new functions.

U.S. Per Capita Tax Burden in 2000 Dollars

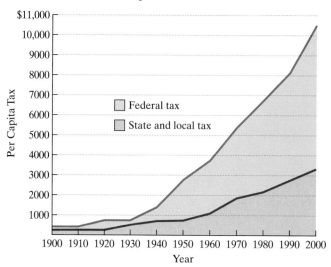

Figure 2.53   *Source:* Tax Foundation

1 Combine functions arithmetically, specifying domains.

Combinations of Functions

To begin our discussion, take a look at the information shown for the year 2000. The total per capita tax burden is approximately $10,500. The per capita state and local tax is approximately $3400. The per capita federal tax is the difference between these amounts.

$$\text{Per capita federal tax} = \$10,500 - \$3400 = \$7100$$

We can think of this subtraction as the subtraction of function values. We do this by introducing the following functions:

Let $T(x)$ = total per capita tax in year x.

Let $S(x)$ = per capita state and local tax in year x.

Using Figure 2.53, we see that

$$T(2000) = \$10,500 \quad \text{and} \quad S(2000) = \$3400.$$

We can subtract these function values by introducing a new function, $T - S$, defined by the subtraction of $T(x)$ and $S(x)$. Thus,

$$(T - S)(x) = T(x) - S(x) = \begin{array}{l}\text{total per capita tax in year x} \\ \text{minus state and local per} \\ \text{capita tax in year x.}\end{array}$$

For example,

$$(T - S)(2000) = T(2000) - S(2000) = \$10,500 - \$3400 = \$7100.$$

In 2000, the difference between total tax and state and local tax was $7100. This is the per capita federal tax.

Figure 2.53 illustrates that information involving differences of functions often appears in graphs seen in newspapers and magazines. Like numbers and algebraic expressions, two functions can be added, subtracted multiplied, or divided as long as there are numbers common to the domains of both functions. The common domain for functions T and S in Figure 2.53 is

$$\{1900, 1901, 1902, 1903, \dots, 2000\}.$$

Because functions are usually given as equations, we perform operations by carrying out these operations with the algebraic expressions that appear on the right side of the equations. For example, we can combine the following two functions using addition:

$$f(x) = 2x + 1 \quad \text{and} \quad g(x) = x^2 - 4.$$

To do so, we add the terms to the right of the equal sign for $f(x)$ to the terms to the right of the equal sign for $g(x)$. Here is how it's done:

$$\begin{aligned}(f + g)(x) &= f(x) + g(x) \\ &= (2x + 1) + (x^2 - 4) \quad \text{Add terms for f(x) and g(x).} \\ &= 2x - 3 + x^2 \quad \text{Combine like terms.} \\ &= x^2 + 2x - 3 \quad \text{Arrange terms in descending powers of x.}\end{aligned}$$

The name of this new function is $f + g$. Thus, the sum $f + g$ is the function defined by $(f + g)(x) = x^2 + 2x - 3$. The domain of $f + g$ consists of the numbers x that are in the domain of f and in the domain of g. Because neither f nor g contains division or even roots, the domain of each function is the set of all real numbers. Thus, the domain of $f + g$ is also the set of all real numbers.

EXAMPLE 1   Finding the Sum of Two Functions

Let $f(x) = x^2 - 3$ and $g(x) = 4x + 5$. Find:

a. $(f + g)(x)$ **b.** $(f + g)(3)$.

Solution

a. $(f + g)(x) = f(x) + g(x) = (x^2 - 3) + (4x + 5) = x^2 + 4x + 2$. Thus, $(f + g)(x) = x^2 + 4x + 2$.

b. We find $(f + g)(3)$ by substituting 3 for x in the equation for $f + g$.

$(f + g)(x) = x^2 + 4x + 2$ This is the equation for $f + g$.

Substitute 3 for x.

$(f + g)(3) = 3^2 + 4 \cdot 3 + 2 = 9 + 12 + 2 = 23$

Check Point 1   Let $f(x) = 3x^2 + 4x - 1$ and $g(x) = 2x + 7$. Find:

a. $(f + g)(x)$ **b.** $(f + g)(4)$.

Here is a general definition for function addition:

The Sum of Functions

Let f and g be two functions. The **sum $f + g$** is the function defined by

$$(f + g)(x) = f(x) + g(x).$$

The domain of $f + g$ is the set of all real numbers that are common to the domain of f and the domain of g.

EXAMPLE 2   Adding Functions and Determining the Domain

Let $f(x) = \sqrt{x + 3}$ and $g(x) = \sqrt{x - 2}$. Find:

a. $(f + g)(x)$ **b.** the domain of $f + g$.

Solution

a. $(f + g)(x) = f(x) + g(x) = \sqrt{x + 3} + \sqrt{x - 2}$

b. The domain of $f + g$ is the set of all real numbers that are common to the domain of f and the domain of g. Thus, we must find the domains of f and g. We will do so for f first.

Note that $f(x) = \sqrt{x + 3}$ is a function involving the square root of $x + 3$. Because the square root of a negative quantity is not a real number, the value of $x + 3$ must be nonnegative. Thus, the domain of f is all x such that $x + 3 \geq 0$. Equivalently, the domain is $\{x | x \geq -3\}$, or $[-3, \infty)$.

Likewise, $g(x) = \sqrt{x - 2}$ is also a square root function. Because the square root of a negative quantity is not a real number, the value of $x - 2$ must be nonnegative. Thus, the domain of g is all x such that $x - 2 \geq 0$. Equivalently, the domain is $\{x | x \geq 2\}$, or $[2, \infty)$.

Now, we can use a number line to determine the domain of $f + g$. Figure 2.54 shows the domain of f in blue and the domain of g in red. Can you see that all real numbers greater than or equal to 2 are common to both domains? This is shown in purple on the number line. Thus, the domain of $f + g$ is $[2, \infty)$.

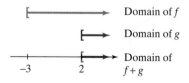

Domain of f

Domain of g

Domain of $f + g$

−3   2

Figure 2.54 Finding the domain of the sum $f + g$

Technology

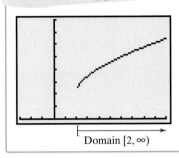

The graph on the left is the graph of
$$y = \sqrt{x + 3} + \sqrt{x - 2}$$
in a $[-3, 10, 1]$ by $[0, 8, 1]$ viewing rectangle. The graph reveals what we discovered algebraically in Example 2(b). The domain of this function is $[2, \infty)$.

Domain $[2, \infty)$

Check Point 2

Let $f(x) = \sqrt{x - 3}$ and $g(x) = \sqrt{x + 1}$. Find:
a. $(f + g)(x)$ **b.** the domain of $f + g$.

We can also combine functions using subtraction, multiplication, and division by performing operations with the algebraic expressions that appear on the right side of the equations. For example, the functions $f(x) = x + 3$ and $g(x) = x - 1$ can be combined to form the difference, product, and quotient of f and g. Here's how it's done.

Difference: f − g
$$(f - g)(x) = f(x) - g(x)$$
$$= (x + 3) - (x - 1) = x + 3 - x + 1 = 4$$

Product: fg
$$(fg)(x) = f(x) \cdot g(x)$$
$$= (x + 3)(x - 1) = x^2 + 2x - 3$$

Quotient: $\frac{f}{g}$
$$\left(\frac{f}{g}\right)(x) = \frac{f(x)}{g(x)} = \frac{x + 3}{x - 1}, \quad x \neq 1$$

Just like the domain for $f + g$, the domain for each of these functions consists of all real numbers that are common to the domains of f and g. In the case of the quotient function $\frac{f(x)}{g(x)}$, we must remember not to divide by 0, so we add the further restriction that $g(x) \neq 0$.

The following definitions summarize our discussion:

Definitions: Sum, Difference, Product, and Quotient of Functions

Let f and g be two functions. The **sum** $f + g$, the **difference** $f - g$, the **product** fg, and the **quotient** $\frac{f}{g}$ are
functions whose domains are the set of all real numbers common to the domains of f and g, defined as follows:

1. Sum: $(f + g)(x) = f(x) + g(x)$
2. Difference: $(f - g)(x) = f(x) - g(x)$
3. Product: $(fg)(x) = f(x) \cdot g(x)$
4. Quotient: $\left(\dfrac{f}{g}\right)(x) = \dfrac{f(x)}{g(x)}$, provided $g(x) \neq 0$

EXAMPLE 3 Combining Functions

If $f(x) = 2x - 1$ and $g(x) = x^2 + x - 2$, find:

a. $(f - g)(x)$ **b.** $(fg)(x)$ **c.** $\left(\dfrac{f}{g}\right)(x)$.

Determine the domain for each function.

Solution

a. $(f - g)(x) = f(x) - g(x)$ This is the definition of the difference $f - g$.

$= (2x - 1) - (x^2 + x - 2)$ Subtract $g(x)$ from $f(x)$.

$= 2x - 1 - x^2 - x + 2$ Perform the subtraction.

$= -x^2 + x + 1$ Combine like terms and arrange terms in descending powers of x.

b. $(fg)(x) = f(x) \cdot g(x)$ This is the definition of the product fg.

$= (2x - 1)(x^2 + x - 2)$ Multiply $f(x)$ and $g(x)$.

$= 2x(x^2 + x - 2) - 1(x^2 + x - 2)$ Multiply each term in the second factor by 2x and −1, respectively.

$= 2x^3 + 2x^2 - 4x - x^2 - x + 2$ Use the distributive property.

$= 2x^3 + (2x^2 - x^2) + (-4x - x) + 2$ Rearrange terms so that like terms are adjacent.

$= 2x^3 + x^2 - 5x + 2$ Combine like terms.

c. $\left(\dfrac{f}{g}\right)(x) = \dfrac{f(x)}{g(x)}$ This is the definition of the quotient $\dfrac{f}{g}$.

$= \dfrac{2x - 1}{x^2 + x - 2}$ Divide the algebraic expressions for $f(x)$ and $g(x)$.

Because the equations for f and g do not involve division or contain even roots, the domain of both f and g is the set of all real numbers. Thus, the domain of $f - g$ and fg is the set of all real numbers. However, for $\dfrac{f}{g}$, the denominator cannot equal zero. We can factor the denominator as follows:

$$\left(\frac{f}{g}\right)(x) = \frac{2x - 1}{x^2 + x - 2} = \frac{2x - 1}{(x + 2)(x - 1)}.$$

Because $x + 2 \neq 0$, $x \neq -2$.   Because $x - 1 \neq 0$, $x \neq 1$.

We see that the domain for $\dfrac{f}{g}$ is the set of all real numbers except -2 and 1: $\{x | x \neq -2, x \neq 1\}$.

Study Tip

If the function $\dfrac{f}{g}$ can be simplified, determine the domain *before* simplifying.

EXAMPLE:

$f(x) = x^2 - 4$ and

$g(x) = x - 2$

$\left(\dfrac{f}{g}\right)(x) = \dfrac{x^2 - 4}{x - 2}$

Domain of $\left(\dfrac{f}{g}\right)$ is $\{x | x \neq 2\}$.

$= \dfrac{\overset{1}{(x + 2)(\cancel{x - 2})}}{\underset{1}{\cancel{(x - 2)}}} = x + 2$

Check Point 3 If $f(x) = x - 5$ and $g(x) = x^2 - 1$, find:

a. $(f - g)(x)$ **b.** $(fg)(x)$ **c.** $\left(\dfrac{f}{g}\right)(x)$.

Determine the domain for each function.

② Form composite functions.

Composite Functions

There is another way of combining two functions. To help understand this new combination, suppose that your computer store is having a sale. The models that are on sale cost either $300 less than the regular price or 85% of the regular price. If x represents the computer's regular price, both discounts can be described with the following functions:

$$f(x) = x - 300 \qquad\qquad g(x) = 0.85x.$$

> The computer is on sale for $300 less than its regular price.

> The computer is on sale for 85% of its regular price.

At the store, you bargain with the salesperson. Eventually, she makes an offer you can't refuse: The sale price is 85% of the regular price followed by a $300 reduction:

$$0.85x - 300.$$

> 85% of the regular price

> followed by a $300 reduction

In terms of functions f and g, this offer can be obtained by taking the output of $g(x) = 0.85x$, namely $0.85x$, and using it as the input of f:

$$f(x) = x - 300$$

> Replace x with 0.85x, the output of g(x) = 0.85x.

$$f(0.85x) = 0.85x - 300.$$

Because $0.85x$ is $g(x)$, we can write this last equation as

$$f(g(x)) = 0.85x - 300.$$

We read this equation as "f of g of x is equal to $0.85x - 300$." We call $f(g(x))$ the *composition of the function f with g*, or a *composite function*. This composite function is written $f \circ g$. Thus,

$$(f \circ g)(x) = f(g(x)) = 0.85x - 300.$$

Like all functions, we can evaluate $f \circ g$ for a specified value of x in the function's domain. For example, here's how to find the value of this function at 1400:

$$(f \circ g)(x) = 0.85x - 300 \qquad \text{This composite function describes the offer you cannot refuse.}$$

> Replace x with 1400.

$$(f \circ g)(1400) = 0.85(1400) - 300 = 1190 - 300 = 890.$$

This means that a computer that regularly sells for $1400 is on sale for $890 subject to both discounts.

Before you run out to buy a new computer, let's generalize our discussion of the computer's double discount and define the composition of any two functions.

The Composition of Functions

The **composition of the function** f **with** g is denoted by $f \circ g$ and is defined by the equation

$$(f \circ g)(x) = f(g(x)).$$

The domain of the **composite function** $f \circ g$ is the set of all x such that
1. x is in the domain of g and
2. $g(x)$ is in the domain of f.

The composition of f with g, $f \circ g$, is pictured as a machine with inputs and outputs in Figure 2.55. The diagram indicates that the output of g, or $g(x)$, becomes the input for "machine" f. If $g(x)$ is not in the domain of f, it cannot be input into machine f, and so $g(x)$ must be discarded.

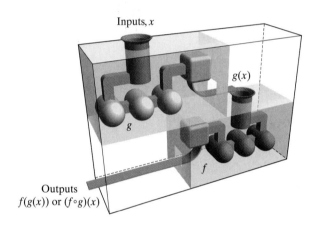

Figure 2.55 Inputting one function into a second function

EXAMPLE 4 Forming Composite Functions

Given $f(x) = 3x - 4$ and $g(x) = x^2 + 6$, find:
a. $(f \circ g)(x)$ **b.** $(g \circ f)(x)$.

Solution

a. We begin with $(f \circ g)(x)$, the composition of f with g. Because $(f \circ g)(x)$ means $f(g(x))$, we must replace each occurrence of x in the equation for f with $g(x)$.

$$f(x) = 3x - 4 \qquad \text{This is the given equation for f.}$$

Replace x with g(x).

$$(f \circ g)(x) = f(g(x)) = 3g(x) - 4$$
$$= 3(x^2 + 6) - 4 \quad \text{Because } g(x) = x^2 + 6, \text{ replace } g(x) \text{ with } x^2 + 6$$
$$= 3x^2 + 18 - 4 \quad \text{Use the distributive property.}$$
$$= 3x^2 + 14 \qquad \text{Simplify.}$$

Thus, $(f \circ g)(x) = 3x^2 + 14$.

b. Next, we find $(g \circ f)(x)$, the composition of g with f. Because $(g \circ f)(x)$ means $g(f(x))$, we must replace each occurrence of x in the equation for g with $f(x)$.

$$g(x) = x^2 + 6 \qquad \text{This is the given equation for g.}$$

Replace x with f(x).

$$(g \circ f)(x) = g(f(x)) = (f(x))^2 + 6$$
$$= (3x - 4)^2 + 6 \qquad \text{Because f(x) = 3x - 4, replace f(x) with 3x - 4.}$$
$$= 9x^2 - 24x + 16 + 6 \qquad \text{Use (A - B)}^2 = A^2 - 2AB + B^2 \text{ to square 3x - 4.}$$
$$= 9x^2 - 24x + 22 \qquad \text{Simplify.}$$

Thus, $(g \circ f)(x) = 9x^2 - 24x + 22$. Notice that $(f \circ g)(x)$ is not the same function as $(g \circ f)(x)$.

Check Point 4 Given $f(x) = 5x + 6$ and $g(x) = x^2 - 1$, find:

a. $(f \circ g)(x)$ **b.** $(g \circ f)(x)$.

3 Determine domains for composite functions.

We need to be careful in determining the domain for the composite function

$$(f \circ g)(x) = f(g(x)).$$

The following values must be excluded from the input x:

- If x is not in the domain of g, it must not be in the domain of $f \circ g$.
- Any x for which $g(x)$ is not in the domain of f must not be in the domain of $f \circ g$.

EXAMPLE 5 **Forming a Composite Function and Finding Its Domain**

Given $f(x) = \dfrac{2}{x - 1}$ and $g(x) = \dfrac{3}{x}$, find:

a. $(f \circ g)(x)$ **b.** the domain of $f \circ g$.

Solution

a. Because $(f \circ g)(x)$ means $f(g(x))$, we must replace x in $f(x) = \dfrac{2}{x - 1}$ with $g(x)$.

Study Tip

The procedure for simplifying complex fractions can be found in Section P.6, pages 66–67.

$$(f \circ g)(x) = f(g(x)) = \frac{2}{g(x) - 1} = \frac{2}{\frac{3}{x} - 1} = \frac{2}{\frac{3}{x} - 1} \cdot \frac{x}{x} = \frac{2x}{3 - x}$$

$g(x) = \dfrac{3}{x}$

Simplify the complex fraction by multiplying by $\dfrac{x}{x}$, or 1.

Thus, $(f \circ g)(x) = \dfrac{2x}{3 - x}$.

b. We determine the domain of $(f \circ g)(x)$ in two steps.

Rules for Excluding Numbers from the Domain of $(f \circ g)(x) = f(g(x))$	Applying the Rules to $f(x) = \dfrac{2}{x-1}$ and $g(x) = \dfrac{3}{x}$
If x is not in the domain of g, it must not be in the domain of $f \circ g$.	The domain of g is $\{x \mid x \neq 0\}$. Thus, 0 must be excluded from the domain of $f \circ g$.
Any x for which $g(x)$ is not in the domain of f must not be in the domain of $f \circ g$.	The domain of f is $\{x \mid x \neq 1\}$. This means we must exclude from the domain of $f \circ g$ any x for which $g(x) = 1$. $\dfrac{3}{x} = 1$ Set g(x) equal to 1. $3 = x$ Multiply both sides by x. 3 must be excluded from the domain of $f \circ g$.

The domain of $f \circ g$ is $\{x \mid x \neq 0 \text{ and } x \neq 3\}$.

Check Point 5 Given $f(x) = \dfrac{4}{x+2}$ and $g(x) = \dfrac{1}{x}$, find:

a. $(f \circ g)(x)$ **b.** the domain of $f \circ g$.

4 Write functions as compositions

Decomposing Functions

When you form a composite function, you "compose" two functions to form a new function. It is also possible to reverse this process. That is, you can "decompose" a given function and express it as a composition of two functions. Although there is more than one way to do this, there is often a "natural" selection that comes to mind first. For example, consider the function h defined by

$$h(x) = (3x^2 - 4x + 1)^5.$$

The function h takes $3x^2 - 4x + 1$ and raises it to the power 5. A natural way to write h as a composition of two functions is to raise the function $g(x) = 3x^2 - 4x + 1$ to the power 5. Thus, if we let

$$f(x) = x^5 \text{ and } g(x) = 3x^2 - 4x + 1, \text{ then}$$
$$(f \circ g)(x) = f(g(x)) = f(3x^2 - 4x + 1) = (3x^2 - 4x + 1)^5.$$

EXAMPLE 6   Writing a Function as a Composition

Express as a composition of two functions:

$$h(x) = \sqrt[3]{x^2 + 1}.$$

Solution The function h takes $x^2 + 1$ and takes its cube root. A natural way to write h as a composition of two functions is to take the cube root of the function $g(x) = x^2 + 1$. Thus, we let

$$f(x) = \sqrt[3]{x} \text{ and } g(x) = x^2 + 1.$$

Study Tip

Suppose the form of function h is $h(x) = (\text{algebraic expression})^{\text{power}}$.

Function h can be expressed as a composition, $f \circ g$, using

$f(x) = x^{\text{power}}$

$g(x) = \text{algebraic expression}$.

We can check this composition by finding $(f \circ g)(x)$. This should give the original function, namely $h(x) = \sqrt[3]{x^2 + 1}$.

$$(f \circ g)(x) = f(g(x)) = f(x^2 + 1) = \sqrt[3]{x^2 + 1} = h(x)$$

Check Point 6   Express as a composition of two functions:
$$h(x) = \sqrt{x^2 + 5}.$$

EXERCISE SET 2.6

 Practice Exercises

1. If $f(x) = 2x^2 - 5$ and $g(x) = 3x + 7$, find:
   a. $(f + g)(x)$ **b.** $(f + g)(4)$.

2. If $f(x) = 3x^2 - 2x + 1$ and $g(x) = 4x - 1$, find:
   a. $(f + g)(x)$ **b.** $(f + g)(5)$.

3. Let $f(x) = \sqrt{x-6}$ and $g(x) = \sqrt{x+2}$, find:
   a. $(f + g)(x)$ **b.** the domain of $f + g$.

4. Let $f(x) = \sqrt{x-8}$ and $g(x) = \sqrt{x+5}$, find:
   a. $(f + g)(x)$ **b.** the domain of $f + g$.

In Exercises 5–16, find $f + g$, $f - g$, fg, and $\frac{f}{g}$. Determine the domain for each function.

5. $f(x) = 2x + 3$, $g(x) = x - 1$

6. $f(x) = 3x - 4$, $g(x) = x + 2$

7. $f(x) = x - 5$, $g(x) = 3x^2$

8. $f(x) = x - 6$, $g(x) = 5x^2$

9. $f(x) = 2x^2 - x - 3$, $g(x) = x + 1$

10. $f(x) = 6x^2 - x - 1$, $g(x) = x - 1$

11. $f(x) = \sqrt{x}$, $g(x) = x - 4$

12. $f(x) = \dfrac{1}{x}$, $g(x) = x - 5$

13. $f(x) = 2 + \dfrac{1}{x}$, $g(x) = \dfrac{1}{x}$

14. $f(x) = 6 - \dfrac{1}{x}$, $g(x) = \dfrac{1}{x}$

15. $f(x) = \sqrt{x + 4}$, $g(x) = \sqrt{x - 1}$

16. $f(x) = \sqrt{x + 6}$, $g(x) = \sqrt{x - 3}$

In Exercises 17–28, find:
   a. $(f \circ g)(x)$
   b. $(g \circ f)(x)$
   c. $(f \circ g)(2)$.

17. $f(x) = 2x$, $g(x) = x + 7$

18. $f(x) = 3x$, $g(x) = x - 5$

19. $f(x) = x + 4$, $g(x) = 2x + 1$

20. $f(x) = 5x + 2$, $g(x) = 3x - 4$

21. $f(x) = 4x - 3$, $g(x) = 5x^2 - 2$

22. $f(x) = 7x + 1$, $g(x) = 2x^2 - 9$

23. $f(x) = x^2 + 2$, $g(x) = x^2 - 2$

24. $f(x) = x^2 + 1$, $g(x) = x^2 - 3$

25. $f(x) = \sqrt{x}$, $g(x) = x - 1$

26. $f(x) = \sqrt{x}$, $g(x) = x + 2$

27. $f(x) = 2x - 3$, $g(x) = \dfrac{x + 3}{2}$

28. $f(x) = 6x - 3$, $g(x) = \dfrac{x + 3}{6}$

In Exercises 29–38, find:
   a. $(f \circ g)(x)$ **b.** *the domain of $f \circ g$.*

29. $f(x) = \dfrac{2}{x + 3}$, $g(x) = \dfrac{1}{x}$

30. $f(x) = \dfrac{5}{x + 4}$, $g(x) = \dfrac{1}{x}$

31. $f(x) = \dfrac{x}{x + 1}$, $g(x) = \dfrac{4}{x}$

32. $f(x) = \dfrac{x}{x + 5}$, $g(x) = \dfrac{6}{x}$

33. $f(x) = \sqrt{x}$, $g(x) = x + 3$

34. $f(x) = \sqrt{x}$, $g(x) = x - 3$

35. $f(x) = x^2 + 4$, $g(x) = \sqrt{1 - x}$

36. $f(x) = x^2 + 1$, $g(x) = \sqrt{2 - x}$

37. $f(x) = 4 - x^2$, $g(x) = \sqrt{x^2 - 4}$

38. $f(x) = 9 - x^2$, $g(x) = \sqrt{x^2 - 9}$

In Exercises 39–46, express the given function h as a composition of two functions f and g so that $h(x) = (f \circ g)(x)$.

39. $h(x) = (3x - 1)^4$ **40.** $h(x) = (2x - 5)^3$

41. $h(x) = \sqrt[3]{x^2 - 9}$ **42.** $h(x) = \sqrt{5x^2 + 3}$

43. $h(x) = |2x - 5|$ **44.** $h(x) = |3x - 4|$

45. $h(x) = \dfrac{1}{2x - 3}$ **46.** $h(x) = \dfrac{1}{4x + 5}$

In Exercises 47–58, use the graphs of f and g to evaluate each function.

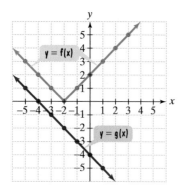

47. $(f + g)(-3)$

48. $(f + g)(-4)$

49. $(f - g)(2)$

50. $(g - f)(2)$

51. $\left(\dfrac{f}{g}\right)(-6)$

52. $\left(\dfrac{f}{g}\right)(-5)$

53. $(fg)(-4)$

54. $(fg)(-2)$

55. $(f \circ g)(2)$

56. $(f \circ g)(1)$

57. $(g \circ f)(0)$

58. $(g \circ f)(-1)$

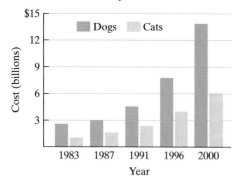

Application Exercises

It seems that Phideau's medical bills are costing us an arm and a paw. The graph shows veterinary costs, in billions of dollars, for dogs and cats in five selected years. Let

$D(x)$ = *veterinary costs, in billions of dollars, for dogs in year x*

$C(x)$ = *veterinary costs, in billions of dollars, for cats in year x.*

Use the graph to solve Exercises 59–62.

Veterinary Costs in the U.S.

Source: American Veterinary Medical Association

59. Find an estimate of $(D + C)(2000)$. What does this mean in terms of the variables in this situation?

60. Find an estimate of $(D - C)(2000)$. What does this mean in terms of the variables in this situation?

61. Using the information shown in the graph, what is the domain of $D + C$?

62. Using the information shown in the graph, what is the domain of $D - C$?

Consider the following functions:

$f(x)$ = *population of the world's more developed regions in year x*

$g(x)$ = *population of the world's less developed regions in year x*

$h(x)$ = *total world population in year x.*

Use these functions and the graph shown to answer Exercises 63–66.

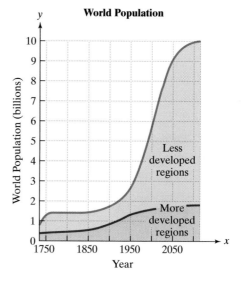

Source: Population Reference Bureau

63. What does the function $f + g$ represent?

64. What does the function $h - g$ represent?

65. Use the graph to estimate $(f + g)(2000)$.

66. Use the graph to estimate $(h - g)(2000)$.

67. A company that sells radios has a yearly fixed cost of $600,000. It costs the company $45 to produce each radio. Each radio will sell for $65. The company's costs and revenue are modeled by the following functions:

$C(x) = 600,000 + 45x$ This function models the company's costs.

$R(x) = 65x.$ This function models the company's revenue.

Find and interpret $(R - C)(20,000)$, $(R - C)(30,000)$ and $(R - C)(40,000)$.

68. A department store has two locations in a city. From 1998 through 2002, the profits for each of the store's two branches are modeled by the functions $f(x) = -0.44x + 13.62$ and $g(x) = 0.51x + 11.14$. In each model, x represents the number of years after 1998 and f and g represent the profit, in millions of dollars.

   a. What is the slope of f? Describe what this means.

   b. What is the slope of g? Describe what this means.

   c. Find $f + g$. What is the slope of this function? What does this mean?

69. The regular price of a computer is x dollars. Let $f(x) = x - 400$ and $g(x) = 0.75x$.

   a. Describe what the functions f and g model in terms of the price of the computer.

   b. Find $(f \circ g)(x)$ and describe what this models in terms of the price of the computer.

   c. Repeat part (b) for $(g \circ f)(x)$.

   d. Which composite function models the greater discount on the computer, $f \circ g$ or $g \circ f$? Explain.

70. The regular price of a pair of jeans is x dollars. Let $f(x) = x - 5$ and $g(x) = 0.6x$.

   a. Describe what functions f and g model in terms of the price of the jeans.

   b. Find $(f \circ g)(x)$ and describe what this models in terms of the price of the jeans.

   c. Repeat part (b) for $(g \circ f)(x)$.

   d. Which composite function models the greater discount on the jeans, $f \circ g$ or $g \circ f$? Explain.

Writing in Mathematics

71. If equations for functions f and g are given, explain how to find $f + g$.

72. If the equations of two functions are given, explain how to obtain the quotient function and its domain.

73. If equations for functions f and g are given, describe two ways to find $(f - g)(3)$.

74. Explain how to use the graphs in Figure 2.53 on page 238 to estimate the per capita federal tax for any one of the years shown on the horizontal axis.

75. Describe a procedure for finding $(f \circ g)(x)$. What is the name of this function?

76. Describe the values of x that must be excluded from the domain of $(f \circ g)(x)$.

Technology Exercises

77. The function $f(t) = -0.14t^2 + 0.51t + 31.6$ models the U.S. population ages 65 and older, $f(t)$, in millions, t years after 1990. The function $g(t) = 0.54t^2 + 12.64t + 107.1$ models the total yearly cost of Medicare, $g(t)$, in billions of dollars, t years after 1990. Graph the function $\frac{g}{f}$ in a $[0, 15, 1]$ by $[0, 60, 1]$ viewing rectangle. What does the shape of the graph indicate about the per capita costs of Medicare for the U.S. population ages 65 and over with increasing time?

78. Graph $y_1 = x^2 - 2x, y_2 = x$, and $y_3 = y_1 \div y_2$ in the same $[-10, 10, 1]$ by $[-10, 10, 1]$ viewing rectangle. Then use the $\boxed{\text{TRACE}}$ feature to trace along y_3. What happens at $x = 0$? Explain why this occurs.

79. Graph $y_1 = x^2 - 4$, $y_2 = \sqrt{4 - x^2}$, and $y_3 = y_2^2 - 4$ in the same $[-5, 5, 1]$ by $[-5, 5, 1]$ viewing rectangle. If y_1 represents f and y_2 represents g, use the graph of y_3 to find the domain of $f \circ g$. Then verify your observation algebraically.

Critical Thinking Exercises

80. Which one of the following is true?

   a. If $f(x) = x^2 - 4$ and $g(x) = \sqrt{x^2 - 4}$, then $(f \circ g)(x) = -x^2$ and $(f \circ g)(5) = -25$.

   b. There can never be two functions f and g, where $f \neq g$, for which $(f \circ g)(x) = (g \circ f)(x)$

   c. If $f(7) = 5$ and $g(4) = 7$ then $(f \circ g)(4) = 35$.

   d. If $f(x) = \sqrt{x}$ and $g(x) = 2x - 1$, then $(f \circ g)(5) = g(2)$.

81. Prove that if f and g are even functions, then fg is also an even function.

82. Define two functions f and g so that $f \circ g = g \circ f$.

83. Use the graphs given in Exercises 63–66 to create a graph that shows the population, in billions, of less developed regions from 1950 through 2050.

Group Exercise

84. Consult an almanac, newspaper, magazine, or the Internet to find data displayed in a graph in the style of Figure 2.53 on page 248. Using the two graphs that group members find most interesting, introduce two functions that are related to the graphs. Then write and solve a problem involving function subtraction for each selected graph. If you are not sure where to begin, reread page 238–239 or look at Exercises 63–66 in this exercise set.

CHAPTER SUMMARY, REVIEW, AND TEST

Summary

DEFINITIONS AND CONCEPTS	EXAMPLES

2.1 Lines and Slope

a. The slope, m, of the line through (x_1, y_1) and (x_2, y_2) is
$$m = \frac{y_2 - y_1}{x_2 - x_1}.$$

Ex. 1, p.167

b. Equations of lines include point-slope form, $y - y_1 = m(x - x_1)$, slope-intercept form, $y = mx + b$, and general form, $Ax + By + C = 0$. The equation of a horizontal line is $y = b$; a vertical line is $x = a$.

Ex. 2 & 3, p.169; Ex. 5 & 6, p.172

c. Parallel lines have equal slopes. Perpendicular lines have slopes that are negative reciprocals.

Ex. 8 & 9, p.174–175

2.2 Distance and Midpoint Formulas; Circles

a. The distance, d, between the points (x_1, y_1) and (x_2, y_2) is given by
$$d = \sqrt{(x_2 - x_1)^2 + (y_2 - y_1)^2}.$$

Ex. 1, p.184

b. The midpoint of the line segment whose endpoints are (x_1, y_1) and (x_2, y_2) is the point with coordinates $\left(\dfrac{x_1 + x_2}{2}, \dfrac{y_1 + y_2}{2}\right)$.

Ex. 2, p.185

c. The standard form of the equation of a circle with center (h, k) and radius r is $(x - h)^2 + (y - k)^2 = r^2$.

Ex. 3, p. 186
Ex. 4 & 5, p. 187

d. The general form of the equation of a circle is $x^2 + y^2 + Dx + Ey + F = 0$.

e. To convert from the general form to the standard form of a circle's equation, complete the square on x and y.

Ex. 6, p. 188

2.3 Basics of Functions

a. A relation is any set of ordered pairs. The set of first components is the domain and the set of second components is the range.

Ex. 1, p. 192

b. A function is a correspondence from a first set, called the domain, to a second set, called the range, such that each element in the domain corresponds to exactly one element in the range. If any element in a relation's domain corresponds to more than one element in the range, the relation is not a function.

Ex. 2, p. 193

c. Functions are usually given in terms of equations involving x and y, in which x is the independent variable and y is the dependent variable. If an equation is solved for y and more than one value of y can be obtained for a given x, then the equation does not define y as a function of x. If an equation defines a function the value of the function at x, $f(x)$, often replaces y.

Ex. 3, p. 195

d. The difference quotient is
$$\frac{f(x + h) - f(x)}{h}, h \neq 0.$$

Ex. 5, p. 197

e. If a function f does not model data or verbal conditions, its domain is the largest set of real numbers for which the value of $f(x)$ is a real number. Exclude from the function's domain real numbers that cause division by zero and real numbers that result in an even root of a negative number.

Fx. 7, p. 200

2.4 Graphs of Functions

a. The graph of a function is the graph of its ordered pairs.

Ex. 1, p. 205

b. The vertical line test for functions: If any vertical line intersects a graph in more than one point, the graph does not define y as a function of x.

Ex. 3, p. 207

c. A function is increasing on intervals where its graph rises, decreasing on intervals where it falls, and constant on intervals where it neither rises nor falls. Precise definitions are given in the box on page 210.

Ex. 5, p. 210

d. If the graph of a function is given, we can often visually locate the number(s) at which the function has a relative maximum or relative minimum. Precise definitions are given in the box on page 211.

Fig 2.32, p. 212

e. The average rate of change of f from x_1 to x_2 is

Ex. 6, p. 212

$$\frac{f(x_2) - f(x_1)}{x_2 - x_1}.$$

f. The graph of an even function in which $f(-x) = f(x)$ is symmetric with respect to the y-axis. The graph of an odd function in which $f(-x) = -f(x)$ is symmetric with respect to the origin.

Ex. 7, p. 214

g. The graph of $f(x) = \text{int}(x)$, where $\text{int}(x)$ is the greatest integer that is less than or equal to x, has function values that form discontinuous steps, shown in Figure 2.39 on page 217. If $n \le x < n + 1$, where n is an integer, then $\text{int}(x) = n$.

2.5 Transformations of Functions

a. Table 2.4 on pages 225–226 shows the graphs of the constant function, $f(x) = c$, the identity function, $f(x) = x$, the standard quadratic function, $f(x) = x^2$, the standard cubic function, $f(x) = x^3$, the square root function, $f(x) = \sqrt{x}$, and the absolute value function, $f(x) = |x|$. The table also lists characteristics of each function.

b. Table 2.5 on page 233 summarizes how to graph a function using vertical shifts, $y = f(x) \pm c$, horizontal shifts, $y = f(x \pm c)$, reflections about the x-axis, $y = -f(x)$, reflections about the y-axis, $y = f(-x)$, vertical stretching, $y = cf(x), c > 1$, and vertical shrinking, $y = cf(x), 0 < c < 1$.

Ex. 1 & 2, p. 227–228; Ex. 3, p. 229; Ex. 4–7, p. 231–233

c. A function involving more than one transformation can be graphed in the following order: (1) horizontal shifting; (2) vertical stretching or shrinking; (3) reflecting; (4) vertical shifting.

Ex. 8, p. 234

2.6 Combinations of Functions; Composite and Inverse Functions

a. When functions are given as equations, they can be added, subtracted, multiplied, or divided by performing operations with the algebraic expressions that appear on the right side of the equations.

Ex. 1, p. 240; Ex. 2, p. 240;

Definitions for the sum $f + g$, the difference $f - g$, the product fg, and the quotient $\dfrac{f}{g}$ functions are given in the box on page 241.

Ex. 3, p. 242

b. The composition of functions f and g, $f \circ g$, is defined by $(f \circ g)(x) = f(g(x))$. The domain of the composite function $f \circ g$ is given in the box on page 246. This composite function is obtained by replacing each occurrence of x in the equation for f with $g(x)$.

Ex. 4, p. 244; Ex. 5, p. 245

Review Exercises

2.1

In Exercises 1–4, find the slope of the line passing through each pair of points or state that the slope is undefined. Then indicate whether the line through the points rises, falls, is horizontal, or is vertical.

1. $(3, 2)$ and $(5, 1)$
2. $(-1, -2)$ and $(-3, -4)$
3. $(-3, \frac{1}{4})$ and $(6, \frac{1}{4})$
4. $(-2, 5)$ and $(-2, 10)$

In Exercises 5–6, use the given conditions to write an equation for each line in point-slope form and slope-intercept form.

5. Passing through $(-3, 2)$ with slope -6
6. Passing through $(1, 6)$ and $(-1, 2)$

In Exercises 7–10, give the slope and y-intercept of each line whose equation is given. Then graph the line.

7. $y = \frac{2}{5}x - 1$
8. $y = -4x + 5$

9. $2x + 3y + 6 = 0$ **10.** $2y - 8 = 0$

11. Corporations in the United States are doing quite well, thank you. The scatter plot in the next column shows corporate profits, in billions of dollars, from 1990 through 2000. Also shown is a line that passes through or near the points.

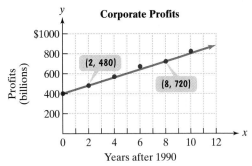

Corporate Profits

Source: U.S Department of Labor

a. Use the two points whose coordinates are shown by the voice balloons to find the point-slope equation of the line that models corporate profits, y, in billions of dollars, x years after 1990.
b. Write the equation in part (a) in slope-intercept form.
c. Use the linear model to predict corporate profits in 2010.

12. The scatter plot on the next page shows the number of minutes each that 16 people exercise per week and the number of headaches per month each person experiences.

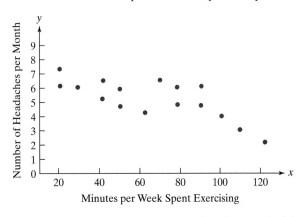

Minutes per Week Spent Exercising

a. Draw a line that fits the data so that the spread of the data points around the line is as small as possible.
b. Use the coordinates of two points along your line to write its point-slope and slope-intercept equations.
c. Use the equation in part (b) to predict the number of headaches per month for a person exercising 130 minutes per week.

In Exercises 13–14, use the given conditions to write an equation for each line in point-slope form and slope-intercept form.

13. Passing through $(4, -7)$ and parallel to the line whose equation is $3x + y - 9 = 0$

14. Passing through $(-3, 6)$ and perpendicular to the line whose equation is $y = \frac{1}{3}x + 4$

2.2

In Exercises 15–16, find the distance between each pair of points. If necessary, round answers to two decimal places.

15. $(-2, -3)$ and $(3, 9)$ **16.** $(-4, 3)$ and $(-2, 5)$

In Exercises 17–18, find the midpoint of each line segment with the given endpoints.

17. $(2, 6)$ and $(-12, 4)$ **18.** $(4, -6)$ and $(-15, 2)$

In Exercises 19–20, write the standard form of the equation of the circle with the given center and radius.

19. Center $(0, 0)$, $r = 3$ **20.** Center $(-2, 4)$, $r = 6$

In Exercises 21–23, give the center and radius of each circle and graph its equation.

21. $x^2 + y^2 = 1$ **22.** $(x + 2)^2 + (y - 3)^2 = 9$

23. $x^2 + y^2 - 4x + 2y - 4 = 0$

2.3

In Exercises 24–26, determine whether each relation is a function. Give the domain and range for each relation.

24. $\{(2, 7), (3, 7), (5, 7)\}$ **25.** $\{(1, 10)\ (2, 500), (13, \pi)\}$

26. $\{(12, 13), (14, 15), (12, 19)\}$

In Exercises 27–29, determine whether each equation defines y as a function of x.

27. $2x + y = 8$ **28.** $3x^2 + y = 14$

29. $2x + y^2 = 6$

In Exercises 30–33, evaluate each function at the given values of the independent variable and simplify.

30. $f(x) = 5 - 7x$
   a. $f(4)$ **b.** $f(x + 3)$ **c.** $f(-x)$

31. $g(x) = 3x^2 - 5x + 2$
   a. $g(0)$ **b.** $g(-2)$
   c. $g(x - 1)$ **d.** $g(-x)$

32. $g(x) = \begin{cases} \sqrt{x - 4} & \text{if } x \geq 4 \\ 4 - x & \text{if } x < 4 \end{cases}$
   a. $g(13)$ **b.** $g(0)$ **c.** $g(-3)$

33. $f(x) = \begin{cases} \dfrac{x^2 - 1}{x - 1} & \text{if } x \neq 1 \\ 12 & \text{if } x = 1 \end{cases}$
   a. $f(-2)$ **b.** $f(1)$ **c.** $f(2)$

In Exercises 34–35, find and simplify the difference quotient

$$\frac{f(x + h) - f(x)}{h}, \quad h \neq 0$$

for the given function.

34. $f(x) = 8x - 11$ **35.** $f(x) = x^2 - 13x + 5$

In Exercises 36–40, find the domain of each function.

36. $f(x) = x^2 + 6x - 3$ **37.** $g(x) = \dfrac{4}{x - 7}$

38. $h(x) = \sqrt{8 - 2x}$ **39.** $f(x) = \dfrac{x}{x^2 - 1}$

40. $g(x) = \dfrac{\sqrt{x - 2}}{x - 5}$

2.4

Graph the functions in Exercises 41–42. Use the integer values of x given to the right of the function to obtain the ordered pairs. Use the graph to specify the function's domain and range.

41. $f(x) = x^2 - 4x + 4 \qquad x = -1, 0, 1, 2, 3, 4$

42. $f(x) = |2 - x| \qquad x = -1, 0, 1, 2, 3, 4$

*In Exercises 43–45, use the graph to determine **a.** the function's domain; **b.** the function's range; **c.** the x-intercepts, if any; **d.** the y-intercept, if any; **e.** intervals on which the function is increasing, decreasing, or constant; and **f.** the function values indicated below the graphs.*

43.

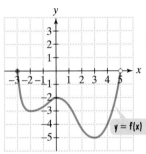

$f(-2) = ? \quad f(3) = ?$

44.

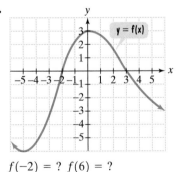

$f(-2) = ? \quad f(6) = ?$

45.

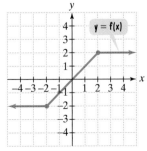

$f(-9) = ? \quad f(14) = ?$

In Exercises 46–47, find:
    a. *The numbers, if any, at which f has a relative maximum. What are these relative maxima?*
    b. *The numbers, if any, at which f has a relative minimum. What are these relative minima?*

46. Use the graph in Exercise 43.

47. Use the graph in Exercise 44.

In Exercises 48–51, use the vertical line test to identify graphs in which y is a function of x.

48.

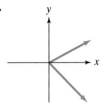

49.

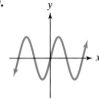

50.

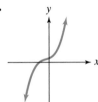

51.

52. Find the average rate of change of $f(x) = x^2 - 4x$ from $x_1 = 5$ to $x_2 = 9$.

53. The graph shows annual spending per uniformed member of the U.S. military in inflation-adjusted dollars. Find the average rate of change of spending per year from 1955 through 2000. Round to the nearest dollar per year.

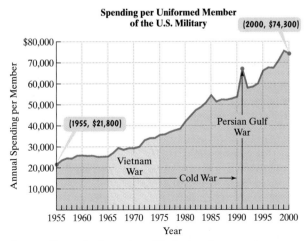

Spending per Uniformed Member of the U.S. Military

Source: Center for Strategic and Budgetary Assessments

In Exercises 54–56, determine whether each function is even, odd, or neither. State each function's symmetry. If you are using a graphing utility, graph the function and verify its possible symmetry.

54. $f(x) = x^3 - 5x$

55. $f(x) = x^4 - 2x^2 + 1$

56. $f(x) = 2x\sqrt{1 - x^2}$

57. The graph shows the height, in meters, of a vulture in terms of its time, in seconds, in flight.

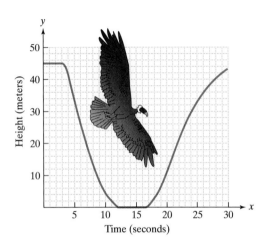

Time (seconds)

a. Is the vulture's height a function of time? Use the graph to explain why or why not.

b. On which interval is the function decreasing? Describe what this means in practical terms.

c. On which intervals is the function constant? What does this mean for each of these intervals?

d. On which interval is the function increasing? What does this mean?

58. A cargo service charges a flat fee of $5 plus $1.50 for each pound or fraction of a pound. Graph shipping cost, $C(x)$, in dollars, as a function of weight, x, in pounds, for $0 < x \le 5$.

2.5

In Exercises 59–61, begin by graphing the standard quadratic function, $f(x) = x^2$. Then use transformations of this graph to graph the given function.

59. $g(x) = x^2 + 2$

60. $h(x) = (x + 2)^2$

61. $r(x) = -(x + 1)^2$

In Exercises 62–64, begin by graphing the square root function, $f(x) = \sqrt{x}$. Then use transformations of this graph to graph the given function.

62. $g(x) = \sqrt{x + 3}$

63. $h(x) = \sqrt{3 - x}$

64. $r(x) = 2\sqrt{x + 2}$

In Exercises 65–67, begin by graphing the absolute value function, $f(x) = |x|$. Then use transformations of this graph to graph the given function.

65. $g(x) = |x + 2| - 3$

66. $h(x) = -|x - 1| + 1$

67. $r(x) = \frac{1}{2}|x + 2|$

In Exercises 68–70, begin by graphing the standard cubic function, $f(x) = x^3$. Then use transformations of this graph to graph the given function.

68. $g(x) = \frac{1}{2}(x - 1)^3$

69. $h(x) = -(x + 1)^3$

70. $r(x) = \frac{1}{4}x^3 - 1$

In Exercises 71–73, use the graph of the function f to sketch the graph of the given function g.

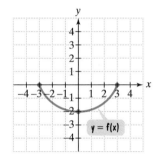

$y = f(x)$

71. $g(x) = f(x + 2) + 3$

72. $g(x) = \frac{1}{2}f(x - 1)$

73. $g(x) = -2 + 2f(x + 2)$

2.6

In Exercises 74–76, find $f + g$, $f - g$, fg, and $\frac{f}{g}$. Determine the domain for each function.

74. $f(x) = 3x - 1$, $g(x) = x - 5$

75. $f(x) = x^2 + x + 1$, $g(x) = x^2 - 1$

76. $f(x) = \sqrt{x + 7}$, $g(x) = \sqrt{x - 2}$

*In Exercises 77–78, find **a.** $(f \circ g)(x)$; **b.** $(g \circ f)(x)$; **c.** $(f \circ g)(3)$.*

77. $f(x) = x^2 + 3$, $g(x) = 4x - 1$

78. $f(x) = \sqrt{x}$, $g(x) = x + 1$

*In Exercises 79–80, find **a.** $(f \circ g)(x)$; **b.** the domain of $(f \circ g)$.*

79. $f(x) = \dfrac{x + 1}{x - 2}$, $g(x) = \dfrac{1}{x}$

80. $f(x) = \sqrt{x - 1}$, $g(x) = x + 3$

In Exercises 81–82, express the given function h as a composition of two functions f and g so that $h(x) = (f \circ g)(x)$.

81. $h(x) = (x^2 + 2x - 1)^4$

82. $h(x) = \sqrt[3]{7x + 4}$

Chapter 2 Test

In Exercises 1–2, use the given conditions to write an equation for each line in point-slope form and slope-intercept form.

1. Passing through $(2, 1)$ and $(-1, -8)$

2. Passing through $(-4, 6)$ and perpendicular to the line whose equation is $y = -\frac{1}{4}x + 5$

3. Strong demand plus higher fuel and labor costs are driving up the price of flying. The graph shows the national averages for one-way fares. Also shown is a line that models that data.

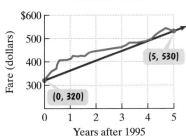

National Averages for One-Way Airline Fares: Business Travel

(5, 530)

(0, 320)

Years after 1995

Source: American Express

   a. Use the two points whose coordinates are shown by the voice balloons to write the slope-intercept equation of the line that models the average one-way fare, y, in dollars, x years after 1995.

   b. According to the model, what will the national average for one-way fares be in 2008?

4. Give the center and radius of the circle whose equation is $x^2 + y^2 + 4x - 6y - 3 = 0$ and graph the equation.

5. List by letter all relations that are not functions.
   a. $\{(7, 5), (8, 5), (9, 5)\}$
   b. $\{(5, 7), (5, 8), (5, 9)\}$
   c.

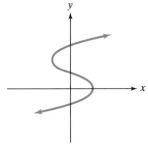

d. $x^2 + y^2 = 100$

e.

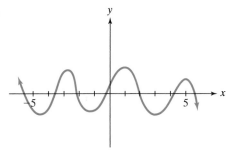

6. If $f(x) = x^2 - 2x + 5$, find $f(x - 1)$ and simplify.

7. If $g(x) = \begin{cases} \sqrt{x - 3} & \text{if } x \geq 3 \\ 3 - x & \text{if } x < 3 \end{cases}$, find $g(-1)$ and $g(7)$.

8. If $f(x) = \sqrt{12 - 3x}$, find the domain of f.

9. If $f(x) = x^2 + 11x - 7$, find and simplify the difference quotient $\dfrac{f(x + h) - f(x)}{h}$.

10. Use the graph of function f to answer the following questions.

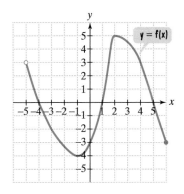

$y = f(x)$

   a. What is $f(4) - f(-3)$?
   b. What is the domain of f?
   c. What is the range of f?
   d. On which interval or intervals is f increasing?
   e. On which interval or intervals is f decreasing?
   f. For what number does f have a relative maximum? What is the relative maximum?
   g. For what number does f have a relative minimum? What is the relative minimum?
   h. What are the x-intercepts?
   i. What is the y-intercept?

11. Find the average rate of change of $f(x) = 3x^2 - 5$ from $x_1 = 6$ to $x_2 = 10$.

12. Determine whether $f(x) = x^4 - x^2$ is even, odd, or neither. Use your answer to explain why the graph in the figure shown cannot be the graph of f.

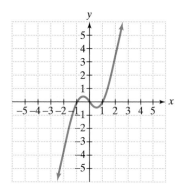

13. The figure at the top of the next column shows how the graph of $h(x) = -2(x - 3)^2$ is obtained from the graph of $f(x) = x^2$. Describe this process, using the graph of g in your description.

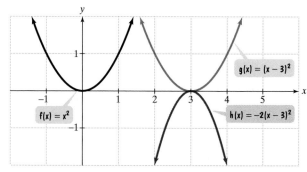

14. Begin by graphing the absolute value function, $f(x) = |x|$. Then use transformations of this graph to graph $g(x) = \frac{1}{2}|x + 1| + 3$.

If $f(x) = x^2 + 3x - 4$ and $g(x) = 5x - 2$, find each function or function value in Exercises 15–19.

15. $(f - g)(x)$

16. $\left(\dfrac{f}{g}\right)(x)$ and its domain

17. $(f \circ g)(x)$

18. $(g \circ f)(x)$

19. $f(g(2))$

20. If $f(x) = \dfrac{7}{x - 4}$ and $g(x) = \dfrac{2}{x}$, find $(f \circ g)(x)$ and the domain of $f \circ g$.

21. Express $h(x) = (2x + 13)^7$ as a composition of two functions f and g so that $h(x) = (f \circ g)(x)$.

Systems of Equations

Chapter 3

Most things in life depend on many variables. Temperature and precipitation are two variables that have a critical effect on whether regions are forests, grasslands, or deserts. Airlines deal with numerous variables during weather disruptions at large connecting airports. They must solve the problem of putting their operation back together again to minimize the cost of the disruption and passenger inconvenience. In this chapter, forests, grasslands, and airline service are viewed in the same way—situations with several variables. You will learn methods for modeling and solving problems in these situations.

A major weather disruption delayed your flight for hours, but you finally made it. You are in Yosemite National Park in California, surrounded by evergreen forests, alpine meadows, and sheer walls of granite. Soaring cliffs, plunging waterfalls, gigantic trees, rugged canyons, mountains and valleys stand in stark contrast to the angry chaos at the airport. This is so different from where you live and attend college, a region in which grasslands predominate.

SECTION 3.1 *Systems of Linear Equations in Two Variables*

Objectives

1. Decide whether an ordered pair is a solution of a linear system.
2. Solve linear systems by substitution.
3. Solve linear systems by addition.
4. Identify systems that do not have exactly one ordered-pair solution.
5. Solve problems using systems of linear equations.

Key West residents Brian Goss (left), George Wallace, and Michael Mooney (right) hold on to each other as they battle 90 mph winds along Houseboat Row in Key West, Fla., on Friday, Sept. 25, 1998. The three had sought shelter behind a Key West hotel as Hurricane Georges descended on the Florida Keys, but were forced to seek other shelter when the storm conditions became too rough. Hundreds of people were killed by the storm when it swept through the Caribbean.

Problems ranging from scheduling airline flights to controlling traffic flow to routing phone calls over the nation's communication network often require solutions in a matter of moments. The solution to these real-world problems can involve solving thousands of equations having thousands of variables. AT&T's domestic long-distance network involves 800,000 variables! Meteorologists describing atmospheric conditions surrounding a hurricane must solve problems involving thousands of equations rapidly and efficiently. The difference between a two-hour warning and a two-day warning is a life-and-death issue for thousands of people in the path of one of nature's most destructive forces.

Although we will not be solving 800,000 equations with 800,000 variables, we will turn our attention to two equations with two variables, such as

$$2x - 3y = -4$$
$$2x + y = 4.$$

The methods that we consider for solving such problems provide the foundation for solving far more complex systems with many variables.

1 Decide whether an ordered pair is a solution of a linear system.

Systems of Linear Equations and Their Solutions

We have seen that all equations in the form $Ax + By = C$ are straight lines when graphed. Two such equations, such as those listed above, are called a **system of linear equations** or a **linear system. A solution to a system of linear equations** is an ordered pair that satisfies all equations in the system. For example, (3, 4) satisfies the system

$$x + y = 7 \qquad (3 + 4 \text{ is, indeed, 7.})$$
$$x - y = -1. \qquad (3 - 4 \text{ is, indeed, } -1.)$$

Thus, $(3, 4)$ satisfies both equations and is a solution of the system. The solution can be described by saying that $x = 3$ and $y = 4$. The solution can also be described using set notation. The solution set to the system is $\{(3, 4)\}$—that is, the set consisting of the ordered pair $(3, 4)$.

A system of linear equations can have exactly one solution, no solution, or infinitely many solutions. We begin with systems that have exactly one solution.

EXAMPLE 1   Determining Whether an Ordered Pair Is a Solution of a System

Determine whether $(4, -1)$ is a solution of the system

$$x + 2y = 2$$
$$x - 2y = 6.$$

Solution   Because 4 is the x-coordinate and -1 is the y-coordinate of $(4, -1)$, we replace x with 4 and y with -1.

$$
\begin{array}{ll}
x + 2y = 2 & \qquad x - 2y = 6 \\
4 + 2(-1) \overset{?}{=} 2 & \qquad 4 - 2(-1) \overset{?}{=} 6 \\
4 + (-2) \overset{?}{=} 2 & \qquad 4 - (-2) \overset{?}{=} 6 \\
2 = 2, \text{ true} & \qquad 4 + 2 \overset{?}{=} 6 \\
& \qquad 6 = 6, \text{ true}
\end{array}
$$

The pair $(4, -1)$ satisfies both equations: It makes each equation true. Thus, the pair is a solution of the system. The solution set to the system is $\{(4, -1)\}$.

The solution of a system of linear equations can be found by graphing both of the equations in the same rectangular coordinate system. For a system with one solution, the **coordinates of the point of intersection give the system's solution.** For example, the system in Example 1,

$$x + 2y = 2$$
$$x - 2y = 6$$

is graphed in Figure 3.1. The solution of the system, $(4, -1)$, corresponds to the point of intersection of the lines.

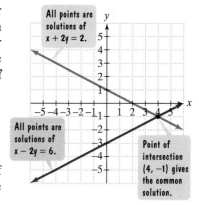

Figure 3.1 Visualizing a system's solution

Check Point 1   Determine whether $(1, 2)$ is a solution of the system

$$2x - 3y = -4$$
$$2x + y = 4.$$

2 Solve linear systems by substitution.

Eliminating a Variable Using the Substitution Method

Finding the solution to a linear system by graphing equations may not be easy to do. For example, a solution of $\left(-\frac{2}{3}, \frac{157}{29}\right)$ would be difficult to "see" as an intersection point on a graph.

Let's consider a method that does not depend on finding a system's solution visually: the substitution method. This method involves converting the system to one equation in one variable by an appropriate substitution.

EXAMPLE 2 Solving a System by Substitution

Solve by the substitution method:

$$y = -x - 1$$
$$4x - 3y = 24.$$

Solution

Step 1 Solve either of the equations for one variable in terms of the other. This step has already been done for us. The first equation, $y = -x - 1$, has y solved in terms of x.

Step 2 Substitute the expression from step 1 into the other equation. We substitute the expression $-x - 1$ for y in the other equation:

$$y = \boxed{-x - 1} \qquad 4x - 3\boxed{y} = 24 \quad \text{Substitute } -x - 1 \text{ for } y.$$

This gives us an equation in one variable, namely

$$4x - 3(-x - 1) = 24.$$

The variable y has been eliminated.

Step 3 Solve the resulting equation containing one variable.

$$
\begin{aligned}
4x - 3(-x - 1) &= 24 && \text{This is the equation containing one variable.} \\
4x + 3x + 3 &= 24 && \text{Apply the distributive property.} \\
7x + 3 &= 24 && \text{Combine like terms.} \\
7x &= 21 && \text{Subtract 3 from both sides.} \\
x &= 3 && \text{Divide both sides by 7.}
\end{aligned}
$$

Step 4 Back-substitute the obtained value into one of the original equations. We now know that the x-coordinate of the solution is 3. To find the y-coordinate, we back-substitute the x-value into either original equation. We will use

$$y = -x - 1.$$

Substitute 3 for x.

$$y = -3 - 1 = -4$$

With $x = 3$ and $y = -4$, the proposed solution is $(3, -4)$.

Step 5 Check the proposed solution in both of the system's given equations. Replace x with 3 and y with -4.

$$
\begin{array}{ll}
y = -x - 1 & 4x - 3y = 24 \\
-4 \stackrel{?}{=} -3 - 1 & 4(3) - 3(-4) \stackrel{?}{=} 24 \\
-4 = -4, \text{ true} & 12 + 12 \stackrel{?}{=} 24 \\
& 24 = 24, \text{ true}
\end{array}
$$

The pair $(3, -4)$ satisfies both equations. The system's solution set is $\{(3, -4)\}$.

Technology

A graphing utility can be used to solve the system in Example 2. Graph each equation and use the intersection feature. The utility displays the solution $(3, -4)$ as $x = 3$, $y = -4$.

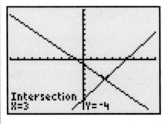
Intersection
X=3 Y=-4

Check Point 2 Solve by the substitution method:

$$y = 5x - 13$$
$$2x + 3y = 12.$$

Before considering additional examples, let's summarize the steps used in the substitution method.

Study Tip

In step 1, you can choose which variable to isolate in which equation. If possible, solve for a variable whose coefficient is 1 or −1 to avoid working with fractions.

Solving Linear Systems by Substitution

1. Solve either of the equations for one variable in terms of the other. (If one of the equations is already in this form, you can skip this step.)
2. Substitute the expression found in step 1 into the other equation. This will result in an equation in one variable.
3. Solve the equation containing one variable.
4. Back-substitute the value found in step 3 into one of the original equations. Simplify and find the value of the remaining variable.
5. Check the proposed solution in both of the system's given equations.

EXAMPLE 3   Solving a System by Substitution

Solve by the substitution method:

$$5x - 4y = 9$$
$$x - 2y = -3.$$

Solution

Step 1   Solve either of the equations for one variable in terms of the other.
We begin by isolating one of the variables in either of the equations. By solving for x in the second equation, which has a coefficient of 1, we can avoid fractions.

$$x - 2y = -3 \qquad \text{This is the second equation in the given system.}$$
$$x = 2y - 3 \qquad \text{Solve for x by adding 2y to both sides.}$$

Step 2   Substitute the expression from step 1 into the other equation.   We substitute $2y - 3$ for x in the first equation.

$$x = \boxed{2y - 3} \qquad 5\boxed{x} - 4y = 9$$

This gives us an equation in one variable, namely

$$5(2y - 3) - 4y = 9.$$

The variable x has been eliminated.

Step 3   Solve the resulting equation containing one variable.

$$5(2y - 3) - 4y = 9 \qquad \text{This is the equation containing one variable.}$$
$$10y - 15 - 4y = 9 \qquad \text{Apply the distributive property.}$$
$$6y - 15 = 9 \qquad \text{Combine like terms.}$$
$$6y = 24 \qquad \text{Add 15 to both sides.}$$
$$y = 4 \qquad \text{Divide both sides by 6.}$$

Study Tip

The equation from step 1, in which one variable is expressed in terms of the other, is equivalent to one of the original equations. It is often easiest to back-substitute an obtained value into this equation to find the value of the other variable. After obtaining both values, get into the habit of checking the ordered-pair solution in *both* equations of the system.

Step 4 Back-substitute the obtained value into one of the original equations. We back-substitute 4 for y into one of the original equations to find x. Let's use both equations to show that we obtain the same value for x in either case.

Using the first equation:

$$5x - 4y = 9$$
$$5x - 4(4) = 9$$
$$5x - 16 = 9$$
$$5x = 25$$
$$x = 5$$

Using the second equation:

$$x - 2y = -3$$
$$x - 2(4) = -3$$
$$x - 8 = -3$$
$$x = 5$$

With $x = 5$ and $y = 4$, the proposed solution is $(5, 4)$.

Step 5 Check. Take a moment to show that $(5, 4)$ satisfies both given equations. The solution set is $\{(5, 4)\}$.

Check Point 3 Solve by the substitution method:

$$3x + 2y = -1$$
$$x - y = 3.$$

Eliminating a Variable Using the Addition Method

The substitution method is most useful if one of the given equations has an isolated variable. A second, and frequently the easiest, method for solving a linear system is the addition method. Like the substitution method, the addition method involves eliminating a variable and ultimately solving an equation containing only one variable. However, this time we eliminate a variable by adding the equations.

For example, consider the following system of linear equations:

$$3x - 4y = 11$$
$$-3x + 2y = -7.$$

When we add these two equations, the x-terms are eliminated. This occurs because the coefficients of the x-terms, 3 and -3, are opposites (additive inverses) of each other:

$$3x - 4y = 11$$
$$-3x + 2y = -7$$

Add: $-2y = 4$ The sum is an equation in one variable.

$$y = -2$$ Solve for y, dividing both sides by -2.

Now we can back-substitute -2 for y into one of the original equations to find x. It does not matter which equation you use; you will obtain the same value for x in either case. If we use either equation, we can show that $x = 1$ and the solution $(1, -2)$ satisfies both equations in the system.

When we use the addition method, we want to obtain two equations whose sum is an equation containing only one variable. The key step is to obtain, for one of the variables, coefficients that differ only in sign. To do this, we may need to multiply one or both equations by some nonzero number so that the coefficients of one of the variables, x or y, become opposites. Then when the two equations are added, this variable is eliminated.

3 Solve linear systems by addition.

EXAMPLE 4 Solving a System by the Addition Method

Solve by the addition method:

$$3x + 2y = 48$$
$$9x - 8y = -24.$$

Solution We must rewrite one or both equations in equivalent forms so that the coefficients of the same variable (either x or y) are opposites of each other. Consider the terms in x in each equation, that is, $3x$ and $9x$. To eliminate x, we can multiply each term of the first equation by -3 and then add the equations.

$$3x + 2y = 48 \quad \underrightarrow{\text{Multiply by } -3.} \quad -9x - 6y = -144$$
$$9x - 8y = -24 \quad \underrightarrow{\text{No change}} \quad \underline{9x - 8y = -24}$$

$$\text{Add:} \qquad -14y = -168$$
$$y = 12 \qquad \text{Solve for } y, \text{ dividing both sides by } -14.$$

Thus, $y = 12$. We back-substitute this value into either one of the given equations. We'll use the first one.

$$3x + 2y = 48 \qquad \text{This the first equation in the given system.}$$
$$3x + 2(12) = 48 \qquad \text{Substitute 12 for } y.$$
$$3x + 24 = 48 \qquad \text{Multiply.}$$
$$3x = 24 \qquad \text{Subtract 24 from both sides.}$$
$$x = 8 \qquad \text{Divide both sides by 3.}$$

The solution $(8, 12)$ can be shown to satisfy both equations in the system. Consequently, the solution set is $\{(8, 12)\}$.

Solving Linear Systems by Addition

1. If necessary, rewrite both equations in the form $Ax + By = C$.
2. If necessary, multiply either equation or both equations by appropriate nonzero numbers so that the sum of the x-coefficients or the sum of the y-coefficients is 0.
3. Add the equations in step 2. The sum is an equation in one variable.
4. Solve the equation in one variable.
5. Back-substitute the value obtained in step 4 into either of the given equations and solve for the other variable.
6. Check the solution in both of the original equations.

Check Point 4 Solve by the addition method:

$$4x + 5y = 3$$
$$2x - 3y = 7.$$

Some linear systems have solutions that are not integers. If the value of one variable turns out to be a "messy" fraction, back-substitution might lead to cumbersome arithmetic. If this happens, you can return to the original system and use addition to find the value of the other variable.

> **EXAMPLE 5** **Solving a System by the Addition Method**

Solve by the addition method:

$$2x = 7y - 17$$
$$5y = 17 - 3x.$$

Solution

Step 1 Rewrite both equations in the form $Ax + By = C$. We first arrange the system so that variable terms appear on the left and constants appear on the right. We obtain

$$2x - 7y = -17 \quad \text{Subtract } 7y \text{ from both sides of the first equation.}$$
$$3x + 5y = 17. \quad \text{Add } 3x \text{ to both sides of the second equation.}$$

Step 2 If necessary, multiply either equation or both equations by appropriate numbers so that the sum of the x-coefficients or the sum of the y-coefficients is 0. We can eliminate x or y. Let's eliminate x by multiplying the first equation by 3 and the second equation by -2.

$$2x - 7y = -17 \quad \underrightarrow{\text{Multiply by 3.}} \quad 3 \cdot 2x - 3 \cdot 7y = 3(-17) \longrightarrow 6x - 21y = -51$$
$$3x + 5y = 17 \quad \underrightarrow{\text{Multiply by } -2.} \quad -2 \cdot 3x + (-2) \cdot 5y = -2(17) \longrightarrow -6x - 10y = -34$$

Steps 3 and 4 Add the equations and solve the equation in one variable.

$$6x - 21y = -51$$
$$\underline{-6x - 10y = -34}$$
Add: $\quad -31y = -85$

$$\frac{-31y}{-31} = \frac{-85}{-31} \quad \text{Divide both sides by } -31.$$

$$y = \frac{85}{31} \quad \text{Simplify.}$$

Step 5 Back-substitute and find the value for the other variable. Back-substitution of $\frac{85}{31}$ for y into either of the given equations results in cumbersome arithmetic. Instead, let's use the addition method on the given system in the form $Ax + By = C$ to find the value for x. Thus, we eliminate y by multiplying the first equation by 5 and the second equation by 7.

$$2x - 7y = -17 \quad \underrightarrow{\text{Multiply by 5.}} \quad 10x - 35y = -85$$
$$3x + 5y = 17 \quad \underrightarrow{\text{Multiply by 7.}} \quad \underline{21x + 35y = 119}$$
Add: $\quad 31x = 34$

$$x = \tfrac{34}{31} \quad \text{Divide both sides by 31.}$$

Step 6 Check. For this system, a calculator is helpful in showing the solution $\left(\frac{34}{31}, \frac{85}{31}\right)$ satisfies both equations. Consequently, the solution set is $\left\{\left(\frac{34}{31}, \frac{85}{31}\right)\right\}$.

Check Point 5 Solve by the addition method:

$$4x = 5 + 2y$$
$$3y = 4 - 2x.$$

4 Identify systems that do not have exactly one ordered-pair solution.

Linear Systems Having No Solution or Infinitely Many Solutions

We have seen that a system of linear equations in two variables represents a pair of lines. The lines either intersect, are parallel, or are identical. Thus, there are three possibilities for the number of solutions to a system of two linear equations.

The Number of Solutions to a System of Two Linear Equations

The number of solutions to a system of two linear equations in two variables is given by one of the following. (See Figure 3.2.)

Number of Solutions	What This Means Graphically
Exactly one ordered-pair solution	The two lines intersect at one point.
No solution	The two lines are parallel.
Infinitely many solutions	The two lines are identical.

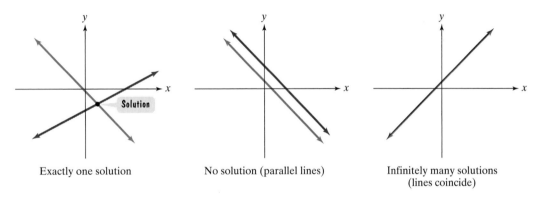

Exactly one solution   No solution (parallel lines)   Infinitely many solutions (lines coincide)

Figure 3.2 Possible graphs for a system of two linear equations in two variables

A linear system with no solution is called an **inconsistent system.** If you attempt to solve such a system by substitution or addition, you will eliminate both variables. A false statement such as $0 = 17$ will be the result.

EXAMPLE 6   A System with No Solution

Solve the system:

$$4x + 6y = 12$$
$$6x + 9y = 12.$$

Solution Because no variable is isolated, we will use the addition method. To obtain coefficients of x that differ only in sign, we multiply the first equation by 3 and multiply the second equation by -2.

$$4x + 6y = 12 \xrightarrow{\text{Multiply by 3.}} 12x + 18y = 36$$
$$6x + 9y = 12 \xrightarrow{\text{Multiply by } -2.} \underline{-12x - 18y = -24}$$
$$\text{Add:} \qquad\qquad\qquad 0 = 12$$

There are no values of x and y for which $0 = 12$.

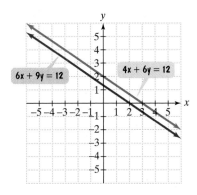

Figure 3.3 The graph of an inconsistent system

The false statement $0 = 12$ indicates that the system is inconsistent and has no solution. The solution set is the empty set, $\varnothing$.

The lines corresponding to the two equations in Example 6 are shown in Figure 3.3. The lines are parallel and have no point of intersection.

Discovery

Show that the graphs of $4x + 6y = 12$ and $6x + 9y = 12$ must be parallel lines by solving each equation for y. What is the slope and y-intercept for each line? What does this mean? If a linear system is inconsistent, what must be true about the slopes and y-intercepts for the system's graphs?

Check Point 6   Solve the system:

$$x + 2y = 4$$
$$3x + 6y = 13.$$

A linear system that has at least one solution is called a **consistent system.** Lines that intersect and lines that coincide both represent consistent systems. If the lines coincide, then the consistent system has infinitely many solutions, represented by every point on the line.

The equations in a linear system with infinitely many solutions are called **dependent.** If you attempt to solve such a system by substitution or addition, you will eliminate both variables. However, a true statement such as $0 = 0$ will be the result.

EXAMPLE 7   A System with Infinitely Many Solutions

Solve the system:

$$y = 3 - 2x$$
$$4x + 2y = 6.$$

Solution   Because the variable y is isolated in the first equation, we can use the substitution method. We substitute the expression for y in the other equation.

$$y = \boxed{3 - 2x} \quad 4x + 2\boxed{y} = 6 \qquad \text{Substitute } 3 - 2x \text{ for } y.$$

$$4x + 2y = 6 \qquad\qquad \text{This is the second equation in the given system.}$$

$$4x + 2(3 - 2x) = 6 \qquad\qquad \text{Substitute } 3 - 2x \text{ for } y.$$

$$4x + 6 - 4x = 6 \qquad\qquad \text{Apply the distributive property.}$$

$$6 = 6 \qquad\qquad \text{Simplify. This statement is true for all values of } x \text{ and } y.$$

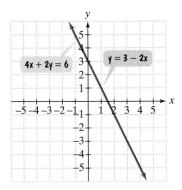

Figure 3.4 The graph of a system with infinitely many solutions

In our final step, both variables have been eliminated, and the resulting statement $6 = 6$ is true. This true statement indicates that the system has infinitely many solutions. The solution set consists of all points (x, y) lying on either of the coinciding lines, $y = 3 - 2x$ or $4x + 2y = 6$, as shown in Figure 3.4.

We express the solution set for the system in one of two equivalent ways:

$$\{(x, y) \mid y = 3 - 2x\} \quad \text{The set of all ordered pairs (x, y) such that y = 3 - 2x}$$

or $\{(x, y) \mid 4x + 2y = 6\}$ The set of all ordered pairs (x, y) such that 4x + 2y = 6

Check Point 7 Solve the system:

$$y = 4x - 4$$
$$8x - 2y = 8.$$

Applications

5 Solve problems using systems of linear equations.

As a young entrepreneur, did you ever try selling lemonade in your front yard? Suppose that you charged 55¢ for each cup and you sold 45 cups. Your **revenue** is your income from selling these 45 units, or $\$0.55(45) = \$24.75$. Your *revenue function* from selling x cups is

$$R(x) = 0.55x.$$

This is the unit price: 55¢ for each cup.   This is the number of units sold.

For any business, the **revenue function,** R, is the money generated by selling x units of the product:

$$R(x) = px.$$

Price per unit   x units sold

Back to selling lemonade and energizing the neighborhood with white sugar: Is your revenue for the afternoon also your profit? No. We need to consider the cost of the business. You estimate that the lemons, white sugar, and bottled water cost 5¢ per cup. Furthermore, mommy dearest is charging you a $\$10$ rental fee for use of your (her?) front yard. The **cost function,** C, for any business is the sum of its fixed and variable costs. Thus, your cost function for selling x cups of lemonade is

$$C(x) = 10 + 0.05x.$$

This is your $10 fixed cost.   This is your variable cost: 5¢ for each cup produced.

Profit

What does every entrepreneur, from a kid selling lemonade to Bill Gates, want to do? Generate profit, of course. The profit function, P, generated after producing and selling x units of a product is the difference between the revenue function, R, and the cost function, C. The profit function for the lemonade business in Figure 8.5 is

$$P(x) = R(x) - C(x)$$

$$= 0.55x - (10 + 0.05x)$$

$$= 0.50x - 10.$$

The graph of this profit function is shown below. The red portion lies below the x-axis and shows a loss when fewer than 20 units are sold. The lemonade business is "in the red." The black portion lies above the x-axis and shows a gain when more than 20 units are sold. The lemonade business is "in the black."

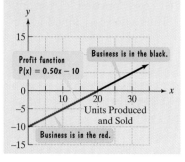

Figure 3.5 shows the graphs of the revenue and cost functions for the lemonade business. Similar graphs and models apply no matter how small or large a business venture may be.

$$R(x) = 0.55x \qquad C(x) = 10 + 0.05x$$

> Revenue is 55¢ times the number of cups sold.

> Cost is $10 plus 5¢ times the number of cups produced.

Figure 3.5

The lines intersect at the point (20, 11). This means that when 20 cups are produced and sold, both cost and revenue are $11. In business, this point of intersection is called the **break-even point.** At the break-even point, the money coming in is equal to the money going out. Can you see what happens for x-values less than 20? The red cost graph is above the blue revenue graph. The cost is greater than the revenue and the business is losing money. Thus, if you sell fewer than 20 cups of lemonade, the result is a *loss*. By contrast, look at what happens for x-values greater than 20. The blue revenue graph is above the red cost graph. The revenue is greater than the cost and the business is making money. Thus, if you sell more than 20 cups of lemonade, the result is a *gain*.

EXAMPLE 8　Finding a Break-Even Point

Technology is now promising to bring light, fast, and beautiful wheelchairs to millions of disabled people. A company is planning to manufacture these radically different wheelchairs. Fixed cost will be $500,000 and it will cost $400 to produce each wheelchair. Each wheelchair will be sold for $600.

　a. Write the cost function, C, of producing x wheelchairs.

　b. Write the revenue function, R, from the sale of x wheelchairs.

　c. Determine the break-even point. Describe what this means.

Solution

　a. The cost function is the sum of the fixed cost and variable cost.

> Fixed cost of $500,000

> plus

> Variable cost: $400 for each chair produced

$$C(x) = 500,000 + 400x$$

b. The revenue function is the money generated from the sale of x wheelchairs.

> Revenue per chair, $600, times   the number of chairs sold

$$R(x) = 600x$$

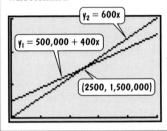
c. The break-even point occurs where the graphs of C and R intersect. Thus, we find this point by solving the system

$$C(x) = 500{,}000 + 400x \qquad y = 500{,}000 + 400x$$
$$R(x) = 600x \qquad\qquad\qquad y = 600x.$$

or

Using substitution, we can substitute $600x$ for y in the first equation.

$$600x = 500{,}000 + 400x \qquad \text{Substitute } 600x \text{ for } y.$$
$$200x = 500{,}000 \qquad\qquad \text{Subtract } 400x \text{ from both sides.}$$
$$x = 2500 \qquad\qquad\qquad \text{Divide both sides by } 200.$$

Back-substituting 2500 for x in either of the system's equations (or functions), we obtain

$$R(2500) = 600(2500) = 1{,}500{,}000.$$

> We used $R(x) = 600x$.

The break-even point is $(2500, 1{,}500{,}000)$. This means that the company will break even if it produces and sells 2500 wheelchairs. At this level, the money coming in is equal to the money going out: $1,500,000.

Check Point 8 A company that manufactures running shoes has a fixed cost of $300,000. Additionally, it costs $30 to produce each pair of shoes. They are sold at $80 per pair.

a. Write the cost function, C, of producing x pairs of running shoes.

b. Write the revenue function, R, from the sale of x pairs of running shoes.

c. Determine the break-even point. Describe what this means.

An important application of systems of equations arises in connection with supply and demand. As the price of a product increases, the demand for that product decreases. However, at higher prices suppliers are willing to produce greater quantities of the product.

EXAMPLE 9   Supply and Demand Models

A chain of video stores specializes in cult films. The weekly demand and supply models for *The Rocky Horror Picture Show* are given by

$$N = -13p + 760 \qquad \text{Demand model}$$
$$N = 2p + 430 \qquad \text{Supply model}$$

in which p is the price of the video and N is the number of copies of the video sold or supplied each week to the chain of stores.

a. How many copies of the video can be sold and supplied at $18 per copy?

b. Find the price at which supply and demand are equal. At this price, how many copies of *Rocky Horror* can be supplied and sold each week?

Solution

a. To find how many copies of the video can be sold and supplied at $18 per copy, we substitute 18 for p in the demand and supply models.

Demand Model	**Supply Model**
$N = -13p + 760$	$N = 2p + 430$

Substitute 18 for p.   Substitute 18 for p.

$$N = -13 \cdot 18 + 760 = 526 \qquad N = 2 \cdot 18 + 430 = 466$$

At $18 per video, the chain can sell 526 copies of *Rocky Horror* in a week. The manufacturer is willing to supply 466 copies per week. This will result in a shortage of copies of the video. Under these conditions, the retail chain is likely to raise the price of the video.

b. We can find the price at which supply and demand are equal by solving the demand-supply linear system. We will use substitution, substituting $-13p + 760$ for N in the second equation.

$$N = \boxed{-13p + 760} \qquad \boxed{N} = 2p + 430 \quad \text{Substitute } -13p + 760 \text{ for N.}$$

$$-13p + 760 = 2p + 430 \qquad \text{The resulting equation contains only one variable.}$$

$$-15p + 760 = 430 \qquad \text{Subtract 2p from both sides.}$$

$$-15p = -330 \qquad \text{Subtract 760 from both sides.}$$

$$p = 22 \qquad \text{Divide both sides by } -15.$$

The price at which supply and demand are equal is $22 per video. To find the value of N, the number of videos supplied and sold weekly at this price, we back-substitute 22 for p into either the demand or the supply model. We'll use both models to make sure we get the same number in each case.

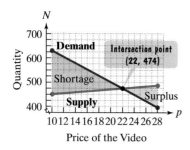

Figure 3.6 Priced at $22 per video, 474 copies of the video can be supplied and sold weekly.

Demand Model	**Supply Model**
$N = -13p + 760$	$N = 2p + 430$

Substitute 22 for p.   Substitute 22 for p.

$$N = -13 \cdot 22 + 760 = 474 \qquad N = 2 \cdot 22 + 430 = 474$$

At a price of $22 per video, 474 units of the video can be supplied and sold weekly. The intersection point, $(22, 474)$, is shown in Figure 3.6.

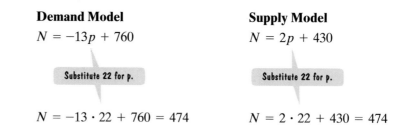

Check Point 9

The demand for a product is modeled by $N = -20p + 1000$ and the supply for the product by $N = 5p + 250$. In these models, p is the price of the product and N is the number supplied or sold weekly. At what price will supply equal demand? At that price, how many units of the product will be supplied and sold each week?

EXERCISE SET 3.1

Practice Exercises

In Exercises 1–4, determine whether the given ordered pair is a solution of the system.

1. $(2, 3)$
$x + 3y = 11$
$x - 5y = -13$

2. $(-3, 5)$
$9x + 7y = 8$
$8x - 9y = -69$

3. $(2, 5)$
$2x + 3y = 17$
$x + 4y = 16$

4. $(8, 5)$
$5x - 4y = 20$
$3y = 2x + 1$

In Exercises 5–18, solve each system by the substitution method.

5. $x + y = 4$
$y = 3x$

6. $x + y = 6$
$y = 2x$

7. $x + 3y = 8$
$y = 2x - 9$

8. $2x - 3y = -13$
$y = 2x + 7$

9. $x = 4y - 2$
$x = 6y + 8$

10. $x = 3y + 7$
$x = 2y - 1$

11. $5x + 2y = 0$
$x - 3y = 0$

12. $4x + 3y = 0$
$2x - y = 0$

13. $2x + 5y = -4$
$3x - y = 11$

14. $2x + 5y = 1$
$-x + 6y = 8$

15. $2x - 3y = 8 - 2x$
$3x + 4y = x + 3y + 14$

16. $3x - 4y = x - y + 4$
$2x + 6y = 5y - 4$

17. $y = \frac{1}{3}x + \frac{2}{3}$
$y = \frac{5}{7}x - 2$

18. $y = -\frac{1}{2}x + 2$
$y = \frac{3}{4}x + 7$

In Exercises 19–30, solve each system by the addition method.

19. $x + y = 1$
$x - y = 3$

20. $x + y = 6$
$x - y = -2$

21. $2x + 3y = 6$
$2x - 3y = 6$

22. $3x + 2y = 14$
$3x - 2y = 10$

23. $x + 2y = 2$
$-4x + 3y = 25$

24. $2x - 7y = 2$
$3x + y = -20$

25. $4x + 3y = 15$
$2x - 5y = 1$

26. $3x - 7y = 13$
$6x + 5y = 7$

27. $3x - 4y = 11$
$2x + 3y = -4$

28. $2x + 3y = -16$
$5x - 10y = 30$

29. $3x = 4y + 1$
$3y = 1 - 4x$

30. $5x = 6y + 40$
$2y = 8 - 3x$

In Exercises 31–42, solve by the method of your choice. Identify systems with no solution and systems with infinitely many solutions, using set notation to express their solution sets.

31. $x = 9 - 2y$
$x + 2y = 13$

32. $6x + 2y = 7$
$y = 2 - 3x$

33. $y = 3x - 5$
$21x - 35 = 7y$

34. $9x - 3y = 12$
$y = 3x - 4$

35. $3x - 2y = -5$
$4x + y = 8$

36. $2x + 5y = -4$
$3x - y = 11$

37. $x + 3y = 2$
$3x + 9y = 6$

38. $4x - 2y = 2$
$2x - y = 1$

39. $\frac{x}{4} - \frac{y}{4} = -1$
$x + 4y = -9$

40. $\frac{x}{6} - \frac{y}{2} = \frac{1}{3}$
$x + 2y = -3$

41. $2x = 3y + 4$
$4x = 3 - 5y$

42. $4x = 3y + 8$
$2x = -14 + 5y$

In Exercises 43–46, let x represent one number and let y represent the other number. Use the given conditions to write a system of equations. Solve the system and find the numbers.

43. The sum of two numbers is 7. If one number is subtracted from the other, their difference is −1. Find the numbers.

44. The sum of two numbers is 2. If one number is subtracted from the other, their difference is 8. Find the numbers.

45. Three times a first number decreased by a second number is 1. The first number increased by twice the second number is 12. Find the numbers.

46. The sum of three times a first number and twice a second number is 8. If the second number is subtracted from twice the first number, the result is 3. Find the numbers.

Application Exercises

Exercises 47–50 describe a number of business ventures. For each exercise,

a. Write the cost function, C.

b. Write the revenue function, R.

c. Determine the break-even point. Describe what this means.

47. A company that manufactures small canoes has a fixed cost of $18,000. It costs $20 to produce each canoe. The selling price is $80 per canoe. (In solving this exercise, let x represent the number of canoes produced and sold.)

48. A company that manufactures bicycles has a fixed cost of $100,000. It costs $100 to produce each bicycle. The selling price is $300 per bike. (In solving this exercise, let x represent the number of bicycles produced and sold.)

49. You invest in a new play. The cost includes an overhead of $30,000, plus production costs of $2500 per performance. A sold-out performance brings in $3125. (In solving this exercise, let x represent the number of sold-out performances.)

50. You invested $30,000 and started a business writing greeting cards. Supplies cost 2¢ per card and you are selling each card for 50¢. (In solving this exercise, let x represent the number of cards produced and sold.)

51. At a price of p dollars per ticket, the number of tickets to a rock concert that can be sold is given by the demand model $N = -25p + 7500$. At a price of p dollars per ticket, the number of tickets that the concert's promoters are willing to make available is given by the supply model $N = 5p + 6000$.

   a. How many tickets can be sold and supplied for $40 per ticket?

   b. Find the ticket price at which supply and demand are equal. At this price, how many tickets will be supplied and sold?

52. The weekly demand and supply models for a particular brand of scientific calculator for a chain of stores are given by the demand model $N = -53p + 1600$, and the supply model $N = 75p + 320$. In these models, p is the price of the calculator and N is the number of calculators sold or supplied each week to the stores.

   a. How many calculators can be sold and supplied at $12 per calculator?

   b. Find the price at which supply and demand are equal. At this price, how many calculators of this type can be supplied and sold each week?

53. In the United States, deaths from car accidents, per 100,000 persons, are decreasing at a faster rate than deaths from gunfire, shown by the blue and red lines that model the data points in the figure.

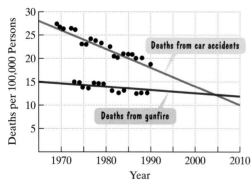

Annual Deaths in the U.S. from Car Accidents and Gunfire

Source: Journal of the American Medical Association

The function $y = -0.4x + 28$ models deaths from car accidents, y, per 100,000 persons, x years after 1965. The function $0.07x + y = 15$ models deaths from gunfire, y, per 100,000 persons, x years after 1965. Use

these models to project when the number of deaths from gunfire will equal the number of deaths from car accidents. Round to the nearest year. How many annual deaths, per 100,000 persons, will there be from gunfire and from car accidents at that time? Describe how this is illustrated by the lines in the figure shown.

54. The June 7, 1999 issue of *Newsweek* presented statistics showing progress African Americans have made in education, health, and finance. Infant mortality for African Americans is decreasing at a faster rate than it is for whites, shown by the graphs below. Infant mortality for African Americans can be modeled by $M = -0.41x + 22$ and for whites by $M = -0.18x + 10$. In both models, x is the number of years after 1980 and M is infant mortality, measured in deaths per 1000 live births. Use these models to project when infant mortality for African Americans and whites will be the same. What is infant mortality rate for both groups at that time?

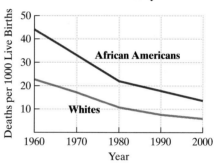

Infant Mortality

Source: National Center for Health Statistics

The graphs show average weekly earnings of full-time wage and salary workers 25 and older, by educational attainment. Exercises 55–56 involve the information in these graphs.

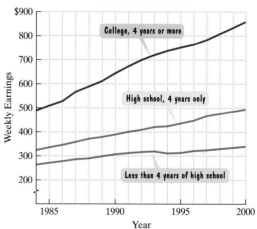

Average Weekly Earnings by Educational Attainment

Source: U.S. Bureau of Labor Statistics

55. In 1985, college graduates averaged $508 in weekly earnings. This amount has increased by approximately $25 in weekly earnings per year. By contrast, in 1985, high school graduates averaged $345 in weekly earnings. This amount has only increased by approximately $9 in weekly earnings per year.

a. Write a function that models weekly earnings, E, for college graduates x years after 1985.

b. Write a function that models weekly earnings, E, for high school graduates x years after 1985.

c. How many years after 1985 will college graduates be earning twice as much per week as high school graduates? In which year will this occur? What will be the weekly earnings for each group at that time?

56. In 1985, college graduates averaged $508 in weekly earnings. This amount has increased by approximately $25 in weekly earnings per year. By contrast, in 1985, people with less than four years of high school averaged $270 in weekly earnings. This amount has only increased by approximately $4 in weekly earnings per year.

a. Write a function that models weekly earnings, E, for college graduates x years after 1985.

b. Write a function that models weekly earnings, E, for people with less than four years of high school x years after 1985.

c. How many years after 1985 will college graduates be earning three times as much per week as people with less than four years of high school? (Round to the nearest whole number.) In which year will this occur? What will be the weekly earnings for each group at that time?

Use a system of linear equations to solve Exercises 57–67.

The graph shows the calories in some favorite fast foods. Use the information in Exercises 57-58 to find the exact caloric content of the specified foods.

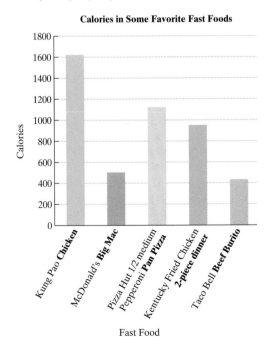

Calories in Some Favorite Fast Foods

Source: Center for Science in the Public Interest

57. One pan pizza and two beef burritos provide 1980 calories. Two pan pizzas and one beef burrito provide 2670 calories. Find the caloric content of each item.

58. One Kung Pao chicken and two Big Macs provide 2620 calories. Two Kung Pao chickens and one Big Mac provide 3740 calories. Find the caloric content of each item.

59. Cholesterol intake should be limited to 300 mg or less each day. One serving of scrambled eggs from McDonalds and one Double Beef Whopper from Burger King exceed this intake by 241 mg. Two servings of scrambled eggs and three Double Beef Whoppers provide 1257 mg of cholesterol. Determine the cholesterol content in each item.

60. Two medium eggs and three cups of ice cream contain 701 milligrams of cholesterol. One medium egg and one cup of ice cream exceed the suggested daily cholesterol intake of 300 milligrams by 25 milligrams. Determine the cholesterol content in each item.

61. A hotel has 200 rooms. Those with kitchen facilities rent for $100 per night and those without kitchen facilities rent for $80 per night. On a night when the hotel was completely occupied, revenues were $17,000. How many of each type of room does the hotel have?

62. In a new development, 50 one- and two-bedroom condominiums were sold. Each one-bedroom condominium sold for $120 thousand and each two bedroom condominium sold for $150 thousand. If sales totaled $7050 thousand, how many of each type of unit was sold?

63. A rectangular lot whose perimeter is 360 feet is fenced along three sides. An expensive fencing along the lot's length costs $20 per foot, and an inexpensive fencing along the two side widths costs only $8 per foot. The total cost of the fencing along the three sides comes to $3280. What are the lot's dimensions?

64. A rectangular lot whose perimeter is 320 feet is fenced along three sides. An expensive fencing along the lot's length costs $16 per foot, and an inexpensive fencing along the two side widths costs only $5 per foot. The total cost of the fencing along the three sides comes to $2140. What are the lot's dimensions?

65. When a crew rows with the current, it travels 16 miles in 2 hours. Against the current, the crew rows 8 miles in 2 hours. Let $x =$ the crew's rowing rate in still water and let $y =$ the rate of the current. The following chart summarizes this information:

	Rate	×	Time	=	Distance
Rowing with current	$x + y$		2		16
Rowing against current	$x - y$		2		8

Find the rate of rowing in still water and the rate of the current.

66. When an airplane flies with the wind, it travels 800 miles in 4 hours. Against the wind, it takes 5 hours to cover the same distance. Find the plane's rate in still air and the rate of the wind.

67. Find the measures of the angles marked $x°$ and $y°$ in the figure.

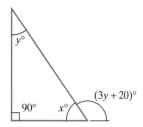

Writing in Mathematics

68. What is a system of linear equations? Provide an example with your description.

69. What is the solution to a system of linear equations?

70. Explain how to solve a system of equations using the substitution method. Use $y = 3 - 3x$ and $3x + 4y = 6$ to illustrate your explanation.

71. Explain how to solve a system of equations using the addition method. Use $3x + 5y = -2$ and $2x + 3y = 0$ to illustrate your explanation.

72. When is it easier to use the addition method rather than the substitution method to solve a system of equations?

73. When using the addition or substitution method, how can you tell if a system of linear equations has infinitely many solutions? What is the relationship between the graphs of the two equations?

74. When using the addition or substitution method, how can you tell if a system of linear equations has no solution? What is the relationship between the graphs of the two equations?

75. Describe the break-even point for a business.

76. The law of supply and demand states that, in a free market economy, a commodity tends to be sold at its equilibrium price. At this price, the amount that the seller will supply is the same amount that the consumer will buy. Explain how systems of equations can be used to determine the equilibrium price.

77. The function $y = 0.94x + 5.64$ models annual U.S. consumption of chicken, y, in pounds per person, x years after 1950. The function $0.74x + y = 146.76$ models annual U.S. consumption of red meat, y, in pounds per person, x years after 1950. What is the most efficient method for solving this system? What does the solution mean in terms of the variables in the functions? (It is not necessary to solve the system.)

78. In Exercise 77, find the slope of each model. Describe what this means in terms of the rate of change of chicken

consumption and the rate of change of red meat consumption. Why must the graphs have an intersection point? What happens to the right of the intersection point?

Technology Exercises

79. Verify your solutions to any five exercises in Exercises 5–42 by using a graphing utility to graph the two equations in the system in the same viewing rectangle. Then use the intersection feature to display the solution.

80. Some graphing utilities can give the solution to a linear system of equations. (Consult your manual for details.) This capability is usually accessed with the $\boxed{\text{SIMULT}}$ (simultaneous equations) feature. First, you will enter 2, for two equations in two variables. With each equation in $Ax + By = C$ form, you will then enter the coefficients for x and y and the constant term, one equation at a time. After entering all six numbers, press $\boxed{\text{SOLVE}}$. The solution will be displayed on the screen. (The x-value may be displayed as $x_1 =$ and the y-value as $x_2 =$.) Use this capability to verify the solution to any five of the exercises you solved in the practice exercises of this exercise set. Describe what happens when you use your graphing utility on a system with no solution or infinitely many solutions.

Critical Thinking Exercises

81. Write a system of equations having $\{(-2, 7)\}$ as a solution set. (More than one system is possible.)

82. Solve the system for x and y in terms of $a_1, b_1, c_1, a_2, b_2,$ and c_2:

$$a_1x + b_1y = c_1$$
$$a_2x + b_2y = c_2.$$

83. Two identical twins can only be recognized by the characteristic that one always tells the truth and the other always lies. One twin tells you of a lucky number pair: "When I multiply my first lucky number by 3 and my second lucky number by 6, the addition of the resulting numbers produces a sum of 12. When I add my first lucky number and twice my second lucky number, the sum is 5." Which twin is talking?

84. A marching band has 52 members, and there are 24 in the pom-pom squad. They wish to form several hexagons and squares like those diagrammed below. Can it be done with no people left over?

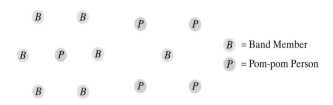

Group Exercise

85. The group should write four different word problems that can be solved using a system of linear equations in two variables. All of the problems should be on different topics. The group should turn in the four problems and their algebraic solutions.

SECTION 3.2   *Systems of Linear Equations in Three Variables*

Objectives

1. Verify the solution of a system of linear equations in three variables.

2. Solve systems of linear equations in three variables.

3. Solve problems using systems in three variables.

All animals sleep, but the length of time they sleep varies widely: Cattle sleep for only a few minutes at a time. We humans seem to need more sleep than other animals. Without enough sleep, we have difficulty concentrating, make mistakes in routine tasks, lose energy, and feel bad-tempered. There is a relationship between hours of sleep and death rate per year per 100,000 people. How many hours of sleep will put you in the group with the minimum death rate? In this section, we will answer this question by solving a system of linear equations with more than two variables.

1 Verify the solution of a system of linear equations in three variables.

Systems of Linear Equations in Three Variables and Their Solutions

An equation such as $x + 2y - 3z = 9$ is called a **linear equation in three variables.** In general, any equation of the form

$$Ax + By + Cz = D$$

where $A, B, C,$ and D are real numbers such that $A, B,$ and C are not all 0, is a linear equation in the variables $x, y,$ and z. The graph of this linear equation in three variables is a plane in three-dimensional space.

The process of solving a system of three linear equations in three variables is geometrically equivalent to finding the point of intersection (assuming that there is one) of three planes in space (see Figure 3.7). A **solution** to a system of linear equations in three variables is an ordered triple of real numbers that satisfies all equations of the system. The **solution set** of the system is the set of all its solutions.

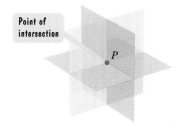

Point of intersection

P

Figure 3.7

EXAMPLE 1 **Determining Whether an Ordered Triple Satisfies a System**

Show that the ordered triple $(-1, 2, -2)$ is a solution of the system:

$$x + 2y - 3z = 9$$
$$2x - y + 2z = -8$$
$$-x + 3y - 4z = 15.$$

Solution Because -1 is the x-coordinate, 2 is the y-coordinate, and -2 is the z-coordinate of $(-1, 2, -2)$, we replace x with -1, y with 2, and z with -2 in each of the three equations.

$$x + 2y - 3z = 9$$
$$-1 + 2(2) - 3(-2) \overset{?}{=} 9$$
$$-1 + 4 + 6 \overset{?}{=} 9$$
$$9 = 9, \text{ true}$$

$$2x - y + 2z = -8$$
$$2(-1) - 2 + 2(-2) \overset{?}{=} -8$$
$$-2 - 2 - 4 \overset{?}{=} -8$$
$$-8 = -8, \text{ true}$$

$$-x + 3y - 4z = 15$$
$$-(-1) + 3(2) - 4(-2) \overset{?}{=} 15$$
$$1 + 6 + 8 \overset{?}{=} 15$$
$$15 = 15, \text{ true}$$

The ordered triple $(-1, 2, -2)$ satisfies the three equations: It makes each equation true. Thus, the ordered triple is a solution of the system.

Check Point 1 Show that the ordered triple $(-1, -4, 5)$ is a solution of the system:

$$x - 2y + 3z = 22$$
$$2x - 3y - z = 5$$
$$3x + y - 5z = -32.$$

2 Solve systems of linear equations in three variables.

Solving Systems of Linear Equations in Three Variables by Eliminating Variables

The method for solving a system of linear equations in three variables is similar to that used on systems of linear equations in two variables. We use addition to eliminate any variable, reducing the system to two equations in two variables. Once we obtain a system of two equations in two variables, we use addition or substitution to eliminate a variable. The result is a single equation in one variable. We solve this equation to get the value of the remaining variable. Other variable values are found by back-substitution.

Solving Linear Systems in Three Variables by Eliminating Variables

1. Reduce the system to two equations in two variables. This is usually accomplished by taking two different pairs of equations and using the addition method to eliminate the same variable from each pair.
2. Solve the resulting system of two equations in two variables using addition or substitution. The result is an equation in one variable that gives the value of that variable.
3. Back-substitute the value of the variable found in step 2 into either of the equations in two variables to find the value of the second variable.
4. Use the values of the two variables from steps 2 and 3 to find the value of the third variable by back-substituting into one of the original equations.
5. Check the proposed solution in each of the original equations.

EXAMPLE 2 **Solving a System in Three Variables**

Solve the system:

$$5x - 2y - 4z = 3 \quad \text{Equation 1}$$
$$3x + 3y + 2z = -3 \quad \text{Equation 2}$$
$$-2x + 5y + 3z = 3. \quad \text{Equation 3}$$

Solution There are many ways to proceed. Because our initial goal is to reduce the system to two equations in two variables, **the central idea is to take two different pairs of equations and eliminate the same variable from each pair.**

Step 1 **Reduce the system to two equations in two variables.** We choose any two equations and use the addition method to eliminate a variable. Let's eliminate z using Equations 1 and 2. We do so by multiplying Equation 2 by 2. Then we add equations.

$$
\begin{array}{lll}
(\text{Equation 1}) \;\; 5x - 2y - 4z = 3 & \xrightarrow{\;\text{No change}\;} & 5x - 2y - 4z = 3 \\
(\text{Equation 2}) \;\; 3x + 3y + 2z = -3 & \xrightarrow{\;\text{Multiply by 2.}\;} & 6x + 6y + 4z = -6 \\
& \text{Add:} & \overline{11x + 4y \quad\;\;\; = -3} \;\; \text{Equation 4}
\end{array}
$$

Now we must eliminate the *same* variable using another pair of equations. We can eliminate z from Equations 2 and 3. First, we multiply Equation 2 by -3. Next, we multiply Equation 3 by 2. Finally, we add equations.

$$
\begin{array}{lll}
(\text{Equation 2}) \;\;\;\; 3x + 3y + 2z = -3 & \xrightarrow{\;\text{Multiply by} -3.\;} & -9x - 9y - 6z = 9 \\
(\text{Equation 3}) \;\; -2x + 5y + 3z = 3 & \xrightarrow{\;\text{Multiply by 2.}\;} & -4x + 10y + 6z = 6 \\
& \text{Add:} & \overline{-13x + \quad y \quad\;\;\; = 15} \;\; \text{Equation 5}
\end{array}
$$

Equations 4 and 5 give us a system of two equations in two variables.

Step 2 **Solve the resulting system of two equations in two variables.** We will use the addition method to solve Equations 4 and 5 for x and y. To do so, we multiply Equation 5 on both sides by -4 and add this to Equation 4.

$$
\begin{array}{lll}
(\text{Equation 4}) \;\; 11x + 4y = -3 & \xrightarrow{\;\text{No change}\;} & 11x + 4y = -3 \\
(\text{Equation 5}) \;\; -13x + y = 15 & \xrightarrow{\;\text{Multiply by} -4.\;} & 52x - 4y = -60 \\
& \text{Add:} & \overline{63x \quad\quad\;\; = -63} \\
& & \quad\quad x \quad\;\; = -1 \quad \text{Divide both sides by 63.}
\end{array}
$$

Step 3 **Use back-substitution in one of the equations in two variables to find the value of the second variable.** We back-substitute -1 for x in either Equation 4 or 5 to find the value of y.

$$
\begin{aligned}
-13x + y &= 15 & \text{Equation 5} \\
-13(-1) + y &= 15 & \text{Substitute } -1 \text{ for x.} \\
13 + y &= 15 & \text{Multiply.} \\
y &= 2 & \text{Subtract 13 from both sides.}
\end{aligned}
$$

Step 4   Back-substitute the values found for two variables into one of the original equations to find the value of the third variable.   We can now use any one of the original equations and back-substitute the values of x and y to find the value for z. We will use Equation 2.

$$3x + 3y + 2z = -3 \quad \text{Equation 2}$$
$$3(-1) + 3(2) + 2z = -3 \quad \text{Substitute } -1 \text{ for } x \text{ and } 2 \text{ for } y.$$
$$3 + 2z = -3 \quad \text{Multiply and then add:}$$
$$3(-1) + 3(2) = -3 + 6 = 3.$$
$$2z = -6 \quad \text{Subtract 3 from both sides.}$$
$$z = -3 \quad \text{Divide both sides by 2.}$$

With $x = -1$, $y = 2$, and $z = -3$, the proposed solution is the ordered triple $(-1, 2, -3)$.

Step 5   Check.   Check the proposed solution, $(-1, 2, -3)$, by substituting the values for x, y, and z into each of the three original equations. These substitutions yield three true statements. Thus, the solution set is $\{(-1, 2, -3)\}$.

Check Point 2   Solve the system:

$$x + 4y - z = 20$$
$$3x + 2y + z = 8$$
$$2x - 3y + 2z = -16.$$

In some examples, one of the variables is already eliminated from a given equation. In this case, the same variable should be eliminated from the other two equations, thereby making it possible to omit one of the elimination steps. We illustrate this idea in Example 3.

EXAMPLE 3   Solving a System of Equations with a Missing Term

Solve the system:

$$x + \quad z = 8 \quad \text{Equation 1}$$
$$x + y + 2z = 17 \quad \text{Equation 2}$$
$$x + 2y + z = 16. \quad \text{Equation 3}$$

Solution

Step 1   Reduce the system to two equations in two variables.   Because Equation 1 contains only x and z, we could omit one of the elimination steps by eliminating y using Equations 2 and 3. This will give us two equations in x and z. To eliminate y using Equations 2 and 3, we multiply Equation 2 by -2 and add Equation 3.

(Equation 2) $x + y + 2z = 17$ $\xrightarrow{\text{Multiply by } -2.}$ $-2x - 2y - 4z = -34$
(Equation 3) $x + 2y + z = 16$ $\xrightarrow{\text{No change}}$ $x + 2y + z = 16$
$$\text{Add:} \quad -x \quad -3z = -18 \quad \text{Equation 4}$$

Equation 4 and the given Equation 1 provide us with a system of two equations in two variables.

$$x + \quad z = 8 \quad \text{Equation 1}$$
$$x + y + 2z = 17 \quad \text{Equation 2}$$
$$x + 2y + z = 16 \quad \text{Equation 3}$$

The system we are solving, repeated

Step 2   Solve the resulting system of two equations in two variables.   We will solve Equations 1 and 4 for x and z.

$$
\begin{array}{rl}
x + z = 8 & \text{Equation 1} \\
-x - 3z = -18 & \text{Equation 4} \\
\hline
\text{Add:} \quad -2z = -10 & \\
z = 5 & \text{Divide both sides by } -2.
\end{array}
$$

Step 3   Use back-substitution in one of the equations in two variables to find the value of the second variable.   To find x, we back-substitute 5 for z in either Equation 1 or 4. We will use Equation 1.

$$
\begin{array}{rl}
x + z = 8 & \text{Equation 1} \\
x + 5 = 8 & \text{Substitute 5 for z.} \\
x = 3 & \text{Subtract 5 from both sides.}
\end{array}
$$

Step 4   Back-substitute the values found for two variables into one of the original equations to find the value of the third variable.   To find y, we back-substitute 3 for x and 5 for z into Equation 2 or 3. We can't use Equation 1 because y is missing in this equation. We will use Equation 2.

$$
\begin{array}{rl}
x + y + 2z = 17 & \text{Equation 2} \\
3 + y + 2(5) = 17 & \text{Substitute 3 for x and 5 for z.} \\
y + 13 = 17 & \text{Multiply and add.} \\
y = 4 & \text{Subtract 13 from both sides.}
\end{array}
$$

We found that $z = 5$, $x = 3$, and $y = 4$. Thus, the proposed solution is the ordered triple $(3, 4, 5)$.

Step 5   Check.   Substituting 3 for x, 4 for y, and 5 for z into each of the three original equations yields three true statements. Consequently, the solution set is $\{(3, 4, 5)\}$.

Check Point 3   Solve the system:

$$
\begin{array}{rl}
2y - z = 7 \\
x + 2y + z = 17 \\
2x - 3y + 2z = -1.
\end{array}
$$

A system of linear equations in three variables represents three planes. The three planes need not intersect at one point. The planes may have no common point of intersection and represent an inconsistent system with no solution. By contrast, the planes may coincide or intersect along a line. In these cases, the planes have infinitely many points in common and represent systems with infinitely many solutions.

3   Solve problems using systems in three variables.

Applications

Systems of equations may allow us to find models for data without using a graphing utility. Three data points that do not lie on or near a line determine the graph of a quadratic function of the form $y = ax^2 + bx + c$, $a \neq 0$. Quadratic functions often model situations in which values of y are decreasing and then increasing, suggesting the cuplike shape of a parabola.

EXAMPLE 4 Modeling Data Relating Sleep and Death Rate

In a study relating sleep and death rate, the following data were obtained. Use the function $y = ax^2 + bx + c$ to model the data.

x (Average Number of Hours of Sleep)	y (Death Rate per Year per 100,000 Males)
4	1682
7	626
9	967

Solution   We need to find values for a, b, and c in $y = ax^2 + bx + c$. We can do so by solving a system of three linear equations in a, b, and c. We obtain the three equations by using the values of x and y from the data as follows:

$y = ax^2 + bx + c$ Use the quadratic function to model the data.

When $x = 4$, $y = 1682$: $1682 = a \cdot 4^2 + b \cdot 4 + c$ or $16a + 4b + c = 1682$
When $x = 7$, $y = 626$: $626 = a \cdot 7^2 + b \cdot 7 + c$ or $49a + 7b + c = 626$
When $x = 9$, $y = 967$: $967 = a \cdot 9^2 + b \cdot 9 + c$ or $81a + 9b + c = 967$.

The easiest way to solve this system is to eliminate c from two pairs of equations, obtaining two equations in a and b. Solving this system gives $a = 104.5$, $b = -1501.5$, and $c = 6016$. We now substitute the values for a, b, and c into $y = ax^2 + bx + c$. The function that models the given data is

$$y = 104.5x^2 - 1501.5x + 6016.$$

We can use the model that we obtained in Example 4 to find the death rate of males who average, say, 6 hours of sleep. First, write the model in function notation:

$$f(x) = 104.5x^2 - 1501.5x + 6016.$$

Substitute 6 for x:

$$f(6) = 104.5(6)^2 - 1501.5(6) + 6016 = 769.$$

According to the model, the death rate for males who average 6 hours of sleep is 769 deaths per 100,000 males.

Technology

The graph of

$y = 104.5x^2 - 1501.5x + 6016$

is displayed in a [3, 12, 1] by [500, 2000, 100] viewing rectangle. The minimum function feature shows that the lowest point on the graph, the vertex, is approximately (7.2, 622.5). Men who average 7.2 hours of sleep are in the group with the lowest death rate, approximately 622.5 per 100,000.

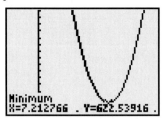

Minimum
X=7.212766 . Y=622.53916 .

Check Point 4   Find the quadratic function $y = ax^2 + bx + c$ whose graph passes through the points $(1, 4)$, $(2, 1)$, and $(3, 4)$.

EXERCISE SET 3.2

Practice Exercises

In Exercises 1–4, determine if the given ordered triple is a solution of the system.

1. $x + y + z = 4$
$x - 2y - z = 1$
$2x - y - 2z = -1$
$(2, -1, 3)$

2. $x + y + z = 0$
$x + 2y - 3z = 5$
$3x + 4y + 2z = -1$
$(5, -3, -2)$

3. $x - 2y = 2$
$2x + 3y = 11$
$ y - 4z = -7$
$(4, 1, 2)$

4. $x - 2z = -5$
$ y - 3z = -3$
$2x - z = -4$
$(-1, 3, 2)$

Solve each system in Exercises 5–18.

5. $x + y + 2z = 11$
$x + y + 3z = 14$
$x + 2y - z = 5$

6. $2x + y - 2z = -1$
$3x - 3y - z = 5$
$x - 2y + 3z = 6$

7. $4x - y + 2z = 11$
$x + 2y - z = -1$
$2x + 2y - 3z = -1$

8. $x - y + 3z = 8$
$3x + y - 2z = -2$
$2x + 4y + z = 0$

9. $3x + 5y + 2z = 0$
$12x - 15y + 4z = 12$
$6x - 25y - 8z = 8$

10. $2x + 3y + 7z = 13$
$3x + 2y - 5z = -22$
$5x + 7y - 3z = -28$

11. $2x - 4y + 3z = 17$
$x + 2y - z = 0$
$4x - y - z = 6$

12. $x + z = 3$
$x + 2y - z = 1$
$2x - y + z = 3$

13. $2x + y = 2$
$x + y - z = 4$
$3x + 2y + z = 0$

14. $x + 3y + 5z = 20$
$y - 4z = -16$
$3x - 2y + 9z = 36$

15. $x + y = -4$
$y - z = 1$
$2x + y + 3z = -21$

16. $x + y = 4$
$x + z = 4$
$y + z = 4$

17. $3(2x + y) + 5z = -1$
$2(x - 3y + 4z) = -9$
$4(1 + x) = -3(z - 3y)$

18. $7z - 3 = 2(x - 3y)$
$5y + 3z - 7 = 4x$
$4 + 5z = 3(2x - y)$

In Exercises 19–20, let x represent the first number, y the second number, and z the third number. Use the given conditions to write a system of equations. Solve the system and find the numbers.

19. The sum of three numbers is 16. The sum of twice the first number, 3 times the second number, and 4 times the third number is 46. The difference between 5 times the first number and the second number is 31. Find the three numbers.

20. The following is known about three numbers: Three times the first number plus the second number plus twice the third number is 5. If 3 times the second number is subtracted from the sum of the first number and 3 times the third number, the result is 2. If the third number is subtracted from 2 times the first number and 3 times the second number, the result is 1. Find the numbers.

In Exercises 21–24, find the quadratic function $y = ax^2 + bx + c$ whose graph passes through the given points.

21. $(-1, 6), (1, 4), (2, 9)$

22. $(-2, 7), (1, -2), (2, 3)$

23. $(-1, -4), (1, -2), (2, 5)$

24. $(1, 3), (3, -1), (4, 0)$

Application Exercises

25. The bar graph shows that the number of gays discharged from the military decreased from 1998 to 1999 and increased from 1999 to 2000.

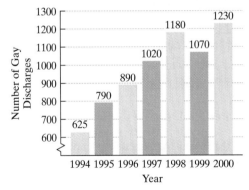

Number of Gay Discharges from the Military Under "Don't Ask, Don't Tell"

Source: New York Times

a. Write the data for 1998, 1999, and 2000 as ordered pairs (x, y), where x is the number of years after 1998 and y is the number of gay discharges from the military.

b. The three data points in part (a) can be modeled by the quadratic function $y = ax^2 + bx + c$. Substitute each ordered pair into this function, one ordered pair at a time, and write a system of three linear equations in three variables that can be used to find values for $a, b,$ and c.

c. Solve the system in part (b). Then write the quadratic function that models the data for 1998 through 2000.

26. The bar graph shows that the percentage of the U.S. population that was foreign-born decreased between 1940 and 1970 and then increased between 1970 and 2000.

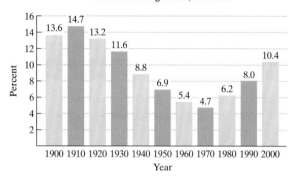

Percentage of U.S. Population That Was Foreign-Born, 1900-2000

Source: U.S. Census Bureau

a. Write the data for 1940, 1970, and 2000 as ordered pairs (x, y), where x is the number of years after 1940 and y is the percentage of the U.S. population that was foreign-born in that year.

b. The three data points in part (a) can be modeled by the quadratic function $y = ax^2 + bx + c$. Substitute each ordered pair into this function, one ordered pair at a time, and write a system of linear equations in three variables that can be used to find values for a, b, and c.

c. Solve the system in part (b). Then write the quadratic function that models the data for 1940 through 2000.

27. You throw a ball straight up from a rooftop. The ball misses the rooftop on its way down and eventually strikes the ground. A mathematical model can be used to describe the relationship for the ball's height above the ground, y, after x seconds. Consider the following data:

x, seconds after the ball is thrown	y, ball's height, in feet, above the ground
1	224
3	176
4	104

a. Find the quadratic function $y = ax^2 + bx + c$ whose graph passes through the given points.

b. Use the function in part (a) to find the value for y when $x = 5$. Describe what this means.

28. A mathematical model can be used to describe the relationship between the number of feet a car travels once the brakes are applied, y, and the number of seconds the car is in motion after the brakes are applied, x. A research firm collects the following data:

x, seconds in motion after brakes are applied	y, feet car travels once the brakes are applied
1	46
2	84
3	114

a. Find the quadratic function $y = ax^2 + bx + c$ whose graph passes through the given points.

b. Use the function in part (a) to find the value for y when $x = 6$. Describe what this means.

Use a system of linear equations in three variables to solve Exercises 29–35.

29. In current U.S. dollars, John D. Rockefeller's 1913 fortune of $900 million would be worth about $189 billion. The bar graph shows that Rockefeller is the wealthiest among the world's five richest people of all time. The combined estimated wealth, in current billions of U.S. dollars, of Andrew Carnegie, Cornelius Vanderbilt, and Bill Gates is $256 billion. The difference between Carnegie's estimated wealth and Vanderbilt's is $4 billion. The difference between Vanderbilt's estimated wealth and Gate's is $36 billion. Find the estimated wealth, in current billions of U.S. dollars, of Carnegie, Vanderbilt, and Gates.

The Richest People of All Time Estimated Wealth, in Current Billions of U.S. Dollars

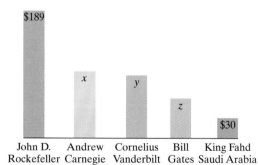

Source: Scholastic Book of World Records

30. The circle graph indicates computers in use for the United States and the rest of the world. The percentage of the world's computers in Europe and Japan combined is 13% less than the percentage of the world's computers in the United States. If the percentage of the world's computers in Europe is doubled, it is only 3% more than the percentage of the world's computers in the United States. Find the percentage of the world's computers in the United States, Europe, and Japan.

Percentage of the World's Computers: U.S. and the World

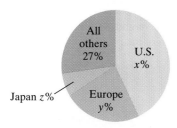

Source: Jupiter Communications

31. At a college production of *Evita*, 400 tickets were sold. The ticket prices were $8, $10, and $12, and the total income from ticket sales was $3700. How many tickets of each type were sold if the combined number of $8 and $10 tickets sold was 7 times the number of $12 tickets sold?

32. A certain brand of razor blades comes in packages of 6, 12, and 24 blades, costing $2, $3, and $4 per package, respectively. A store sold 12 packages containing a total of 162 razor blades and took in $35. How many packages of each type were sold?

33. A person invested $6700 for one year, part at 8%, part at 10%, and the remainder at 12%. The total annual income from these investments was $716. The amount of money invested at 12% was $300 more than the amount invested at 8% and 10% combined. Find the amount invested at each rate.

34. A person invested $17,000 for one year, part at 10%, part at 12%, and the remainder at 15%. The total annual income from these investments was $2110. The amount of money invested at 12% was $1000 less than the amount invested at 10% and 15% combined. Find the amount invested at each rate.

35. Find the measures of the angles marked $x°$, $y°$, and $z°$ in the following triangle.

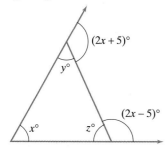

Writing in Mathematics

36. What is a system of linear equations in three variables?

37. How do you determine whether a given ordered triple is a solution of a system in three variables?

38. Describe in general terms how to solve a system in three variables.

39. AIDS is taking a deadly toll on southern Africa. Describe how to use the techniques that you learned in this section to obtain a model for African life span using projections with AIDS. Let x represent the number of years after 1985 and let y represent African life span in that year.

African Life Span

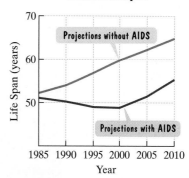

Source: United Nations

Technology Exercises

40. Does your graphing utility have a feature that allows you to solve linear systems by entering coefficients and constant terms? If so, use this feature to verify the solutions to any five exercises that you worked by hand from Exercises 5–16.

41. Verify your results in Exercises 21–24 by using a graphing utility to graph the resulting parabola. Trace along the curve and convince yourself that the three points given in the exercise lie on the parabola.

42. Some graphing utilities will do three-dimensional graphing. For example, on the TI-92, press MODE, go to GRAPH, press the arrow to the right, select 3D, then ENTER. When you display the Y = screen, you will see the equations are functions of x and y. Thus, you must solve each of a linear system's equations for z before entering the equation. For example,

$$x + y + z = 19$$

is solved for z, giving

$$z = 19 - x - y.$$

(Consult your manual.) If your utility does three-dimensional graphing, graph five of the systems in Exercises 5–16 and trace along the planes to find their common point of intersection.

Critical Thinking Exercises

43. Describe how the system

$$x + y - z - 2w = -8$$
$$x - 2y + 3z + w = 18$$
$$2x + 2y + 2z - 2w = 10$$
$$2x + y - z + w = 3$$

could be solved. Is it likely that in the near future a graphing utility will be available to provide a geometric solution (using intersecting graphs) to this system? Explain.

44. A modernistic painting consists of triangles, rectangles, and pentagons, all drawn so as to not overlap or share sides. Within each rectangle are drawn 2 red roses, and each pentagon contains 5 carnations. How many triangles, rectangles, and pentagons appear in the painting if the painting contains a total of 40 geometric figures, 153 sides of geometric figures, and 72 flowers?

Group Exercise

45. Group members should develop appropriate functions that model each of the projections shown in Exercise 39.

SECTION 3.3 Matrix Solutions to Linear Systems

Objectives

1. Write the augmented matrix for a linear system.
2. Perform matrix row operations.
3. Use matrices and Gaussian elimination to solve systems.
4. Use matrices and Gauss-Jordan elimination to solve systems.

Yes, we overindulged, but it was delicious. Anyway, a few hours of moderate activity and we'll just burn off those extra calories. The following chart should help. We see that the number of calories burned per hour depends on our weight. Four hours of tennis and we'll be as good as new!

How Fast You Burn Off Calories

Activity	Weight (pounds)					
	110	132	154	176	187	209
	Calories Burned per Hour for a Given Weight					
Housework	175	210	245	285	300	320
Cycling	190	215	245	270	280	295
Tennis	335	380	425	470	495	520
Watching TV	60	70	80	85	90	95

The 24 numbers inside the red brackets are arranged in four rows and six columns. This rectangular array of 24 numbers, arranged in rows and columns and placed in brackets, is an example of a **matrix** (plural: **matrices**). The numbers inside the brackets are called **elements** of the matrix. Matrices are used to display information and to solve systems of linear equations. Because systems involving two equations in two variables can easily be solved by substitution or addition, we will focus on matrix solutions to systems of linear equations in three or more variables.

1 Write the augmented matrix for a linear system.

Solving Linear Systems by Using Matrices

A matrix gives us a shortened way of writing a system of equations. The first step in solving a system of linear equations using matrices is to write the augmented matrix. An **augmented matrix** has a vertical bar separating the columns of the matrix into two groups. The coefficients of each variable are placed to the left of the vertical line, and the constants are placed to the right. If any variable is missing, its coefficient is 0.

System of Linear Equations	Augmented Matrix

$$
\begin{aligned}
3x + y + 2z &= 31 \\
x + y + 2z &= 19 \\
x + 3y + 2z &= 25
\end{aligned}
\qquad
\left[\begin{array}{ccc|c}
3 & 1 & 2 & 31 \\
1 & 1 & 2 & 19 \\
1 & 3 & 2 & 25
\end{array}\right]
$$

$$
\begin{aligned}
x + 2y - 5z &= -19 \\
y + 3z &= 9 \\
z &= 4
\end{aligned}
\qquad
\left[\begin{array}{ccc|c}
1 & 2 & -5 & -19 \\
0 & 1 & 3 & 9 \\
0 & 0 & 1 & 4
\end{array}\right]
$$

Notice how the second matrix contains 1s down the diagonal from upper left to lower right and 0s below the 1s. This arrangement makes it easy to find the solution of the system of equations, as Example 1 shows.

EXAMPLE 1   Solving a System Using a Matrix

Write the solution set for a system of equations represented by the matrix

$$
\left[\begin{array}{ccc|c}
1 & 2 & -5 & -19 \\
0 & 1 & 3 & 9 \\
0 & 0 & 1 & 4
\end{array}\right].
$$

Solution   The system represented by the given matrix is

$$
\left[\begin{array}{ccc|c}
1 & 2 & -5 & -19 \\
0 & 1 & 3 & 9 \\
0 & 0 & 1 & 4
\end{array}\right]
\rightarrow
\begin{aligned}
1x + 2y - 5z &= -19 \\
0x + 1y + 3z &= 9 \\
0x + 0y + 1z &= 4
\end{aligned}.
$$

This system can be simplified as follows.

$$
\begin{aligned}
x + 2y - 5z &= -19 & &\text{Equation 1} \\
y + 3z &= 9 & &\text{Equation 2} \\
z &= 4 & &\text{Equation 3}
\end{aligned}
$$

The value of z is known. We can find y by back-substitution.

$$
\begin{aligned}
y + 3z &= 9 & &\text{Equation 2} \\
y + 3(4) &= 9 & &\text{Substitute 4 for z.} \\
y + 12 &= 9 & &\text{Multiply.} \\
y &= -3 & &\text{Subtract 12 from both sides.}
\end{aligned}
$$

With values for y and z, we can now use back-substitution to find x.

$$x + 2y - 5z = -19 \qquad \text{Equation 1}$$
$$x + 2(-3) - 5(4) = -19 \qquad \text{Substitute } -3 \text{ for } y \text{ and } 4 \text{ for } z.$$
$$x - 6 - 20 = -19 \qquad \text{Multiply.}$$
$$x - 26 = -19 \qquad \text{Add.}$$
$$x = 7 \qquad \text{Add 26 to both sides.}$$

We see that $x = 7$, $y = -3$, and $z = 4$. The solution set for the system is $\{(7, -3, 4)\}$.

Check Point 1 Write the solution set for a system of equations represented by the matrix

$$\begin{bmatrix} 1 & -1 & 1 & \bigm| & 8 \\ 0 & 1 & -12 & \bigm| & -15 \\ 0 & 0 & 1 & \bigm| & 1 \end{bmatrix}.$$

Our goal in solving a system of linear equations in three variables using matrices is to produce a matrix similar to the one in Example 1. In general, the matrix will be of the form

$$\begin{bmatrix} 1 & a & b & \bigm| & c \\ 0 & 1 & d & \bigm| & e \\ 0 & 0 & 1 & \bigm| & f \end{bmatrix}$$

where a through f represent real numbers. The third row of this matrix gives us the value of one variable. The other variables can then be found by back-substitution.

A matrix with 1s down the diagonal from upper left to lower right and 0s below the 1s is said to be in **row-echelon form.** How do we produce a matrix in this form? We use **row operations** on the augmented matrix. These row operations are just like what you did when solving a linear system by the addition method. The difference is that we no longer write the variables, usually represented by x, y, and z.

2 Perform matrix row operations.

Matrix Row Operations

These row operations produce matrices that lead to systems with the same solution set as the original system.

1. Two rows of a matrix may be interchanged. This is the same as interchanging two equations in the linear system.
2. The elements in any row may be multiplied by a nonzero number. This is the same as multiplying both sides of an equation by a nonzero number.
3. The elements in any row may be multiplied by a nonzero number, and these products may be added to the corresponding elements in any other row. This is the same as multiplying both sides of an equation by a nonzero number and then adding equations to eliminate a variable.

Two matrices are **row equivalent** if one can be obtained from the other by a sequence of row operations.

Study Tip

When performing the row operation

$$kR_i + R_j$$

we use row i to find the products. However, **elements in row i do not change. It is the elements in row j that change:** Add k times the elements in row i to the corresponding elements in row j. Replace elements in row j by these sums.

Study Tip

As you read the solution, keep looking back at the given matrix.

$$\begin{bmatrix} 3 & 18 & -12 & | & 21 \\ 1 & 2 & -3 & | & 5 \\ -2 & -3 & 4 & | & -6 \end{bmatrix}$$

Each matrix row operation in the preceding box can be expressed symbolically as follows:

1. Interchange the elements in the ith and jth rows: $R_i \leftrightarrow R_j$.
2. Multiply each element in the ith row by k: kR_i.
3. Add k times the elements in row i to the corresponding elements in row j: $kR_i + R_j$.

EXAMPLE 2   Performing Matrix Row Operations

Use the matrix

$$\begin{bmatrix} 3 & 18 & -12 & | & 21 \\ 1 & 2 & -3 & | & 5 \\ -2 & -3 & 4 & | & -6 \end{bmatrix}$$

and perform each indicated row operation:

a. $R_1 \leftrightarrow R_2$ **b.** $\frac{1}{3}R_1$ **c.** $2R_2 + R_3$.

Solution

a. The notation $R_1 \leftrightarrow R_2$ means to interchange the elements in row 1 and row 2. This results in the row-equivalent matrix

$$\begin{bmatrix} 1 & 2 & -3 & | & 5 \\ 3 & 18 & -12 & | & 21 \\ -2 & -3 & 4 & | & -6 \end{bmatrix}$$

This was row 2; now it's row 1.
This was row 1; now it's row 2.

b. The notation $\frac{1}{3}R_1$ means to multiply each element in row 1 by $\frac{1}{3}$. This results in the row-equivalent matrix

$$\begin{bmatrix} \frac{1}{3}(3) & \frac{1}{3}(18) & \frac{1}{3}(-12) & | & \frac{1}{3}(21) \\ 1 & 2 & -3 & | & 5 \\ -2 & -3 & 4 & | & -6 \end{bmatrix} = \begin{bmatrix} 1 & 6 & -4 & | & 7 \\ 1 & 2 & -3 & | & 5 \\ -2 & -3 & 4 & | & -6 \end{bmatrix}$$

c. The notation $2R_2 + R_3$ means to add 2 times the elements in row 2 to the corresponding elements in row 3. Replace the elements in row 3 by these sums. First, we find 2 times the elements in row 2:

$$2(1) \text{ or } 2, \quad 2(2) \text{ or } 4, \quad 2(-3) \text{ or } -6, \quad 2(5) \text{ or } 10.$$

Now we add these products to the corresponding elements in row 3. Although we use row 2 to find the products, row 2 does not change. It is the elements in row 3 that change, resulting in the row-equivalent matrix

$$\begin{bmatrix} 3 & 18 & -12 & | & 21 \\ 1 & 2 & -3 & | & 5 \\ -2+2=0 & -3+4=1 & 4+(-6)=-2 & | & -6+10=4 \end{bmatrix}$$

$$= \begin{bmatrix} 3 & 18 & -12 & | & 21 \\ 1 & 2 & -3 & | & 5 \\ 0 & 1 & -2 & | & 4 \end{bmatrix}.$$

Check Point 2

Use the matrix

$$\begin{bmatrix} 4 & 12 & -20 & | & 8 \\ 1 & 6 & -3 & | & 7 \\ -3 & -2 & 1 & | & -9 \end{bmatrix}$$

and perform each indicated row operation:

a. $R_1 \leftrightarrow R_2$ **b.** $\frac{1}{4}R_1$ **c.** $3R_2 + R_3$.

3 Use matrices and Gaussian elimination to solve systems.

The process that we use to solve linear systems using matrix row operations is called **Gaussian elimination,** after the German mathematician Carl Friedrich Gauss (1777–1855). Here are the steps used in Gaussian elimination:

Solving Linear Systems Using Gaussian Elimination

1. Write the augmented matrix for the system.
2. Use matrix row operations to simplify the matrix to one with 1s down the diagonal from upper left to lower right, and 0s below the 1s.

$$\begin{bmatrix} 1 & * & * & | & * \\ * & * & * & | & * \\ * & * & * & | & * \end{bmatrix} \rightarrow \begin{bmatrix} 1 & * & * & | & * \\ 0 & * & * & | & * \\ 0 & * & * & | & * \end{bmatrix} \rightarrow \begin{bmatrix} 1 & * & * & | & * \\ 0 & 1 & * & | & * \\ 0 & * & * & | & * \end{bmatrix} \rightarrow \begin{bmatrix} 1 & * & * & | & * \\ 0 & 1 & * & | & * \\ 0 & 0 & * & | & * \end{bmatrix} \rightarrow \begin{bmatrix} 1 & * & * & | & * \\ 0 & 1 & * & | & * \\ 0 & 0 & 1 & | & * \end{bmatrix}$$

Get 1 in the upper left-hand corner.

Use the 1 in the first column to get 0s below it.

Get 1 in the second row, second column position.

Use the 1 in the second column to get 0 below it.

Get 1 in the third row, third column position.

3. Write the system of linear equations corresponding to the matrix in step 2, and use back-substitution to find the system's solution.

EXAMPLE 3 Gaussian Elimination with Back-Substitution

Use matrices to solve the system:

$$3x + y + 2z = 31$$
$$x + y + 2z = 19$$
$$x + 3y + 2z = 25.$$

Solution

Step 1 Write the augmented matrix for the system.

Linear System

$$3x + y + 2z = 31$$
$$x + y + 2z = 19$$
$$x + 3y + 2z = 25$$

Augmented Matrix

$$\begin{bmatrix} 3 & 1 & 2 & | & 31 \\ 1 & 1 & 2 & | & 19 \\ 1 & 3 & 2 & | & 25 \end{bmatrix}$$

Step 2 Use matrix row operations to simplify the matrix to one with 1s down the diagonal from upper left to lower right, and 0s below the 1s. Our goal is to obtain a matrix of the form

$$\left[\begin{array}{ccc|c} 1 & a & b & c \\ 0 & 1 & d & e \\ 0 & 0 & 1 & f \end{array}\right].$$

Our first step in achieving this goal is to get 1 in the top position of the first column.

We want 1 in this position.
$$\left[\begin{array}{ccc|c} 3 & 1 & 2 & 31 \\ 1 & 1 & 2 & 19 \\ 1 & 3 & 2 & 25 \end{array}\right]$$

To get 1 in this position, we interchange rows 1 and 2. $R_1 \leftrightarrow R_2$. (We could also interchange rows 1 and 3 to attain our goal.)

$$\left[\begin{array}{ccc|c} 1 & 1 & 2 & 19 \\ 3 & 1 & 2 & 31 \\ 1 & 3 & 2 & 25 \end{array}\right]$$
This was row 2; now it's row 1.
This was row 1; now it's row 2.

Now we want to get 0s below the 1 in the first column.

We want 0 in these positions.
$$\left[\begin{array}{ccc|c} 1 & 1 & 2 & 19 \\ 3 & 1 & 2 & 31 \\ 1 & 3 & 2 & 25 \end{array}\right]$$

To get a 0 where there is now a 3, multiply the top row of numbers by -3 and add these products to the second row of numbers: $-3R_1 + R_2$. To get a 0 where there is now a 1, multiply the top row of numbers multiplied by -1 and add these products to the third row of numbers: $-1R_1 + R_3$. Although we are using row 1 to find the products, the numbers in row 1 do not change.

$-3R_1 + R_2$
$-1R_1 + R_3$
$$\left[\begin{array}{ccc|c} 1 & 1 & 2 & 19 \\ -3(1)+3 & -3(1)+1 & -3(2)+2 & -3(19)+31 \\ -1(1)+1 & -1(1)+3 & -1(2)+2 & -1(19)+25 \end{array}\right]$$

$$= \left[\begin{array}{ccc|c} 1 & 1 & 2 & 19 \\ 0 & -2 & -4 & -26 \\ 0 & 2 & 0 & 6 \end{array}\right]$$

We move on to the second column. We want 1 in the second row, second column.

We want 1 in this position.
$$\left[\begin{array}{ccc|c} 1 & 1 & 2 & 19 \\ 0 & -2 & -4 & -26 \\ 0 & 2 & 0 & 6 \end{array}\right]$$

To get 1 in the desired position, we multiply -2 by its reciprocal, $-\frac{1}{2}$. Therefore, we multiply all the numbers in the second row by $-\frac{1}{2}$: $-\frac{1}{2} R_2$.

$$-\frac{1}{2} R_2 \quad \begin{bmatrix} 1 & 1 & 2 & \bigm| & 19 \\ -\frac{1}{2}(0) & -\frac{1}{2}(-2) & -\frac{1}{2}(-4) & \bigm| & -\frac{1}{2}(-26) \\ 0 & 2 & 0 & \bigm| & 6 \end{bmatrix} = \begin{bmatrix} 1 & 1 & 2 & \bigm| & 19 \\ 0 & 1 & 2 & \bigm| & 13 \\ 0 & 2 & 0 & \bigm| & 6 \end{bmatrix}.$$

We want 0 in this position.

We are not yet done with the second column. The voice balloon shows that we want to get a 0 where there is now a 2. If we multiply the second row of numbers by -2 and add these products to the third row of numbers, we will get 0 in this position: $-2R_2 + R_3$. Although we are using the numbers in row 2 to find the products, the numbers in row 2 do not change.

$$-2R_2 + R_3 \quad \begin{bmatrix} 1 & 1 & 2 & \bigm| & 19 \\ 0 & 1 & 2 & \bigm| & 13 \\ -2(0) + 0 & -2(1) + 2 & -2(2) + 0 & \bigm| & -2(13) + 6 \end{bmatrix} = \begin{bmatrix} 1 & 1 & 2 & \bigm| & 19 \\ 0 & 1 & 2 & \bigm| & 13 \\ 0 & 0 & -4 & \bigm| & -20 \end{bmatrix}$$

We move on to the third column. We want 1 in the third row, third column.

We want 1 in this position.

$$\begin{bmatrix} 1 & 1 & 2 & \bigm| & 19 \\ 0 & 1 & 2 & \bigm| & 13 \\ 0 & 0 & -4 & \bigm| & -20 \end{bmatrix}$$

To get 1 in the desired position, we multiply -4 by its reciprocal, $-\frac{1}{4}$. Therefore, we multiply all the numbers in the third row by $-\frac{1}{4}$: $-\frac{1}{4} R_3$.0

$$-\frac{1}{4} R_3 \quad \begin{bmatrix} 1 & 1 & 2 & \bigm| & 19 \\ 0 & 1 & 2 & \bigm| & 13 \\ -\frac{1}{4}(0) & -\frac{1}{4}(0) & -\frac{1}{4}(-4) & \bigm| & -\frac{1}{4}(-20) \end{bmatrix} = \begin{bmatrix} 1 & 1 & 2 & \bigm| & 19 \\ 0 & 1 & 2 & \bigm| & 13 \\ 0 & 0 & 1 & \bigm| & 5 \end{bmatrix}$$

We now have the desired matrix with 1s down the diagonal and 0s below the 1s.

Step 3 Write the system of linear equations corresponding to the matrix in step 2, and use back-substitution to find the system's solution. The system represented by the matrix in step 2 is

$$\begin{bmatrix} 1 & 1 & 2 & \bigm| & 19 \\ 0 & 1 & 2 & \bigm| & 13 \\ 0 & 0 & 1 & \bigm| & 5 \end{bmatrix} \rightarrow \begin{array}{l} 1x + 1y + 2z = 19 \\ 0x + 1y + 2z = 13 \\ 0x + 0y + 1z = 5 \end{array} \quad \text{or} \quad \begin{array}{r} x + y + 2z = 19 \\ y + 2z = 13. \\ z = 5 \end{array}$$

We immediately see that the value for z is 5. To find y, we back-substitute 5 for z in the second equation.

$$y + 2z = 13 \qquad \text{Equation 2}$$

$$y + 2(5) = 13 \qquad \text{Substitute 5 for z.}$$

$$y = 3 \qquad \text{Solve for y.}$$

Technology

Most graphing utilities can convert an augmented matrix to one with 1s down the diagonal from upper left to lower right, and 0s below the 1s. Recall that this is called row-echelon form. However, row-echelon form is not unique. Your graphing utility might give a row-echelon form different from the one you obtained by hand. However, all row-echelon forms for a given system's augmented matrix produce the same solution to the system. Enter the augmented matrix and name it A. Then use the $\boxed{\text{REF}}$ (row-echelon form) command on matrix A.

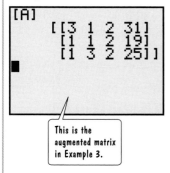

```
[A]
    [[3 1 2 31]
     [1 1 2 19]
     [1 3 2 25]]
■
```

This is the augmented matrix in Example 3.

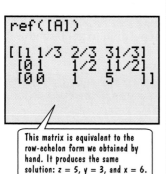

```
ref([A])
[[1 1/3 2/3 31/3]
 [0 1   1/2 11/2]
 [0 0   1   5   ]]
```

This matrix is equivalent to the row-echelon form we obtained by hand. It produces the same solution: $z = 5$, $y = 3$, and $x = 6$.

Finally, back-substitute 3 for y and 5 for z in the first equation:

$$x + y + 2z = 19 \quad \text{Equation 1}$$
$$x + 3 + 2(5) = 19 \quad \text{Substitute 3 for y and 5 for z.}$$
$$x + 13 = 19 \quad \text{Multiply and add.}$$
$$x = 6 \quad \text{Subtract 13 from both sides.}$$

The solution set for the original system is $\{(6, 3, 5)\}$. Check to see that the solution satisfies all three equations in the given system.

Check Point 3 Use matrices to solve the system:

$$2x + y + 2z = 18$$
$$x - y + 2z = 9$$
$$x + 2y - z = 6.$$

Modern supercomputers are capable of solving systems with more than 600,000 variables. The augmented matrices for such systems are huge, but the solution using matrices is exactly like what we did in Example 3. Work with the augmented matrix, one column at a time. First, get 1 in the desired position. Then get 0s below the 1. Let's see how this works for a linear system involving four equations in four variables.

EXAMPLE 4 Gaussian Elimination with Back-Substitution

Use matrices to solve the system:

$$2w + x + 3y - z = 6$$
$$w - x + 2y - 2z = -1$$
$$w - x - y + z = -4$$
$$-w + 2x - 2y - z = -7.$$

Solution

Step 1 Write the augmented matrix for the system.

Linear System	Augmented Matrix

$$
\begin{array}{rrrrr}
2w + & x + 3y - & z = & 6 \\
w - & x + 2y - 2z = & -1 \\
w - & x - & y + & z = & -4 \\
-w + 2x - 2y - & z = & -7
\end{array}
\qquad
\left[\begin{array}{rrrr|r}
2 & 1 & 3 & -1 & 6 \\
1 & -1 & 2 & -2 & -1 \\
1 & -1 & -1 & 1 & -4 \\
-1 & 2 & -2 & -1 & -7
\end{array}\right]
$$

Step 2 Use matrix row operations to simplify the matrix to one with 1s down the diagonal from upper left to lower right, and 0s below the 1s. Working one column at a time, we must obtain 1 in the diagonal position. Then we use this 1 to get 0s below it. Thus, our first step in achieving this goal is to get 1 in the top position of the first column. To do this, we interchange rows 1 and 2: $R_1 \leftrightarrow R_2$.

We want 0s in these positions.

$$\begin{bmatrix} 1 & -1 & 2 & -2 & | & -1 \\ 2 & 1 & 3 & -1 & | & 6 \\ 1 & -1 & -1 & 1 & | & -4 \\ -1 & 2 & -2 & -1 & | & -7 \end{bmatrix}$$

This was row 2; now it's row 1.

This was row 1; now it's row 2.

Now we use the 1 at the top of the first column to get 0s below it.

Use the previous matrix and:

Replace row 2 by $-2R_1 + R_2$.

Replace row 3 by $-1R_1 + R_3$.

Replace row 4 by $1R_1 + R_4$.

$$\begin{bmatrix} 1 & -1 & 2 & -2 & | & -1 \\ 0 & 3 & -1 & 3 & | & 8 \\ 0 & 0 & -3 & 3 & | & -3 \\ 0 & 1 & 0 & -3 & | & -8 \end{bmatrix}$$

We want 1 in this position.

We move on to the second column. We can obtain 1 in the desired position by multiplying the numbers in the second row by $\frac{1}{3}$, the reciprocal of 3.

$$\begin{bmatrix} 1 & -1 & 2 & -2 & | & -1 \\ \frac{1}{3}(0) & \frac{1}{3}(3) & \frac{1}{3}(-1) & \frac{1}{3}(3) & | & \frac{1}{3}(8) \\ 0 & 0 & -3 & 3 & | & -3 \\ 0 & 1 & 0 & -3 & | & -8 \end{bmatrix} = \begin{bmatrix} 1 & -1 & 2 & -2 & | & -1 \\ 0 & 1 & -\frac{1}{3} & 1 & | & \frac{8}{3} \\ 0 & 0 & -3 & 3 & | & -3 \\ 0 & 1 & 0 & -3 & | & -8 \end{bmatrix}$$ $\frac{1}{3}R_2$

We want 0s in these positions. The top position already has a 0.

Now we use the 1 in the second row, second column position to get 0s below it.

Replace row 4 in the previous matrix by $-1R_2 + R_4$.

$$\begin{bmatrix} 1 & -1 & 2 & -2 & | & -1 \\ 0 & 1 & -\frac{1}{3} & 1 & | & \frac{8}{3} \\ 0 & 0 & -3 & 3 & | & -3 \\ 0 & 0 & \frac{1}{3} & -4 & | & -\frac{32}{3} \end{bmatrix}$$

We want 1 in this position.

We move on to the third column. We can obtain 1 in the desired position by multiplying the numbers in the third row by $-\frac{1}{3}$, the reciprocal of -3.

Now we use the 1 in the third column to get 0 below it.

$$\begin{bmatrix} 1 & -1 & 2 & -2 & | & -1 \\ 0 & 1 & -\frac{1}{3} & 1 & | & \frac{8}{3} \\ -\frac{1}{3}(0) & -\frac{1}{3}(0) & -\frac{1}{3}(-3) & -\frac{1}{3}(3) & | & -\frac{1}{3}(-3) \\ 0 & 0 & \frac{1}{3} & -4 & | & -\frac{32}{3} \end{bmatrix} = \begin{bmatrix} 1 & -1 & 2 & -2 & | & -1 \\ 0 & 1 & -\frac{1}{3} & 1 & | & \frac{8}{3} \\ 0 & 0 & 1 & -1 & | & 1 \\ 0 & 0 & \frac{1}{3} & -4 & | & -\frac{32}{3} \end{bmatrix}$$ $-\frac{1}{3}R_3$

We want 0 in this position.

$$\begin{bmatrix} 1 & -1 & 2 & -2 & | & -1 \\ 0 & 1 & -\frac{1}{3} & 1 & | & \frac{8}{3} \\ 0 & 0 & 1 & -1 & | & 1 \\ 0 & 0 & 0 & -\frac{11}{3} & | & -11 \end{bmatrix}$$

> Replace row 4 in the previous matrix by $-\frac{1}{3}R_3 + R_4$.

> We want 1 in this position.

We move on to the fourth column. Because we want 1s down the diagonal from upper left to lower right, we want 1 where there is now $-\frac{11}{3}$. We can obtain 1 in this position by multiplying the numbers in the fourth row by $-\frac{3}{11}$.

$$\begin{bmatrix} 1 & -1 & 2 & -2 & | & -1 \\ 0 & 1 & -\frac{1}{3} & 1 & | & \frac{8}{3} \\ 0 & 0 & 1 & -1 & | & 1 \\ -\frac{3}{11}(0) & -\frac{3}{11}(0) & -\frac{3}{11}(0) & -\frac{3}{11}\left(-\frac{11}{3}\right) & | & -\frac{3}{11}(-11) \end{bmatrix}$$

$$= \begin{bmatrix} 1 & -1 & 2 & -2 & | & -1 \\ 0 & 1 & -\frac{1}{3} & 1 & | & \frac{8}{3} \\ 0 & 0 & 1 & -1 & | & 1 \\ 0 & 0 & 0 & 1 & | & 3 \end{bmatrix}$$

> $-\frac{3}{11}R_4$

We now have the desired matrix in row-echelon form, with 1s down the diagonal and 0s below the 1s. An equivalent row-echelon matrix can be obtained using a graphing utility and the REF command on the augmented matrix.

Step 3 Write the system of linear equations corresponding to the matrix in step 2, and use back-substitution to find the system's solution. The system represented by the matrix in step 2 is

$$\begin{bmatrix} 1 & -1 & 2 & -2 & | & -1 \\ 0 & 1 & -\frac{1}{3} & 1 & | & \frac{8}{3} \\ 0 & 0 & 1 & -1 & | & 1 \\ 0 & 0 & 0 & 1 & | & 3 \end{bmatrix} \rightarrow \begin{array}{l} 1w - 1x + 2y - 2z = -1 \\ 0w + 1x - \frac{1}{3}y + 1z = \frac{8}{3} \\ 0w + 0x + 1y - 1z = 1 \\ 0w + 0x + 0y + 1z = 3 \end{array} \text{ or } \begin{array}{rcr} w - x + 2y - 2z &=& -1 \\ x - \frac{1}{3}y + z &=& \frac{8}{3} \\ y - z &=& 1 \\ z &=& 3. \end{array}$$

We immediately see that the value for z is 3. We can now use back-substitution to find the values for y, x, and w.

> These are the four equations from the last column on the previous page.

$$z = 3 \quad \begin{array}{l} y - z = 1 \\ y - 3 = 1 \\ y = 4 \end{array} \quad \begin{array}{l} x - \frac{1}{3}y + z = \frac{8}{3} \\ x - \frac{1}{3}(4) + 3 = \frac{8}{3} \\ x + \frac{5}{3} = \frac{8}{3} \\ x = 1 \end{array} \quad \begin{array}{l} w - x + 2y - 2z = -1 \\ w - 1 + 2(4) - 2(3) = -1 \\ w - 1 + 8 - 6 = -1 \\ w + 1 = -1 \\ w = -2 \end{array}$$

Let's agree to write the solution set for the system in the alphabetical order in which the variables for the given system appeared from left to right, namely (w, x, y, z). Thus, the solution set is $\{(-2, 1, 4, 3)\}$. We can verify this solution set by substituting the value for each variable into the original system of equations.

Check
Point
4 Use matrices to solve the system:

$$w - 3x - 2y + z = -3$$
$$2w - 7x - y + 2z = 1$$
$$3w - 7x - 3y + 3z = -5$$
$$5w + x + 4y - 2z = 18.$$

4 Use matrices and Gauss-Jordan elimination to solve systems.

Gauss-Jordan Elimination

Using Gaussian elimination, we obtain a matrix in row-echelon form, with 1s down the diagonal from upper left to lower right and 0s below the 1s. A second method, called **Gauss-Jordan elimination,** after Carl Friedrich Gauss and Wilhelm Jordan (1842–1899), continues the process until a matrix with 1s down the diagonal from upper left to lower right and 0s in every position *above and below* each 1 is found. Such a matrix is said to be in **reduced row-echelon form.** For a system of linear equations in three variables, x, y, and z, we must get the augmented matrix into the form

$$\left[\begin{array}{ccc|c} 1 & 0 & 0 & a \\ 0 & 1 & 0 & b \\ 0 & 0 & 1 & c \end{array}\right].$$

Based on this matrix, we conclude that $x = a$, $y = b$, and $z = c$.

Solving Linear Systems Using Gauss-Jordan Elimination

1. Write the augmented matrix for the system.
2. Use matrix row operations to simplify the matrix to one with 1s down the diagonal from upper left to lower right, and 0s above and below the 1s.
   a. Get 1 in the upper left-hand corner.
   b. Use the 1 in the first column to get 0s below it.
   c. Get 1 in the second row, second column.
   d. Use the 1 in the second column to make the remaining entries in the second column 0.
   e. Get 1 in the third row, third column.
   f. Use the 1 in the third column to make the remaining entries in the third column 0.
   g. Continue this procedure as far as possible.
3. Use the reduced row-echelon form of the matrix in step 2 to write the system's solution set. (Back-substitution is not necessary.)

EXAMPLE 5   Using Gauss-Jordan Elimination

Use Gauss-Jordan elimination to solve the system:

$$3x + y + 2z = 31$$
$$x + y + 2z = 19$$
$$x + 3y + 2z = 25.$$

Technology

Most graphing utilities can convert a matrix to reduced row-echelon form. Enter the system's augmented matrix and name it A. Then use the [REF] (reduced row-echelon form) command on matrix A.

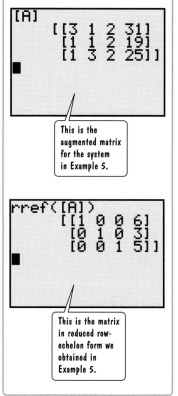

This is the augmented matrix for the system in Example 5.

This is the matrix in reduced row-echelon form we obtained in Example 5.

Solution   In Example 3, we used Gaussian elimination to obtain the following matrix:

$$\left[\begin{array}{ccc|c} 1 & 1 & 2 & 19 \\ 0 & 1 & 2 & 13 \\ 0 & 0 & 1 & 5 \end{array}\right].$$

To use Gauss-Jordan elimination, we need 0s both below and above the 1s in the diagonal position. We use the 1 in the second row, second column to get a 0 above it.

Replace row 1 in the previous matrix by $-1R_2 + R_1$

$$\left[\begin{array}{ccc|c} 1 & 0 & 0 & 6 \\ 0 & 1 & 2 & 13 \\ 0 & 0 & 1 & 5 \end{array}\right]$$

We want 0s in these positions. The top position already has a 0.

We use the 1 in the third column to get 0s above it.

$$\left[\begin{array}{ccc|c} 1 & 0 & 0 & 6 \\ 0 & 1 & 0 & 3 \\ 0 & 0 & 1 & 5 \end{array}\right]$$

Replace row 2 in the previous matrix by $-2R_3 + R_2$.

This last matrix corresponds to

$$x = 6, \quad y = 3, \quad z = 5.$$

As we found in Example 3, the solution set is $\{(6, 3, 5)\}$.

Check Point 5   Solve the system in Check Point 3 using Gauss-Jordan elimination. Begin by working with the matrix that you obtained in Check Point 3.

EXERCISE SET 3.3

Practice Exercises

In Exercises 1–8, write the augmented matrix for each system of linear equations.

1. $\begin{aligned} 2x + y + 2z &= 2 \\ 3x - 5y - z &= 4 \\ x - 2y - 3z &= -6 \end{aligned}$

2. $\begin{aligned} 3x - 2y + 5z &= 31 \\ x + 3y - 3z &= -12 \\ -2x - 5y + 3z &= 11 \end{aligned}$

3. $\begin{aligned} x - y + z &= 8 \\ y - 12z &= -15 \\ z &= 1 \end{aligned}$

4. $\begin{aligned} x - 2y + 3z &= 9 \\ y + 3z &= 5 \\ z &= 2 \end{aligned}$

5. $\begin{aligned} 5x - 2y - 3z &= 0 \\ x + y &= 5 \\ 2x - 3z &= 4 \end{aligned}$

6. $\begin{aligned} x - 2y + z &= 10 \\ 3x + y &= 5 \\ 7x + 2z &= 2 \end{aligned}$

7. $\begin{aligned} 2w + 5x - 3y + z &= 2 \\ 3x + y &= 4 \\ w - x + 5y &= 9 \\ 5w - 5x - 2y &= 1 \end{aligned}$

8. $\begin{aligned} 4w + 7x - 8y + z &= 3 \\ 5x + y &= 5 \\ w - x - y &= 17 \\ 2w - 2x + 11y &= 4 \end{aligned}$

In Exercises 9–12, write the system of linear equations represented by the augmented matrix. Use x, y, z, and, if necessary, w, x, y, and z, for the variables.

9. $\begin{bmatrix} 5 & 0 & 3 & | & -11 \\ 0 & 1 & -4 & | & 12 \\ 7 & 2 & 0 & | & 3 \end{bmatrix}$ 10. $\begin{bmatrix} 7 & 0 & 4 & | & -13 \\ 0 & 1 & -5 & | & 11 \\ 2 & 7 & 0 & | & 6 \end{bmatrix}$

11. $\begin{bmatrix} 1 & 1 & 4 & 1 & | & 3 \\ -1 & 1 & -1 & 0 & | & 7 \\ 2 & 0 & 0 & 5 & | & 11 \\ 0 & 0 & 12 & 4 & | & 5 \end{bmatrix}$ 12. $\begin{bmatrix} 4 & 1 & 5 & 1 & | & 6 \\ 1 & -1 & 0 & -1 & | & 8 \\ 3 & 0 & 0 & 7 & | & 4 \\ 0 & 0 & 11 & 5 & | & 3 \end{bmatrix}$

In Exercises 13–18, write the system of linear equations represented by the augmented matrix. Use x, y, z, and, if necessary, w, x, y, and z, for the variables. Once the system is written, use back-substitution to find its solution.

13. $\begin{bmatrix} 1 & 0 & -4 & | & 5 \\ 0 & 1 & -12 & | & 13 \\ 0 & 0 & 1 & | & -\frac{1}{2} \end{bmatrix}$ 14. $\begin{bmatrix} 1 & 2 & 1 & | & 0 \\ 0 & 1 & 0 & | & -2 \\ 0 & 0 & 1 & | & 3 \end{bmatrix}$

15. $\begin{bmatrix} 1 & \frac{1}{2} & 1 & | & \frac{11}{2} \\ 0 & 1 & \frac{3}{2} & | & 7 \\ 0 & 0 & 1 & | & 4 \end{bmatrix}$ 16. $\begin{bmatrix} 1 & 1 & 0 & | & 3 \\ 0 & 1 & \frac{3}{2} & | & -2 \\ 0 & 0 & 1 & | & 0 \end{bmatrix}$

17. $\begin{bmatrix} 1 & -1 & 1 & 1 & | & 3 \\ 0 & 1 & -2 & -1 & | & 0 \\ 0 & 0 & 1 & 6 & | & 17 \\ 0 & 0 & 0 & 1 & | & 3 \end{bmatrix}$ 18. $\begin{bmatrix} 1 & 2 & -1 & 0 & | & 2 \\ 0 & 1 & 1 & -2 & | & -3 \\ 0 & 0 & 1 & -1 & | & -2 \\ 0 & 0 & 0 & 1 & | & 3 \end{bmatrix}$

In Exercises 19–24, perform each matrix row operation and write the new matrix.

19. $\begin{bmatrix} 2 & -6 & 4 & | & 10 \\ 1 & 5 & -5 & | & 0 \\ 3 & 0 & 4 & | & 7 \end{bmatrix}$ $\frac{1}{2}R_1$

20. $\begin{bmatrix} 3 & -12 & 6 & | & 9 \\ 1 & -4 & 4 & | & 0 \\ 2 & 0 & 7 & | & 4 \end{bmatrix}$ $\frac{1}{3}R_1$

21. $\begin{bmatrix} 1 & -3 & 2 & | & 0 \\ 3 & 1 & -1 & | & 7 \\ 2 & -2 & 1 & | & 3 \end{bmatrix}$ $-3R_1 + R_2$

22. $\begin{bmatrix} 1 & -1 & 5 & | & -6 \\ 3 & 3 & -1 & | & 10 \\ 1 & 3 & 2 & | & 5 \end{bmatrix}$ $-3R_1 + R_2$

23. $\begin{bmatrix} 1 & -1 & 1 & 1 & | & 3 \\ 0 & 1 & -2 & -1 & | & 0 \\ 2 & 0 & 3 & 4 & | & 11 \\ 5 & 1 & 2 & 4 & | & 6 \end{bmatrix}$ $\begin{matrix} \\ \\ -2R_1 + R_3 \\ -5R_1 + R_4 \end{matrix}$

24. $\begin{bmatrix} 1 & -5 & 2 & -2 & | & 4 \\ 0 & 1 & -3 & -1 & | & 0 \\ 3 & 0 & 2 & -1 & | & 6 \\ -4 & 1 & 4 & 2 & | & -3 \end{bmatrix}$ $\begin{matrix} \\ \\ -3R_1 + R_3 \\ 4R_1 + R_4 \end{matrix}$

In Exercises 25–26, a few steps in the process of simplifying the given matrix to one with 1s down the diagonal from upper left to lower right, and 0s below the 1s, are shown. Fill in the missing numbers in the steps that are shown.

25. $\begin{bmatrix} 1 & -1 & 1 & | & 8 \\ 2 & 3 & -1 & | & -2 \\ 3 & -2 & -9 & | & 9 \end{bmatrix} \rightarrow \begin{bmatrix} 1 & -1 & 1 & | & 8 \\ 0 & 5 & \blacksquare & | & \blacksquare \\ 0 & 1 & \blacksquare & | & \blacksquare \end{bmatrix}$

$\rightarrow \begin{bmatrix} 1 & -1 & 1 & | & 8 \\ 0 & 1 & \blacksquare & | & \blacksquare \\ 0 & 1 & \blacksquare & | & \blacksquare \end{bmatrix}$

26. $\begin{bmatrix} 1 & -2 & 3 & | & 4 \\ 2 & 1 & -4 & | & 3 \\ -3 & 4 & -1 & | & -2 \end{bmatrix} \rightarrow \begin{bmatrix} 1 & -2 & 3 & | & 4 \\ 0 & 5 & \blacksquare & | & \blacksquare \\ 0 & -2 & \blacksquare & | & \blacksquare \end{bmatrix}$

$\rightarrow \begin{bmatrix} 1 & -2 & 3 & | & 4 \\ 0 & 1 & \blacksquare & | & \blacksquare \\ 0 & -2 & \blacksquare & | & \blacksquare \end{bmatrix}$

In Exercises 27–44, solve each system of equations using matrices. Use Gaussian elimination with back-substitution or Gauss-Jordan elimination.

27. $\begin{aligned} x + y - z &= -2 \\ 2x - y + z &= 5 \\ -x + 2y + 2z &= 1 \end{aligned}$ 28. $\begin{aligned} x - 2y - z &= 2 \\ 2x - y + z &= 4 \\ -x + y - 2z &= -4 \end{aligned}$

29. $\begin{aligned} x + 3y &= 0 \\ x + y + z &= 1 \\ 3x - y - z &= 11 \end{aligned}$ 30. $\begin{aligned} 3y - z &= -1 \\ x + 5y - z &= -4 \\ -3x + 6y + 2z &= 11 \end{aligned}$

31. $\begin{aligned} 2x - y - z &= 4 \\ x + y - 5z &= -4 \\ x - 2y &= 4 \end{aligned}$ 32. $\begin{aligned} x - 3z &= -2 \\ 2x + 2y + z &= 4 \\ 3x + y - 2z &= 5 \end{aligned}$

33. $\begin{aligned} x + y + z &= 4 \\ x - y - z &= 0 \\ x - y + z &= 2 \end{aligned}$ 34. $\begin{aligned} 3x + y - z &= 0 \\ x + y + 2z &= 6 \\ 2x + 2y + 3z &= 10 \end{aligned}$

35. $\begin{aligned} x + 2y &= z - 1 \\ x &= 4 + y - z \\ x + y - 3z &= -2 \end{aligned}$ 36. $\begin{aligned} 2x + y &= z + 1 \\ 2x &= 1 + 3y - z \\ x + y + z &= 4 \end{aligned}$

37. $\begin{aligned} 3a - b - 4c &= 3 \\ 2a - b + 2c &= -8 \\ a + 2b - 3c &= 9 \end{aligned}$ 38. $\begin{aligned} 3a + b - c &= 0 \\ 2a + 3b - 5c &= 1 \\ a - 2b + 3c &= -4 \end{aligned}$

39. $\begin{aligned} 2x + 2y + 7z &= -1 \\ 2x + y + 2z &= 2 \\ 4x + 6y + z &= 15 \end{aligned}$ 40. $\begin{aligned} 3x + 2y + 3z &= 3 \\ 4x - 5y + 7z &= 1 \\ 2x + 3y - 2z &= 6 \end{aligned}$

41. $\begin{aligned} w + x + y + z &= 4 \\ 2w + x - 2y - z &= 0 \\ w - 2x - y - 2z &= -2 \\ 3w + 2x + y + 3z &= 4 \end{aligned}$ 42. $\begin{aligned} w + x + y + z &= 5 \\ w + 2x - y - 2z &= -1 \\ w - 3x - 3y - z &= -1 \\ 2w - x + 2y - z &= -2 \end{aligned}$

43. $\begin{aligned} 3w - 4x + y + z &= 9 \\ w + x - y - z &= 0 \\ 2w + x + 4y - 2z &= 3 \\ -w + 2x + y - 3z &= 3 \end{aligned}$ 44. $\begin{aligned} 2w + y - 3z &= 8 \\ w - x + 4z &= -10 \\ 3w + 5x - y - z &= 20 \\ w + x - y - z &= 6 \end{aligned}$

Application Exercises

45. The graph shows the alligator population, $P(x)$, in a national park after x years of a protection program. A quadratic function

$$P(x) = ax^2 + bx + c$$

can be used to model the data.

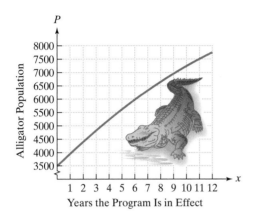

Years the Program Is in Effect

a. Use the points shown in the graph to find the values of a, b, and c. Solve the system of linear equations involving a, b, and c using matrices.

b. Find and interpret $P(12)$. Identify your solution on the graph shown.

46. A football is kicked straight upward. A position function

$$s(t) = \tfrac{1}{2}at^2 + v_0 t + s_0$$

can be used to describe the ball's height, $s(t)$, in feet, after t seconds.

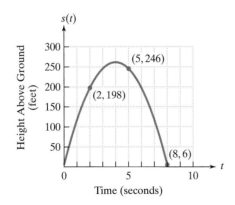

Time (seconds)

a. Use the points labeled in the graph to find the values of a, v_0, and s_0. Solve the system of linear equations involving a, v_0, and s_0 using matrices.

b. Find and interpret $s(7)$. Identify your solution on the graph shown.

Write a system of linear equations in three variables to solve Exercises 47–50. Then use matrices to solve the system. Exercises 47–48 are based on a Time/CNN telephone poll that included never-married single women between the ages of 18 and 49 and never-married men between the ages of 18 and 49. The circle graphs show the results for one of the questions in the poll.

If You Couldn't Find the Perfect Mate, Would You Marry Someone Else?

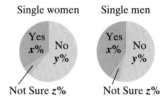

47. For single women in the poll, the percentage who said no exceeded the combined percentages for those who said yes and those who said not sure by 22%. If the percentage who said yes is doubled, it is 7% more than the percentage who said no. Find the percentage of single women who responded yes, no, and not sure.

48. For single men in the poll, the percentage who said no exceeded the combined percentages for those who said yes and those who said not sure by 8%. If the percentage who said yes is doubled, it is 28% more than the percentage who said no. Find the percentage of single men who responded yes, no, and not sure.

49. Three foods have the following nutritional content per ounce.

	Calories	Protein (in grams)	Vitamin C (in milligrams)
Food A	40	5	30
Food B	200	2	10
Food C	400	4	300

If a meal consisting of the three foods allows exactly 660 calories, 25 grams of protein, and 425 milligrams of vitamin C, how many ounces of each kind of food should be used?

50. A furniture company produces three types of desks: a children's model, an office model, and a deluxe model. Each desk is manufactured in three stages: cutting, construction, and finishing. The time requirements for each model and manufacturing stage are given in the following table.

	Children's model	Office model	Deluxe model
Cutting	2 hr	3 hr	2 hr
Construction	2 hr	1 hr	3 hr
Finishing	1 hr	1 hr	2 hr

Each week the company has available a maximum of 100 hours for cutting, 100 hours for construction, and 65 hours for finishing. If all available time must be used, how many of each type of desk should be produced each week?

Writing in Mathematics

51. What is a matrix?

52. Describe what is meant by the augmented matrix of a system of linear equations.

53. In your own words, describe each of the three matrix row operations. Give an example with each of the operations.

54. Describe how to use row operations and matrices to solve a system of linear equations.

55. What is the difference between Gaussian elimination and Gauss-Jordan elimination?

56. The graphs show the percentage of recorded music on CDs, cassettes, and LPs from 1981–2001. For this time period, which of these three forms of recorded music would you be most inclined to model using a quadratic function? Explain your answer.

**Percentage of Recorded Music on
CDs, Cassettes, and LPs**

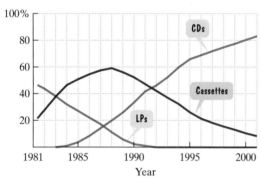

Source: Recording Industry Association of America

57. In Exercise 56, assume that you plan to obtain the quadratic model by hand. Explain how to use the graph for the form that you selected to find a, b, and c in $y = ax^2 + bx + c$, where x represents the number of years after 1981 and y represents the percentage of recorded music on this form. Describe the role that matrices can play in the process of obtaining the model.

Technology Exercises

58. Most graphing utilities can perform row operations on matrices. Consult the owner's manual for your graphing utility to learn proper keystrokes for performing these operations. Then duplicate the row operations of any three exercises that you solved from Exercises 19–24.

59. If your graphing utility has a REF (row-echelon form) command or a RREF (reduced row-echelon form) command, use this feature to verify your work with any five systems from Exercises 27–44.

60. Solve using a graphing utility's REF or RREF command:

$$
\begin{aligned}
2x_1 - 2x_2 + 3x_3 - x_4 \quad\quad &= 12 \\
x_1 + 2x_2 - x_3 + 2x_4 - x_5 &= -7 \\
x_1 + \quad\quad x_3 + x_4 - 5x_5 &= 1 \\
-x_1 + x_2 - x_3 - 2x_4 - 3x_5 &= 0 \\
x_1 - x_2 - \quad\quad x_4 + x_5 &= 4.
\end{aligned}
$$

Critical Thinking Exercises

61. Find a cubic function whose graph passes through the points $(0, -3)$, $(1, 5)$, $(-1, -7)$, and $(-2, -13)$. (*Hint:* Use the equation $y = ax^3 + bx^2 + cx + d$.)

62. The table shows the daily production level and profit for a business.

x (Number of units Produced Daily)	30	50	100
y (Daily Profit)	$5900	$7500	$4500

Use the quadratic function $y = ax^2 + bx + c$ to determine the number of units that should be produced each day for maximum profit. What is the maximum daily profit?

Group Exercise

63. In Chapter 3, you learned how to fit a quadratic function of the form $y = ax^2 + bx + c$ to data without using the regression feature of a graphing utility (see pages 278–279). Each group member should find an interesting data set. Group members should select the two sets of data that are most interesting and relevant.

a. For one of the data sets selected, use the function $y = ax^3 + bx^2 + cx + d$ and four ordered pairs of values (x, y) to find the cubic function that models the data. Use matrices or a graphing utility to solve the resulting system in four variables for $a, b, c,$ and d.

b. For the other data set selected, fit a higher-degree polynomial function to the data. Use a graphing utility to solve the resulting system in five or more variables.

SECTION 3.4 *Determinants and Cramer's Rule*

Objectives

1. Evaluate a second-order determinant.
2. Solve a system of linear equations in two variables using Cramer's rule.
3. Evaluate a third-order determinant.
4. Solve a system of linear equations in three variables using Cramer's rule.
5. Use determinants to identify inconsistent systems and systems with dependent equations.
6. Evaluate higher-order determinants.

A portion of Charles Babbage's unrealized Difference Engine

As cyberspace absorbs more and more of our work, play, shopping, and socializing, where will it all end? Which activities will still be offline in 2025?

Our technologically transformed lives can be traced back to the English inventor Charles Babbage (1792–1871). Babbage knew of a method for solving linear systems called *Cramer's rule,* in honor of the Swiss geometer Gabriel Cramer (1704–1752). Cramer's rule was simple, but involved numerous multiplications for large systems. Babbage designed a machine, called the "difference engine," that consisted of toothed wheels on shafts for performing these multiplications. Despite the fact that only one-seventh of the functions ever worked, Babbage's invention demonstrated how complex calculations could be handled mechanically. In 1944, scientists at IBM used the lessons of the difference engine to create the world's first computer.

Those who invented computers hoped to relegate the drudgery of repeated computation to a machine. In this section, we look at a method for solving linear systems that played a critical role in this process. The method uses arrays of numbers, called *determinants.* As with matrix methods, solutions are obtained by writing down the coefficients and constants of a linear system and performing operations with them.

1 Evaluate a second-order determinant.

The Determinant of a 2 × 2 Matrix

Associated with every square matrix is a real number, called its **determinant.** The determinant for a 2 × 2 square matrix is defined as follows:

Study Tip

To evaluate a second-order determinant, find the difference of the product of the two diagonals.

$$\begin{vmatrix} a_1 & b_1 \\ a_2 & b_2 \end{vmatrix} = a_1b_2 - a_2b_1$$

Definition of the Determinant of a 2 × 2 Matrix

The determinant of the matrix $\begin{bmatrix} a_1 & b_1 \\ a_2 & b_2 \end{bmatrix}$ is denoted by $\begin{vmatrix} a_1 & b_1 \\ a_2 & b_2 \end{vmatrix}$ and is defined by

$$\begin{vmatrix} a_1 & b_1 \\ a_2 & b_2 \end{vmatrix} = a_1b_2 - a_2b_1.$$

We also say that the **value** of the **second-order determinant** $\begin{vmatrix} a_1 & b_1 \\ a_2 & b_2 \end{vmatrix}$ is $a_1 b_2 - a_2 b_1$.

Example 1 illustrates that the determinant of a matrix may be positive or negative. The determinant can also have 0 as its value.

EXAMPLE 1 Evaluating the Determinant of a 2 × 2 Matrix

Evaluate the determinant of:

a. $\begin{bmatrix} 5 & 6 \\ 7 & 3 \end{bmatrix}$ **b.** $\begin{bmatrix} 2 & 4 \\ -3 & -5 \end{bmatrix}$.

Solution We multiply and subtract as indicated.

a. $\begin{vmatrix} 5 & 6 \\ 7 & 3 \end{vmatrix} = 5 \cdot 3 - 7 \cdot 6 = 15 - 42 = -27$ The value of the second-order determinant is -27.

b. $\begin{vmatrix} 2 & 4 \\ -3 & -5 \end{vmatrix} = 2(-5) - (-3)(4) = -10 + 12 = 2$ The value of the second-order determinant is 2.

Discovery

Write and then evaluate three determinants, one whose value is positive, one whose value is negative, and one whose value is 0.

Check Point 1 Evaluate the determinant of:

a. $\begin{bmatrix} 10 & 9 \\ 6 & 5 \end{bmatrix}$ **b.** $\begin{bmatrix} 4 & 3 \\ -5 & -8 \end{bmatrix}$.

2 Solve a system of linear equations in two variables using Cramer's rule.

Solving Systems of Linear Equations in Two Variables Using Determinants

Determinants can be used to solve a linear system in two variables. In general, such a system appears as

$$a_1 x + b_1 y = c_1$$
$$a_2 x + b_2 y = c_2.$$

Let's first solve this system for x using the addition method. We can solve for x by eliminating y from the equations. Multiply the first equation by b_2 and the second equation by $-b_1$. Then add the two equations:

$$a_1 x + b_1 y = c_1 \quad \text{Multiply by } b_2. \quad a_1 b_2 x + b_1 b_2 y = c_1 b_2$$
$$a_2 x + b_2 y = c_2 \quad \text{Multiply by } -b_1. \quad -a_2 b_1 x - b_1 b_2 y = -c_2 b_1$$
$$\text{Add:} \quad (a_1 b_2 - a_2 b_1)x = c_1 b_2 - c_2 b_1$$
$$x = \frac{c_1 b_2 - c_2 b_1}{a_1 b_2 - a_2 b_1}$$

Because

$$\begin{vmatrix} c_1 & b_1 \\ c_2 & b_2 \end{vmatrix} = c_1 b_2 - c_2 b_1 \quad \text{and} \quad \begin{vmatrix} a_1 & b_1 \\ a_2 & b_2 \end{vmatrix} = a_1 b_2 - a_2 b_1$$

we can express our answer for x as the quotient of two determinants:

$$x = \frac{\begin{vmatrix} c_1 & b_1 \\ c_2 & b_2 \end{vmatrix}}{\begin{vmatrix} a_1 & b_1 \\ a_2 & b_2 \end{vmatrix}}.$$

In a similar way, we could use the addition method to solve our system for y, again expressing y as the quotient of two determinants. This method of using determinants to solve the linear system, called **Cramer's rule**, is summarized in the box.

Solving a Linear System in Two Variables Using Determinants

Cramer's Rule

If

$$a_1 x + b_1 y = c_1$$
$$a_2 x + b_2 y = c_2$$

then

$$x = \frac{\begin{vmatrix} c_1 & b_1 \\ c_2 & b_2 \end{vmatrix}}{\begin{vmatrix} a_1 & b_1 \\ a_2 & b_2 \end{vmatrix}} \quad \text{and} \quad y = \frac{\begin{vmatrix} a_1 & c_1 \\ a_2 & c_2 \end{vmatrix}}{\begin{vmatrix} a_1 & b_1 \\ a_2 & b_2 \end{vmatrix}}$$

where

$$\begin{vmatrix} a_1 & b_1 \\ a_2 & b_2 \end{vmatrix} \neq 0.$$

Here are some helpful tips when solving

$$a_1 x + b_1 y = c_1$$
$$a_2 x + b_2 y = c_2$$

using determinants:

1. Three different determinants are used to find x and y. The determinants in the denominators for x and y are identical. The determinants in the numerators for x and y differ. In abbreviated notation, we write

$$x = \frac{D_x}{D} \quad \text{and} \quad y = \frac{D_y}{D}, \text{ where } D \neq 0.$$

2. The elements of D, the determinant in the denominator, are the coefficients of the variables in the system.

$$D = \begin{vmatrix} a_1 & b_1 \\ a_2 & b_2 \end{vmatrix}$$

3. D_x, the determinant in the numerator of x, is obtained by replacing the x-coefficients, in D, a_1 and a_2, with the constants on the right side of the equations, c_1 and c_2.

$$D = \begin{vmatrix} a_1 & b_1 \\ a_2 & b_2 \end{vmatrix} \quad \text{and} \quad D_x = \begin{vmatrix} c_1 & b_1 \\ c_2 & b_2 \end{vmatrix} \quad \begin{array}{l} \text{Replace the column with } a_1 \text{ and } a_2 \text{ with} \\ \text{the constants } c_1 \text{ and } c_2 \text{ to get } D_x. \end{array}$$

4. D_y, the determinant in the numerator for y, is obtained by replacing the y-coefficients, in D, b_1 and b_2, with the constants on the right side of the equations, c_1 and c_2.

$$D = \begin{vmatrix} a_1 & b_1 \\ a_2 & b_2 \end{vmatrix} \quad \text{and} \quad D_y = \begin{vmatrix} a_1 & c_1 \\ a_2 & c_2 \end{vmatrix} \quad \begin{array}{l} \text{Replace the column with } b_1 \text{ and } b_2 \text{ with} \\ \text{the constants } c_1 \text{ and } c_2 \text{ to get } D_y. \end{array}$$

EXAMPLE 2 **Using Cramer's Rule to Solve a Linear System**

Use Cramer's rule to solve the system:

$$5x - 4y = 2$$
$$6x - 5y = 1.$$

Solution Because

$$x = \frac{D_x}{D} \quad \text{and} \quad y = \frac{D_y}{D},$$

we will set up and evaluate the three determinants $D, D_x,$ and D_y.

1. D, the determinant in both denominators, consists of the x- and y-coefficients.

$$D = \begin{vmatrix} 5 & -4 \\ 6 & -5 \end{vmatrix} = (5)(-5) - (6)(-4) = -25 + 24 = -1$$

Because this determinant is not zero, we continue to use Cramer's rule to solve the system.

2. D_x, the determinant in the numerator for x, is obtained by replacing the x-coefficients in $D, 5$ and 6, by the constants on the right side of the equation, 2 and 1.

$$D_x = \begin{vmatrix} 2 & -4 \\ 1 & -5 \end{vmatrix} = (2)(-5) - (1)(-4) = -10 + 4 = -6$$

3. D_y, the determinant in the numerator for y, is obtained by replacing the y-coefficients in $D, -4$ and -5, by the constants on the right side of the equation, 2 and 1.

$$D_y = \begin{vmatrix} 5 & 2 \\ 6 & 1 \end{vmatrix} = (5)(1) - (6)(2) = 5 - 12 = -7$$

4. Thus,

$$x = \frac{D_x}{D} = \frac{-6}{-1} = 6 \quad \text{and} \quad y = \frac{D_y}{D} = \frac{-7}{-1} = 7.$$

As always, the solution $(6, 7)$ can be checked by substituting these values into the original equations. The solution set is $\{(6, 7)\}$.

Check Point 2 Use Cramer's rule to solve the system:

$$5x + 4y = 12$$
$$3x - 6y = 24.$$

3 Evaluate a third-order determinant.

The Determinant of a 3 × 3 Matrix

Associated with every square matrix is a real number called its determinant. The determinant for a 3 × 3 matrix is defined on the next page.

Definition of a Third-Order Determinant

$$\begin{vmatrix} a_1 & b_1 & c_1 \\ a_2 & b_2 & c_2 \\ a_3 & b_3 & c_3 \end{vmatrix} = a_1b_2c_3 + b_1c_2a_3 + c_1a_2b_3 - a_3b_2c_1 - b_3c_2a_1 - c_3a_2b_1$$

The six terms and the three factors in each term in this complicated evaluation formula can be rearranged, and then we can apply the distributive property. We obtain

$$a_1b_2c_3 - a_1b_3c_2 - a_2b_1c_3 + a_2b_3c_1 + a_3b_1c_2 - a_3b_2c_1$$
$$= a_1(b_2c_3 - b_3c_2) - a_2(b_1c_3 - b_3c_1) + a_3(b_1c_2 - b_2c_1)$$
$$= a_1\begin{vmatrix} b_2 & c_2 \\ b_3 & c_3 \end{vmatrix} - a_2\begin{vmatrix} b_1 & c_1 \\ b_3 & c_3 \end{vmatrix} + a_3\begin{vmatrix} b_1 & c_1 \\ b_2 & c_2 \end{vmatrix}.$$

You can evaluate each of the second-order determinants and obtain the three expressions in parentheses in the second step.

In summary, we now have arranged the definition of a third-order determinant as follows:

Definition of the Determinant of a 3 × 3 Matrix

A third-order determinant is defined by

$$\begin{vmatrix} a_1 & b_1 & c_1 \\ a_2 & b_2 & c_2 \\ a_3 & b_3 & c_3 \end{vmatrix} = a_1\begin{vmatrix} b_2 & c_2 \\ b_3 & c_3 \end{vmatrix} - a_2\begin{vmatrix} b_1 & c_1 \\ b_3 & c_3 \end{vmatrix} + a_3\begin{vmatrix} b_1 & c_1 \\ b_2 & c_2 \end{vmatrix}.$$

The a's on the right come from the first column.

Here are some tips that may be helpful when evaluating the determinant of a 3 × 3 matrix:

Evaluating the Determinant of a 3 × 3 Matrix

1. Each of the three terms in the definition contains two factors—a numerical factor and a second-order determinant.

2. The numerical factor in each term is an element from the first column of the third-order determinant.

3. The minus sign precedes the second term.

4. The second-order determinant that appears in each term is obtained by crossing out the row and the column containing the numerical factor.

$$a_1\begin{vmatrix} b_2 & c_2 \\ b_3 & c_3 \end{vmatrix} - a_2\begin{vmatrix} b_1 & c_1 \\ b_3 & c_3 \end{vmatrix} + a_3\begin{vmatrix} b_1 & c_1 \\ b_2 & c_2 \end{vmatrix}$$

The **minor** of an element is the determinant that remains after deleting the row and column of that element. For this reason, we call this method **expansion by minors**.

EXAMPLE 3   Evaluating the Determinant of a 3 × 3 Matrix

Evaluate the determinant of

$$\begin{bmatrix} 4 & 1 & 0 \\ -9 & 3 & 4 \\ -3 & 8 & 1 \end{bmatrix}.$$

Solution   We know that each of the three terms in the determinant contains a numerical factor and a second-order determinant. The numerical factors are from the first column of the determinant of the given matrix. They are highlighted in the following matrix:

$$\begin{vmatrix} 4 & 1 & 0 \\ -9 & 3 & 4 \\ -3 & 8 & 1 \end{vmatrix}.$$

We find the minor for each numerical factor by deleting the row and column of that element:

The minor for 4 is $\begin{vmatrix} 3 & 4 \\ 8 & 1 \end{vmatrix}$.

The minor for −9 is $\begin{vmatrix} 1 & 0 \\ 8 & 1 \end{vmatrix}$.

The minor for −3 is $\begin{vmatrix} 1 & 0 \\ 3 & 4 \end{vmatrix}$.

Now we have three numerical factors, 4, −9, and −3, and three second-order determinants. We multiply each numerical factor by its second-order determinant to find the three terms of the third-order determinant:

$$4\begin{vmatrix} 3 & 4 \\ 8 & 1 \end{vmatrix}, \quad -9\begin{vmatrix} 1 & 0 \\ 8 & 1 \end{vmatrix}, \quad -3\begin{vmatrix} 1 & 0 \\ 3 & 4 \end{vmatrix}.$$

Based on the preceding definition, we subtract the second term from the first term and add the third term:

Technology

A graphing utility can be used to evaluate the determinant of a matrix. Enter the matrix and call it *A*. Then use the determinant command. The screen below verifies our result in Example 3.

```
[A]
      [[4  1  0]
       [-9 3  4]
       [-3 8  1]]
det([A])
           -119
```

Don't forget to supply the minus sign.

$$\begin{vmatrix} 4 & 1 & 0 \\ -9 & 3 & 4 \\ -3 & 8 & 1 \end{vmatrix} = 4\begin{vmatrix} 3 & 4 \\ 8 & 1 \end{vmatrix} - (-9)\begin{vmatrix} 1 & 0 \\ 8 & 1 \end{vmatrix} - 3\begin{vmatrix} 1 & 0 \\ 3 & 4 \end{vmatrix}$$ Evaluate the three second-order determinants.

$$= 4(3 \cdot 1 - 8 \cdot 4) + 9(1 \cdot 1 - 8 \cdot 0) - 3(1 \cdot 4 - 3 \cdot 0)$$

$$= 4(3 - 32) + 9(1 - 0) - 3(4 - 0)$$

$$= 4(-29) + 9(1) - 3(4)$$ Subtract within parentheses.

$$= -116 + 9 - 12$$ Multiply.

$$= -119$$ Add and subtract as indicated.

Evaluate the determinant of

$$\begin{bmatrix} 2 & 1 & 7 \\ -5 & 6 & 0 \\ -4 & 3 & 1 \end{bmatrix}.$$

The six terms in the definition of a third-order determinant can be rearranged and factored in a variety of ways. Thus, it is possible to expand a determinant by minors about any row or any column. *Minus signs must be supplied preceding any element appearing in a position where the sum of its row and its column is an odd number.* For example, expanding about the elements in column 2 gives us

$$\begin{vmatrix} a_1 & b_1 & c_1 \\ a_2 & b_2 & c_2 \\ a_3 & b_3 & c_3 \end{vmatrix} = -b_1\begin{vmatrix} a_2 & c_2 \\ a_3 & c_3 \end{vmatrix} + b_2\begin{vmatrix} a_1 & c_1 \\ a_3 & c_3 \end{vmatrix} - b_3\begin{vmatrix} a_1 & c_1 \\ a_2 & c_2 \end{vmatrix}.$$

Minus sign is supplied because b_1 appears in row 1 and column 2; $1+2=3$, an odd number.

Minus sign is supplied because b_3 appears in row 3 and column 2; $3+2=5$, an odd number.

Study Tip

Keep in mind that you can expand a determinant by minors about any row or column. Use alternating plus and minus signs to precede the numerical factors of the minors according to the following sign array:

$$\begin{vmatrix} + & - & + \\ - & + & - \\ + & - & + \end{vmatrix}.$$

Expanding by minors about column 3, we obtain

$$\begin{vmatrix} a_1 & b_1 & c_1 \\ a_2 & b_2 & c_2 \\ a_3 & b_3 & c_3 \end{vmatrix} = c_1\begin{vmatrix} a_2 & b_2 \\ a_3 & b_3 \end{vmatrix} - c_2\begin{vmatrix} a_1 & b_1 \\ a_3 & b_3 \end{vmatrix} + c_3\begin{vmatrix} a_1 & b_1 \\ a_2 & b_2 \end{vmatrix}.$$

Minus sign must be supplied because c_2 appears in row 2 and column 3; $2+3=5$, an odd number.

When evaluating a 3 × 3 determinant using expansion by minors, you can expand about any row or column. To simplify the arithmetic, if a row or column contains one or more 0s, expand about that row or column.

EXAMPLE 4 Evaluating a Third-Order Determinant

Evaluate:

$$\begin{vmatrix} 9 & 5 & 0 \\ -2 & -3 & 0 \\ 1 & 4 & 2 \end{vmatrix}.$$

Solution Note that the last column has two 0s. We will expand the determinant about the elements in that column.

$$\begin{vmatrix} 9 & 5 & 0 \\ -2 & -3 & 0 \\ 1 & 4 & 2 \end{vmatrix} = 0\begin{vmatrix} -2 & -3 \\ 1 & 4 \end{vmatrix} - 0\begin{vmatrix} 9 & 5 \\ 1 & 4 \end{vmatrix} + 2\begin{vmatrix} 9 & 5 \\ -2 & -3 \end{vmatrix}$$

$$= 0 - 0 + 2[9(-3) - (-2) \cdot 5]$$ Evaluate the second-order determinant whose numerical factor is not 0.

$$= 2(-27 + 10)$$

$$= 2(-17)$$

$$= -34$$

Check Point 4   Evaluate:

$$\begin{vmatrix} 6 & 4 & 0 \\ -3 & -5 & 3 \\ 1 & 2 & 0 \end{vmatrix}.$$

4 Solve a system of linear equations in three variables using Cramer's rule.

Solving Systems of Linear Equations in Three Variables Using Determinants

Cramer's rule can be applied to solving systems of linear equations in three variables. The determinants in the numerator and denominator of all variables are third-order determinants.

Solving Three Equations in Three Variables Using Determinants

Cramer's Rule

If

$$a_1 x + b_1 y + c_1 z = d_1$$
$$a_2 x + b_2 y + c_2 z = d_2$$
$$a_3 x + b_3 y + c_3 z = d_3$$

then

$$x = \frac{D_x}{D}, \; y = \frac{D_y}{D}, \; \text{and} \; z = \frac{D_z}{D}.$$

These four third-order determinants are given by:

$$D = \begin{vmatrix} a_1 & b_1 & c_1 \\ a_2 & b_2 & c_2 \\ a_3 & b_3 & c_3 \end{vmatrix}$$ These are the coefficients of the variables x, y, and z. $D \neq 0$.

$$D_x = \begin{vmatrix} d_1 & b_1 & c_1 \\ d_2 & b_2 & c_2 \\ d_3 & b_3 & c_3 \end{vmatrix}$$ Replace x-coefficients in D with the **constants at the right** of the three equations.

$$D_y = \begin{vmatrix} a_1 & d_1 & c_1 \\ a_2 & d_2 & c_2 \\ a_3 & d_3 & c_3 \end{vmatrix}$$ Replace y-coefficients in D with the **constants at the right** of the three equations.

$$D_z = \begin{vmatrix} a_1 & b_1 & d_1 \\ a_2 & b_2 & d_2 \\ a_3 & b_3 & d_3 \end{vmatrix}.$$ Replace z-coefficients in D with the **constants at the right** of the three equations.

EXAMPLE 5   **Using Cramer's Rule to Solve a Linear System in Three Variables**

Use Cramer's rule to solve:

$$x + 2y - z = -4$$
$$x + 4y - 2z = -6$$
$$2x + 3y + z = 3.$$

Solution   Because

$$x = \frac{D_x}{D}, \quad y = \frac{D_y}{D}, \quad \text{and} \quad z = \frac{D_z}{D},$$

we need to set up and evaluate four determinants.

$x + 2y - z = -4$

$x + 4y - 2z = -6$

$2x + 3y + z = 3$

The given linear system, repeated

Step 1   Set up the determinants.

1. D, the determinant in all three denominators, consists of the x-, y-, and z-coefficients.

$$D = \begin{vmatrix} 1 & 2 & -1 \\ 1 & 4 & -2 \\ 2 & 3 & 1 \end{vmatrix}$$

2. D_x, the determinant in the numerator for x, is obtained by replacing the x-coefficients in D, 1, 1, and 2, with the constants on the right side of the equation, -4, -6, and 3.

$$D_x = \begin{vmatrix} -4 & 2 & -1 \\ -6 & 4 & -2 \\ 3 & 3 & 1 \end{vmatrix}$$

3. D_y, the determinant in the numerator for y, is obtained by replacing the y-coefficients in D, 2, 4, and 3, with the constants on the right side of the equation, -4, -6, and 3.

$$D_y = \begin{vmatrix} 1 & -4 & -1 \\ 1 & -6 & -2 \\ 2 & 3 & 1 \end{vmatrix}$$

4. D_z, the determinant in the numerator for z, is obtained by replacing the z-coefficients in D, -1, -2, and 1, with the constants on the right side of the equation, -4, -6, and 3.

$$D_z = \begin{vmatrix} 1 & 2 & -4 \\ 1 & 4 & -6 \\ 2 & 3 & 3 \end{vmatrix}$$

Step 2   Evaluate the four determinants.

Study Tip

To find D_x, D_y, and D_z, you'll need to apply the evaluation process for 3×3 determinant three times. The values of D_x, D_y, and D_z, cannot be obtained from the numbers that occur in the computation of D.

$$D = \begin{vmatrix} 1 & 2 & -1 \\ 1 & 4 & -2 \\ 2 & 3 & 1 \end{vmatrix} = 1 \begin{vmatrix} 4 & -2 \\ 3 & 1 \end{vmatrix} - 1 \begin{vmatrix} 2 & -1 \\ 3 & 1 \end{vmatrix} + 2 \begin{vmatrix} 2 & -1 \\ 4 & -2 \end{vmatrix}$$

$$= 1(4 + 6) - 1(2 + 3) + 2(-4 + 4)$$

$$= 1(10) - 1(5) + 2(0) = 5$$

Using the same technique to evaluate each determinant, we obtain

$$D_x = -10, \quad D_y = 5, \quad \text{and} \quad D_z = 20.$$

Step 3   Substitute these four values and solve the system.

$$x = \frac{D_x}{D} = \frac{-10}{5} = -2$$

$$y = \frac{D_y}{D} = \frac{5}{5} = 1$$

$$z = \frac{D_z}{D} = \frac{20}{5} = 4$$

The solution $(-2, 1, 4)$ can be checked by substitution into the original three equations. The solution set is $\{(-2, 1, 4)\}$.

> **Check Point 5** Use Cramer's rule to solve the system:
>
> $$\begin{aligned} 3x - 2y + z &= 16 \\ 2x + 3y - z &= -9. \\ x + 4y + 3z &= 2 \end{aligned}$$

5 Use determinants to identify inconsistent systems and systems with dependent equations.

Cramer's Rule with Inconsistent and Dependent Systems

If D, the determinant in the denominator, is 0, the variables described by the quotient of determinants are not real numbers. However, when $D = 0$, this indicates that the system is inconsistent or contains dependent equations. This gives rise to the following two situations:

Discovery

Write a system of two equations that is inconsistent. Now use determinants and the result boxed on the right to verify that this is truly an inconsistent system. Repeat the same process for a system with two dependent equations.

> **Determinants: Inconsistent and Dependent-Systems**
>
> 1. If $D = 0$ and at least one of the determinants in the numerator is not 0, then the system is inconsistent. The solution set is $\varnothing$.
>
> 2. If $D = 0$ and all the determinants in the numerators are 0, then the equations in the system are dependent. The system has infinitely many solutions.

Although we have focused on applying determinants to solve linear systems, they have other applications, some of which we consider in the exercise set that follows.

6 Evaluate higher-order determinants.

The Determinant of Any $n \times n$ Matrix

A determinant with n rows and n columns is said to be an **nth-order determinant.** The value of an nth-order determinant $(n > 2)$ can be found in terms of determinants of order $n - 1$. For example, we found the value of a third-order determinant in terms of determinants of order 2.

We can generalize this idea for fourth-order determinants and higher. We have seen that the **minor** of the element a_{ij} is the determinant obtained by deleting the ith row and the jth column in the given array of numbers. The **cofactor** of the element a_{ij} is $(-1)^{i+j}$ times the minor of the a_{ij}th entry. If the sum of the row and column $(i + j)$ is even, the cofactor is the same as the minor. If the sum of the row and column $(i + j)$ is odd, the cofactor is the opposite of the minor.

Let's see what this means in the case of a fourth-order determinant.

EXAMPLE 6   Evaluating the Determinant of a 4 × 4 Matrix

Evaluate the determinant of

$$A = \begin{bmatrix} 1 & -2 & 3 & 0 \\ -1 & 1 & 0 & 2 \\ 0 & 2 & 0 & -3 \\ 2 & 3 & -4 & 1 \end{bmatrix}.$$

Cramer's Rule and the World's Fastest Computer

In 2002, the fastest super-computer was the *ASCI White*, built by IBM and capable of performing 12 trillion (12×10^{12}) calculations per second. To solve a linear system with a "mere" 20 equations using Cramer's rule requires over 5×10^{19} multiplications. Although the *ASCI White* can solve a problem in one second that would take one person with a calculator 10 million years to complete, it would take the supercomputer more than 48 days to solve a system with 20 equations using Cramer's rule. Might the *ASCI White* be interested in this challenge? Absolutely not. Its purpose is to allow the testing of nuclear weapons using computer simulation rather than detonating actual bombs.

Solution

$$|A| = \begin{vmatrix} 1 & -2 & 3 & 0 \\ -1 & 1 & 0 & 2 \\ 0 & 2 & 0 & -3 \\ 2 & 3 & -4 & 1 \end{vmatrix}$$

With two 0s in the third column, we will expand along the third column.

$$= (-1)^{1+3}(3) \begin{vmatrix} -1 & 1 & 2 \\ 0 & 2 & -3 \\ 2 & 3 & 1 \end{vmatrix} + (-1)^{4+3}(-4) \begin{vmatrix} 1 & -2 & 0 \\ -1 & 1 & 2 \\ 0 & 2 & -3 \end{vmatrix}$$

3 is in row 1, column 3.

−4 is in row 4, column 3.

$$= 3 \begin{vmatrix} -1 & 1 & 2 \\ 0 & 2 & -3 \\ 2 & 3 & 1 \end{vmatrix} + 4 \begin{vmatrix} 1 & -2 & 0 \\ -1 & 1 & 2 \\ 0 & 2 & -3 \end{vmatrix}$$

The determinant that follows 3 is obtained by crossing out the row and the column (row 1, column 3) in the original determinant. The minor for −4 is obtained in the same manner.

Evaluate the two third-order determinants to get

$$|A| = 3(-25) + 4(-1) = -79.$$

Check Point 6 Evaluate the determinant of

$$A = \begin{bmatrix} 0 & 4 & 0 & -3 \\ -1 & 1 & 5 & 2 \\ 1 & -2 & 0 & 6 \\ 3 & 0 & 0 & 1 \end{bmatrix}.$$

If a linear system has n equations, Cramer's rule requires you to compute $n + 1$ determinants of nth order. The excessive number of calculations required to perform Cramer's rule for systems with four or more equations makes it an inefficient method for solving large systems.

EXERCISE SET 3.4

Practice Exercises

Evaluate each determinant in Exercises 1–10.

1. $\begin{vmatrix} 5 & 7 \\ 2 & 3 \end{vmatrix}$ 2. $\begin{vmatrix} 4 & 8 \\ 5 & 6 \end{vmatrix}$

3. $\begin{vmatrix} -4 & 1 \\ 5 & 6 \end{vmatrix}$ 4. $\begin{vmatrix} 7 & 9 \\ -2 & -5 \end{vmatrix}$

5. $\begin{vmatrix} -7 & 14 \\ 2 & -4 \end{vmatrix}$ 6. $\begin{vmatrix} 1 & -3 \\ -8 & 2 \end{vmatrix}$

7. $\begin{vmatrix} -5 & -1 \\ -2 & -7 \end{vmatrix}$ 8. $\begin{vmatrix} \frac{1}{5} & \frac{1}{6} \\ -6 & 5 \end{vmatrix}$

9. $\begin{vmatrix} \frac{1}{2} & \frac{1}{2} \\ \frac{1}{8} & -\frac{3}{4} \end{vmatrix}$ 10. $\begin{vmatrix} \frac{2}{3} & \frac{1}{3} \\ -\frac{1}{2} & \frac{3}{4} \end{vmatrix}$

For Exercises 11–26, use Cramer's rule to solve each system or to determine that the system is inconsistent or contains dependent equations.

11. $x + y = 7$
    $x - y = 3$

12. $2x + y = 3$
    $x - y = 3$

13. $12x + 3y = 15$
$2x - 3y = 13$

14. $x - 2y = 5$
$5x - y = -2$

15. $4x - 5y = 17$
$2x + 3y = 3$

16. $3x + 2y = 2$
$2x + 2y = 3$

17. $x + 2y = 3$
$5x + 10y = 15$

18. $2x - 9y = 5$
$3x - 3y = 11$

19. $3x - 4y = 4$
$2x + 2y = 12$

20. $3x = 7y + 1$
$2x = 3y - 1$

21. $2x = 3y + 2$
$5x = 51 - 4y$

22. $y = -4x + 2$
$2x = 3y + 8$

23. $3x = 2 - 3y$
$2y = 3 - 2x$

24. $x + 2y - 3 = 0$
$12 = 8y + 4x$

25. $4y = 16 - 3x$
$6x = 32 - 8y$

26. $2x = 7 + 3y$
$4x - 6y = 3$

Evaluate each determinant in Exercises 27–32.

27. $\begin{vmatrix} 3 & 0 & 0 \\ 2 & 1 & -5 \\ 2 & 5 & -1 \end{vmatrix}$

28. $\begin{vmatrix} 4 & 0 & 0 \\ 3 & -1 & 4 \\ 2 & -3 & 5 \end{vmatrix}$

29. $\begin{vmatrix} 3 & 1 & 0 \\ -3 & 4 & 0 \\ -1 & 3 & -5 \end{vmatrix}$

30. $\begin{vmatrix} 2 & -4 & 2 \\ -1 & 0 & 5 \\ 3 & 0 & 4 \end{vmatrix}$

31. $\begin{vmatrix} 1 & 1 & 1 \\ 2 & 2 & 2 \\ -3 & 4 & -5 \end{vmatrix}$

32. $\begin{vmatrix} 1 & 2 & 3 \\ 2 & 2 & -3 \\ 3 & 2 & 1 \end{vmatrix}$

In Exercises 33–40, use Cramer's rule to solve each system.

33. $x + y + z = 0$
$2x - y + z = -1$
$-x + 3y - z = -8$

34. $x - y + 2z = 3$
$2x + 3y + z = 9$
$-x - y + 3z = 11$

35. $4x - 5y - 6z = -1$
$x - 2y - 5z = -12$
$2x - y = 7$

36. $x - 3y + z = -2$
$x + 2y = 8$
$2x - y = 1$

37. $x + y + z = 4$
$x - 2y + z = 7$
$x + 3y + 2z = 4$

38. $2x + 2y + 3z = 10$
$4x - y + z = -5$
$5x - 2y + 6z = 1$

39. $x + 2z = 4$
$2y - z = 5$
$2x + 3y = 13$

40. $3x + 2z = 4$
$5x - y = -4$
$4y + 3z = 22$

Evaluate each determinant in Exercises 41–44.

41. $\begin{vmatrix} 4 & 2 & 8 & -7 \\ -2 & 0 & 4 & 1 \\ 5 & 0 & 0 & 5 \\ 4 & 0 & 0 & -1 \end{vmatrix}$

42. $\begin{vmatrix} 3 & -1 & 1 & 2 \\ -2 & 0 & 0 & 0 \\ 2 & -1 & -2 & 3 \\ 1 & 4 & 2 & 3 \end{vmatrix}$

43. $\begin{vmatrix} -2 & -3 & 3 & 5 \\ 1 & -4 & 0 & 0 \\ 1 & 2 & 2 & -3 \\ 2 & 0 & 1 & 1 \end{vmatrix}$

44. $\begin{vmatrix} 1 & -3 & 2 & 0 \\ -3 & -1 & 0 & -2 \\ 2 & 1 & 3 & 1 \\ 2 & 0 & -2 & 0 \end{vmatrix}$

Application Exercises

Determinants are used to find the area of a triangle whose vertices are given by three points in a rectangular coordinate system. The area of a triangle with vertices $(x_1, y_1), (x_2, y_2),$ and (x_3, y_3) is

$$\text{Area} = \pm \frac{1}{2} \begin{vmatrix} x_1 & y_1 & 1 \\ x_2 & y_2 & 1 \\ x_3 & y_3 & 1 \end{vmatrix}$$

where the $\pm$ symbol indicates that the appropriate sign should be chosen to yield a positive area. Use this information to work Exercises 45–46.

45. Use determinants to find the area of the triangle whose vertices are $(3, -5), (2, 6),$ and $(-3, 5)$.

46. Use determinants to find the area of the triangle whose vertices are $(1, 1), (-2, -3),$ and $(11, -3)$.

Determinants are used to show that three points lie on the same line (are collinear). If

$$\begin{vmatrix} x_1 & y_1 & 1 \\ x_2 & y_2 & 1 \\ x_3 & y_3 & 1 \end{vmatrix} = 0,$$

then the points $(x_1, y_1), (x_2, y_2),$ and (x_3, y_3) are collinear. If the determinant does not equal 0, then the points are not collinear. Use this information to work Exercises 47–48.

47. Are the points $(3, -1), (0, -3),$ and $(12, 5)$ collinear?

48. Are the points $(-4, -6), (1, 0),$ and $(11, 12)$ collinear?

Determinants are used to write an equation of a line passing through two points. An equation of the line passing through the distinct points (x_1, y_1) and (x_2, y_2) is given by

$$\begin{vmatrix} x & y & 1 \\ x_1 & y_1 & 1 \\ x_2 & y_2 & 1 \end{vmatrix} = 0.$$

Use this information to work Exercises 49–50.

49. Use the determinant to write an equation of the line passing through $(3, -5)$ and $(-2, 6)$. Then expand the determinant, expressing the line's equation in slope-intercept form.

50. Use the determinant to write an equation of the line passing through $(-1, 3)$ and $(2, 4)$. Then expand the determinant, expressing the line's equation in slope-intercept form.

Writing in Mathematics

51. Explain how to evaluate a second-order determinant.

52. Describe the determinants D_x and D_y in terms of the coefficients and constants in a system of two equations in two variables.

53. Explain how to evaluate a third-order determinant.

54. When expanding a determinant by minors, when is it necessary to supply minus signs?

55. Without going into too much detail, describe how to solve a linear system in three variables using Cramer's rule.

56. In applying Cramer's rule, what does it mean if $D = 0$?

57. The process of solving a linear system in three variables using Cramer's rule can involve tedious computation. Is there a way of speeding up this process, perhaps using Cramer's rule to find the value for only one of the variables? Describe how this process might work, presenting a specific example with your description. Remember that your goal is still to find the value for each variable in the system.

58. If you could use only one method to solve linear systems in three variables, which method would you select? Explain why this is so.

Technology Exercises

59. Use the feature of your graphing utility that evaluates the determinant of a square matrix to verify any five of the determinants that you evaluated by hand in Exercises 1–10, 27–32, or 41–44.

In Exercises 60–61, use a graphing utility to evaluate the determinant for the given matrix.

60. $\begin{bmatrix} 3 & -2 & -1 & 4 \\ -5 & 1 & 2 & 7 \\ 2 & 4 & 5 & 0 \\ -1 & 3 & -6 & 5 \end{bmatrix}$

61. $\begin{bmatrix} 8 & 2 & 6 & -1 & 0 \\ 2 & 0 & -3 & 4 & 7 \\ 2 & 1 & -3 & 6 & -5 \\ -1 & 2 & 1 & 5 & -1 \\ 4 & 5 & -2 & 3 & -8 \end{bmatrix}$

62. What is the fastest method for solving a linear system with your graphing utility?

Critical Thinking Exercises

63. a. Evaluate: $\begin{vmatrix} a & a \\ 0 & a \end{vmatrix}$.

b. Evaluate: $\begin{vmatrix} a & a & a \\ 0 & a & a \\ 0 & 0 & a \end{vmatrix}$.

c. Evaluate: $\begin{vmatrix} a & a & a & a \\ 0 & a & a & a \\ 0 & 0 & a & a \\ 0 & 0 & 0 & a \end{vmatrix}$.

d. Describe the pattern in the given determinants.

e. Describe the pattern in the evaluations.

64. Evaluate: $\begin{vmatrix} 2 & 0 & 0 & 0 & 0 \\ 0 & 3 & 0 & 0 & 0 \\ 0 & 0 & 2 & 0 & 0 \\ 0 & 0 & 0 & 1 & 0 \\ 0 & 0 & 0 & 0 & 4 \end{vmatrix}$.

65. What happens to the value of a second-order determinant if the two columns are interchanged?

66. Consider the system

$$a_1 x + b_1 y = c_1$$
$$a_2 x + b_2 y = c_2.$$

Use Cramer's rule to prove that if the first equation of the system is replaced by the sum of the two equations, the resulting system has the same solution as the original system.

67. Show that the equation of a line through (x_1, y_1) and (x_2, y_2) is given by the determinant equation in Exercises 49–50.

Group Exercise

68. We have seen that determinants can be used to solve linear equations, give areas of triangles in rectangular coordinates, and determine equations of lines. Not impressed with these applications? Members of the group should research an application of determinants that they find intriguing. The group should then present a seminar to the class about this application.

CHAPTER SUMMARY, REVIEW, AND TEST

Summary

DEFINITIONS AND CONCEPTS	EXAMPLES

3.1 Systems of Linear Equations in Two Variables

a. Two equations in the form $Ax + By = C$ are called a system of linear equations. A solution to the system is an ordered pair that satisfies both equations in the system.

Ex. 1, p. 259

b. Systems of linear equations in two variables can be solved by eliminating a variable, using the substitution method (see the box on page 261) or the addition method (see the box on page 263).

Ex. 2, p. 260;
Ex. 3, p. 261;
Ex. 4, p. 263;
Ex. 5, p. 264

c. Some linear systems have no solution and are called inconsistent systems; others have infinitely many solutions. The equations in a linear system with infinitely many solutions are called dependent. For details, see the box on page 265.

Ex. 6, p. 265;
Ex. 7, p. 266

3.2 Systems of Linear Equations in Three Variables

a. Three equations in the form $Ax + By + Cz = D$ are called a system of linear equations in three variables. A solution to the system is an ordered triple that satisfies all three equations in the system.

Ex. 1, p. 276

b. A system of linear equations in three variables can be solved by eliminating variables. Use the addition method to eliminate any variable, reducing the system to two equations in two variables.

Ex. 2, p. 277;
Ex. 3, p. 278

3.3 Matrix Solutions to Linear Systems

a. Matrix row operations are described in the box on page 286.

Ex. 2, p. 287

b. To solve a linear system using Gaussian elimination, begin with the system's augmented matrix. Use matrix operations to get 1s down the diagonal from upper left to lower right and 0s below the 1s. Such a matrix is in row-echelon form. Details are in the box on page 288.

Ex. 3, p. 288;
Ex. 4, p. 291

c. To solve a linear system using Gauss-Jordan elimination, use the procedure of Gaussian elimination, but obtain 0s above and below the 1s in the diagonal from upper left to lower right. Such a matrix is in reduced row-echelon form. Details are in the box on page 293.

Ex. 5, p.294

3.4 Determinants and Cramer's Rule

a. Value of a Second-Order Determinant:

$$\begin{vmatrix} a_1 & b_1 \\ a_2 & b_2 \end{vmatrix} = a_1 b_2 - a_2 b_1$$

Ex. 1, p. 300

b. Cramer's rule for solving systems of linear equations in two variables uses three second-order determinants and is stated in the box on page 301.

Ex. 2, p. 302

c. To evaluate an nth-order determinant, where $n > 2$,

   1. Select a row or column about which to expand.

Ex. 3, p. 304;

   2. Multiply each element a_{ij} in the row or column, by $(-1)^{i+j}$ times the determinant obtained by deleting the ith row and the jth column in the given array of numbers.

Ex. 4, p. 305;
Ex. 6, p. 308

   3. The value of the determinant is the sum of the products found in step 2.

d. Cramer's rule for solving systems of linear equations in three variables uses four third-order determinants and is stated in the box on page 307.

Ex. 5, p. 306

e. Cramer's rule with inconsistent and dependent systems is summarized by the two situations in the box on page 309.

Review Exercises

3.1

In Exercises 1–5, solve by the method of your choice. Identify systems with no solution and systems with infinitely many solutions, using set notation to express their solution sets.

1. $y = 4x + 1$
$3x + 2y = 13$

2. $x + 4y = 14$
$2x - y = 1$

3. $5x + 3y = 1$
$3x + 4y = -6$

4. $2y - 6x = 7$
$3x - y = 9$

5. $4x - 8y = 16$
$3x - 6y = 12$

6. A company is planning to manufacture computer desks. The fixed cost will be $60,000 and it will cost $200 to produce each desk. Each desk will be sold for $450.
   a. Write the cost function, C, of producing x desks.
   b. Write the revenue function, R, from the sale of x desks.
   c. Determine the break-even point. Describe what this means.

7. The weekly demand and supply models for the video *Pearl Harbor* at a chain of stores that sells videos are given by the demand model $N = -60p + 1000$ and the supply model $N = 4p + 200$, in which p is the price of the video and N is the number of videos sold or supplied each week to the chain of stores. Find the price at which supply and demand are equal. At this price, how many copies of *Pearl Harbor* can be supplied and sold each week?

8. The graph makes Super Bowl Sunday look like a day of snack food binging in the United States. The number of pounds of guacamole consumed is ten times the difference between the number of pounds of potato and tortilla chips eaten on the same day. On Super Bowl Sunday, Americans also eat a total quantity of potato and tortilla chips that exceeds popcorn consumption by 7.3 million pounds. How many millions of pounds of potato chips and tortilla chips are consumed on Super Bowl Sunday?

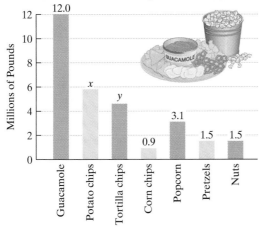

Millions of Pounds of Snack Food Consumed on Super Bowl Sunday

Source: Association of American Snack Foods

9. A travel agent offers two package vacation plans. The first plan costs $360 and includes 3 days at a hotel and a rental car for 2 days. The second plan costs $500 and includes 4 days at a hotel and a rental car for 3 days. The daily charge for the hotel is the same under each plan, as is the daily charge for the car. Find the cost per day for the hotel and for the car.

10. The calorie-nutrient information for an apple and an avocado is given in the table. How many of each should be eaten to get exactly 1000 calories and 100 grams of carbohydrates?

	One Apple	One Avocado
Calories	100	350
Carbohydrates (grams)	24	14

3.2

Solve each system in Exercises 11–12.

11. $2x - y + z = 1$
$3x - 3y + 4z = 5$
$4x - 2y + 3z = 4$

12. $x + 2y - z = 5$
$2x - y + 3z = 0$
$2y + z = 1$

13. Find the quadratic function $y = ax^2 + bx + c$ whose graph passes through the points $(1, 4)$, $(3, 20)$, and $(-2, 25)$.

14. The bar graph shows that the U.S. divorce rate increased between 1970 and 1985 and then decreased between 1985 and 1999.

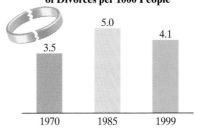

U.S. Divorce Rates: Number of Divorces per 1000 People

Source: U.S. Census Bureau

   a. Write the data for 1970, 1985, and 1999 as ordered pairs (x, y), where x is the number of years after 1970 and y is that year's divorce rate.
   b. The three data points in part (a) can be modeled by the quadratic function $y = ax^2 + bx + c$. Write a system of linear equations in three variables that can be used to find values for a, b, and c. It is not necessary to solve the system.

15. The bar graph indicates countries in which ten or more languages have become extinct. The number of extinct languages in the United States, Colombia, and India combined is 50. The number of extinct languages in the United States exceeds the number in Colombia by 4 and is 2 more than twice that for India. How many languages have become extinct in the United States, Colombia, and India?

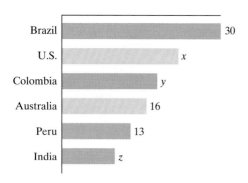

Countries Where Ten or More Laguages Have Become Extinct (Number of Languages)

Brazil 30
U.S. x
Colombia y
Australia 16
Peru 13
India z

Source: Grimes

3.3

In Exercises 1–2, write the system of linear equations represented by the augmented matrix. Use x, y, z, and, if necessary, w ,x, y, and z, for the variables. Once the system is written, use back-substitution to find its solution.

16.
$$\begin{bmatrix} 1 & 1 & 3 & | & 12 \\ 0 & 1 & -2 & | & -4 \\ 0 & 0 & 1 & | & 3 \end{bmatrix}$$

17.
$$\begin{bmatrix} 1 & 0 & -2 & 2 & | & 1 \\ 0 & 1 & 1 & -1 & | & 0 \\ 0 & 0 & 1 & -\frac{7}{3} & | & -\frac{1}{3} \\ 0 & 0 & 0 & 1 & | & 1 \end{bmatrix}$$

In Exercises 3–4, perform each matrix row operation and write the new matrix.

18.
$$\begin{bmatrix} 1 & 2 & 2 & | & 2 \\ 0 & 1 & -1 & | & 2 \\ 0 & 5 & 4 & | & 1 \end{bmatrix} \quad -5R_2 + R_3$$

19.
$$\begin{bmatrix} 2 & -2 & 1 & | & -1 \\ 1 & 2 & -1 & | & 2 \\ 6 & 4 & 3 & | & 5 \end{bmatrix} \quad \frac{1}{2}R_1$$

In Exercises 5–7, solve each system of equations using matrices. Use Gaussian elimination with back-substitution or Gauss-Jordan elimination.

20.
$$\begin{aligned} x + 2y + 3z &= -5 \\ 2x + y + z &= 1 \\ x + y - z &= 8 \end{aligned}$$

21.
$$\begin{aligned} x - 2y + z &= 0 \\ y - 3z &= -1 \\ 2y + 5z &= -2 \end{aligned}$$

22.
$$\begin{aligned} 3x_1 + 5x_2 - 8x_3 + 5x_4 &= -8 \\ x_1 + 2x_2 - 3x_3 + x_4 &= -7 \\ 2x_1 + 3x_2 - 7x_3 + 3x_4 &= -11 \\ 4x_1 + 8x_2 - 10x_3 + 7x_4 &= -10 \end{aligned}$$

23. The table shows the pollutants in the air in a city on a typical summer day.

x (Hours after 6 A.M.)	y (Amount of Pollutants in the Air, in parts per million)
2	98
4	138
10	162

a. Use the function $y = ax^2 + bx + c$ to model the data. Use either Gaussian elimination with back-substitution or Gauss-Jordan elimination to find the values for a, b, and c.

b. Use the function to find the time of day at which the city's air pollution level is at a maximum. What is the maximum level?

3.4

In Exercises 24–29, evaluate each determinant.

24.
$$\begin{vmatrix} 3 & 2 \\ -1 & 5 \end{vmatrix}$$

25.
$$\begin{vmatrix} -2 & -3 \\ -4 & -8 \end{vmatrix}$$

26.
$$\begin{vmatrix} 2 & 4 & -3 \\ 1 & -1 & 5 \\ -2 & 4 & 0 \end{vmatrix}$$

27.
$$\begin{vmatrix} 4 & 7 & 0 \\ -5 & 6 & 0 \\ 3 & 2 & -4 \end{vmatrix}$$

28.
$$\begin{vmatrix} 1 & 1 & 0 & 2 \\ 0 & 3 & 2 & 1 \\ 0 & -2 & 4 & 0 \\ 0 & 3 & 0 & 1 \end{vmatrix}$$

29.
$$\begin{vmatrix} 2 & 2 & 2 & 2 \\ 0 & 2 & 2 & 2 \\ 0 & 0 & 2 & 2 \\ 0 & 0 & 0 & 2 \end{vmatrix}$$

In Exercises 30–33, use Cramer's rule to solve each system.

30.
$$\begin{aligned} x - 2y &= 8 \\ 3x + 2y &= -1 \end{aligned}$$

31.
$$\begin{aligned} 7x + 2y &= 0 \\ 2x + y &= -3 \end{aligned}$$

32.
$$\begin{aligned} x + 2y + 2z &= 5 \\ 2x + 4y + 7z &= 19 \\ -2x - 5y - 2z &= 8 \end{aligned}$$

33.
$$\begin{aligned} 2x + y &= -4 \\ y - 2z &= 0 \\ 3x - 2z &= -11 \end{aligned}$$

34. Use the quadratic function $y = ax^2 + bx + c$ to model the following data:

x (Age of a Driver)	y (Average Number of Automobile Accidents per Day in the United States)
20	400
40	150
60	400

Use Cramer's rule to determine values for a, b, and c. Then use the model to write a statement about the average number of automobile accidents in which 30-year-olds and 50-year-olds are involved daily.

Chapter 3 Test

In Exercises 1–5, solve the system.

1. $x = y + 4$
$3x + 7y = -18$

2. $2x + 5y = -2$
$3x - 4y = 20$

3. $x + y + z = 6$
$3x + 4y - 7z = 1$
$2x - y + 3z = 5$

4. $x^2 + y^2 = 25$
$x + y = 1$

5. $2x^2 - 5y^2 = -2$
$3x^2 + 2y^2 = 35$

In Exercises 6–7, solve each system of equations using matrices.

6. $x + 2y - z = -3$
$2x - 4y + z = -7$
$-2x + 2y - 3z = 4$

7. $x - 2y + z = 2$
$2x - y - z = 1$

8. Evaluate: $\begin{vmatrix} 4 & -1 & 3 \\ 0 & 5 & -1 \\ 5 & 2 & 4 \end{vmatrix}$.

9. Solve for x only using Cramer's rule:
$3x + y - 2z = -3$
$2x + 7y + 3z = 9$
$4x - 3y - z = 7.$

Trigonometric Functions

H ave you had days where your physical, intellectual, and emotional potentials were all at their peak? Then there are those other days when we feel we should not even bother getting out of bed. Do our potentials run in oscillating cycles like the tides? Can they be described mathematically? In this chapter you will encounter functions that enable us to model phenomena that occur in cycles.

What a day! It started when you added two miles to your morning run. You've experienced a feeling of peak physical well-being ever since. College was wonderful: You actually enjoyed two difficult lectures and breezed through a math test that had you worried. Now you're having dinner with an old group of friends. You experience the warmth from bonds of friendship filling the room.

SECTION 4.1 *Angles and Their Measure*

Objectives

1. Recognize and use the vocabulary of angles.
2. Use degree measure.
3. Draw angles in standard position.
4. Find coterminal angles.
5. Find complements and supplements.
6. Use radian measure.
7. Convert between degrees and radians.
8. Find the length of a circular arc.
9. Use linear and angular speed to describe motion on a circular path.

The San Francisco Museum of Modern Art was constructed in 1995 to illustrate how art and architecture can enrich one another. The exterior involves geometric shapes, symmetry, and unusual facades. Although there are no windows, natural light streams in through a truncated cylindrical skylight that crowns the building. The architect worked with a scale model of the museum at the site and observed how light hit it during different times of the day. These observations were used to cut the cylindrical skylight at an angle that maximizes sunlight entering the interior.

Angles play a critical role in creating modern architecture. They are also fundamental in trigonometry. In this section, we begin our study of trigonometry by looking at angles and methods for measuring them.

1 Recognize and use the vocabulary of angles.

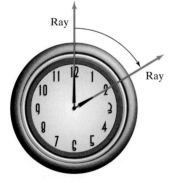

Figure 4.1 Clock with hands forming an angle

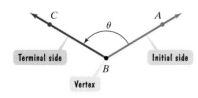

Figure 4.2 An angle; two rays with a common endpoint

Angles

The hour hand of a clock suggests a **ray,** a part of a line that has only one endpoint and extends forever in the opposite direction. An **angle** is formed by two rays that have a common endpoint. One ray is called the **initial side** and the other the **terminal side.**

A rotating ray is often a useful way to think about angles. The ray in Figure 4.1 rotates from 12 to 2. The ray pointing to 12 is the **initial side** and the ray pointing to 2 is the **terminal side.** The common endpoint of an angle's initial side and terminal side is the **vertex** of the angle.

Figure 4.2 shows an angle. The arrow near the vertex shows the direction and the amount of rotation from the initial side to the terminal side. Several methods can be used to name an angle. Lowercase Greek letters, such as α (alpha), β (beta), γ (gamma), and θ (theta), are often used.

An angle is in **standard position** if

- its vertex is at the origin of a rectangular coordinate system

and

- its initial side lies along the positive *x*-axis.

The angles in Figure 4.3 are both in standard position.

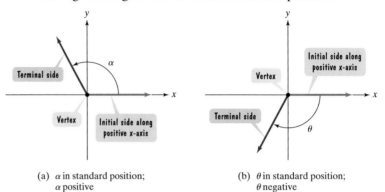

(a) α in standard position; α positive

(b) θ in standard position; θ negative

Figure 4.3 Two angles in standard position

When we see an initial side and a terminal side in place, there are two kinds of rotation that could have generated it. The arrow in Figure 4.3(a) indicates that the rotation from the initial side to the terminal side is in the counterclockwise direction. **Positive angles** are generated by counterclockwise rotation. Thus, angle α is positive. By contrast, the arrow in Figure 4.3(b) shows that the rotation from the initial side to the terminal side is in the clockwise direction. **Negative angles** are generated by clockwise rotation. Thus, angle θ is negative.

When an angle is in standard position, its terminal side can lie in a quadrant. We say that the angle **lies in that quadrant.** For example, in Figure 4.3(a), the terminal side of angle α lies in quadrant II. Thus, angle α lies in quadrant II. By contrast, in Figure 4.3(b), the terminal side of angle θ lies in quadrant III. Thus, angle θ lies in quadrant III.

Must all angles in standard position lie in a quadrant? The answer is no. The terminal side can lie on the x-axis or the y-axis. For example, angle β in Figure 4.4 has a terminal side that lies on the negative y-axis. An angle is called a **quadrantal angle** if its terminal side lies on the x-axis or the y-axis. Angle β in Figure 4.4 is an example of a quadrantal angle.

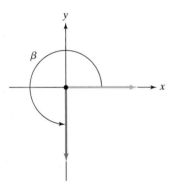

Figure 4.4 β is a quadrantal angle.

2 Use degree measure.

Measuring Angles Using Degrees

Angles are measured by determining the amount of rotation from the initial side to the terminal side. One way to measure angles is in **degrees,** symbolized by a small, raised circle °. Think of the hour hand of a clock. From 12 noon to 12 midnight, the hour hand moves around in a complete circle. By definition, the ray has rotated through 360 degrees, or 360°. Using 360° as the amount of rotation of a ray back onto itself, a degree, 1°, is $\frac{1}{360}$ of a complete rotation.

Figure 4.5 shows angles classified by their degree measurement. An **acute angle** measures less than 90° [see Figure 4.5(a)]. A **right angle,** one quarter of a complete rotation, measures 90° [Figure 4.5(b)]. Examine the right angle—do you see a small square at the vertex? This symbol is used to indicate a right angle. An **obtuse angle** measures more than 90°, but less than 180° [Figure 4.5(c)]. Finally, a **straight angle,** one-half a complete rotation, measures 180° [Figure 4.5(d)].

A complete 360° rotation

Figure 4.5 Classifying angles by their degree measurement

(a) **Acute angle**
$(0° < \theta < 90°)$

(b) **Right angle**
$(\frac{1}{4}$ rotation$)$

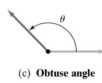

(c) **Obtuse angle**
$(90° < \theta < 180°)$

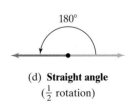

(d) **Straight angle**
$(\frac{1}{2}$ rotation$)$

3 Draw angles in standard position.

We will be using notation such as $\theta = 60°$ to refer to an angle θ whose measure is $60°$. We also refer to *an angle of 60°* or a *60° angle*, rather than using the more precise (but cumbersome) phrase *an angle whose measure is 60°*.

Technology

Fractional parts of degrees are measured in minutes and seconds. One minute, written $1'$, is $\frac{1}{60}$ degree: $1' = \frac{1}{60}°$.

One second, written $1''$, is $\frac{1}{3600}$ degree: $1'' = \frac{1}{3600}°$.

For example,

$$31° \ 47' \ 12''$$

$$= \left(31 + \frac{47}{60} + \frac{12}{3600} \right)°$$

$$\approx 31.787°.$$

Many calculators have keys for changing an angle from degree, minute, second notation (D°M'S") to a decimal form and vice versa.

EXAMPLE 1 Drawing Angles in Standard Position

Draw each angle in standard position:

a. a $45°$ angle **b.** a $225°$ angle **c.** a $-135°$ angle **d.** a $405°$ angle.

Solution Because we are drawing angles in standard position, each vertex is at the origin and each initial side lies along the positive x-axis.

a. A $45°$ angle is half of a right angle. The angle lies in quadrant I and is shown in Figure 4.6(a).

b. A $225°$ angle is a positive angle. It has a counterclockwise rotation of $180°$ followed by a counterclockwise rotation of $45°$. The angle lies in quadrant III and is shown in Figure 4.6(b).

c. A $-135°$ angle is negative angle. It has a clockwise rotation of $90°$ followed by a clockwise rotation of $45°$. The angle lies in quadrant III and is shown in Figure 4.6(c).

d. A $405°$ angle is a positive angle. It has a counterclockwise rotation of $360°$, one complete rotation, followed by a counterclockwise rotation of $45°$. The angle lies in quadrant I and is shown in Figure 4.6(d).

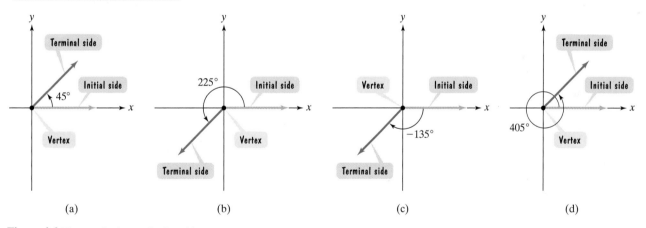

(a)   (b)   (c)   (d)

Figure 4.6 Four angles in standard position

Check Point 1 Draw each angle in standard position:

a. a $30°$ angle **b.** a $210°$ angle **c.** a $-120°$ angle **d.** a $390°$ angle.

4 Find coterminal angles.

Look at Figure 4.6 again. The $45°$ and $405°$ angles in parts (a) and (d) have the same initial and terminal sides. Similarly, the $225°$ and $-135°$ angles in parts (b) and (c) have the same initial and terminal sides. Two angles with the same initial and terminal sides are called **coterminal angles.**

Every angle has infinitely many coterminal angles. Why? Think of an angle in standard position. One or more complete rotations of 360°, clockwise or counterclockwise, result in angles with the same initial and terminal sides as the original angle.

> **Coterminal Angles**
>
> An angle of $x°$ is coterminal with angles of
> $$x° + k \cdot 360°$$
> where k is an integer.

Two coterminal angles for an angle of $x°$ can be found by adding 360° to $x°$ and subtracting 360° from $x°$.

Counterclockwise Clocks

The counterclockwise rotation associated with positive angles was used in England to manufacture counterclockwise clocks. They ran backward but told the time perfectly correctly.

EXAMPLE 2   Finding Coterminal Angles

Assume the following angles are in standard position. Find a positive angle less than 360° that is coterminal with:

a. a 420° angle   **b.** a −120° angle.

Solution   We obtain the coterminal angle by adding or subtracting 360°. The requirement to obtain a positive angle less than 360° determines whether we should add or subtract.

a. For a 420° angle, subtract 360° to find a positive coterminal angle.
$$420° - 360° = 60°$$

A 60° angle is coterminal with a 420° angle. Figure 4.7(a) illustrates that these angles have the same initial and terminal sides.

b. For a −120° angle, add 360° to find a positive coterminal angle.
$$-120° + 360° = 240°$$

A 240° angle is coterminal with a −120° angle. Figure 4.7(b) illustrates that these angles have the same initial and terminal sides.

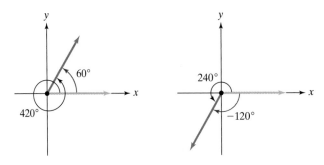

(a) Angles of 420° and 60° are coterminal.

(b) Angles of −120° and 240° are coterminal.

Figure 4.7 Pairs of coterminal angles

Check Point 2 Find a positive angle less than 360° that is coterminal with:
a. a 400° angle   **b.** a −135° angle.

5 Find complements and supplements.

Two positive angles are **complements** if their sum is 90°. For example, angles of 70° and 20° are complements because 70° + 20° = 90°.

Two positive angles are **supplements** if their sum is 180°. For example, angles of 130° and 50° are supplements because 130° + 50° = 180°.

Finding Complements and Supplements

- For an $x°$ angle, the complement is a $90° - x°$ angle. Thus, the complement's measure is found by subtracting the angle's measure from 90°.
- For an $x°$ angle, the supplement is a $180° - x°$ angle. Thus, the supplement's measure is found by subtracting the angle's measure from 180°.

Because we use only positive angles for complements and supplements, some angles do not have complements and supplements.

EXAMPLE 3 Complements and Supplements

If possible, find the complement and the supplement of the given angle:
a. $\theta = 62°$ **b.** $\alpha = 123°$.

Solution We find the complement by subtracting the angle's measure from 90°. We find the supplement by subtracting the angle's measure from 180°.

a. We begin with $\theta = 62°$.

$$\text{complement} = 90° - 62° = 28°$$
$$\text{supplement} = 180° - 62° = 118°$$

For a 62° angle, the complement is a 28° angle and the supplement is a 118° angle.

b. Now we turn to $\alpha = 123°$. For the angle's complement, we consider subtracting 123° from 90°. The difference is negative. Because we use only positive angles for complements, a 123° angle has no complement. It does, however, have a supplement.

$$\text{supplement} = 180° - 123° = 57°$$

The supplement of a 123° angle is a 57° angle.

Check Point 3 If possible, find the complement and the supplement of the given angle:
a. $\theta = 78°$ **b.** $\alpha = 150°$.

6 Use radian measure.

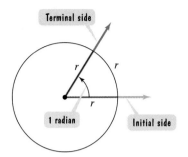

Figure 4.8 For a 1-radian angle, the intercepted arc and the radius are equal.

Measuring Angles Using Radians

Another way to measure angles is in *radians*. Let's first define an angle measuring **1 radian.** We use a circle of radius r. In Figure 4.8, we've constructed an angle whose vertex is at the center of the circle. Such an angle is called a **central angle.** Notice that this central angle intercepts an arc along the circle measuring r units. The radius of the circle is also r units. The measure of such an angle is 1 radian.

> ### Definition of a Radian
>
> **One radian** is the measure of the central angle of a circle that intercepts an arc equal in length to the radius of the circle.

The **radian measure** of any central angle is the length of the intercepted arc divided by the circle's radius. In Figure 4.9(a), the length of the arc intercepted by angle β is double the radius, r. We find the measure of angle β in radians by dividing the length of the intercepted arc by the radius.

$$\beta = \frac{\text{length of the intercepted arc}}{\text{radius}} = \frac{2r}{r} = 2$$

Thus, angle β measures 2 radians.

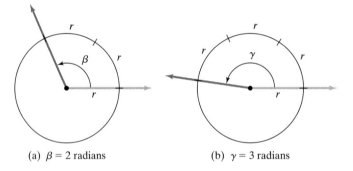

(a) $\beta = 2$ radians   (b) $\gamma = 3$ radians

Figure 4.9 Two central angles measured in radians

In Figure 4.9(b), the length of the intercepted arc is triple the radius, r. Let us find the measure of angle γ:

$$\gamma = \frac{\text{length of the intercepted arc}}{\text{radius}} = \frac{3r}{r} = 3.$$

Thus, angle γ measures 3 radians.

> ### Radian Measure
>
> Consider an arc of length s on a circle of radius r. The measure of the central angle, θ, that intercepts the arc is
>
> $$\theta = \frac{s}{r} \text{ radians.}$$

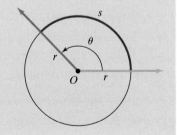

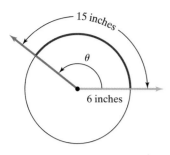

Figure 4.10

EXAMPLE 4 Computing Radian Measure

A central angle, θ, in a circle of radius 6 inches intercepts an arc of length 15 inches. What is the radian measure of θ?

Solution Angle θ is shown in Figure 4.10. The radian measure of a central angle is the length of the intercepted arc, s, divided by the circle's radius, r. The length of the intercepted arc is 15 inches: $s = 15$ inches. The circle's radius is 6 inches: $r = 6$ inches. Now we use the formula for radian measure to find the radian measure of θ.

$$\theta = \frac{s}{r} = \frac{15 \text{ inches}}{6 \text{ inches}} = 2.5$$

Thus, the radian measure of θ is 2.5.

Study Tip

Before applying the formula for radian measure, be sure that the same unit of length is used for the intercepted arc, s, and the radius, r.

In Example 4, notice that the units (inches) cancel when we use the formula for radian measure. We are left with a number with no units. Thus, if an angle θ has a measure of 2.5 radians, we can write $\theta = 2.5$ radians or $\theta = 2.5$. We will often include the word *radians* simply for emphasis. There should be no confusion as to whether radian or degree measure is being used. Why is this so? If θ has a degree measure of, say, 2.5°, we must include the degree symbol and write $\theta = 2.5°$, and *not* $\theta = 2.5$.

> **Check Point 4** A central angle, θ, in a circle of radius 12 feet intercepts an arc of length 42 feet. What is the radian measure of θ?

7 Convert between degrees and radians.

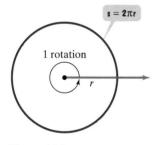

Figure 4.11 A complete rotation

Relationship between Degrees and Radians

How can we obtain a relationship between degrees and radians? We compare the number of degrees and the number of radians in one complete rotation, shown in Figure 4.11. We know that 360° is the amount of rotation of a ray back onto itself. The length of the intercepted arc is equal to the circumference of the circle. Thus, the radian measure of this central angle is the circumference of the circle divided by the circle's radius, r. The circumference of a circle of radius r is $2\pi r$. We use the formula for radian measure to find the radian measure of the 360° angle.

$$\theta = \frac{s}{r} = \frac{\text{the circle's circumference}}{r} = \frac{2\pi r}{r} = 2\pi$$

Because one complete rotation measures 360° and 2π radians,

$$360° = 2\pi \text{ radians.}$$

Dividing both sides by 2, we have

$$180° = \pi \text{ radians.}$$

Dividing this last equation by 180° or π gives the conversion rules that appear on the next page.

Study Tip

The unit you are converting *to* appears in the *numerator* of the conversion factor.

Conversion between Degrees and Radians

Using the basic relationship π radians $= 180°$,

1. To convert degrees to radians, multiply degrees by $\dfrac{\pi \text{ radians}}{180°}$.

2. To convert radians to degrees, multiply radians by $\dfrac{180°}{\pi \text{ radians}}$.

Angles that are fractions of a complete rotation are usually expressed in radian measure as fractional multiples of π, rather than as decimal approximations. For example, we write $\theta = \dfrac{\pi}{2}$ rather than using the decimal approximation $\theta \approx 1.57$.

EXAMPLE 5 Converting from Degrees to Radians

Convert each angle in degrees to radians:

a. $30°$ **b.** $90°$ **c.** $-135°$.

Solution To convert degrees to radians, multiply by $\dfrac{\pi \text{ radians}}{180°}$. Observe how the degree units cancel.

a. $30° = 30° \cdot \dfrac{\pi \text{ radians}}{180°} = \dfrac{30\pi}{180} \text{ radians} = \dfrac{\pi}{6} \text{ radians}$

b. $90° = 90° \cdot \dfrac{\pi \text{ radians}}{180°} = \dfrac{90\pi}{180} \text{ radians} = \dfrac{\pi}{2} \text{ radians}$

c. $-135° = -135° \cdot \dfrac{\pi \text{ radians}}{180°} = -\dfrac{135\pi}{180} \text{ radians} = -\dfrac{3\pi}{4} \text{ radians}$

> Divide the numerator and denominator by 45.

Check Point 5 Convert each angle in degrees to radians:

a. $60°$ **b.** $270°$ **c.** $-300°$.

EXAMPLE 6 Converting from Radians to Degrees

Convert each angle in radians to degrees:

a. $\dfrac{\pi}{3}$ radians **b.** $-\dfrac{5\pi}{3}$ radians **c.** 1 radian.

Solution To convert radians to degrees, multiply by $\dfrac{180°}{\pi \text{ radians}}$. Observe how the radian units cancel.

Study Tip

In Example 6(c), we see that 1 radian is approximately 57°. Keep in mind that a radian is much larger than a degree.

a. $\dfrac{\pi}{3}$ radians $= \dfrac{\pi \text{ radians}}{3} \cdot \dfrac{180°}{\pi \text{ radians}} = \dfrac{180°}{3} = 60°$

b. $-\dfrac{5\pi}{3}$ radians $= -\dfrac{5\pi \text{ radians}}{3} \cdot \dfrac{180°}{\pi \text{ radians}} = -\dfrac{5 \cdot 180°}{3} = -300°$

c. 1 radian $= 1 \text{ radian} \cdot \dfrac{180°}{\pi \text{ radians}} = \dfrac{180°}{\pi} \approx 57.3°$

Check Point 6

Convert each angle in radians to degrees:

a. $\dfrac{\pi}{4}$ radians   **b.** $-\dfrac{4\pi}{3}$ radians   **c.** 6 radians.

Figure 4.12 illustrates the degree and radian measures of angles that you will commonly see in trigonometry. Each angle is in standard position, so that the initial side lies along the positive *x*-axis. We will be using both degree and radian measure for these angles.

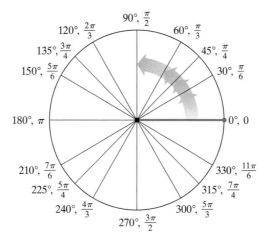

Figure 4.12 Degree and radian measures of selected angles

8 Find the length of a circular arc.

The Length of a Circular Arc

We can use the radian measure formula, $\theta = \dfrac{s}{r}$, to find the length of the arc of a circle. How do we do this? Remember that *s* represents the length of the arc intercepted by the central angle θ. Thus, by solving the formula for *s*, we have an equation for arc length.

The Length of a Circular Arc

Let *r* be the radius of a circle and θ the nonnegative radian measure of a central angle of the circle. The length of the arc intercepted by the central angle is

$$s = r\theta.$$

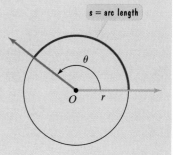

EXAMPLE 7 Finding the Length of a Circular Arc

A circle has a radius of 10 inches. Find the length of the arc intercepted by a central angle of 120°.

Study Tip

The unit used to describe the length of a circular arc is the same unit that is given in the circle's radius.

Solution The formula $s = r\theta$ can be used only when θ is expressed in radians. Thus, we begin by converting 120° to radians. Multiply by $\frac{\pi \text{ radians}}{180°}$.

$$120° = 120° \cdot \frac{\pi \text{ radians}}{180°} = \frac{120\pi}{180} \text{ radians} = \frac{2\pi}{3} \text{ radians}$$

Now we can use the formula $s = r\theta$ to find the length of the arc. The circle's radius is 10 inches: $r = 10$ inches. The measure of the central angle, in radians, is $\frac{2\pi}{3}$: $\theta = \frac{2\pi}{3}$. The length of the arc intercepted by this central angle is

$$s = r\theta = (10 \text{ inches})\left(\frac{2\pi}{3}\right) = \frac{20\pi}{3} \text{ inches} \approx 20.94 \text{ inches.}$$

Check Point 7 A circle has a radius of 6 inches. Find the length of the arc intercepted by a central angle of 45°. Express arc length in terms of π. Then round your answer to two decimal places.

9 Use linear and angular speed to describe motion on a circular path.

Linear and Angular Speed

A carousel contains four circular rows of animals. As the carousel revolves, the animals in the outer row travel a greater distance per unit of time than those in the inner rows. These animals have a greater *linear speed* than those in the inner rows. By contrast, all animals, regardless of the row, complete the same number of revolutions per unit of time. All animals in the four circular rows travel at the same *angular speed*.

Using v for linear speed and ω (omega) for angular speed, we define these two kinds of speeds along a circular path as follows:

Definitions of Linear and Angular Speed

If a point is in motion on a circle of radius r through an angle of θ radians in time t, then its **linear speed** is

$$v = \frac{s}{t}$$

where s is the arc length given by $s = r\theta$, and its **angular speed** is

$$\omega = \frac{\theta}{t}.$$

The hard drive in a computer rotates at 3600 revolutions per minute. This angular speed, expressed in revolutions per minute, can also be expressed in revolutions per second, radians per minute, and radians per second. Using 2π radians $= 1$ revolution, we express the angular speed of a hard drive in radians per minute as follows:

3600 revolutions per minute

$$= \frac{3600 \text{ revolutions}}{1 \text{ minute}} \cdot \frac{2\pi \text{ radians}}{1 \text{ revolution}} = \frac{7200\pi \text{ radians}}{1 \text{ minute}}$$

$= 7200\pi$ radians per minute.

We can establish a relationship between the two kinds of speed by dividing both sides of the arc length formula, $s = r\theta$, by t:

$$\frac{s}{t} = \frac{r\theta}{t} = r\frac{\theta}{t}.$$

This expression defines linear speed.

This expression defines angular speed.

Thus, linear speed is the product of the radius and the angular speed.

Linear Speed in Terms of Angular Speed

The linear speed, v, of a point a distance r from the center of rotation is given by

$$v = r\omega$$

where ω is the angular speed in radians per unit of time.

EXAMPLE 8 **Finding Linear Speed**

A wind machine used to generate electricity has blades that are 10 feet in length (see Figure 4.13). The propeller is rotating at four revolutions per second. Find the linear speed, in feet per second, of the tips of the blades.

10 feet

Figure 4.13

Figure 4.13, repeated

Solution   We are given ω, the angular speed.

$$\omega = 4 \text{ revolutions per second}$$

We use the formula $v = r\omega$ to find v, the linear speed. Before applying the formula, we must express ω in radians per second.

$$\omega = \frac{4 \text{ revolutions}}{1 \text{ second}} \cdot \frac{2\pi \text{ radians}}{1 \text{ revolution}} = \frac{8\pi \text{ radians}}{1 \text{ second}} \quad \text{or} \quad \frac{8\pi}{1 \text{ second}}$$

The angular speed of the propeller is 8π radians per second. The linear speed is

$$v = r\omega = 10 \text{ feet} \cdot \frac{8\pi}{1 \text{ second}} = \frac{80\pi \text{ feet}}{\text{second}}.$$

The linear speed of the tips of the blades is 80π feet per second, which is approximately 251 feet per second.

Check Point 8   A 45-rpm record has an angular speed of 45 revolutions per minute. Find the linear speed, in inches per minute, at the point where the needle is 1.5 inches from the record's center.

EXERCISE SET 4.1

Practice Exercises

In Exercises 1–6, each angle is in standard position. Determine the quadrant in which the angle lies.

1. $145°$ **2.** $285°$

3. $-100°$ **4.** $-110°$

5. $362°$ **6.** $364°$

In Exercises 7–10, classify the angle as acute, right, straight, or obtuse.

7.

8.

9.

10.

In Exercises 11–18, draw each angle in standard position.

11. $135°$ **12.** $120°$

13. $-150°$ **14.** $-240°$

15. $420°$ **16.** $450°$

17. $-90°$ **18.** $-270°$

In Exercises 19–24, find a positive angle less than 360° that is coterminal with the given angle.

19. $395°$ **20.** $415°$

21. $-150°$ **22.** $-160°$

23. $-45°$ **24.** $-40°$

In Exercises 25–30, if possible, find the complement and the supplement of the given angle.

25. $52°$ **26.** $85°$

27. $37.4°$ **28.** $47.6°$

29. $111°$ **30.** $95°$

In Exercises 31–36, find the radian measure of the central angle of a circle of radius r that intercepts an arc of length s.

Radius, *r*	Arc length, *s*
31. 10 inches	40 inches
32. 5 feet	30 feet
33. 6 yards	8 yards
34. 8 yards	18 yards
35. 1 meter	400 centimeters
36. 1 meter	600 centimeters

In Exercises 37–44, convert each angle in degrees to radians. Express your answer as a multiple of π.

37. $45°$ **38.** $18°$

39. $135°$ **40.** $150°$

41. $300°$ **42.** $330°$

43. $-225°$ **44.** $-270°$

In Exercises 45–52, convert each angle in radians to degrees.

45. $\dfrac{\pi}{2}$ **46.** $\dfrac{\pi}{9}$

47. $\dfrac{2\pi}{3}$ **48.** $\dfrac{3\pi}{4}$

49. $\dfrac{7\pi}{6}$ **50.** $\dfrac{11\pi}{6}$

51. -3π **52.** -4π

In Exercises 53–58, convert each angle in degrees to radians. Round to two decimal places.

53. $18°$ **54.** $76°$

55. $-40°$ **56.** $-50°$

57. $200°$ **58.** $250°$

In Exercises 59–64, convert each angle in radians to degrees. Round to two decimal places.

59. 2 radians   **60.** 3 radians

61. $\dfrac{\pi}{13}$ radians   **62.** $\dfrac{\pi}{17}$ radians

63. -4.8 radians   **64.** -5.2 radians

In Exercises 65–68, find the length of the arc on a circle of radius r intercepted by a central angle θ. Express arc length in terms of π. Then round your answer to two decimal places.

Radius, *r*	Central angle, *θ*
65. 12 inches	$\theta = 45°$
66. 16 inches	$\theta = 60°$
67. 8 feet	$\theta = 225°$
68. 9 yards	$\theta = 315°$

In Exercises 69–70, express each angular speed in radians per second.

69. 6 revolutions per second

70. 20 revolutions per second

Application Exercises

71. The minute hand of a clock moves from 12 to 2 o'clock, or $\frac{1}{6}$ of a complete revolution. Through how many degrees does it move? Through how many radians does it move?

72. The minute hand of a clock moves from 12 to 4 o'clock, or $\frac{1}{3}$ of a complete revolution. Through how many degrees does it move? Through how many radians does it move?

73. The minute hand of a clock is 8 inches long and moves from 12 to 2 o'clock. How far does the tip of the minute hand move? Express your answer in terms of π and then round to two decimal places.

74. The minute hand of a clock is 6 inches long and moves from 12 to 4 o'clock. How far does the tip of the minute hand move? Express your answer in terms of π and then round to two decimal places.

75. The figure shows a highway sign that warns of a railway crossing. The lines that form the cross pass through the circle's center and intersect at right angles. If the radius of the circle is 24 inches, find the length of each of the four arcs formed by the cross. Express your answer in terms of π and then round to two decimal places.

76. The radius of a wheel is 80 centimeters. If the wheel rotates through an angle of $60°$, how many centimeters does it move? Express your answer in terms of π and then round to two decimal places.

How do we measure the distance between two points, A and B, on Earth? We measure along a circle with a center, C, at the center of Earth. The radius of the circle is equal to the distance from C to the surface. Use the fact that Earth is a sphere of radius equal to approximately 4000 miles to solve Exercises 77–80.

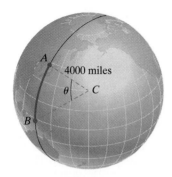

77. If two points, *A* and *B*, are 8000 miles apart, express angle θ in radians and in degrees.

78. If two points, *A* and *B*, are 10,000 miles apart, express angle θ in radians and in degrees.

79. If $\theta = 30°$, find the distance between *A* and *B* to the nearest mile.

80. If $\theta = 10°$, find the distance between *A* and *B* to the nearest mile.

81. The angular speed of a point on Earth is $\dfrac{\pi}{12}$ radians per hour. The Equator lies on a circle of radius approximately 4000 miles. Find the linear velocity, in miles per hour, of a point on the Equator.

82. A ferris wheel has a radius of 25 feet. The wheel is rotating at three revolutions per minute. Find the linear speed, in feet per minute, of this ferris wheel.

83. A water wheel has a radius of 12 feet. The wheel is rotating at 20 revolutions per minute. Find the linear speed, in feet per minute, of the water.

84. On a carousel, the outer row of animals is 20 feet from the center. The inner row of animals is 10 feet from the center. The carousel is rotating at 2.5 revolutions per minute. What is the difference, in feet per minute, in the linear speeds of the animals in the outer and inner rows? Round to the nearest foot per minute.

Writing in Mathematics

85. What is an angle?

86. What determines the size of an angle?

87. Describe an angle in standard position.

88. Explain the difference between positive and negative angles. What are coterminal angles?

89. Explain what is meant by one radian.

90. Explain how to find the radian measure of a central angle.

91. Describe how to convert an angle in degrees to radians.

92. Explain how to convert an angle in radians to degrees.

93. Explain how to find the length of a circular arc.

94. If a carousel is rotating at 2.5 revolutions per minute, explain how to find the linear speed of a child seated on one of the animals.

95. The angular velocity of a point on Earth is $\dfrac{\pi}{12}$ radians per hour. Describe what happens every 24 hours.

96. Have you ever noticed that we use the vocabulary of angles in everyday speech? Here is an example:

    My opinion about art museums took a 180° turn after visiting the San Francisco Museum of Modern Art.

    Explain what this means. Then give another example of the vocabulary of angles in everyday use.

Technology Exercises

In Exercises 97–100, use the keys on your calculator or graphing utility for converting an angle in degrees, minutes, and seconds ($D°M'S''$) into decimal form, and vice versa.

In Exercises 97–98, convert each angle to a decimal in degrees. Round your answer to two decimal places.

97. $30°15'10''$ 98. $65°45'20''$

In Exercises 99–100, convert each angle to $D°M'S''$ form. Round your answer to the nearest second.

99. $30.42°$ 100. $50.42°$

Critical Thinking Exercises

101. If $\theta = \frac{3}{2}$, is this angle larger or smaller than a right angle?

102. A railroad curve is laid out on a circle. What radius should be used if the track is to change direction by 20° in a distance of 100 miles? Round your answer to the nearest mile.

103. Assuming Earth to be a sphere of radius 4000 miles, how many miles north of the Equator is Miami, Florida, if it is 26° north from the Equator? Round your answer to the nearest mile.

SECTION 4.2 *Right Triangle Trigonometry*

Objectives

1. Use right triangles to evaluate trigonometric functions.
2. Find function values for $30°\left(\dfrac{\pi}{6}\right)$, $45°\left(\dfrac{\pi}{4}\right)$, and $60°\left(\dfrac{\pi}{3}\right)$.
3. Recognize and use fundamental identities.
4. Use equal cofunctions of complements.
5. Evaluate trigonometric functions with a calculator.
6. Use right triangle trigonometry to solve applied problems.

In the last century, Ang Rita Sherpa climbed Mount Everest ten times, all without the use of bottled oxygen.

Mountain climbers have forever been fascinated by reaching the top of Mount Everest, sometimes with tragic results. The mountain, on Asia's Tibet-Nepal border, is Earth's highest, peaking at an incredible 29,035 feet. The heights of mountains can be found using **trigonometry.** The word *trigonometry* means *measurement of triangles*. Trigonometry is used in navigation, building, and engineering. For centuries, Muslims used trigonometry and the stars to navigate across the Arabian desert to Mecca, the birthplace of the prophet Muhammad, the founder of Islam. The ancient Greeks used trigonometry to record the locations of thousands of stars and worked out the motion of the Moon relative to Earth. Today, trigonometry is used to study the structure of DNA, the master molecule that determines how we grow from a single cell to a complex, fully developed adult.

1 Use right triangles to evaluate trigonometric functions.

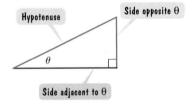

Figure 4.14 Naming a right triangle's sides from the point of view of an acute angle θ

The Six Trigonometric Functions

We begin the study of trigonometry by defining six functions, the six *trigonometric functions*. The inputs for these functions are measures of acute angles in right triangles. The outputs are the ratios of the lengths of the sides of right triangles.

Figure 4.14 shows a right triangle with one of its acute angles labeled θ. The side opposite the right angle is known as the **hypotenuse.** The other sides of the triangle are described by their position relative to the acute angle θ. One side is opposite θ and one is adjacent to θ.

The trigonometric functions have names that are words, rather than single letters such as f, g, and h. For example, the **sine of** θ is the length of the side opposite θ divided by the length of the hypotenuse:

$$\sin\theta = \frac{\text{length of side opposite } \theta}{\text{length of hypotenuse}}.$$

Input is the measure of an acute angle.

Output is the ratio of the lengths of the sides.

The ratio of lengths depends on angle θ and thus is a function of θ. The expression $\sin\theta$ really means $\sin(\theta)$, where sine is the name of the function and θ, the measure of an acute angle, is an input.

Here are the names of the six trigonometric functions, along with their abbreviations:

Name	Abbreviation	Name	Abbreviation
sine	sin	cosecant	csc
cosine	cos	secant	sec
tangent	tan	cotangent	cot

Now, let θ be an acute angle in a right triangle, shown in Figure 4.15. The length of the side opposite θ is a, the length of the side adjacent to θ is b, and the length of the hypotenuse is c.

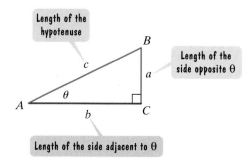

Figure 4.15

Right Triangle Definitions of Trigonometric Functions

See Figure 4.15. The six **trigonometric functions of the acute angle θ** are defined as follows:

$$\sin\theta = \frac{\text{length of side opposite angle } \theta}{\text{length of hypotenuse}} = \frac{a}{c} \qquad \csc\theta = \frac{\text{length of hypotenuse}}{\text{length of side opposite angle } \theta} = \frac{c}{a}$$

$$\cos\theta = \frac{\text{length of side adjacent to angle } \theta}{\text{length of hypotenuse}} = \frac{b}{c} \qquad \sec\theta = \frac{\text{length of hypotenuse}}{\text{length of side adjacent to angle } \theta} = \frac{c}{b}$$

$$\tan\theta = \frac{\text{length of side opposite angle } \theta}{\text{length of side adjacent to angle } \theta} = \frac{a}{b} \qquad \cot\theta = \frac{\text{length of side adjacent to angle } \theta}{\text{length of side opposite angle } \theta} = \frac{b}{a}$$

Each of the trigonometric functions of the acute angle θ is positive. Observe that the functions in the second column in the box are the reciprocals of the corresponding functions in the first column.

Figure 4.16 on the next page shows four right triangles of varying sizes. In each of the triangles, θ is the same acute angle, measuring approximately 56.3°. All four of these similar triangles have the same shape and the lengths of corresponding sides are in the same ratio. In each triangle, the tangent function has the same value: $\tan\theta = \frac{3}{2}$.

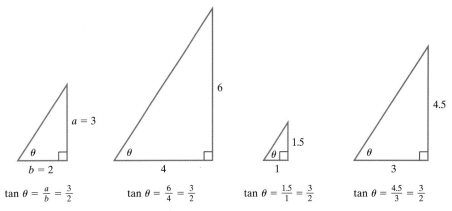

$$\tan \theta = \frac{a}{b} = \frac{3}{2} \qquad \tan \theta = \frac{6}{4} = \frac{3}{2} \qquad \tan \theta = \frac{1.5}{1} = \frac{3}{2} \qquad \tan \theta = \frac{4.5}{3} = \frac{3}{2}$$

Figure 4.16 A particular acute angle always gives the same ratio of opposite to adjacent sides.

In general, **the trigonometric function values of θ depend only on the size of angle θ, and not on the size of the triangle.**

Figure 4.17

EXAMPLE 1   Evaluating Trigonometric Functions

Find the value of each of the six trigonometric functions of θ in Figure 4.17.

Solution   We need to find the values of the six trigonometric functions of θ. However, we must know the lengths of all three sides of the triangle (a, b, and c) to evaluate all six functions. The values of a and b are given. We can use the Pythagorean Theorem, $c^2 = a^2 + b^2$, to find c.

$$a = 5 \qquad b = 12$$

$$c^2 = a^2 + b^2 = 5^2 + 12^2 = 25 + 144 = 169$$

$$c = \sqrt{169} = 13$$

Now that we know the lengths of the three sides of the triangle, we apply the definitions of the six trigonometric functions of θ. Referring to these lengths as opposite, adjacent, and hypotenuse, we have

$$\sin \theta = \frac{\text{opposite}}{\text{hypotenuse}} = \frac{5}{13} \qquad \csc \theta = \frac{\text{hypotenuse}}{\text{opposite}} = \frac{13}{5}$$

$$\cos \theta = \frac{\text{adjacent}}{\text{hypotenuse}} = \frac{12}{13} \qquad \sec \theta = \frac{\text{hypotenuse}}{\text{adjacent}} = \frac{13}{12}$$

$$\tan \theta = \frac{\text{opposite}}{\text{adjacent}} = \frac{5}{12} \qquad \cot \theta = \frac{\text{adjacent}}{\text{opposite}} = \frac{12}{5}.$$

Study Tip

The functions in the second column are reciprocals of those in the first column. You can obtain their values by exchanging the numerator and denominator of the corresponding ratios in the first column.

Check Point 1   Find the value of each of the six trigonometric functions of θ in the figure.

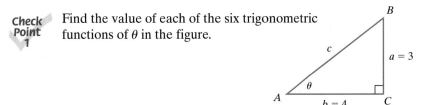

2 Find function values for $30° \left(\dfrac{\pi}{6}\right)$, $45° \left(\dfrac{\pi}{4}\right)$, and $60° \left(\dfrac{\pi}{3}\right)$.

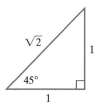

Figure 4.18 An isosceles right triangle

Function Values for Some Special Angles

A 45°, or $\dfrac{\pi}{4}$ radian, angle occurs frequently in trigonometry. How do we find the values of the trigonometric functions of 45°? We construct a right triangle with a 45° angle, shown in Figure 4.18. The triangle actually has two 45° angles. Thus, the triangle is isosceles—that is, it has two sides of the same length. Assume that each leg of the triangle has a length equal to 1. We can find the length of the hypotenuse using the Pythagorean Theorem.

$$(\text{length of hypotenuse})^2 = 1^2 + 1^2 = 2$$

$$\text{length of hypotenuse} = \sqrt{2}$$

With Figure 4.18, we can determine the trigonometric function values for 45°.

EXAMPLE 2 Evaluating Trigonometric Functions of 45°

Use Figure 4.18 to find $\sin 45°$, $\cos 45°$, and $\tan 45°$.

Solution We apply the definitions of these three trigonometric functions.

$$\sin 45° = \frac{\text{length of side opposite } 45°}{\text{length of hypotenuse}} = \frac{1}{\sqrt{2}}$$

$$\cos 45° = \frac{\text{length of side adjacent to } 45°}{\text{length of hypotenuse}} = \frac{1}{\sqrt{2}}$$

$$\tan 45° = \frac{\text{length of side opposite } 45°}{\text{length of side adjacent to } 45°} = \frac{1}{1} = 1$$

Check Point 2 Use Figure 4.18 to find $\csc 45°$, $\sec 45°$, and $\cot 45°$.

When you worked Check Point 2, did you actually use Figure 4.18 or did you use reciprocals to find the values?

$$\csc 45° = \sqrt{2} \qquad \sec 45° = \sqrt{2} \qquad \cot 45° = 1$$

Take the reciprocal of $\sin 45° = \dfrac{1}{\sqrt{2}}$.   Take the reciprocal of $\cos 45° = \dfrac{1}{\sqrt{2}}$.   Take the reciprocal of $\tan 45° = \dfrac{1}{1}$.

We found that $\sin 45° = \dfrac{1}{\sqrt{2}}$ and $\cos 45° = \dfrac{1}{\sqrt{2}}$. This value is often expressed by rationalizing the denominator:

$$\frac{1}{\sqrt{2}} = \frac{1}{\sqrt{2}} \cdot \frac{\sqrt{2}}{\sqrt{2}} = \frac{\sqrt{2}}{2}.$$

We are multiplying by 1 and not changing the value of $\dfrac{1}{\sqrt{2}}$.

Thus, $\sin 45° = \dfrac{\sqrt{2}}{2}$ and $\cos 45° = \dfrac{\sqrt{2}}{2}$.

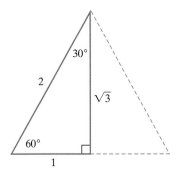

Figure 4.19 30°–60°–90° triangle

Two other angles that occur frequently in trigonometry are 30°, or $\dfrac{\pi}{6}$ radian, and 60°, or $\dfrac{\pi}{3}$ radian, angles. We can find the values of the trigonometric functions of 30° and 60° by using a right triangle. To form this right triangle, draw an equilateral triangle—that is a triangle with all sides the same length. Assume that each side has a length equal to 2. Now take half of the equilateral triangle. We obtain the right triangle in Figure 4.19. This right triangle has a hypotenuse of length 2 and a leg of length 1. The other leg has length a, which can be found using the Pythagorean Theorem.

$$a^2 + 1^2 = 2^2$$
$$a^2 + 1 = 4$$
$$a^2 = 3$$
$$a = \sqrt{3}$$

With the right triangle in Figure 4.19, we can determine the trigonometric functions for 30° and 60°.

EXAMPLE 3 Evaluating Trigonometric Functions of 30° and 60°

Use Figure 4.19 to find $\sin 60°$, $\cos 60°$, $\sin 30°$, and $\cos 30°$.

Solution   We begin with 60°. Use the angle on the lower left in Figure 4.19.

$$\sin 60° = \frac{\text{length of side opposite } 60°}{\text{length of hypotenuse}} = \frac{\sqrt{3}}{2}$$

$$\cos 60° = \frac{\text{length of side adjacent to } 60°}{\text{length of hypotenuse}} = \frac{1}{2}$$

To find $\sin 30°$ and $\cos 30°$, use the angle on the upper right in Figure 4.19.

$$\sin 30° = \frac{\text{length of side opposite } 30°}{\text{length of hypotenuse}} = \frac{1}{2}$$

$$\cos 30° = \frac{\text{length of side adjacent to } 30°}{\text{length of hypotenuse}} = \frac{\sqrt{3}}{2}$$

Check Point 3   Use Figure 4.19 to find $\tan 60°$ and $\tan 30°$. If a radical appears in a denominator, rationalize the denominator.

Because we will often use the function values of 30°, 45°, and 60°, you should learn to construct the right triangles shown in Figures 4.18 and 4.19. With sufficient practice, you will memorize the values in the box on the next page.

Sines, Cosines, and Tangents of Special Angles

$$\sin 30° = \sin \frac{\pi}{6} = \frac{1}{2} \qquad \cos 30° = \cos \frac{\pi}{6} = \frac{\sqrt{3}}{2} \qquad \tan 30° = \tan \frac{\pi}{6} = \frac{\sqrt{3}}{3}$$

$$\sin 45° = \sin \frac{\pi}{4} = \frac{\sqrt{2}}{2} \qquad \cos 45° = \cos \frac{\pi}{4} = \frac{\sqrt{2}}{2} \qquad \tan 45° = \tan \frac{\pi}{4} = 1$$

$$\sin 60° = \sin \frac{\pi}{3} = \frac{\sqrt{3}}{2} \qquad \cos 60° = \cos \frac{\pi}{3} = \frac{1}{2} \qquad \tan 60° = \tan \frac{\pi}{3} = \sqrt{3}$$

3 Recognize and use fundamental identities.

Fundamental Identities

Many relationships exist among the six trigonometric functions. These relationships are described using **trigonometric identities.** For example, $\csc \theta$ is defined as the reciprocal of $\sin \theta$. This relationship can be expressed by the identity

$$\csc \theta = \frac{1}{\sin \theta}.$$

This identity is one of six **reciprocal identities.**

Reciprocal Identities

$$\sin \theta = \frac{1}{\csc \theta} \qquad \cos \theta = \frac{1}{\sec \theta} \qquad \tan \theta = \frac{1}{\cot \theta}$$

$$\csc \theta = \frac{1}{\sin \theta} \qquad \sec \theta = \frac{1}{\cos \theta} \qquad \cot \theta = \frac{1}{\tan \theta}$$

Two other relationships that follow from the definitions of the trigonometric functions are called the **quotient identities.**

Quotient Identities

$$\tan \theta = \frac{\sin \theta}{\cos \theta} \qquad \cot \theta = \frac{\cos \theta}{\sin \theta}$$

If $\sin \theta$ and $\cos \theta$ are known, a quotient identity and three reciprocal identities make it possible to find the value of each of the four remaining trigonometric functions.

EXAMPLE 4 **Using Quotient and Reciprocal Identities**

Given $\sin\theta = \dfrac{1}{2}$ and $\cos\theta = \dfrac{\sqrt{3}}{2}$, find the value of each of the four remaining trigonometric functions.

Solution We can find $\tan\theta$ by using the quotient identity that describes $\tan\theta$ as the quotient of $\sin\theta$ and $\cos\theta$.

$$\tan\theta = \frac{\sin\theta}{\cos\theta} = \frac{\dfrac{1}{2}}{\dfrac{\sqrt{3}}{2}} = \frac{1}{2}\cdot\frac{2}{\sqrt{3}} = \frac{1}{\sqrt{3}} = \frac{1}{\sqrt{3}}\cdot\frac{\sqrt{3}}{\sqrt{3}} = \frac{\sqrt{3}}{3}$$

> Rationalize the denominator.

We use the reciprocal identities to find the value of each of the remaining three functions.

$$\csc\theta = \frac{1}{\sin\theta} = \frac{1}{\dfrac{1}{2}} = 2$$

$$\sec\theta = \frac{1}{\cos\theta} = \frac{1}{\dfrac{\sqrt{3}}{2}} = \frac{2}{\sqrt{3}} = \frac{2}{\sqrt{3}}\cdot\frac{\sqrt{3}}{\sqrt{3}} = \frac{2\sqrt{3}}{3}$$

> Rationalize the denominator.

$$\cot\theta = \frac{1}{\tan\theta} = \frac{1}{\dfrac{1}{\sqrt{3}}} = \sqrt{3}$$

We found $\tan\theta = \dfrac{1}{\sqrt{3}}$. We could use $\tan\theta = \dfrac{\sqrt{3}}{3}$, but then we would have to rationalize the denominator.

> **Check Point 4** Given $\sin\theta = \dfrac{2}{3}$ and $\cos\theta = \dfrac{\sqrt{5}}{3}$, find the value of each of the four remaining trigonometric functions.

Other relationships among trigonometric functions follow from the Pythagorean Theorem. Using Figure 4.20, the Pythagorean Theorem states that

$$a^2 + b^2 = c^2.$$

To obtain ratios that correspond to trigonometric functions, divide both sides of this equation by c^2.

$$\frac{a^2}{c^2} + \frac{b^2}{c^2} = 1 \quad\text{or}\quad \left(\frac{a}{c}\right)^2 + \left(\frac{b}{c}\right)^2 = 1$$

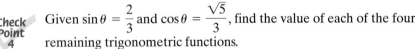

In Figure 4.20, $\sin\theta = \dfrac{a}{c}$, so this is $(\sin\theta)^2$.   In Figure 4.20, $\cos\theta = \dfrac{b}{c}$, so this is $(\cos\theta)^2$.

Based on the observations in the voice balloons, we see that

$$(\sin\theta)^2 + (\cos\theta)^2 = 1.$$

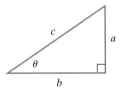

Figure 4.20

We will use the notation $\sin^2\theta$ for $(\sin\theta)^2$ and $\cos^2\theta$ for $(\cos\theta)^2$. With this notation, we can write the identity as

$$\sin^2\theta + \cos^2\theta = 1.$$

Two additional identities can be obtained from $a^2 + b^2 = c^2$ by dividing both sides by b^2 and a^2, respectively. The three identities are called the **Pythagorean identities.**

> ### Pythagorean Identities
>
> $$\sin^2\theta + \cos^2\theta = 1 \qquad 1 + \tan^2\theta = \sec^2\theta \qquad 1 + \cot^2\theta = \csc^2\theta$$

EXAMPLE 5 Using a Pythagorean Identity

Given that $\sin\theta = \frac{3}{5}$ and θ is an acute angle, find the value of $\cos\theta$ using a trigonometric identity.

Solution   We can find the value of $\cos\theta$ by using the Pythagorean identity

$$\sin^2\theta + \cos^2\theta = 1.$$

$$\left(\frac{3}{5}\right)^2 + \cos^2\theta = 1 \qquad \textit{We are given that } \sin\theta = \frac{3}{5}.$$

$$\frac{9}{25} + \cos^2\theta = 1 \qquad \textit{Square } \frac{3}{5}: \left(\frac{3}{5}\right)^2 = \frac{3^2}{5^2} = \frac{9}{25}.$$

$$\cos^2\theta = 1 - \frac{9}{25} \qquad \textit{Subtract } \frac{9}{25} \textit{ from both sides.}$$

$$\cos^2\theta = \frac{16}{25} \qquad \textit{Simplify: } 1 - \frac{9}{25} = \frac{25}{25} - \frac{9}{25} = \frac{16}{25}.$$

$$\cos\theta = \sqrt{\frac{16}{25}} = \frac{4}{5} \qquad \textit{Because } \theta \textit{ is an acute angle, } \cos\theta \textit{ is positive.}$$

Thus, $\cos\theta = \frac{4}{5}$.

> **Check Point 5**   Given that $\sin\theta = \frac{1}{2}$ and θ is an acute angle, find the value of $\cos\theta$ using a trigonometric identity.

4 Use equal cofunctions of complements.

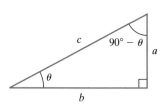

Figure 4.21

Trigonometric Functions and Complements

Another relationship among trigonometric functions is based on angles that are complements. Refer to Figure 4.21. Because the sum of the angles of any triangle is 180°, in a right triangle the sum of the acute angles is 90°. Thus, the acute angles are complements. If the degree measure of one acute angle is θ, then the degree measure of the other acute angle is $(90° - \theta)$. This angle is shown on the upper right in Figure 4.21.

Let's use Figure 4.21 to compare $\sin\theta$ and $\cos(90° - \theta)$.

$$\sin\theta = \frac{\text{length of side opposite } \theta}{\text{length of hypotenuse}} = \frac{a}{c}$$

$$\cos(90° - \theta) = \frac{\text{length of side adjacent to } (90° - \theta)}{\text{length of hypotenuse}} = \frac{a}{c}$$

Thus, $\sin\theta = \cos(90° - \theta)$. If two angles are complements, the sine of one equals the cosine of the other. Because of this relationship, the sine and cosine are called *cofunctions* of each other. The name *cosine* is a shortened form of the phrase *complement's sine.*

Any pair of trigonometric functions f and g for which

$$f(\theta) = g(90° - \theta) \quad \text{and} \quad g(\theta) = f(90° - \theta)$$

are called **cofunctions.** Using Figure 4.21, we can show that the tangent and cotangent are also cofunctions of each other. So are the secant and cosecant.

Cofunction Identities

The value of a trigonometric function of θ is equal to the cofunction of the complement of θ.

$$\sin\theta = \cos(90° - \theta) \qquad \cos\theta = \sin(90° - \theta)$$
$$\tan\theta = \cot(90° - \theta) \qquad \cot\theta = \tan(90° - \theta)$$
$$\sec\theta = \csc(90° - \theta) \qquad \csc\theta = \sec(90° - \theta)$$

If θ is in radians, replace 90° with $\dfrac{\pi}{2}$.

EXAMPLE 6

Find a cofunction with the same value as the given expression:

a. $\sin 72°$ **b.** $\csc \dfrac{\pi}{3}.$

Solution Because the value of a trigonometric function of θ is equal to the cofunction of the complement of θ, we need to find the complement of each angle. We do this by subtracting the angle's measure from 90° or its radian equivalent, $\dfrac{\pi}{2}$.

a. $\sin 72° = \cos(90° - 72°) = \cos 18°$

> We have a function and its cofunction.

b. $\csc \dfrac{\pi}{3} = \sec\left(\dfrac{\pi}{2} - \dfrac{\pi}{3}\right) = \sec\left(\dfrac{3\pi}{6} - \dfrac{2\pi}{6}\right) = \sec \dfrac{\pi}{6}$

> We have a cofunction and its function.

> Perform the subtraction using the least common denominator, 6.

Check Point 6 Find a cofunction with the same value as the given expression:

a. $\sin 46°$ **b.** $\cot \dfrac{\pi}{12}.$

5 Evaluate trigonometric functions with a calculator.

Using a Calculator to Evaluate Trigonometric Functions

The values of the trigonometric functions obtained with the special triangles are exact values. For most angles other than 30°, 45°, and 60°, we approximate the value of each of the trigonometric functions using a calculator. The first step is to set the calculator to the correct *mode*, degrees or radians, depending on how the acute angle is measured.

Most calculators have keys marked [SIN], [COS], and [TAN]. For example, to find the value of sin 30°, set the calculator to the degree mode and enter 30 [SIN] on most scientific calculators and [SIN] 30 [ENTER] on most graphing calculators. Consult the manual for your calculator.

To evaluate the cosecant, secant, and cotangent functions, use the key for the respective reciprocal function, [SIN], [COS], or [TAN], and then use the reciprocal key. The reciprocal key is [1/x] on many scientific calculators and [x⁻¹] on many graphing calculators. For example, we can evaluate $\sec \frac{\pi}{12}$ using the following reciprocal relationship:

$$\sec \frac{\pi}{12} = \frac{1}{\cos \frac{\pi}{12}}.$$

Using the radian mode, enter one of the following keystroke sequences:

Many Scientific Calculators

$$\boxed{\pi}\;\boxed{\div}\;\boxed{12}\;\boxed{=}\;\boxed{\text{COS}}\;\boxed{1/x}$$

Many Graphing Calculators

$$\boxed{(}\;\boxed{\text{COS}}\;\boxed{(}\;\boxed{\pi}\;\boxed{\div}\;\boxed{12}\;\boxed{)}\;\boxed{)}\;\boxed{x^{-1}}\;\boxed{\text{ENTER}}.$$

Rounding the display to four decimal places, we obtain $\sec \frac{\pi}{12} = 1.0353$.

EXAMPLE 7   Evaluating Trigonometric Functions with a Calculator

Use a calculator to find the value to four decimal places:

    a. cos 48.2°   **b.** cot 1.2.

Solution

Scientific Calculator Solution

Function	Mode	Keystrokes	Display, rounded to four decimal places
a. cos 48.2°	Degree	48.2 [COS]	0.6665
b. cot 1.2	Radian	1.2 [TAN] [1/x]	0.3888

Graphing Calculator Solution

Function	Mode	Keystrokes	Display, rounded to four decimal places
a. cos 48.2°	Degree	[COS] 48.2 [ENTER]	0.6665
b. cot 1.2	Radian	[(] [TAN] 1.2 [)] [x⁻¹] [ENTER]	0.3888

<table>
<tr><td>Check Point 7</td><td>Use a calculator to find the value to four decimal places:

a. $\sin 72.8°$ **b.** $\csc 1.5$.</td></tr>
</table>

6 Use right triangle trigonometry to solve applied problems.

Applications

Many applications of right triangle trigonometry involve the angle made with an imaginary horizontal line. As shown in Figure 4.22, an angle formed by a horizontal line and the line of sight to an object that is above the horizontal line is called the **angle of elevation.** The angle formed by a horizontal line and the line of sight to an object that is below the horizontal line is called the **angle of depression.** Transits and sextants are instruments used to measure such angles.

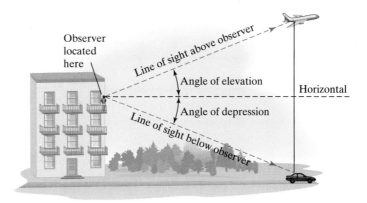

Figure 4.22

EXAMPLE 8   Problem Solving Using an Angle of Elevation

Sighting the top of a building, a surveyor measured the angle of elevation to be 22°. The transit is 5 feet above the ground and 300 feet from the building. Find the building's height.

Solution   The situation is illustrated in Figure 4.23. Let a be the height of the portion of the building that lies above the transit. The height of the building is the transit's height, 5 feet, plus a. Thus, we need to identify a trigonometric function that will make it possible to find a. In terms of the 22° angle, we are looking for the side opposite the angle. The transit is 300 feet from the building, so the side adjacent to the 22° angle is 300 feet. Because we have a known angle, an unknown opposite side, and a known adjacent side, we select the tangent function.

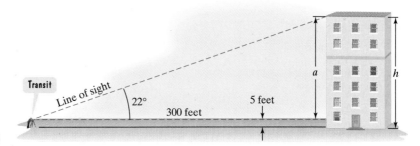

Figure 4.23

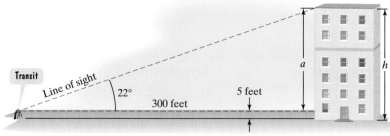

Figure 4.23, repeated

$$\tan 22° = \frac{a}{300}$$

Length of side opposite the 22° angle

Length of side adjacent to the 22° angle

$$a = 300 \tan 22°$$ Multiply both sides of the equation by 300.

$$a \approx 300(0.4040) \approx 121$$ Find tan 22° with a calculator in the degree mode.

The height of the part of the building above the transit is approximately 121 feet. Thus, the height of the building is determined by adding the transit's height, 5 feet, to 121 feet.

$$h \approx 5 + 121 = 126$$

The building's height is approximately 126 feet.

Check Point 8

The irregular blue shape in Figure 4.24 represents a lake. The distance across the lake, a, is unknown. To find this distance, a surveyor took the measurements shown in the figure. What is the distance across the lake?

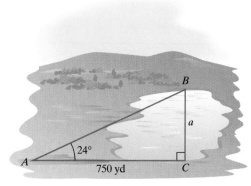

Figure 4.24

If two sides of a right triangle are known, an appropriate trigonometric function can be used to find an acute angle θ in the triangle. You will also need to use the *inverse key* on a calculator. This key uses a function value to display the acute angle θ. For example, suppose that $\sin \theta = 0.866$. We can find θ in the degree mode by using the secondary *inverse sine* key, usually labeled $\boxed{\text{SIN}^{-1}}$.

Many Scientific Calculators:

.866 $\boxed{\text{2nd}}$ $\boxed{\text{SIN}^{-1}}$

Many Graphing Calculators:

$\boxed{\text{2nd}}$ $\boxed{\text{SIN}^{-1}}$ .866 $\boxed{\text{ENTER}}$

The display should show approximately 59.99, which can be rounded to 60. Thus, if $\sin \theta = 0.866$, then $\theta \approx 60°$.

EXAMPLE 9   Determining the Angle of Elevation

A building that is 21 meters tall casts a shadow 25 meters long. Find the angle of elevation of the sun to the nearest degree.

Solution   The situation is illustrated in Figure 4.25. We are asked to find θ. We begin with the tangent function.

$$\tan \theta = \frac{\text{side opposite } \theta}{\text{side adjacent to } \theta} = \frac{21}{25}$$

We use a calculator in the degree mode to find θ.

Many Scientific Calculators:

$$\boxed{(}\;\boxed{21}\;\boxed{\div}\;\boxed{25}\;\boxed{)}\;\boxed{\text{2nd}}\;\boxed{\text{TAN}^{-1}}$$

Many Graphing Calculators:

$$\boxed{\text{2nd}}\;\boxed{\text{TAN}^{-1}}\;\boxed{(}\;\boxed{21}\;\boxed{\div}\;\boxed{25}\;\boxed{)}\;\boxed{\text{ENTER}}$$

The display should show approximately 40. Thus, the angle of elevation of the sun is approximately 40°.

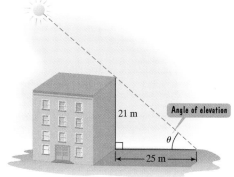

21 m

Angle of elevation

θ

25 m

Figure 4.25

Check Point 9   A flagpole that is 14 meters tall casts a shadow 10 meters long. Find the angle of elevation of the sun to the nearest degree.

The Mountain Man

In the 1930s, a *National Geographic* team headed by Brad Washburn used trigonometry to create a map of the 5000-square-mile region of the Yukon, near the Canadian border. The team started with aerial photography. By drawing a network of angles on the photographs, the approximate locations of the major mountains and their rough heights were determined. The expedition then spent three months on foot to find the exact heights. Team members established two base points a known distance apart, one directly under the mountain's peak. By measuring the angle of elevation from one of the base points to the peak, the tangent function was used to determine the peak's height. The Yukon expedition was a major advance in the way maps are made.

EXERCISE SET 4.2

Practice Exercises

In Exercises 1–8, use the Pythagorean Theorem to find the length of the missing side of each right triangle. Then find the value of each of the six trigonometric functions of θ.

1.
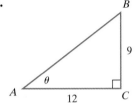

2.
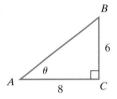

3.
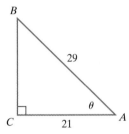

4.
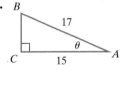

5.
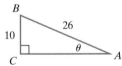

6.

7.
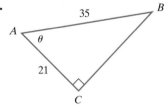

8.

In Exercises 9–16, use the given triangles to evaluate each expression. If necessary, express the value without a square root in the denominator by rationalizing the denominator.

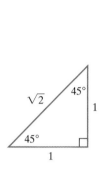
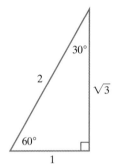

9. $\cos 30°$ **10.** $\tan 30°$

11. $\sec 45°$ **12.** $\csc 45°$

13. $\tan \dfrac{\pi}{3}$ **14.** $\cot \dfrac{\pi}{3}$

15. $\sin \dfrac{\pi}{4} - \cos \dfrac{\pi}{4}$ **16.** $\tan \dfrac{\pi}{4} + \csc \dfrac{\pi}{6}$

In Exercises 17–20, θ is an acute angle and sin θ and cos θ are given. Use identities to find tan θ, csc θ, sec θ, and cot θ. Where necessary, rationalize denominators.

17. $\sin \theta = \dfrac{8}{17}, \quad \cos \theta = \dfrac{15}{17}$

18. $\sin \theta = \dfrac{3}{5}, \quad \cos \theta = \dfrac{4}{5}$

19. $\sin \theta = \dfrac{1}{3}, \quad \cos \theta = \dfrac{2\sqrt{2}}{3}$

20. $\sin \theta = \dfrac{2}{3}, \quad \cos \theta = \dfrac{\sqrt{5}}{3}$

In Exercises 21–24, θ is an acute angle and sin θ is given. Use the Pythagorean identity $\sin^2 \theta + \cos^2 \theta = 1$ to find cos θ.

21. $\sin \theta = \dfrac{6}{7}$ **22.** $\sin \theta = \dfrac{7}{8}$

23. $\sin \theta = \dfrac{\sqrt{39}}{8}$ **24.** $\sin \theta = \dfrac{\sqrt{21}}{5}$

In Exercises 25–30, use an identity to find the value of each expression. Do not use a calculator.

25. $\sin 37° \csc 37°$ **26.** $\cos 53° \sec 53°$

27. $\sin^2 \dfrac{\pi}{9} + \cos^2 \dfrac{\pi}{9}$ **28.** $\sin^2 \dfrac{\pi}{10} + \cos^2 \dfrac{\pi}{10}$

29. $\sec^2 23° - \tan^2 23°$ **30.** $\csc^2 63° - \cot^2 63°$

In Exercises 31–38, find a cofunction with the same value as the given expression.

31. $\sin 7°$

32. $\sin 19°$

33. $\csc 25°$

34. $\csc 35°$

35. $\tan \dfrac{\pi}{9}$

36. $\tan \dfrac{\pi}{7}$

37. $\cos \dfrac{2\pi}{5}$

38. $\cos \dfrac{3\pi}{8}$

In Exercises 39–48, use a calculator to find the value of the trigonometric function to four decimal places.

39. $\sin 38°$

40. $\cos 21°$

41. $\tan 32.7°$

42. $\tan 52.6°$

43. $\csc 17°$

44. $\sec 55°$

45. $\cos \dfrac{\pi}{10}$

46. $\sin \dfrac{3\pi}{10}$

47. $\cot \dfrac{\pi}{12}$

48. $\cot \dfrac{\pi}{18}$

In Exercises 49–54, find the measure of the side of the right triangle whose length is designated by a lowercase letter. Round answers to the nearest whole number.

49.

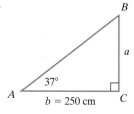

50.

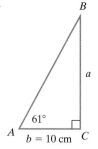

51.

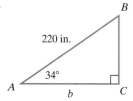

52.

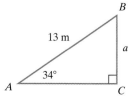

53.

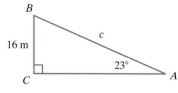

54.

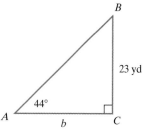

In Exercises 55–58, use a calculator to find the value of the acute angle θ to the nearest degree.

55. $\sin \theta = 0.2974$

56. $\cos \theta = 0.8771$

57. $\tan \theta = 4.6252$

58. $\tan \theta = 26.0307$

In Exercises 59–62, use a calculator to find the value of the acute angle θ in radians, rounded to three decimal places.

59. $\cos \theta = 0.4112$

60. $\sin \theta = 0.9499$

61. $\tan \theta = 0.4169$

62. $\tan \theta = 0.5117$

Application Exercises

63. To find the distance across a lake, a surveyor took the measurements in the figure shown. Use these measurements to determine how far it is across the lake. Round to the nearest yard.

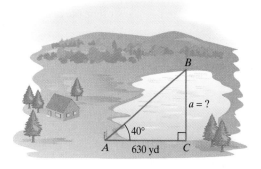

64. At a certain time of day, the angle of elevation of the sun is 40°. To the nearest foot, find the height of a tree whose shadow is 35 feet long.

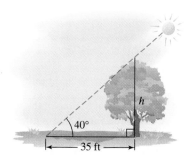

65. A tower that is 125 feet tall casts a shadow 172 feet long. Find the angle of elevation of the sun to the nearest degree.

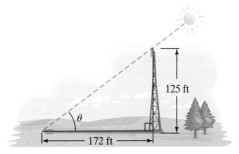

125 ft

172 ft

θ

66. The Washington Monument is 555 feet high. If you stand one quarter of a mile, or 1320 feet, from the base of the monument and look to the top, find the angle of elevation to the nearest degree.

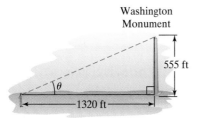

Washington Monument

555 ft

1320 ft

θ

67. A plane rises from take-off and flies at an angle of 10° with the horizontal runway. When it has gained 500 feet, find the distance, to the nearest foot, the plane has flown.

B

c = ?

10°

500 ft

A

C

68. A road is inclined at an angle of 5°. After driving 5000 feet along this road, find the driver's increase in altitude. Round to the nearest foot.

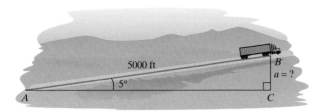

5000 ft

5°

B

a = ?

A

C

69. A telephone pole, shown at the top of the next column, is 60 feet tall. A guy wire 75 feet long is attached from the ground to the top of the pole. Find the angle between the wire and the pole to the nearest degree.

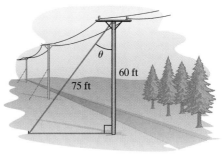

θ

60 ft

75 ft

70. A telephone pole is 55 feet tall. A guy wire 80 feet long is attached from the ground to the top of the pole. Find the angle between the wire and the pole to the nearest degree.

Writing in Mathematics

71. If you are given the lengths of the sides of a right triangle, describe how to find the sine of either acute angle.

72. Describe one similarity and one difference between the definitions of $\sin \theta$ and $\cos \theta$, where θ is an acute angle of a right triangle.

73. Describe the triangle used to find the trigonometric functions of 45°.

74. Describe the triangle used to find the trigonometric functions of 30° and 60°.

75. What is a trigonometric identity?

76. Use words (not an equation) to describe one of the reciprocal identities.

77. Use words (not an equation) to describe one of the quotient identities.

78. Use words (not an equation) to describe one of the Pythagorean identities.

79. Describe a relationship among trigonometric functions that is based on angles that are complements.

80. Describe what is meant by an angle of elevation and an angle of depression.

81. Stonehenge, the famous "stone circle" in England, was built between 2750 B.C. and 1300 B.C. using solid stone blocks weighing over 99,000 pounds each. It required 550 people to pull a single stone up a ramp inclined at a 9° angle. Describe how right triangle trigonometry can be used to determine the distance the 550 workers had to drag a stone in order to raise it to a height of 30 feet.

Technology Exercises

82. Use a calculator in the radian mode to fill in the values in the following table. Then draw a conclusion about $\dfrac{\sin\theta}{\theta}$ as θ approaches 0.

θ	0.4	0.3	0.2	0.1	0.01	0.001	0.0001	0.00001
$\sin\theta$								
$\dfrac{\sin\theta}{\theta}$								

83. Use a calculator in the radian mode to fill in the values in the following table. Then draw a conclusion about $\dfrac{\cos\theta - 1}{\theta}$ as θ approaches 0.

θ	0.4	0.3	0.2	0.1	0.01	0.001	0.0001	0.00001
$\cos\theta$								
$\dfrac{\cos\theta - 1}{\theta}$								

Critical Thinking Exercises

84. Which one of the following is true?

a. $\dfrac{\tan 45°}{\tan 15°} = \tan 3°$

b. $\tan^2 15° - \sec^2 15° = -1$

c. $\sin 45° + \cos 45° = 1$

d. $\tan^2 5° = \tan 25°$

85. Explain why the sine or cosine of an acute angle cannot be greater than or equal to 1.

86. Describe what happens to the tangent of an acute angle as the angle gets close to 90°. What happens at 90°?

87. From the top of a 250-foot lighthouse, a plane is sighted overhead and a ship is observed directly below the plane. The angle of elevation of the plane is 22° and the angle of depression of the ship is 35°. Find **a.** the distance of the ship from the lighthouse; **b.** the plane's height above the water. Round to the nearest foot.

SECTION 4.3   *Trigonometric Functions of Any Angle*

Objectives

1. Use the definitions of trigonometric functions of any angle.
2. Use the signs of the trigonometric functions.
3. Find reference angles.
4. Use reference angles to evaluate trigonometric functions.

There is something comforting in the repetition of some of nature's patterns. The ocean level at a beach varies between high and low tide approximately every 12 hours. The number of hours of daylight oscillates from a maximum on the summer solstice, June 21, to a minimum on the winter solstice, December 21. Then it increases to the same maximum the following June 21. Some believe that cycles, called biorhythms, represent physical, emotional, and intellectual aspects of our lives. Throughout the remainder of this chapter, we will see how the trigonometric functions are used to model phenomena that occur again and again. To do this, we need to move beyond right triangles.

1 Use the definitions of trigonometric functions of any angle.

Trigonometric Functions of Any Angle

In the last section, we evaluated trigonometric functions of acute angles, such as that shown in Figure 4.26(a). Note that this angle is in standard position. The point $P = (x, y)$ is a point r units from the origin on the terminal side of θ. A right triangle is formed by drawing a perpendicular from $P = (x, y)$ to the x-axis. Note that y is the length of the side opposite θ and x is the length of the side adjacent to θ.

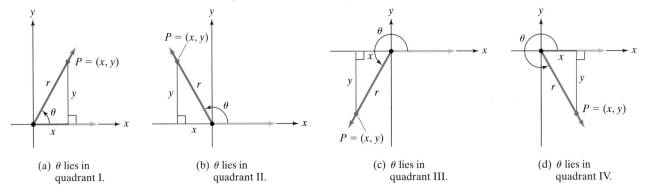

(a) θ lies in quadrant I.

(b) θ lies in quadrant II.

(c) θ lies in quadrant III.

(d) θ lies in quadrant IV.

Figure 4.26

Figures 4.26(b), (c), and (d) show angles in standard position, but they are not acute. We can extend our definitions of the six trigonometric functions to include such angles, as well as quadrantal angles. (Recall that a quadrantal angle has its terminal side on the x-axis or y-axis; such angles are *not* shown in Figure 4.26.) The point $P = (x, y)$ may be any point on the terminal side of the angle θ other than the origin, $(0, 0)$.

Study Tip

If θ is acute, we have the right triangle shown in Figure 4.26(a). In this situation, the definitions in the box are the right triangle definitions of the trigonometric functions. This should make it easier for you to remember the six definitions.

Definitions of Trigonometric Functions of Any Angle

Let θ be any angle in standard position, and let $P = (x, y)$ be a point on the terminal side of θ. If $r = \sqrt{x^2 + y^2}$ is the distance from $(0, 0)$ to (x, y), as shown in Figure 4.26, the **six trigonometric functions of θ** are defined by the following ratios:

$$\sin \theta = \frac{y}{r} \qquad \cos \theta = \frac{x}{r} \qquad \tan \theta = \frac{y}{x}, x \neq 0$$

$$\csc \theta = \frac{r}{y}, y \neq 0 \qquad \sec \theta = \frac{r}{x}, x \neq 0 \qquad \cot \theta = \frac{x}{y}, y \neq 0.$$

Because the point $P = (x, y)$ is any point on the terminal side of θ other than the origin, $(0, 0), r = \sqrt{x^2 + y^2}$ cannot be zero. Examine the six trigonometric functions defined previously. Note that the denominator of the sine and cosine functions is r. Because $r \neq 0$, the sine and cosine functions are defined for any real value of the angle θ. This is not true for the other four trigonometric functions. Note that the denominator of the tangent and secant functions is x. These functions are not defined if $x = 0$. If the point $P = (x, y)$ is on the y-axis, then $x = 0$. Thus, the tangent and secant functions are undefined for all quadrantal angles with terminal sides on the positive or negative y-axis. Likewise, if $P = (x, y)$ is on the x-axis, then $y = 0$, and the cotangent and cosecant functions are undefined. The cotangent and cosecant functions are undefined for all quadrantal angles with terminal sides on the positive or negative x-axis.

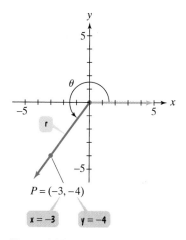

Figure 4.27

x = −3   y = −4

EXAMPLE 1 Evaluating Trigonometric Functions

Let $P = (-3, -4)$ be a point on the terminal side of θ. Find each of the six trigonometric functions of θ.

Solution The situation is shown in Figure 4.27. We need values for x, y, and r to evaluate all six trigonometric functions. We are given the values of x and y. Because $P = (-3, -4)$ is a point on the terminal side of θ, $x = -3$ and $y = -4$. Furthermore,

$$r = \sqrt{x^2 + y^2} = \sqrt{(-3)^2 + (-4)^2} = \sqrt{9 + 16} = \sqrt{25} = 5.$$

Now that we know x, y, and r, we can find the six trigonometric functions of θ.

$$\sin\theta = \frac{y}{r} = \frac{-4}{5} = -\frac{4}{5}, \quad \cos\theta = \frac{x}{r} = \frac{-3}{5} = -\frac{3}{5}, \quad \tan\theta = \frac{y}{x} = \frac{-4}{-3} = \frac{4}{3}$$

$$\csc\theta = \frac{r}{y} = \frac{5}{-4} = -\frac{5}{4}, \quad \sec\theta = \frac{r}{x} = \frac{5}{-3} = -\frac{5}{3}, \quad \cot\theta = \frac{x}{y} = \frac{-3}{-4} = \frac{3}{4}$$

These ratios are the reciprocals of those shown directly above.

Check Point 1 Let $P = (4, -3)$ be a point on the terminal side of θ. Find each of the six trigonometric functions of θ.

How do we find the values of the trigonometric functions for a quadrantal angle? First, draw the angle in standard position. Second, choose a point P on the angle's terminal side. The trigonometric function values of θ depend only on the size of θ and not on the distance of point P from the origin. Thus, we choose a point that is 1 unit from the origin. Finally, apply the definition of the appropriate trigonometric function.

EXAMPLE 2 Trigonometric Functions of Quadrantal Angles

Evaluate, if possible, the sine function and the tangent function at the following four quadrantal angles:

a. $\theta = 0° = 0$ **b.** $\theta = 90° = \dfrac{\pi}{2}$ **c.** $\theta = 180° = \pi$ **d.** $\theta = 270° = \dfrac{3\pi}{2}$.

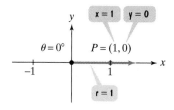

x = 1   y = 0

Solution

a. If $\theta = 0° = 0$ radians, then the terminal side of the angle is on the positive x-axis. Let us select the point $P = (1, 0)$ with $x = 1$ and $y = 0$. This point is 1 unit from the origin, so $r = 1$. Now that we know x, y, and r, we can apply the definitions of the sine and tangent functions. (The figure on the left is repeated at the top of the next page.)

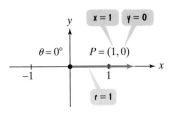

$$\sin 0° = \sin 0 = \frac{y}{r} = \frac{0}{1} = 0$$

$$\tan 0° = \tan 0 = \frac{y}{x} = \frac{0}{1} = 0$$

b. If $\theta = 90° = \frac{\pi}{2}$ radians, then the terminal side of the angle is on the positive y-axis. Let us select the point $P = (0, 1)$ with $x = 0$ and $y = 1$. This point is 1 unit from the origin, so $r = 1$. Now that we know x, y, and r, we can apply the definitions of the sine and tangent functions.

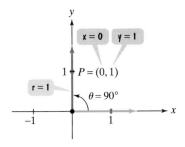

$$\sin 90° = \sin \frac{\pi}{2} = \frac{y}{r} = \frac{1}{1} = 1$$

$$\tan 90° = \tan \frac{\pi}{2} = \frac{y}{x} = \frac{1}{0}$$

Because division by 0 is undefined, $\tan 90°$ is undefined.

c. If $\theta = 180° = \pi$ radians, then the terminal side of the angle is on the negative x-axis. Let us select the point $P = (-1, 0)$ with $x = -1$ and $y = 0$. This point is 1 unit from the origin, so $r = 1$. Now that we know x, y, and r, we can apply the definitions of the sine and tangent functions.

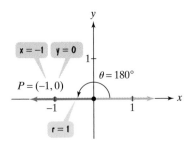

$$\sin 180° = \sin \pi = \frac{y}{r} = \frac{0}{1} = 0$$

$$\tan 180° = \tan \pi = \frac{y}{x} = \frac{0}{-1} = 0$$

Discovery

Try finding tan 90° and tan 270° with your calculator. Describe what occurs.

d. If $\theta = 270° = \dfrac{3\pi}{2}$ radians, then the terminal side of the angle is on the negative y-axis. Let us select the point $P = (0, -1)$ with $x = 0$ and $y = -1$. This point is 1 unit from the origin, so $r = 1$. Now that we know x, y, and r, we can apply the definitions of the sine and tangent functions.

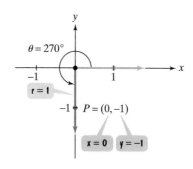

$$\sin 270° = \sin \frac{3\pi}{2} = \frac{y}{r} = \frac{-1}{1} = -1$$

$$\tan 270° = \tan \frac{3\pi}{2} = \frac{y}{x} = \frac{-1}{0}$$

Because division by 0 is undefined, tan 270° is undefined.

Check Point 2 Evaluate, if possible, the cosine function and the cosecant function at the following four quadrantal angles:

a. $\theta = 0° = 0$ **b.** $\theta = 90° = \dfrac{\pi}{2}$

c. $\theta = 180° = \pi$ **d.** $\theta = 270° = \dfrac{3\pi}{2}$.

2 Use the signs of the trigonometric functions.

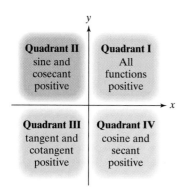

Figure 4.28 The signs of the trigonometric functions

The Signs of the Trigonometric Functions

In Example 2, we evaluated trigonometric functions of quadrantal angles. However, we will now return to the trigonometric functions of nonquadrantal angles. **If θ is not a quadrantal angle, the sign of a trigonometric function depends on the quadrant in which θ lies.** In all four quadrants, r is positive. However, x and y can be positive or negative. For example, if θ lies in quadrant II, x is negative and y is positive. Thus, the only positive ratios in this quadrant are $\dfrac{y}{r}$ and its reciprocal, $\dfrac{r}{y}$. These ratios are the function values for the sine and cosecant, respectively. In short, if θ lies in quadrant II, $\sin \theta$ and $\csc \theta$ are positive. The other four trigonometric functions are negative.

Figure 4.28 summarizes the signs of the trigonometric functions. If θ lies in quadrant I, all six functions are positive. If θ lies in quadrant II, only $\sin \theta$ and $\csc \theta$ are positive. If θ lies in quadrant III, only $\tan \theta$ and $\cot \theta$ are positive. Finally, if θ lies in quadrant IV, only $\cos \theta$ and $\sec \theta$ are positive. Observe that the positive functions in each quadrant occur in reciprocal pairs.

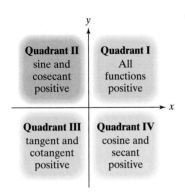

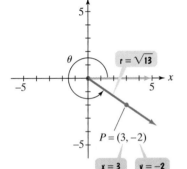

Figure 4.28 The signs of the trigonometric functions, repeated

Figure 4.29 $\tan\theta = -\frac{2}{3}$ and $\cos\theta > 0$

3 Find reference angles.

EXAMPLE 3 Finding the Quadrant in Which an Angle Lies

If $\tan\theta < 0$ and $\cos\theta > 0$, name the quadrant in which angle θ lies.

Solution Because $\tan\theta < 0$, θ cannot lie in quadrant I; all the functions are positive in quadrant I. Furthermore, θ cannot lie in quadrant III; $\tan\theta$ is positive in quadrant III. Thus, with $\tan\theta < 0$, θ lies in quadrant II or quadrant IV. We are also given that $\cos\theta > 0$. Because quadrant IV is the only quadrant in which the cosine is positive and the tangent is negative, we conclude that θ lies in quadrant IV.

Check Point 3 If $\sin\theta < 0$ and $\cos\theta < 0$, name the quadrant in which angle θ lies.

EXAMPLE 4 Evaluating Trigonometric Functions

Given $\tan\theta = -\frac{2}{3}$ and $\cos\theta > 0$, find $\cos\theta$ and $\csc\theta$.

Solution Because the tangent is negative and the cosine is positive, θ lies in quadrant IV. This will help us to determine whether the negative sign in $\tan\theta = -\frac{2}{3}$ should be associated with the numerator or the denominator. Keep in mind that in quadrant IV, x is positive and y is negative. Thus,

> In quadrant IV, y is negative.

$$\tan\theta = -\frac{2}{3} = \frac{y}{x} = \frac{-2}{3}.$$

(See Figure 4.29.) Thus, $x = 3$ and $y = -2$. Furthermore,

$$r = \sqrt{x^2 + y^2} = \sqrt{3^2 + (-2)^2} = \sqrt{9 + 4} = \sqrt{13}.$$

Now that we know x, y, and r, we can find $\cos\theta$ and $\csc\theta$.

$$\cos\theta = \frac{x}{r} = \frac{3}{\sqrt{13}} = \frac{3}{\sqrt{13}} \cdot \frac{\sqrt{13}}{\sqrt{13}} = \frac{3\sqrt{13}}{13} \qquad \csc\theta = \frac{r}{y} = \frac{\sqrt{13}}{-2} = -\frac{\sqrt{13}}{2}$$

Check Point 4 Given $\tan\theta = -\frac{1}{3}$ and $\cos\theta < 0$, find $\sin\theta$ and $\sec\theta$.

Reference Angles

We will often evaluate trigonometric functions of positive angles greater than 90° and all negative angles by making use of a positive acute angle. This positive acute angle is called a *reference angle*.

> **Definition of a Reference Angle**
>
> Let θ be a nonacute angle in standard position that lies in a quadrant. Its **reference angle** is the positive acute angle θ' formed by the terminal side of θ and the x-axis.

Figure 4.30 shows the reference angle for θ lying in quadrants II, III, and IV. Notice that the formula used to find θ', the reference angle, varies according to the quadrant in which θ lies. You may find it easier to find the reference angle for a given angle by making a figure that shows the angle in standard position. The acute angle formed by the terminal side of this angle and the x-axis is the reference angle.

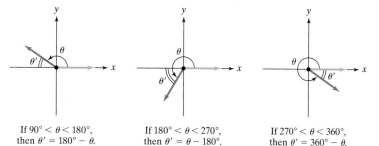

Figure 4.30 Reference angles, θ', for positive angles, θ, in quadrants II, III, and IV

If $90° < \theta < 180°$, then $\theta' = 180° - \theta$.

If $180° < \theta < 270°$, then $\theta' = \theta - 180°$.

If $270° < \theta < 360°$, then $\theta' = 360° - \theta$.

EXAMPLE 5   Finding Reference Angles

Find the reference angle, θ', for each of the following angles:

a. $\theta = 345°$ **b.** $\theta = \dfrac{5\pi}{6}$ **c.** $\theta = -135°$ **d.** $\theta = 2.5$.

Solution

a. A $345°$ angle in standard position is shown in Figure 4.31. Because $345°$ lies in quadrant IV, the reference angle is

$$\theta' = 360° - 345° = 15°.$$

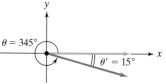

Figure 4.31

b. Because $\dfrac{5\pi}{6}$ lies between $\dfrac{\pi}{2} = \dfrac{3\pi}{6}$ and

$\pi = \dfrac{6\pi}{6}$, $\theta = \dfrac{5\pi}{6}$ lies in quadrant II.

The angle is shown in Figure 4.32. The reference angle is

$$\theta' = \pi - \frac{5\pi}{6} = \frac{6\pi}{6} - \frac{5\pi}{6} = \frac{\pi}{6}.$$

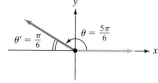

Figure 4.32

c. A $-135°$ angle in standard position is shown in Figure 4.33. The figure indicates that the positive acute angle formed by the terminal side of θ and the x-axis is $45°$. The reference angle is

$$\theta' = 45°.$$

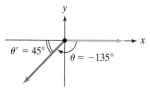

Figure 4.33

d. The angle $\theta = 2.5$ lies between $\dfrac{\pi}{2} \approx 1.57$

and $\pi \approx 3.14$. This means that $\theta = 2.5$ is in quadrant II, shown in Figure 4.34. The reference angle is

$$\theta' = \pi - 2.5 \approx 0.64.$$

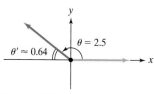

Figure 4.34

Check Point 5 Find the reference angle, θ', for each of the following angles:

a. $\theta = 210°$ **b.** $\theta = \dfrac{7\pi}{4}$ **c.** $\theta = -240°$ **d.** $\theta = 3.6$

The way that reference angles are defined makes them useful in evaluating trigonometric functions.

4 Use reference angles to evaluate trigonometric functions.

Using Reference Angles to Evaluate Trigonometric Functions

The values of the trigonometric functions of a given angle, θ, are the same as the values of the trigonometric functions of the reference angle, θ', except possibly for the sign. A function value of the acute reference angle, θ', is always positive. However, the same function value for θ may be positive or negative.

For example, we can use a reference angle, θ', to obtain an exact value for $\tan 120°$. The reference angle for $\theta = 120°$ is $\theta' = 180° - 120° = 60°$. We know the exact value of the tangent function of the reference angle: $\tan 60° = \sqrt{3}$. We also know that the value of a trigonometric function of a given angle, θ, is the same as that of its reference angle, θ', except possibly for the sign. Thus, we can conclude that $\tan 120°$ equals $-\sqrt{3}$ or $\sqrt{3}$.

What sign should we attach to $\sqrt{3}$? A $120°$ angle lies in quadrant II, where only the sine and cosecant are positive. Thus, the tangent function is negative for a $120°$ angle. Therefore,

> Prefix by a negative sign to show tangent is negative in quadrant II.

$$\tan 120° = -\tan 60° = -\sqrt{3}.$$

> The reference angle for $120°$ is $60°$.

In the previous section, we used two right triangles to find exact trigonometric values of $30°, 45°,$ and $60°$. Using a procedure similar to finding $\tan 120°$, we can now find the function values of all angles for which $30°, 45°,$ or $60°$ are reference angles.

A Procedure for Using Reference Angles to Evaluate Trigonometric Functions

The value of a trigonometric function of any angle θ is found as follows:

1. Find the associated reference angle, θ', and the function value for θ'.
2. Use the quadrant in which θ lies to prefix the appropriate sign to the function value in step 1.

Discovery

Draw the two right triangles involving $30°, 45°,$ and $60°$. Indicate the length of each side. Use these lengths to verify the function values for the reference angles in the solution to Example 6.

EXAMPLE 6 Using Reference Angles to Evaluate Trigonometric Functions

Use reference angles to find the exact value of each of the following trigonometric functions:

a. $\sin 135°$ **b.** $\cos \dfrac{4\pi}{3}$ **c.** $\cot\left(-\dfrac{\pi}{3}\right)$.

Solution

a. We use our two-step procedure to find $\sin 135°$.

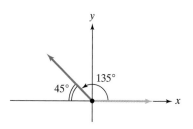

Figure 4.35 Reference angle for 135°

Step 1 Find the reference angle, θ', and $\sin\theta'$. Figure 4.35 shows 135° lies in quadrant II. The reference angle is

$$\theta' = 180° - 135° = 45°.$$

The function value for the reference angle is $\sin 45° = \dfrac{\sqrt{2}}{2}$.

Step 2 Use the quadrant in which θ lies to prefix the appropriate sign to the function value in step 1. The angle $\theta = 135°$ lies in quadrant II. Because the sine is positive in quadrant II, we put a $+$ sign before the function value of the reference angle. Thus,

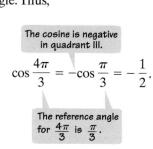

The sine is positive in quadrant II.

$$\sin 135° = +\sin 45° = \dfrac{\sqrt{2}}{2}.$$

The reference angle for 135° is 45°.

b. We use our two-step procedure to find $\cos\dfrac{4\pi}{3}$.

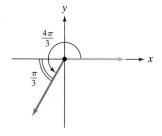

Figure 4.36 Reference angle for $\dfrac{4\pi}{3}$

Step 1 Find the reference angle, θ', and $\cos\theta'$. Figure 4.36 shows that $\theta = \dfrac{4\pi}{3}$ lies in quadrant III. The reference angle is

$$\theta' = \dfrac{4\pi}{3} - \pi = \dfrac{4\pi}{3} - \dfrac{3\pi}{3} = \dfrac{\pi}{3}.$$

The function value for the reference angle is

$$\cos\dfrac{\pi}{3} = \dfrac{1}{2}.$$

Step 2 Use the quadrant in which θ lies to prefix the appropriate sign to the function value in step 1. The angle $\theta = \dfrac{4\pi}{3}$ lies in quadrant III. Because only the tangent and cotangent are positive in quadrant III, the cosine is negative in this quadrant. We put a $-$ sign before the function value of the reference angle. Thus,

The cosine is negative in quadrant III.

$$\cos\dfrac{4\pi}{3} = -\cos\dfrac{\pi}{3} = -\dfrac{1}{2}.$$

The reference angle for $\dfrac{4\pi}{3}$ is $\dfrac{\pi}{3}$.

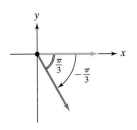

Figure 4.37 Reference angle for $-\dfrac{\pi}{3}$

c. We use our two-step procedure to find $\cot\left(-\dfrac{\pi}{3}\right)$.

Step 1 Find the reference angle, θ', and $\cot\theta'$. Figure 4.37 shows that $\theta = -\dfrac{\pi}{3}$ lies in quadrant IV. The reference angle is $\theta' = \dfrac{\pi}{3}$. The function value for the reference angle is $\cot\dfrac{\pi}{3} = \dfrac{\sqrt{3}}{3}$.

Step 2 Use the quadrant in which θ lies to prefix the appropriate sign to the function value in step 1. The angle $\theta = -\dfrac{\pi}{3}$ lies in quadrant IV. Because only the cosine and secant are positive in quadrant IV, the cotangent is negative in this quadrant. We put a $-$ sign before the function value of the reference angle. Thus,

> The cotangent is negative in quadrant IV.

$$\cot\left(-\frac{\pi}{3}\right) = -\cot\frac{\pi}{3} = -\frac{\sqrt{3}}{3}.$$

> The reference angle for $-\frac{\pi}{3}$ is $\frac{\pi}{3}$.

Check Point 6 Use reference angles to find the exact value of the following trigonometric functions:

a. $\sin 300°$ **b.** $\tan\dfrac{5\pi}{4}$ **c.** $\sec\left(-\dfrac{\pi}{6}\right)$.

EXERCISE SET 4.3

Practice Exercises

In Exercises 1–8, a point on the terminal side of angle θ is given. Find the exact value of each of the six trigonometric functions of θ.

1. $(-4, 3)$ **2.** $(-12, 5)$
3. $(2, 3)$ **4.** $(3, 7)$
5. $(3, -3)$ **6.** $(5, -5)$
7. $(-2, -5)$ **8.** $(-1, -3)$

In Exercises 9–16, evaluate the trigonometric function at the quadrantal angle, or state that the expression is undefined.

9. $\cos\pi$ **10.** $\tan\pi$
11. $\sec\pi$ **12.** $\csc\pi$
13. $\tan\dfrac{3\pi}{2}$ **14.** $\cos\dfrac{3\pi}{2}$
15. $\cot\dfrac{\pi}{2}$ **16.** $\tan\dfrac{\pi}{2}$

In Exercises 17–22, let θ be an angle in standard position. Name the quadrant in which θ lies.

17. $\sin\theta > 0$, $\cos\theta > 0$
18. $\sin\theta < 0$, $\cos\theta > 0$
19. $\sin\theta < 0$, $\cos\theta < 0$
20. $\tan\theta < 0$, $\sin\theta < 0$
21. $\tan\theta < 0$, $\cos\theta < 0$
22. $\cot\theta > 0$, $\sec\theta < 0$

In Exercises 23–34, find the exact value of each of the remaining trigonometric functions of θ.

23. $\cos\theta = -\frac{3}{5}$, θ in quadrant III
24. $\sin\theta = -\frac{12}{13}$, θ in quadrant III
25. $\sin\theta = \frac{5}{13}$, θ in quadrant II
26. $\cos\theta = \frac{4}{5}$, θ in quadrant IV
27. $\cos\theta = \frac{8}{17}$, $270° < \theta < 360°$
28. $\cos\theta = \frac{1}{3}$, $270° < \theta < 360°$
29. $\tan\theta = -\frac{2}{3}$, $\sin\theta > 0$
30. $\tan\theta = -\frac{1}{3}$, $\sin\theta > 0$
31. $\tan\theta = \frac{4}{3}$, $\cos\theta < 0$
32. $\tan\theta = \frac{5}{12}$, $\cos\theta < 0$
33. $\sec\theta = -3$, $\tan\theta > 0$
34. $\csc\theta = -4$, $\tan\theta > 0$

In Exercises 35–50, find the reference angle for each angle.

35. 160°

36. 170°

37. 205°

38. 210°

39. 355°

40. 351°

41. $\dfrac{7\pi}{4}$

42. $\dfrac{5\pi}{4}$

43. $\dfrac{5\pi}{6}$

44. $\dfrac{5\pi}{7}$

45. −150°

46. −250°

47. −335°

48. −359°

49. 4.7

50. 5.5

In Exercises 51–66, use reference angles to find the exact value of each expression. Do not use a calculator.

51. $\cos 225°$

52. $\sin 300°$

53. $\tan 210°$

54. $\sec 240°$

55. $\tan 420°$

56. $\tan 405°$

57. $\sin \dfrac{2\pi}{3}$

58. $\cos \dfrac{3\pi}{4}$

59. $\csc \dfrac{7\pi}{6}$

60. $\cot \dfrac{7\pi}{4}$

61. $\tan \dfrac{9\pi}{4}$

62. $\tan \dfrac{9\pi}{2}$

63. $\sin(-240°)$

64. $\sin(-225°)$

65. $\tan\left(-\dfrac{\pi}{4}\right)$

66. $\tan\left(-\dfrac{\pi}{6}\right)$

Writing in Mathematics

67. If you are given a point on the terminal side of angle θ, explain how to find $\sin \theta$.

68. Explain why $\tan 90°$ is undefined.

69. If $\cos \theta > 0$ and $\tan \theta < 0$, explain how to find the quadrant in which θ lies.

70. What is a reference angle? Give an example with your description.

71. Explain how reference angles are used to evaluate trigonometric functions. Give an example with your description.

SECTION 4.4 Trigonometric Functions of Real Numbers; Periodic Functions

Objectives

1. Use a unit circle to define trigonometric functions of real numbers.
2. Recognize the domain and range of sine and cosine functions.
3. Use even and odd trigonometric functions.
4. Use periodic properties.

Cycles govern many aspects of life—heartbeats, sleep patterns, seasons, and tides all follow regular, predictable cycles. In this section, we will see why trigonometric functions are used to model phenomena that occur in cycles. To do this, we need to move beyond angles and consider trigonometric functions of real numbers.

1 Use a unit circle to define trigonometric functions of real numbers.

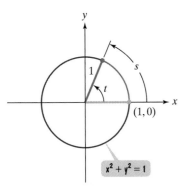

Figure 4.38 Unit circle with a central angle measuring t radians

Trigonometric Functions of Real Numbers

Thus far, we have considered trigonometric functions of angles measured in degrees or radians. To define trigonometric functions of real numbers, rather than angles, we use a unit circle. A **unit circle** is a circle of radius 1, with its center at the origin of a rectangular coordinate system. The equation of this unit circle is $x^2 + y^2 = 1$. Figure 4.38 shows a unit circle in which the central angle measures t radians. We can use the formula for the length of a circular arc, $s = r\theta$, to find the length of the intercepted arc.

$$s = r\theta = 1 \cdot t = t$$

| The radius of a unit circle is 1. | The radian measure of the central angle is t. |

Thus, the length of the intercepted arc is t. This is also the radian measure of the central angle. Thus, **in a unit circle, the radian measure of the angle is equal to the measure of the intercepted arc.** Both are given by the same *real number t*.

In Figure 4.39, the radian measure of the angle and the length of the intercepted arc are both shown by t. Let $P = (x, y)$ denote the point on the unit circle that has arc length t from $(1, 0)$. Figure 4.39(a) shows that if t is positive, point P is reached by moving counterclockwise along the unit circle from $(1, 0)$. Figure 4.39(b) shows that if t is negative, point P is reached by moving clockwise along the unit circle from $(1, 0)$. For each real number t, there corresponds a point $P = (x, y)$ on the unit circle.

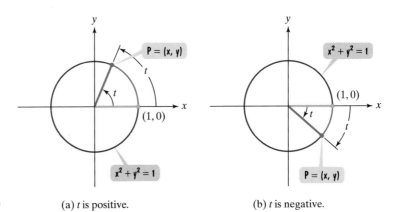

Figure 4.39   (a) t is positive.   (b) t is negative.

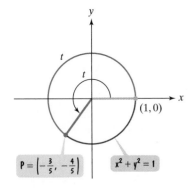

Figure 4.40

Using Figure 4.39, we define the cosine function at t as the x-coordinate of P and the sine function at t as the y-coordinate of P. Thus,

$$x = \cos t \quad \text{and} \quad y = \sin t.$$

For example, a point $P = (x, y)$ on the unit circle corresponding to a real number t is shown in Figure 4.40 for $\pi < t < \dfrac{3\pi}{2}$. We see that the coordinates of $P = (x, y)$ are $x = -\frac{3}{5}$ and $y = -\frac{4}{5}$. Because the cosine function is the x-coordinate of P and the sine function is the y-coordinate of P, the values of these trigonometric functions at the real number t are

$$\cos t = -\frac{3}{5} \quad \text{and} \quad \sin t = -\frac{4}{5}.$$

> **Definitions of the Trigonometric Functions in Terms of a Unit Circle**
> If t is a real number and $P = (x, y)$ is a point on the unit circle that corresponds to t, then
>
> $$\sin t = y \qquad\qquad \cos t = x \qquad\qquad \tan t = \frac{y}{x}, x \neq 0$$
>
> $$\csc t = \frac{1}{y}, y \neq 0 \qquad\qquad \sec t = \frac{1}{x}, x \neq 0 \qquad\qquad \cot t = \frac{x}{y}, y \neq 0.$$

Because this definition expresses function values in terms of coordinates of a point on a unit circle, the trigonometric functions are sometimes called the **circular functions.**

EXAMPLE 1 Finding Values of the Trigonometric Functions

Use Figure 4.41 to find the values of the trigonometric functions at $t = \dfrac{\pi}{2}$.

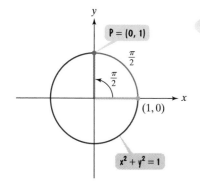

Figure 4.41

Solution   The point P on the unit circle that corresponds to $t = \dfrac{\pi}{2}$ has coordinates $(0, 1)$. We use $x = 0$ and $y = 1$ to find the values of the trigonometric functions.

$$\sin \frac{\pi}{2} = y = 1 \qquad\qquad \cos \frac{\pi}{2} = x = 0$$

$$\csc \frac{\pi}{2} = \frac{1}{y} = \frac{1}{1} = 1 \qquad\qquad \cot \frac{\pi}{2} = \frac{x}{y} = \frac{0}{1} = 0$$

By definition, $\tan t = \dfrac{y}{x}$ and $\sec t = \dfrac{1}{x}$. Because $x = 0$, $\tan \dfrac{\pi}{2}$ and $\sec \dfrac{\pi}{2}$, are undefined.

> **Check Point 1**   Use the figure on the right to find the values of the trigonometric functions at $t = \pi$.

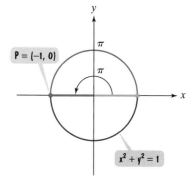

Domain and Range of Sine and Cosine Functions

2 Recognize the domain and range of sine and cosine functions.

The value of a trigonometric function at the real number t is its value at an angle of t radians. However, using real number domains, we can observe properties of trigonometric functions that are not as apparent using the angle approach. For example, the domain and range of each trigonometric function can be found from the unit circle definition. At this point, let's look only at the sine and cosine functions,

$$\sin t = y \quad \text{and} \quad \cos t = x.$$

Because t can be the radian measure of any angle or, equivalently, the measure of any intercepted arc, the domain of the sine function and the cosine function is the set of all real numbers. Because the radius of the unit circle is 1, we have

$$-1 \leq x \leq 1 \quad \text{and} \quad -1 \leq y \leq 1.$$

Therefore, with $x = \cos t$ and $y = \sin t$, we obtain

$$-1 \leq \cos t \leq 1 \quad \text{and} \quad -1 \leq \sin t \leq 1.$$

The range of the cosine and sine functions is $[-1, 1]$.

The Domain and Range of the Sine and Cosine Functions

The domain of the sine function and the cosine function is the set of all real numbers. The range of these functions is the set of all real numbers from -1 to 1, inclusive.

3 Use even and odd trigonometric functions.

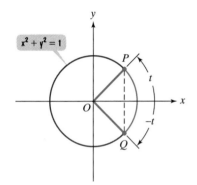

Figure 4.42

Even and Odd Trigonometric Functions

In Chapter 2, we saw that a function is even if $f(-t) = f(t)$ and odd if $f(-t) = -f(t)$. We can use Figure 4.42 to show that the cosine function is an even function and the sine function is an odd function. By definition, the coordinates of the points P and Q in Figure 4.42 are as follows:

$$P\text{: } (\cos t, \sin t)$$
$$Q\text{: } (\cos(-t), \sin(-t)).$$

In Figure 4.42, the x-coordinates of P and Q are the same. Thus,

$$\cos(-t) = \cos t.$$

This shows that the cosine function is an even function. By contrast, the y-coordinates of P and Q are negatives of each other. Thus,

$$\sin(-t) = -\sin t.$$

This shows that the sine function is an odd function.

This argument is valid regardless of the length of t. Thus, the arc may terminate in any of the four quadrants or on any axis. Using the unit circle definition of the trigonometric functions, we obtain the following results:

Even and Odd Trigonometric Functions

The cosine and secant functions are *even*.

$$\cos(-t) = \cos t \qquad\qquad \sec(-t) = \sec t$$

The sine, cosecant, tangent, and cotangent functions are *odd*.

$$\sin(-t) = -\sin t \qquad\qquad \csc(-t) = -\csc t$$
$$\tan(-t) = -\tan t \qquad\qquad \cot(-t) = -\cot t$$

EXAMPLE 2 **Using Even and Odd Functions to Find Exact Values**

Find the exact value of:

    a. $\cos(-45°)$ **b.** $\tan\left(-\dfrac{\pi}{3}\right)$.

Solution

    a. $\cos(-45°) = \cos 45° = \dfrac{\sqrt{2}}{2}$ **b.** $\tan\left(-\dfrac{\pi}{3}\right) = -\tan\dfrac{\pi}{3} = -\sqrt{3}$

Check Point 2 Find the exact value of:

    a. $\cos(-60°)$ **b.** $\tan\left(-\dfrac{\pi}{6}\right)$.

4 Use periodic properties.

Periodic Functions

Certain patterns in nature repeat again and again. For example, the ocean level at a beach varies from low tide to high tide and then back to low tide approximately every 12 hours. If low tide occurs at noon, then high tide will be around 6 P.M. and low tide will occur again around midnight, and so on infinitely. If $f(t)$ represents the ocean level at the beach at any time t, then the level is the same 12 hours later. Thus,

$$f(t + 12) = f(t).$$

The word *periodic* means that this tidal behavior repeats infinitely. The *period*, 12 hours, is the time it takes to complete one full cycle.

Definition of a Periodic Function

A function f is **periodic** if there exists a positive number p such that

$$f(t + p) = f(t)$$

for all t in the domain of f. The smallest number p for which f is periodic is called the **period** of f.

    The trigonometric functions are used to model periodic phenomena. Why? If we begin at any point P on the unit circle and travel a distance of 2π units along the perimeter, we will return to the same point P. Because the trigonometric functions are defined in terms of the coordinates of that point P, we obtain the following results:

Periodic Properties of the Sine and Cosine Functions

$$\sin(t + 2\pi) = \sin t \quad \text{and} \quad \cos(t + 2\pi) = \cos t$$

The sine and cosine functions are periodic functions and have period 2π.

EXAMPLE 3 Using Periodic Properties to Find Exact Values

Find the exact value of: **a.** $\tan 420°$ **b.** $\sin \dfrac{9\pi}{4}$.

Solution

  a. $\tan 420° = \tan(60° + 360°) = \tan 60° = \sqrt{3}$

  b. $\sin \dfrac{9\pi}{4} = \sin\left(\dfrac{\pi}{4} + 2\pi\right) = \sin \dfrac{\pi}{4} = \dfrac{\sqrt{2}}{2}$

> **Check Point 3** Find the exact value of:
>
>   **a.** $\cos 405°$ **b.** $\tan \dfrac{7\pi}{3}$.

Like the sine and cosine functions, the secant and cosecant functions have period 2π. However, the tangent and cotangent functions have a smaller period. If we begin at any point $P(x, y)$ on the unit circle and travel a distance of π units along the perimeter, we arrive at the point $(-x, -y)$. The tangent function, defined in terms of the coordinates of a point, is the same at (x, y) and $(-x, -y)$.

$$\underset{\substack{\text{Tangent function} \\ \text{at } (x, y)}}{\dfrac{y}{x}} = \underset{\substack{\text{Tangent function} \\ \pi \text{ radians later}}}{\dfrac{-y}{-x}}$$

We see that $\tan(t + \pi) = \tan t$. The same observations apply to the cotangent function.

Periodic Properties of the Tangent and Cotangent Functions

$$\tan(t + \pi) = \tan t \quad \text{and} \quad \cot(t + \pi) = \cot t$$

The tangent and cotangent functions are periodic functions and have period π.

Why do the trigonometric functions model phenomena that repeat *indefinitely*? By starting at point P on the unit circle and traveling a distance of 2π units, 4π units, 6π units, and so on, we return to the starting point P. Because the trigonometric functions are defined in terms of the coordinates of that point P, if we add (or subtract) multiples of 2π, the trigonometric values do not change. Furthermore, the trigonometric values for the tangent and cotangent functions do not change if we add (or subtract) multiples of π.

> **Repetitive Behavior of the Sine, Cosine, and Tangent Functions**
>
> For any integer n and real number t,
>
> $$\sin(t + 2\pi n) = \sin t, \quad \cos(t + 2\pi n) = \cos t, \quad \text{and} \quad \tan(t + \pi n) = \tan t.$$

EXERCISE SET 4.4

Practice Exercises

In Exercises 1–4, a point $P(x, y)$ is shown on the unit circle corresponding to a real number t. Find the values of the trigonometric functions at t.

1.

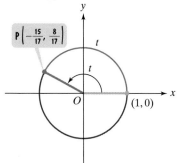

2.

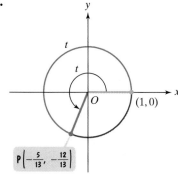

3.

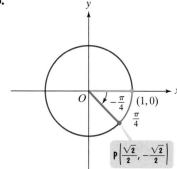

4.

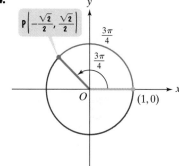

In Exercises 5–8, use even and odd properties of the trigonometric functions to find the exact value of each expression.

5. $\sin(-45°)$ **6.** $\tan(-45°)$

7. $\sec\left(-\dfrac{\pi}{3}\right)$ **8.** $\sec\left(-\dfrac{\pi}{6}\right)$

In Exercises 9–12, use periodic properties to find the exact value of each expression.

9. $\cos 585°$

10. $\cos 570°$

11. $\cot \dfrac{7\pi}{3}$

12. $\cot \dfrac{9\pi}{4}$

Application Exercises

13. The number of hours of daylight, H, on day t of any given year (on January 1, $t = 1$) in Fairbanks, Alaska, can be modeled by the function

$$H(t) = 12 + 8.3 \sin\left[\frac{2\pi}{365}(t - 80)\right].$$

   a. March 21, the 80th day of the year, is the spring equinox. Find the number of hours of daylight in Fairbanks on this day.

   b. June 21, the 172nd day of the year, is the summer solstice, the day with the maximum number of hours of daylight. To the nearest tenth of an hour, find the number of hours of daylight in Fairbanks on this day.

   c. December 21, the 355th day of the year, is the winter solstice, the day with the minimum number of hours of daylight. Find, to the nearest tenth of an hour, the number of hours of daylight in Fairbanks on this day.

14. The number of hours of daylight, H, on day t of any given year (on January 1, $t = 1$) in San Diego, California, can be modeled by the function

$$H(t) = 12 + 2.4 \sin\left[\frac{2\pi}{365}(t - 80)\right].$$

   a. March 21, the 80th day of the year, is the spring equinox. Find the number of hours of daylight in San Diego on this day.

   b. June 21, the 172nd day of the year, is the summer solstice, the day with the maximum number of hours of daylight. Find, to the nearest tenth of an hour, the number of hours of daylight in San Diego on this day.

   c. December 21, the 355th day of the year, is the winter solstice, the day with the minimum number of hours of daylight. To the nearest tenth of an hour, find the number of hours of daylight in San Diego on this day.

15. People who believe in biorhythms claim that there are three cycles that rule our behavior—the physical, emotional, and mental. Each is a sine function of a certain period. The function for our emotional fluctuations is

$$E = \sin \frac{\pi}{14} t$$

where t is measured in days starting at birth. Emotional fluctuations, E, are measured from -1 to 1, inclusive, with 1 representing peak emotional well-being, -1 representing the low for emotional well-being, and 0 representing feeling neither emotionally high nor low.

   a. Find E corresponding to $t = 7$, 14, 21, 28, and 35. Describe what you observe.

   b. What is the period of the emotional cycle?

16. The height of the water, H, in feet, at a boat dock t hours after 6 A.M. is given by

$$H = 10 + 4 \sin \frac{\pi}{6} t.$$

   a. Find the height of the water at the dock at 6 A.M., 9 A.M., noon, 6 P.M., midnight, and 3 A.M.

   b. When is low tide and when is high tide?

   c. What is the period of this function and what does this mean about the tides?

Writing in Mathematics

17. Why are the trigonometric functions sometimes called circular functions?

18. What is the range of the sine function? Use the unit circle to explain where this range comes from.

19. What do we mean by even trigonometric functions? Which of the six functions fall into this category?

20. What is a periodic function? Why are the sine and cosine functions periodic?

21. Explain how you can use the function for emotional fluctuations in Exercise 15 to determine good days for having dinner with your moody boss.

22. Describe a phenomenon that repeats infinitely. What is its period?

Critical Thinking Exercises

23. Find the exact value of $\cos 0° + \cos 1° + \cos 2° + \cos 3° + \cdots + \cos 179° + \cos 180°$.

24. If $f(x) = \sin x$ and $f(a) = \frac{1}{4}$, find the value of

$$f(a) + f(a + 2\pi) + f(a + 4\pi) + f(a + 6\pi).$$

25. If $f(x) = \sin x$ and $f(a) = \frac{1}{4}$, find the value of $f(a) + 2f(-a)$.

26. The seats of a ferris wheel are 40 feet from the wheel's center. When you get on the ride, your seat is 5 feet above the ground. How far above the ground are you after rotating through an angle of 765°? Round to the nearest foot.

Chapter Summary, Review, and Test

Summary

DEFINITIONS AND CONCEPTS	EXAMPLES

4.1 Angles and Their Measure

a. An angle consists of two rays with a common endpoint, the vertex.

b. An angle is in standard position if its vertex is at the origin and its initial side lies along the positive x-axis. Figure 4.3 on page 318 shows positive and negative angles in standard position.
Ex. 1, p. 319

c. A quadrantal angle is one with its terminal side on the x-axis or the y-axis.

d. Angles can be measured in degrees. $1°$ is $\frac{1}{360}$ of a complete rotation.

e. Acute angles measure less than $90°$, right angles $90°$, obtuse angles more than $90°$ but less than $180°$, and straight angles $180°$.

f. Two angles with the same initial and terminal sides are called coterminal angles.
Ex. 2, p. 320

g. Two angles are complements if their sum is $90°$ and supplements if their sum is $180°$. Only positive angles are used.
Ex. 3, p. 321

h. Angles can be measured in radians. One radian is the measure of the central angle when the intercepted arc and radius have the same length. In general, the radian measure of a central angle is the length of the intercepted arc divided by the circle's radius: $\theta = \frac{s}{r}$.
Ex. 4, p. 323

i. To convert from degrees to radians, multiply degrees by $\frac{\pi \text{ radians}}{180°}$. To convert from radians to degrees, multiply radians by $\frac{180°}{\pi \text{ radians}}$.
Ex. 5, p. 324;
Ex. 6, p. 324

j. The arc length formula, $s = r\theta$, is described in the box on page 325.
Ex. 7, p. 326

k. The definitions of linear speed, $v = \frac{s}{t}$, and angular speed, $\omega = \frac{\theta}{t}$, are given in the box on page 326.

l. Linear speed is expressed in terms of angular speed by $v = r\omega$, where v is the linear speed of a point a distance r from the center of rotation and ω is the angular speed in radians per unit of time.
Ex. 8, p. 327

4.2 Right Triangle Trigonometry

a. The right triangle definitions of the six trigonometric functions are given in the box on page 332.
Ex. 1, p. 333

b. Function values for $30°, 45°,$ and $60°$ can be obtained using these special triangles.
Ex. 2, p. 334;
Ex. 3, p. 335

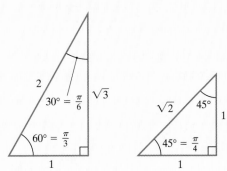

DEFINITIONS AND CONCEPTS	EXAMPLES

c. Fundamental Identities

1. Reciprocal Identities

$$\sin\theta = \frac{1}{\csc\theta} \quad \cos\theta = \frac{1}{\sec\theta} \quad \tan\theta = \frac{1}{\cot\theta}$$

Ex. 4, p. 337;
Ex. 5, p. 338

$$\csc\theta = \frac{1}{\sin\theta} \quad \sec\theta = \frac{1}{\cos\theta} \quad \cot\theta = \frac{1}{\tan\theta}$$

2. Quotient Identities

$$\tan\theta = \frac{\sin\theta}{\cos\theta} \quad \cot\theta = \frac{\cos\theta}{\sin\theta}$$

3. Pythagorean Identities

$$\sin^2\theta + \cos^2\theta = 1$$
$$1 + \tan^2\theta = \sec^2\theta$$
$$1 + \cot^2\theta = \csc^2\theta$$

d. The value of a trigonometric function of θ is equal to the cofunction of the complement of θ. Cofunction identities are listed in the box on page 339.

Ex. 6, p. 339

4.3 Trigonometric Functions of Any Angle

a. Definitions of the trigonometric functions of any angle are given in the box on page 348.

Ex. 1, p. 349;
Ex. 2, p. 349

b. Signs of the trigonometric functions: All functions are positive in quadrant I. If θ lies in quadrant II, $\sin\theta$ and $\csc\theta$ are positive. If θ lies in quadrant III, $\tan\theta$ and $\cot\theta$ are positive. If θ lies in quadrant IV, $\cos\theta$ and $\sec\theta$ are positive.

Ex. 3, p. 352;
Ex. 4, p. 352

c. If θ is a nonacute angle in standard position that lies in a quadrant, its reference angle is the positive acute angle θ' formed by the terminal side of θ and the x-axis. The reference angle for a given angle can be found by making a sketch that shows the angle in standard position. Figure 4.30 on page 353 shows reference angles for θ in quadrants II, III, and IV.

Ex. 5, p. 353

d. The values of the trigonometric functions of a given angle are the same as the values of the functions of the reference angle, except possibly for the sign. A procedure for using reference angles to evaluate trigonometric functions is given in the box on page 354.

Ex. 6, p. 354

4.4 Trigonometric Functions of Real Numbers; Periodic Functions

a. Definitions of the trigonometric functions in terms of a unit circle are given in the box on page 359.

Ex. 1, p. 359

b. The cosine and secant functions are even:

Ex. 2, p. 361

$$\cos(-t) = \cos t, \quad \sec(-t) = \sec t.$$

The other trigonometric functions are odd:

$$\sin(-t) = -\sin t, \quad \csc(-t) = -\csc t,$$
$$\tan(-t) = -\tan t, \quad \cot(-t) = -\cot t.$$

c. If $f(t + p) = f(t)$, function f is periodic. The smallest p for which f is periodic is the period of f. The tangent and cotangent functions have period π. The other four trigonometric functions have period 2π.

Ex. 3, p. 362

Review Exercises

4.1

In Exercises 1–4, draw each angle in standard position.

1. $190°$

2. $-135°$

3. $\dfrac{5\pi}{6}$

4. $-\dfrac{2\pi}{3}$

In Exercises 5–6, find a positive angle less than $360°$ that is coterminal with the given angle.

5. $400°$

6. $-85°$

In Exercises 7–8, if possible, find the complement and the supplement of the given angle.

7. $73°$

8. $\dfrac{2\pi}{3}$

9. Find the radian measure of the central angle of a circle of radius 6 centimeters that intercepts an arc of length 27 centimeters.

In Exercises 10–12, convert each angle in degrees to radians. Express your answer as a multiple of π.

10. $15°$ **11.** $120°$ **12.** $315°$

In Exercises 13–15, convert each angle in radians to degrees.

13. $\dfrac{5\pi}{3}$ **14.** $\dfrac{7\pi}{5}$ **15.** $-\dfrac{5\pi}{6}$

16. Find the length of the arc on a circle of radius 10 feet intercepted by a $135°$ central angle. Express arc length in terms of π. Then round your answer to two decimal places.

17. The angular speed of a propeller on a wind generator is 10.3 revolutions per minute. Express this angular speed in radians per minute.

18. The propeller of an airplane has a radius of 3 feet. The propeller is rotating at 2250 revolutions per minute. Find the linear speed, in feet per minute, of the tip of the propeller.

4.2

19. Use the triangle to find each of the six trigonometric functions of θ.

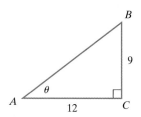

In Exercises 20–23, find the exact value of each expression. Do not use a calculator.

20. $\tan 60°$ **21.** $\cos \dfrac{\pi}{4}$

22. $\sec \dfrac{\pi}{6}$ **23.** $\sin^2 \dfrac{\pi}{5} + \cos^2 \dfrac{\pi}{5}$

24. If θ is an acute angle and $\sin \theta = \dfrac{2}{\sqrt{7}}$, use the identity $\sin^2 \theta + \cos^2 \theta = 1$ to find $\cos \theta$.

In Exercises 25–26, find a cofunction with the same value as the given expression.

25. $\sin 70°$ **26.** $\cos \dfrac{\pi}{2}$

In Exercises 27–29, find the measure of the side of the right triangle whose length is designated by a lowercase letter. Round answers to the nearest whole number.

27.

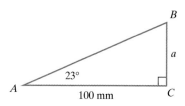

28.

29.

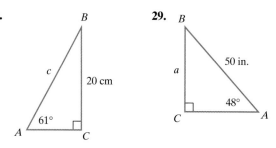

30. A hiker climbs for a half mile up a slope whose inclination is $17°$. How many feet of altitude, to the nearest foot, does the hiker gain?

31. To find the distance across a lake, a surveyor took the measurements in the figure shown. What is the distance across the lake? Round to the nearest meter.

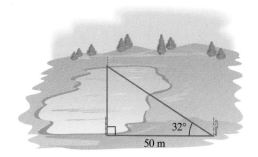

32. When a six-foot pole casts a four-foot shadow, what is the angle of elevation of the sun? Round to the nearest whole degree.

4.3 and 4.4

In Exercises 33–34, a point on the terminal side of angle θ is given. Find the exact value of each of the six trigonometric functions of θ, or state that the function is undefined.

33. $(-1, -5)$ **34.** $(0, -1)$

In Exercises 35–36, let θ be an angle in standard position. Name the quadrant in which θ lies.

35. $\tan \theta > 0$ and $\sec \theta > 0$

36. $\tan \theta > 0$ and $\cos \theta < 0$

In Exercises 37–38, find the exact value of each of the remaining trigonometric functions of θ.

37. $\cos \theta = \frac{2}{5}$, $\sin \theta < 0$ **38.** $\tan \theta = -\frac{1}{3}$, $\sin \theta > 0$

In Exercises 39–41, find the reference angle for each angle.

39. $265°$ **40.** $\dfrac{5\pi}{8}$ **41.** $-410°$

In Exercises 42–50, find the exact value of each expression. Do not use a calculator.

42. $\sin 240°$ **43.** $\tan 120°$ **44.** $\sec \dfrac{7\pi}{4}$

45. $\cos \dfrac{11\pi}{6}$ **46.** $\cot(-210°)$ **47.** $\csc\left(-\dfrac{2\pi}{3}\right)$

48. $\sin\left(-\dfrac{\pi}{3}\right)$ **49.** $\sin 495°$ **50.** $\tan \dfrac{13\pi}{4}$

Chapter 4 Test

1. Convert $135°$ to exact radian measure.

2. Find the supplement of the angle whose radian measure is $\dfrac{9\pi}{13}$. Express the answer in terms of π.

3. Find the length of the arc on a circle of radius 20 feet intercepted by a $75°$ central angle. Express arc length in terms of π. Then round your answer to two decimal places.

4. If $(-2, 5)$ is a point on the terminal side of angle θ, find the exact value of each of the six trigonometric functions of θ.

5. Determine the quadrant in which θ lies if $\cos\theta < 0$ and $\cot\theta > 0$.

6. If $\cos\theta = \frac{1}{3}$ and $\tan\theta < 0$, find the exact value of each of the remaining trigonometric functions of θ.

In Exercises 7–9, find the exact value of each expression. Do not use a calculator.

7. $\tan \dfrac{\pi}{6} \cos \dfrac{\pi}{3} - \cos \dfrac{\pi}{2}$ **8.** $\tan 300°$

9. $\sin \dfrac{7\pi}{4}$

Answers to Selected Exercises

CHAPTER P

Section P.1

Check Point Exercises

1. a. $\sqrt{2} - 1$ **b.** $\pi - 3$ **c.** 1   **2.** 9   **3.** 250; In 1990, the population of the United States was 250 million.   **4.** $38x - 19y$

Exercise Set P.1

1. a. $\sqrt{100}$ **b.** $0, \sqrt{100}$ **c.** $-9, 0, \sqrt{100}$ **d.** $-9, -\frac{4}{5}, 0, 0.25, 9.2, \sqrt{100}$ **e.** $\sqrt{3}$ **3. a.** $\sqrt{64}$ **b.** $0, \sqrt{64}$ **c.** $-11, 0, \sqrt{64}$

d. $-11, -\frac{5}{6}, 0, 0.75, \sqrt{64}$ **e.** $\sqrt{5}, \pi$ **5.** 0   **7.** Answers may vary.   **9.** true   **11.** true   **13.** true   **15.** 300   **17.** $12 - \pi$

19. $5 - \sqrt{2}$ **21.** -1 **23.** 4   **25.** 3   **27.** 7   **29.** -1 **31.** $|17 - 2|; 15$ **33.** $|5 - (-2)|; 7$ **35.** $|-4 - (-19)|; 15$
37. $|-1.4 - (-3.6)|; 2.2$ **39.** 27   **41.** -19 **43.** 25   **45.** 10   **47.** -8 **49.** commutative property of addition
51. associative property of addition   **53.** commutative property of addition   **55.** distributive property of multiplication over addition
57. inverse property of multiplication   **59.** $15x + 16$ **61.** $27x - 10$ **63.** $29y - 29$ **65.** $8y - 12$ **67.** $16y - 25$
69. $14x$ **71.** $-2x + 3y + 6$ **73.** x **75.** yes   **77.** Answers may vary.   **79.** 21; In 2000, approximately 21% of American adults
smoked cigarettes.   **81. a.** $132 - 0.6a$ **b.** 120   **89.** (c) is true.   **91.** $<$ **93.** $>$

Section P.2

Check Point Exercises

1. -256 **2. a.** $\frac{1}{8}$ **b.** 36   **3. a.** 243   **b.** $\frac{1}{8}$ **c.** x^6 **4. a.** 729   **b.** y^{28} **c.** $\frac{1}{x^8}$ **5. a.** 9   **b.** $\frac{1}{x^7}$ **c.** y^9 **6.** $-64x^3$

7. a. $\frac{27}{64}$ **b.** $-\frac{32}{y^5}$ **8. a.** $16x^{12}y^{24}$ **b.** $-18x^3y^8$ **c.** $\frac{5y^6}{x^4}$ **d.** $\frac{y^8}{25x^2}$ **9. a.** 7,400,000,000   **b.** 0.000003017

10. a. 7.41×10^9 **b.** 9.2×10^{-8} **11.** \$12.86

Exercise Set P.2

1. 50   **3.** 64   **5.** -64 **7.** 1   **9.** -1 **11.** $\frac{1}{64}$ **13.** 32   **15.** 64   **17.** 16   **19.** $\frac{1}{9}$ **21.** $\frac{1}{16}$ **23.** $\frac{y}{x^2}$ **25.** y^5 **27.** x^{10}

29. x^5 **31.** x^{21} **33.** x^{-15} **35.** x^7 **37.** x^{21} **39.** $64x^6$ **41.** $-\frac{64}{x^3}$ **43.** $9x^4y^{10}$ **45.** $6x^{11}$ **47.** $18x^9y^5$ **49.** $4x^{16}$

51. $-5a^{11}b$ **53.** $\frac{2}{b^7}$ **55.** $\frac{1}{16x^6}$ **57.** $\frac{3y^{14}}{4x^4}$ **59.** $\frac{y^2}{25x^6}$ **61.** $-\frac{27\,b^{15}}{a^{18}}$ **63.** 1   **65.** 4700   **67.** 4,000,000   **69.** 0.000786

71. 0.00000318   **73.** 3.6×10^3 **75.** 2.2×10^8 **77.** 2.7×10^{-2} **79.** 7.63×10^{-4} **81.** 600,000   **83.** 0.123   **85.** 30,000

87. 0.021   **89.** $\frac{4.8 \times 10^{11}}{1.2 \times 10^{-4}}; 4 \times 10^{15}$ **91.** $\frac{(7.2 \times 10^{-4})(3 \times 10^{-3})}{2.4 \times 10^{-4}}; 9 \times 10^{-3}$ **93.** \$6800   **95.** 1.12×10^{12} **97.** 1.06×10^{-18} gram

107. (b) is true.   **109.** $A = C + D$

Section P.3

Check Point Exercises

1. a. 3   **b.** $5x\sqrt{2}$ **2. a.** $\frac{5}{4}$ **b.** $5x\sqrt{3}$ **3. a.** $17\sqrt{13}$ **b.** $-19\sqrt{17x}$ **4. a.** $17\sqrt{3}$ **b.** $10\sqrt{2x}$ **5. a.** $\frac{5\sqrt{3}}{3}$ **b.** $\sqrt{3}$

6. $\frac{32 - 8\sqrt{5}}{11}$ **7. a.** $2\sqrt[3]{5}$ **b.** $2\sqrt[5]{2}$ **c.** $\frac{5}{3}$ **8.** $5\sqrt[3]{3}$ **9. a.** 9   **b.** 3   **c.** $\frac{1}{2}$ **10. a.** 8   **b.** $\frac{1}{4}$ **11. a.** $10x^4$ **b.** $4x^{5/2}$ **12.** $\sqrt{x}$

Exercise Set P.3

1. 6   **3.** not a real number   **5.** 13   **7.** $5\sqrt{2}$ **9.** $3|x|\sqrt{5}$ **11.** $2x\sqrt{3}$ **13.** $x\sqrt{x}$ **15.** $2x\sqrt{3x}$ **17.** $\frac{1}{9}$ **19.** $\frac{7}{4}$ **21.** $4x$

23. $5x\sqrt{2x}$ **25.** $2x^2\sqrt{5}$ **27.** $13\sqrt{3}$ **29.** $-2\sqrt{17x}$ **31.** $5\sqrt{2}$ **33.** $3\sqrt{2x}$ **35.** $34\sqrt{2}$ **37.** $20\sqrt{2} - 5\sqrt{3}$ **39.** $\frac{\sqrt{7}}{7}$

41. $\frac{\sqrt{10}}{5}$ **43.** $\frac{13(3 - \sqrt{11})}{-2}$ **45.** $7(\sqrt{5} + 2)$ **47.** $3(\sqrt{5} - \sqrt{3})$ **49.** 5   **51.** -2 **53.** not a real number   **55.** 3   **57.** -3

59. $-\frac{1}{2}$ **61.** $2\sqrt[3]{4}$ **63.** $x\sqrt[3]{x}$ **65.** $3\sqrt[3]{2}$ **67.** $2x$ **69.** $7\sqrt[5]{2}$ **71.** $13\sqrt[3]{2}$ **73.** $-y\sqrt[3]{2x}$ **75.** $\sqrt{2} + 2$ **77.** 6   **79.** 2

81. 25   **83.** $\frac{1}{16}$ **85.** $14x^{7/12}$ **87.** $4x^{1/4}$ **89.** x^2 **91.** $5x^2|y|^3$ **93.** $27y^{2/3}$ **95.** $\sqrt{5}$ **97.** x^2 **99.** $\sqrt[3]{x^2}$ **101.** $\sqrt[3]{x^2 y}$

103. $20\sqrt{2}$ mph   **105.** $\frac{\sqrt{5} + 1}{2} \approx 1.62$ **107.** $\frac{7\sqrt{2\cdot2\cdot3}}{6} = \frac{7\sqrt{2^2\cdot3}}{6} = \frac{7\sqrt{2^2}\sqrt{3}}{6} = \frac{7\cdot2\sqrt{3}}{6} = \frac{7}{3}\sqrt{3}$

109. The duration of a storm whose diameter is 9 miles is 1.89 hours.   **117.** 45.00, 23.76, 15.68, 11.33, 8.59, 6.70, 5.31, 4.25, 3.41, 2.73, 2.17, 1.70, 1.30, 0.95, 0.65, 0.38; The percentage of potential employees testing positive for illegal drugs is decreasing over time.
119. (d) is true.   **121.** Let $\square = 25$ and $\square = 14$.   **123. a.** $>$ **b.** $>$

Section P.4

Check Point Exercises

1. a. $-x^3 + x^2 - 8x - 20$ **b.** $20x^3 - 11x^2 - 2x - 8$ **2.** $15x^3 - 31x^2 + 30x - 8$ **3.** $28x^2 - 41x + 15$
4. a. $49x^2 - 64$ **b.** $4y^6 - 25$ **5. a.** $x^2 + 20x + 100$ **b.** $25x^2 + 40x + 16$ **6. a.** $x^2 - 18x + 81$ **b.** $49x^2 - 42x + 9$
7. $2x^2y + 5xy^2 - 2y^3$ **8. a.** $21x^2 - 25xy + 6y^2$ **b.** $x^4 + 10x^2y + 25y^2$

Exercise Set P.4

1. yes; $3x^2 + 2x - 5$ **3.** no   **5.** 2   **7.** 4   **9.** $11x^3 + 7x^2 - 12x - 4$; 3   **11.** $12x^3 + 4x^2 + 12x - 14$; 3   **13.** $6x^2 - 6x + 2$; 2
15. $x^3 + 1$ **17.** $2x^3 - 9x^2 + 19x - 15$ **19.** $x^2 + 10x + 21$ **21.** $x^2 - 2x - 15$ **23.** $6x^2 + 13x + 5$ **25.** $10x^2 - 9x - 9$
27. $15x^4 - 47x^2 + 28$ **29.** $8x^5 - 40x^3 + 3x^2 - 15$ **31.** $x^2 - 9$ **33.** $9x^2 - 4$ **35.** $25 - 49x^2$ **37.** $16x^4 - 25x^2$ **39.** $1 - y^{10}$
41. $x^2 + 4x + 4$ **43.** $4x^2 + 12x + 9$ **45.** $x^2 - 6x + 9$ **47.** $16x^4 - 8x^2 + 1$ **49.** $4x^2 - 28x + 49$ **51.** $x^3 + 3x^2 + 3x + 1$
53. $8x^3 + 36x^2 + 54x + 27$ **55.** $x^3 - 9x^2 + 27x - 27$ **57.** $27x^3 - 108x^2 + 144x - 64$ **59.** $7x^2y - 4xy$ is of degree 3
61. $2x^2y + 13xy + 13$ is of degree 3   **63.** $-5x^3 + 8xy - 9y^2$ is of degree 3   **65.** $x^4y^2 + 8x^3y + y - 6x$ is of degree 6
67. $7x^2 + 38xy + 15y^2$ **69.** $2x^2 + xy - 21y^2$ **71.** $15x^2y^2 + xy - 2$ **73.** $49x^2 + 70xy + 25y^2$ **75.** $x^4y^4 - 6x^2y^2 + 9$
77. $x^3 - y^3$ **79.** $9x^2 - 25y^2$ **81.** $49x^2y^4 - 100y^2$ **83.** 7.567; A person earning $40,000 feels underpaid by $7567.
85. 527.53; The number of violent crimes in the United States was 527.53 per 100,000 inhabitants in 2000. The calculated value is a good
approximation to the actual value, 524.7.   **87.** $\frac{2}{3}t^3 - 2t^2 + 4t$ **89.** $6x + 22$ **99.** 61.2, 59.0, 56.8, 54.8, 52.8, 50.9, 49.3, 47.7, 46.4, 45.2,
44.3, 43.6, 43.1, 43.0, 43.1, 43.6, 44.4, 45.5, 47.0, 48.9, 51.2; The percentage of U.S. high school seniors who had ever used marijuana decreased
from 1980, reached a low in 1993, then increased through 2000.   **101.** $49x^2 + 70x + 25 - 16y^2$ **103.** $x^4 - y^4$

Section P.5

Check Point Exercises

1. a. $2x^2(5x - 2)$ **b.** $(x - 7)(2x + 3)$ **2.** $(x + 5)(x^2 - 2)$ **3. a.** $(x + 8)(x + 5)$ **b.** $(x - 7)(x + 2)$ **4.** $(3x - 1)(2x + 7)$
5. a. $(x + 9)(x - 9)$ **b.** $(6x + 5)(6x - 5)$ **6.** $(9x^2 + 4)(3x + 2)(3x - 2)$ **7. a.** $(x + 7)^2$ **b.** $(4x - 7)^2$
8. a. $(x + 1)(x^2 - x + 1)$ **b.** $(5x - 2)(25x^2 + 10x + 4)$ **9.** $3x(x - 5)^2$ **10.** $(x + 10 + 6a)(x + 10 - 6a)$ **11.** $\frac{2x - 1}{(x - 1)^{1/2}}$

Exercise Set P.5

1. $9(2x + 3)$ **3.** $3x(x + 2)$ **5.** $9x^2(x^2 - 2x + 3)$ **7.** $(x + 5)(x + 3)$ **9.** $(x - 3)(x^2 + 12)$ **11.** $(x^2 + 5)(x - 2)$
13. $(x - 1)(x^2 + 2)$ **15.** $(3x - 2)(x^2 - 2)$ **17.** $(x + 2)(x + 3)$ **19.** $(x - 5)(x + 3)$ **21.** $(x - 5)(x - 3)$
23. $(3x + 2)(x - 1)$ **25.** $(3x - 28)(x + 1)$ **27.** $(2x - 1)(3x - 4)$ **29.** $(2x + 3)(2x + 5)$ **31.** $(x + 10)(x - 10)$
33. $(6x + 7)(6x - 7)$ **35.** $(3x + 5y)(3x - 5y)$ **37.** $(x^2 + 4)(x + 2)(x - 2)$ **39.** $(4x^2 + 9)(2x + 3)(2x - 3)$ **41.** $(x + 1)^2$
43. $(x - 7)^2$ **45.** $(2x + 1)^2$ **47.** $(3x - 1)^2$ **49.** $(x + 3)(x^2 - 3x + 9)$ **51.** $(x - 4)(x^2 + 4x + 16)$
53. $(2x - 1)(4x^2 + 2x + 1)$ **55.** $(4x + 3)(16x^2 - 12x + 9)$ **57.** $3x(x + 1)(x - 1)$ **59.** $4(x + 2)(x - 3)$
61. $2(x^2 + 9)(x + 3)(x - 3)$ **63.** $(x - 3)(x + 3)(x + 2)$ **65.** $2(x - 8)(x + 7)$ **67.** $x(x - 2)(x + 2)$ **69.** prime
71. $(x - 2)(x + 2)^2$ **73.** $y(y^2 + 9)(y + 3)(y - 3)$ **75.** $5y^2(2y + 3)(2y - 3)$ **77.** $(x - 6 + 7y)(x - 6 - 7y)$

79. $(x + y)(3b + 4)(3b - 4)$ **81.** $(y - 2)(x + 4)(x - 4)$ **83.** $2x(x + 6 + 2a)(x + 6 - 2a)$ **85.** $x^{1/2}(x - 1)$ **87.** $\dfrac{4(1 + 2x)}{x^{2/3}}$

89. $-(x + 3)^{1/2}(x + 2)$ **91.** $\dfrac{x + 4}{(x + 5)^{3/2}}$ **93.** $-\dfrac{4(4x - 1)^{1/2}(x - 1)}{3}$ **95. a.** $0.36\,x$ **b.** no; It is selling at 36% of the original price.

97. $16(4 + t)(4 - t)$ **99.** $(3x + 2)(3x - 2)$ **109.** $(x^n + 4)(x^n + 2)$ **111.** $(x - y)^3(x + y)$ **113.** $b = 8, -8, 16, -16$

Section P.6

Check Point Exercises

1. a. -5 **b.** $6, -6$ **2. a.** $x^2, x \neq -3$ **b.** $\dfrac{x - 1}{x + 1}, x \neq -1$ **3.** $\dfrac{x - 3}{(x - 2)(x + 3)}, x \neq 2, x \neq -2, x \neq -3$

4. $\dfrac{3(x - 1)}{x(x + 2)}, x \neq 1, x \neq 0, x \neq -2$ **5.** $-2, x \neq -1$ **6.** $\dfrac{2(4x + 1)}{(x + 1)(x - 1)}, x \neq 1, x \neq -1$ **7.** $(x - 3)(x - 3)(x + 3)$

8. $\dfrac{-x^2 + 11x - 20}{2(x - 5)^2}, x \neq 5$ **9.** $\dfrac{2(2 - 3x)}{4 + 3x}, x \neq 0, x \neq -\dfrac{4}{3}$

Exercise Set P.6

1. 3   **3.** $5, -5$ **5.** $-1, -10$ **7.** $\dfrac{3}{x - 3}, x \neq 3$ **9.** $\dfrac{x - 6}{4}, x \neq 6$ **11.** $\dfrac{y + 9}{y - 1}, y \neq 1, 2$ **13.** $\dfrac{x + 6}{x - 6}, x \neq 6, -6$ **15.** $\dfrac{1}{3}, x \neq 2, -3$

17. $\dfrac{(x - 3)(x + 3)}{x(x + 4)}, x \neq 0, -4, 3$ **19.** $\dfrac{x - 1}{x + 2}, x \neq -2, -1, 2, 3$ **21.** $\dfrac{x^2 + 2x + 4}{3x}, x \neq -2, 0, 2$ **23.** $\dfrac{7}{9}, x \neq -1$

25. $\dfrac{(x - 2)^2}{x}, x \neq 0, -2, 2$ **27.** $\dfrac{2(x + 3)}{3}, x \neq 3, -3$ **29.** $\dfrac{x - 5}{2}, x \neq 1, -5$ **31.** $\dfrac{(x + 2)(x + 4)}{x - 5}, x \neq -6, -3, -1, 3, 5$

33. $2, x \neq -\dfrac{5}{6}$ **35.** $\dfrac{2x - 1}{x + 3}, x \neq 0, -3$ **37.** $3, x \neq 2$ **39.** $\dfrac{3}{x - 3}, x \neq 3, -4$ **41.** $\dfrac{9x + 39}{(x + 4)(x + 5)}, x \neq -4, -5$

43. $-\dfrac{3}{x(x + 1)}, x \neq -1, 0$ **45.** $\dfrac{3x^2 + 4}{(x + 2)(x - 2)}, x \neq -2, 2$ **47.** $\dfrac{2x^2 + 50}{(x - 5)(x + 5)}, x \neq -5, 5$ **49.** $\dfrac{4x + 16}{(x + 3)^2}, x \neq -3$

51. $\dfrac{x^2 - x}{(x + 5)(x - 2)(x + 3)}, x \neq -5, 2, -3$ **53.** $\dfrac{x - 1}{x + 2}, x \neq -2, -1$ **55.** $\dfrac{1}{3}, x \neq 3$ **57.** $\dfrac{x + 1}{3x - 1}, x \neq 0, \dfrac{1}{3}$

59. $\dfrac{1}{xy}, x \neq 0, y \neq 0, x \neq -y$ **61.** $\dfrac{x}{x + 3}, x \neq -2, -3$ **63.** $-\dfrac{x - 14}{7}, x \neq -2, 2$ **65. a.** $86.67, 520, 1170$; It costs \$86,670,000 to inoculate 40% of the population against this strain of flu, \$520,000,000 to inoculate 80% of the population, and \$1,170,000,000 to inoculate 90% of the population.   **b.** $x = 100$ **c.** increases rapidly; impossible to inoculate 100% of the population.

67. a. $\dfrac{100W}{L}$ **b.** round   **69.** $\dfrac{2r_1r_2}{r_1 + r_2}$; 24 mph   **83. a.** $\dfrac{Pi(1 + i)^n}{(1 + i)^n - 1}$ **b.** \$527   **85.** $-4x - 1$ **87.** It cubes x.

Chapter P Review Exercises

1. a. $\sqrt{81}$ **b.** $0, \sqrt{81}$ **c.** $-17, 0, \sqrt{81}$ **d.** $-17, -\dfrac{9}{13}, 0, 0.75, \sqrt{81}$ **e.** $\sqrt{2}, \pi$ **2.** 103   **3.** $\sqrt{2} - 1$ **4.** $\sqrt{17} - 3$

5. $|4 - (-17)|$; 21   **6.** 20   **7.** 4   **8.** commutative property of addition   **9.** associative property of multiplication   **10.** distributive property of multiplication over addition   **11.** commutative property of multiplication   **12.** commutative property of multiplication   **13.** commutative property of addition   **14.** $23x - 23y - 2$ **15.** $2x$ **16.** -108 **17.** $\dfrac{5}{16}$ **18.** $\dfrac{1}{25}$ **19.** $\dfrac{1}{27}$

20. $-8x^{12}y^9$ **21.** $\dfrac{10}{x^8}$ **22.** $\dfrac{1}{16x^{12}}$ **23.** $\dfrac{y^8}{4x^{10}}$ **24.** 37,400   **25.** 0.0000745   **26.** 3.59×10^6 **27.** 7.25×10^{-3} **28.** 3.9×10^5

29. 2.3×10^{-2} **30.** 10^3 or 1000 yr   **31.** $\$4.2 \times 10^{10}$ **32.** $10\sqrt{3}$ **33.** $2|x|\sqrt{3}$ **34.** $2x\sqrt{5}$ **35.** $r\sqrt{r}$ **36.** $\dfrac{11}{2}$ **37.** $4x\sqrt{3}$

38. $20\sqrt{5}$ **39.** $16\sqrt{2}$ **40.** $24\sqrt{2} - 8\sqrt{3}$ **41.** $6\sqrt{5}$ **42.** $\dfrac{\sqrt{6}}{3}$ **43.** $\dfrac{5(6 - \sqrt{3})}{33}$ **44.** $7(\sqrt{7} + \sqrt{5})$ **45.** 5   **46.** -2

47. not a real number   **48.** 5   **49.** $3\sqrt[3]{3}$ **50.** $y\sqrt[3]{y^2}$ **51.** $2\sqrt[4]{5}$ **52.** $13\sqrt[3]{2}$ **53.** $x\sqrt[4]{2}$ **54.** 4

55. $\dfrac{1}{5}$ **56.** 5   **57.** $\dfrac{1}{3}$ **58.** 16   **59.** $\dfrac{1}{81}$ **60.** $20x^{11/12}$ **61.** $3x^{1/4}$ **62.** $25x^4$ **63.** $\sqrt{y}$ **64.** $8x^3 + 10x^2 - 20x - 4$; degree 3

65. $8x^4 - 5x^3 + 6$; degree 4   **66.** $12x^3 + x^2 - 21x + 10$ **67.** $6x^2 - 7x - 5$ **68.** $16x^2 - 25$ **69.** $4x^2 + 20x + 25$

70. $9x^2 - 24x + 16$ **71.** $8x^3 + 12x^2 + 6x + 1$ **72.** $125x^3 - 150x^2 + 60x - 8$ **73.** $-x^2 - 17xy - 3y^2$; degree 2

74. $24x^3y^2 + x^2y - 12x^2 + 4$; degree 5   **75.** $3x^2 + 16xy - 35y^2$ **76.** $9x^2 - 30xy + 25y^2$ **77.** $9x^4 + 12x^2y + 4y^2$

78. $49x^2 - 16y^2$ **79.** $a^3 - b^3$ **80.** $3x^2(5x + 1)$ **81.** $(x - 4)(x - 7)$ **82.** $(3x + 1)(5x - 2)$ **83.** $(8 - x)(8 + x)$ **84.** prime

85. $3x^2(x - 5)(x + 2)$ **86.** $4x^3(5x^4 - 9)$ **87.** $(x + 3)(x - 3)^2$ **88.** $(4x - 5)^2$ **89.** $(x^2 + 4)(x + 2)(x - 2)$

90. $(y - 2)(y^2 + 2y + 4)$ **91.** $(x + 4)(x^2 - 4x + 16)$ **92.** $3x^2(x - 2)(x + 2)$ **93.** $(3x - 5)(9x^2 + 15x + 25)$

94. $x(x - 1)(x + 1)(x^2 + 1)$ **95.** $(x^2 - 2)(x + 5)$ **96.** $(x + 9 + y)(x + 9 - y)$ **97.** $\dfrac{16(1 + 2x)}{x^{3/4}}$

98. $(x + 2)(x - 2)(x^2 + 3)^{1/2}(-x^4 + x^2 + 13)$ **99.** $\dfrac{6(2x + 1)}{x^{3/2}}$ **100.** $x^2, x \neq -2$ **101.** $\dfrac{x - 3}{x - 6}, x \neq -6, 6$ **102.** $\dfrac{x}{x + 2}, x \neq -2$

103. $\dfrac{(x + 3)^3}{(x - 2)^2(x + 2)}, x \neq 2, -2$ **104.** $\dfrac{2}{x(x + 1)}, x \neq 0, 1, -1, -\dfrac{1}{3}$ **105.** $\dfrac{x + 3}{x - 4}, x \neq -3, 4, 2, 8$ **106.** $\dfrac{1}{x - 3}, x \neq 3, -3$

107. $\dfrac{4x(x - 1)}{(x + 2)(x - 2)}, x \neq 2, -2$ **108.** $\dfrac{2x^2 - 3}{(x - 3)(x + 3)(x - 2)}, x \neq 3, -3, 2$ **109.** $\dfrac{11x^2 - x - 11}{(2x - 1)(x + 3)(3x + 2)}, x \neq \dfrac{1}{2}, -3, -\dfrac{2}{3}$

110. $\dfrac{3}{x}, x \neq 0, 2$ **111.** $\dfrac{3x}{x - 4}, x \neq 0, 4, -4$ **112.** $\dfrac{3x + 8}{3x + 10}, x \neq -3, -\dfrac{10}{3}$

Chapter P Test

1. $-7, -\dfrac{4}{5}, 0, 0.25, \sqrt{4}, \dfrac{22}{7}$ **2.** commutative property of addition   **3.** distributive property of multiplication over addition

4. 7.6×10^{-4} **5.** $85x + 2y - 15$ **6.** $\dfrac{5y^8}{x^6}$ **7.** $3r\sqrt{2}$ **8.** $11\sqrt{2}$ **9.** $\dfrac{3(5 - \sqrt{2})}{23}$ **10.** $2x\sqrt[3]{2x}$ **11.** $\dfrac{x + 3}{x - 2}, x \neq 2, 1$ **12.** $\dfrac{1}{243}$

13. $2x^3 - 13x^2 + 26x - 15$ **14.** $25x^2 + 30xy + 9y^2$ **15.** $(x - 3)(x - 6)$ **16.** $(x^2 + 3)(x + 2)$ **17.** $(5x - 3)(5x + 3)$

18. $(6x - 7)^2$ **19.** $(y - 5)(y^2 + 5y + 25)$ **20.** $(x + 5 + 3y)(x + 5 - 3y)$ **21.** $\dfrac{2x + 3}{(x + 3)^{3/5}}$ **22.** $\dfrac{2(x + 3)}{x + 1}, x \neq 3, -1, -4, -3$

23. $\dfrac{x^2 + 2x + 15}{(x + 3)(x - 3)}, x \neq 3, -3$ **24.** $\dfrac{5}{(x - 3)(x - 4)}, x \neq 3, 4$ **25.** $\dfrac{3 - x}{3}, x \neq 0$

CHAPTER 1

Section 1.1

Check Point Exercises

1.
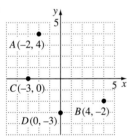

2.
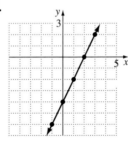

3. The minimum x-value is -100 and the maximum x-value is 100. The distance between consecutive tick marks is 50. The minimum y-value is -80 and the maximum y-value is 80. The distance between consecutive tick marks is 10.

4. $21\dfrac{1}{2}$; 1900

Exercise Set 1.1

1.
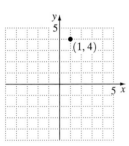

3.
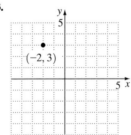

5.
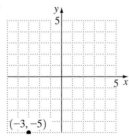

7.
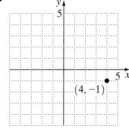

9.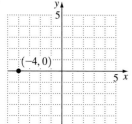

11.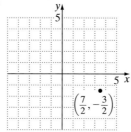

13.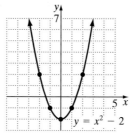

15.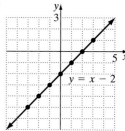

17.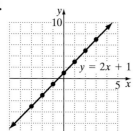

19.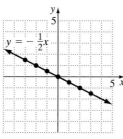

21.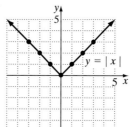

23.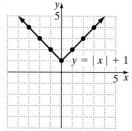

25.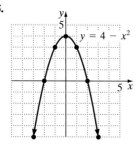

27.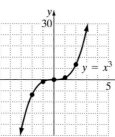

29. (c) **31.** (b) **33. a.** 2 **b.** −4 **35. a.** 1, −2 **b.** 2
37. a. −1 **b.** None **39.** A $(2, 7)$; The football is 7 feet high when it is 2 yards from the quarterback.

41. $C\left(6, 9\frac{1}{2}\right)$ **43.** 12 feet; 15 yards **45.** 0–4 years

47. year 4; 8% **57.** (c) gives a complete graph.
59. (c) gives a complete graph. **61.** (a) **63.** (b)

Section 1.2

Check Point Exercises

1. $\{16\}$ **2.** $\{5\}$ **3.** $\{-2\}$ **4.** $\{3\}$ **5.** $\varnothing$ **6.** identity

Exercise Set 1.2

1. $\{11\}$ **3.** $\{7\}$ **5.** $\{13\}$ **7.** $\{2\}$ **9.** $\{9\}$ **11.** $\{-5\}$ **13.** $\{6\}$ **15.** $\{-2\}$ **17.** $\{12\}$ **19.** $\{24\}$ **21.** $\{-15\}$

23. $\{5\}$ **25.** $\left\{\frac{33}{2}\right\}$ **27.** $\{-12\}$ **29.** $\left\{\frac{46}{5}\right\}$ **31. a.** 0 **b.** $\left\{\frac{1}{2}\right\}$ **33. a.** 0 **b.** $\{-2\}$ **35. a.** 0 **b.** $\{2\}$ **37. a.** 0

b. $\{4\}$ **39. a.** 1 **b.** $\{3\}$ **41. a.** −1 **b.** $\varnothing$ **43. a.** 1 **b.** $\{2\}$ **45. a.** −2, 2 **b.** $\varnothing$ **47. a.** −1, 1 **b.** $\{-3\}$
49. a. −2, 4 **b.** $\varnothing$ **51.** identity **53.** inconsistent equation **55.** conditional equation **57.** inconsistent equation
59. $\{-7\}$ **61.** not true for any real number, $\varnothing$ **63.** $\{-4\}$ **65.** $\{8\}$ **67.** $\{-1\}$ **69.** not true for any real number, $\varnothing$

71. a. 250 mg/dl **b.** 375,000 annual deaths; 350,000 saved lives **73.** $409\frac{1}{5}$ ft **87.** inconsistent **89.** conditional; $\{-5\}$

91. $x = \dfrac{c - b}{a}$ **93.** Answers may vary. **95.** 20

Section 1.3

Check Point Exercises

1. 2008 **2.** *Saturday Night Fever* sold 11 million albums; *Jagged Little Pill* sold 16 million albums. **3.** 300 min

4. $15,000 at 9%; $10,000 at 12% **5.** width = 50 ft; length = 94 ft **6.** $m = \dfrac{y - b}{x}$ **7.** $C = \dfrac{P}{1 + M}$

Exercise Set 1.3

1. $x + 9$ **3.** $20 - x$ **5.** $8 - 5x$ **7.** $15 \div x$ **9.** $2x + 20$ **11.** $7x - 30$ **13.** $4(x + 12)$ **15.** $x + 40 = 450;\ \{410\}$
17. $5x - 7 = 123;\ \{26\}$ **19.** $9x = 3x + 30;\ \{5\}$ **21.** 40 years old; It is shown by the point $(40, 117)$ on the line for females.
23. approximately 41 years after 1960 in 2001 **25.** 196 lb **27.** $Waterworld = \$160$ million; $Titanic = \$200$ million
29. Miami $= 57$ hr; Los Angeles $= 82$ hr **31.** 800 mi **33.** 2005 **35. a.** total monthly cost with coupon book $= 21 + 0.50x$; total
monthly cost without coupon book $= 1.25x$ **b.** 28 times **37.** $\$600; \$580$ **39.** $\$31,250$ in noninsured bonds; $\$18,750$ in
government-insured certificates of deposit **41.** $\$6000$ at 12%; $\$2000$ at a 5% loss **43.** length $= 78$ ft; width $= 36$ ft
45. length $= 2$ ft; height $= 5$ ft **47.** 11 hr **49.** $\$31,000$ **51.** 7 oz **53.** $\$20,000$ **55.** 5 ft 7 in. **57.** $\omega = \dfrac{A}{l}$ **59.** $b = \dfrac{2A}{h}$
61. $p = \dfrac{I}{rt}$ **63.** $m = \dfrac{E}{c^2}$ **65.** $p = \dfrac{T - D}{m}$ **67.** $a = \dfrac{2A}{h} - b$ **69.** $r = \dfrac{S - P}{Pt}$ **71.** $S = \dfrac{F}{B} + V$ **73.** $I = \dfrac{E}{R + r}$
75. $f = \dfrac{pq}{p + q}$ **81.**

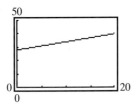

The trace feature shows x to be about 15
when $y = 37$, so 2005. The trace feature
shows x to be 20 when $y = 40$, so 2010.

83. North campus had 600 students; South campus had 400 students.
85. Coburn $= 60$ years old; woman $= 20$ years old
87. $\$4000$ for the mother; $\$8000$ for the boy; $\$2000$ for the girl

Section 1.4

Check Point Exercises

1. a. $8 + i$ **b.** $-10 + 10i$ **2. a.** $63 + 14i$ **b.** $58 - 11i$ **3.** $\dfrac{3}{5} + \dfrac{13}{10}i$ **4. a.** $7i\sqrt{3}$ **b.** $1 - 4i\sqrt{3}$ **c.** $-7 + i\sqrt{3}$

Exercise Set 1.4

1. $8 - 2i$ **3.** $-2 + 9i$ **5.** $24 + 7i$ **7.** $-14 + 17i$ **9.** $21 + 15i$ **11.** $-43 - 23i$ **13.** $-29 - 11i$ **15.** 34 **17.** 34
19. $-5 + 12i$ **21.** $\dfrac{3}{5} + \dfrac{1}{5}i$ **23.** $1 + i$ **25.** $-\dfrac{24}{25} + \dfrac{32}{25}i$ **27.** $\dfrac{7}{5} + \dfrac{4}{5}i$ **29.** $3i$ **31.** $47i$ **33.** $-8i$ **35.** $2 + 6i\sqrt{7}$
37. $-\dfrac{1}{3} + \dfrac{\sqrt{2}}{6}i$ **39.** $-\dfrac{1}{8} - \dfrac{\sqrt{3}}{24}i$ **41.** $-2\sqrt{6} - 2i\sqrt{10}$ **43.** $24\sqrt{15}$ **53.** (d) is true. **55.** $\dfrac{14}{25} - \dfrac{2}{25}i$ **57.** 0

Section 1.5

Check Point Exercises

1. a. $\{0, 3\}$ **b.** $\left\{-1, \dfrac{1}{2}\right\}$ **2. a.** $\{-\sqrt{7}, \sqrt{7}\}$ **b.** $\{-5 + \sqrt{11}, -5 - \sqrt{11}\}$ **3.** $49; (x - 7)^2$ **4.** $\{1 + \sqrt{3}, 1 - \sqrt{3}\}$
5. $\left\{\dfrac{-1 + \sqrt{3}}{2}, \dfrac{-1 - \sqrt{3}}{2}\right\}$ **6.** $\{1 + i, 1 - i\}$ **7.** -56; two complex imaginary solutions **8.** 1998; a good approximation **9.** 12 in.

Exercise Set 1.5

1. $\{-2, 5\}$ **3.** $\{3, 5\}$ **5.** $\left\{-\dfrac{5}{2}, \dfrac{2}{3}\right\}$ **7.** $\left\{-\dfrac{4}{3}, 2\right\}$ **9.** $\{-4, 0\}$ **11.** $\left\{0, \dfrac{1}{3}\right\}$ **13.** $\{-3, 1\}$ **15.** $\{-3, 3\}$
17. $\{-\sqrt{10}, \sqrt{10}\}$ **19.** $\{-7, 3\}$ **21.** $\left\{-\dfrac{5}{3}, \dfrac{1}{3}\right\}$ **23.** $\left\{\dfrac{1 - \sqrt{7}}{5}, \dfrac{1 + \sqrt{7}}{5}\right\}$ **25.** $\left\{\dfrac{4 - 2\sqrt{2}}{3}, \dfrac{4 + 2\sqrt{2}}{3}\right\}$
27. $36; x^2 + 12x + 36 = (x + 6)^2$ **29.** $25; x^2 - 10x + 25 = (x - 5)^2$ **31.** $\dfrac{9}{4}; x^2 + 3x + \dfrac{9}{4} = \left(x + \dfrac{3}{2}\right)^2$
33. $\dfrac{49}{4}; x^2 - 7x + \dfrac{49}{4} = \left(x - \dfrac{7}{2}\right)^2$ **35.** $\dfrac{1}{9}; x^2 - \dfrac{2}{3}x + \dfrac{1}{9} = \left(x - \dfrac{1}{3}\right)^2$ **37.** $\dfrac{1}{36}; x^2 - \dfrac{1}{3}x + \dfrac{1}{36} = \left(x - \dfrac{1}{6}\right)^2$ **39.** $\{-7, 1\}$
41. $\{1 + \sqrt{3}, 1 - \sqrt{3}\}$ **43.** $\{3 + 2\sqrt{5}, 3 - 2\sqrt{5}\}$ **45.** $\{-2 + \sqrt{3}, -2 - \sqrt{3}\}$ **47.** $\left\{\dfrac{-3 + \sqrt{13}}{2}, \dfrac{-3 - \sqrt{13}}{2}\right\}$

49. $\left\{\dfrac{1}{2}, 3\right\}$ **51.** $\left\{\dfrac{1 + \sqrt{2}}{2}, \dfrac{1 - \sqrt{2}}{2}\right\}$ **53.** $\left\{\dfrac{1 + \sqrt{7}}{3}, \dfrac{1 - \sqrt{7}}{3}\right\}$ **55.** $\{-5, -3\}$ **57.** $\left\{\dfrac{-5 + \sqrt{13}}{2}, \dfrac{-5 - \sqrt{13}}{2}\right\}$

59. $\left\{\dfrac{3 + \sqrt{57}}{6}, \dfrac{3 - \sqrt{57}}{6}\right\}$ **61.** $\left\{\dfrac{1 + \sqrt{29}}{4}, \dfrac{1 - \sqrt{29}}{4}\right\}$ **63.** $\{3 + i, 3 - i\}$ **65.** 36; 2 unequal real solutions

67. 97; 2 unequal real solutions   **69.** 0; 1 real solution   **71.** 37; 2 unequal real solutions   **73.** $\left\{-\dfrac{1}{2}, 1\right\}$ **75.** $\left\{\dfrac{1}{5}, 2\right\}$

77. $\{-2\sqrt{5}, 2\sqrt{5}\}$ **79.** $\{1 + \sqrt{2}, 1 - \sqrt{2}\}$ **81.** $\left\{\dfrac{-11 + \sqrt{33}}{4}, \dfrac{-11 - \sqrt{33}}{4}\right\}$ **83.** $\left\{0, \dfrac{8}{3}\right\}$ **85.** $\{2\}$ **87.** $\{-2, 2\}$

89. $\{3 + 2i, 3 - 2i\}$ **91.** $\{2 + i\sqrt{3}, 2 - i\sqrt{3}\}$ **93.** $\left\{0, \dfrac{7}{2}\right\}$ **95.** $\{2 + \sqrt{10}, 2 - \sqrt{10}\}$ **97.** $\{-5, -1\}$

99. 19 year olds and 72 year olds; fairly well   **101.** 1994   **103.** (4, 27); This is the graph's highest point; During this time period, the greatest number of recipients was 27 million in 1994.   **105.** 1990; (10, 740)   **107.** 127.28 ft   **109.** 34 ft   **111.** width = 15 ft; length = 20 ft   **113.** 10 in.   **115.** 9.3 in. and 0.7 in.   **117.** 2 in.   **129.** (c) is true.   **131.** $x^2 - 2x - 15 = 0$ **133.** 2.4 m; Yes

Section 1.6

Check Point Exercises

1. $\{-\sqrt{3}, 0, \sqrt{3}\}$ **2.** $\left\{-2, -\dfrac{3}{2}, 2\right\}$ **3.** $\{-1, 3\}$ **4.** $\{4\}$ **5. a.** $\{\sqrt[3]{25}\}$ or $\{5^{2/3}\}$ **b.** $\{-8, 8\}$ **6.** $\{-\sqrt{3}, -\sqrt{2}, \sqrt{2}, \sqrt{3}\}$

7. $\left\{-\dfrac{1}{27}, 64\right\}$ **8.** $\{-2, 3\}$

Exercise Set 1.6

1. $\{-4, 0, 4\}$ **3.** $\left\{-2, -\dfrac{2}{3}, 2\right\}$ **5.** $\left\{-\dfrac{1}{2}, \dfrac{1}{2}, \dfrac{3}{2}\right\}$ **7.** $\left\{-2, -\dfrac{1}{2}, \dfrac{1}{2}\right\}$ **9.** $\{0, 2, -1 + i\sqrt{3}, -1 - i\sqrt{3}\}$ **11.** $\{6\}$ **13.** $\{6\}$

15. $\{-6\}$ **17.** $\{10\}$ **19.** $\{12\}$ **21.** $\{8\}$ **23.** $\varnothing$ **25.** $\varnothing$ **27.** $\left\{\dfrac{13 + \sqrt{105}}{6}\right\}$ **29.** $\{4\}$ **31.** $\{13\}$ **33.** $\{\sqrt[5]{4}\}$

35. $\{-60, 68\}$ **37.** $\{-4, 5\}$ **39.** $\{-2, -1, 1, 2\}$ **41.** $\left\{-\dfrac{4}{3}, -1, 1, \dfrac{4}{3}\right\}$ **43.** $\{25, 64\}$ **45.** $\left\{-\dfrac{1}{4}, \dfrac{1}{5}\right\}$ **47.** $\{-8, 27\}$ **49.** $\{1\}$

51. $\left\{\dfrac{1}{4}, 1\right\}$ **53.** $\{2, 12\}$ **55.** $\{-3, -1, 2, 4\}$ **57.** $\{-8, -2, 1, 4\}$ **59.** $\{-8, 8\}$ **61.** $\{-5, 9\}$ **63.** $\{-2, 3\}$ **65.** $\left\{-\dfrac{5}{3}, 3\right\}$

67. $\left\{-\dfrac{2}{5}, \dfrac{2}{5}\right\}$ **69.** $\varnothing$ **71.** $\left\{\dfrac{1}{2}\right\}$ **73.** $\{-1, 3\}$ **75.** $\{1\}$ **77.** $\{0\}$ **79.** $\left\{\dfrac{5}{2}\right\}$ **81.** $\{-8, -6, 4, 6\}$ **83.** $\{-1, 1, 2\}$

85. 2018   **87.** 36 years old; (36, 40,000)   **89.** 149 million km   **91.** either 1.2 feet or 7.5 feet from the base of the 6 foot pole

101. $\{-3, -1, 1\}$ **103.** $\{-2\}$ **105.** (d) is true.   **107.** $\left\{\dfrac{2}{5}, \dfrac{1}{2}\right\}$ **109.** $\{0, 1\}$

Section 1.7

Check Point Exercises

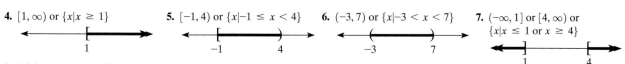

1. a.
b.
c.

2. a. $\{x | -2 \le x < 5\}$ **b.** $\{x | 1 \le x \le 3.5\}$ **c.** $\{x | x < -1\}$ **3.** $[-1, \infty)$ or $\{x | x \ge -1\}$

4. $[1, \infty)$ or $\{x | x \ge 1\}$ **5.** $[-1, 4)$ or $\{x | -1 \le x < 4\}$ **6.** $(-3, 7)$ or $\{x | -3 < x < 7\}$ **7.** $(-\infty, 1]$ or $[4, \infty)$ or $\{x | x \le 1 \text{ or } x \ge 4\}$

8. driving more than 720 mi per week

Exercise Set 1.7

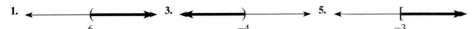

1.
6

3.
−4

5.
−3

7.
4

9.
−2   5

11.
−1   4

13. $1 < x \le 6$
1   6

15. $-5 \le x < 2$
−5   2

17. $-3 \le x \le 1$
−3   1

19. $x > 2$
2

21. $x \ge -3$
−3

23. $x < 3$
3

25. $x < 5.5$
5.5

27. $(-\infty, 3)$
3

29. $\left[\dfrac{20}{3}, \infty\right)$
$\dfrac{20}{3}$

31. $(-\infty, -4]$
−4

33. $\left(-\infty, -\dfrac{2}{5}\right]$
$-\dfrac{2}{5}$

35. $[0, \infty)$
0

37. $(-\infty, 1)$
1

39. $[6, \infty)$
6

41. $\left[-\dfrac{32}{5}, \infty\right)$
$-\dfrac{32}{5}$

43. $(-\infty, -6)$
−6

45. $[13, \infty)$
13

47. $(-\infty, \infty)$
0

49. $(3, 5)$
3   5

51. $[-1, 3)$
−1   3

53. $(-5, -2]$
−5   −2

55. $[3, 6)$
3   6

57. $(-3, 3)$
−3   3

59. $[-1, 3]$
−1   3

61. $(-1, 7)$
−1   7

63. $[-5, 3]$
−5   3

65. $(-6, 0)$
−6   0

67. $(-\infty, -3)$ or $(3, \infty)$
−3   3

69. $(-\infty, -1]$ or $[3, \infty)$
−1   3

71. $\left(-\infty, \dfrac{1}{3}\right)$ or $(5, \infty)$
$\dfrac{1}{3}$ 5

73. $(-\infty, -5]$ or $[3, \infty)$
−5   3

75. $(-\infty, -3)$ or $(12, \infty)$
−3   12

77. $(-\infty, -1]$ or $[3, \infty)$
−1   3

79. $(-\infty, -1)$ or $(2, \infty)$
−1   2

81. $\left(-\infty, -\dfrac{75}{14}\right)$ or $\left(\dfrac{87}{14}, \infty\right)$
$-\dfrac{75}{14}$ $\dfrac{87}{14}$

83. $(-\infty, -6]$ or $[24, \infty)$
−6   24

85. sports events and playing sports   **87.** amusement parks, gardening, movies, and exercise   **89.** gardening and movies
91. home improvement, amusement parks, and gardening   **93.** $x > 20$; all years after 2008   **95.** between 59°F and 95°F inclusive
97. $58.6 \le x \le 61.8$; Between 58.6% and 61.8% of U.S. households watched the "M*A*S*H" episode.   **99.** $h \le 41$ or $h \ge 59$
101. $50 + 0.20x < 20 + 0.50x$; more than 100 mi   **103.** $1800 + 0.03x < 200 + 0.08x$; greater than $32,000
105. $2x > 10,000 + 0.40x$; more than 6250 tapes   **107.** $265 + 65x \le 2800$; at most 39 bags

109. a. $\dfrac{86 + 88 + x}{3} \ge 90$; at least a 96   **b.** $\dfrac{86 + 88 + x}{3} < 80$; a grade less than 66

121.

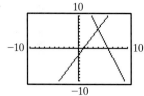

$x < 4$

123.

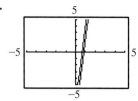

The graph of the left side of the inequality is never above the graph of the right side, therefore there is no solution; You get a statement that is always false.

125. a. $C = 4 + 0.10x$; $C = 2 + 0.15x$

b.

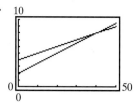

c. 41 or more checks
d. $x > 40$

127. Because $x > y$, $y - x$ represents a negative number, so when both sides are multiplied by $(y - x)$, the inequality must be reversed.
129. at least $500, but no more than $2500

Chapter 1 Review Exercises

1.

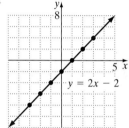

$y = 2x - 2$

2.

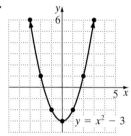

$y = x^2 - 3$

3.

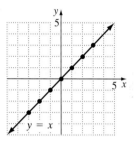

$y = x$

4.

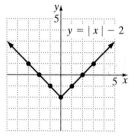

$y = |x| - 2$

5.

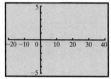

6. x-intercept: -2; y-intercept: 2 **7.** x-intercepts: $2, -2$; y-intercept: -4
8. x-intercept: 5; y-intercept: none   **9.** 20%   **10.** 85 years
11. The percentage of Americans with Alzheimer's disease increases with age.
12. $\{6\}$ **13.** $\{-10\}$ **14.** $\{5\}$ **15.** $\{-13\}$ **16.** $\{-3\}$ **17.** $\{-1\}$ **18.** $\{2\}$ **19.** $\{2\}$

20. $\left\{\dfrac{72}{11}\right\}$ **21.** $\{-12\}$ **22.** $\left\{\dfrac{77}{15}\right\}$ **23. a.** 0 **b.** $\{2\}$ **24. a.** 5 **b.** $\varnothing$ **25. a.** $-1, 1$ **b.** all real numbers except 1 and -1

26. a. $-2, 4$ **b.** $\{7\}$ **27.** inconsistent equation   **28.** identity   **29.** conditional equation   **30.** 2005   **31.** 2000

32. low $= $174 thousand, middle $= $237 thousand, high $= $345 thousand   **33.** 9 years; 2009   **34.** 500 min

35. $6250 at 8%; $3750 at 12%   **36.** length $= 120$ m; width $= 53$ m   **37.** 20 times   **38.** $10,000   **39.** 95 concerts   **40.** $h = \dfrac{3V}{B}$

41. $M = \dfrac{f - F}{f}$ **42.** $g = \dfrac{T}{r + vt}$ **43.** $-9 + 4i$ **44.** $-12 - 8i$ **45.** $29 + 11i$ **46.** $-7 - 24i$ **47.** 113 **48.** $\dfrac{15}{13} - \dfrac{3}{13}i$

49. $\dfrac{1}{5} + \dfrac{11}{10}i$ **50.** $i\sqrt{2}$ **51.** $-96 - 40i$ **52.** $2 + i\sqrt{2}$ **53.** $\left\{-8, \dfrac{1}{2}\right\}$ **54.** $\{-4, 0\}$ **55.** $\{-8, 8\}$ **56.** $\left\{\dfrac{4 + 3\sqrt{2}}{3}, \dfrac{4 - 3\sqrt{2}}{3}\right\}$

57. $100; (x + 10)^2$ **58.** $\dfrac{9}{4}; \left(x - \dfrac{3}{2}\right)^2$ **59.** $\{3, 9\}$ **60.** $\left\{2 + \dfrac{\sqrt{3}}{3}, 2 - \dfrac{\sqrt{3}}{3}\right\}$ **61.** $\{1 + \sqrt{5}, 1 - \sqrt{5}\}$

62. $\{1 + 3i\sqrt{2}, 1 - 3i\sqrt{2}\}$ **63.** $\left\{\dfrac{-2 + \sqrt{10}}{2}, \dfrac{-2 - \sqrt{10}}{2}\right\}$ **64.** -36; 2 complex imaginary solutions   **65.** 81; 2 unequal real solutions

66. $\left\{\dfrac{1}{2}, 5\right\}$ **67.** $\left\{-2, \dfrac{10}{3}\right\}$ **68.** $\left\{\dfrac{7 + \sqrt{37}}{6}, \dfrac{7 - \sqrt{37}}{6}\right\}$ **69.** $\{-3, 3\}$ **70.** $\{-2, 8\}$ **71.** $\left\{\dfrac{1}{6} + i\dfrac{\sqrt{23}}{6}, \dfrac{1}{6} - i\dfrac{\sqrt{23}}{6}\right\}$

72. 20 weeks   **73.** 10 years   **74.** $(10, 7250)$ **75.** length $= 5$ yd; width $= 3$ yd   **76.** approximately 134 m   **77.** $\{-5, 0, 5\}$

78. $\left\{-3, \dfrac{1}{2}, 3\right\}$ **79.** $\{2\}$ **80.** $\{8\}$ **81.** $\{16\}$ **82.** $\{132\}$ **83.** $\{-2, -1, 1, 2\}$ **84.** $\{16\}$ **85.** $\{-4, 3\}$ **86.** $\{-5, 11\}$

87. $\left\{-1, -\dfrac{2\sqrt{6}}{9}, \dfrac{2\sqrt{6}}{9}, 1\right\}$ **88.** $\{2\}$ **89.** $\{1, 4\}$ **90.** $\{-3, -2, 3\}$ **91.** 1250 ft

92.   **93.**    **94.** 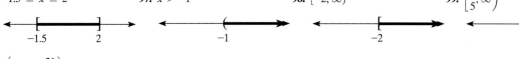   **95.** $-2 < x \le 3$

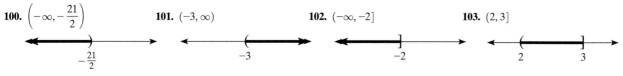

96. $-1.5 \le x \le 2$ **97.** $x > -1$ **98.** $[-2, \infty)$ **99.** $\left[\dfrac{3}{5}, \infty\right)$

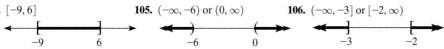

100. $\left(-\infty, -\dfrac{21}{2}\right)$ **101.** $(-3, \infty)$ **102.** $(-\infty, -2]$ **103.** $(2, 3]$

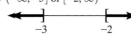

104. $[-9, 6]$ **105.** $(-\infty, -6)$ or $(0, \infty)$ **106.** $(-\infty, -3]$ or $[-2, \infty)$

107. Most people sleep between 5.5 and 7.5 hours. **108.** between 50°F and 77°F inclusively **109.** more than 50 checks
110. at least 93

Chapter 1 Test

1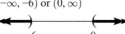

2. x-intercept: 2; y-intercept: 3 **3.** 1992; 7.8%
4. $\{-1\}$ **5** $\{-6\}$ **6.** $\{5\}$
7. $\left\{-\dfrac{1}{2}, 2\right\}$ **8.** $\left\{\dfrac{1 - 5\sqrt{3}}{3}, \dfrac{1 + 5\sqrt{3}}{3}\right\}$ **9.** $\{1 - \sqrt{5}, 1 + \sqrt{5}\}$
10. $\left\{1 + \dfrac{1}{2}i, 1 - \dfrac{1}{2}i\right\}$ **11.** $\{-1, 1, 4\}$ **12.** $\{7\}$ **13.** $\{5\}$
14. $\{\sqrt[3]{4}\}$ **15.** $\{1, 512\}$ **16.** $\{6, 12\}$

17. $(-\infty, 12]$ **18.** $\left[\dfrac{21}{8}, \infty\right)$ **19.** $\left[-7, \dfrac{13}{2}\right)$

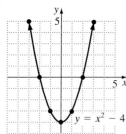

20. $\left(-\infty, -\dfrac{5}{3}\right]$ or $\left[\dfrac{1}{3}, \infty\right)$ **21.** $(-3, 4)$ **22.** $(3, 10)$

      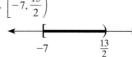

23. $47 + 16i$ **24.** $2 + i$ **25.** $38i$ **26.** $h = \dfrac{3V}{lw}$ **27.** $x = x_1 + \dfrac{y - y_1}{m}$ **28.** 2004; very well **29.** 2007; very well
30. New York City: 55 days; Los Angeles: 213 days **31.** 26 yr; $33,600 **32.** $3000 at 8%; $7000 at 10%
33. length = 12 ft; width = 4 ft **34.** 10 ft **35.** $47,500

CHAPTER 2

Section 2.1

Check Point Exercises

1. a. 6   **b.** $-\dfrac{7}{5}$ **2.** $y + 5 = 6(x - 2); y = 6x - 17$ **3.** $y + 1 = -5(x + 2); y = -5x - 11$

4.
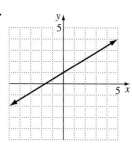

5.
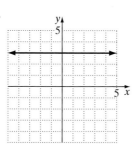

6.
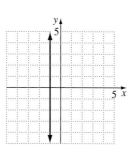

7. slope: $-\dfrac{1}{2}$; y-intercept: 2
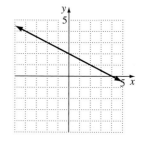

Exercise Set 2.1

1. $\dfrac{3}{4}$; rises   **3.** $\dfrac{1}{4}$; rises   **5.** 0; horizontal   **7.** −5; falls   **9.** undefined; vertical   **11.** $y - 5 = 2(x - 3); y = 2x - 1$

13. $y - 5 = 6(x + 2); y = 6x + 17$ **15.** $y + 3 = -3(x + 2); y = -3x - 9$ **17.** $y - 0 = -4(x + 4); y = -4x - 16$

19. $y + 2 = -1\left(x + \dfrac{1}{2}\right); y = -x - \dfrac{5}{2}$ **21.** $y - 0 = \dfrac{1}{2}(x - 0); y = \dfrac{1}{2}x$ **23.** $y + 2 = -\dfrac{2}{3}(x - 6); y = -\dfrac{2}{3}x + 2$

25. using $(1, 2), y - 2 = 2(x - 1); y = 2x$ **27.** using $(-3, 0), y - 0 = 1(x + 3); y = x + 3$

29. using $(-3, -1), y + 1 = 1(x + 3); y = x + 2$ **31.** using $(-3, -2), y + 2 = \dfrac{4}{3}(x + 3); y = \dfrac{4}{3}x + 2$

33. using $(-3, -1), y + 1 = 0(x + 3); y = -1$ **35.** using $(2, 4), y - 4 = 1(x - 2); y = x + 2$

37. using $(0, 4), y - 4 = 8(x - 0); y = 8x + 4$

39. $m = 2; b = 1$ **41.** $m = -2; b = 1$ **43.** $m = \dfrac{3}{4}; b = -2$ **45.** $m = -\dfrac{3}{5}; b = 7$

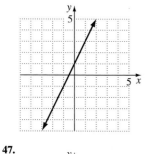
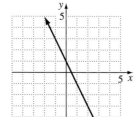
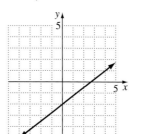
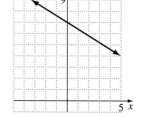

47.
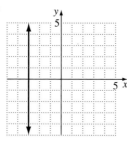

49.
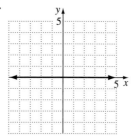

51.
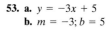

53. a. $y = -3x + 5$
b. $m = -3; b = 5$
c.
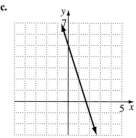

55. a. $y = -\dfrac{2}{3}x + 6$

b. $m = -\dfrac{2}{3}; b = 6$

c.

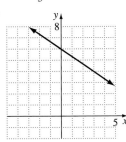

57. a. $y = 2x - 3$

b. $m = 2; b = -3$

c.

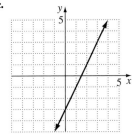

59. a. $x = 3$

b. m is undefined; no y-intercept

c.

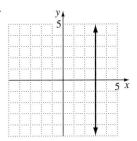

61. $y + 10 = -4(x + 8); y = -4x - 42$ **63.** $y + 3 = -5(x - 2); y = -5x + 7$ **65.** $y - 2 = \dfrac{2}{3}(x + 2); y = \dfrac{2}{3}x + \dfrac{10}{3}$

67. $y + 7 = -2(x - 4); y = -2x + 1$ **69.** $y = 15$ **71.** 111; The federal budget surplus is increasing \$111 billion each year.

73. a. 16, In 1950, there were 16 workers per Social Security beneficiary.   **b.** −0.24; The number of workers per Social Security beneficiary is decreasing by 0.24 workers each year.   **c.** $y = -0.24x + 16$ **d.** 1.6; 5   **75. a.** $y - 30 = 4(x - 2)$ **b.** $y = 4x + 22$ **c.** 74   **77.** $y = -2.3x + 255$, where x is the percentage of adult females who are literate and y is under-five mortality per thousand; For each percent increase is adult female literacy, under-five mortality decreases by 2.3 per thousand.   **79.** $y = -0.7x + 60$; y represents the percentage of U.S. adults who read a newspaper x years after 1995.   **81.** $y = -500x + 29,500$; 4500 shirts

93. $m = -3$

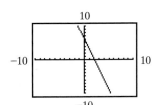

95. $m = \dfrac{3}{4}$

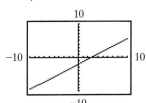

97. (c) is true.

99. a. m_1, m_3, m_2, m_4
    b. b_2, b_1, b_4, b_3

Section 2.2

Check Point Exercises

1. 5   **2.** $\left(4, -\dfrac{1}{2}\right)$ **3.** $x^2 + y^2 = 16$ **5.** center: $(-3, 1)$; radius: 2   **6.** $(x + 2)^2 + (y - 2)^2 = 9$

4. $(x - 5)^2 + (y + 6)^2 = 100$

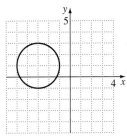

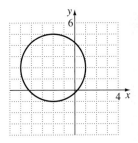

Exercise Set 2.2

1. 13   **3.** $2\sqrt{2} \approx 2.83$ **5.** 5   **7.** $\sqrt{29} \approx 5.39$ **9.** $4\sqrt{2} \approx 5.66$ **11.** $2\sqrt{5} \approx 4.47$ **13.** $2\sqrt{2} \approx 2.83$ **15.** $\sqrt{93} \approx 9.64$

17. $\sqrt{5} \approx 2.24$ **19.** $(4, 6)$ **21.** $(-4, -5)$ **23.** $\left(\dfrac{3}{2}, -6\right)$ **25.** $(-3, -2)$ **27.** $(1, 5\sqrt{5})$ **29.** $(2\sqrt{2}, 0)$ **31.** $x^2 + y^2 = 49$

33. $(x - 3)^2 + (y - 2)^2 = 25$ **35.** $(x + 1)^2 + (y - 4)^2 = 4$ **37.** $(x + 3)^2 + (y + 1)^2 = 3$ **39.** $(x + 4)^2 + (y - 0)^2 = 100$

41. center: $(0, 0)$
radius: 4

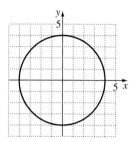

43. center: $(3, 1)$
radius: 6

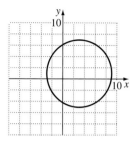

45. center: $(-3, 2)$
radius: 2

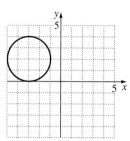

47. center: $(-2, -2)$
radius: 2

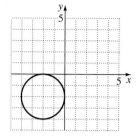

49. $(x + 3)^2 + (y + 1)^2 = 4$
center: $(-3, -1)$
radius: 2

51. $(x - 5)^2 + (y - 3)^2 = 64$
center: $(5, 3)$
radius: 8

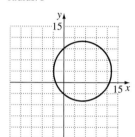

53. $(x + 4)^2 + (y - 1)^2 = 25$
center: $(-4, 1)$
radius: 5

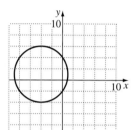

55. $(x - 1)^2 + (y - 0)^2 = 16$
center: $(1, 0)$
radius: 4

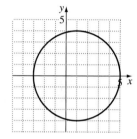

57. 0.5hr; 30 min   **59.** $x^2 + (y - 82)^2 = 4624$ **69.**

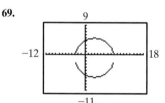

71. (d) is true.

73. a. Distance between (x_1, y_1) and $\left(\dfrac{x_1 + x_2}{2}, \dfrac{y_1 + y_2}{2}\right)$

$$= \sqrt{\left(\frac{x_1 + x_2}{2} - x_1\right)^2 + \left(\frac{y_1 + y_2}{2} - y_1\right)^2}$$

$$= \sqrt{\left(\frac{x_1 + x_2 - 2x_1}{2}\right)^2 + \left(\frac{y_1 + y_2 - 2y_1}{2}\right)^2}$$

$$= \sqrt{\left(\frac{x_2 - x_1}{2}\right)^2 + \left(\frac{y_2 - y_1}{2}\right)^2}$$

$$= \sqrt{\frac{x_2^2 - 2x_1x_2 + x_1^2}{4} + \frac{y_2^2 - 2y_1y_2 + y_1^2}{4}}$$

$$= \sqrt{\frac{x_1^2 - 2x_1x_2 + x_2^2}{4} + \frac{y_1^2 - 2y_1y_2 + y_2^2}{4}}$$

$$= \sqrt{\left(\frac{x_1 - x_2}{2}\right)^2 + \left(\frac{y_1 - y_2}{2}\right)^2}$$

$$= \sqrt{\left(\frac{x_1 + x_2 - 2x_2}{2}\right)^2 + \left(\frac{y_1 + y_2 - 2y_2}{2}\right)^2}$$

$$= \sqrt{\left(\frac{x_1 + x_2}{2} - x_2\right)^2 + \left(\frac{y_1 + y_2}{2} - y_2\right)^2}$$

$$= \text{Distance between } (x_2, y_2) \text{ and } \left(\frac{x_1 + x_2}{2}, \frac{y_1 + y_2}{2}\right)$$

b. $\sqrt{\left(\dfrac{x_2 - x_1}{2}\right)^2 + \left(\dfrac{y_2 - y_1}{2}\right)^2} + \sqrt{\left(\dfrac{x_2 - x_1}{2}\right)^2 + \left(\dfrac{y_2 - y_1}{2}\right)^2}$

$$= 2\sqrt{\left(\frac{x_2 - x_1}{2}\right)^2 + \left(\frac{y_2 - y_1}{2}\right)^2}$$

$$= 2\sqrt{\frac{(x_2 - x_1)^2 + (y_2 - y_1)^2}{4}}$$

$$= \sqrt{(x_2 - x_1)^2 + (y_2 - y_1)^2}$$

$$= \text{Distance from } (x_1, y_1) \text{ to } (x_2, y_2)$$

75. $(x + 3)^2 + (y - 2)^2 = 16$; $x^2 + y^2 + 6x - 4y - 3 = 0$ **77.** $y + 4 = \dfrac{3}{4}(x - 3)$

Section 2.3

Check Point Exercises

1. domain: $\{5, 10, 15, 20, 25\}$; range: $\{12.8, 16.2, 18.9, 20.7, 21.8\}$ **2. a.** not a function **b.** function **3. a.** $y = 6 - 2x$; function
b. $y = \pm\sqrt{1 - x^2}$, not a function **4. a.** 42 **b.** $x^2 + 6x + 15$ **c.** $x^2 + 2x + 7$ **5. a.** $x^2 + 2hx + h^2 - 7x - 7h + 3$
b. $2x + h - 7$ **6. a.** 28 **b.** 33 **7. a.** $(-\infty, \infty)$ **b.** $\{x | x \neq -7, x \neq 7\}$ **c.** $[3, \infty)$.

Exercise Set 2.3

1. function; $\{1, 3, 5\}$; $\{2, 4, 5\}$ **3.** not a function; $\{3, 4\}$; $\{4, 5\}$ **5.** function; $\{-3, -2, -1, 0\}$; $\{-3, -2, -1, 0\}$
7. not a function; $\{1\}$; $\{4, 5, 6\}$ **9.** y is a function of x. **11.** y is a function of x. **13.** y is not a function of x.
15. y is not a function of x. **17.** y is a function of x. **19.** y is a function of x. **21. a.** 29 **b.** $4x + 9$ **c.** $-4x + 5$
23. a. 2 **b.** $x^2 + 12x + 38$ **c.** $x^2 - 2x + 3$ **25. a.** 13 **b.** 1 **c.** $x^4 - x^2 + 1$ **d.** $81a^4 - 9a^2 + 1$ **27. a.** 3 **b.** 7
c. $\sqrt{x} + 3$ **29. a.** $\dfrac{15}{4}$ **b.** $\dfrac{15}{4}$ **c.** $\dfrac{4x^2 - 1}{x^2}$ **31. a.** 1 **b.** -1 **c.** 1 **33.** $4, h \neq 0$ **35.** $3, h \neq 0$ **37.** $2x + h, h \neq 0$
39. $2x + h - 4, h \neq 0$ **41.** $0, h \neq 0$ **43.** $-\dfrac{1}{x(x + h)}, h \neq 0$ **45. a.** -1 **b.** 7 **c.** 19 **47. a.** 3 **b.** 3 **c.** 0
49. a. 8 **b.** 3 **c.** 6 **51.** $(-\infty, \infty)$ **53.** $(-\infty, 4)$ or $(4, \infty)$ **55.** $(-\infty, -4)$ or $(-4, 4)$ or $(4, \infty)$
57. $(-\infty, -3)$ or $(-3, 7)$ or $(7, \infty)$ **59.** $(-\infty, -8)$ or $(-8, -3)$ or $(-3, \infty)$ **61.** $(-\infty, \infty)$ **63.** $[3, \infty)$ **65.** $(3, \infty)$
67. $[-7, \infty)$ **69.** $(-\infty, 12]$ **71.** $(-\infty, -2]$ or $[7, \infty)$ **73.** $[2, 5)$ or $(5, \infty)$
75. $\{(1, 31), (2, 53), (3, 70), (4, 86), (5, 86)|\}$; $\{1, 2, 3, 4, 5\}$; $\{31, 53, 70, 86\}$; Yes; Each member of the domain corresponds to exactly one
member of the range. **77.** No; There is a member of the domain that corresponds to more than one member of the range.
79. 1713; There were 1713 gray wolves in the U.S. in 1990; Very well. **81.** 19; Very well. **83.** 5; Okay.
85. $f(0) = 200$; There were 200 thousand lawyers in the United States in 1951. **87.** $f(50) = 1058$; There were 1058 thousand or
1,058,000 lawyers in the United States in the year 2001. **89.** 8873; A person earning $40,000 owed $8873 in taxes.
91. $C = 100,000 + 100x$, where x is the number of bicycles produced; $C(90) = 109,000$; It cost $109,000 to produce 90 bicycles.
93. $T = \dfrac{40}{x} + \dfrac{40}{x + 30}$, where x is the rate on the outgoing trip; $T(30) = 2$; It takes 2 hours, traveling 30 mph outgoing and 60 mph returning.
103. $[1, \infty)$ **105.** $(-\infty, 5]$ **107.** Answers may vary. **109.** $f(r_1) = 0$; r_1 is a solution to the equation $ax^2 + bx + c = 0$.

Section 2.4

Check Point Exercises

1. $(-3, 7), (-2, 2), (-1, -1),$
$(0, -2), (1, -1), (2, 2), (3, 7)$

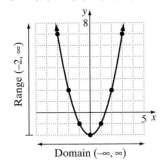

2. $f(4) = 1$; domain: $[0, 6)$; range: $(-2, 2]$
3. a. function
 b. function
 c. not a function
4. a. $f(10) \approx 16$ **b.** $x \approx 8$
5. increasing on $(-\infty, -1)$, decreasing on $(-1, 1)$, increasing on $(1, \infty)$
6. a. 1
 b. 7
 c. 4
7. a. even
 b. odd
 c. neither

Exercise Set 2.4

1. $(-3, 11), (-2, 6), (-1, 3),$
$(0, 2), (1, 3), (2, 6), (3, 11)$

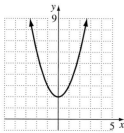

Domain: $(-\infty, \infty)$
Range: $[2, \infty)$

3. $(0, -1), (1, 0), (4, 1), (9, 2)$

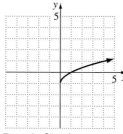

Domain: $[0, \infty)$
Range: $[-1, \infty)$

5. $(1, 0), (2, 1), (5, 2), (10, 3)$

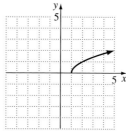

Domain: $[1, \infty)$
Range: $[0, \infty)$

7. $(-3, 2), (-2, 1), (-1, 0),$
$(0, -1), (1, 0), (2, 1), (3, 2)$

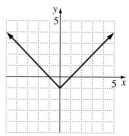

Domain: $(-\infty, \infty)$
Range: $[-1, \infty)$

9. $(-3, 4), (-2, 3), (-1, 2),$
$(0, 1), (1, 0), (2, 1), (3, 2)$

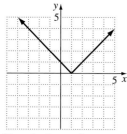

Domain: $(-\infty, \infty)$
Range: $[0, \infty)$

11. $(-3, 5), (-2, 5), (-1, 5),$
$(0, 5), (1, 5), (2, 5), (3, 5)$

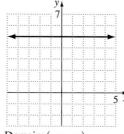

Domain: $(-\infty, \infty)$
Range: $\{5\}$

13. $(-2, -10), (-1, -3),$
$(0, -2), (1, -1), (2, 6)$

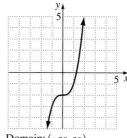

Domain: $(-\infty, \infty)$
Range: $(-\infty, \infty)$

15. a. $(-\infty, \infty)$ **b.** $[-4, \infty)$ **c.** -3 and 1 **d.** -3 **17. a.** $(-\infty, \infty)$ **b.** $[1, \infty)$ **c.** none **d.** 1
e. $f(-1) = 2$ and $f(3) = 4$ **19. a.** $[0, 5)$ **b.** $[-1, 5)$ **c.** 2 **d.** -1 **e.** $f(3) = 1$ **21. a.** $[0, \infty)$ **b.** $[1, \infty)$ **c.** none
d. 1 **e.** $f(4) = 3$ **23. a.** $[-2, 6]$ **b.** $[-2, 6]$ **c.** 4 **d.** 4 **e.** $f(-1) = 5$ **25. a.** $(-\infty, \infty)$ **b.** $(-\infty, -2]$ **c.** none
d. -2 **e.** $f(-4) = -5$ and $f(4) = -2$ **27. a.** $(-\infty, \infty)$ **b.** $(0, \infty)$ **c.** none **d.** 1 **29. a.** $\{-5, -2, 0, 1, 3\}$ **b.** $\{2\}$
c. none **d.** 2 **31.** function **33.** function **35.** not a function **37.** function **39. a.** increasing: $(-1, \infty)$
b. decreasing: $(-\infty, -1)$ **c.** constant: none **41. a.** increasing: $(0, \infty)$ **b.** decreasing: none **c.** constant: none
43. a. increasing: none **b.** decreasing: $(-2, 6)$ **c.** constant: none **45. a.** increasing: $(-\infty, -1)$ **b.** decreasing: none
c. constant: $(-1, \infty)$ **47. a.** increasing: $(-\infty, 0)$ or $(1.5, 3)$ **b.** decreasing: $(0, 1.5)$ or $(3, \infty)$ **c.** constant: none
49. a. increasing: $(-2, 4)$ **b.** decreasing: none **c.** constant: $(-\infty, -2)$ or $(4, \infty)$ **51. a.** $0; f(0) = 4$

b. $-3, 3; f(-3) = f(3) = 0$ **53. a.** $-2; f(-2) = 21$ **b.** $1; f(1) = -6$ **55.** 3 **57.** 10 **59.** $\dfrac{1}{5}$ **61.** odd **63.** neither

65. even **67.** even **69.** even **71.** odd **73.** even **75.** odd

77. $f(1.06) = 1$ **79.** $f\left(\dfrac{1}{3}\right) = 0$ **81.** $f(-2.3) = -3$ **83.** $f(60) \approx 3.1$; In 1960, Jewish Americans made up about 3.1% of the U.S.

population. **85.** $x \approx 19$ and $x \approx 64$; In 1919 and 1964, Jewish Americans made up about 3% of the U.S. population. **87.** 1940; 3.7%
89. Each year corresponds to only one percentage. **91.** increasing: $(45, 74)$; decreasing: $(16, 45)$; The number of accidents occurring per
50,000 miles driven increases with age starting at age 45, while it decreases with age starting at age 16. **93.** Answers will vary; an example
is 16 and 74 years old. For those ages, the number of accidents is 526.4 per 50 million miles.

95.

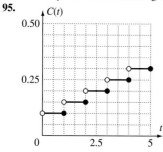

97. Answers may vary.
109. a.

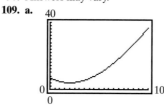

The number of doctor visits decreases during childhood
and then increases as you get older. The minimum is
$(20.29, 3.99)$, which means that the minimum number of
annual doctor visits, about 4, occurs at around age 20.

111.
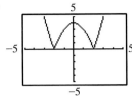
Increasing: $(-2, 0)$ or $(2, \infty)$
Decreasing: $(-\infty, -2)$ or $(0, 2)$

113.
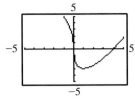
Increasing: $(1, \infty)$
Decreasing: $(-\infty, 1)$

115.
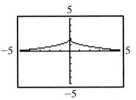
Increasing: $(-\infty, 0)$
Decreasing: $(0, \infty)$

117. (c) is true.
119. Answers may vary.

121.

Weight at least	Cost
0 oz.	$0.37
1	0.60
2	0.83
3	1.06
4	1.29

Section 2.5

Check Point Exercises

1.
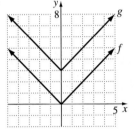

2.
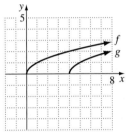

3.
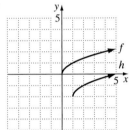

4.
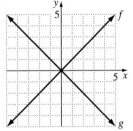

5.
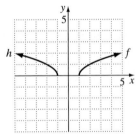

6.
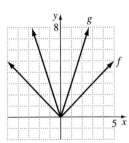

7.
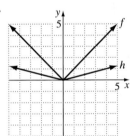

8.
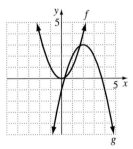

Exercise Set 2.5

1.
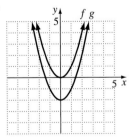

3.
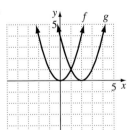

5.
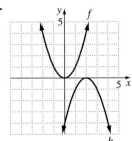

7.
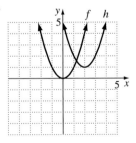

9.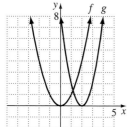

11.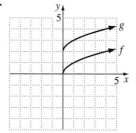

13.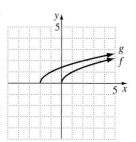

15.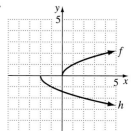

17.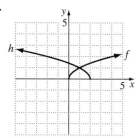

19.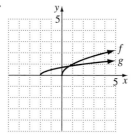

21.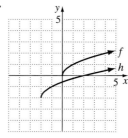

23.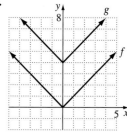

25.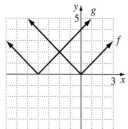

27.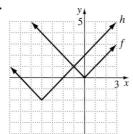

29.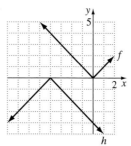

31.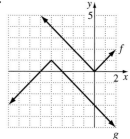

33.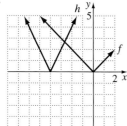

35.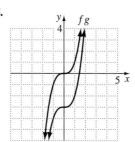

37.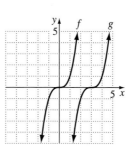

39.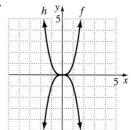

41.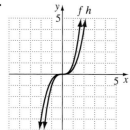

43.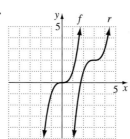

45.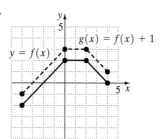

47.

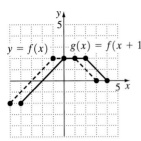

$y = f(x)$ $g(x) = f(x + 1)$

49.

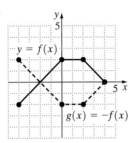

$y = f(x)$

$g(x) = -f(x)$

51.

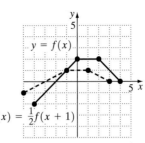

$y = f(x)$

$g(x) = \frac{1}{2}f(x + 1)$

53. $y = \sqrt{x - 2}$
55. $y = (x + 1)^2 - 4$

57. a. First, vertically stretch the graph of $f(x) = \sqrt{x}$ by the factor 2.9; then, vertically shift the result up 20.1 units.
b. 40.2 in.; Very well.   **c.** 0.9 in. per month   **d.** 0.2 in. per month; This is a much smaller rate of change; The graph is not as steep between 50 and 60 as it is between 0 and 10.

65. a.

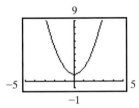

b.

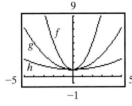

f

g

h

c. Answers may vary.
d. Answers may vary.
e. Answers may vary.

67. $g(x) = -(x + 4)^2$
69. $g(x) = -\sqrt{x - 2} + 2$
71. $(-a, b)$
73. $(a + 3, b)$

Section 2.6

Check Point Exercises

1. a. $(f + g)(x) = 3x^2 + 6x + 6$ **b.** $(f + g)(4) = 78$ **2. a.** $(f + g)(x) = \sqrt{x - 3} + \sqrt{x + 1}$ **b.** $[3, \infty)$

3. a. $(f - g)(x) = -x^2 + x - 4$ **b.** $(fg)(x) = x^3 - 5x^2 - x + 5$ \ **5. a.** $(f \circ g)(x) = \dfrac{4x}{1 + 2x}$ **b.** $\left\{ x \Big| x \neq \text{ and } x \neq -\dfrac{1}{2} \right\}$

6. $f(x) = \sqrt{x}$ and $g(x) = x^2 + 5$, then $h(x) = (f \circ g)(x)$

Exercise Set 2.6

1. a. $(f + g)(x) = 2x^2 + 3x + 2$ **b.** $(f + g)(4) = 46$ **3. a.** $(f + g)(x) = \sqrt{x - 6} + \sqrt{x + 2}$ **b.** Domain: $[6, \infty)$

5. $(f + g)(x) = 3x + 2$; Domain: $(-\infty, \infty)$; $(f - g)(x) = x + 4$; Domain: $(-\infty, \infty)$; $(fg)(x) = 2x^2 + x - 3$;

Domain: $(-\infty, \infty)$; $\left(\dfrac{f}{g}\right)(x) = \dfrac{2x + 3}{x - 1}$; Domain: $(-\infty, 1)$ or $(1, \infty)$ **7.** $(f + g)(x) = 3x^2 + x - 5$;

Domain: $(-\infty, \infty)$; $(f - g)(x) = -3x^2 + x - 5$; Domain: $(-\infty, \infty)$; $(fg)(x) = 3x^3 - 15x^2$; Domain: $(-\infty, \infty)$; $\left(\dfrac{f}{g}\right)(x) = \dfrac{x - 5}{3x^2}$;

Domain: $(-\infty, 0)$ or $(0, \infty)$ **9.** $(f + g)(x) = 2x^2 - 2$; Domain: $(-\infty, \infty)$; $(f - g)(x) = 2x^2 - 2x - 4$;

Domain: $(-\infty, \infty)$; $(fg)(x) = 2x^3 + x^2 - 4x - 3$; Domain: $(-\infty, \infty)$; $\left(\dfrac{f}{g}\right)(x) = 2x - 3$; Domain: $(-\infty, -1)$ or $(-1, \infty)$

11. $(f + g)(x) = \sqrt{x} + x - 4$; Domain: $[0, \infty)$; $(f - g)(x) = \sqrt{x} - x + 4$; Domain: $[0, \infty)$; $(fg)(x) = \sqrt{x}(x - 4)$;

Domain: $[0, \infty)$; $\left(\dfrac{f}{g}\right)(x) = \dfrac{\sqrt{x}}{x - 4}$; Domain: $[0, 4)$ or $(4, \infty)$ **13.** $(f + g)(x) = \dfrac{2x + 2}{x}$; Domain: $(-\infty, 0)$ or $(0, \infty)$; $(f - g)(x) = 2$;

Domain: $(-\infty, 0)$ or $(0, \infty)$; $(fg)(x) = \dfrac{2x + 1}{x^2}$; Domain: $(-\infty, 0)$ or $(0, \infty)$; $\left(\dfrac{f}{g}\right)(x) = 2x + 1$; Domain: $(-\infty, 0)$ or $(0, \infty)$

15. $(f + g)(x) = \sqrt{x + 4} + \sqrt{x - 1}$; Domain: $[1, \infty)$; $(f - g)(x) = \sqrt{x + 4} - \sqrt{x - 1}$; Domain: $[1, \infty)$; $(fg)(x) = \sqrt{x^2 + 3x - 4}$;

Domain: $[1, \infty)$; $\left(\dfrac{f}{g}\right)(x) = \dfrac{\sqrt{x + 4}}{\sqrt{x - 1}}$; Domain: $(1, \infty)$ **17. a.** $(f \circ g)(x) = 2x + 14$ **b.** $(g \circ f)(x) = 2x + 7$ **c.** $(f \circ g)(2) = 18$

19. a. $(f \circ g)(x) = 2x + 5$ **b.** $(g \circ f)(x) = 2x + 9$ **c.** $(f \circ g)(2) = 9$ **21. a.** $(f \circ g)(x) = 20x^2 - 11$

b. $(g \circ f)(x) = 80x^2 - 120x + 43$ **c.** $(f \circ g)(2) = 69$ **23. a.** $(f \circ g)(x) = x^4 - 4x^2 + 6$ **b.** $(g \circ f)(x) = x^4 + 4x^2 + 2$

c. $(f \circ g)(2) = 6$ **25. a.** $(f \circ g)(x) = \sqrt{x - 1}$ **b.** $(g \circ f)(x) = \sqrt{x} - 1$ **c.** $(f \circ g)(2) = 1$ **27. a.** $(f \circ g)(x) = x$

b. $(g \circ f)(x) = x$ **c.** $(f \circ g)(2) = 2$ **29. a.** $(f \circ g)(x) = \dfrac{2x}{1 + 3x}$ **b.** $\left\{ x \Big| x \neq 0 \text{ and } x \neq -\dfrac{1}{3} \right\}$ **31. a.** $(f \circ g)(x) = \dfrac{4}{4 + x}$

b. $\{x | x \neq 0 \text{ and } x \neq -4\}$ **33. a.** $(f \circ g)(x) = \sqrt{x + 3}$ **b.** $\{x | x \geq 0\}$ **35. a.** $(f \circ g)(x) = 5 - x$ **b.** $\{x | x \leq 1\}$

37. a. $(f \circ g)(x) = 8 - x^2$ **b.** $\{x|x < -2 \text{ or } x > 2\}$ **39.** $f(x) = x^4, g(x) = 3x - 1$ **41.** $f(x) = \sqrt[3]{x}, g(x) = x^2 - 9$

43. $f(x) = |x|, g(x) = 2x - 5$ **45.** $f(x) = \dfrac{1}{x}, g(x) = 2x - 3$ **47.** 0 **49.** 10 **51.** 2 **53.** 0 **55.** 4 **57.** −6 **59.** 20; In

2000, veterinary costs in the U.S. for dogs and cats were about $20 billion. **61.** Domain of $D + C = \{1983, 1987, 1991, 1996, 2000\}$
63. $f + g$ represents the total world population in year x. **65.** $(f + g)(2000) \approx 6$ billion people **67.** $(R - C)(20,000) = -200,000$;
The company lost $200,000 since costs exceeded revenues; $(R - C)(30,000) = 0$; The company broke even since revenues equaled cost;
$(R - C)(40,000) = 200,000$; The company made a profit of $200,000. **69. a.** f gives the price of the computer after a $400 discount. g
gives the price of thecomputer after a 25% discount. **b.** $(f \circ g)(x) = 0.75x - 400$. This models the price of a computer after first a 25%
discount and then a $400 discount. **c.** $(g \circ f)(x) = 0.75(x - 400)$. This models the price of a computer after first a $400 discount and
then a 25% discount. **d.** The function $f \circ g$ models the greater discount, since the 25% discount is taken on the regular price first.

77.
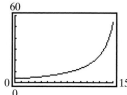
The per capita costs are
increasing over time.

79.
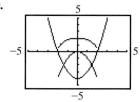
Domain of $f \circ g$ is $[-2, 2]$.

81. Assume f and g are even; then $f(-x) = f(x)$ and
$g(-x) = g(x)$. $(fg)(-x) = f(-x) \cdot g(-x) = f(x) \cdot g(x)$
$= (fg)(x)$, so fg is even.

83.
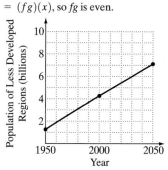

Chapter 2 Review Exercises

1. $m = -\dfrac{1}{2}$; falls **2.** $m = 1$; rises **3.** $m = 0$; horizontal **4.** $m =$ undefined; vertical **5.** $y - 2 = -6(x + 3); y = -6x - 16$

6. using $(1, 6), y - 6 = 2(x - 1); y = 2x + 4$

7. Slope: $\dfrac{2}{5}$; y-intercept: −1 **8.** Slope: −4; y-intercept: 5 **9.** Slope: $-\dfrac{2}{3}$; y-intercept: −2 **10.** Slope: 0; y-intercept: 4

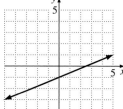 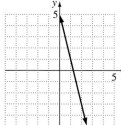 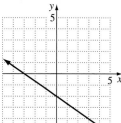 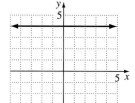

11. a. $y - 480 = 40(x - 2)$ **b.** $y = 40x + 400$ **c.** $1200 billion. **12. a.** Answers may vary. **b.** Answers may vary.
c. Answers may vary. **13.** $y + 7 = -3(x - 4); y = -3x + 5$ **14.** $y - 6 = -3(x + 3); y = -3x - 3$ **15.** 13

16. $2\sqrt{2} \approx 2.83$ **17.** $(-5, 5)$ **18.** $\left(-\dfrac{11}{2}, -2\right)$ **19.** $x^2 + y^2 = 9$ **20.** $(x + 2)^2 + (y - 4)^2 = 36$

21. Center: $(0, 0)$; radius: 1 **22.** Center: $(-2, 3)$; radius: 3 **23.** Center: $(2, -1)$; radius: 3

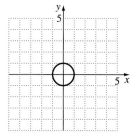 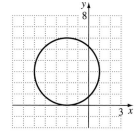 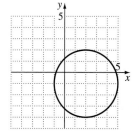

24. Function; Domain: $\{2, 3, 5\}$; Range: $\{7\}$ **25.** Function; Domain: $\{1, 2, 13\}$; Range: $\{10, 500, \pi\}$

26. Not a function; Domain: $\{12, 14\}$; Range: $\{13, 15, 19\}$ **27.** y is a function of x.   **28.** y is a function of x.

29. y is not a function of x.   **30. a.** $f(4) = -23$ **b.** $f(x + 3) = -7x - 16$ **c.** $f(-x) = 5 + 7x$

31. a. $g(0) = 2$ **b.** $g(-2) = 24$ **c.** $g(x - 1) = 3x^2 - 11x + 10$ **d.** $g(-x) = 3x^2 + 5x + 2$

32. a. $f(a) = 4a - 3$ **b.** $f(a + h) = 4a + 4h - 3$ **c.** $\dfrac{f(a + h) - f(a)}{h} = 4$ **d.** $f(a) + f(h) = 4a + 4h - 6$

33. a. $g(13) = 3$ **b.** $g(0) = 4$ **c.** $g(-3) = 7$ **34.** 8   **35.** $2x + h - 13$ **c.** $f(2) = 3$ **36.** $(-\infty, \infty)$

37. $(-\infty, 7)$ or $(7, \infty)$ **38.** $(-\infty, 4]$ **39.** $(-\infty, -1)$ or $(-1, 1)$ or $(1, \infty)$ **40.** $[2, 5)$ or $(5, \infty)$

41. Ordered pairs: $(-1, 9), (0, 4),$
$(1, 1), (2, 0), (3, 1), (4, 4)$.

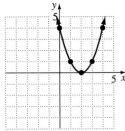

Domain: $(-\infty, \infty)$
Range: $[0, \infty)$

42. Ordered pairs: $(-1, 3), (0, 2),$
$(1, 1), (2, 0), (3, 1), (4, 2)$.

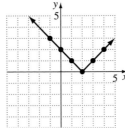

Domain: $(-\infty, \infty)$
Range: $[0, \infty)$

43. a. Domain: $[-3, 5)$
b. Range: $[-5, 0]$
c. x-intercept: -3
d. y-intercept: -2
e. increasing: $(-2, 0)$ or $(3, 5)$
    decreasing: $(-3, -2)$ or $(0, 3)$
f. $f(-2) = -3$ and $f(3) = -5$

44. a. Domain: $(-\infty, \infty)$
b. Range: $(-\infty, \infty)$
c. x-intercepts: -2 and 3
d. y-intercept: 3
e. increasing: $(-5, 0)$;
    decreasing: $(-\infty, -5)$ or $(0, \infty)$
f. $f(-2) = 0$ and $f(6) = -3$

45. a. Domain: $(-\infty, \infty)$ **b.** Range: $[-2, 2]$ **c.** x-intercept: 0 **d.** y-intercept: 0 **e.** increasing: $(-2, 2)$; constant: $(-\infty, -2)$
or $(2, \infty)$ **f.** $f(-9) = -2$ and $f(14) = 2$ **46. a.** $0; f(0) = -2$ **b.** $-2, 3; f(-2) = -3, f(3) = -5$

47. a. $0; f(0) = 3$ **b.** $-5; f(-5) = -6$ **48.** not a function   **49.** function   **50.** function   **51.** not a function   **52.** 10

53. about $1167   **54.** odd; symmetric with respect to the origin   **55.** even; symmetric with respect to the y-axis

56. odd; symmetric with respect to the origin   **57. a.** yes; The graph passes the vertical line test.   **b.** Decreasing: $(3, 12)$;
The vulture descended.   **c.** Constant: $(0, 3)$ and $(12, 17)$; The vulture's height held steady during the first 3 seconds and the vulture
was on the ground for 5 seconds.   **d.** Increasing: $(17, 30)$; The vulture was ascending.

58.

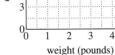

59.

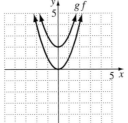

60.

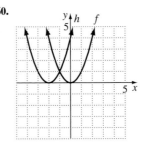

61.

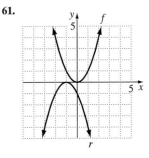

62.

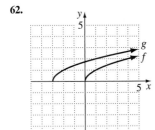

63.

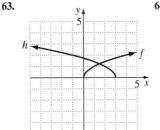

64.

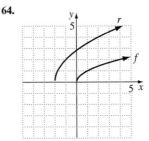

65.

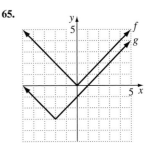

66.

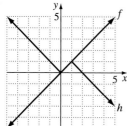

67.

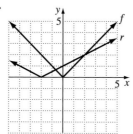

68.

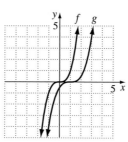

69.

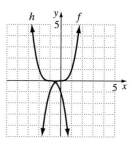

70.

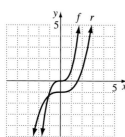

71.

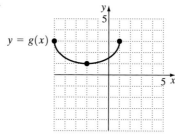

72.

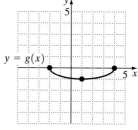

73.

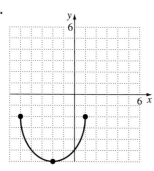

74. $(f + g)(x) = 4x - 6$; Domain: $(-\infty, \infty)$; $(f - g)(x) = 2x + 4$; Domain: $(-\infty, \infty)$;
$(fg)(x) = 3x^2 - 16x + 5$; Domain: $(-\infty, \infty)$; $\left(\dfrac{f}{g}\right)(x) = \dfrac{3x - 1}{x - 5}$; Domain: $(-\infty, 5)$ or $(5, \infty)$

75. $(f + g)(x) = 2x^2 + x$; Domain: $(-\infty, \infty)$; $(f - g)(x) = x + 2$; Domain: $(-\infty, \infty)$;
$(fg)(x) = x^4 + x^3 - x - 1$; Domain: $(-\infty, \infty)$; $\left(\dfrac{f}{g}\right)(x) = \dfrac{x^2 + x + 1}{x^2 - 1}$;
Domain: $(-\infty, -1)$ or $(-1, 1)$ or $(1, \infty)$

76. $(f + g)(x) = \sqrt{x + 7} + \sqrt{x - 2}$; Domain: $[2, \infty)$; $(f - g)(x) = \sqrt{x + 7} - \sqrt{x - 2}$;
Domain: $[2, \infty)$; $(fg)(x) = \sqrt{x^2 + 5x - 14}$; Domain: $[2, \infty)$; $\left(\dfrac{f}{g}\right)(x) = \dfrac{\sqrt{x + 7}}{\sqrt{x - 2}}$;
Domain: $(2, \infty)$

77. a. $(f \circ g)(x) = 16x^2 - 8x + 4$ **b.** $(g \circ f)(x) = 4x^2 + 11$ **c.** $(f \circ g)(3) = 124$ **78. a.** $(f \circ g)(x) = \sqrt{x + 1}$
b. $(g \circ f)(x) = \sqrt{x} + 1$ **c.** $(f \circ g)(3) = 2$ **79. a.** $\dfrac{1 + x}{1 - 2x}$ **b.** $\{x | x \neq 0 \text{ and } x \neq \frac{1}{2}\}$ **80. a.** $\sqrt{x + 2}$ **b.** $\{x | x \geq -2\}$

81. $f(x) = x^4$, $g(x) = x^2 + 2x - 1$ **82.** $f(x) = \sqrt[3]{x}$, $g(x) = 7x + 4$

Chapter 2 Test

1. using $(2, 1)$, $y - 1 = 3(x - 2)$; $y = 3x - 5$ **2.** $y - 6 = 4(x + 4)$; $y = 4x + 22$ **3. a.** $y = 42x + 320$ **b.** $866
4. Center: $(-2, 3)$; radius: 4   **5.** b, c, d   **6.** $f(x - 1) = x^2 - 4x + 8$ **7.** $g(-1) = 4$; $g(7) = 2$ **8.** Domain: $(-\infty, 4]$
9. $2x + h + 11$ **10. a.** $f(4) - f(-3) = 5$ **b.** Domain: $(-5, 6]$ **c.** Range: $[-4, 5]$ **d.** Increasing: $(-1, 2)$
e. Decreasing: $(-5, -1)$ or $(2, 6)$ **f.** 2; $f(2) = 5$ **g.** -1; $f(-1) = -4$ **h.** $-4, 1,$ and 5 **i.** -3 **11.** 48   **12.** $f(x)$ is even and is
symmetric with respect to the y-axis. The graph in the figure is symmetric with respect to the origin.   **13.** The graph of f is shifted 3 to
the right to obtain the graph of g. Then the graph of g is stretched by a factor of 2 and reflected about the x-axis to obtain the graph of h.

14.

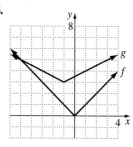

15. $(f - g)(x) = x^2 - 2x - 2$.   **16.** $\left(\dfrac{f}{g}\right)(x) = \dfrac{x^2 + 3x - 4}{5x - 2}$; Domain: $\left(-\infty, \dfrac{2}{5}\right)$ or $\left(\dfrac{2}{5}, \infty\right)$

17. $(f \circ g)(x) = 25x^2 - 5x - 6$ **18.** $(g \circ f)(x) = 5x^2 + 15x - 22$.

19. $f(g(2)) = 84$.   **20.** $\dfrac{7x}{2 - 4x}$; $\{x | x \neq 0 \text{ or } x \neq \frac{1}{2}\}$.   **21.** $f(x) = x^7$, $g(x) = 2x + 13$

CHAPTER 3

Section 3.1

Check Point Exercises

1. solution   **2.** $\{(3,2)\}$ **3.** $\{(1,-2)\}$ **4.** $\{(2,-1)\}$ **5.** $\left\{\left(\dfrac{23}{16},\dfrac{3}{8}\right)\right\}$ **6.** $\varnothing$ **7.** $\{(x,y)|y=4x-4\}$ **8. a.** $C(x)=300{,}000+30x$

b. $R(x)=80x$ **c.** $(6000,480{,}000)$; The company will break even if it produces and sells 6000 pairs of shoes.   **9.** $\$30$; 400 units

Exercise Set 3.1

1. solution   **3.** not a solution   **5.** $\{(1,3)\}$ **7.** $\{(5,1)\}$ **9.** $\{(-22,-5)\}$ **11.** $\{(0,0)\}$ **13.** $\{(3,-2)\}$ **15.** $\{(5,4)\}$

17. $\{(7,3)\}$ **19.** $\{(2,-1)\}$ **21.** $\{(3,0)\}$ **23.** $\{(-4,3)\}$ **25.** $\{(3,1)\}$ **27.** $\{(1,-2)\}$ **29.** $\left\{\left(\dfrac{7}{25},-\dfrac{1}{25}\right)\right\}$ **31.** $\varnothing$

33. $\{(x,y)|y=3x-5\}$ **35.** $\{(1,4)\}$ **37.** $\{(x,y)|x+3y=2\}$ **39.** $\{(-5,-1)\}$ **41.** $\left\{\left(\dfrac{29}{22},-\dfrac{5}{11}\right)\right\}$

43. $x+y=7$; $x-y=-1$; 3 and 4   **45.** $3x-y=1$; $x+2y=12$; 2 and 5   **47. a.** $C(x)=18{,}000+20x$ **b.** $R(x)=80x$
c. $(300,24{,}000)$; This means the company will break even if it produces and sells 300 canoes.   **49. a.** $C(x)=30{,}000+2500x$
b. $R(x)=3125$ **c.** $(48,150{,}000)$; The play will break even if 48 sold-out performances are produced.   **51. a.** 6500 tickets can be sold.

6200 tickets can be supplied.   **b.** $\$50$; 6250 tickets   **53.** 2004; $12\dfrac{8}{33}$; The lines intersect at $\left(39\dfrac{13}{33},12\dfrac{8}{33}\right)$.   **55. a.** $E(x)=508+25x$

b. $E(x)=345+9x$ **c.** 26; 2011; $\$1158$ for college graduates, $\$579$ for high school graduates   **57.** Pan pizza: 1120 calories; beef
burrito: 430 calories   **59.** Scrambled eggs: 366 mg cholesterol; Double Beef Whopper: 175 mg cholesterol   **61.** 50 rooms with kitchen
facilities, 150 rooms without kitchen facilities   **63.** 100 ft long by 80 ft wide   **65.** Rate rowing in still water: 6 mph; rate of the current:
2 mph   **67.** $x=55$, $y=35$ **81.** Answers may vary.   **83.** the twin who always lies

Section 3.2

Check Point Exercises

1. $(-1)-2(-4)+3(5)=22$; $2(-1)-3(-4)-5=5$; $3(-1)+(-4)-5(5)=-32$ **2.** $\{(1,4,-3)\}$ **3.** $\{(4,5,3)\}$
4. $y=3x^2-12x+13$

Exercise Set 3.2

1. solution   **3.** solution   **5.** $\{(2,3,3)\}$ **7.** $\{(2,-1,1)\}$ **9.** $\left\{\left(\dfrac{1}{3},-\dfrac{2}{5},\dfrac{1}{2}\right)\right\}$ **11.** $\{(3,1,5)\}$ **13.** $\{(1,0,-3)\}$

15. $\{(1,-5,-6)\}$ **17.** $\left\{\left(\dfrac{1}{2},\dfrac{1}{3},-1\right)\right\}$ **19.** 7, 4 and 5   **21.** $y=2x^2-x+3$ **23.** $y=2x^2+x-5$

25. a. $(0,1180)$, $(1,1070)$, $(2,1230)$ **b.** $c=1180$ $a+b+c=1070$ $4a+2b+c=1230$ **c.** $y=135x^2-245x+1180$
27. a. $y=-16x^2+40x+200$ **b.** $y=0$ when $x=5$; The ball hit the ground after 5 seconds   **29.** Carnegie: $\$100$ billion; Vanderbilt:
$\$96$ billion; Gates: $\$60$ billion   **31.** 200 $\$8$ tickets; 150 $\$10$ tickets; 50 $\$12$ tickets   **33.** $\$1200$ at 8%, $\$2000$ at 10%, and $\$3500$ at 12%
35. $x=60$, $y=55$, $z=65$ **43.** Answers may vary.

Section 3.3

Check Point Exercises

1. $\{(4,-3,1)\}$ **2. a.** $\left[\begin{array}{rrr|r} 1 & 6 & -3 & 7 \\ 4 & 12 & -20 & 8 \\ -3 & -2 & 1 & -9 \end{array}\right]$ **b.** $\left[\begin{array}{rrr|r} 1 & 3 & -5 & 2 \\ 1 & 6 & -3 & 7 \\ -3 & -2 & 1 & -9 \end{array}\right]$ **c.** $\left[\begin{array}{rrr|r} 4 & 12 & -20 & 8 \\ 1 & 6 & -3 & 7 \\ 0 & 16 & -8 & 12 \end{array}\right]$

3. $\{(5,2,3)\}$ **4.** $\{(1,-1,2,-3)\}$ **5.** $\{(5,2,3)\}$

Exercise Set 3.3

1. $\left[\begin{array}{rrr|r} 2 & 1 & 2 & 2 \\ 3 & -5 & -1 & 4 \\ 1 & -2 & -3 & -6 \end{array}\right]$ **3.** $\left[\begin{array}{rrr|r} 1 & -1 & 1 & 8 \\ 0 & 1 & -12 & -15 \\ 0 & 0 & 1 & 1 \end{array}\right]$ **5.** $\left[\begin{array}{rrr|r} 5 & -2 & -3 & 0 \\ 1 & 1 & 0 & 5 \\ 2 & 0 & -3 & 4 \end{array}\right]$ **7.** $\left[\begin{array}{rrrr|r} 2 & 5 & -3 & 1 & 2 \\ 0 & 3 & 1 & 0 & 4 \\ 1 & -1 & 5 & 0 & 9 \\ 5 & -5 & -2 & 0 & 1 \end{array}\right]$

9. $5x + 3z = -11$
$y - 4z = 12$
$7x + 2y = 3$

11. $w + x + 4y + z = 3$
$-w + x - y = 7$
$2w + 5z = 11$
$12y + 4z = 5$

13. $x - 4z = 5$; $\left\{\left(3, 7, -\dfrac{1}{2}\right)\right\}$
$y - 12z = 13$
$z = -\dfrac{1}{2}$

15. $x + \dfrac{1}{2}y + z = \dfrac{11}{2}$; $(\{1, 1, 4\})$
$y + \dfrac{3}{2}z = 7$
$z = 4$

17. $w - x + y + z = 3$; $\{(2, 1, -1, 3)\}$
$x - 2y - z = 0$
$y + 6z = 17$
$z = 3$

19. $\begin{bmatrix} 1 & -3 & 2 & | & 5 \\ 1 & 5 & -5 & | & 0 \\ 3 & 0 & 4 & | & 7 \end{bmatrix}$

21. $\begin{bmatrix} 1 & -3 & 2 & | & 0 \\ 0 & 10 & -7 & | & 7 \\ 2 & -2 & 1 & | & 3 \end{bmatrix}$

23. $\begin{bmatrix} 1 & -1 & 1 & 1 & | & 3 \\ 0 & 1 & -2 & -1 & | & 0 \\ 0 & 2 & 1 & 2 & | & 5 \\ 0 & 6 & -3 & -1 & | & -9 \end{bmatrix}$

25. $R_2: -3, -18$; $R_3: -12, -15$; $R_2: -\dfrac{3}{5}, -\dfrac{18}{5}$; $R_3: -12, -15$ **27.** $\{(1, -1, 2)\}$ **29.** $\{(3, -1, -1)\}$ **31.** $\{2, -1, 1\}$ **33.** $\{(2, 1, 1)\}$

35. $\{(2, -1, 1)\}$ **37.** $\{(-1, 2, -2)\}$ **39.** $\{(1, 2, -1)\}$ **41.** $\{(1, 2, 3, -2)\}$ **43.** $\{(0, -3, 0, -3)\}$ **45. a.** $\{(-10, 475, 3500)\}$

b. 7760; 12 years into the program, there are 7760 alligators.   **47.** $x + y + z = 100$; yes: 34%; no: 61%; not sure: 5%
$x + z = y - 22$
$2x = y + 7$

49. $40x + 200y + 400z = 660$; 4 oz of Food A; $\dfrac{1}{2}$ oz of Food B; 1 oz of Food C **61.** $y = x^3 + 2x^2 + 5x - 3$
$5x + 2y + 4z = 25$
$30x + 10y + 300z = 425$

Section 3.4

Check Point Exercises

1. a. -4 **b.** -17 **2.** $\{(4, -2)\}$ **3.** 80   **4.** -24 **5.** $\{(2, -3, 4)\}$ **6.** -250

Exercise Set 3.4

1. 1   **3.** -29 **5.** 0   **7.** 33   **9.** $-\dfrac{7}{16}$ **11.** $\{(5, 2)\}$ **13.** $\{(2, -3)\}$ **15.** $\{(3, -1)\}$ **17.** The system is dependent.

19. $\{(4, 2)\}$ **21.** $\{(7, 4)\}$ **23.** The system is inconsistent.   **25.** The system is dependent.   **27.** 72   **29.** -75 **31.** 0

33. $\{(-5, -2, 7)\}$ **35.** $\{(2, -3, 4)\}$ **37.** $\{(3, -1, 2)\}$ **39.** $\{(2, 3, 1)\}$ **41.** -200 **43.** 195   **45.** 28 sq units   **47.** yes

49. The equation of the line is $y = -\dfrac{11}{5}x + \dfrac{8}{5}$.   **61.** 13,200

63. a. a^2 **b.** a^3 **c.** a^4 **d.** Each determinant has zeros below the main diagonal and a's everywhere else.
e. Each determinant equals a raised to the power equal to the order of the determinant.
65. The sign of the value is changed when 2 columns are interchanged in a 2nd order determinant.

67. $\begin{vmatrix} x & y & 1 \\ x_1 & y_1 & 1 \\ x_2 & y_2 & 1 \end{vmatrix} = x(y_1 - y_2) - y(x_1 - x_2) + (x_1y_2 - x_2y_1) = 0$; solving for y,

$y = \dfrac{y_1 - y_2}{x_1 - x_2}x + \dfrac{x_1y_2 - x_2y_1}{x_1 - x_2}$, and $m = \dfrac{y_1 - y_2}{x_1 - x_2}$ and $b = \dfrac{x_1y_2 - x_2y_1}{x_1 - x_2}$.

Chapter 3 Review Exercises

1. $\{(1, 5)\}$ **2.** $\{(2, 3)\}$ **3.** $\{(2, -3)\}$ **4.** $\varnothing$ **5.** $\{(x, y) | 3x - 6y = 12\}$ **6. a.** $C(x) = 60,000 + 200x$ **b.** $R(x) = 450x$
c. $(240, 108,000)$; This means the company will break even if it produces and sells 240 desks.   **7.** 250 copies can be supplied and sold for
$12.50 each.   **8.** 5.8 million pounds of potato chips, 4.6 million pounds of tortilla chips   **9.** $80 per day for the room, $60 per day for the car
10. 3 apples and 2 avocados   **11.** $\{(0, 1, 2)\}$ **12.** $\{(2, 1, -1)\}$ **13.** $y = 3x^2 - 4x + 5$ **14. a.** $(0, 3.5), (15, 5.0), (29, 4.1)$
b. $c = 3.5$ $225a + 15b + c = 5.0$ $841a + 29b + c = 4.1$ **15.** United States: 22; Colombia: 18; India: 10

16. $x + y + 3z = 12$; $\{(1, 2, 3)\}$ **17.** $w - 2y + 2z = 1$; $\{(3, -1, 2, 1)\}$ **18.** $\begin{bmatrix} 1 & 2 & 2 & | & 2 \\ 0 & 1 & -1 & | & 2 \\ 0 & 0 & 9 & | & -9 \end{bmatrix}$ **19.** $\begin{bmatrix} 1 & -1 & \frac{1}{2} & | & -\frac{1}{2} \\ 1 & 2 & -1 & | & 2 \\ 6 & 4 & 3 & | & 5 \end{bmatrix}$
$y - 2z = -4$ $x + y - z = 0$
$z = 3$ $y - \dfrac{7}{3}z = -\dfrac{1}{3}$
$z = 1$

20. $\{(1, 3, -4)\}$ **21.** $\{(-2, -1, 0)\}$ **22.** $\{(2, -2, 3, 4)\}$ **23. a.** $a = -2; b = 32; c = 42$ **b.** 2:00 P.M.; 170 parts per million

24. 17 **25.** 4 **26.** −86 **27.** −236 **28.** 4 **29.** 16 **30.** $\left\{\left(\frac{7}{4}, -\frac{25}{8}\right)\right\}$ **31.** $\{(2, -7)\}$

32. $\{(23, -12, 3)\}$ **33.** $\{(-3, 2, 1)\}$ **34.** $a = \frac{5}{8}; b = -50; c = 1150$; 30- and 50-year-olds are involved in an average of 212.5 automobile accidents per day.

Chapter 3 Test

1. $\{(1, -3)\}$ **2.** $\{(4, -2)\}$ **3.** $\{(1, 3, 2)\}$ **4.** $\{(4, -3), (-3, 4)\}$ **5.** $\{(3, 2), (3, -2), (-3, 2), (-3, -2)\}$

6. $\left\{\left(-3, \frac{1}{2}, 1\right)\right\}$ **7.** $\{(z, z - 1, z)\}$ **8.** 18 **9.** $x = 2$

CHAPTER 4

Section 4.1

Check Point Exercises

1. a. **b.** **c.** **d.**

2. a. 40° **b.** 225° **3. a.** 12°; 102° **b.** no complementary angle; 30° **4.** 3.5 radians **5. a.** $\frac{\pi}{3}$ radians **b.** $\frac{3\pi}{2}$ radians

c. $-\frac{5\pi}{3}$ radians **6. a.** 45° **b.** −240° **c.** 343.8° **7.** $\frac{3\pi}{2}$ in. ≈ 4.71 in. **8.** 135π in./min ≈ 424 in./min

Exercise Set 4.1

1. quadrant II **3.** quadrant III **5.** quadrant I **7.** obtuse **9.** straight

11. **13.** **15.** **17.**

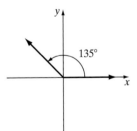

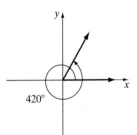

19. 35° **21.** 210° **23.** 315° **25.** 38°; 128° **27.** 52.6°; 142.6° **29.** no complement; 69° **31.** 4 radians **33.** $\frac{4}{3}$ radians

35. 4 radians **37.** $\frac{\pi}{4}$ radians **39.** $\frac{3\pi}{4}$ radians **41.** $\frac{5\pi}{3}$ radians **43.** $-\frac{5\pi}{4}$ radians **45.** 90° **47.** 120° **49.** 210° **51.** −540°

53. 0.31 radians **55.** −0.70 radians **57.** 3.49 radians **59.** 114.59° **61.** 13.85° **63.** −275.02° **65.** 3π in. ≈ 9.42 in.

67. 10π ft ≈ 31.42 ft. **69.** $\frac{12\pi \text{ radians}}{\text{second}}$ **71.** 60°; $\frac{\pi}{3}$ radians **73.** $\frac{8\pi}{3}$ in. ≈ 8.38 in. **75.** 12π in. ≈ 37.70 in. **77.** 2 radians; 114.59°

79. 2094 mi **81.** 1047 mph **83.** 1508 ft/min **97.** 30.25° **99.** 30°25′12″ **101.** smaller than a right angle **103.** 1815 mi

Section 4.2

Check Point Exercises

1. $\sin\theta = \dfrac{3}{5}$; $\cos\theta = \dfrac{4}{5}$; $\tan\theta = \dfrac{3}{4}$; $\csc\theta = \dfrac{5}{3}$; $\sec\theta = \dfrac{5}{4}$; $\cot\theta = \dfrac{4}{3}$ **2.** $\sqrt{2}$; $\sqrt{2}$; 1 **3.** $\sqrt{3}$; $\dfrac{\sqrt{3}}{3}$ **4.** $\tan\theta = \dfrac{2\sqrt{5}}{5}$; $\csc\theta = \dfrac{3}{2}$;

$\sec\theta = \dfrac{3\sqrt{5}}{5}$; $\cot\theta = \dfrac{\sqrt{5}}{2}$ **5.** $\dfrac{\sqrt{3}}{2}$ **6. a.** $\cos 44°$ **b.** $\tan\dfrac{5\pi}{12}$ **7. a.** 0.9553 **b.** 1.0025 **8.** 333.9 yd **9.** $54°$

Exercise Set 4.2

1. 15; $\sin\theta = \dfrac{3}{5}$; $\cos\theta = \dfrac{4}{5}$; $\tan\theta = \dfrac{3}{4}$; $\csc\theta = \dfrac{5}{3}$; $\sec\theta = \dfrac{5}{4}$; $\cot\theta = \dfrac{4}{3}$ **3.** 20; $\sin\theta = \dfrac{20}{29}$; $\cos\theta = \dfrac{21}{29}$; $\tan\theta = \dfrac{20}{21}$; $\csc\theta = \dfrac{29}{20}$;

$\sec\theta = \dfrac{29}{21}$; $\cot\theta = \dfrac{21}{20}$ **5.** 24; $\sin\theta = \dfrac{5}{13}$; $\cos\theta = \dfrac{12}{13}$; $\tan\theta = \dfrac{5}{12}$; $\csc\theta = \dfrac{13}{5}$; $\sec\theta = \dfrac{13}{12}$; $\cot\theta = \dfrac{12}{5}$

7. 28; $\sin\theta = \dfrac{4}{5}$; $\cos\theta = \dfrac{3}{5}$; $\tan\theta = \dfrac{4}{3}$; $\csc\theta = \dfrac{5}{4}$; $\sec\theta = \dfrac{5}{3}$; $\cot\theta = \dfrac{3}{4}$ **9.** $\dfrac{\sqrt{3}}{2}$ **11.** $\sqrt{2}$ **13.** $\sqrt{3}$ **15.** 0

17. $\tan\theta = \dfrac{8}{15}$; $\csc\theta = \dfrac{17}{8}$; $\sec\theta = \dfrac{17}{15}$; $\cot\theta = \dfrac{15}{8}$ **19.** $\tan\theta = \dfrac{\sqrt{2}}{4}$; $\csc\theta = 3$; $\sec\theta = \dfrac{3\sqrt{2}}{4}$; $\cot\theta = 2\sqrt{2}$ **21.** $\dfrac{\sqrt{13}}{7}$

23. $\dfrac{5}{8}$ **25.** 1 **27.** 1 **29.** 1 **31.** $\cos 83°$ **33.** $\sec 65°$ **35.** $\cot\dfrac{7\pi}{18}$ **37.** $\sin\dfrac{\pi}{10}$ **39.** 0.6157 **41.** 0.6420 **43.** 3.4203

45. 0.9511 **47.** 3.7321 **49.** 188 cm **51.** 182 in. **53.** 41 m **55.** $17°$ **57.** $78°$ **59.** 1.147 radians **61.** 0.3950 radians

63. 529 yd **65.** $36°$ **67.** 2879 ft **69.** $37°$

83. $0.92106, -0.19735$; $0.95534, -0.148878$; $0.98007, -0.099667$; $0.99500, -0.04996$; $0.99995, -0.005$; $0.9999995, -0.0005$; 0.999999995, -0.00005; $0.99999999995, -0.000005$; $\dfrac{\cos\theta - 1}{\theta}$ approaches 0 as θ approaches 0.

85. In a right triangle, the hypotenuse is greater than either other side. Therefore, both $\dfrac{\text{opposite}}{\text{hypotenuse}}$ and $\dfrac{\text{adjacent}}{\text{hypotenuse}}$ must be less than 1 for an acute angle in a right triangle.

87. a. 357 ft **b.** 394 ft

Section 4.3

Check Point Exercises

1. $\sin\theta = -\dfrac{3}{5}$; $\cos\theta = \dfrac{4}{5}$; $\tan\theta = -\dfrac{3}{4}$; $\csc\theta = -\dfrac{5}{3}$; $\sec\theta = \dfrac{5}{4}$; $\cot\theta = -\dfrac{4}{3}$ **2. a.** 1; undefined **b.** 0; 1 **c.** -1; undefined

d. 0; -1 **3.** quadrant III **4.** $\dfrac{\sqrt{10}}{10}$; $-\dfrac{\sqrt{10}}{3}$ **5. a.** $30°$ **b.** $\dfrac{\pi}{4}$ **c.** $60°$ **d.** 0.46 **6. a.** $-\dfrac{\sqrt{3}}{2}$ **b.** 1 **c.** $\dfrac{2\sqrt{3}}{3}$

Exercise Set 4.3

1. $\sin\theta = \dfrac{3}{5}$; $\cos\theta = -\dfrac{4}{5}$; $\tan\theta = -\dfrac{3}{4}$; $\csc\theta = \dfrac{5}{3}$; $\sec\theta = -\dfrac{5}{4}$; $\cot\theta = -\dfrac{4}{3}$ **3.** $\sin\theta = \dfrac{3\sqrt{13}}{13}$; $\cos\theta = \dfrac{2\sqrt{13}}{13}$; $\tan\theta = \dfrac{3}{2}$; $\csc\theta = \dfrac{\sqrt{13}}{3}$;

$\sec\theta = \dfrac{\sqrt{13}}{2}$; $\cot\theta = \dfrac{2}{3}$ **5.** $\sin\theta = -\dfrac{\sqrt{2}}{2}$; $\cos\theta = \dfrac{\sqrt{2}}{2}$; $\tan\theta = -1$; $\csc\theta = -\sqrt{2}$; $\sec\theta = \sqrt{2}$; $\cot\theta = -1$ **7.** $\sin\theta = -\dfrac{5\sqrt{29}}{29}$;

$\cos\theta = -\dfrac{2\sqrt{29}}{29}$; $\tan\theta = \dfrac{5}{2}$; $\csc\theta = -\dfrac{\sqrt{29}}{5}$; $\sec\theta = -\dfrac{\sqrt{29}}{2}$; $\cot\theta = \dfrac{2}{5}$ **9.** -1 **11.** -1 **13.** undefined **15.** 0 **17.** quadrant I

19. quadrant III **21.** quadrant II **23.** $\sin\theta = -\dfrac{4}{5}$; $\tan\theta = \dfrac{4}{3}$; $\csc\theta = -\dfrac{5}{4}$; $\sec\theta = -\dfrac{5}{3}$; $\cot\theta = \dfrac{3}{4}$ **25.** $\cos\theta = -\dfrac{12}{13}$; $\tan\theta = -\dfrac{5}{12}$;

$\csc\theta = \dfrac{13}{5}$; $\sec\theta = -\dfrac{13}{12}$; $\cot\theta = -\dfrac{12}{5}$ **27.** $\sin\theta = -\dfrac{15}{17}$; $\tan\theta = -\dfrac{15}{8}$; $\csc\theta = -\dfrac{17}{15}$; $\sec\theta = \dfrac{17}{8}$; $\cot\theta = -\dfrac{8}{15}$ **29.** $\sin\theta = \dfrac{2\sqrt{13}}{13}$;

$\cos\theta = -\dfrac{3\sqrt{13}}{13}$; $\csc\theta = \dfrac{\sqrt{13}}{2}$; $\sec\theta = -\dfrac{\sqrt{13}}{3}$; $\cot\theta = -\dfrac{3}{2}$ **31.** $\sin\theta = -\dfrac{4}{5}$; $\cos\theta = -\dfrac{3}{5}$; $\csc\theta = -\dfrac{5}{4}$; $\sec\theta = -\dfrac{5}{3}$; $\cot\theta = \dfrac{3}{4}$

33. $\sin\theta = -\dfrac{2\sqrt{2}}{3}$; $\cos\theta = -\dfrac{1}{3}$; $\tan\theta = 2\sqrt{2}$; $\csc\theta = -\dfrac{3\sqrt{2}}{4}$; $\cot\theta = \dfrac{\sqrt{2}}{4}$ **35.** $20°$ **37.** $25°$ **39.** $5°$ **41.** $\dfrac{\pi}{4}$ **43.** $\dfrac{\pi}{6}$ **45.** $30°$

47. $25°$ **49.** 1.56 **51.** $-\dfrac{\sqrt{2}}{2}$ **53.** $\dfrac{\sqrt{3}}{3}$ **55.** $\sqrt{3}$ **57.** $\dfrac{\sqrt{3}}{2}$ **59.** -2 **61.** 1 **63.** $\dfrac{\sqrt{3}}{2}$ **65.** -1

Section 4.4

Check Point Exercises

1. $\sin \pi = 0$; $\cos \pi = -1$; $\tan \pi = 0$; $\csc \pi$ is undefined; $\sec \pi = -1$; $\cot \pi$ is undefined **2. a.** $\dfrac{1}{2}$ **b.** $-\dfrac{\sqrt{3}}{3}$ **3. a.** $\dfrac{\sqrt{2}}{2}$ **b.** $\sqrt{3}$

Exercise Set 4.4

1. $\sin t = \dfrac{8}{17}$; $\cos t = -\dfrac{15}{17}$; $\tan t = -\dfrac{8}{15}$; $\csc t = \dfrac{17}{8}$; $\sec t = -\dfrac{17}{15}$; $\cot t = -\dfrac{15}{8}$ **3.** $\sin\left(-\dfrac{\pi}{4}\right) = -\dfrac{\sqrt{2}}{2}$; $\cos\left(-\dfrac{\pi}{4}\right) = \dfrac{\sqrt{2}}{2}$;

$\tan\left(-\dfrac{\pi}{4}\right) = -1$; $\csc\left(-\dfrac{\pi}{4}\right) = -\sqrt{2}$; $\sec\left(-\dfrac{\pi}{4}\right) = \sqrt{2}$; $\cot\left(-\dfrac{\pi}{4}\right) = -1$ **5.** $-\dfrac{\sqrt{2}}{2}$ **7.** 2 **9.** $-\dfrac{\sqrt{2}}{2}$ **11.** $\dfrac{\sqrt{3}}{3}$ **13. a.** 12 hr

b. 20.3 hr **c.** 3.7 hr **15. a.** 1; 0; −1; 0; 1 **b.** 28 days **23.** 0 **25.** $-\dfrac{1}{4}$ **c.** 9.6hr

Chapter 4 Review Exercises

1.   **2.**   **3.**   **4.**

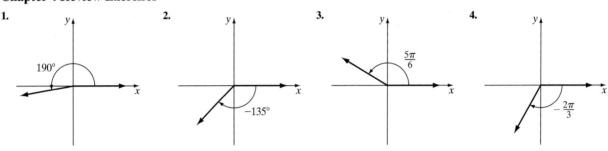

5. 40° **6.** 275° **7.** 17°; 107° **8.** no complement; $\dfrac{\pi}{3}$ radians **9.** 4.5 radians **10.** $\dfrac{\pi}{12}$ radians **11.** $\dfrac{2\pi}{3}$ radians **12.** $\dfrac{7\pi}{4}$ radians

13. 300° **14.** 252° **15.** −150° **16.** $\dfrac{15\pi}{2}$ ft ≈ 23.56 ft **17.** 20.6π radians per min **18.** 42,412 ft per min **19.** $\sin \theta = \dfrac{3}{5}$;

$\cos \theta = \dfrac{4}{5}$; $\tan \theta = \dfrac{3}{4}$; $\csc \theta = \dfrac{5}{3}$; $\sec \theta = \dfrac{5}{4}$; $\cot \theta = \dfrac{4}{3}$ **20.** $\sqrt{3}$ **21.** $\dfrac{\sqrt{2}}{2}$ **22.** $\dfrac{2\sqrt{3}}{3}$ **23.** 1 **24.** $\dfrac{\sqrt{21}}{7}$ **25.** $\cos 20°$

26. $\sin 0$ **27.** 42 mm **28.** 23 cm **29.** 37 in. **30.** 772 ft **31.** 31 m **32.** 56° **33.** $\sin \theta = -\dfrac{5\sqrt{26}}{26}$; $\cos \theta = -\dfrac{\sqrt{26}}{26}$; $\tan \theta = 5$;

$\csc \theta = -\dfrac{\sqrt{26}}{5}$; $\sec \theta = -\sqrt{26}$; $\cot \theta = \dfrac{1}{5}$ **34.** $\sin \theta = -1$; $\cos \theta = 0$; $\tan \theta$ is undefined; $\csc \theta = -1$; $\sec \theta$ is undefined; $\cot \theta = 0$

35. quadrant I **36.** quadrant III **37.** $\sin \theta = -\dfrac{\sqrt{21}}{5}$; $\tan \theta = -\dfrac{\sqrt{21}}{2}$; $\csc \theta = -\dfrac{5\sqrt{21}}{21}$; $\sec \theta = \dfrac{5}{2}$; $\cot \theta = -\dfrac{2\sqrt{21}}{21}$

38. $\sin \theta = \dfrac{\sqrt{10}}{10}$; $\cos \theta = -\dfrac{3\sqrt{10}}{10}$; $\csc \theta = \sqrt{10}$; $\sec \theta = -\dfrac{\sqrt{10}}{3}$; $\cot \theta = -3$ **39.** 85° **40.** $\dfrac{3\pi}{8}$ **41.** 50° **42.** $-\dfrac{\sqrt{3}}{2}$ **43.** $-\sqrt{3}$

44. $\sqrt{2}$ **45.** $\dfrac{\sqrt{3}}{2}$ **46.** $-\sqrt{3}$ **47.** $-\dfrac{2\sqrt{3}}{3}$ **48.** $-\dfrac{\sqrt{3}}{2}$ **49.** $\dfrac{\sqrt{2}}{2}$ **50.** 1

Chapter 4 Test

1. $\dfrac{3\pi}{4}$ radians **2.** $\dfrac{4\pi}{13}$ **3.** $\dfrac{25\pi}{3}$ ft ≈ 26.18 ft **4.** $\sin \theta = \dfrac{5\sqrt{29}}{29}$; $\cos \theta = -\dfrac{2\sqrt{29}}{29}$; $\tan \theta = -\dfrac{5}{2}$; $\csc \theta = \dfrac{\sqrt{29}}{5}$; $\sec \theta = -\dfrac{\sqrt{29}}{2}$; $\cot \theta = -\dfrac{2}{5}$

5. quadrant III **6.** $\sin \theta = -\dfrac{2\sqrt{2}}{3}$; $\tan \theta = -2\sqrt{2}$; $\csc \theta = -\dfrac{3\sqrt{2}}{4}$; $\sec \theta = 3$; $\cot \theta = -\dfrac{\sqrt{2}}{4}$ **7.** $\dfrac{\sqrt{3}}{6}$ **8.** $-\sqrt{3}$ **9.** $-\dfrac{\sqrt{2}}{2}$

Subject Index

Photo Credits

About the Author   Robert F. Blitzer

CHAPTER P   cmcd/Getty Images, Inc.   **p2** SuperStock, Inc.   **p13** Tom Stewart/Corbis/Stock Market   **p24** William Sallaz/Duomo Photography Incorporated   **p35** PEANUTS reprinted by permission of United Feature Syndicate, Inc.   **p36** Purdue News Service/AP/Wide World Photos   **p48** Gabe Palmer/Mug Shots/Corbis/Stock Market   **p59** Telegraqph Colour Library/Getty Images, Inc.

CHAPTER 1   Nita Winter Photography   **p76** S.S. Archives/Shooting Star International. ©All rights reserved.   **p84** A. Ramu/Stock Boston   **p86** Squeak Carnwath "Equations" 1981, oil on cotton canvas 96 in. h x 72 in. w.   **p95** Getty Images Inc.—Stone   **p106** PEANUTS reprinted by permission of United Features Syndicate, Inc.   **p108** ©2001 Roz Chast from Cartoonbank.com. All rights reserved.   **p111** Stamp from the private collection of Professor C. M. Lang, photography by Gary J. Shulfer, University of Wisconsin, Stevens Point. "Germany: #5"; Scott Standard Postage Stamp Catalogue, Scott Pub. Co., Sidney, Ohio.   **p114** Paramount/Getty Images Inc.—Hulton Archive Photos   **p122** CORBIS   **p131** Fred Bavendam/Peter Arnold, Inc.   **p136** Paul Katz   **p144** CORBIS

CHAPTER 2   Chris Salvo/Getty Images, Inc.   **p166** David Schmidt/Masterfile Corporation   **p167** Carol Simowitz/San Francisco Convention and Visitors Bureau   **p183** Skip Moody/Dembinsky Photo Associates   **p191** Photofest   **p204** Hans Neleman/Getty Images, Inc.   **p225** Douglas Kirkland/Corbis/Sygma   **p230** SuperStock, Inc.   **p238** Graham French/Masterfile Corporation   **p260** Reuters/Fred Prouser/Getty Images Inc.—Hulton Archive Photos

CHAPTER 3   Travelpix/Getty Images, Inc.   **p258** Dave Martin/AP/Wide World Photos   **p268** Esbin-Anderson/Photo Network; Richard Falco/Black Star   **p275** David W. Hamilton/Getty Images, Inc.   **p284** Steven Needham/Envision   **p299** David Parker/Science Museum/Science Photo Library/Photo Researchers, Inc.

CHAPTER 4   Peter Langone/ImageState/International Stock Photography Ltd.   **p317** San Francisco MOMA/Olivier Laude/Getty Images, Inc.—Liaison   **p326** Pictor/ImageState/International Stock Photography Ltd.   **p331** Chris Noble/Getty Images Inc.—Stone   **p343** Janet Foster/Masterfile Corporation   **p346** Hugh Sitton/Getty Images Inc.—Stone   **p347** Gary Kufner/Corbis Sharpshooters   **p357** Nature Source/Raphael Macia/Photo Researchers, Inc.